To Make Our World Anew

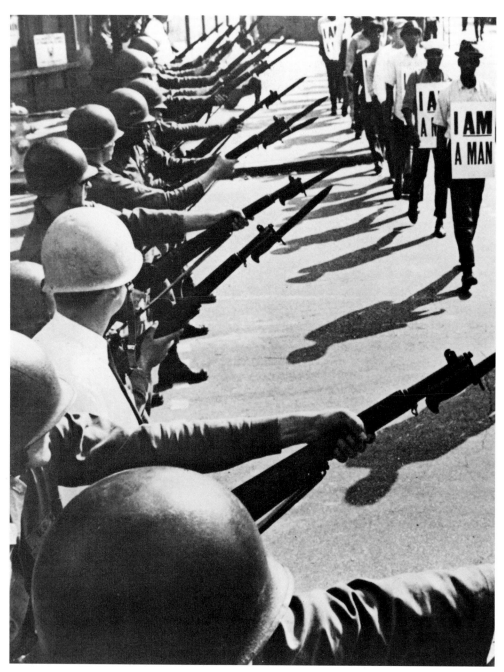

National Guardsmen confront marchers on Beale Street, Memphis, in 1968.

To Make Our World Anew

A History of African Americans

edited by

Robin D. G. Kelley

and

Earl Lewis

OXFORD
UNIVERSITY PRESS

OXFORD
UNIVERSITY PRESS

Oxford   New York
Athens   Auckland   Bangkok   Bogotá   Buenos Aires   Calcutta
Cape Town   Chennai   Dar es Salaam   Delhi   Florence   Hong Kong
Istanbul   Karachi   Kuala Lumpur   Madrid   Melbourne   Mexico City
Mumbai   Nairobi   Paris   São Paulo   Singapore   Taipei   Tokyo
Toronto   Warsaw

and associated companies in
Berlin   Ibadan

Copyright © 2000 by Oxford University Press, Inc.

Preface © 2000 by Oxford University Press, Inc.
"The First Passage" © 1995, 2000 by Colin A. Palmer
"Strange New Land" © 1996, 2000 by Peter H. Wood
"Revolutionary Citizens" © 1997, 2000 by Daniel C. Littlefield
"Let My People Go" © 1996, 2000 by Deborah Gray White
"Breaking the Chains" © 1996, 2000 by Noralee Frankel
"Though Justice Sleeps" © 1997, 2000 by Barbara Bair
"A Chance to Make Good" © 1997, 2000 by James R. Grossman
"From a Raw Deal to a New Deal?" © 1996, 2000 by Joe William Trotter Jr.
"We Changed the World" © 1997, 2000 by Vincent Harding,
Robin D. G. Kelley, and Earl Lewis
"Into the Fire" © 1996, 2000 by Robin D. G. Kelley

"To You" is reproduced from COLLECTED POEMS by Langston Hughes
Copyright © 1994 by the Estate of Langston Hughes
Reprinted by permission of Alfred A. Knopf, a Division of Random House, Inc.

Published by Oxford University Press, Inc.,
198 Madison Avenue, New York, New York 10016
www.oup.com

Oxford is a registered trademark of Oxford University Press

Library of Congress Cataloging-in-Publication Data
To make our world anew : a history of African Americans / edited by Robin
D. G. Kelley and Earl Lewis.
    p.   cm.
Includes bibliographical references (p.) and index.
ISBN 0-19-513945-3
    1. Afro-Americans—History.   I. Kelley, Robin D. G.   II. Lewis, Earl.
E185 .T68 2000
973'.0496073—dc21   00-021131

1 3 5 7 9 10 8 6 4 2

Printed in the United States of America
on acid-free paper

Contents

To You

To sit and dream, to sit and read,
To sit and learn about the world
Outside our world of here and now—
        Our problem world—
To dream of vast horizons of the soul
Through dreams made whole,
Unfettered free—help me!
All you who are dreamers, too,
Help me make our world anew
I reach out my hands to you.

—Langston Hughes

To live with and care for one's family without fear of separation—something that had been denied to slaves—was a goal for blacks after the Civil War. This family was photographed in 1886.

Preface

Robin D. G. Kelley and *Earl Lewis*

T he history of African Americans is nothing less than the dramatic saga of a
people attempting to remake the world. Brought to the Americas against
their will as commodities to be bought and sold, Africans and their descendants struggled to change their conditions and thus turn the New World of their
European masters upside down. Even when they did not succeed, the actions,
thoughts, and dreams of Africans are responsible for some of the most profound
economic, political, and cultural developments in the modern West. Black labor
generated unprecedented wealth and helped give birth to capitalism; black resistance slowly destroyed the system of slavery and prompted new methods of coercion and punishment; black creativity influenced virtually all forms of Western
art—from music and dance to theater and the plastic arts; black visions of freedom
and efforts to realize them not only transformed American politics but inspired
uprisings the world over—from South Africa to Tiananmen Square. Indeed, by in-
voking Langston Hughes's call to "make our world anew," we recognize that African
Americans historically understood their plight and their possibilities in global
terms. For if this book demonstrates anything, it is that African Americans saw
themselves as both Americans and part of a larger, international black diaspora. *To
Make Our World Anew* tells the story of the nation, but places the struggles and
achievements of black people in a larger international framework.

The history of African Americans begins on the African continent, a huge and
varied land bounded by the Atlantic and Indian Oceans. It was home to people
with different languages, traditions, histories, and religions. They called themselves
Twi, Yoruba, Ethiopian, Zulu, Ashanti, and Kumba, among other names. Some
lived in ancient kingdoms as old as the annals of recorded history, and others lived
in small family groupings. Some lived in societies headed by powerful men, and
others by powerful women. Whether in cities or rural areas, whether Muslim,
Christian, or other, the peoples of this amazing continent had long played a central role in world affairs. Egyptian advances in medicine, language, and architec-
ture greatly influenced the Greek and Roman worlds. Gold from the Bure and

Bambuk goldfields of West Africa made its way into the Mediterranean world, where the accumulation of significant quantities enabled the merchants of Genoa (Italy) to underwrite European exploration and expansion. Likewise, notable learning centers like Timbuktu attracted vistors from Europe and the Orient, and greatly enriched the Islamic world.

The roles of Africans in world affairs changed significantly with the rise of the South Atlantic System. As European explorers made their way to the Americas, they expected to find streets paved with gold. The Americas were indeed rich in natural resoures, but the bounty had to be excavated, cultivated, and processed. Labor was needed. The Europeans had already begun exploiting African labor on plantations in the Mediterranean and off the coast of West Africa, so the modern world's turn to Africa as a reservoir of slaves was not surprising. What followed was the forced migration and enslavement of several million Africans of varied ethnic backgrounds. Although scholars debate the exact numbers, it is understood that somewhere between ten and twenty million people became part of the system of enslavement that ultimately led to the making of an African diaspora and African Americans. Many died in the trek from the interior to the coast, others during the wait for a slave ship, and scores of others during the harsh middle passage. Out of the crucible of their sufffering was forged a new people—no longer simply Twi, Yoruba, Ashanti, or Kumba. In the Americas, they first became Africans and then African Americans. This process of people-making is central to a complete understanding of African-American history.

To the countless numbers of Africans who survived the trans-Atlantic journey and were forced to disembark at one of the many ports along the coast of Britain's North American colonies, what lay before them was indeed a "strange new land." The seemingly infinite landscape, the cooler climate, the European settlers whose station in society ranged from vagabond to plantation owner, and their new neighbors—the native peoples who had occupied the land for centuries—were all unfamiliar to these new arrivals. More than the land itself, the relationships they entered into must have seemed especially peculiar. Although forms of bondage had existed in West and Central Africa long before the trans-Atlantic slave trade, human beings were rarely the main commodity at the marketplace. Here in the modern world, the enslaved African was inspected, assessed, auctioned, bought, sold, bartered, and treated in any manner the auctioneer or owner saw fit.

By the end of the 18th century, African slaves came to be property, pure and simple, and the color of their skin had everything to do with their unique status. This had not always been the case, however. During the first half of the 17th century, the planters and colonial administrators had few hard and fast rules about what it meant to be a slave. Some Africans were treated like European indentured servants and emancipated after a designated period of time. Others were slaves for life, but their children were born free. Over time, however, the owners realized how valuable their investments were and proceeded to support laws that tightened the bonds of racial slavery—most notably laws that made African slavery an inherited condition and denied black people the most rudimentary human rights.

The slaves did not always cooperate, however. They fought the masters and overseers, ran away, and made the business of commercial farming more difficult by not working efficiently. Some white indentured servants supported their fellow laborers, especially at the beginning of the 17th century, but as the laws changed and blackness became the primary mark of slavery, most poor white servants learned that the consequences of interracial solidarity had become much more severe. Being white, even a poor white, meant immunity from absolute slavery.

Yet, in spite of their condition, enslaved Africans were still thinking and feeling human beings endowed with intellect, creativity, and vision. They came to these shores from various ethnic groups and speaking many languages, but through it all they forged a strong sense of community. Here in this strange new land the Africans learned the English language and made it their own. They learned Christianity and transformed it. Others held fast to Islam or combined their own spiritual beliefs with the faith of the master. Sometimes the master's words served as their sharpest weapons, for all around them, especially into the late 18th century, they heard talk of liberty and freedom, of the rights of man. Not surprisingly, many enslaved Africans embraced the idea of liberty as a fundamental right, and some even presented petitions to colonial administrators insisting on their right to be free. But nobody had to read a declaration or a treatise to have a yearning for freedom. Indeed, the slaves themselves authored the earliest declarations of freedom, and they were written in blood in the form of slave insurrections. The majority simply stole themselves to freedom.

In the 150 years since their forced arrival in the 17th century, little exposed the contradiction between slavery and freedom for Africans as much as this nation's fight for independence from Great Britain. It was a contradiction many resolved to settle. Some, such as Crispus Attucks, joined with other colonists in striking direct blows for liberty. Others, meanwhile, heard the pleas for loyalty to the British crown, and with the promise of emancipation as their reward, remained faithful to the old order only to see it vanish before them. But whether in the poems of Phillis Wheatley, the legal action of Qouk Walker, or the efforts of Paul Cuffee, Americans of African descent helped define what it meant to be revolutionary citizens.

In fact, as the clamor for independence from Great Britain intensified, so too did the debate over slavery. Many who participated recognized that slavery remained a central form of labor in both the North and the South. Although it was a minority view, some American colonists favored emancipation. They ably pointed to the few blacks who purchased their freedom and gained an economic foothold before the 1760s. But in a land where dark skin signaled a subordinate social position, the few who lived as other than slaves represented the exception. For the enslaved, independence was not a philosophical debate, it stood as an alternative to permanent bondage.

As a result African Americans took a keen interest in public affairs. A small group of Africans in Massachusetts, for example, vigorously asserted their right to freedom, telling the provisional House of Representatives so as early as 1773. Such petitions increased in frequency and cogency after the Declaration of Independence. Others acted individually, suing their masters for manumission and thereby insisting that they were citizens with the right to seek redress. And after five generations on North American soil, the promise of freedom seemed tantalizingly close, so a few clung to the potential for British citizenship, trading loyalty to the crown for freedom. Irrespective of which side they supported, African people saw in the war an opportunity to escape slavery, pursuing different routes to possible full citizenship.

The Revolutionary era did more than accelerate the push for freedom. It also midwifed the birth of a people called African Americans. In the crucible of the United States' birth, Africans claimed they too were Americans. They emphasized the role they played in building the infant nation and in securing its freedom. From their embrace of the religious awakening to the formation of independent institutions, they inserted themselves into the social and cultural life of the country. Ever aware of the implication of freedom, they spread word of their own efforts throughout the Americas, and took pleasure as other members of the African diaspora liberated themselves in Haiti.

The age of revolution ended with a tightening of the Southern slave regime along with an intensification of resistance to slavery. As the industrial revolution got under way in the Northeastern states and England, the market for cotton was more profitable than ever. And after inventor Eli Whitney created a machine that could easily remove the seeds from cotton bolls—a slow and tedious chore slaves had to do by hand—plantation owners were able to grow even more cotton with the same number of hands. They were not about to give up the slave system so easily. Even after the United States abolished the slave trade in 1808, plantation owners in the less fertile "upper South" added a new twist to the business of human bondage by breeding their slaves like cattle and selling them to the growing cotton plantations of the South and Southwest.

Not surprisingly, the African-American struggle to be free—and remain free—in the United States clashed with the slaveholders' efforts to keep the system alive and profitable. Indeed, the central goal of free blacks in antebellum America, beyond their very survival as a people, was to fight for the complete abolition of slavery. And fight they did, often in concert with fellow slaves, sometimes in alliance with progressive white abolitionists, sometimes all alone. Free and enslaved African Americans, including such notable figures as Gabriel Prosser, Denmark Vesey, and Nat Turner, attempted to launch slave rebellions against the system. David Walker, Frederick Douglass, Maria Stewart, Henry Highland Garnet, and a host of others wrote militant books, pamphlets, and speeches calling for the abolition of slavery and condemning the United States for its hypocritical claim to being a "land of the free."

The clash between slaveholders and their opponents (most notably, the slaves themselves) ultimately escalated into a full-scale war. The years of Civil War and reconstruction challenged the very foundations of American democracy and established the place of African Americans in that democracy. The war raised the intriguing question of whether a state or collection of states had the right to leave the union when residents felt their way of life was under attack. It eventually raised the question of whether a nation founded on the deep belief in freedom could deny those same rights and privileges to others because of a difference in color and status.

When southern forces fired on Fort Sumter, South Carolina, in 1861, sparking a confrontation between the federal government and southerners, the end of a way of life was at hand. The country had grown increasingly polarized over the issue of slavery. Some favored total abolition; others simply wished to contain slavery, halting its further spread. Yet, after the start of the war, and over the pleas of prominent African Americans such as Frederick Douglass, President Lincoln and members of Congress hesitated to make the struggle a referendum on slavery. Initially, Lincoln sought to reunite the country. But with growing pressures from some whites, after several important defeats, and in light of African American agitation, the freedom of African Americans became a paramount concern.

The emancipation of slaves and the abolition of slavery was neither immediate nor universally applied. And the shift from slavery to freedom introduced a number of searching questions for Southern blacks. Although the majority favored freedom over enslavement, a few feared such a dramatic change in status. Many, for example, ran away to join army units, where they encountered Northern blacks heading south to aid in their liberation. Others filled the contraband camps—so called because fleeing slaves had no legal status and were considered contraband— that flanked Northern encampments. And even after Lincoln signed the Emancipation Proclamation in 1863, blacks living in border states such as West Virginia were not freed until passage of the 13th Amendment to the Constitution in 1865. Still, a few served in the Confederate army, which is not surprising because a few blacks had been slave owners.

When the war ended in 1865, many African Americans anticipated their inclusion into the nation's civic culture. With ratification of the 14th Amendment in 1868, which granted blacks citizenship and the 15th (1870), which extended the franchise, they were free and optimistic. Scores anxiously searched for family members sold during slavery; others exercised their right to form labor associations, and to build schools, churches, and other institutions. Families withdrew women and children from the labor force, thereby asserting a right to be treated as paid, free labor. Although continued racial violence tempered some of this optimism, blacks voted and played an active role in the affairs of the nation. African Americans were free at last! They were finally full-fledged members of the republic.

So they thought. "The slave went free; stood a brief moment in the sun; then moved back again toward slavery." This is how W. E. B. DuBois, the great black scholar and activist, described the plight of black people in 1877—the year reconstruction officially came to a close. Federal troops were withdrawn from the South, freed slaves were not given the land promised them, white terrorist groups ran rampant, and the same defenders of slavery who led the Civil War against the North returned to positions of power. It was a sad moment, for it marked the end of a decade and a half of efforts to create a true democracy in the South. And during the next fifteen years, things only got worse. It didn't have to be this way, DuBois argued. If only poor whites recognized that their own freedom was tied to the freedom of black people. If they only understood the power of united action, of black and white working together to overthrow the landlords, the merchants, and money-hungry factory owners. Instead, tragically, white people barely able to make ends meet chose allegiance to their race over their class—in other words, they identified more with being white than being a worker or a farmer who shared common interests with black workers and farmers. Thus begins what black historian Rayford Logan calls "the nadir," or low point, of African American history.

Low point, indeed. Lynchings increased, racial segregation became law, and African American citizens who worked so hard for the Republican party in the days of Reconstruction found themselves without the right to vote. Many, many emancipated black people found themselves with no property, working for white landlords under conditions reminiscent of slavery. These rural folk had to rent their land, grow the crops the market demanded, and give half or more of what they produced to their landlords. This system of sharecropping, sometimes called the new slavery, kept most African Americans in debt and poverty. Yet, it did not destroy their fighting spirit. Africans Americans were more than victims of "Jim Crow" laws and racial violence. They organized, fought back, moved around, thought, wrote, and created works of art. They connected their struggles with the rest of the world, turning to Africa, Europe, and the Caribbean for guidance and inspiration. And in many respects, they kept alive a vision of justice and equality born during Reconstruction. Some African Americans joined interracial movements such as the Populists or the Knights of Labor; others turned inward and built religious, fraternal, educational, and political institutions that ultimately became sources of power and inspiration for the stony road ahead. Others simply left, finding refuge as far away as Liberia (West Africa), Canada, and Haiti, or as close as Kansas and Oklahoma. There African American men and women founded all-black towns such as Mound Bayou in Mississippi, or Langston and Boley in Oklahoma, and imagined a promised land free of white terrorism. A handful followed the advice of black educator Booker T. Washington, who called on Southern black folk to "cast down their buckets where they are" and carve out a life on the land. Proving that African Americans are a productive people, he believed, would reduce the terror and eliminate racism. Then there were those, such as Ida B. Wells, who believed blacks should cast down the gauntlet and punch it out with white supremacists. Wells, one of many leading black women activists of that era, declared war on lynching and sexual violence against black women.

If you can't beat them, leave. And this is what more than one million Southern blacks did around the time war broke out in Europe. With the wartime economy booming and European immigration at a virtual standstill because of the conflict, the demand for labor attracted hundreds of thousands of black folk to the Northern metropolises of Chicago, New York, Philadelphia, Milwaukee, Cleveland, and Detroit, to name a few. For some, the move North was a version of Exodus. They sought refuge and possibility in the North; they sought security and safety in the burgeoning ghettos of the midwestern and eastern seaboard cities. Many found what they were looking for; others only found more misery. Most experienced a combination of exhilaration and disappointment. And everyone, whether they stayed in the South or joined the Great Migration, confronted a society in flux: the world during and immediately following the Great War was a world marked by destruction, international migrations, rapid industrialization, a wave of anticolonial uprisings in Africa and the Caribbean, revolutions in Russia, Germany, Mexico, Ireland, and elsewhere, and racial violence at home. Black men returned from a war fought to make the world safe for democracy ready to demand democracy for themselves. For their militance they paid a dear price—black men were lynched in uniform, black institutions were attacked by racist white mobs, the ranks of black industrial workers, which had swelled during the war, were rapidly downsized. On the other hand, while the 1920s looked pretty bad for ordinary African Americans, the "artists of the race" experienced a renaissance. Popular fascination with blackness meant that the cultural achievements of African Americans—in literature, music, theater, dance, visual arts—would have an audience.

By the end of the decade, however, things looked bad for everybody. When the Great Depression hit America, African Americans were feeling it even before the stock market crash of 1929. But they had hardly given up hope. On the contrary, the crisis was seen by some as yet another opportunity to "make the world anew." Hope in the midst of crisis is a major theme in the history of the 1930s and '40s. Alongside images of bank closings, endless soup lines, jobless men selling apples, unemployed workers begging for work, hard-working middle class Americans losing everything, we find newsreel footage of families glued to radios listening to the President's inspirational speeches, labor leaders declaring victory in the aftermath of militant strikes, radical protesters fighting tenaciously to transform the country. This sense of hope and high expectation was also evident in the many letters ordinary people sent to President Franklin Delano Roosevelt, the man Americans sent to the White House three times in a row beginning in 1932. They believed things would change, that the nation would rise up out of the Depression. And Roosevelt himself reinforced their hopes by promising a New Deal for all Americans. For African Americans, in particular, the era was simultaneously an inferno and an eden: black workers had the highest unemployment rate at a time when black leaders held important positions in Roosevelt's administration; New Deal legislation threw hundreds of thousands of black sharecroppers off the land while the same federal government provided unprecedented opportunities for black writers and artists; dramatic episodes of racist violence against African Americans opened the decade just when communists and other radicals launched a nationwide campaign against racial injustice.

This sense of hope amid crisis became even more pronounced once the United States entered the Second World War in 1941. For African Americans, the horrors of war provided an opportunity to demand equal treatment. They criticized the United States for fighting for democracy overseas while black people at home were treated like second-class citizens. Unlike the First World War, this time around black leaders called for a "Double Victory"—a victory against fascism abroad and racism at home. The war also created employment opportunities for many black working people, many of whom left the South permanently for the sprawling factories of the urban North. It was a replay of the same social and economic phenomena of World War I. Hopeful that the northern metropolises would be the "promised land," a good number of these migrants found only frustration and disappointment, since a comparatively small proportion of African Americans gained access to industrial jobs and training programs. Those who did obtain well-paying jobs often experienced violent reprisals from disgruntled white workers who refused to work with blacks. Thus, throughout the war white workers waged "hate strikes" to protest the promotion of blacks, and black workers frequently retaliated with their own strikes to protest discrimination. And in many instances, racial tensions spread beyond the workplace, erupting in riots in several major U.S. cities. Spurred by poor housing and living conditions in ghettos, competition between blacks and whites over the use of public parks, and police treatment of black citizens, these riots resulted in several deaths, thousands of injuries, and millions of dollars in property damage. Indeed, it might be said that while U.S. troops invaded Normandy and bombed Okinawa, African Americans in the urban ghettos fought their own war at home.

It was only the beginning. Despite a long and noble history of black resistance to racism and oppression in the United States, the period from 1945 to 1970 might be described as a protracted war for freedom. Black Americans were determined to be the architects of an inclusive America, one that championed human rights for all. Moreover, they openly linked local efforts to global conditions. The fight for economic and racial justice in Baton Rouge, Montgomery, and other southern towns and cities became part of a worldwide fight for human rights. In song, word, and deed, anticolonial efforts in Africa became connected to human rights struggles in the United States; opposition to the war in Vietnam became linked to the oppression of third-world peoples everywhere. In that sense the black struggle in the United States became a beacon for the world.

The Second World War had exposed the persistent contradictions between the American ideal and the American reality. Black Americans resolved to eliminate that contradiction. They would not only fight for democracy abroad, they would pursue democracy at home. In communities large and small they organized after the war, often aided by World War II veterans who had resolved to return home and change things.

They used institutions such as churches, fraternal orders, and civil rights organizations, and created new ones to funnel their efforts. In cadences of black ministers, the lyrics of gospel and civil rights songs, the energies of college students, the noble dreams of ordinary folk, they plotted their strategies.

Lest it be forgotten, however, it took community organizing and mobilizing; it took poor and middle class, young and old, college educated and school dropouts to organize the communities for social change. Some resisted, fearing beatings, job loss, and even murder. And for good reason—African Americans who organized the civil rights movement experienced the range of negative response. After all, the federal government only reluctantly backed civil rights workers and aggressively investigated black leaders when they complained about the war in Vietnam and social inequities elsewhere. It is also important to understand that while African Americans generally shared a vision of changing the world, they did disagree at times over strategies, procedures, and timing. In time, southern activists came to realize that the challenges faced by northern and western urban dwellers required new emphases. Members of the Student Nonviolent Coordinating Committee (SNCC) publicly and quietly feuded with elders in organizations such as the NAACP and the Southern Christian Leadership Committee (SCLC).

When the 1960s came to a close most black people were surprisingly optimistic. The civil rights movement had made remarkable gains, and many people believed that the Black Power movement might achieve for African Americans the self-determination they had been seeking for the past three centuries. And there were some stunning victories, especially in the arena of electoral politics. Several major cities elected black mayors, African American representation in Congress increased significantly, and a black man named Jesse Jackson actually became a serious contender for the Presidency. The black middle class expanded, as corporate board rooms became slightly more integrated and black college–educated professionals moved to newly built suburban homes.

The majority were not so lucky. After 1970, massive economic changes adversely affected black workers: the disappearance of heavy industry, the flight of American industry to foreign lands, and the displacement of millions of workers across the country. Permanent unemployment and underemployment became a way of life. A few years after the War on Poverty had been declared a victory, the number of black poor grew dramatically. And despite the growing presence of African Americans in political office, city services declined, federal spending on cities dried up, affirmative action programs were dismantled, blatant acts of racism began to rise again, and the U.S. entered a seemingly endless economic recession.

Economic decline, poverty, and rising racism in the "post segregation" age is only part of the story. The final chapters of this book tell yet another story of how black people are still fighting for change. It is the story of how an increasingly diverse and always complicated black community resisted oppression, struggled for power, dealt with internal tensions, conflicts, and differences, and profoundly shaped American culture. It is the story of the resurgence of black nationalism, the rise of black neoconservatism, the challenge of black feminism, the impact of Caribbean immigration on African American communities, the escalation of interethnic tensions, and the roots of rap music and hip-hop culture. It is a story whose final chapters will have to be written by all of us.

To Make Our World Anew is truly a collective endeavor. We have combined the efforts of eleven leading historians to write the chapters of this volume, and each of them deserves full credit as a co-author of this book: Colin A. Palmer, Peter H. Wood, Daniel C. Littlefield, Deborah Gray White, Noralee Frankel, Barbara Bair, James R. Grossman, Joe William Trotter, Jr., Vincent Harding, Robin D. G. Kelley, and Earl Lewis.

To Make Our World Anew

CHAPTER 1

The First Passage

1502–1619

Colin A. Palmer

Without exception, the contemporary societies of North and South America and the Caribbean include peoples of African descent. They form the numerical majority in the Caribbean, are about one half of Brazil's population, and make up a significant minority in the United States. In other countries, such as Canada, Mexico, Venezuela, and Colombia, blacks are present in smaller numbers. Regardless of the societies in which they live, these peoples share a common historical origin and ancestral homeland. Their experiences in the Americas have also been remarkably similar since the sixteenth century, when they began to arrive from Africa in ever-increasing numbers.

Black Africans were brought as slaves into the Caribbean islands and the mainland colonies of Central and South America, first by the Spaniards and later by the Portuguese. Beginning in 1502, the slave trade gathered momentum as white colonists came to rely on this forced black labor. During the early years of the trade, Africans passed through Spain (where many remained) to the Americas. By 1518, however, a direct trade route from Africa to the Americas was introduced.

Not all Africans in the Americas, even in the sixteenth century, served as slaves for the duration of their lives. Some managed to achieve their freedom; others were born free. In 1617 the first town or settlement controlled by free blacks in the Americas was established in Mexico. This was a major development in black life in the Western Hemisphere; it was the first time that a group of Africans gained the right to live as free people. These pioneers had successfully thrown off the yoke of slavery through their own efforts, setting the stage for the eventual liberation of other enslaved Africans. But almost three centuries passed before this goal would be accomplished everywhere in the Americas.

Two years after this free Mexican town—San Lorenzo de los Negros—received its charter, about twenty Africans disembarked from a Dutch ship at Jamestown, Virginia. These people were the first Africans shipped to the new and permanent settlement that the English colonists had established in North America. They came 117 years after Africans were first enslaved in the Americas, in Hispaniola.

From Africa to the Americas

Modern archaeological research has established that Africa was the birthplace of human life. No precise date can be given for the emergence of early humans, or the hominid species, but it may have taken place about two million years ago. The earliest of these hominid fossils were discovered at Lake Turkana in Kenya, at Olduvai Gorge in Tanzania, and the river Omo in Ethiopia. Consequently, it is possible to claim that east and northeast Africa formed the cradle of human society. In time, over hundreds of thousands of years, early humans moved to other parts of Africa and to other continents.

The first Africans were nomadic peoples who made simple stone tools to aid them in their struggles for survival. With the passage of time, these tools became more sophisticated. The hand ax, for example, appeared around a million years ago. Its sharp cutting edges were more effective in the killing of prey than the earlier tools. Probably about sixty thousand years ago, Africans started using fire. This development meant that meat could be cooked, and fire may even have been used to clear land for settlement or other purposes.

Human life in Africa, or elsewhere for that matter, was always changing. The people developed new tools, moved around, and organized their lives and societies in a variety of ways. There was much diversity among the African peoples in terms of their culture and skin color. In northeastern Africa, for example, the people tended to be lighter in complexion than those who lived in the tropical areas. Much of this difference in skin color was a result of living in different climates. Individuals who lived in areas of intense heat and sunlight developed the kind of dark skin pigmentation that provided more effective protection against the ravages of heat and allowed them to survive.

The black peoples of Africa, however, should not be characterized as belonging to a single race. In fact, many scholars have abandoned the use of the concept of "race" as a way of categorizing peoples. Skin color and other physical features do not reveal much about the genetic makeup of an individual or group. Two individuals with the same skin color and hair texture may be more genetically different from one another than they are from two persons with another pigmentation. For this reason, scholars have concluded that Africans, and other peoples as well, are so internally different that the old way of classifying people according to physical appearance or "race" is no longer useful.

It is more useful to look at the African peoples according to language groupings. Different languages make up a family if their structures are basically similar. In most cases, the similarities in these languages result from the interaction among the speakers and the mutual borrowing of words. Using this method of studying languages, scholars have fitted the African peoples into five language families. These are the Afro-Asiatic family in North Africa, the Nilo-Saharan languages spoken in areas south and east of the Sahara and around the Nile River valley, the Congo-Kordofanian family spoken in West and West Central Africa, and the Khoisan group of languages spoken in southern Africa and parts of East Africa. A sixth family, the Austronesian, is found in Madagascar but is not native of Africa (having originated in Southeast Asia).

African societies varied in the pace of their development and the nature of the changes that they experienced over time. Egypt, for example, was the first society to begin cultivating food crops, probably about 5500 B.C. Other societies followed. By 3000 B.C., the people living in the savanna were producing a variety of grains and yams. The development of agriculture made it possible to support larger populations and contributed to the rise of settlements.

Throughout the continent, the people organized themselves in political units of various sizes and degrees of complexity. Egypt was the first great African civilization. Located in an area fertilized by the Nile River, Egypt made rapid strides in agriculture and commerce by 3000 B.C. Before 3100 B.C., however, several small states existed in the area. These political divisions came to an end when the states formed one kingdom ruled by the pharaohs. This national unity paved the way for an impressive civilization that would last for several centuries.

Egyptian civilization was characterized by a hieroglyphic writing system, complex religious ideas, and monumental stone pyramids. Although historians disagree on this matter, it appears that the Egyptian peoples consisted of black Afri cans as well as lighter-skinned peoples from the Mediterranean area. Their civilization had a major impact on Greek culture and ultimately on Western civilization.

Ancient Egypt is the best known of the early African societies, but it did not stand alone. Elsewhere, Africans developed a variety of states ranging from a few hundred people to large kingdoms and empires. These states were not all alike; there were variations in their political and social structures, the nature of the power exercised by the rulers, their religions, and so on. Many Africans believed that the authority and power of their ruler derived from the gods. Most of these societies had their own bureaucracies, taxation systems, and armed forces.

Some of the best-known states and empires were located in the western and central Sudan. Ghana, located in West Africa north of the Niger and Senegal valleys, was probably the earliest of them all. Noted for its great wealth and the power of its ruler, Ghana was said to have had an army of more than 200,000 soldiers around A.D. 1068. Later, the empire of Mali rose to prominence in the fourteenth century, occupying areas that are now part of Nigeria and the Guinea forests.

Mali's most famous ruler was Mansa Kankan Musa, who came to the throne in 1312. Bold and aggressive, he extended the frontiers of the Mali Empire to the Atlantic Ocean, incorporating several smaller states along the way. A Muslim, Mansa Musa undertook a pilgrimage to Mecca, which was then a part of Egypt, in 1324. On this journey, Mansa Musa made a lavish display of his wealth. He was

ANCIENT KINGDOMS OF THE WESTERN SUDAN

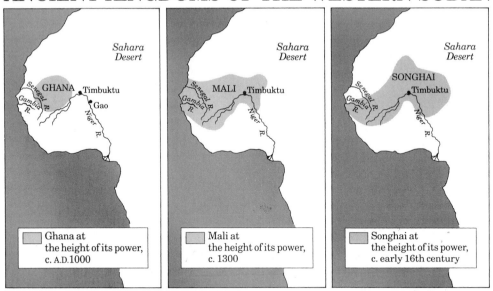

In the western Sudan, the kingdom of Ghana was the first important African empire to emerge. The Mali empire came to power in the fourteenth century and later, in the early sixteenth century, the Songhai kingdom dominated the region.

accompanied by five hundred slaves, each one bearing a staff of gold that weighed six pounds. In addition, one hundred camels carried thirty thousand pounds of gold. Mansa Musa's extravagance in Egypt created an accurate perception that his empire was one of the wealthiest then in existence.

The African peoples also developed cultural traditions that met their needs. The family was the basis of their social organization. Kinship ties, which united members of an ethnic group, were particularly strong. African societies were also deeply religious; most had a supreme god and other lesser deities. There was hardly any distinction between the religious and the secular, or civil, aspects of life. Religious beliefs determined when almost all activities, such as the planting seasons, harvest time, or the naming of children, would take place. Not surprisingly, the African peoples who came to the Americas brought very strong family and religious traditions with them.

African societies were never free from influences that originated outside of the continent. The Egyptian civilization enjoyed much interaction with the societies of the Mediterranean. There was a great deal of contact between the East African societies and those of Asia. Ethiopians had lived in Greece from about the fifth century B.C. Other Africans, usually traders, had visited various European countries for centuries.

In the eighth century, the new and aggressive Islamic religion began to gain converts in North and sub-Saharan Africa. With the embrace of Islam came important changes in the beliefs of the Africans and the nature of their legal systems. The Islamization of West Africa was aided by traders who converted to Islam in the north and brought their new religious ideas across the Sahara to the south. The pace of religious conversion and the number of converts varied, but few states remained untouched by Islam at the start of the Atlantic slave trade in the early sixteenth century. This did not mean, however, that most West Africans became Muslims and abandoned their traditional religious ideas. For many of the converts to Islam, ancient beliefs existed alongside the new ones, although these beliefs were undoubtedly modified in some way over time. Some of the Africans who were enslaved in the Americas were Muslims, but most were not.

Some scholars think that some West African peoples had established trading relationships with the native peoples of the Americas before the arrival of Columbus in 1492. Such contacts may have begun as early as the seventh century B.C. This conclusion is based on skeletal remains found in Central America that appear to be African, representations of African features in the art of some of the first Americans, as well as similarities in some African languages and those spoken in the Americas before Columbus. Because these kinds of evidence are subject to different interpretations, it cannot yet be established conclusively that Africans arrived in the Americas before the Europeans did.

Historians can never be certain of the number of Africans who were brought to the Americas as slaves. Reliable records were often not kept, some have disappeared, and there is no firm data on those persons who were imported illegally. Those Europeans and Americans who engaged in illegal slave trading did so in order to avoid paying taxes on the slaves that they carried. Others traded without receiving permission to do so from the authorities or began smuggling slaves after laws were passed abolishing the human traffic. In spite of these difficulties, most historians now estimate that the number of Africans who arrived as slaves from 1502 to the mid-nineteenth century amounted to between ten and twelve million. Most of these people were shipped to Latin America and the Caribbean.

The foundations of the Atlantic slave trade were established in the sixteenth century by Spanish colonists, who were no strangers to the institution of slavery. Prior to Columbus's voyages to the Americas, the Spaniards held Muslims, black Africans, Slavs, and even other Spaniards as slaves. In fact, the number of African slaves in Spain and Portugal was increasing during the years preceding Columbus's voyages, reflecting a decline in the use of other groups as slaves.

Under the circumstances, it is not surprising that the Spaniards in Hispaniola, the first colony in the Caribbean, asked the Crown to send them African slaves once the need for labor arose. This request was made in 1501, a mere seven years after the island had been colonized. Unwilling to perform menial and backbreaking tasks, the Spaniards had expected to depend on the forced labor of the native peoples. The Indians, at least those who fell under the control of the colonists, were enslaved and required to work in the fields, households, and mines. But many Indians soon died from mistreatment and disease, which created a shortage of labor.

Faced with a declining supply of Indian laborers, the Spanish colonists pondered their options and decided to introduce African slavery. Not only were Africans performing unpaid labor in Spain and elsewhere in Europe at the time, but as a group they were placed at the bottom of the social order as well. The terms *black* and *slave* had become increasingly interchangeable in Spain in the fifteenth century. The country's moral climate justified African slavery. In other words, black Africans had occupied a decidedly inferior place in Spanish society prior to Columbus's expeditions. In addition, the notion that Africans could be enslaved and were suited for that condition had become widely accepted and deeply rooted in Spanish society.

It is not entirely clear why this was the case. Spaniards, and by extension the Portuguese and other Europeans, may have attributed negative qualities to the Africans because they were different culturally, had black skins, and were not Christians. Africans were people set apart as the "other," persons whose differences the Europeans neither appreciated, respected, nor understood. Not until the nineteenth century, however, did a full-blown racist ideology develop to promote the biological claims to superiority by whites and to defend the treatment of blacks by alleging that they were inferior members of the human species. No such "scientific" claims were made at the time of Columbus. Perhaps none was needed. By purchasing Africans and using them as slaves, the Europeans were already asserting power over them. In time, the Africans' inferior place in society came to be seen as normal, and few voices were raised to challenge their treatment and condition.

In response to the request from the governor of Hispaniola for African slave labor in 1501, the Spanish Crown authorized the shipment of slaves in 1502. The slaves in this first cargo had lived in Spain for some time before they were shipped to the Caribbean. Not until 1518 would slaves be transported to the Americas directly from Africa.

The Portuguese were the pioneering European slave traders. Portugal was the first country in Europe that had developed the technology to conduct a seafaring trade. Unlike some of the other European countries, Portugal was politically united by the fifteenth century and free from the sorts of serious internal conflicts that weakened its neighbors. As a result, its leaders could focus their energies on overseas expansion and trade. Situated on the Atlantic Ocean, the Portuguese had also made significant advances in shipbuilding, thereby giving them the ability to participate actively in overseas trading ventures. Portugal had also developed a class of merchants and entrepreneurs with the wealth, skill, and experience to conduct a slave trade.

Prince Henry, who would later be called "the Navigator," was one of the earliest of the Portuguese explorers. His explorations along the African coast in the 1420s opened the way for the development of a European-African trade in black slaves. The first organized Portuguese expedition to capture black Africans and enslave them appears to have occurred in 1441. Led by Antão Gonçalves and Nuno Tristão, the members of the expedition captured twelve Africans off the coast of northern Mauritania and presented them at the Portuguese court.

This initial Portuguese success at people-stealing encouraged additional attempts. A few kidnapped Africans were brought to Portugal in succeeding months, but the single largest group was unloaded in Lisbon on August 8, 1444. There were between 235 and 240 captives in this party. In time, Genoese, Florentine, and Castilian traders joined the Portuguese kidnappers on the West African coast. But the Portuguese remained the principal carriers of Africans to Europe for the next century and more. The process by which these Africans were acquired in the early years cannot be characterized as a trade. The evidence does not show that the Europeans bargained with anyone; the Africans were simply abducted. Portuguese authorities, however, imposed a tax on all Africans sold in their country.

Not surprisingly, the Europeans could not continue to kidnap Africans indefinitely, and a trade with its own rules would have to be developed. To this end, the Portuguese built a fort on the island of Arguin to serve as a base for trade with the Africans. This did not mean that raids for African slaves ceased; it indicated that the contact with Africa was being placed on a more formal footing and that the abductions decreased even if they did not disappear. By 1450 the Portuguese had begun to transport an average of one thousand to two thousand African slaves to Europe each year. Most of these people came from the Senegambia, but a few were from other nearby areas.

Portugal's domination of the Euro-African trade deepened as the fifteenth century wore on. In 1452, Pope Nicholas V granted the Portuguese king the authority to attack and enslave "the Moors, heathens and other enemies of Christ" who lived south of Cape Bojador. Although this and other papal grants did not necessarily lead to an increase in the number of slaves, they gave the approval of the church to the institution of slavery and paved the way for Portuguese conquest and occupation of societies that were not Christian. In 1479, Spain recognized Portugal's supremacy in the slave trade by signing the Treaty of Aláçovas. The treaty granted Portugal the right to supply Spain with African slaves and accepted its monopoly of the African trade. Three years later, in 1482, the Portuguese built a fort on the Gold Coast (modern Ghana) to encourage, assist, and protect the expanding African commerce. Known as Elmina Castle, the fort could hold hundreds of slaves.

Clearly, when the Spanish Crown agreed to send African slaves to Hispaniola in 1502, the bureaucratic machinery of treaties and established practices was already in place to acquire them. Under the terms of the 1479 treaty, the Portuguese had already agreed to supply African slaves to the Spaniards. So the decline of the

This drawing shows the layout of a European slave-trading center in West Africa. By the mid-seventeenth century, Portugal, England, France, Holland, and other European countries were involved in the trade of African slaves.

Indian population of the Americas and the Spanish colonists' insistence on a new labor force did not create the African slave trade and slavery. Both were already in existence. The demand for slaves in the Americas did, however, lead to an expansion of the trade and a change in its direction. Instead of going up to Europe, the majority of the Africans would soon be sent across the Atlantic to the Americas.

The increase in the demand for slaves, coupled with the expectation that huge profits could be made, led several other European nations to participate in the slave trade. By 1650, the Dutch, the English, and the French, among others, had joined the Portuguese in this human commerce. Spain, whose colonies consumed most of the African slaves during the first century and a half of the slave trade, did no trading on the African coast until the late eighteenth century. This was not by design. It was a consequence of another treaty signed by Spain and Portugal in 1494. Known as the Treaty of Tordesillas, the agreement permitted the Portuguese to trade on the African coast and in Asia and Brazil. The Spaniards were confined to the rest of what became known as the Americas. The other European nations, however, were not parties to this division of the known world. They did not feel themselves bound by the treaty, and they ignored it.

Once the Spanish Crown authorized the introduction of African slaves in the Americas, it issued licenses, for a fee, to individual traders to supply the slaves. These traders were likely to be either Portuguese, Genoese, or Spaniards. The license specified the number of slaves that would be delivered and the destination. A new license was required for each slave-trading journey because the Crown wanted to exercise control over the supply of slaves and to receive the tax revenue that the trade generated. Most traders received permission to deliver fewer than twenty or thirty slaves. There were exceptions, of course, and some traders were allowed to ship hundreds of slaves at one time. Spaniards who intended to settle in the colonies were also allowed to take with them any slaves that they already owned.

The system of awarding licenses did not satisfy the growing demand for unfree African labor. Some traders did not fulfill their contractual obligations for one reason or another. Slave deliveries were often delayed, and Africans never arrived in adequate numbers to meet the demand.

In spite of the bureaucratic and other problems that the licensing system produced, it was not replaced until 1595. In that year, the Spanish Crown introduced a monopoly system known as the *Asiento,* or "contract." Under this system, a trader or a trading company was granted the sole right to supply a given number of slaves, usually several thousand each year, to the colonies for a specified number of years. These contracts were awarded only after the Crown received bids from prospective traders. The traders who were chosen had to pay a sizeable fee when they received the contract.

Most, if not all, of these traders failed to meet the terms of their agreements. Some ran into financial difficulties, and others were more interested in engaging in other forms of commerce, such as trading in silver and other precious metals or in textiles. The failure of the *Asentistas* to meet their contractual obligations paved the way for other traders to smuggle slaves into the colonies. The smugglers were likely to be Portuguese, Spanish, Dutch, or English traders.

The business of the Atlantic slave trade was helped by the existence of slavery and a slave trade inside Africa. As was the case with various societies in Asia, Europe, and the Americas, forms of servitude existed among African ethnic groups. Captives taken in war, debtors, and persons convicted of certain crimes, such as homicides, could lose their liberty. These people still had some rights, however. They could marry, inherit property, and participate extensively in the life of the host society. Over time, most slaves could expect to receive their freedom. The pace at which this occurred must have varied, but the expectation that freedom was within reach probably made their condition more endurable.

Still, the Atlantic slave trade did not develop *because* slavery already existed in Africa. Such a claim would place the primary responsibility for the human traffic on the shoulders of the African peoples. The European and American traders joined hands with their African counterparts to conduct a mutually beneficial

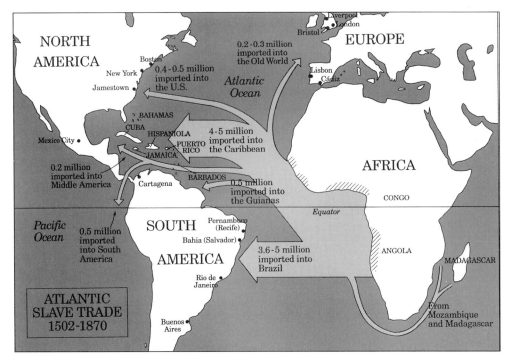

This map shows where African slaves were shipped during the Atlantic slave trade. Between 10 and 12 million African slaves were imported into the Americas.

commerce. It was a trade like any other, bound by the rules of supply and demand, profit and loss. But the slave trade differed from other forms of business in one important respect: the trading goods were other human beings. It is this crucial difference that explains the horror of the slave trade and the moral revulsion that it would later produce.

The rules governing the slave trade took their distinctive shape during the second half of the fifteenth century. Once the external demand for African workers began to increase, the process by which they were acquired fell under the control of the local traders. Although European traders continued to abduct unsuspecting Africans, the number of such raids diminished. The African leaders and their peoples had to assert control over what was taking place in their territory and could not allow foreigners to kidnap their citizens at will. Such atrocities undermined the stability of the society and constituted an assault on the people. The African rulers also realized that if the developing trade were organized and regulated, they could make money from it. Among other things, a tax was imposed on the sale of each slave.

Portuguese traders obtained their slave cargoes for the Americas from West Africa as well as from the Congo and Angola, which are located in West Central Africa. Until about 1600, the majority of the slaves came from West Africa, from a vast area north of the equator. This region includes modern Senegal, Gambia, Guinea-Bissau, and Sierra Leone. The ethnic groups that made up these slave cargoes included the Wolof and the Serer from Senegal; the Mandinka from the Gambia; the Bram, Banyun, and Biafada from Guinea-Bissau. The Baga, Temne, and Landuma peoples came from Sierra Leone. The Congo-Angola region provided the Bakongo, Teke, and Ambundu peoples. Probably about one-third of the slaves originated in the Congo-Angola region, and about twenty-five percent each came from the Senegambia and Guinea-Bissau.

The sources for the supply of slaves kept shifting throughout the entire history of the African slave trade. Much depended on political developments in the various societies. Whenever states were at war, and if these wars continued for long periods of time, the captives would be made available for sale to European traders. Such was the case of the states in the Senegambia in the sixteenth century and of the kingdom of Kongo during the same period. Angola increasingly became the chief source of slaves as the sixteenth century progressed. This was the result of the political disorder that wracked the various states in the area. By 1600, slave cargoes also included the Akan from the Gold Coast (modern Ghana), the Fon from coastal Dahomey, and the Ibo from eastern Nigeria. A few persons also came from southeastern Africa, principally from Mozambique. Overall, West Central Africa supplied about forty percent of the slaves between the sixteenth and nineteenth centuries.

The political divisions among the African peoples largely account for the availability of slaves for the Atlantic market. Africa has never been a politically united continent whose peoples had a common identity and consciousness—either during the sixteenth century, or at any time during the course of the slave trade, or later. Hardly anyone would have described himself or herself as an "African." Residents of the continent were more likely to think of themselves as belonging to specific ethnic groups, such as the Ibo, Biafada, Bram, or Mandinka. The concept of an African identity above and beyond ethnic and geographic boundaries is a relatively recent development.

West and West Central Africa, from which most of the captives were taken, consisted of a large number of states. Some of these were relatively small, while others, such as the kingdom of Kongo and the Jolof Empire in the Senegambia, were very large and included various mini-states that they had absorbed. These states frequently had disputes that led to warfare. In some cases, larger and more powerful states attempted to overrun their smaller neighbors. These instances of territorial expansion often led to prolonged conflicts and the taking of prisoners. Other conflicts between states arose from commercial rivalries, struggles to control trade routes, and even efforts to determine who would succeed to the leadership of bordering states. The political fragmentation of the different regions, coupled with the varieties of conflicts that led to war, created a constant flow of human victims for the trade.

The vast majority of the slaves were prisoners of war. The seller and the victim usually belonged to different states and were enemies. Accordingly, Africans did not "sell their own people," as some historians have maintained. Such a claim ignores the culturally and politically diverse nature of the regions from which the slaves came as well as the diversity of the African continent as a whole. The overwhelming majority—perhaps eighty percent—of the victims of the human traffic were likely to be persons who had no ties to the state of their sellers, had no rights, and were vulnerable to the traditional fate of wartime prisoners—imprisonment, enslavement, or death.

Little is known about the process by which the slaves were traded during the early years. (Information is much more readily available for the years after 1650.) Still, it is known that the European traders exchanged textile products, guns, gunpowder, alcohol, pots and pans, and a range of other consumer goods for the slaves. The value of each slave was arrived at after much bargaining between the black and the white traders. The process evidently became more complicated in the seventeenth century, when more Europeans entered the trade, bringing a wider variety of products with values expressed in their own currency. Thus, in addition to the Portuguese escudo, the Africans had to get accustomed to the English pound sterling, the Dutch guilder, and the French franc. The Africans, too, had different monetary systems. There was the iron bar in Sierra Leone, gold in Ghana, cowrie shells in Dahomey, and Loango cloth in Angola.

Once the African was sold, he or she was usually branded with the identification mark of the purchaser. Whether this was a regular practice in the early years is uncertain, but it would become so in the seventeenth century and later. A slave who was branded could be identified in the event of escape or if the individual were stolen by a European competitor. There was, understandably, not much honor in the slave-trading business.

The slaves' journey to the coast and to the waiting ships could be quite hazardous. Prodded by their captors, some perished along the way as a consequence of disease and wounds infected by branding. Death was an ever-present feature of the trade. Many more would die as they awaited departure on the coast for the Americas, and others would succumb during the Atlantic crossing.

The length of time that the human cargoes waited in the forts on the coast prior to their departure for the Americas varied. Much depended on the supply of slaves to be purchased. This, in turn, was related to whether the states were at war, which would generate captives who could be sold. Once the traders had acquired their full cargo, the long and terrible journey to the Americas began.

The journey from Africa to the Americas was known as the middle passage. It derived its name from the second, or middle, segment of a European-based slave ship's triangular route. The first leg was the trip from Europe to Africa, and the third was the ship's return journey from the Americas to Europe. The middle passage, however, remains the most horrible symbol of the traffic in human beings. Chained together and confined to the cramped, hot, and humid holds of the ships, these Africans were lucky if they survived the ordeal. The sanitary conditions aboard these slave ships were appalling, producing the perfect environment for the spread of disease. Some slaves were already ill before they embarked, and others were tormented by disease on board the ship. Dysentery, measles, smallpox, yellow fever, dehydration, and a variety of "fevers" proved to be the scourge of every journey.

It was, of course, impossible to predict how many slaves would die during the crossing. The *Asiento* contracts that the Spaniards awarded usually made allowances for a death rate of between ten percent and forty percent on each cargo. But it is not entirely clear whether this was an accurate estimate for the sixteenth century.

The death rate not only reflected the sanitary conditions aboard the ships, but it was also related to the general health of the slaves before the journey began. Chance, or luck, played a part as well. If there was no one on board who carried an infectious disease, such as smallpox, the cargo would most likely experience a lower than average death rate.

There was also a relationship between the time the ship took to cross the Atlantic and the death toll. The faster the sailing time, the lower the death rate. During the sixteenth century it took anywhere from twelve to twenty weeks to reach the American ports. Such a long confinement at sea in close quarters aided the spread of disease. With the construction of faster ships in the eighteenth and nineteenth centuries, the sailing time ranged between five and eight weeks. The average death rate in the eighteenth century was between ten percent and fifteen percent; by the nineteenth century it had fallen to somewhere between five percent and ten percent. Sanitary conditions had improved aboard the ships, and better medical care was provided.

Thoughtful captains took care to provide their human cargoes with a diet consisting of the foods to which they were accustomed. The composition of these foods varied, depending on the part of Africa from which the slaves came. In general, however, such foods included corn, yams, palm oil, rice, and potatoes. Slave ships also stocked foodstuffs that they brought from Europe, such as bread, cheese, beef, beans, and flour. However, these supplies sometimes proved inadequate to feed a cargo of slaves, particularly if the journey to the Americas lasted longer than had been expected. Reports from the eighteenth century and later described voyages that ran out of food and slaves who arrived thin and hungry.

The slaves must have engaged in forms of resistance on board ships during this early period, but the surviving records shed no light on this issue. Ships did, however, carry a variety of gadgets—such as mouth openers, thumb screws, chains, and whips—to punish those who resisted their condition. During the eighteenth and nineteenth centuries slaves participated in rebellions and hunger strikes, jumped overboard, and verbally abused the crew. Such physical challenges to slavery on the high seas were seldom successful, but they often resulted in considerable loss of life.

The arrival of the slaves in such places as Hispaniola, Lima, and Vera Cruz signaled the end of one awful experience and the beginning of another. The Africans were purchased yet again and became the property of strange people in a strange land. Their prospects of returning to their homeland were virtually nonexistent. Their ties with their kith and kin were severed forever, and their sense of alienation in their new lands must have been paralyzing.

Where did the slaves who arrived in the Americas go? The vast majority, approximately ninety-five percent, were distributed to the societies of Latin America and the Caribbean. Only about five percent ended up in the British colonies of North America, or what is now the United States. The following figures are a reasonably accurate accounting of the distribution patterns of the trade based upon present knowledge:

British North America	550,000
Spanish America	2,000,000
British Caribbean	2,500,000 to 3,000,000
French Caribbean	1,600,000
Dutch Caribbean	50,000
Brazil	4,000,000 to 5,000,000
Danish Caribbean	50,000

Almost all of the slaveholding societies of the Americas experienced an annual decrease in population as the Africans fell victim to hard work and disease. As a result, they had to depend on the slave trade to replenish their labor supply. The only exception to this pattern was English North America. By the first decades of the eighteenth century, the North American slave population began to reproduce itself, and it sustained this growth until emancipation came in the 1860s. For this reason, North America was much less dependent on the slave trade than the other slave societies of the Americas, which had a profound influence on the culture of the black population in this region. The North American slave population by the nineteenth century was essentially a creole, or locally born, population. Although only about 500,000 Africans had been imported into that society, the slave population numbered almost four million in 1860, just before the outbreak of the Civil War.

The Worlds of Slavery and Work

African slaves were first brought to the Americas in the sixteenth century to meet the economic needs of Spanish and Portuguese colonists. The first slaves arrived in Hispaniola in 1502; thousands more would experience a similar fate as the century progressed. From Hispaniola the institution of slavery spread to the other islands in the Caribbean that were colonized by the Spaniards—Puerto Rico, Cuba, and Jamaica. Eventually, such mainland colonies as Mexico, Peru, Venezuela, Bolivia, and those in Central America became the new homes of thousands of unfree African workers. Brazil, a Portuguese colony, was no exception; by 1600 it joined Mexico and Peru as one of the three largest slaveholding societies.

The Spaniards and the Portuguese were not the only slaveholders in the Americas. In time, African slaves were used in all of the European colonies. By 1650, for example, the English had begun to use enslaved Africans in their Caribbean and North American colonies. The Dutch, the French, and the Danes would soon do likewise. So great was the demand for African labor that an average of 60,000 slaves were imported annually during the eighteenth century.

Of the 300,000 Africans who arrived before 1620, the greatest number, probably around 80,000, went to Mexico. This colony received most of its slaves after 1570, when the Indian population began a rapid decline. Once the local population began to recover in the mid seventeenth century and a racially mixed group emerged (mestizos, the children of Spaniards and Indians), fewer Africans were imported. The other mainland colonies and the Caribbean islands received another eighty thousand to ninety thousand slaves before 1620. Portuguese Brazil did not begin to import Africans until the mid sixteenth century, but it received an ever-increasing number throughout the rest of that century and in succeeding years. By 1620 that colony had imported an estimated 130,000 slaves.

Regardless of where the slaves went, the colonial authorities introduced laws that defined their status and regulated their behavior. Because the Spaniards and the Portuguese owned slaves before they came to the Americas, they had already developed rules governing their behavior, rights, and treatment. The Spanish slave laws were a part of a larger body of laws and moral principles that formed the basis of the Spanish legal system. Known as *Las Siete Partidas* (the Seven Parts), these laws granted slaves the right to marry, inherit property, and to be freed under certain conditions. The *Partidas* imposed limits on the masters' ability to mistreat their slaves, and slaves could appeal to the local authorities if their rights were violated. It is not known whether the law was always enforced.

The situation in Portugal, at least in theory, was somewhat different. At the time when Brazil was colonized in the sixteenth century, the mother country did not have a body of laws similar to the *Siete Partidas*. Rather, each town had its own rules, and there does not appear to have been much uniformity in content or enforcement. Accordingly, the Crown filled the breach by issuing appropriate laws when the need arose. The English, French, and Dutch had no preexisting law of slavery. As a result, these nations developed their colonial slave laws in a piecemeal fashion, as the need arose.

The slave laws that the Spanish colonists introduced in the sixteenth century in Hispaniola, Mexico, Peru, and elsewhere shared many features. In general, these laws were much harsher than those existing in Spain. Outnumbered by a servile population of Indians and Africans in the sixteenth century, the colonists tried to impose rigid controls over those whom they exploited and enslaved. Essentially, the laws were designed to protect the slaveholding class from the angry reprisals of their human property.

The earliest legislation concerning black slaves that the colonial governments introduced prohibited them from owning or carrying weapons. In Mexico, for example, such laws were placed on the books at various times beginning in 1537. Peru issued its first series of restrictive measures in 1545 and repeated the measures in succeeding years to ensure enforcement. Such restrictive legislation also established the punishment for assaulting whites. According to a 1552 law, slaves who took up arms against a Spaniard in Mexico were liable to receive one hundred lashes in addition to having a nail driven through their hands. Slaves would have their hands cut off if they repeated the offense.

As the slave populations increased, colonial authorities imposed a series of controls on almost every aspect of the Africans' public lives. Although the details varied, slaves were forbidden to be out of doors after dark, and could not travel freely or gather in large groups except for religious purposes. Insecure masters wanted to take no chances; they had to ensure that their human property lacked the opportunity or the means to launch movements to claim their freedom. But such restrictions did not always have the desired results.

Although the slave owners and other whites feared black slaves, colonial society increasingly became dependent on them for a variety of services. As soon as blacks began to arrive in the colonies, the Spaniards used them to help subjugate the native peoples and to explore for new territories to seize. Hernan Cortés, who defeated the Aztecs, is said to have had three hundred African slaves with him in Mexico in 1522. African slaves accompanied the Spaniards on their various military invasions of Peru beginning in 1524. A number of them participated in explorations into Chile and other areas on the coast and in the interior. A black man was among the four Spanish soldiers chosen by the Spanish conquistador Francisco Pizarro to be in the advance party to survey the Inca capital at Cuzco, Peru. Slaves also participated in the Spanish military expeditions against the Indians in Honduras in the 1550s.

The role of blacks in such military expeditions, however, paled in comparison to their sustained importance as workers. As soon as they began to arrive in Hispaniola in 1502, slaves assumed the most strenuous tasks, setting a precedent for other slaveholding societies. The colonists in these early years were particularly interested in mining for precious metals and constantly appealed for black slaves. The Crown was willing to agree because it received a one-fifth share of the proceeds of the mines. In 1505, for example, King Ferdinand informed the governor of Hispaniola that "I will send more Negro slaves as you request. I think there may be a hundred. At each time a trustworthy person will go with them who may share in the gold they may collect."

Without a doubt, black slaves played the most important roles in the mining industry during the sixteenth century. Mining was a particularly hazardous activity, and the death rate of those involved in it tended to be quite high. The Indian workers died quickly, and the Spaniards as a group did not find the occupation attractive. African slaves were imported as substitutes, and they, too, suffered a high death rate.

The Africans were used first in the copper and gold mines of Hispaniola, but these metals were not abundant there. The industry soon collapsed. On the other hand, the mainland colonies of Mexico and Peru were extremely rich in silver deposits. By 1550 the colonists had found silver in northern Mexico at Zacatecas, Guanajuato, and Pachuca. Deposits of silver were also uncovered at Michoacan, Tasco, Temascaltepec, and other places. In Peru, silver veins were struck in the highland areas of Potosí and Porco, and rich gold deposits were discovered at Chachapoyas and Carabaya.

Shortly after the discovery of the first silver veins in Mexico, Viceroy Antonio de Mendoza requested that the authorities in Spain send Africans because "the silver mines are increasing, as each day more and more are discovered while the [Indian] slaves continue to decrease." A sympathetic Crown responded favorably to these pleas, but the supply of Africans could not keep abreast of the demand for them in the mines and other economic enterprises. The high death rate of the Africans and Indians employed in the mining industry from accidents (such as collapsing underground roofs) and lung diseases also made the labor problem more severe.

Some of those who advocated the importation of Africans wanted to relieve the Indians of the burdensome labor of the mines. Another Mexican viceroy, the Marques de Villamanrique, was one such person. In 1586, for example, he noted the "dangerous" and "excessive" nature of the work in which the Indians were engaged in the mines. In order to protect them from such exploitation he asked that three thousand or four thousand Africans be sent. Four years later, in an attempt to increase the servile labor force, the viceroy recommended that all free blacks and mulattoes (children of Spaniards and blacks) in the colony be forced to labor in the mines. Not only would they serve as a substitute for Indian workers, the viceroy reasoned, but they would also earn wages and "their children growing up in that life would become fond of it."

Black slaves also played critically important roles in the textile factories of Mexico and, to a lesser extent, Peru. These workshops, known as *obrajes,* manufactured cloth for the residents of the colonies. The workers in these factories were often physically abused and forced to labor for long hours in cramped, hot, and humid quarters. The Crown was concerned about the poor working conditions in these hell houses and wanted to protect the Indians in Mexico from being employed in them. In 1601 the Crown prohibited Indian workers from laboring in the Mexican *obrajes* and repeated the ban in 1609, probably because it was not being enforced. In both instances, the Crown decreed that black slaves should replace the Indians. Clearly, the Crown saw black workers as suited for the most difficult tasks in society and seemed unconcerned about the inhumane conditions under which they worked. There was nothing particularly new about this attitude; black workers in Spain had experienced a similar fate.

As soon as it became clear that the early mining economy in the islands would collapse because of the depletion of the mineral resources, the Spanish colonists embraced other pursuits. The climate and soil of the Caribbean proved ideal for sugarcane cultivation, and in 1506 the colonists in Hispaniola began to experiment with growing that crop. The Spaniards and the Portuguese had been familiar with sugarcane cultivation for centuries before the Columbus voyages. By the mid fifteenth century, the Portuguese had begun to use African slaves on their sugarcane plantations in the Atlantic islands of Madeira, São Tomé, the Azores, the Canaries, and Cape Verde. Africans who were experienced in the techniques of sugarcane cultivation and the sugar industry must have comprised some of the slave cargoes to the Americas.

The first sugar mill (*ingenio*) in the Caribbean was constructed in Hispaniola in 1516, and by 1548 the island had thirty-five of them, the most that would exist there at any one time in the sixteenth century. Sugarcane cultivation also spread to the other islands of Puerto Rico, Jamaica, and Cuba. Although Hispaniola began to export sugar in 1521, the sugar industry did not flourish anywhere in the Caribbean in the sixteenth century. Not until after 1650 did sugar become "king" in the islands, particularly in the English, Dutch, and French colonies.

Sugarcane cultivation, aided by the extensive use of African slave labor, underwent its greatest expansion on the mainland during the sixteenth century. Mexico and Brazil became particularly important as sugar-producing colonies, but cane was also cultivated in Peru, Venezuela, and elsewhere. Because the Portuguese dominated the slave trade, Brazil received an ever-expanding supply of African labor. By 1580, this colony not only boasted a large black population but was the principal supplier of sugar to European markets.

Mexico was the earliest of the mainland colonies to grow sugarcane. Because of their agreeable climates, the tropical areas surrounding Vera Cruz and the warm valleys of Michoacan, Huatusco, Córdoba, and Oaxaca quickly became major centers of sugarcane cultivation. Historians are not certain when the colonists first started to grow the cane; contemporary sources indicate that it began between 1524 and 1530. African slaves seemed to have been used in the industry from the outset.

Sugarcane plantations in sixteenth-century Mexico were of various sizes, depending on the availability of capital, land, and labor. There were some extremely large ones by the last decades of the sixteenth century, employing scores of African

This seventeenth-century French engraving shows slaves laboring at an outdoor sugar mill in the Caribbean. Most sugar mills were actually inside buildings.

workers. In 1580, a plantation at Orizaba reported the presence of 123 African slaves, and in 1606 the Santísima Trinidad plantation in Jalapa had two hundred. Most plantations probably employed fewer Africans, and almost all appear to have had Indian workers as well.

The Crown did not take kindly to the use of Indians on the sugar plantations. The work was demanding, and it was believed that the native peoples lacked the physical strength to do the work. In fact, Spanish colonists on the mainland and in the Caribbean islands believed that one African could do the work of four Indians. This kind of mythology ensured that blacks would not only be in great demand but would be assigned the most strenuous tasks.

Work on the sugar plantations in Mexico and elsewhere extracted a heavy toll from the Africans. At the Xochimaneas hacienda in southern Mexico, owned by the Society of Jesus,

> slaves were generally awakened at four in the morning and worked until ten
> or eleven o'clock at night. Upon arising, the slaves went to the sugar mill
> where they ground eight, nine, or ten caldrons of sugar "depending on the

cane and the season." At daybreak the sound of a bell summoned the slaves to take the sugar from the boiling house (casa de calderas) to the refinery (casa de purgar) and to put the "white sugar" in the sun to be dried. When there was no sugar to be sunned, the slaves occupied themselves with other tasks. When this work was completed, they returned to their homes for breakfast and to ready themselves for the fields.

Accidents occurred in the *ingenios* and the overall death rate in the sugar plantations seemed to have been as high as that in the mines, if not higher. The Mexican viceroy confessed in 1599 that African slaves who worked in the sugar industry had a death rate in excess of "that in any other kind of work."

As in Mexico, the cultivation of the sugarcane began in Brazil shortly after the Europeans settled there. The exact date is uncertain, but it may have started as early as 1516. There is some evidence that Brazilian sugar was being exported to Europe in 1519. By the 1540s sugar plantations existed all along the coastal area extending from Pernambuco in the north to São Vicente in the south. Pernambuco would become the most important sugar-producing area in the colony by the 1580s, and by 1600 it had two hundred sugar mills. In fact, by the beginning of the seventeenth century, Pernambuco produced more sugar than any other place in the world.

African slaves played an important role in the latter part of the sixteenth century in Pernambuco's (and Brazil's) rise to prominence in the sugar industry. It is believed that Africans first came to Brazil with the Portuguese explorer Pedro Álvares Cabral in 1500. Brazil was sparsely populated by the native peoples, and it did not, at first, appear very attractive to the Portuguese as a place to settle and accumulate wealth. A few colonists trickled in after 1500, some bringing one or two African slaves, mostly domestic servants and artisans. Not until 1539 did the Crown receive a request from a colonist for permission to import Africans to work on his sugar plantation.

The Crown did not approve Duarte Coelhós's request, and he repeated it in 1542. This time, the colonist emphasized that the success of the sugar industry depended upon black labor. Up until that point, and for the next four or five decades, Indians provided most of the labor services on the sugar plantations. But the colonists would, at various times, press their argument that Africans were superior and hardier workers.

The first groups of slaves to arrive in Brazil directly from Africa, as opposed to being sent from Portugal, arrived at the city of Salvador in 1550. This was a momentous development, because it was the start of a formal slave trade between Brazil and Africa that would last for the next three hundred years. In response to the increasing demand for African workers as a result of the expansion of the sugar industry, the Crown issued a decree in 1559 allowing the owners of sugar plantations to import a maximum of 120 slaves for each sugar mill that they owned.

This *Alvará,* or decree, gave a tremendous boost to the slave trade. Accurate records are lacking, but it is clear that Portuguese traders responded to this demand for Africans with considerable vigor. In time, African workers would replace the Indians on the plantations, and Brazil's human and cultural landscape would be irreversibly transformed. It has been estimated that after about 1580 between 10,000 and 15,000 slaves landed in Brazil annually. Most were destined to serve on the sugar plantations, and most would come from Angola. The lot of the African on a Brazilian sugar plantation in the sixteenth century and later was a difficult one. With extremely hard work, long working hours, inadequate diet, and exposure to debilitating diseases, slaves faced an early death.

The work in the mines, *obrajes,* and sugar plantations must rank as the most demanding of the tasks that slaves had to perform in the sixteenth century and later. Their death rates were higher than those of slaves engaged in other tasks. This was a consequence of the terrible working conditions that prevailed in them. The sugar, mining, and textile industries were capitalist enterprises that were driven by the profit motive. Each used a combination of free and slave labor, and each depended on a great deal of labor and capital for its survival. Each was a form of industrial slavery. These enterprises, because of the need for profits, drove the slaves to their maximum, extracting as much labor from them as possible. Poorly fed and overworked, these human machines were wracked by ill health and suffered an early death.

Slaves who were used in the pearl-fishing business also faced an early death as a result of the hazardous nature of their work. They seemed to have been assigned this task in all of the coastal areas where the waters were considered particularly rich in pearls. But the divers frequently ran the risk of drowning or colliding with underwater objects. An order issued by the authorities in Vera Cruz, Mexico, in the 1550s unwittingly shows the relationship between pearl fishing and the incidence of death by drowning. The order was designed to clear the waters of sharks, not to protect the slaves. It noted that "because the bodies of drowned Negroes have not been removed from [the waters of] oyster fisheries, many sharks are present and haunt the places with grave danger to life." Given the risks involved, the colonial authorities sought to prevent Indians from pearl fishing for the colonists. In 1572, for example, Indians were forbidden to dive for pearls off the Venezuelan coast. Statistics are not available for the sixteenth century on the number of Africans who died while engaged in pearl fishing, but its dangerous nature was widely recognized.

African slaves were also used extensively as artisans. Many were already skilled in metalworking, cloth making, leatherwork, arts and crafts, and carpentry, to name a few skills, before they were brought to the Americas. Some acquired specialized skills in the Americas by virtue of the tasks that they were assigned. The *maestro de azucar* (sugar master) was one of the most highly respected slaves because he was in charge of processing the cane in the *ingenios*. Such skilled workers determined the success or failure of the sugarmaking industry.

Not all colonists, whether in Brazil or Spanish America, welcomed the participation of African slaves—or even free persons—in the skilled trades. They feared that the competition from slave labor would lower the wages that they received. In addition, skilled whites wanted to confine blacks to manual labor, believing that the prestige of their trades would be lessened if they were open to slaves. As a result, several guilds that licensed tradesmen or provided specialized training excluded blacks from membership. Those that admitted blacks frequently confined them to the rank of journeyman, denying them the privilege of becoming masters.

Still, colonists who were hard-pressed for skilled labor used their slaves in a variety of capacities. Black carpenters, for example, were used extensively in the construction industry. They helped build houses, churches, monasteries, hospitals, bridges, shops, and public buildings. Others served as bricklayers, plasterers, and blacksmiths. African slaves engaged in iron working, made hats, baked bread, and sewed clothes, in addition to other skilled tasks. The image of Africans confined exclusively to field work, mining, or household chores is not accurate for the sixteenth or for any other century. During the sixteenth century most skilled slaves appear to have been located primarily in urban areas, such as Santo Domingo, Mexico City, Lima, and Salvador. Most of the European colonists were also urban residents, and they were the ones who depended on the specialized skills of the free and unfree African labor force. Black slaves and free persons were also used significantly in their households. Domestic workers, who were chiefly women, cooked, washed, cleaned, and cared for the children. Some scholars maintain that slaves in the urban areas had an easier life than those in the rural areas, particularly in the case of those who were engaged in sugar cultivation or mining.

Not all slaves in the rural areas were agricultural workers, although most of them were during the sixteenth century and later. In Hispaniola, Cuba, and Jamaica, blacks helped to grow the foods, such as maize and plantains, that sustained the islands' populations. They were also engaged in cultivating ginger on the three islands, but chiefly in Hispaniola.

There was also much diversity in the agricultural activities of the slaves on the mainland. In Mexico, for example, slaves were engaged in the cultivation of the cocoa bean in Colima, Oaxaca, and Huatulco. Others grew crops on haciendas everywhere. In Peru, slaves worked in the vineyards in the south; others grew wheat, olives, and other foodstuffs. The colonists in Venezuela used their African labor to produce cacao, cotton, vegetables, and other provisions. Most Brazilian slaves were involved in the sugar industry during the period, but some must have cultivated the crops that would feed them.

Rural slaves everywhere had to engage in pastoral activities, usually tending sheep and cattle. By 1550, the colonists in the Caribbean islands had developed a vibrant grazing economy. In Hispaniola, some families owned as many as thirty thousand head of cattle by the 1540s. Slaves also worked on Mexican ranches during the sixteenth century, although they were not as numerous as the free workers. Slaves seem to have been more important in Peru and may even have constituted the majority of the herdsmen on some of the larger ranches. Ranching may have afforded the slaves a greater degree of control over their lives than some of the other occupations. Charged with tending livestock over huge areas of land, the slaves were quite likely free from the constant supervision of their owners.

Because slaves were expensive property, most colonists lacked the resources to purchase them. But they still needed the services of additional hands from time to time. In order to supply such colonists with the labor that they wanted, the practice of hiring out slaves developed in the sixteenth century. Those who needed slave labor contracted with the owners to use their human property for a fixed period of time and for a determined rental fee. As property, slaves probably had no choice in the matter; they had to go where they were sent and to work for whoever hired them. Some people bought Africans for the sole purpose of renting them to others.

It appears that the slave owners in Spanish and Portuguese America assigned tasks in accordance with the gender of the workers. Males were more likely to be employed in the mining industry, in the *ingenios,* and as artisans and pearl fishers. Women were used primarily as domestics and performed the same duties as the men on the plantations. There is also some suspicion that women formed the majority of the labor force in the textile factories. Because the majority of the slaves in the early period were males, women appear less frequently in the records.

Africans, both men and women, played a crucial role in building the economies of the Americas in the sixteenth century. They endured the terrible conditions of the *obrajes,* the heat of the *ingenios,* and the physical hazards of the mines. Many engaged in the skilled trades and planted the food that would help feed the society as a whole. The sugar that they manufactured and the silver and other metals that they mined would cross the ocean to Europe with profound consequences for the diets and economies of the importing countries. The African presence would continue to grow in these societies in succeeding centuries. But the sixteenth-century pioneers laid the foundations of the new societies then in formation. Africans were present at the birth of the Americas as we know them today, not as colonizers but as the coerced hewers of wood and drawers of water.

Slave Society and Culture

European colonists in every part of the Americas came to depend on the labor of Indians and Africans in the sixteenth century. The Indians were enslaved as soon as the Spaniards established effective control of the Caribbean islands. When Mexico, Peru, and other areas fell under Spanish control, the colonists converted the Indians on the mainland into a servile labor force. The Portuguese would do the same once they settled Brazil. In effect, the European outsiders became the ruling elite in these societies, imposing their will on the original residents and taking their land in the process. Not all of the Indians were enslaved, however. Some simply lived beyond the reach of the colonists and refused to submit to them, and in Mexico and Peru, at least in the immediate aftermath of the colonial occupation, the sheer size of the Indian population made complete control by the European conquerors impossible.

Slavery was only one of the labor systems that the Europeans employed. The Spaniards also introduced the *encomienda*. Under this system, a number of Indians were assigned by colonial authorities to work for the Spaniards without receiving wages. In return, the colonists were expected to teach the workers Spanish customs, language, and religion. These Indians were not slaves because they were not owned; the Spaniards had access only to their labor, and the condition was not hereditary. But in time, the colonists began to treat these Indians as if they were slaves, abusing them and denying them basic rights.

Faced with mounting criticism of Indian slavery and the *encomienda* system from humanitarians, the Spanish Crown abolished both in 1542. They were replaced with a system that rotated Indian workers among the Spanish colonists who needed their labor. Workers would be assigned to employers for a specified period of time, for designated tasks, and for a wage. Once the time had expired and the duties had been completed, the Indians could be allocated to other colonists. This system was called the *repartimiento* (or *mita* in Peru). It, too, proved to be an unsatisfactory response to the labor problem. Workers were often not paid, and some were held by the colonists longer than they were supposed to work.

The *repartimiento* system all but disappeared by the seventeenth century. In some societies, a system of debt passage emerged. Under this system, Indian workers borrowed money from their employers to purchase necessities but could not leave their job until the debt was repaid. Many people fell further and further behind because their wages were so low. Because these debts were considered hereditary, generations of Indian workers were tied to the colonists and had no option but to work for them. Not all labor services in the Spanish empire were coerced, however. Wage labor existed alongside the various unfree systems.

Like the Spanish, the Portuguese in Brazil also enslaved the Indian peoples who fell under their control. Portuguese colonists received grants of land from the Crown, under which they could enslave the Indians who resided on them. Other Indians were simply pursued, captured, and enslaved. Before 1600 almost no one doubted the right of the Portuguese colonists to treat the native peoples in this fashion. With the Indian population diminishing and the sugar industry expanding in the second half of the sixteenth century, Africans would come to form the dominant group of exploited workers by 1600.

Thus, Africans were not the only peoples whom the Europeans would enslave or exploit in one fashion or another. But they were the only peoples imported as permanent, unfree laborers. The sixteenth century was a particularly ugly one in the Americas. It saw the military defeat of the Indian peoples, their colonization, the astounding decline in their number, the introduction of oppressive labor systems, and the start of African slavery. It was a century of chaos, disaster, and crises for the native peoples. For the Africans, it was the beginning of an awful odyssey in these societies. Arriving as involuntary workers, African slaves confronted the challenge of helping to build societies in which they were, and would continue to be, persons with few if any rights. They also had to struggle to maintain, as best they could, a measure of human dignity, and to develop the social institutions that would sustain them.

African slaves occupied the lowest rank in the social order of the colonial societies. Imported as human property, their sole function was to work for those who had purchased them. Though the colonists valued Africans for the agricultural and craft skills that they possessed, they were nevertheless considered of "bad race" and "bad caste" by those who had come to depend on their labor. Such unflattering descriptions originated in Europe, but they assumed an added intensity and strength in the Americas as slavery expanded.

The European colonists also embraced negative images of the Indians whom they encountered. There was no inclination to see them as equals and to treat them accordingly. In fact, there was some doubt among the Spanish colonists whether the Indians were rational beings. But the pope resolved these doubts in 1537 by declaring that "the Indians are truly men."

The papal pronouncement did not lead to an end to the mistreatment of the Indians, nor did it mean that the colonists embraced them as equals. Driven by the desire to acquire wealth, the colonists wanted only to be left alone to exploit the native peoples. Still, there were some voices raised to denounce the colonists for their behavior. Chief among them was Bishop Bartolomé de las Casas, a member of the Dominican religious order who became enraged at Spanish cruelty toward the Indians. He was not the first, however, to publicly chastise his fellow Spaniards. That honor fell to Friar Antonio de Montesinos. In 1511, he denounced the mistreatment of the Indians in Hispaniola and questioned the moral basis for their inhumane treatment.

Although the Crown introduced measures to protect the Indians, or at least reduce the level of their mistreatment, these laws were never adequately enforced. Las Casas never lost his concern for the plight of the Indian peoples and kept up an active campaign to promote their rights and reduce the degree of their exploitation. He debated one of the foremost proponents of the view that the Spaniards were superior to the Indians and were entitled to exercise control over them. This important debate was held in Valladolid, Spain, beginning in late 1550. Juan Ginés de Sepúlveda, a noted scholar, was Las Casas's opponent. The two men debated

Bartolomé de las Casas, who appears as the savior of the Indians in this heroic depiction, argued that Indians were not inferior to Spaniards.

before a panel of judges and addressed the question, "What rights do the Indians have and what are the obligations of the Spaniards to them?"

A fervent admirer of the Indians, Las Casas argued that the Indians were not inferior to the Spaniards in any way. He maintained that they were "prudent and rational beings, of as good ability and judgment as other men and more able, discreet, and of better understanding than the peoples of many other nations." He believed that the Spaniards should do their own work and cease their exploitation of the Indians. Sepúlveda, on the other hand, was certain that the Spaniards were superior to the Indian peoples. The Indians lacked the capacity, he argued, to attain the level of development that the Spaniards had reached. They should be forced to work for the Spaniards and, in time, they would acquire some of the customs and habits of their superiors.

We do not know who won the debate, but the Spanish Crown seemed to have been more influenced by Las Casas's arguments. Subsequent laws were more respectful of the rights of the Indians and often limited the power of the colonists over them. Yet such laws were often not enforced, and the colonists still abused the Indians. There was a considerable difference between what the law said and how it was applied.

The debate at Valladolid and the spirit of the Spanish legislation concerning Indians underscores the fact that there was no similar concern shown by Spanish officials toward the fate of the Africans. The Indians were new peoples to the Spaniards. Africans, by contrast, had long been familiar to the Spaniards, and their image of Africans had already been framed. Even Las Casas recommended in 1517 that black slaves should be imported to replace Indian workers. He would later renounce this position.

The society that the Spaniards and the Portuguese created in the sixteenth century recognized racial and class distinctions. Everyone knew his or her place in the social order. Whites as a group formed the elite, followed by the mixed peoples—mestizos and mulattoes. Then came the Indians and the Africans. Africans may have been set apart from the other groups because of their status as property and their racial heritage. Colonial society reserved the most difficult and hazardous jobs for Africans, sanctioned the most horrendous forms of punishment for them, and for three hundred years held generations of them as property.

Black slaves consisted of three principal groups, the distinctions based primarily on the place of their birth. First, there were people who were born in Africa but spent time in Europe before they were transported to the Americas. The Spaniards called them *ladinos*. They knew some Spanish and, in varying degrees, were familiar with Spanish culture. The second category consisted of people who were born in Africa and came directly to the Americas. Known as *bozales*, these individuals had little or no familiarity with the ways of the Europeans. As soon as they began to speak the languages of the Europeans and accepted Christianity, they could be called *ladinos*. The third major group of slaves comprised those who were born in the Americas. They were called *criollos* (creoles). Unlike the *bozales,* they were exposed to the cultural influences of the Europeans and other groups, such as Indians and mestizos, from birth. The *bozales* formed the majority of the slave populations once a direct slave trade with Africa was instituted in 1518. Although the *bozales* were called *ladinos* once they became accustomed to the ways of their owners, no one can say how long this process lasted. Some *bozales* probably never became *ladinos.* In any event, *ladinos* probably never lost all of their African heritage, even though they embraced aspects of the way of life in the Americas.

Early records show that the African-born slaves were renamed in the Spanish colonies and elsewhere in the Americas. These persons had no say in the selection of a new name because it was forced upon them by the person who purchased them. In some cases, they may have been renamed by the priest who baptized them. The Africans who were renamed had to begin the difficult process of adjusting to a new identity. Their previous names had deep emotional, cultural, and ceremonial meanings, so the loss of their names must have resulted in much anguish. These Africans probably never abandoned their former names and used them among their friends and peers.

In renaming the Africans, the colonists seemed to have confined their choices to the most popular first names in usage. Thus, males were named Fernando, Juan, Jaime, Ricardo, José, Cristobal, and so on. Women were frequently called Mariá, Catarina, Luisa, Margarita, and Ana, to name just a few. Most slaves were given only one name; only a small minority had a last name, usually that of the person who owned them. In order to make their identification easier, the designation *"criollo," "ladino,"* or *"bozal"* would be listed after the slaves' names on official documents. In other cases, their ethnic or national origin would be added. Thus, official documents would list a slave as María Biafada, Ricardo Congo, or Juan Angola.

The imposition of a new name was just one of the many changes that the Africans had to endure. In order to communicate with their owners, they had to learn Spanish or Portuguese, depending on the colony. Africans spoke many different languages, but some of these languages were similar enough that the speakers could usually understand one another. In the Americas, however, the Africans had to learn the languages of the Europeans, which was the primary means of communication. Some slaves became reasonably fluent in these languages, although they probably spoke their own languages whenever possible. The African languages spoken by the slaves must also have had an impact on Spanish and Portuguese— on the vocabulary, the meanings of words, and the intonation. The slaves must have Africanized these languages, particularly in those colonies, such as Brazil, where they formed a large share of the population.

Torn from their homeland, ethnic group, family, and kin, the Africans experienced a sense of profound shock, loss, and alienation in the Americas. Kinship ties were the core of the societies from which the slaves came. Marriages united not only the husband and the wife but also the lineages to which they belonged. In most instances, the bond between the two lineages was more important than that which existed between the couple. To be without ties of kinship was to be socially dead; an individual could exist meaningfully only as part of a network of blood relationships. The slave trade and slavery destroyed these bonds, and the individual faced the enormous challenge of re-creating them in the Americas.

The task of developing new relationships in the Americas was made more difficult by the very wide geographic distribution of the slaves in the sixteenth century. Few slave owners owned more than two or three Africans, although there would be very large concentrations of them in the mines, *obrajes,* and on the sugar plantations as the century wore on. There were, however, enough Africans living in easy reach of one another in some places so that extensive family relationships were reconstructed by 1580. In addition, strong emotional bonds united the Africans who crossed the Atlantic in the same ship. They had endured terrible times together, and those experiences fostered strong ties among the survivors. These shipboard bonds formed the beginnings of the struggle by the Africans to create relationships among themselves and to replace those that had been severed.

As a rule, the colonial authorities did not oppose formal marriages of their slaves. In fact, the church and the state in Spain's colonies encouraged unions among the population at large, including slaves. The family was seen as the foundation stone of society. In theory, at least, once slaves were married they could not be separated through sale. Slaves whose marriages were broken up by their masters could appeal to the civil or religious authorities for redress.

This did not mean that African slaves waited for the state or the Catholic church to sanction their intimate relationships. Most slaves probably chose their partners whenever and wherever they could and had their own marriage ceremonies in accordance with their own customs and practices. Africans came from societies with complex traditions and rules that governed all aspects of human relationships, including family life, and there is no reason to believe that these were abandoned quickly, if at all, in the Americas. In their choices of marriage partners and in other ways, they responded to universal human tugs and emotions.

Beginning in the sixteenth century there are numerous examples of Africans getting married in Catholic ceremonies. But such marriages probably represented a minority of the unions that the slaves made. Most of them, it can be guessed, did not accept the authority of the church in this matter, because they still maintained their own traditions. Marriages that did not receive the approval of the church were, of course, considered illegal—and therefore nonexistent—by the colonial authorities.

In order to have a marriage sanctioned according to colonial rules, the Africans had to apply for a license. The prospective bride and groom had to appear with two

This document contains an application for marriage by two slaves, whose names are at the top, and a grant of permission by an official (bottom). African slaves had to make such applications to have their marriage recognized by colonial authorities.

witnesses before an official to make the request. They had to declare their ethnic backgrounds, stating whether they were Mandinka, Bram, Biafada, and so on. Creole slaves also had to indicate where they were born. The witnesses had to verify the accuracy of the statements made by the couple, and they also had to state how long and under what circumstances they had known the man and woman. The authorities were not interested in whether the bride and the groom had ever been married in Africa. Such prior unions were never recognized by the church as valid because they had not occurred under Christian authority. The bride and groom had only to establish that they had never been married in the Americas or that they had been widowed.

An analysis of the surviving marriage licenses from Mexico and Peru suggests that Africans tended to marry individuals from the same ethnic group or from the same geographic area. Such a pattern of ethnically based choices should not be particularly surprising. As foreigners in strange lands, these Africans sought to reconstruct and nurture their ethnic ties and heritage. They chose partners with whom they shared a cultural heritage and who had similar life experiences. For the same reasons, creole slaves were also more likely to marry other creoles. Ethnicity, as reflected through marriage choices, remained an important part of the lives of African slaves.

Slave owners were not always respectful of the marriages of the Africans. The unions were sometimes broken up and families separated through sale. The church opposed such atrocities, railing against these practices from time to time but with little effect.

Africans who avoided the Catholic marriage ceremonies simply lived together as man and wife, if the circumstances allowed. The Spanish colonial and religious authorities frowned on this practice, declaring it worthy of punishment. The Holy Office of the Inquisition, an institution created to pursue religious offenders of all sorts, was established in Mexico in 1570. It had been in existence in Spain for a century, and its principal targets included Jews, Muslims, and others accused of a variety of religious crimes. In Mexico, in addition to its customary victims, the Holy Office pursued blacks accused of concubinage (unmarried couples living together), bigamy, witchcraft, sorcery, and other offenses. Individuals convicted of *amancebado* relationships (concubinage) could be flogged, imprisoned, or humiliated in various ways. Bigamists received similar punishments.

By punishing those accused of bigamy and *amancebado* relationships, the Holy Office and other colonial authorities failed to understand the meanings of such behavior for the Africans. The Catholic authorities viewed church-approved marriages as the norm and refused to recognize any other form of marital arrangement as legitimate. Thus Africans who may have had private marriage ceremonies according to their own rules ran the risk of being accused of *amancebado* and punished.

Similarly, the frequency of what the Spaniards called bigamy shows how African cultural traditions endured in the New World. It was the norm in many African societies for one man to have several wives. In others, it was acceptable if the number of women of marriageable age exceeded the number of men. Because having children was the highest service one could render in many African societies, men and women faced enormous pressure to marry and start families. If there were not enough men to go around, polygyny (having more than one wife) was a culturally proper way of solving the problem. These cultural obligations did not die in the Americas of the sixteenth century. African men continued to take several wives whenever that was possible. Failing to understand the larger meaning of such a practice, the colonial authorities responded in horror, broke up the unions, and punished the individuals involved. In this way they applied Western and Catholic norms to a people whose traditions and values were fundamentally different. Creoles who were accused of bigamy, particularly in the seventeenth century, may not have been immune to the continuing influences of their African ancestry. Judging from the testimony offered at their trials, however, some of them understood the Christian precepts against two spouses but chose to engage in that practice anyway.

Like their family arrangements, the traditional religious ideas and beliefs of the Africans were very much alive in sixteenth-century America. Regardless of their ethnic origins, African peoples came from societies where religious beliefs influenced all aspects of the life of individuals and the community. Unlike Western societies, there was no distinction between secular and religious spheres. Religious ideas determined the timing of important occasions, naming ceremonies, planting seasons, harvesting practices, the nature of art and dance, and a thousand other aspects of life. The African who converted to Christianity would have to undergo a profound internal rebirth as well as changes in his everyday life. In other words, the religious ideas of Africans were deeply imbedded in their human fabric, forming an central part of their being and profoundly influencing and shaping their behavior. To embrace Christianity meant, in effect, the acceptance of a new identity.

The Catholic church, with the support of the Crown and other state officials, believed that its duty was to Christianize the Africans. They had no respect for the Africans' religious ideas and practices. Muslim slaves were particularly feared, and their importation into the Americas was discouraged. The Spaniards and other Catholics had been the foes of the Muslims for centuries, and they did not want religious competition and conflicts to arise in the Americas. In addition, the Spaniards believed that Muslim slaves would indoctrinate the Indians with their religious ideas.

Both the Spanish Crown and the religious authorities required that Africans be baptized prior to their departure for the Americas. It is doubtful whether this had anything more than a symbolic value because the Africans would not have received much, if any, instruction in the Catholic faith. A few slaves who came from the

Two Catholics of African descent worship in Peru. Many Africans became formal members of the Catholic church in Latin America.

Congo-Angola region may have already been exposed to Christianity, because Portuguese missionaries and citizens had arrived there in the fifteenth century. From the complaints that the priests in the Americas made throughout the sixteenth century, it is clear that many slaves, contrary to what the Crown wanted, left the African coast without being baptized. The situation was not much better in the Americas. There were frequent reports that some Africans had not been baptized even after they had been in residence for several years.

This was probably a welcome development for the Africans. Undoubtedly, most of them would have preferred to continue to practice their religious beliefs without the interference of the Christians. Conscientious priests and friars, however, wanted to do their duty as Christians to instruct the Africans about their faith and to baptize them. With the permission of the owners, they conducted classes for the slaves on Sundays or at other mutually convenient times. Not all slaveholders cooperated, some believing that the time that their human property spent receiving religious instructions should be devoted to working at their various tasks.

Still, many Africans were baptized and became formal members of the church. They participated in the various festivals and had marriages and funerals performed by a priest. Some Africans became active members of the religious brotherhoods known as the *cofradía*. In essence, these were mutual aid organizations that were devoted to the memory of a particular saint. The members paid dues and received financial help in times of difficulty. *Cofradías* took part in the various religious processions that occurred from time to time.

The authorities in the colonies kept a careful watch on the activities of black *cofradías*. The spectacle of hundreds of blacks congregating to hold meetings or to participate in processions raised white fears of conspiracy and insurrection. In 1572, for example, the Mexican viceroy was concerned that "recently the negroes have had a *cofradía* and have assembled and held processions with their members as the others do, and these are always increasing . . . and it seems that they may create problems." On occasion, intoxicated members did create problems in Mexico and Peru and probably elsewhere. In 1612, members of a black *cofradía* in Mexico City played a leading role in a rebellion that slaves and free persons had planned. Such rebellious activity led to the temporary suspension of the organization by the authorities. The potential of the *cofradías* to lead violent assaults on slavery must have led to an increase in their surveillance. In general, however, *cofradías* were more likely to meet the needs of the slaves for social interaction and communal activities.

The first black *cofradías* may have been established as soon as enough Africans were baptized in a particular colony and lived close to one another. The church encouraged the formation of separate *cofradías* for Africans, probably for racial reasons. The Africans may also have wanted their own organizations, free from the direct control of whites and reflecting their own needs and bearing their cultural stamp. In fact, the *cofradías* in Peru, and perhaps in other colonies as well, were organized along African ethnic lines in the sixteenth century. This could only have occurred in those places where individuals from particular ethnic groups existed in significant numbers. The existence of ethnic-based *cofradías* clearly suggests the continuing strength of an African heritage in the Americas.

Although the Catholic church succeeded in making converts among the slaves, Christianity did not replace African religious beliefs in the sixteenth century or at later times. Christianized Africans did not abandon their core religious beliefs. In other words, their African religious ideas existed alongside the dogma of the Christianity that they embraced. African slaves could draw upon their Christian beliefs when it suited their purposes. On other occasions, they drew upon their African beliefs.

Practitioners of African religions used a variety of charms and amulets in their rituals. These could be herbs, sticks, bags, cloth, or bones. Africans believed that these objects carried certain mystical powers or were the objects through which the supernatural operated. Dirt from cemeteries, perhaps because of its association with the ancestors, also possessed revered qualities. When used in the appropriate fashion and accompanied by the relevant ceremonies, the charms, objects, and dirt could be used to avenge a wrong, win the affections of a man or woman, solve a crime, get a slave owner to treat his slaves well, and accomplish a variety of other objectives.

The use of these objects and charms was based on the belief that certain forces or events could be manipulated and controlled by resorting to the appropriate ritual acts. This is similar in some respects to the Christian belief that prayer can be used effectively to achieve a desired end. What is important, however, is not any perceived similarity to Christianity, but the persistence of African beliefs and ways of influencing the supernatural in the Americas. Over time, of course, some of these ideas and practices would be modified or altered in some fashion.

In addition to their kinship systems and religious ideas, Africans brought their music, songs, dances, art forms, and cooking methods with them. The colonists viewed many of these cultural practices negatively, and tried to suppress them. Slaves danced in the streets on festive occasions, drawing upon their African styles of movement. Others were skilled at drumbeating and played such stringed musical instruments as the banjo and marimba.

We possess little information on the diet of the slaves during their early years in the Americas. The principal ingredients appear to be corn, sweet potatoes, plantains, beef, and a variety of legumes. The nutritional adequacy of the diet is also unknown because of the absence of information about the quantity of the foods provided to each slave. Similarly, we can make no definite comment on the relationship between diet, disease, and the death rates of the slaves. Slaves, like other members of society, fell victim to the frequent epidemics of measles and smallpox. Workers in the mines and the *ingenios* had a higher death rate than other blacks, a result of the physical hazards of such employment and perhaps of overwork and a poor diet. The unhealthy climate of such places as Vera Cruz may also have taken its toll on the health of the slaves.

Medical care, such as it was, was available for sick slaves, particularly those who lived in urban areas. In Lima, for example, a hospital run by the Jesuits welcomed slaves and gave them the same care that they provided to whites. Hospitals run by municipalities also accepted slaves in Mexico City and Lima. Some large plantations in the rural areas had infirmaries attached to them. Given the state of medical knowledge during the sixteenth century, it is doubtful whether these hospital stays did any good if serious illnesses were involved. African slaves had their own traditional remedies, and many of them may not have availed themselves of the services that the hospitals offered. They also seemed to have borrowed freely from the medical lore of the Indians. This is hardly surprising, given their often close interaction with one another.

Indians and Africans also fell in love with each other, got married, or lived together without the approval of the church or the state. The Spanish Crown, in particular, opposed such unions, preferring that individuals choose partners from among their own "races" or groups. But such a restriction was impossible to enforce. Male Africans greatly outnumbered the females, so Indian women often became the sexual partners of black men. Because the Indian women were likely to be free, the children of such unions, known as *zambos,* took the mother's legal status and were born free. This was probably an added incentive for male slaves to choose Indian women as partners.

The early colonial records indicate, however, that there was some tension in the relationship between the Africans and the native peoples of the Americas. It may very well be that colonial officials focused much more on the difficulties between them, ignoring the many areas and instances of cooperation. In particular, the Peruvian and Mexican authorities accused blacks of physically assaulting Indians, taking their possessions, and generally mistreating them.

In order to correct this problem, the Crown and the local authorities attempted to prevent the two peoples from living in the same communities. These restrictions were sometimes not enforced, and they were repeated with regularity throughout the sixteenth century. The Crown also forbade blacks from trading with Indians on the grounds that they took advantage of them. It is doubtful, however, that the commercial activity between the two groups ceased.

Regardless of the colony in which they lived, Africans were placed at the bottom of the social order. Forced to work for others, they nevertheless tried to maintain their humanity, doing the things that gave meaning to their lives. They toiled, married, reproduced, worshiped their gods, and made the best of their situation. Their burdens were never easy, and the forced separation from their homeland created much physical suffering and emotional anguish. But those Africans who arrived in the sixteenth century faced, in retrospect, an additional challenge. It was they who had to lay the cultural and institutional foundations of the modern black societies of the Americas.

The Struggle for Freedom

Perhaps the Africans could have eased their emotional pain in that terrible first century of their enslavement in the Americas if they had been present in larger

numbers in the various colonies. This would have provided them with the opportunity to associate more intimately with one another and establish meaningful
support systems. But even when relatively large numbers of slaves arrived in such
colonies as Mexico, Peru, and Hispaniola, they were widely scattered. Most lived in
small groups of their peers. Not until the mid seventeenth century did the large
sugar plantations, with their huge concentrations of slaves, become increasingly
regular features of the Caribbean islands. The silver mines of Mexico and Peru and
a few sugar plantations had employed high numbers of slaves before 1600, but
most blacks still lived in smaller communities.

An African population living in larger groups would not have automatically
ended the alienation that its members felt or have fostered a sense of community
among them. The African-born slaves were divided along ethnic lines, which was
an obstacle to cooperative relationships between them and the development of a
sense of oneness. In addition, there were cultural differences between those people
who had become familiar with the ways of Europeans and those who were newly
arrived from Africa bearing their traditional culture.

Thus, the slave population had to overcome many obstacles before it could pose
an organized challenge to the institution under whose control it lived. Such challenges took different forms, depending on the local circumstances, the size of the
slave population, the degree of interaction among its members, and their level of
political consciousness. Slaves who lived within easy reach of wooded, mountainous, or other inaccessible areas often chose flight as their principal means of resistance. Where their numbers permitted, others conspired and participated in
revolts. Still others engaged in day-to-day acts of sabotage, such as working slowly,
that punctured the efficiency of the institution of slavery.

Slaves were inclined to resist their condition when they came to the recognition
that a profound wrong had been committed against them. Resistance occurred
when the individual had decided to reclaim control over his or her life. Such a decision could come after much careful thought, or it could occur in a moment of passion, such as when the person was being mistreated. Once a decision to resist had
been made, whether individually or collectively, the slave had reached an important turning point, and his or her life would not be the same again.

During the seventeenth century, when black cultures in the Americas were taking firm shape, slaves engaged in flight more frequently than any other form of
physical resistance. This was the case in all of the colonies, and there were several
reasons for its appeal. Regardless of whether the slaves were shipped from Spain or
came directly from Africa, the overwhelming majority were African-born. They
were, therefore, unaccustomed to the demands and rigors of plantation, mining,
and other forms of labor that they were required to perform. Not surprisingly, they
sought to escape from the sources of their oppression as soon as the opportunity
presented itself. Often few in numbers and separated from their peers by long dis-

tances, flight also had a certain practicality. It did not depend significantly on the cooperation of others for its success. Slaves could escape alone or in a group. Small groups were best because slaves ran the risk of detection and capture if the number in the escape party was too large.

The physical environment of the colonies also aided escape. Hispaniola, Jamaica, Cuba, Mexico, and Brazil, to name just a few places, all had mountainous, inaccessible, and wooded areas—the ideal terrain for those who wanted to create sanctuaries away from their pursuers. The Sierra Maestra mountain range in eastern Cuba, the densely wooded Cockpit Country in central Jamaica, the hilly Orizaba zone adjacent to Vera Cruz in Mexico, and the densely forested regions of northeastern Brazil beckoned and protected the escapees.

Adult males were the most likely to escape. Women constituted a minority of the slave population, so it is not surprising that they remained a small proportion of those who fled. Perhaps women were less inclined to risk the hazards of the escape than the men. They may also have chosen to remain behind with their children. Because infants and older children slowed the pace of escape and increased the risk of capture, parents had to face difficult choices in this regard.

The incidence of escape began as soon as the first slaves arrived in Hispaniola in 1502. In 1503, the governor of the colony, Nicolás de Ovando, reported to the Crown that a number of slaves had fled. There is no additional information on this first group of runaways, but they probably fled to a remote area of the colony. Whatever their fate, these people established a pattern that would be followed by other slaves everywhere in the Americas.

These escaped slaves were called *cimarrones* by the Spaniards. The origin of this term is not entirely clear, but some scholars believe that the word *cimarrón* originally referred to cattle that roamed in the hills of Hispaniola. Eventually, it was applied to Indians who had fled from slavery. As Indian slavery declined and blacks arrived in increasing numbers, the word came to be associated with those who escaped. It is not certain, however, when *cimarrón* began to be applied exclusively to black runaways, but it appears that was the case by the 1530s. In time, the English equivalent became *maroon,* and the French used the word *marron.* The word *cimarrón,* at least in the eyes of the Spaniards, had negative connotations. It was generally a synonym for "wild," "fierce," or "untamed." On the other hand, the escapees may have worn it as a badge of honor, in the same way that the descendants of the maroons in the English-speaking Caribbean do today.

There was a close relationship between the number of escapes and the size of the black population. As more and more Africans arrived, the flight to an uncertain freedom in the mountains and other remote areas accelerated. Slaves who were inclined to escape probably ran off quietly, perhaps not even telling friends of their plans for fear of betrayal. The colonists may even have come to expect that some of their slaves would flee. The surviving documents from these early years often mention *cimarrones* in an offhand manner. It is only when the escaped slaves began to attack their former masters or entice other slaves to escape that their existence became a matter of grave public concern.

It was not until the 1520s that the references to *cimarrones* in the letters of the colonists and in official reports became more frequent and urgent. There were reports of *cimarrones* not only in Hispaniola, but also in Mexico in 1523, in Puerto Rico in 1529, and in Cuba in 1534. By the 1550s, additional reports of the presence of *cimarrones* had come from Panama, Venezuela, Peru, and Honduras. In general, the *cimarrones* were accused of murdering Spaniards, participating in rebellions, and theft. In 1546, a Spanish official in Hispaniola, for example, noted that the *cimarrones* in one part of the island were so dangerous that "no one dared to venture out unless he was in a group of fifteen to twenty people."

Colonial authorities everywhere saw the *cimarrones* as a threat to public order. As a result, the descriptions of them in the records are overwhelmingly negative. Given the fact that the *cimarrones* in all of the colonies were depicted as assaulting the colonists and, in some cases, the Indians, such charges must have had some merit. Because such accusations were often followed by requests for resources to strengthen the law-enforcement agencies, it is also conceivable that the reports gave exaggerated accounts of the behavior of the escapees.

Some historians have attempted to make distinctions between the motivations of the *cimarrones* and those who remained in slavery but participated in revolts. They suggest that the *cimarrones* did not pose much of a threat to slavery because they escaped from the institution and returned only now and then to carry out hit-and-run attacks on it. On the other hand, slave revolts threatened slavery from within and were designed to destroy it. This distinction does not hold for the early years, when *cimarrones* played the most significant roles in a large number of the early challenges to slavery.

With the possible exception of a few urban areas such as Mexico City and Lima, slaves were so sparsely distributed in the sixteenth century that they lacked the numbers necessary to organize and launch rebellions. Slaves apparently escaped individually or in small groups and eventually formed maroon communities of varying sizes. In 1542, one estimate in Hispaniola placed the number of *cimarrones* at "about two thousand or three thousand." Several hundred were reported to be in Puerto Rico at various times in the sixteenth century. The same could be said of Mexico, particularly in the mountainous area between Mount Orizaba and Vera Cruz. Accounts from Peru, Cuba, and Venezuela also suggest significant runaway populations in those early years.

The existence of these communities gave the *cimarrones* the confidence to challenge the slave owners and their colonial society. The *cimarrones* were, for the most part, interested not only in preserving their own freedom, but in destroying slavery as well. The first slave rebellion in the Americas occurred in Hispaniola in 1522. Three years earlier, in 1519, Indians were reported to have been joined by escaped slaves in an attack on the Spaniards. But when the first all-black revolt occurred in 1522, it included *cimarrones* and slaves who had never fled. The 40 slaves and *cimarrones* who participated were, however, defeated by the Spaniards. Several lost their lives in the fighting, and the Spaniards hanged those who were captured.

This early assault on the Spaniards was followed by others. It is doubtful, however, that the runaways always united with the slaves. Nor is it entirely clear if all of the disturbances were designed to destroy slavery or whether they were a consequence of the *cimarrones* defending their communities from invasions by the Spanish authorities. It is certain, nonetheless, that there were serious confrontations between the Spaniards and the *cimarrones* in Puerto Rico in 1529; Cuba in 1534; Mexico, Columbia, Hispaniola in the 1540s; and Panama in the 1550s.

The Mexican *cimarrones* were probably the most active during the sixteenth and early seventeenth centuries. Mexico's slave population steadily increased after the Spanish occupation, and the native peoples declined in number. There were about twenty thousand African slaves in Mexico by 1570 and perhaps as many as fifty thousand by 1600. The Mexican terrain, with its numerous mountain slopes, provided ideal sanctuaries for escaped slaves. The number of escapes increased after the 1550s, and there were frequent reports from the silver mines in the north and the east that *cimarrones* were engaged in attacks on the colonists. In some cases, Indians joined the *cimarrones* in acts of arson and theft. By 1580, *cimarrones* could be found almost everywhere in rural Mexico.

Relatively speaking, a great deal is known about a community of *cimarrones* that lived in the area of Mount Orizaba adjacent to Vera Cruz during the late sixteenth and early seventeenth centuries. The community had developed a reputation for attacking the Spaniards, taking their possessions, and enticing other slaves to flee. Their leader was Yanga, an African-born man who had escaped shortly after arriving in Mexico. Evidently a skilled military tactician, he had successfully repulsed several attempts by the Spaniards to destroy his settlement and return the residents to slavery. By 1608 there were about five hundred *cimarrones* in the community. They supported themselves by planting such crops as corn and potatoes and by rearing animals.

Despite their best efforts, the *cimarrones* were unable to withstand an aggressive assault on their camp in 1609. An invading army of 450 men forced Yanga and his people to accept a truce. Under the terms of the agreement, the Spanish authorities recognized the freedom of the *cimarrones* and allowed them to establish and govern their own town. Yanga would become governor of the town, and the position could only be held by those descended from him. The *cimarrones* promised to defend the colony if it were ever attacked by Spain's enemies and agreed to return all future runaways to their owners. It is not clear whether this part of the agreement was kept. In accordance with the terms of the agreement, the town of San Lorenzo de los Negros received its charter in 1617.

SOULEVEMENT DES NEGRES
à la Jamaïque.

Cimarrones kill colonists in a revolt against the English in 1758. Starting in the early seventeenth century, large communities of escaped slaves were powerful enough to sign peace treaties with colonial authorities in Mexico, Jamaica, and other colonies.

The treaty that these *cimarrones* signed with the Spanish set a model for other societies. In later years, maroons signed peace treaties with the authorities in Jamaica, Cuba, Suriname, Venezuela, and other places. Many of these large maroon communities came into existence after 1600. In Jamaica, for example, one group of maroons signed a peace treaty with the English in 1739 that affirmed their freedom. Similar treaties would be signed with other maroon groups in succeeding years.

The slaves in Brazil also embraced escape as an effective form of resistance. Portuguese assaults on some of their settlements killed many of the residents but failed to destroy them. The most resilient of these early maroons were those who established a settlement known as Palmares in Pernambuco. In 1612 a Portuguese official noted that "some thirty leagues inland, there is a site between mountains called Palmares which harbors runaway slaves . . . whose attack and raids force the whites into armed pursuits which amount to little for they return to raid again."

Palmares had between eleven thousand and twenty thousand residents at its peak in the seventeenth century. After maintaining their freedom for almost a century, however, the residents of the settlement were finally defeated by the Portuguese in 1694. The disappearance of Palmares as an organized community of maroons did not end this form of resistance in Brazil. Known as *quilombos,* such settlements became more numerous as the slave population increased. Some of these communities still survive in contemporary Brazil.

Slave owners and the colonial authorities attempted to curb the incidence of runaways. Several colonies, such as Mexico and Peru, established civil militias primarily to catch runaways and prevent their attacks on Spanish life and property. In addition, the authorities introduced a series of measures for the punishment of those who escaped and were recaptured. Some of these laws permitted the castration of the *cimarrones* and even authorized their deaths if they had escaped for long periods of time. According to a 1535 law passed in Lima, an absence of more than six days carried the death penalty. Runaways could also be whipped, chained, imprisoned, tortured, or have a foot or hand cut off. Such horrible punishments reflected the seriousness with which the authorities viewed the slaves' efforts to claim their freedom. On the other hand, by escaping in the face of such reprisals, the slaves demonstrated the powerful nature of their desire to live as free people.

Although the *cimarrones* and the slaves who did not flee joined together sometimes to challenge slavery, there were occasions on which this was evidently not the case. In fact, several slave revolts during this early period and later do not appear to have involved the participation of *cimarrones*. There were organizational difficulties that stood in the way of such collaboration. Maroons lived in remote areas, and communication between them and the slaves was usually not easy. Nor should it be assumed that the *cimarrones* always wanted to involve themselves in such conflicts. They had fled from slavery; the struggle to destroy it remained the primary responsibility of those who were left behind.

The first major conspiracy involving slaves acting alone occurred in Mexico City in 1537. The conspirators elected a king and planned to kill the Spaniards, liberate themselves, and seize control of the colony. The plot, however, was discovered by the authorities, and those involved were arrested. A frightened government extracted confessions from the accused and hanged them. The threat of rebellion never declined in Mexico, and the Spaniards always feared that the Indians would join the black slaves in any confrontation.

Spanish fears were fulfilled in 1608 when thirty-one free blacks and slaves gathered in Mexico City to elect a king and queen and to plot a revolt. One of the conspirators reported the details to the authorities. Predictably, the participants were arrested, although it is not clear what punishment they received. Four years later, in 1612, blacks in Mexico City once again planned a revolt. When the authorities heard of the plans they arrested a large number of people and tortured them to obtain more information on the conspiracy. In the end, 35 blacks were hanged and others were sent out of the colony.

Slaves continued to escape in all societies of the Americas, and many were successful in building their own communities and maintaining their freedom. Maroon communities united slaves from different African ethnic groups as well as the creoles. The first settlements, however, consisted almost exclusively of African-born persons. These communities probably saw the breaking down of ethnic divisions as the Ibos, the Coromantee, the Mandinka, and others had to cooperate with one another in order to survive. These communities of runaway slaves represented the first truly black societies in the Americas. Free from white control and responsible for their own decisions, these societies were the first attempts by African peoples in this hemisphere to order their lives in their own way. Their societies were always insecure, however, because they faced the constant threat of invasions from the outside. Yet many of them survived for long periods of time because the desire for freedom gave them the necessary resolve to confront, and in many cases overcome, the obstacles that stood in their path.

The communities that these maroons established appear to have been patterned along the lines of African societies. Although information on this subject is still rather sketchy, such communities could be characterized as centralized kingdoms with a ruler, such as Yanga, wielding absolute or near-absolute power. These communities, of course, were also influenced by the conditions the escapees encountered in the Americas. Consequently, they were never exact copies of the Africa that they remembered. In any event, the maroons created communities that met their needs and bore their own cultural and political stamp.

No slave revolt, however, achieved any success during this first century. The slaves could not successfully contest the armed might of the colonial states. Not

Wearing Spanish clothes and native jewelry, *zambos* from Esmeraldas (in present-day Ecuador) visit Quito in 1599. Some *zambos,* children of blacks and Indians, were among the many free Africans in the Americas.

until two centuries later were slaves in Haiti able to claim their freedom through their own efforts. Still, the incidence of revolts and conspiracies shows that the enslaved never resigned themselves to their condition and never saw it as just. Although relatively few in number, these individuals gave slave owners everywhere notice that they could never be taken for granted.

The enslavement of the African peoples in the Americas finally ended in 1888. In that year, Brazil became the last society to emancipate its slaves, bringing to an end a process that had begun in the first decades of the nineteenth century. The Haitian slaves began a successful revolution in 1791 and finally defeated the French slave-owning colonists in 1803. When they achieved their independence from Spain in the early 19th century, the former Spanish colonies began a slow process of liberating their slaves. The British passed an Emancipation Act in 1833, and the French followed suit in 1848. In North America, all of the slaves were freed in 1865 as a result of a bloody civil war. Puerto Rico ended the institution in 1873, and Cuba acted similarly in 1886.

There were, of course, a number of slaves who managed to become legally free before slavery formally ended in the various societies. This process began in the sixteenth century, but its extent varied, depending on the society and the forces that encouraged freedom for some slaves. In all of the slaveholding societies of the Americas, a child born to a free woman but fathered by a male slave was legally free. Some slave owners freed their own children born of slave women and some-times those women as well. Others liberated slaves who had grown too old to work or who had served faithfully for a period of time. Some slaves purchased their freedom; others had it done on their behalf by a sympathetic citizen or humanitarian. Children born to parents who were already free also added to the size of the free black population.

The Spanish legal code, the *Siete Partidas,* encouraged liberty for slaves. It stated that slavery was "the most evil and the most despicable thing that can be found among men." As a result, according to the *Siete Partidas,* "all of the laws of the world should lead toward freedom." Owners who freed their slaves, the document maintained, rendered a service to God. In 1540, the Crown echoed these sentiments and advised its officials in the Americas that if slaves "should publicly demand their liberty, they should be heard and justice done to them, and care be taken that they should not on that account ... be maltreated by their Masters." There was, of course, a tremendous gulf between these ideals and actual practice both in Spain and in the colonies. The Portuguese never produced a document similar to the *Siete Partidas* and did not embrace, at least in legal theory, the notion that property in persons was not to be encouraged.

In general, the enslavement of the Africans in the Americas was not an issue about which sixteenth-century Spaniards and Portuguese worried. Only a few enlightened voices raised questions about the morality of African slavery, but their objections had no effect. One of the first people to do so was Alonso de Montufár, the archbishop of Mexico. In 1560 he wrote to the king of Spain complaining that "we do not know what reason exists that the Negroes should be enslaved more than the Indians ... because they receive the holy faith and do not make war against the Christians." Nine years later, Friar Tomás de Mercado denounced the abuses of the slave trade and urged his fellow Spaniards not to participate in it. In 1573, Bartolomé de Albornoz, a professor who lived in Mexico, wrote a well-known treatise condemning slavery. He pointed out that the institution violated natural law, or the basic "natural" rights of all human beings. These were lonely voices; it was not until the second half of the eighteenth century that a movement to abolish the slave trade—and eventually slavery—gathered momentum, particularly in England and France.

The slaves who gained their freedom in the sixteenth century, therefore, benefited from individual arrangements and not from any formal end of slavery. While some slaves were freed by their owners, others worked hard, saved whatever money came their way and, if the master were agreeable, bought their freedom. On occasion, slaves could not readily meet the price the master asked, so they purchased their freedom over a period of years.

Young men between the ages of fourteen and twenty-five were the group least likely to be freed. They were in the most productive years of their lives physically, and slave owners were not particularly eager to part with their strongest and healthiest workers. At the other extreme, the mulatto children of the slave masters and the mistresses of these men stood the best chance of acquiring their freedom. Liberty was clearly not within the reach of everyone in quite the same way. Most African-born slaves and their children could expect to spend their entire lives in bondage.

It is impossible to say how many persons received their freedom in the Spanish empire and in Portuguese Brazil in the sixteenth century. The proportions probably never exceeded five percent to ten percent of the black population at any time. It may be guessed, however, that the number of freed persons in the Spanish colonies increased steadily after 1550 simply because of the continuing growth of the black population, the incidence of owners freeing their children and mistresses, and the fact that some slaves by that time had been in the colonies long enough and received their freedom because of advancing age.

There were no laws in the colonies that prevented slaves from being freed. This did not mean, however, that free blacks were accorded equal rights with whites. The white colonists dominated the colonies, and blacks and Indians, regardless of their legal status, occupied subordinate places. The free peoples of African descent were expected to pay taxes, serve in the armed forces, and generally assume the responsibilities of full citizenship, but they were the victims of discriminatory legislation because of their racial heritage.

As soon as the numbers of free blacks began to increase, the Spanish Crown and the colonial authorities sought to control their lives and limit their opportunities. Such actions were based on the racist notion that blacks needed white supervision. Unlike the slaves, free blacks could, at least in theory, choose their employers and move from place to place. The colonists feared the loss of control over them, as well as loss of access to their labor. Beginning in the 1570s free blacks were ordered to live with Spaniards and work for them for a wage. This was a serious curtailment of their liberty and made them little better than slaves. Other measures required that all freed persons be registered with the local authorities in order to make it easier to collect taxes from them. Failure to be registered brought severe physical punishments. The order was repeated from time to time, an indication that some free persons successfully evaded it.

Most free blacks performed menial and unskilled tasks during the period, but some were artisans much in demand. The various guilds—associations of craftsmen, such as carpenters—either refused membership to free blacks or allowed them to become only apprentices. They were also excluded from high schools and universities, a fact that also limited their economic and social opportunities.

The Spanish-American societies went to extraordinary lengths throughout the period to emphasize the inferior status of the free persons of African descent. In 1614, for example, the authorities in Lima ruled that free blacks should be buried without coffins. Evidently, burial in a coffin blurred the social distinctions between whites and blacks. The authorities in Mexico and Peru also prevented free black women from adorning themselves with gold and other jewelry and wearing silk. Such finery was the preserve of white women, as a mark of their social superiority.

Very little is known about the texture of the lives of the free peoples of African descent in this early period or about the social institutions that they created. Scattered evidence suggests that as a group they were likely to choose their marriage partners from among their peers. Few males married slave women, probably because their children would take the mother's status. There was considerable interaction at other levels, however. Free blacks and slaves often belonged to the same *cofradías,* or mutual aid organizations, participated in conspiracies, established friendships, and worked together in *obrajes,* households, on sugar plantations, and so on.

The relationships of the free peoples with one another, however, was not always harmonious. There is some evidence that some of them adopted the racist views of Spanish society and gave a higher value to those who had a lighter skin color by virtue of a mixed ancestry. Some *cofradías* that free persons established in Lima, for example, admitted only mulattoes. Yet, in spite of such divisions, a similar heritage bound the free and the slave—a fact that none could forget. Slavery and discriminatory treatment in the Americas produced enormous stresses and strains in the lives of the freed people, but their common identity was never destroyed.

Shaping America

For the black populations in the Americas, the sixteenth century represented the start of their unique historical odyssey. The estimated 300,000 Africans who arrived during that first century made crucial contributions to the shaping of the colonial societies. They also laid the foundations of the present-day black societies of the Americas. Whether they came in groups large or small, Africans brought their languages, religious beliefs, musical styles, cooking practices, and a thousand other aspects of their societies with them. Because Africans came from many different ethnic groups, they did not all share the same culture or ways of doing things. As a result, a variety of African beliefs and cultural forms went into the making and shaping of the societies of the Americas.

Although their number was small at first, the labor of the Africans was indispensable in the mining industries, textile factories, and in sugar cultivation and other agricultural enterprises. By the second half of the eighteenth century, African workers had helped make sugarcane "king" in the Caribbean and Brazil. Vast numbers of slaves would by that time, or shortly thereafter, be used on the coffee plantations in Haiti and Brazil and in the cotton industry in the southern United States.

In terms of labor, African slaves made the principal contribution to the construction of the plantation economies of the Americas. But they were not the beneficiaries of their efforts. They formed an exploited labor force, and their energies went into the creation of wealth for those who owned them. Because they did not benefit materially from what they produced, the slaves really had no stake in the economic systems. Their labor was both forced and unpaid. Still, the roles that they played as workers in the building of the American societies must be recognized, even as the slave systems that defined Africans and their children as property and tried to debase them at every turn should be condemned.

The economic benefits of slavery and the slave trade, even in the sixteenth century, went beyond the Americas. The European slave traders, slave owners, and their societies reaped economic rewards as well. These rewards increased as the slave trade and slavery expanded in the seventeenth and eighteenth centuries.

Starting in the sixteenth century, a number of European-produced goods—such as guns, textiles, woolen products, and pots and pans—were used in the African trade. The increased demand for these products benefited the economies of the areas that manufactured them. The construction of slave ships created jobs for carpenters, sail makers, painters, and other artisans. Slave traders brought African gold, ivory, and redwood back to Europe, imports that were in great demand. Then, too, the profits from the slave trade were frequently invested in other areas of the European economies.

Historians are not in agreement on the degree to which the slave trade was profitable. Several joint stock companies went bankrupt in the first two hundred years. But the independent traders who dominated the human traffic after about 1700 seemed to have done much better. The rate of profit or loss varied from trader to trader or from voyage to voyage. A great deal depended on the business sense and skills of the trader, the price of slaves on the African coast, their selling price in the Americas, the number who perished during the Atlantic crossing, and the state of their health upon arrival. With these qualifications in mind, most of the existing studies show a return of somewhere between five percent and twenty percent on the investment made by the traders.

In the end, it may not be possible to separate the profitability of the slave trade from that of slavery. The two business practices were intricately interrelated. The funds that the slave trade generated were used to purchase the products that were produced with slave labor. Thus, a slave trader would sell his slaves in the Caribbean and use the funds to buy sugar, which he would then sell in Europe.

There are no reliable estimates of the returns that slave owners made on their investments in slaves in Latin America and the Caribbean. Investments in slaves in the United States in the nineteenth century yielded an average rate of profitability of ten percent, making for a very healthy business. Some Caribbean slave owners were heavily in debt by the beginning of the nineteenth century, but others must have continued to turn a profit. In fact, some scholars have argued that the economies of European countries owed their expansion to the slave trade and the financial benefits of slave labor.

The impact of the slave trade on the African societies is also a highly controversial issue. Some scholars maintain that the removal of millions of people from West and West Central Africa led to the depopulation of certain societies. Others conclude that the African populations did not decline during the almost four centuries that the slave trade existed. They suggest that new food crops introduced during the period led to improved diets and helped to account for a steady increase in the population, even though millions were being drained away by the trade. These two points of view do not necessarily rule each other out.

The slave trade did not affect all African societies in the same way, and its impact varied over time. Some weaker societies disappeared, while the stronger ones with access to guns and gunpowder increased their power and size. They were able to incorporate other societies into their own, often selling the captives whom they took in the process. The fact that most of the slaves who were sold were young males must have had severe negative consequences in some societies. There were probably imbalances in the number of men to women in some societies and a shortage of persons available for such male-assigned duties as defense.

The slave trade may also have increased the incidence of wars in the African societies. African societies in the sixteenth century and later went to war for their own local reasons. The popular view that the Europeans created wars between the Africans for the purpose of acquiring slaves is highly exaggerated. Nor is it generally true that the Africans fought primarily for the purpose of obtaining captives to be sold as slaves. It is very likely, however, that the availability of European-supplied weapons led to an increase in the frequency of wars.

The slave trade, according to most scholars, had a negative economic effect on the African societies that were involved in it. This was because the Africans developed a taste for the consumer goods provided by the Europeans in exchange for the slaves. Because these goods could be obtained without undue difficulty and the prices were not excessive, some Africans developed a dependence on them and neglected their own local industries. In the long run, the Africans' failure to develop their own industries helps to account for their falling behind the Europeans in manufacturing.

The Atlantic slave trade left a lasting and bitter legacy for all groups involved in it. It has remained a source of embarrassment and guilt for them. Some have sought to establish blame and responsibility for its origins and continuation. The unpleasant fact is that there were African sellers and European and American buyers. The African sellers came from many different societies and so did the purchasers. The contemporary reader looks back in horror at human beings buying and selling other members of the human family. But most people at the time did not see anything wrong with the slave trade. Still, there were others, undoubtedly a small minority, who denounced the human traffic and reacted to it with disgust.

Blame and accusation aside, the extraordinary burdens that the enslaved endured must be recognized. They were human property, subjected to the whims of their owners, humiliated, and abused. As unfree workers, they labored long hours, often at dangerous tasks. Overworked and underfed, many died prematurely. Their life chances were limited, and few could expect to acquire their freedom. Yet, there is ample evidence that the enslaved called upon their inner strength to survive their ordeal. Beginning in the sixteenth century, they escaped and rebelled, challenging the power of those who denied them freedom. The enslaved everywhere established the cultural institutions that became the core of black life in the Americas. Theirs is a tale of extraordinary suffering; but it is also a timeless lesson in endurance and survival.

CHAPTER 2

Strange New Land

1619–1776

Peter H. Wood

I n the summer of 1619, a 160-ton ship from the port of Flushing in Holland sailed into Chesapeake Bay. This Dutch vessel was under the command of Captain Jope and piloted by an Englishman named Marmaduke Raynor. They were seeking to obtain provisions after a season of raiding in the West Indies. In exchange for supplies, Jope and his crew sold more than twenty Negroes to the local authorities in the struggling English colony of Virginia. These black newcomers came ashore twelve years after the founding of Jamestown and one year before the *Mayflower* arrived at Plymouth in New England. The people brought to Virginia by the Dutch man-of-war are often cited as the first persons of African ancestry to set foot on North America. But, in fact, others had come before them and had traveled widely through the southern part of the continent.

Africans were present in the early Spanish forays onto the continent of North America, as Juan Ponce de León and his successors probed Florida and the Gulf Coast in search of slaves, wealth, and a passage to the Pacific. In August 1526, for example, six Spanish ships landed on the coast of what is now South Carolina. Their commander, Lucas Vásquez de Ayllón, brought at least five hundred people—men, women, and children—along with one hundred horses and enough cattle, sheep, and pigs to start a settlement. They pushed south along the coast to find a suitable location, and they constructed a small village of thatched-roof huts. But within months Ayllón died, and bitter tensions arose over who should succeed him. In the midst of this struggle for control, African slaves set fire to some of the houses at night. Divided and embittered, 150 survivors straggled back to the Caribbean as winter set in. Almost all the rest—more than 350 people—died because of sickness, violence, hunger, or cold. But it was rumored that some of the Africans had escaped their bondage and remained to live among the coastal Indians.

That same winter the Spanish king approved another expedition to the Florida region, and five ships, commanded by Pánfilo de Narváez, set sail from Spain in June 1527. The following spring more than four hundred soldiers and servants, including some men of African descent, landed near Tampa Bay and marched northwest. They hoped to make great conquests, but they were poorly prepared and badly led. The Indians fought fiercely to defend their own lands, and soon the invaders were separated from their supply boats and from each other. Most died in the Gulf Coast wilderness, but a few survived long enough to be taken in by local tribes. Miraculously, four such men encountered one another on the Texas coast in 1534. They evaded the tribes with whom they were living and set off across the Southwest in hopes of reaching Mexico City, the capital of the Spanish colony of New Spain.

One of these four survivors was a Spanish-speaking African named Esteban—the first African to emerge clearly in the pages of North American history. Another survivor was a Spanish officer named Álvar Núñez Cabeza de Vaca who wrote down their incredible story. He told how they had been enslaved by Indians and forced to haul wood and water, living on nuts, rabbits, spiders, and the juice of prickly pears. Heading west, they viewed the rolling Texas prairie with its herds of buffalo. "Over all the region," they reported, "we saw vast and beautiful plains that would make good pasture." They also marveled at the variety of languages they encountered among Southwestern Indians. Cabeza de Vaca noted that "there are a thousand dialectical differences," adding that Esteban served as their primary go-between. "He was constantly in conversation, finding out about routes, towns, and other matters we wished to know."

After eight years in America, including two years traveling together through the Southwest, the four men finally reached Mexico City in 1536—the first newcomers from Europe and Africa to cross the huge expanse of North America. When they described the massive Indian apartment dwellings they had seen (known as *pueblos*), gold-hungry listeners assumed they had glimpsed the legendary and wealthy Seven Cities of Cíbola. Soon the Spanish viceroy, Governor Antonio de Mendoza, organized a new exploration to seek out these seven mythical towns, which were supposedly surrounded by turquoise-studded walls of gold. Since the black man was a skilled translator and a seasoned guide who remained enslaved, Mendoza purchased Esteban and presented him to a Spanish friar named Marcos de Niza, who had been selected to lead the expedition. In March 1539, the friar's party, "with the Negro and other slaves, and Indians," headed northward toward what is now Arizona in search of Cíbola. According to an official report:

> The Lord Viceroy having . . . news and notice of such land sent a friar and a negro, the latter having come from Florida with the others . . . as survivors of the party taken there by Pánfilo Narváez. These set out with the knowledge the negro had in order to go to a very rich country, as the latter declared, and told the friar . . . that there are seven very populous cities with great buildings. . . . They have houses built of stone and lime, being of three stories, and with great quantities of turquoises set in doors and windows.

Esteban, familiar with the region, proceeded ahead with his two dogs and a number of Indians. As the summer heat increased, he sent wooden crosses back to the Christian friar to assure him of their progress. Finally he approached a large community—probably the pueblo of Zuni in western New Mexico. Hoping to have reached "Cíbola" at last, Esteban sent messengers ahead as usual, carrying "his great Mace made of a gourd," which "had a string of belles upon it, and two feathers one white and another red, in token that he demanded safe conduct, and that he came peaceably." But the Zunis quickly recognized the bells as Spanish. They linked this party advancing from the south with rumors of Spanish slave raiding and violence that were already circulating in the Indian markets of the region. Zuni leaders blamed the appearance of foreigners for deaths that had already occurred, and they feared a plot by which "neither man nor woman of them shall remaine unslaine."

When Esteban's messengers returned, they reported handing over the "great gourd" to the Indian magistrate. He "tooke the same in his hands, and after he had spyed the belles, in a great rage and fury hee cast it to the ground, and willed the messengers to get them packing with speed, for he knew well ynough what people they were, and that they should . . . in no case enter the citie, for if they did hee would put them all to death." Determined in his course and confident that diplomacy could prevail, Esteban dismissed this initial rejection as "no great matter" and proceeded to approach the town. But armed men blocked his entrance to the city and confined him to an outlying building. They denied him food and water overnight, and they confiscated his trade goods. Negotiations proved unsuccessful, and when Esteban emerged the next morning, he and most of his company were attacked and killed by an angry crowd. Though "bloody and wounded in many places," several of his Indian companions managed to survive. They returned southward to inform Fray Marcos of the death of his experienced black guide.

The failure of the expeditions of Ayllón, Narváez, and Fray Marcos only increased the ambitions of other explorers. Their ventures into the American interior would also include the presence of Africans at every stage. Even before the death of Esteban at the Zuni pueblo, other black Hispanic soldiers and slaves were among those preparing to accompany Francisco Vázquez de Coronado into the Southwest and Hernando de Soto into the Southeast, and a few remain visible in the surviving accounts. Among those marching with de Soto, for example, was a man named "Gomez, a negro belonging to Vasco Gonçalez who spoke good Spanish." In 1537, de Soto had received permission to invade Florida and carve out a province for himself and his followers in the southern interior. The Spanish crown had authorized him to raise an army, to establish three fortified towns, and to include as many as fifty enslaved Negroes in his plans. Gomez was among the black men forced to take part in this ambitious design.

When the expedition landed in Florida in May 1539, it contained 330 foot soldiers and almost as many others—artisans, carpenters, cooks, servants, and priests. They also brought herds of hogs and other livestock that would accompany their army to provide fresh meat. De Soto had taken part in Pizarro's successful campaign against the golden cities of the Incas in Peru. Now he was anxious to discover an equally wealthy kingdom of his own. But long marches through the swamps and forests of the Deep South revealed no such prize, even when he tortured local leaders for information and pushed his own company to extremes. The more de Soto's ambition was frustrated, the more ruthless his invasion became. At the Indian town of Cofitachequi near the Savannah River, he finally received gifts of pearls in the spring of 1540. But he thanked the young woman leader (or *cacica*) who had presented the pearls by making her a captive in her own region and obliging her to march with his soldiers to assure their safe passage in her domain.

De Soto's repeated cruelty toward the Native Americans ensured that few would give him a kindly reception. His ruthlessness with his own army meant that many were willing to risk desertion in a strange land, especially slaves who stood to gain nothing from the entire enterprise. Several weeks after de Soto's departure from Cofitachequi, his royal Indian prisoner stepped off the path with several servants and made good her escape. Several members of de Soto's company also disappeared, including three Spanish-speaking slaves: an Indian boy from Cuba, a Berber from North Africa, and a West African—Gomez. The first two slaves eventually returned to camp and begged forgiveness, reporting that Gomez had elected to remain behind with the young Indian.

Regarding the black man and the Native American woman, these informants said, "it was very certain that they held communication as husband and wife, and that both had made up their minds" to go to Cofitachequi.

So by 1540, less than fifty years after the arrival of Columbus in the Caribbean, an African ex-slave and an Indian *cacica* were living together in the southern forest. By now other European countries, jealous of Spanish wealth in the New World, were beginning to show an interest in the coast of North America. Several explorers sailing for the French king envisioned the possibility of discovering a short "Northwest Passage" from the Atlantic to the Pacific. Giovanni da Verrazzano hoped to find a route to the Orient when he examined the Outer Banks of Carolina and the mouth of New York harbor in 1524. Jacques Cartier had similar ambitions when he sailed up the broad St. Lawrence River in 1535. Even if they could not discover access to the Pacific, Spain's rivals could take advantage of the excellent fishing grounds in the North Atlantic. Or, if they dared, they could go after grander targets, attacking the Spanish galleons that sailed homeward regularly from Mexico.

The annual Spanish fleet, carrying gold and silver from the New World to Seville, followed the currents of the Gulf Stream northward along the Florida Peninsula. Foreign ships, lying in wait along that coastline, could easily attack and capture stray vessels before they headed across the Atlantic. In 1565, therefore, the Spanish established a garrison at St. Augustine on the east coast of Florida. The purpose of this small port town was to help protect the passing gold fleet from marauders and to secure Spain's claim to the Florida region against European rivals. It became the first permanent non-Indian settlement in North America, and Africans were present there from the beginning.

By 1600, roughly forty Africans had been transported to the small outpost of St. Augustine as property of the royal garrison; another sixty had arrived in the households of private individuals. These early African Americans—mostly men and mostly Spanish-speaking—were involved in erecting more than one hundred Spanish-owned shops and houses and in building Fort San Marcos on the northern edge of town. They planted gardens and fished in the Matanzas River, selling their catch in the local fish market. Those who had accepted Christianity worshipped at the local Catholic church, and some drew token pay for themselves and their owners as drummers, fifers, and flag bearers in the local militia.

But living conditions were harsh, and controls at the remote outpost were limited. So some Africans escaped to live among the Indians, as Gomez and others had done several generations earlier. A Spanish document from 1605 complained that slaves had slipped away toward the south and intermarried with the Ais tribe living along the Florida coast. Those who remained in town had little reason for allegiance to their owners. The authorities feared that they would support any invader who offered them their freedom, and one official, writing in 1606, warned others to be wary of "persons of their kind, who are the worst enemies we can have." More than a century later St. Augustine would be viewed as a potential haven by a later generation of black Southerners, but that day was still far in the future.

Just as blacks, both enslaved and free, took part in the exploration and colonization of Spanish Florida, they also participated in the creation of a new colony in the Southwest. There, from the time of Esteban, Spanish raiding parties had carried Indian captives back to Mexico to work in the silver mines alongside enslaved Africans. Before the end of the sixteenth century, Mexican adventurers pushed to gain control of the populated region along the upper Rio Grande. Their reasons for immigrating to this region were many and varied: Some hoped to limit the exploitation of local Indians; some hoped to convert the Indians to Christianity; some hoped to control them and extract a profit. Government officials hoped to prevent rival Europeans from discovering wealth that had so far eluded the Spanish. But most of the settlers simply hoped to escape harsh conditions in *old* Mexico and take their chances on the rough frontier in a colony to be called *New* Mexico.

In 1595, a contract for this northern venture was awarded to Don Juan de Oñate, one of the last in a long line of ambitious and violent conquistadors stretching back to Cortés and Pizarro, de Soto and Coronado. Oñate put up the enormous wealth his father had gained from silver mining (largely with Indian and African labor) in exchange for the right to conquer, control, and exploit a vast region. His tactics proved strikingly ruthless, even in an era known for its brutality, and his grandest ambitions were never realized. In 1599 he crushed a desperate Indian revolt at the pueblo of Acoma so ferociously that he was reprimanded for his acts, and eventually he was forced to withdraw from his newly founded colony. By 1608 there was serious talk of abandoning the settlement of New Mexico altogether.

Nevertheless, by 1610 a permanent mission had been established at Santa Fe, and many of those who had accompanied Oñate had demonstrated their determination to remain in New Mexico.

In 1598, the first contingent of 500 colonists heading north included persons of varied racial backgrounds and social ranks. These newcomers to the Southwest included black and mulatto men and women, both enslaved and free. Authorities in Mexico, anxious to prevent runaways from escaping to another province, ordered the death penalty for any Indian or mulatto attempting to migrate without presenting clear identification. So when several hundred reinforcements headed north in 1600, nonwhites had to obtain clearance to depart.

In the century before the first Dutch slave-trading ship arrived in Virginia, Africans in North America had experienced all of the hardships and some of the opportunities associated with transatlantic colonization.

The Uncertain Century

During the first half of the sixteenth century, while Gomez and Esteban encountered the wilderness of America, Europe was shaken by a religious upheaval. The disruption was so large that its shock waves had a lasting influence on all parts of the Atlantic world, including Africa and North America. Members of Europe's Catholic church, led by German minister Martin Luther, "protested" against practices of the established priesthood and challenged the authority of the Pope. These dissenters, called Protestants, broke away from the Catholic church in Rome and organized their own Christian churches. Their mass movement, aiming to "reform" Christianity to a purer and simpler pattern of earlier times, became known as the Reformation. Encouraged by the theologian John Calvin in Geneva, this rebellion against papal authority soon gained its strongest support in northern Europe.

There were more than religious motivations for defying papal power in Rome. The Catholic church was also a major economic and political force across Europe. Its large cathedrals and numerous monasteries made it a dominant landholder throughout the continent, and the Pope supported, and benefited from, the enormous spoils that flowed to Europe as a result of Spanish conquest in the New World. Both England and the Netherlands, two lands caught up in the Reformation, were small countries with excellent ports and long seagoing traditions. By the second half of the sixteenth century they each had enough ships and sailors, backed by private capital and encouraged by government leaders, to dare to challenge the awesome sea power of Catholic Spain. The Protestant Reformation's ideas about humanity's relationship to God and about papal authority added a religious and political dimension to this challenge.

Defending its economic power and its religious ties, Spain emerged as the leader of an extended "Counter-Reformation," and by the 1580s this struggle had erupted into international warfare in Europe. Among the Dutch, the northern provinces rebelled successfully against Spanish control (becoming the country we know as Holland or the Netherlands). Among the English, Queen Elizabeth's seamen, led by Sir Francis Drake, repelled a huge invasion by an armada of Spanish ships in 1588. Emboldened by such triumphs and jealous of Spanish and Portuguese success overseas, Dutch and English sea captains became increasingly active in Atlantic waters and beyond.

As a result, these religious and political rivalries in Europe took on a much wider and more lasting significance, reaching out to touch and shape the lives of many distant peoples, including early African Americans. Reformation rivalries helped determine where Africans would be transported in the New World and by whom, as well as which new languages they would hear and what forms of Christianity they would encounter. Most importantly, these struggles meant that for an entire uncertain century, from the 1560s to the 1660s and beyond, it was by no means clear how many Africans would reach North America or what their exact status would be when they arrived.

One way for Englishmen to gain access to Spain's closely guarded dominions and profits in the New World was to seek a role in shipping non-Christians between Africa and Latin America. Englishmen first tried transporting Africans across the Atlantic for gain in the 1560s, when an Elizabethan "sea dog" named John Hawkins made several slaving voyages from Africa to the Caribbean. Spanish reluctance, not English scruples, cut short this approach. Alternative ways for England to undermine the powerful Spaniards involved plundering their gold fleet in the waters of the Gulf Stream, or—even more dangerously—attacking their Central American ports and inciting discontented Indians and enslaved Africans to revolt against their Spanish overlords. Raiding Panama for treasure in 1572, Francis Drake received valuable aid from the *cimarrones,* several thousand "valiant" Negroes living in the mountains who had, according to one English account, "fled from their cruel masters the Spaniards."

When Drake returned to the Spanish Caribbean on a similar mission in 1585, his countryman Sir Walter Raleigh sent a related expedition to the Atlantic Coast. Raleigh's men established an outpost at Roanoke Island. The spot (in modern-day North Carolina) was not far from Florida and was protected by the Outer Banks. From there, the colonists hoped to support raids against the Spaniards. In addition, the Protestant Englishmen intended to treat neighboring Indians and imported Africans with greater respect and humanity than their Catholic rivals had shown. The opportunity came sooner than they expected. Drake, having narrowly missed the Spanish treasure fleet, attacked several major Spanish ports, siding openly with local *cimarrones* and embittered slaves. In Santo Domingo and Cartagena he extracted huge ransoms, captured valuable ships, and liberated hundreds of enslaved men and women—Indians, Africans, Turks, and Moors. Frightened Spanish officials reported "the pains he took to carry off launches and frigates, implements, locks and all sorts of hardware and negro labourous who in his country are free."

Drake's next stop was at St. Augustine, where his men attacked the fort and encouraged local Indians to burn the town. The victorious little fleet, carrying people from three different continents, then headed north up the coast to Roanoke. Three black men who remained behind at St. Augustine confirmed to authorities that their liberator "meant to leave all the negroes he had in a fort and settlement established . . . by the English who went there a year ago." But when Drake reached Roanoke in June 1586, he found the officers and men ready to give up their enterprise as a failure. Before he could unload his newly freed reinforcements and captured hardware, a summer storm scattered his fleet from its unprotected anchorage. Within days Drake sailed for England in his remaining ships, taking most of the garrison with him. A further settlement effort on the same spot the following year with more than one hundred new colonists had disappeared by 1590, largely because boats carrying much-needed supplies were held in England to help resist the Spanish Armada.

The real mystery of this so-called "Lost Colony" is not what became of the English settlers; evidence suggests that most were absorbed peacefully into neighboring tribes. Instead, the most fascinating, and unanswerable, question concerns several hundred ex-slaves from the Caribbean. These people, mostly Africans, apparently vanished in the sudden storm, and records give no indication of their fate. But one wonders: what might have become of these "lost colonists" if they had managed to go ashore before the tempest struck? They would certainly have been put to work along with everyone else, for the outpost was short on supplies and needed additional hands. But the English, to score a propaganda victory, might have gone out of their way to convert these men and women to the Protestant religion and to make sure they lived more freely than under Spanish rule. Grateful for liberation and relative independence, these newcomers might have served in future Caribbean ventures, eager to gain revenge upon the Spanish, liberate fellow Africans, and share in possible spoils.

The transition to rigid and unwavering racial enslavement in North America still lay in the future. Black arrivals before 1680, several thousand in number, came from varied backgrounds and often had extensive Caribbean experience. Most had been denied their freedom in the West Indies and had been forced to work as slaves, but this did not mean that their status was fixed for life in the fledgling colonies of the mainland. Frequently they spoke one or more European languages; often they were of mixed European and African ancestry. They entered a world where religious identity and the practical demands of daily survival still counted for far more than one's physical appearance or ethnic background. Between 1600 and the 1670s, the status of Africans in North America remained varied and uncertain, as the Protestant English and Dutch pushed to establish new settlements along a coastline that the Spanish had once claimed as their own.

In 1609, the Dutch laid claim to the area now known as New York when Henry Hudson sailed up the river that now bears his name. Their colony, called New

During the seventeenth century, Dutch ships transported several thousand Africans to the New World each year. Most were enslaved on Brazilian and Caribbean sugar plantations, but a few hundred labored in New Amsterdam.

Netherland, began as a fur trading outpost, and African Americans appeared there aboard the earliest ships.

By 1628, the Dutch had constructed a crude fort at the tip of Manhattan Island. They planned to import enslaved Africans to augment the supply of farm laborers in the little village of New Amsterdam, which had a population of fewer than three hundred people. Several years later the Dutch West India Company imported additional slaves from the Caribbean to rebuild the fort, and by 1639, a company map showed a slave camp five miles north of the town housing newcomers from the West Indies. Though most black settlers were legally enslaved and some apparently lived in a separate settlement, these few initial Afro-Dutch residents did not lead a life totally apart from other colonists in New Amsterdam. Some were granted "half-freedom" (they lived independently but continued to pay an annual tax); others were manumitted, or freed, by their owners and possessed their own land and labor. Indeed, it was possible for a European woman to work for an African freeman as an indentured servant.

Early Dutch records make clear that blacks were active in the courts. In June 1639, for example, a freeman named Pedro Negretto, who worked as a day laborer alongside Dutch farmhands, sued Jan Celes for failing to pay him for taking care of his hogs. Similarly, religious documents show that the few Africans who professed Christianity were permitted to marry within the Dutch Reformed church. Among fifty marriages recorded by the New Amsterdam church from 1639 to 1652, thirteen involved unions between black men and black women. When Indian wars threatened, as in 1641, Africans found themselves recruited by the governor and council to venture out in teams against Indian hunting parties.

Though Holland steadily expanded its role in transporting Africans to the Americas, the population of New Netherland grew slowly at first. For the most part, the powerful Dutch confined their major traffic to the burgeoning plantation economies of the South Atlantic. They focused particularly on Portuguese Brazil, seizing temporary control there in 1637. They also took from the Portuguese several ports in Africa (Elmina on the Gold Coast and Luanda in Angola), and soon they were transporting 2,500 Africans per year west across the South Atlantic. A few of these people eventually ended up in New Amsterdam, as suggested by the presence in the records of such names as Paulo d'Angola, Simon Congo, and Anthony Portuguese.

In 1654, the Dutch lost control of Brazil, where they had been shipping thousands of Africans, so distant New Netherland suddenly became a more attractive destination for Dutch slavers from the South Atlantic. The first shipload of several hundred people brought directly from Africa arrived at the mouth of the Hudson in 1655. More shipments followed, and many of the enslaved passengers were promptly resold to English planters in the Chesapeake colonies seeking additional workers. By this time the Dutch had made peace with the Spanish and found themselves at war with their former ally, England. In 1664, when the English seized New Netherland and renamed it New York, there may have been as many as seven hundred Dutch-speaking black residents in a population of nine thousand. The Dutch soon turned their colonizing attention to other places—such as South Africa, where they had established a colony at the Cape of Good Hope in 1652.

It would be the English who expanded their hold on the Atlantic Coast of North America and steadily increased the number of blacks living there. As more black newcomers appeared in the English mainland colonies, racial designations gradually took on new significance. Eventually, legal codes would impose hereditary enslavement, and profit-conscious traders would undertake the importation of slaves directly from Africa.

An early muster roll from the Plymouth Colony in New England, founded by the Pilgrims in 1620, shows that at least one African—or "blackamoor," the old English term for a dark-skinned African—was present in the community by the early 1630s and was serving in the militia. The journal of John Winthrop, governor of the larger Massachusetts Bay Colony (founded in 1630), makes clear that in 1638, not long after the English defeat of the neighboring Pequot Indians, a Boston sea captain carried Native American captives to the West Indies and brought back "salt, cotton, tobacco, and Negroes." Six years later, in 1644, Boston merchants sent several ships directly to the West African coast, a small beginning to a pattern of New England slave trading that would continue for a century and a half.

At the start of the seventeenth century, Christian Europeans still tended to see political and religious, not physical, differences as the key divisions among mankind. Enemies in foreign wars and adherents to different faiths could be captured and enslaved. For this reason, John Smith, a leader of the English colony at Jamestown, had been forced briefly into slavery by the Muslims when fighting in Eastern Europe as a young man; "infidel" Pequots who opposed Winthrop's men in New England were sold into bondage in the Caribbean. Such enslavement was not always for life; conversion to the religion of the captor and other forms of good behavior could result in freedom. A law passed in the colony of Rhode Island in 1652 even attempted to limit the term of involuntary servitude to ten years.

By mid-century, however, the condition of unfree colonists in North America had started to change. In the older colonies of the Spanish New World to the south, a pattern of hereditary servitude based upon race had long ago evolved into a powerful and irresistible system of exploitation. Now, slowly, this destructive institution began to gain a substantial foothold in the small colonies of the North American mainland as well. Its emergence would have a devastating effect on the next generation of Africans to cross the Atlantic, and upon all of their descendants for several long centuries to come.

The Terrible Transformation

During the second half of the seventeenth century, a terrible transformation, the enslavement of people solely on the basis of race, occurred in the lives of African Americans living in North America. These newcomers still numbered only a few thousand, but the bitter reversals they experienced—first subtle, then drastic—would shape the lives of all those who followed them, generation after generation.

The timing and nature of the change varied considerably from colony to colony, and even from family to family. Gradually, the terrible transformation took on a momentum of its own, numbing and burdening everything in its path, like a disastrous winter storm. Unlike the changing seasons, however, the encroachment of racial slavery in the colonies of North America was certainly not a natural process. It was highly unnatural—the work of powerful competitive governments and many thousands of human beings spread out across the Atlantic world. Nor was it inevitable that people's legal status would come to depend upon their racial background and that the condition of slavery would be passed down from parent to child. Numerous factors combined to bring about this disastrous shift. It is worth exploring how all these human forces swirled together during the decades after 1650, to create an enormously destructive storm.

This Indenture

Witnesseth, That I *Jaques Rapalje, of New York*

Hath put himself, and by these Presents, *and* — — — —

— — — — — — — — — — — — doth voluntarily, and of his own free Will and Accord, put himself Apprentice to *William Faulkner of Brookland in Kings County* — — — — to learn the Art, Trade and Mystery of *Brewing Malting & Fining Bar* and after the Manner of an Apprentice, to serve from the Day of the Date hereof, for and during, and until the full End and Term of *five Years then* — — — — — — — next ensuing; during all which Time, the said Apprentice his said Master faithfully shall serve, his Secrets keep, his lawful Commands every where readily obey: He shall do no Damage to his said Master, nor see it to be done by others, without letting or giving Notice thereof to his said Master: He shall not waste his said Master's Goods, nor lend them unlawfully to any: He shall not commit Fornication, nor contract Matrimony within the said Term: At Cards, Dice, or any other unlawful Game, he shall not play, whereby his said Master may have Damage: With his own Goods, nor the Goods of others, without Licence from his said Master, he shall neither buy nor sell: He shall not absent himself Day nor Night from his said Master's Service, without his Leave; nor haunt Ale houses, Taverns, or Play-houses; but in all Things behave himself as a faithful Apprentice ought to do, during the said Term. And the said Master shall use the utmost of his Endeavour to teach, or cause to be taught, or instructed, the said Apprentice in the Trade or Mystery of *Brewing Malting & Fining Bar* and procure and provide for him sufficient Meat, Drink,

Lodging and Washing, fitting for an Apprentice, during the said Term of *five Years To be found by Garret Rapalje,*

AND for the true Performance of all and singular the Covenants and Agreements aforesaid, the said Parties bind themselves each unto the other firmly by these Presents. In Witness whereof the said Parties have interchangeably set their Hands and Seals hereunto. Dated the *First* Day of *August* — — — in the *Sixteenth* Year of the Reign of our Sovereign Lord GEORGE the Third, King of Great-Britain, &c. Annoq; Domini, One Thousand Seven Hundred and *50*

Sealed and delivered in the Presence of

Robt Wilson

Andrew Van Tuye

Jaques Rapalje

The indenture papers of Jacques Rapalje, a white immigrant who agreed to work for a New York brewer for five years. Many Europeans arrived in America as indentured servants. Their labor belonged to their master for a set number of years, after which they were free.

Consider the situation at mid-century along the Atlantic Coast. Except for St. Augustine in Florida, there were no colonial settlements south of Chesapeake Bay. The English and Dutch colonies remained extremely small. As growing communities, they felt a steady need for additional hands, but their first priority was to add persons of their own religion and nationality. Many newcomers labored for others, but most of them were "indentured"—they had signed contracts to work under fixed conditions for a limited number of years. Their term could be shortened for good service or lengthened for disobeying the laws, but when their indenture expired they looked forward to having land of their own. Ships sailing back to England and Holland regularly carried letters describing the pluses and minuses of each colony. As a result of this continuous feedback, European migrants learned to avoid the settlements that had the longest indentures, the poorest working conditions, and the least amount of available land.

Conditions in the Caribbean and Latin America were strikingly different. There, for well over a century, Spanish and Portuguese colonizers had enslaved "infidels": first Indians and then Africans. At first, they relied for justification upon the Mediterranean tradition that persons of a different religion, or persons captured in war, could be enslaved for life. But hidden in this idea of slavery was the notion that persons who converted to Christianity should receive their freedom. Wealthy planters in the tropics, afraid that their cheap labor would be taken away from them because of this loophole, changed the reasoning behind their exploitation. Even persons who could prove that they were not captured in war and that they accepted the Catholic faith still could not change their appearance. So by making color the key factor behind enslavement, dark-skinned people brought from Africa to work in silver mines and on sugar plantations could be exploited for life. Indeed, the condition could be made hereditary, so enslaved people's children automatically inherited the same unfree status.

By 1650, hereditary enslavement based upon color, not upon religion, was a bitter reality in the older Catholic colonies of the New World. But this cruel and self-perpetuating system had not yet taken firm hold in North America for a variety of reasons. The same anti-Catholic propaganda that had led Sir Francis Drake to liberate Negro slaves in Central America in the 1580s still prompted many colonists to believe that it was the Protestant mission to convert non-Europeans rather than enslave them. Apart from such moral concerns, there were simple matters of cost and practicality. Workers subject to longer terms and coming from further away would require a larger initial investment.

By 1650, however, conditions were already beginning to change. For one thing, both the Dutch and the English had started using enslaved Africans to produce sugar in the Caribbean and the tropics. English experiments at Barbados and Providence Island showed that Protestant investors could easily overcome their moral scruples. Large profits could be made if foreign rivals could be held in check. After agreeing to peace with Spain and giving up control of Northeast Brazil at mid-century, Dutch slave traders were actively looking for new markets. In England, after Charles II was restored to the throne in 1660 he rewarded supporters by creating the Royal African Company to enter aggressively into the slave trade. The English king also chartered a new colony in Carolina. He hoped it would be close enough to the Spanish in Florida and the Caribbean to challenge them in economic and military terms. Many of the first English settlers in Carolina after 1670 came from Barbados. They brought enslaved Africans with them. They also brought the beginnings of a legal code and a social system that accepted race slavery.

While new colonies with a greater acceptance of race slavery were being founded, the older colonies continued to grow. Early in the seventeenth century no tiny North American port could absorb several hundred workers arriving at one time on a large ship. Most Africans—such as those reaching Jamestown in 1619—arrived several dozen at a time aboard small boats and privateers from the Caribbean. Like Mingo, who was working among white indentured servants on a Virginia farm in 1648, they tended to mix with other unfree workers on small plantations. All of these servants, no matter what their origin, could hope to obtain their own land and the personal independence that goes with private property. In 1645, in Northampton County on Virginia's Eastern Shore, Captain Philip Taylor, after complaining that "Anthony the negro" did not work hard enough for him, agreed to set aside part of the corn field where they worked as Anthony's plot. "I am very glad of it," the black man told a local clerk, "now I know myne owne ground and I will worke when I please and play when I please."

Gradually, it was becoming harder to obtain English labor in the mainland colonies. Civil War and a great plague reduced England's population, and the Great Fire of London created fresh demands for workers at home. Stiff penalties were imposed on sea captains who grabbed young people in England and sold them in the colonies as indentured servants. (This common practice was given a new name: "kidnapping.") English servants already at work in the colonies demanded shorter indentures, better working conditions, and suitable farmland when their contracts expired. Officials feared they would lose future English recruits to rival colonies if bad publicity filtered back to Europe, so they could not ignore this pressure, even when it undermined colonial profits.

Nor could colonial planters turn instead to Indian labor. Native Americans captured in frontier wars continued to be enslaved, but each act of aggression by European colonists made future diplomacy with neighboring Indians more difficult. Native American captives could easily escape into the familiar wilderness and return to their original tribe. Besides, their numbers were limited. African Americans, in contrast, were thousands of miles from their homeland, and their availability increased as the scope of the Atlantic slave trade expanded. More European countries competed to transport and exploit African labor; more West African leaders proved willing to engage in profitable trade with them; more New World planters had the money to purchase new workers from across the ocean. It seemed as though every decade the ships became larger, the contacts more regular, the departures more frequent, the routes more familiar, the sales more efficient.

As the size and efficiency of this brutal traffic increased, so did its rewards for European investors. Their ruthless competition pushed up the volume of transatlantic trade from Africa and drove down the relative cost of individual Africans in the New World at a time when the price of labor from Europe was rising. As their profits increased, slave merchants and their captains continued to look for fresh markets. North America, on the fringe of this expanding and infamous Atlantic system, represented a likely target. As the small mainland colonies grew and their trade with one another and with England increased, their capacity to purchase large numbers of new laborers from overseas expanded. By the end of the century, Africans were arriving aboard large ships directly from Africa as well as on smaller boats from the West Indies. In 1698, the monopoly held by England's Royal African Company on this transatlantic business came to an end, and independent traders from England and the colonies stepped up their voyages, intending to capture a share of the profits.

All these large and gradual changes would still not have brought about the terrible transformation to race slavery, had it not been for several other crucial factors. One ingredient was the mounting fear among colonial leaders regarding signs of discontent and cooperation among poor and unfree colonists of all sorts. Europeans and Africans worked together, intermarried, ran away together, and shared common resentments toward the well-to-do. Both groups were involved in a series of bitter strikes and servant uprisings among tobacco pickers in Virginia, culminating in an open rebellion in 1676. Greatly outnumbered by these armed workers, authorities were quick to sense the need to divide their labor force in order to control it. Stressing cultural and ethnic divisions would be one way to do that.

A second crucial ingredient contributing to worsening conditions was the total lack of feedback within the stream of African arrivals. If masters mistreated their English servants, word of such abuses could reach England and influence future migration. Whether this information traveled by letter or by word of mouth, it provided an incentive for fair treatment that did not exist for migrants brought from Africa. Once deported across the Atlantic, Africans had no prospect of returning to their homeland, and few European sailors possessed the will, or the language skill, to carry the full story of New World enslavement back to the seaports of West Africa. Therefore, when an English master misused his African workers, it had no influence upon the future supply of labor from that continent. He was therefore tempted to hold them for life, reasoning that they had been enslaved for life long before he ever saw them. Once they were held for life, he could not extend their term of service for bad behavior (the usual punishment for indentured servants), so he resorted increasingly to harsh physical punishments, knowing that this year's brutality would not effect next year's supply of African labor.

Lifetime servitude could be enforced only by removing the prospect that a person might gain freedom through Christian conversion. One approach was to outlaw this traditional route to freedom. As early as 1664, a Maryland statute specified that Christian baptism could have no effect upon the legal status of a slave. A more sweeping solution, however, involved removing religion altogether as a factor in determining servitude. Therefore, a third and fundamental key to the terrible transformation was the shift from changeable spiritual faith to unchangeable physical appearance as a measure of status. Increasingly, the dominant English came to view Africans not as "heathen people" but as "black people." They began, for the first time, to describe themselves not as Christians but as whites. And they gradually wrote this shift into their colonial laws. Within a generation, the English definition of who could be made a slave had shifted from someone who was not a Christian to someone who was not European in appearance. Indeed, the transition for self-interested Englishmen went further. It was a small but momentous step from saying that black persons *could* be enslaved to saying that Negroes *should* be enslaved. One Christian minister was dismayed by this rapid change to slavery based on race: "these two words, *Negro* and *Slave*," wrote the Reverend Morgan Godwyn in 1680, are "by custom grown Homogeneous and Convertible"—that is, interchangeable.

As if this momentous shift were not enough, it was accompanied by another. Those who wrote the colonial laws not only moved to make slavery *racial*; they also made it *hereditary*. Under English common law, a child inherited the legal status of the father. As Virginia officials put it when looking into the case of Elizabeth Key in 1655: "by the Comon Law the Child of a Woman slave begott by a freeman ought to bee free." Elizabeth, called Black Bess by her neighbors, was the mulatto daughter of Thomas Key and his Negro servant. As a child, she had been indentured by her father for nine years to Colonel Humphrey Higginson, but after Thomas Key died others had attempted to extend her term of service indefinitely.

Now Bess was in her mid-twenties and anxious to prove her free status in court before marrying William Greensted. After hearing sworn testimony, the authorities ruled that "the said Elizabeth ought to bee free and that her last Master should give her Corne and Cloathes and give her satisfaction for the time shee hath served longer than Shee ought to have done." Bess did indeed have the same status as her father and was free to marry William. But within seven years that option had been removed. Faced with similar cases of "whether children got by any Englishman upon a negro woman should be slave or Free," the Virginia Assembly in 1662 decided in favor of the master demanding service rather than the child claiming freedom. In this special circumstance, the Assembly ignored all English precedents that children inherited the name and status of their father. Instead, the men in the colonial legislature declared that all such children "borne in this country shal be held bond or free only according to the condition of the mother." In Virginia, and soon elsewhere, the children of slave mothers would be slaves forever.

This 1680 document contains a land grant at the top, and at the bottom a manumission document for "Negro Harry" from South Carolina. As the nature of slavery in the colonies changed, such routes to freedom became less available.

To satisfy their huge demand for labor in America, colonial empires developed the vicious circle depicted here. Europeans offered guns, rum, and trade goods to Africans for enemies captured in local wars. With profits from reselling these enslaved workers in the New World, they imported more guns and rum to encourage further conflict, which in turn provided additional African captives.

Now the terrible transformation was almost complete, with the colony of Virginia leading the way. An additional legal sleight of hand by the land-hungry Virginia gentry helped speed the process. For several generations, as an incentive toward immigration, newcomers had received title to a parcel of land, called a "headright," for every family member or European servant they brought to the struggling colony. By expanding this system to include Africans, self-interested planter-magistrates, who were rich enough to make the initial investment in enslaved workers, managed to obtain free land, as well as valuable labor, every time they purchased an African worker.

A Nation of Newcomers

In 1976, the African-American writer Alex Haley traced the story of his black family in the popular book *Roots*. He discovered that his "furthest-back-person" in America was Kunte Kinte, a Gambian who had been brought in chains from West Africa to Annapolis, Maryland, in the 1760s aboard the English slave ship *Lord Ligonier*. Haley was fortunate in knowing the name of his first American forebear and in being able to locate the exact ship on which he arrived. But the facts themselves are remarkably typical. On average, the furthest-back New World ancestor for any African American today would have reached these shores shortly before the American Revolution, just as Kunte Kinte did. (By comparison, the largest migrations of Europeans and Asians to the United States began in the late nineteenth century and grew larger in the twentieth century.)

Newcomers like Kunte Kinte were part of a large forced migration that started in earnest shortly before 1700 and ended, for the most part, shortly after 1800. By the time the government of the young United States prohibited further importation of enslaved Africans in 1807, well over 400,000 people had been brought to North America directly from Africa or indirectly via the Caribbean. (Most of these people were transported to English-speaking settlements on the East Coast, although some entered Florida and Louisiana; many fewer entered Canada and the Spanish Southwest.) Roughly 100,000 of these enslaved people arrived during the final generation of the slave trade, between 1776 and 1807. This means that more than 300,000 Africans reached North America during the century stretching between 1675 and 1775. They were described at the time as "Saltwater Negroes," Africans who had endured the Atlantic crossing. This diverse group of men and women occupies an important place in American history.

Even though these black ancestors arrived in North America *early* compared to most white ancestors, they arrived *late* in comparison with Africans elsewhere in the New World. In addition, these ancestors represent a surprisingly small part— less than five percent—of the entire transatlantic movement from Africa.

Moreover, even within the British portion of the vast African trade, Africans sent to North American ports represented only a small portion of the total exodus. Between 1690 and 1807, English captains deported nearly 2.75 million slaves from Africa. Most were sold in foreign ports, but English planters on the tiny island of Barbados purchased more African slaves than all the mainland British colonies combined, and English-controlled Jamaica absorbed fully twice as many workers. Finally, unlike their countrymen dispersed through the sugar cultures of the tropics, the Africans transported to North America managed to live longer on average and bear more children. Almost from the start, the number of births regularly exceeded the number of deaths in most places over the course of each year, meaning that the black population grew steadily, regardless of new importations from Africa.

The conditions faced by these saltwater slaves were less horrendous than those encountered by their black contemporaries entering the sugar colonies of Latin America. But they were decidedly worse than those faced by the few thousand Africans reaching North America before 1675 (or by the numerous Europeans who arrived in increasing numbers throughout the eighteenth century). Diverse forces combined in the late seventeenth century to slowly and terribly transform the status of African arrivals from bad to worse.

Two further adjustments assured that this system of race-based exploitation would endure across North America for generations—and in some regions for more than 150 years. The first shift involved the creation of strict legal codes in one colony after another, spelling out the organized practice of discrimination and giving it the full force of the law. Wealthy white assemblymen, representing the landowning gentry who would benefit the most financially from these changes, enacted statutes that destroyed the legal standing of African Americans. The laws of the land they had entered viewed them not as humans with rights but as property to be controlled by others. Specific statutes prohibited enslaved blacks from earning wages, moving about freely, congregating in groups, seeking education, marrying whites, carrying firearms, resisting punishment, or testifying in court. In 1705, Virginia legislators gathered diverse laws aimed against blacks into a single comprehensive "slave code," and other colonies followed this example.

English colonists took another step as well—less formal but equally destructive. Brutal and dehumanizing treatment of African newcomers was approved not only in the colonial courts of law, but also in the broad court of white public opinion. The phenomenon all Americans know as "racism"—which peaked in the nineteenth century and persists even at the end of the twentieth century—first emerged as a solid feature of North American society in the early eighteenth century. In Boston, the prominent Puritan minister Cotton Mather (himself a slaveholder) generalized about what he viewed as the "stupidity" of Negroes. In 1701, another Bostonian refused to free his African slave on the grounds that the "character" of every black person was innately deficient.

Unquestionably, signs of European prejudice and discrimination toward Indians and Africans had been present in the English colonies from the start. But this poisonous pattern of mistrust and abuse became widespread and central within the culture only after 1700, as race slavery rapidly expanded. One indication of this racism was the increased hostility toward marriages between Africans and Europeans. Such interracial unions became illegal in Virginia in 1691, in Massachusetts in 1705, in Maryland in 1715, and soon after in most other colonies.

Another indication was the sharp prejudice exhibited toward free blacks. A law passed in Virginia in 1699 required black persons receiving their freedom to leave the colony within six months. The assembly argued that additional free blacks would represent "great inconveniences ... by their either entertaining negro slaves ..., or receiving stolen goods, or being grown old bringing a charge upon the country."

City of New-York, *fs.*

A LAW,

For Regulating Negroes and Slaves in the Night Time.

BE *It Ordained by the Mayor, Recorder, Aldermen and Affiftants of the City of* New-York, *convened in Common-Council, and it is hereby Ordained by the Authority of the fame,* That from hence-forth no Negro, Mulatto or Indian Slave, above the Age of Fourteen Years, do prefume to be or appear in any of the Streets. of this City, on the South-fide of the Frefh-Water, in the Night time, above an hour after Sun-fet; And that if any fuch Negro, Mulatto or Indian Slave or Slaves, as aforefaid, fhall be found in any of the Streets of this City, or in any other Place, on the South fide of the Frefh-Water, in the Night-time, above one hour after Sun-fet, without a Lanthorn and lighted Candle in it, fo as the light thereof may be plainly feen (and not in company with his, her or their Mafter or Miftrefs, or fome White Perfon or White Servant belonging to the Family whofe Slave he or fhe is, or in whofe Service he or fhe then are) That then and in fuch cafe it fhall and may be lawful for any of his Majefty's Subjects within the faid City to apprehend fuch Slave or Slaves, not having fuch Lanthorn and Candle, and forth-with carry him, her or them before the Mayor or Recorder, or any one of the Aldermen of the faid City (if at a feafonable hour) and if at an unfeafonable hour, to the Watch-houfe, there to be confined until the next Morning) who are hereby authorized, upon Proof of the Offence, to commit fuch Slave or Slaves to the common Goal, for fuch his, her or their Contempt, and there to remain uptil the Mafter, Miftrefs or Owner of every fuch Slave or Slaves, fhall pay to the Perfon or Perfons who apprehended and committed every fuch Slave or Slaves, the Sum of *Four Shillings* current *Money of New-York,* for his, her or their pains and Trouble therein, with Reafonable Charges of Profecution.

And be it further Ordained by the Authority aforefaid, That every Slave or Slaves that fhall be convicted of the Offence aforefaid, before he, fhe or they be difcharged out of Cuftody, fhall be Whipped at the Publick Whipping-Poft (not exceeding *Forty Lashes*) if defired by the Mafter or Owner of fuch Slave or Slaves.

Provided always, and it is the intent hereof, That if two or more Slaves (Not exceeding the Number of Three) be together in any lawful Employ or Labour for the Service of their Mafter or Miftrefs (and not otherwife) and only one of them have and carry fuch Lanthorn with a lighted Candle therein, the other Slaves in fuch Compay not carrying a Lanthorn and lighted Candle, fhall not be conftrued and intended to be within the meaning and Penalty of this Law, any thing in this Law contained to the contrary hereof in any wife notwithftanding. *Dated at the City-Hall this Two and Twentieth Day of* April, *in the fourth year of His Majefty's Reign,* Annoq; Domini **1731**.

By Order of Common Council,

Will. Sharpas, Cl.

Towns and colonies drafted elaborate legislation controlling the activities and limiting the mobility of enslaved workers. This law, passed by the Common Council of New York City in 1731, prohibited any "Negro, Mulatto or Indian slave" above the age of fourteen from appearing on the streets of the city at night alone without a lantern. Those caught breaking this law could receive as many a forty lashes at the public whipping post.

Ironically, as the situation worsened and the options diminished for African Americans, their population in certain English mainland colonies rose dramatically. In the forty years between 1680 and 1720, the proportion of blacks in Virginia's population jumped from seven percent to thirty percent, as white landowners shifted from a labor system of indentured servitude to one of chattel slavery. "They import so many Negros hither," observed planter William Byrd II, "that I fear this Colony will some time or other be confirmed by the Name of New Guinea." In South Carolina during the same four decades the African increase was even more pronounced: from seventeen percent to seventy percent. During the 1740s and 1750s, an average of five thousand Africans per year were being sold into bondage on American docks. In 1760, Virginia had more than 130,000 black residents, and fifteen years later the number had jumped beyond 185,000. By the eve of the American Revolution, the proportion of African Americans in the population of North America was higher than it would ever be in any subsequent generation.

Several hundred thousand Africans appear as nameless statistics in ship logs and port records from eighteenth-century North America. Only in exceptional cases can we reconstruct the life of an individual saltwater slave with much certainty. Ayuba Suleiman Diallo, best known as Job ben Solomon, is one such exception. He was born around 1702 to Tanomata, the wife of a Fula high priest named Solomon Diallo in the region of Bondou between the Senegal and Gambia rivers of West Africa, more than two hundred miles inland from the Atlantic Ocean.

Raised as a Muslim, Job could read and write Arabic easily; by the time he was fifteen this exceptional student had committed the Koran to memory and could copy it by heart. His education proved his salvation after March 1, 1731, when he suddenly found himself in chains aboard an English slave ship. He was no stranger to the slave trade, for French captains on the Senegal and English captains on the Gambia further south bartered regularly for captives, and merchant families like the Diallos often took advantage of this stiff competition to drive profitable bargains. Indeed, by his own later account, Job had just sold two persons into slavery in exchange for twenty-eight cattle. He was beginning the long trek home with his new herd when he was suddenly kidnapped by a group of Mandingo men and sold to an Englishman on the Gambia, Captain Pyke of the *Arabella*. Job sent a message to his wealthy father asking for help, but before the distant priest could ransom his son (by providing two replacement slaves), the *Arabella* had set sail across the Atlantic.

For Captain Pyke, the transit from Africa to America was the middle leg of a three-part voyage that began and ended in England and was designed to bring profit to investors Henry and William Hunt. But for the Africans crammed below decks, this middle passage was a terrifying one-way journey from which no one could expect to return. The voyage from James Fort on the Gambia River to Annapolis, Maryland, on Chesapeake Bay was long and hard, as Kunte Kinte would discover three decades later. The men and women were kept in separate, foul-smelling holds. They were given terrible food and almost no chance to move about. For some, the endless motion of the ship brought seasickness; for others, the constant chafing against hard boards created open sores that could not heal. The threat of infection and epidemic disease hung over the captives constantly, made worse by their crowded conditions and the daily changes in temperature below decks, from scorching heat to damp chill.

When the crew, in its daily inspections, found that some had died, their bodies were literally "thrown to the sharks." This prompted further despair, and some, if they shared a common language, spoke of violent revolt. They were physically weakened, narrowly confined, and closely watched. Moreover, they were totally unarmed, uncertain of their whereabouts, and innocent of the workings of the large ship, so an uprising seemed nearly suicidal. Despite these odds, a shipload of passengers occasionally attempted to rebel. But most, however desperate, struggled simply to endure, praying to be saved from this nightmare into the unknown.

For Job ben Solomon, almost alone among more than 100,000 prisoners transported from the Senegambia region to the New World aboard British ships, this prayer would eventually be answered. When Pyke reached Annapolis, he turned over saltwater slaves to Vachell Denton, a local "factor," or agent, who was paid by merchant William Hunt of London to sell the *Arabella*'s human cargo at a profit. When Denton put Job on the auction block, he was purchased for forty-five pounds by Alexander Tolsey, a planter from Queen Anne's County. Job's new master attempted to change his name to Simon and put him to work picking tobacco and herding cattle. This latter task was a thoroughly familiar one, and it gave him time to pray regularly in the woods and also to plan an escape. But when he ran away in desperation, he was captured easily and confined to jail in the back of a local tavern. While there he was visited by an elderly saltwater slave who could still speak Wolof, Job's native language, and the old man explained to Job the full outlines of his predicament.

The ingenious young Fula now wrote a note in Arabic to his important father, explaining his dilemma and requesting Captain Pyke to deliver the letter on his next voyage to the Gambia River. Against all odds, Job sent it to Mr. Denton in Annapolis, who forwarded the curiosity to Mr. Hunt in London, who in turn showed a copy to friends until a translation was obtained from a professor of Arabic at Oxford University. Officials of the Royal African Company, including James Oglethorpe, the idealistic founder of the Georgia colony, took an immediate interest in the note. The author clearly had powerful relatives in Africa who might be of use in future trading ventures, if only the captive could be located in Maryland and returned safely to Gambia. Tediously, the sum of forty-five pounds passed from Oglethorpe to Hunt to Denton to Tolsey, and by the spring of 1733 Job was aboard a ship sailing from Annapolis to London. During the eight-week voyage, between bouts of seasickness, he practiced his English and mastered the European alphabet.

In London, officials of the Royal African Company prepared a certificate "setting forth that Simon otherwise called Job the Gambia black lately brought from Maryland, is . . . to be a free man; and that he is at liberty to take his passage to Africa in any of the Company's ships." They assured Job they would avoid taking Muslim slaves in the future. In return, he agreed to assist them in their competition with the French to gain access to his homeland and its traffic in gold, gum, and non-Muslim slaves. He reached the Gambia River in August 1734, after four years away from Africa, and was met by Francis Moore, the Royal African Company's agent at James Fort.

Moore was eager to benefit from Job's return, so he sent a messenger to Bondou. The man returned in several weeks with disheartening news. According to Moore, he reported that Job's father had recently died and his prosperous country, once noted for its "numerous herds of large cattle," had been ravaged by such a terrible war "that there is not so much as one cow left in it." On top of all that, one of Job's wives had given him up for lost and had married another man. As Moore recorded in his journal, Job "wept grievously for his father's death, and the misfortunes of his country. He forgave his wife, and the man that had taken her; for, says he, Mr. Moore, she could not help thinking I was dead, for I was gone to a land from whence no Pholey [Fula] ever yet returned; therefore she is not to be blamed, nor the man neither."

Though Job ben Solomon's personal sorrows seemed heavy, his biographer rightly calls him "the fortunate slave." Thousands upon thousands were less fortunate, torn away from Africa unwillingly and sold into bondage overseas, with no hope of return. Some of these men and women had already been slaves in their own lands—captured in war, condemned for a crime, or purchased for a price. But they had been treated as people, not as property. They had been allowed to marry and raise families, and their children did not face continuous servitude. Captives deported across the ocean faced a new kind of slavery. They entered a system driven by enormous profits, tolerated by the Christian churches, bolstered by increasing racism, and backed by the full sanction of the law. Very few found ways to tell their story, but one who did was named Olaudah Equiano, who was seized with his sister at age eleven and shipped to Virginia via Barbados.

Equiano was born in 1745 among the Ibo people living near the lower Niger River, an area under the loose control of the king of Benin. Like Job ben Solomon, Olaudah grew up in a slave-owning family. Like Job, he was captured in his native land and shipped to Chesapeake Bay, eventually gaining his freedom and making his way to England. Unlike Job, he did not return to Africa and become a participant in the slave trade from which he had escaped. Instead, he sailed extensively during the era of the American Revolution—to Jamaica, Portugal, Turkey, Greenland. He spoke frequently in Britain about the evils of slavery, and in 1789 he published a vivid autobiography, in which he described the circumstances of his arrival in the New World.

At last we came in sight of the island of Barbadoes, at which the whites on board gave a great shout, and made many signs of joy to us. We did not know what to think of this; but as the vessel drew nearer, we plainly saw the harbor, and other ships of different kinds and sizes, and we anchored amongst them, off Bridgetown. Many merchants and planters now came on board, though it was in the evening. They put us in separate parcels, and examined us attentively. They also made us jump, and pointed to the land, signifying we were to go there. We thought by this, we should be eaten by these ugly men, as they appeared to us; and, when soon after we were all put down under the deck again, there was much dread and trembling among us, and nothing but bitter cries to be heard all the night from these apprehensions, insomuch, that at last the white people got some old slaves from the land to pacify us. They told us we were not to be eaten, but to work, and were soon to go on land, where we should see many of our country people. This report eased us much. And sure enough, soon after we were landed, there came to us Africans of all languages.

We were conducted immediately to the merchant's yard, where we were all pent up together, like so many sheep in a fold, without regard to sex or age. As every object was new to me, everything I saw filled me with surprise. What struck me first, was, that the houses were built with bricks and stories, and in every other respect different from those I had seen in Africa.

We were not many days in the merchant's custody, before we were sold after their usual manner. . . . I now totally lost the small remains of comfort I had enjoyed in conversing with my countrymen; the women too, who used to wash and take care of me were all gone different ways, and I never saw one of them afterwards.

I stayed in this island for a few days, I believe it could not be above a fortnight, when I, and some few more slaves, that were not saleable amongst the rest, from very much fretting, were shipped off in a sloop for North America. On the passage we were better treated than when we were coming from Africa, and we had plenty of rice and fat pork. We were landed up a river a good way from the sea, about Virginia county, where we saw few or none of our native Africans, and not one soul who could talk to me. I was a few weeks weeding grass and gathering stones in a plantation; and at last my companions were distributed different ways, and only myself was left. I was now exceedingly miserable.

Those Africans like Equiano who were shipped to North America made up only one small portion of an enormous stream. But their numbers grew rapidly, particularly in the Southern colonies. Between 1770 and 1775, Charleston, South Carolina, was receiving four thousand Africans per year. All of them were held for several weeks at the so-called pest house on Sullivan's Island, a quarantine station designed to prevent the arrival of epidemics from overseas. So many people arrived there that it has been called "the Ellis Island of black America." Yet unlike the Europeans who poured into New York City through Ellis Island in the late nineteenth and early twentieth centuries, the saltwater slaves of the eighteenth century could have little hope for a life that was more self-sufficient or humane than the one they left behind.

A World of Work

Most immigrants coming to North America arrive with high hopes. They expect to work hard, and they assume their efforts will somehow yield tangible rewards for themselves or their children. Over the centuries the dream has not always been fulfilled, but the dream exists. It did not exist, however, for Africans arriving in colonial North America after the terrible transformation. They had no choice in their deportation and no knowledge of their destination. From the hold of a slave ship, they could only speculate about the reason for their abduction and the nature of their impending fate.

What awaited them was a world of work—lifetimes of unending labor, rigidly controlled. Equiano and thousands of other people like him soon came to the realization that they were to be kept alive, but only in order to work. Their labor would benefit others, rather than themselves. They would be granted minimal food and clothing and shelter in exchange for their toil; there would be no wages and no possibility to save for a better future. Indeed, it seemed clear there would be no better future. The incentive for parents to work hard so that their children could enjoy a better life had been removed for almost all Africans by the terrible transformation to race slavery, which obliged each generation to inherit the same unfree status as the last.

The servitude facing African newcomers was the horrible outgrowth of unprecedented economic warfare on an international scale. With the rise of European exploration overseas, the battles for supremacy among a few rival monarchies had spread far beyond Europe. Their struggles to establish profitable colonies abroad took on new intensity after the religious Reformation divided Europe into competing Protestant and Catholic powers. By creating diverse colonial settlements, each country hoped to provide itself with a steady flow of resources—gold and silver, furs and fish, timber and tobacco, sugar and rice. At the same time, they would prevent rivals from obtaining access to the same goods, unless they were willing to pay a high price.

By 1700, mounting competition had led to the creation of numerous New World colonies, and during the eighteenth century rival European powers would establish additional outposts in all corners of North America. In successive generations the French colonized Louisiana, the English settled Georgia, the Spanish entered California, and the Russians laid claim to Alaska. Though very different in location and purpose, each new European settlement demanded a steady supply of labor in order to survive and grow as a profitable colony. In many places accessible to the transatlantic slave trade, it was Africans who filled that growing demand for labor during the century before the American Revolution.

Work, therefore, dominated the lives of all enslaved African Americans—men and women, young and old. But the nature of that work varied significantly from one place to the next, from one season to the next, and from one generation to the next. Cotton agriculture, though present in Africa, did not yet exist in North America. Later generations of African Americans would be obliged to pick cotton all across the Deep South after 1800, but their ancestors in colonial times faced a very different array of tasks. Most lived in the Chesapeake region and the coastal southeast, where the lengthy growing season promised enormous profits to aggressive white investors once the land had been cleared for plantation agriculture. African newcomers—women as well as men—soon found themselves cutting and burning trees, splitting rails and building fences. Using an axe and a hatchet, each individual was expected to clear several acres of southern wilderness in a single season.

For some, the work with wood never ended. Buildings were needed, and workers spent long hours felling trees and then squaring the logs with an adze. Guided by an African parent or a white overseer, a skilled black youth might learn to be a wheelwright, a house carpenter, a shingle cutter, a boat builder, or a cabinetmaker. But he was most likely to make barrels, for these huge containers were crucial to the safe shipment of valuable products over long distances. Barrels pieced together from separate staves of wood were needed for fish and rum in New England, for grain and tobacco in the Chesapeake, for rice and indigo in South Carolina. By the eighteenth century, timber, which had been cleared to make room for plantations, was scarce on Caribbean islands, so staves shaped from American trees were sold to the West Indies, where they were assembled into barrels for shipping Caribbean sugar and molasses.

The transportation needs of the expanding colonies demanded various sorts of labor. Africans found themselves pressed into service building wagons, hammering horseshoes, stitching saddles, and mending harnesses. Amos Fortune, an African who ended his days as a free leatherworker in Jaffrey, New Hampshire, worked for a tanner in Woburn, Massachusetts, for two decades before gaining his freedom. Black South Carolinians built dugout canoes from cypress logs and fashioned larger boats to float the rice crop to Charleston via the winding rivers. After crops were harvested every fall, planters in South Carolina's coastal low country were required to send enslaved workers to dig ditches. Over several generations they created an amazing network of canals—a web of waterways linking local rivers for travel and irrigation. Near Chesapeake Bay, slaves constructed roads along which huge round wooden "hogsheads" of tobacco could be rolled to ships waiting at harbor docks and riverside piers. In Maryland one of these thoroughfares is still known as "Rolling Road" after more than two hundred years.

Sooner or later, all colonial roads led down to the sea and ships. England's North American colonists clustered around rivers and ports. They sold their surplus produce to Europe and received a steady supply of manufactured goods in return—everything from hats and hatchets to china and window glass. They also sent to the West Indies quantities of salt fish, to be used as food for enslaved workers, and supplies of firewood, to be used in boiling sugarcane into molasses. In return, they brought back slaves who had not yet been sold in Caribbean markets, along with barrels of molasses to be made into rum and shipped to Africa as a commodity in the slave trade. In North Carolina, slaves cut pine trees filled with resin and then burned the wood in closed ovens to produce tar and pitch for use by English sailors. French seamen needed similar materials for protecting the hulls and rigging of their ships. In 1724, an English report suggested that rival French colonists in Louisiana were producing pitch and tar and had "already settled four Plantations with fifty Negroes on each to carry on that Work."

Besides working in the dangerous production of tar and pitch, African-American artisans were involved in all aspects of the colonial boat-building trade. It was one thing to build ships, but quite another to sail on them. Numerous ingenious colonial slaves found ways to leave shore and become harbor pilots and deep-sea sailors. Equiano, for example, was purchased by the captain of a British merchant ship shortly after his arrival in Virginia, and he spent decades sailing the Atlantic, working for different owners on various ships, before finally securing his freedom.

Equiano had never seen the ocean, or even a large river, before being taken from his small village as a boy, but many Africans arrived in America with a knowledge of the sea. Those from coastal regions were experienced swimmers, not as afraid of bathing and diving as most eighteenth-century Europeans. Others were expert fishermen, and they put their skills to good use in the fish-filled bays and rivers of the American coast. Black newcomers in South Carolina and Georgia found an abundance of shrimp (a delicacy well-known to many Africans but foreign to Europeans) in the waters surrounding the coastal Sea Islands. They wove casting nets and hauled in schools of tasty shrimp just as they had done in West Africa. In Southern swamps and rivers, the Europeans proved frightened by the strange alligators. Africans, on the other hand, were familiar with killing and eating crocodiles, so many of them knew how to confront such dangerous reptiles without fear.

Black women often worked in the fields, as many of them had done in Africa, but they also assumed primary responsibility for a great deal of domestic labor. House servants were forced to cook and clean, wash and press, sew and mend, to suit the demands of their colonial mistress. With varying degrees of oversight, a plantation cook handled all aspects of food preparation, from tending the garden or visiting the town market to washing the dishes and throwing leftovers to the pigs. Indeed, when it came time to slaughter the hogs and cure their meat, she supervised that complex process as well. Day after day, year after year, she was obliged to balance the endless demands of the white household and the ongoing needs of her own family. Nothing illustrates this conflict more dramatically than the fact that the mother of a black infant was sometimes required to stop suckling her own baby and to serve instead as the wet nurse to a newborn child in the family of her master.

Southern planters noted approvingly that African women were generally experienced agriculturalists, while women coming from Europe usually were not. They also realized that Africans were less troubled by the seasonal bouts of malaria that often sickened European workers (though no one yet understood that a distinctive blood trait now known as sickle cell contributed to this difference). In addition, they observed an obvious benefit in the fact that West Africans were generally familiar with survival in a warm and humid climate. They knew how to take advantage of shade trees and summer breezes in locating their dwellings, and they were familiar with many of the plants and animals that existed in the subtropics.

Where the flora and fauna differed from the Old World, enslaved Africans could turn to local Indians for knowledge. Indian slaves still made up a portion of the colonial work force in the early eighteenth century. Moreover, Africans were involved in the early Indian wars on the frontier and participated in the extensive fur trade.

These frontier activities brought black men into frequent contact with Native Americans, and eventually this aroused the fears of white authorities. They worried about any black person who was carrying a gun, exploring the countryside, and gaining the acquaintance of Indians willing to harbor runaways. Therefore, they passed laws limiting the participation of enslaved Africans in frontier warfare and the Indian trade. They even went so far as to offer handsome rewards to Indians who brought back runaway slaves, dead or alive. By the 1720s, of course, African Americans had already been in contact with Indians for more than two hundred years, and this complex and important relationship would continue throughout North America regardless of such laws.

The extent of Indian-African contact in the eighteenth century is evident in the way the Southern diet evolved in colonial times. Such African foods as okra, yams, peanuts, and sesame seeds made their way into Southern cooking. Often they were combined with traditional Indian delicacies, as in gumbo, the famous specialty of Louisiana cuisine. The thick base is made by cooking sliced okra (an African dish) or powdered sassafras (a Choctaw Indian staple) in slowly heated oil. Even the word *gumbo* may come from the Angolan *guingombo* for okra or the Choctaw *kombo ashish* for sassafras powder.

Food containers and utensils also revealed traditions from Africa, reinforced by New World Indian practices. The palmetto tree of coastal Carolina, which appeared strange and exotic to Europeans, was familiar to African newcomers as well as Indian residents. Soon black Carolinians were using strips from the long palmetto leaves to bind together circular baskets of all shapes and sizes, much as they had in Africa. Gourds, like palmetto trees, were familiar to Africans and Indians, as the experience of Esteban in an earlier century made clear. Southern Indians had long used light, durable gourds for bowls, dippers, and storage containers, as had arriving Africans. In contrast, English colonists, coming from a cool climate, had little familiarity with gourds and their practical possibilities. In addition, we now know that African-American artisans were fashioning their own clay pots and bowls, which were different from European earthenware but similar to much Native American pottery. These simple vessels, now known as "colonoware," have been correctly identified only in recent years.

In short, the Africans who survived the middle passage brought numerous skills with them and acquired others from Indian neighbors, who already knew which local plants were edible and which had special medicinal value. Ironically, the slaves' ability to persevere and subsist under harsh conditions often benefited their self-styled "owners." Obviously, workers who raised their own food in small garden plots and caught fish in the local stream saved a planter the expense of supplying provisions. A strong man who had hammered iron in Africa needed little instruction in metalworking at a colonial forge. Occasionally Europeans seized and exploited much more than African labor; they took advantage of superior African knowledge as well. The story of profitable rice cultivation in colonial South Carolina is a good example.

After the founding of Carolina in 1670, English colonists spent a full generation seeking a suitable staple crop. In order to have enough food, a few of the earliest enslaved Africans in the settlement began growing rice in the wet swampland, as they had done in their homeland. English planters, who were largely unfamiliar with rice, realized that conditions were excellent for this crop and began to learn more. Production grew rapidly as Africans showed them how to irrigate the plants in the field, pound the rice kernels with a wooden mortar and pestle, and winnow the chaff with a "fanner" basket. Soon slave merchants were advertising workers from the so-called Rice Coast of West Africa, and profits from the sale of Carolina rice were making local plantation owners the richest gentry in North America. French Louisiana began importing Africans aggressively around 1718—the year New Orleans was founded. French officials promptly urged captains to import several Africans "who know how to cultivate rice," along with "hogsheads of rice suitable for planting."

By 1775, roughly half a million African Americans were living and laboring in North America. Throughout the colonies a small proportion were free blacks, but most were legally enslaved, and most lived in the South. As their numbers increased, so did the profits from their work. Wealthy planters acquired more land and bought additional slaves, so an increasing number of enslaved black colonists found themselves working on large plantations. This was especially true in the Chesapeake region, where nearly half of the entire African-American population labored in the tobacco fields of Virginia and Maryland. Thomas Jefferson, still in his early thirties, owned nearly four hundred black Virginians on the eve of the Revolution, and George Washington's enslaved labor force was even larger.

A Division *of the Negros made, and agreed to by between* Col.º George Lee, *and the Brothers of the deceas'd Maj.ʳ Lawrence* Washington *the 10ᵗʰ day of Decemᵇʳ Anno Domini* 1754 —

Col.º Lee's part		The Estates Part	
Old Moll	£25	Phebe	£25
Lawrence	60	Peter	60
Ben	40	Pharo	40
Will	40	Abram	40
Frank	40	Couta	40
Barbara	40	Nell	40
Moll	25	Sall	25
Milly	20	Bella	20
Hannah	15	Barbara	15
Jenny	10	Antene	10
Will	10	Dicer	10
Nan	15	Aaron	15
Nan	35	Judah	35
James	40	Ned	40
Dula	40	Camero	40
Dublin	40	Sambo	40
Acco	40	Sando	40
Harry	35	Scipio	35
Roger	40	Tomboy	40
Grace	40	Lett	40
Phillis	40	Jenny	40
Kate	40	Judah	40
Cesar	25	Tom	15
Sarra 1 mᵗʰ old	F. S	Phill	F. S
Charles	A. 7½	Tom	A. 1
Doll	C. 4	Prince	3 - 7½
Sue	2 - 11½	Betty	3 - 1
George	3 - 7½	Lucy	4 - 1

When Lawrence Washington died in 1754, his African slaves, including infants, were divided "evenly"—with regard to market value rather than family or kinship. Half went to Colonel George Lee and the other half ("the estate's part," right column) went to his brothers, including twenty-two-year-old George Washington.

Washington, Jefferson, and other members of the Virginia gentry were dismayed to see so much of the wealth generated by their African workers passing into the hands of London merchants instead of into their own pockets. The grievances of white colonists would eventually prompt their demands for freedom from English rule. But eighteenth-century African Americans gained few rewards from the revolutionary struggle. Nevertheless, black Americans had been engaged in a successful revolutionary battle of their own over several generations. Throughout the eighteenth century they had been struggling, against tremendous odds, to build the cultural framework that would allow their survival in a harsh and alien land.

Building a Culture

The growing number of black colonists in America varied dramatically in their backgrounds and experiences. Gambians differed from Angolans, and "saltwater" slaves differed from "country-born." Obvious and important contrasts emerged between field hands and house servants, Northerners and Southerners, town dwellers and rural residents—not to mention the gulf often separating the many who were enslaved from the few who were legally free. Among most of these very different people, however, there began to appear during the eighteenth century one identifiable African-American culture.

In certain ways, the emergence of African-American culture can be compared with the later appearance of other ethnic cultures in pluralistic America. All newcomers—from the earliest African Americans down to the most recent immigrants from Asia, Latin America, the Caribbean or the Middle East—try to hold on to certain elements of life from their "old country." In addition, all newcomers confront the hard questions posed by American geography. Is the land hotter or colder, wetter or drier, than the home they left behind? How different are the foods and smells, the hills and rivers, the cities and towns? Each group, in short, must adapt to the possibilities and limits of the varied American landscape and climate. Moreover, all new arrivals must confront the world of white, English-speaking Protestants. This portion of the diverse American population gained the upper hand during the colonial era, grew with the country in the nineteenth century, and has dominated the nation's mainstream culture from its beginning.

In other ways, however, the emergence of black culture is unique in American history, for the influx of Africans was *early, large,* and *involuntary.* The fact that most Africans, in contrast to other distinctive racial, ethnic, or religious groups, arrived during the eighteenth century means that their roots in America are older and deeper. Black culture has had more than two centuries to influence other parts of the society. Though later migrations to North America have been bigger, none has been so large in comparison to the total American population of the time. Most important of all, no other migration to America was involuntary and based entirely upon exploitation. Black immigrants to the strange new land of North America faced lives of physical hardship and constant psychological hurt from one generation to the next. In order to endure in this isolated and confining world of work, it was necessary to forge links that would allow families to form and communities to develop.

Racial slavery as practiced in colonial North America made the creation of stable families extremely hard. Slave captains usually purchased their captives one by one from several African ports. If a husband and wife or mother and daughter somehow managed to stay together and survive until they reached America, they were likely to be separated at the auction block. Creating new families proved almost as difficult as preserving old ones. Newcomers who overcame the deep sense of grief and loss created by the middle passage had to weigh the risk of fresh relationships in the New World. Intimacy was difficult in a realm where neither husbands nor wives controlled their own lives.

Nevertheless, durable families and extensive networks of kinfolk gradually came into being. Masters realized that people with vulnerable and needy loved ones depending on them often proved more obedient and hardworking than single people who lacked local ties. Because it would have limited their power, masters did not recognize legal marriage among slaves, but they encouraged long-term relationships from which they expected to benefit, both through the work of the couple and the labor of their eventual children.

More important than the pressures of the masters were the desires of the people themselves. The harshness and insecurity of their situation increased the need to share the numerous sufferings and rare pleasures with another person. Raising one's own children, even under trying circumstances, could be a greater affirmation than living without children at all. If family members could suddenly be killed or disappear, there was all the more reason to honor each new union, delight in every healthy birth, and extend the network of relations as widely as possible.

Extended slave families reached across generations and linked separate plantations. They were constantly being broken apart and reformed in new ways, adapting to meet the changing and unkind circumstances of plantation life. These emerging family networks played an important role in transmitting cultural patterns and conserving African values. Many slaveowners welcomed these ties as a way to limit black independence, but family bonds were not always such a conservative force for preserving the slavery system as most masters thought. After all, families fostered loyalty and trust; they conveyed information and belief; they provided a strong shelter within which to hide and a reliable launching pad from which to venture forth.

By providing much-needed solace and support, the positive ties of family gave encouragement to individuals and groups who were coming together, against formidable odds, to forge the beginnings of a common culture. Over time, they built a unique and varied way of life of their own that gave them the faith to carry on.

Music undoubtedly provided one crucial starting point for this complex process of cultural building. Certainly no element was more central, or illustrates the process more clearly. Recognizable African harmonies, intonations, and rhythms sounded familiar to strangers from different regions who could not converse with one another. This shared musical background drew together people who still spoke different languages. Songs of grief, worship, love, and work could reassure listeners even before they discovered other common ground. A musical tradition that stressed improvisation provided a welcome hearth where the sharing process could begin. Eventually, a similar sharing process would touch almost every aspect of cultural life, but for many the earliest common links were through music.

Drums, universal among African societies, served as one common denominator, and different styles of drumming and diverse ways of making drums were soon shared. Moreover, this kind of exchange through an emphasis on percussion instruments reached beyond diverse Africans. Native Americans found that the use of drums and rattles represented one of many cultural elements they shared with people from sub-Saharan Africa. Europeans, startled by the extent of African drumming and fearful that this skill sometimes provided a secret means of communication, outlawed the use of drums by slaves in various colonies. South Carolina's strict Negro Code of 1740 prohibited slaves from "using or keeping drums, horns, or other loud instruments, which may call together, or give sign or notice to one another of their wicked designs and purposes."

Such fears did not prevent white colonists from recruiting free blacks to serve as military musicians (as they were already doing in England). Virginia's Militia Act of 1723 allowed that "Such free Negroes, Mulattos or Indians, as are capable, may be listed and emploied as Drummers or Trumpeters." Learning to play European instruments allowed a black person to gain status in the community, avoid harsh tasks, and travel widely. Notices in colonial newspapers suggest such slave musicians were in constant demand.

For each person who learned to make and play European instruments, there were many others who recalled how to make and play African instruments. Besides manufacturing a variety of drums, African Americans also re-created various string and percussion instruments used on the other side of the Atlantic. The most popular import was the banjo (often called a bandore, banjer, or banjar). "The instrument proper to them is the Banjar," wrote Thomas Jefferson, "which they brought hither from Africa."

When William Smith visited West Africa as a surveyor for Britain's Royal African Company in the 1720s, he described the xylophone known as a balafo (also ballafoe, barrafou, or barrafoo) and later published a picture of it. The instrument consisted of eleven thin planks of differing lengths, supported over large gourd resonators of various sizes. The music of this unusual instrument was well known locally, as suggested by a sarcastic comment in the *Virginia Gazette* the following year, when many blacks were joining the British rather than supporting their masters' push for independence. With obvious irritation, the editor observed that these people expected to "be gratified with the use of the sprightly and enlivening *bar-*

rafoo" behind British lines, rather than being stirred by "the drowsy fife and drum" of the patriot cause.

The pattern is clear. Black colonists learned from one another and from non-Africans as well. They recalled old songs and sounds and instruments, and they borrowed new ones. Over several generations, they gave birth to a fresh and changing musical tradition. They drew heavily upon their varied Old World heritage, but they also built, necessarily, on the novel influences and sorrowful circumstances of their strange new land. The result was a range of musical expression that was both African and American. It varied widely in its forms from New Orleans to Philadelphia, or from a Georgia slave cabin to a Boston kitchen. But it contained unifying threads that became stronger over time. After 1800 this consolidation would become clearer still, as access to African roots diminished, communication among black Americans increased, and full entry into the dominant culture remained off limits.

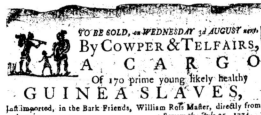

African newcomers to America, such as those reaching Savannah from Angola in July 1774, would learn the strange language of their oppressors from earlier arrivals such as Billy and Quamina, who were said to "speak good English."

The same conditions applied to much more than music. All elements of life in the strange new land seemed to depend upon involvement with other Africans and with non-Africans as well. Language provides a dramatic case in point. Even before they reached America, enslaved Africans began to learn words and phrases from one another. Shipmates from the same area often found they could comprehend portions of their neighbors' languages. In the New World, black newcomers were soon forced to assimilate at least one European language—whether English, French, German, Dutch, Spanish, or Portuguese—and often learned more than one. If an African girl lived on a large plantation in South Carolina, where blacks were in a majority and contact with whites was limited, she might speak Gullah, a complex blend of African languages and English. But if she lived in a white household in New England, she would learn the English of that region.

Certain African words were especially likely to survive. Some, for example, were common to numerous African tongues, such as *Cudjo*, the day name for a boy born on Monday. Others happened to coincide closely in sound with an English word.

An African girl born on Thursday and given the traditional day name *Abba* become known in America as *Abby*. A few terms overlapped in both sound and meaning and therefore had a strong chance of survival. In the Mende language of West Africa, *sasi* could mean "a prideful boaster," or "to ridicule contemptuously." In the Gullah speech of the South Carolina low country, therefore, *sasi* continued to mean "proud one" or "to ridicule," but this matched so closely the common English term "saucy" that it probably reinforced the use of "sassy" and "to sass" in American English. Other words endured simply because they were used so often. In the Congo region, *tota* means "to pick up," and enslavement involved so much lifting and carrying that "to tote" became a universal Southern term.

The same factors that shaped how newcomers might speak also determined other aspects of life. The clothes they wore and the homes they built, how they styled their hair and cooked their food—all these things were influenced by many forces, even in the confining world of enslavement. Obviously one powerful force—though not always the most important one—was the rule of the masters. Colonial assemblies passed laws defining the cheap fabrics suitable for slave clothing and forbidding fancier apparel. But appearance was difficult to legislate. When Peter Deadfoot ran away in Virginia in 1768, his master advertised that this versatile man (a shoemaker, butcher, plowman, sawyer, boatman, and "one of the best scythemen . . . in America") was also "extremely fond of dress."

On certain holidays, colonial blacks were allowed to dress in extravagant English finery. By the 1770s, for instance, a tradition of black celebrations had grown up around the annual white election day in such New England towns as Newport, Rhode Island; Hartford, Connecticut; and Salem, Massachusetts. Once a year, during these sanctioned "Negro Election Days," elegantly dressed black "kings" and "governors" borrowed fine horses, large hats, or dress swords from the whites who endorsed the entertainment. On other special occasions, particularly in the South, blacks often chose to dress in styles and colors and materials that invoked their free African past. By the nineteenth century, and perhaps even earlier on some plantations, slaves in certain localities were dressing in African costumes and dancing to African rhythms during the event that would become known as Jonkonnu. These festivities usually occurred during the Christmas season, and the lead dancer often wore an elaborate mask or headdress and had colorful rags and ribbons swirling from his costume.

Like clothing, hairstyles also represented a complex area for cultural negotiation. Some black men became barbers for whites, learning to cut the hair and powder the wigs of their master; some black women attended to the hair of their mistress and her children, according to the latest European fashions. But how African Americans wore their own hair depended upon the individual's preference, an owner's rules, and the limits of time. For girls to braid their hair in elaborate cornrows—then as now—was satisfying and attractive, but also very time-consuming.

For men to tease their hair into swelling "Afros" drew comments—and even pun-ishments—from white masters who were often offended by such "foreign" styles. Hats and bonnets, bandannas and braids often provided varied and colorful com-promises in the realm of hairdressing.

In some areas, necessity may have agreed with preference. Many early slave cab-ins, for example, had dirt floors and yards without grass. Did this represent simply an unwillingness of the planter to provide boards for floors and seeds for grass? Probably not, for many blacks preferred the African tradition of a clay floor, pound-ed hard and kept clean, just as they valued a carefully swept yard, even though these practices demanded considerable work. Similarly, the thatching of houses with palmetto leaves and the weaving of baskets with coils of sweet grass represent cherished traditions remembered from Africa and practiced in America. What are we to make of the presence of simple handmade pottery at eighteenth-century slave sites across the South? Though iron cooking pots and cracked dishes and pitchers from the big house are also evident, archaeologists now believe many African Americans may have preferred to fashion their own bowls for cooking in a more traditional way.

Finally, consider how these early African Americans fashioned the mental and moral aspects of their emerging culture. In short, what did they think and believe? The question is challenging, and the full answer remains to be found. But in the realm of ideas, as in the material domain, their lives seem to have been varied and creative, despite overwhelming constraints. At the center of black thought through-out the eighteenth century, a crucial debate was occurring over the acceptance of European Christianity. Many "saltwater slaves"—including some, like Job ben Solomon, who had been raised in the Muslim faith—held firmly to their African religious beliefs. A white missionary in South Carolina recalled the answer of one elderly African when asked why he refused to take part in the rituals of the Church of England. The old man replied simply, "I prefer to live by that which I remember."

On the other hand, certain slaves who had left Africa at an early age or had been born in the New World, accepted the Protestant Christian faith of the whites around them. But most African Americans fell somewhere in the middle. Torn between the remembered belief systems of their ancestors and the dominant reli-gion of their masters, they combined these two worlds in a process of evolution that took many generations.

Over time, white masters increasingly demanded, and even rewarded, an out-ward profession of Christianity among many second- and third-generation African Americans. But they had little control over the forms that religion might take, and black colonists, slave and free, gradually began to shape a faith that gave special meaning to traditional Protestant beliefs. Black Christians favored music and song; they emphasized baptism and down-to-earth preaching. Denied the right to read, they stressed Old Testament stories that suited their situation, such as the Hebrew captivity in Egypt. Most of all, they considered carefully the New Testament portrait of Jesus Christ as a friend of the afflicted and a redeemer of the weak. We know that George Liele, the slave of a Baptist deacon in Burke County, Georgia, used to preach to fellow slaves on the text: "Come unto me all ye that labour, and are heavy laden, and I will give you rest."

By the mid-eighteenth century—during a period of revitalized Protestant zeal among whites known as the Great Awakening—a minority of black Americans were beginning to embrace Christianity. Black preachers appeared as early as 1743, and by the mid-1770s, George Liele and a small group of converted slaves along the Savannah River established the Silver Bluff Baptist Church, the first black Protestant church in America. Under the influence of both white and black itinerant Methodist and Baptist ministers, the number of African-American converts would grow during the next generation. But even those who accepted Christianity retained certain African spirit beliefs and burial customs that would become vital aspects of the emerging African-American culture.

Breaking the Bonds

Challenging arbitrary rule is the world's most difficult task, especially when undemocratic control has become firmly established. Faced with overwhelming odds, many in bondage elect survival over open resistance, and their choice is as logical and understandable as it is painful. For those who choose to defy the odds and test the boundaries of their confinement, no one effective model exists. Therefore, they try all imaginable modes of resistance: calculated and spontaneous, covert and direct, psychological and physical, individual and collective. Despite the monotony of enslavement, no two circumstances are ever exactly alike, so the best tactic yesterday may be the most costly or foolhardy today. Adaptability is crucial, and bravery is a constant ingredient, for even the smallest gesture of defiance can result in cruel punishment and lasting consequences.

Small acts of resistance, though dangerous, were regular events in the house of bondage. The slightest command could be wrongly interpreted or carelessly carried out. The easiest task could be purposely bungled or endlessly extended. By breaking a tool or pretending to be sick, slaves could avoid a whole day's work, gaining needed rest for themselves and undercutting steady profits for their owner. Workers forced to labor to support the life of a master often felt justified in appropriating some of the food they had grown and prepared, even if the planter viewed this activity as stealing. Elaborate trading and marketing networks grew up to exchange such goods. Though the owner might encourage slave gardens to reduce his own expense in feeding his work force, he objected when these gardens received more attention than his fields or when the slaves sold their own produce and defiantly pocketed the profits.

No act of defiance was more commonplace than running away. Even brief departures could provide relief from an oppressive overseer. But such disappear-

When he arrived in Virginia from Africa, Equiano was shocked to see a black woman forced to wear an iron muzzle "which locked her mouth so fast that she could scarcely speak; and could not eat nor drink."

ances also deprived the owners of their daily profits, so penalties were often harsh, especially for repeat offenders. Magistrates could not assess fines against persons who were forbidden to own property. Therefore, minor acts of defiance prompted harsh physical punishment, such as whipping, branding, or the wearing of shackles. Moreover, masters were free to inflict their own forms of retribution. Equiano never forgot the horrible sight that confronted him the first time he entered a white dwelling, just days after he had arrived in Virginia:

> I had seen a black woman slave as I came through the house, who was cooking the dinner, and the poor creature was cruelly loaded with various kinds of iron machines; she had one particularly on her head, which locked her mouth so fast that she could scarcely speak; and could not eat nor drink. I was much astonished and shocked at this contrivance, which I afterwards learned was called the iron muzzle.

Seeing or experiencing such inhuman treatment could only sharpen the resentments and deepen the bitterness of a worker in bondage. The resulting rage often found expression in acts of extreme violence. Overseers were beaten to death by angry workhands in the fields; masters and their families were poisoned by desperate servants in the kitchen. Setting fires also became a favored act of defiance, since arson, like poisoning food, was difficult to prove and easy to deny.

Burning a loaded barn at harvest time was a way to avoid unwelcome work and deprive the owner of a year's profits. Even the desperate act of suicide took on a double meaning, for it freed the black worker from bondage and deprived the white owner of a valuable investment.

Black violence against the system of slavery ranged from spontaneous individual acts to elaborate conspiracies involving numerous people. Among enslaved African Americans, as among any people living under totalitarian control, thought of rebellion was universal; open talk of such matters was far more guarded; and the undertaking itself was the bold and rare exception, for a variety of reasons. Urban slaves were closely watched, and rural slaves were widely dispersed; organized patrols were commonplace, and informants were everywhere. Long working hours and wide distances made communication difficult, as did forced illiteracy and diverse ethnic backgrounds. Despite such huge obstacles, brave individuals joined in risky coalitions to attempt mass escape or armed insurrection.

Occasionally, an event took on a life of its own, as rumors of revolt fueled fears among whites and raised hopes among African Americans. Word of a foreign war, a heavenly sign, or a slave rebellion in some other colony could quickly bring matters to a head, increasing the sense of urgency among enslaved blacks and the feelings of paranoia among those who exploited them. In New York City, in 1712, workers desiring their freedom set fire to a building and attacked those summoned to put out the blaze. They managed to kill nine persons and wound seven others, but they failed to spark a larger revolt. Half a dozen accused conspirators committed suicide after their capture, and more than twenty were put to death, some by being burned alive.

Capital punishment was also used in the small French colony of Louisiana, when several hundred Bambara people, who had recently been brought from Africa, planned a revolt that was to begin in late June 1731. The rebellion might have succeeded, but a remark by a defiant African woman tipped off authorities. They were surprised to learn that the leader was a man known as Samba Bambara, who had worked as an interpreter for the slave traders at Galam on the Senegal River in West Africa. After falling out of favor with French authorities there, he had been thrown aboard the slave ship *Annibal* in 1726 and shipped to Louisiana, where he was soon put to work as a trusted overseer. According to Le Page du Pratz, who investigated the case, eight suspected leaders, including Samba, were "clapt in irons" by authorities and then "were put to the torture of burning matches; which, though several times repeated, could not bring them to make any confession." When further evidence prompted an admission of guilt, du Pratz reported that "the eight Negroes were condemned to be broken alive on the wheel"—tied to a wagon wheel and battered severely until they gradually died of shock. Meanwhile, the woman who had revealed the plot was sentenced "to be hanged before their eyes; which was accordingly done." Even then, rumors of revolt continued, but an uprising predicted to begin during midnight mass on Christmas 1731 never materialized.

Meanwhile, slaves had been escaping occasionally from South Carolina and making their way to St. Augustine in northeast Florida. Spanish officials had bestowed freedom on some of the refugees, in hopes of disrupting the neighboring English colony, while others, such as a Mandingo man named Francisco Menendez, were resold into servitude. In 1728, Menendez was made captain of the slave militia, a unit organized to help protect St. Augustine from English attack. In 1733, the Spanish king issued an edict granting freedom to runaway slaves reaching St. Augustine, and in 1738, the local governor granted these newcomers a townsite several miles north of the port city. In return, dozens of converted freedmen pledged to shed their "last drop of blood in defense of the Great Crown of Spain and the Holy Faith, and to be the most cruel enemies of the English." With Menendez as their leader, they constructed a fortification known as Mose (or Moosa or Mosa). Two decades later this small fort (which has recently been located and excavated) still sheltered a community of sixty-seven men, women, and children.

By 1739, a great many of the forty thousand African Americans in bondage in South Carolina were aware that the Spaniards in Florida had offered freedom to slaves from English colonies. In September, when word reached Charleston of the outbreak of open war between England and Spain, the news helped trigger an uprising at Stono Landing south of the city. During the brief and bloody Stono Rebellion, scores of slaves killed their English masters and began marching toward Fort Mose and Spanish St. Augustine, only to be intercepted before their numbers could swell. Fearful of the colony's expanding black majority, officials displayed the heads of executed rebels on poles to discourage future revolts. In addition, they placed a prohibitive duty, or tax, on slaves imported from abroad for several years, and they passed a new Negro Act further restricting the movement and assembly of black South Carolinians. A suspected slave plot in New York in 1741 led to even more fearsome reprisals, fueled by suggestions of underground support and encouragement from Spanish Jesuits and local poor whites.

British conflict with Spain had given hope to slaves in England's North American colonies. Similarly, when England and France became locked in an all-out imperial war in the 1750s, white colonists again became anxious. They feared that enslaved African Americans would take advantage of warfare on the frontiers and seek to challenge their miserable condition. In 1755, British troops under General Edward Braddock suffered a shocking defeat in the backcountry at the hands of the French and their Indian allies. When word of the setback at Fort Duquesne reached the governor of Maryland, he immediately circulated a notice that slaves should be "well observed & watched," and he ordered the colony's militia units "to be prepared to quell it in case any Insurrection should be occasioned by this Stroke."

Officials in Virginia also worried about the potential for rebellion. More than 100,000 blacks now made up well over a third of the total population in that province, and many of the white militiamen were absent in the war. The lieutenant governor reported that local slaves had become "very audacious" in the wake of

Braddock's defeat in the Ohio Valley. In South Carolina, where blacks outnumbered whites by roughly three to two, authorities made plans to separate Charleston from the mainland with a canal (to be dug by slaves), so the city might be somewhat "protected against an Insurrection of the Negroes" in the surrounding countryside or an attack by Indians from the frontier.

The end of the great war of empire brought dramatic changes to the colonies. In Paris in 1762, British representatives sat down with envoys from France and Spain to negotiate a final peace. Their treaty, completed the following year, gave decisive advantages to the victorious British under their young monarch, George III. From the king of France, they received control over Canada. From Spain, the Catholic ally of France, they gained hold of what had for two hundred years been Spanish Florida. These sweeping shifts in the colonial landscape had an immediate impact on all the peoples of eastern North America. Among Indians, for example, it is no coincidence that a major uprising known as Pontiac's Rebellion began in 1763, as Native Americans in the Great Lakes region lost their strategic bargaining position between French and English colonizers.

Many African Americans also felt an immediate impact from the peace settlement. In Florida, hundreds of blacks had been imported as laborers from the West Indies or had escaped from slavery in the neighboring English colonies. Most of them departed with the Spanish as they evacuated St. Augustine in 1763. At the same time, thousands of African Americans enslaved in nearby Georgia and South Carolina saw a sudden end to their dream of escaping to Fort Mose. Florida quickly changed from an outpost of possible black liberty to a new frontier for English plantations. Rich investors in Charleston and Savannah transported several thousand workers to British Florida in hopes of earning quick profits from slave labor. A few of these African Americans managed to escape and join bands of Creek Indians in what would soon be known as the Seminole nation. The rest died in bondage.

Elsewhere on the British colonial frontier, the end of the so-called French and Indian War also brought immediate change for African Americans. In the North, numerous servants and free blacks had taken advantage of the turmoil of war to travel more freely. Some served white officers, while others cut roads, built fortifications, and transported supplies. Still others enlisted as soldiers. Garshom Prince, for example, had been born in New England in 1733 and apparently went to war with Captain Robert Durkee. He must have been issued a musket to fight, for he inscribed a traditional powder container made from a cow's horn, when the soldiers paused at Crown Point in 1761 following their victory over the French. Seventeen years later, at age forty-five, Prince was back in service in the American Revolution, fighting for the patriot side. When he was killed in the Battle of Wyoming, Pennsylvania, in 1778, he was once again carrying his carved powder horn. The years between the end of one great war and the beginning of another would be eventful ones for African Americans in their strange new land.

To the west of the English colonies, the end of the war with France also brought change for African Americans. George III and his government ministers were fearful that expanding settlement would encroach on Native American lands and provoke an expensive Indian war. Britain, deeply in debt after the struggle with France, wanted to avoid such a costly undertaking. So the king proclaimed a boundary line running along the top of the Appalachian mountains to divide the Atlantic colonies from Indian nations living in the Ohio and Mississippi river valleys. This so-called Proclamation Line, plus the willingness of colonial officials to pay bounties to Native Americans for capturing runaways, held down the number of enslaved blacks who risked seeking freedom in Indian country. An act by the Virginia Assembly "thought it good Policy . . . to keep up and increase that natural aversion which happily subsists between Negroes and Indians."

Efforts to prohibit interracial mixing on the frontier were not new. When a German named Christian Priber had gone to live among the Cherokees in the 1730s, announcing his plans for an interracial utopia without private property where all races would be welcome, he was hunted down by authorities and imprisoned in Georgia until he died in 1744. Nevertheless, the backcountry was so large and so thinly populated that it was impossible for white authorities to prevent non-whites from settling together along the frontier. In 1740, Molly Barber, daughter of a wealthy white New England family, eloped with James Chaugham, a Narragansett Indian. The couple established the small community of Barkhamsted in northwest Connecticut, which soon drew a number of Indians, poor whites, and free blacks. In 1758, Mary Jamison, a Scots-Irish immigrant girl, was captured by Indians and lived most of her life among the Senecas in what is now upstate New York. She later told of staying briefly with two African-American runaways at their remote cabin near the Genesee River. She and her children helped harvest their corn crop and passed the winter in their frontier homestead.

Besides affecting African Americans on the borders of the empire, Britain's dramatic triumph over France also had a swift impact upon blacks living in the heart of the mainland colonies. Soon after 1763, the political climate began to change dramatically.

"Liberty! Liberty!"

England's war with France had been a long and expensive struggle; it had taken place on land and sea, and it had extended to several continents. As a result, the British crown had built up an enormous public debt. Therefore, no sooner had victory celebrations ended than the government in London began pressing for new taxes to replenish empty coffers. With residents of England already heavily taxed, Parliament turned its attention to the colonies. Their economies had grown and prospered under the protection of the British crown and had benefited directly from the recent war. In the past, England had asked its colonists to pay only duties designed to regulate trade. Now, however, officials suggested that perhaps it was

THE

Massachusetts Spy

Or, AMERICAN ORACLE of LIBERTY.

"Undaunted by TYRANTS we'll DIE or be FREE."

WHEREAS the NEGROES in the counties of Bristol and Worcester, the 24th of March last, petitioned the Committees of Correspondence for the county of Worcester (then convened in Worcester) to assist them in obtaining their freedom. THEREFORE,

In County Convention, June 14th, 1775.

RESOLVED, That we abhor the enslaving of any of the human race, and particularly of the NEGROES in this country. And that whenever there shall be a door opened, or opportunity present, for any thing to be done toward the emancipating the NEGROES; we will use our influence and endeavour that such a thing may be effected.

Attest. WILLIAM HENSHAW, Clerk.

Although African Americans had dreamed of liberty for generations, it took the idealism of the revolutionary era to prompt some white Americans to accept the political goal of black emancipation. In the June 21, 1775, issue of the *Massachusetts Spy,* the Committee of Correspondence for Worcester County published this notice stating its desire to see an end to slavery.

time to levy taxes to raise revenues, even if the colonists were not directly represented in the English Parliament.

In 1765, Parliament approved the controversial Stamp Act, taxing the colonists by obliging them to purchase a government stamp for such simple transactions as buying a newspaper, filing a will, or selling a piece of property. Extensive protests forced the law to be repealed, but it was followed by other revenue measures that intensified debate. British soldiers and sailors used to maintain order became objects of scorn, and the king's troops were frequently attacked. When Parliament passed the Tea Act in 1773, suspicious local leaders saw the offer of cheap tea as a device to trick the colonies into accepting the principle of taxation by Parliament. Colonists vowed not to purchase English tea and even threw boxes of tea into Boston harbor. In 1774, an irate Parliament responded with a series of "Coercive

Acts," prompting colonial leaders to organize a Continental Congress that would work out the American response to the intrusive British legislation. British troops met armed resistance when they attempted to secure government powder supplies in Lexington, Massachusetts, in April 1775, and in July 1776 the Continental Congress voted to declare independence from Great Britain.

As participants or observers, African Americans were close to all these important events leading up to the American Revolution. They witnessed firsthand the mounting pressures for an armed revolt against the strongest empire on earth. During a Stamp Act protest in Wilmington, North Carolina, for example, the royal governor sent food and drink in an effort to placate white demonstrators. Not willing to be bought off, the crowd "immediately broke in the heads of the Barrels of Punch and let it run into the street." According to a firsthand account, they refused to roast the ox offered to them by the governor. Instead, they put its head on display "in the Pillory and gave the Carcass to the Negroes" who were looking on. Equiano was working as a slave on a small vessel in the Caribbean when word reached America that such protests had brought an end to the Stamp Act. He recalled sailing into Charleston harbor at night and seeing "the town illuminated; the guns were fired, and bonfires and other demonstrations of joy shown, on account of repeal of the stamp act."

Crispus Attucks, son of a black man and an Indian woman, played a central role in the Boston Massacre of 1770, in which British redcoats killed five colonists. Described as "Six Feet two Inches high" with "short curl'd hair," Attucks had run away from his master in Framingham, Massachusetts, in 1750. Twenty years later, at age forty-seven, he was working as a sailor out of the Bahamas, aboard a boat bound from Boston to North Carolina. On the evening of March 5, 1770, Attucks played a leading part in the bloody skirmish on King Street. When attorney John Adams (later the second President of the United States) defended the British soldiers at their trial, he argued they had been provoked by a "mob" made up of "a motley rabble of saucy boys, negroes and mulattoes, Irish teagues [slang for Irishmen] and outlandish jack tarrs [sailors from foreign ports]." "Attucks," he told the court, "appears to have undertaken to be the hero of the night, and to lead this army with banners, to form them in the first place in Dock square, and march them up to King street with their clubs."

Andrew, a slave witness who testified at the same trial, recalled seeing Attucks and his band arrive on the scene, where a bitter scuffle was already in progress. The new contingent was shouting loudly and crying, "Damn them, they dare not fire, we are not afraid of them." According to Andrew, "one of these people, a stout man with a long cordwood stick," whom he later identified as Attucks, "threw himself in, and made a blow at the officer," crying out, "kill the dogs, knock them over." Similarly, John Adams argued that the "stout Molatto fellow" waded into the fray "and with one hand took hold of a bayonet, and with the other knocked the man down." Attucks's actions cost him his life. According to published accounts, he was the first to fall—"killed on the Spot, two Balls entering his Breast." When Boston staged an elaborate public funeral for the martyrs killed in this clash, "all the Bells tolled in solemn Peal" throughout the town. In subsequent years colonial radicals invoked the name of Crispus Attucks as the first person who had given his life for the patriot cause.

Other African Americans would risk their lives, even before the Declaration of Independence. When Paul Revere summoned the Minutemen to oppose British troops at Concord and Lexington in April 1775, a number of black men living in Massachusetts responded to the call. They included Cato Stedman, Cuff Whitemore, and Cato Boardman from Cambridge, Job Potama and Isaiah Bayoman from Stoneham, Peter Salem from Braintree, Prince Easterbrooks from Lexington, Pompy from Brookline, and David Lamson, an elderly mulatto who had fought in the French and Indian War. Later that same year, at the Battle of Bunker Hill, Cuff Whitemore and Peter Salem again saw action, along with nearly twenty other African Americans. Salem Poor, a black freeman from Andover, fought so bravely that some of his white colleagues later petitioned that this "Brave & gallent Soldier" deserved a reward, since he had "behaved like an Experienced officer" throughout the conflict.

Crispus Attucks has become a remembered figure in American history, and a picture of Peter Salem at Bunker Hill has appeared on a U.S. postage stamp. But there are other black men and women from the decade before the revolution who are less well known and who deserve greater recognition. Individually and collectively, they were involved in their own struggle for liberty. They faced tremendous odds and they took enormous risks. Loyal to the principle of freedom, they listened to the competing rhetoric of white patriots and the British crown. Would either side in the mounting debate include African Americans as free and equal members of society? Unfortunately, the response turned out to be "no." But during the decade before 1776 (and the decade after as well) this fateful answer remained uncertain.

After all, there were moral and logical arguments why Englishmen on one or both sides of the Atlantic might finally decide to renounce race slavery. For one thing, a few whites, led by pioneering Quakers such as John Woolman and Anthony Benezet, were showing an interest in abolishing the institution of slavery—an idea that enslaved African Americans had supported unanimously for more than a century. Not only were notions of human equality beginning to gain favor, but politicians and strategists on both sides of the Atlantic were anxious to appear consistent in arguing over "British liberties." White colonists who claimed they were being "enslaved" by British tyranny were frequently reminded of their hypocrisy. How could they pretend to be "advocates for the liberties of mankind," one critic asked, when they were "trampling on the sacred natural rights and privileges of Africans" at the same moment? How indeed, wondered Abigail Adams in

Boston. She reminded her husband, John Adams, that white colonists were preparing to fight for the same liberty that "we are daily robbing and plundering from those who have as good a right to freedom as we have."

Black colonists were ready to fight for their own freedom. They knew they might gain from any dissent that divided the whites who dominated their lives. Even distant events could provide rays of hope. In 1772, a judge in London ruled, in the well-publicized case of a slave named Somerset, that it was illegal to hold anyone in bondage in England, regardless of race. While this case did not actually end slavery in England, word of this stunning decision reached the southern colonies, and created a predictable stir among enslaved workers. Virginia newspapers soon carried ads for black runaways who had disappeared in hopes of securing passage to England.

A year later, four slaves in Boston seeking independence for blacks in Massachusetts had petitioned the colonial legislature. Whether out of irony or flattery, they began by stating: "We expect great things from men who have made such a noble stand against the designs of their *fellow-men* to enslave them." They asked for the right to "leave the province" as soon as they could earn enough money to buy passage "to some part of the coast of *Africa,* where we propose a settlement." At the same time other black New Englanders, both slave and free, were petitioning successive governors, hoping to induce the British crown to show sympathy to their cause. In 1774, African Americans in Massachusetts reminded Governor Thomas Gage, "we have in common with all other men a naturel right to our freedoms." They asked him to abolish slavery and to provide them with "some part of the unimproved land, belonging to the province, for a settlement."

In the Southern colonies, with enslavement more widespread and black literacy generally forbidden, the chances for a petition or public appeal remained slim—unless it came from an outspoken visitor. In the tumultuous spring of 1775, an African-born preacher named David visited Charleston. The young evangelist spoke to a private gathering of black and white Christians, and he refused to utter gentle pieties. Instead, David assured his audience that "God would send Deliverance to the Negroes, from the power of their Masters, as He freed the Children of Israel from Egyptian Bondage." White listeners suspected that "he meant to raise rebellion amongst the negroes," and David had to flee the town rapidly to avoid being hanged.

If enslaved Africans were finally to win deliverance in 1775, perhaps it would be with the aid of British forces. When shots were fired at Lexington in April, and later at Bunker Hill, blacks like Peter Salem joined the patriot forces, and eventually thousands more would follow during the course of the Revolutionary War. But many more, particularly in the South, saw the British as their likely ally, as court testimony reveals. In April, Thomas Jeremiah, a free black who worked as a pilot in Charleston harbor, took aside an enslaved dockworker named Sambo and told him

BOSTON, APRIL 20th, 1773.

SIR,

THE efforts made by the legislative of this province in their last sessions to free themselves from slavery, gave us, who are in that deplorable state, a high degree of satisfaction. We expect great things from men who have made such a noble stand against the designs of their *fellow-men* to enslave them. We cannot but wish and hope Sir, that you will have the same grand object, we mean civil and religious liberty, in view in your next session. The divine spirit of *freedom*, seems to fire every humane breast on this continent, except such as are bribed to assist in executing the execrable plan.

WE are very sensible that it would be highly detrimental to our present masters, if we were allowed to demand all that of *right* belongs to us for past services ; this we disclaim. Even the *Spaniards*, who have not those sublime ideas of freedom that English men have, are conscious that they have no right to all the services of their fellow-men, we mean the *Africans*, whom they have purchased with their money ; therefore they allow them one day in a week to work for themselve, to enable them to earn money to purchase the residue of their time, which they have a right to demand in such portions as they are able to pay for (a due appraizment of their services being first made, which always stands at the purchase money.) We do not pretend to dictate to you Sir, or to the honorable Assembly, of which you are a member : We acknowledge our obligations to you for what you have already done, but as the people of this province seem to be actuated by the principles of equity and justice, we cannot but expect your house will again take our deplorable case into serious confideration, and give us that ample relief which, *as men*, we have a natural right to.

BUT since the wise and righteous governor of the universe, has permitted our fellow men to make us slaves, we bow in submission to him, and determine to behave in such a manner, as that we may have reason to expect the divine approbation of, and assistance in, our peaceable and lawful attempts to gain our freedom.

WE are willing to submit to such regulations and laws, as may be made relative to us, until we leave the province, which we determine to do as soon as we can from our joynt labours procure money to transport ourselves to some part of the coast of *Africa*, where we propose a settlement. We are very desirous that you should have instructions relative to us, from your town, therefore we pray you to communicate this letter to them, and ask this favor for us.

In behalf of our fellow slaves in this province,
And by order of their Committee.

PETER BESTES,
SAMBO FREEMAN,
FELIX HOLBROOK,
CHESTER JOIE.

For the REPRESENTATIVE of the town of *Thompson*

A committee of slaves circulated this carefully worded request to the Colonial Assembly of Massachusetts in 1773. They applauded the anti-British legislature's "noble stand against the designs of their fellow-men to enslave them" and went on to request their own release from bondage and the chance to return to Africa.

"there is a great war coming soon." He urged Sambo to "join the soldiers," because the impending war "was come to help the poor Negroes." Several months later Jeremiah was accused of smuggling guns from a British warship to slaves in the Charleston vicinity. Fearful of black rebellion, patriot leaders in control of the town had Jeremiah publicly hanged and then burned as a brutal example to other African American freedom fighters.

In other Southern colonies black hopes for successful armed rebellion also ran high during 1775, and white fears of a slave uprising proved equally strong. In eastern North Carolina, rumors of revolt were widespread. When a plot was discovered in early July, the patriot Committees of Safety rounded up scores of African Americans, many of them armed. Suspected slaves were severely whipped in public, and some had their ears cut off. All those who spoke to their captors told a similar story. According to Colonel John Simpson, they said they were to rise up on the night of July 8, destroy the local community, and march toward the backcountry, where they expected to be met by armed British officials and "settled in a free government of their own." Blacks in Maryland had similar hopes of overthrowing their bondage. Their bold talk and actions infuriated the patriot leaders in Dorchester County, who finally moved to confiscate their weapons. In one day, they claimed to have taken up "about eighty guns, some bayonets, swords, etc."

As 1775 unfolded, black aspirations for freedom and English desires to frighten white radicals in America seemed to coincide. "Things are coming to that crisis," wrote British commander Thomas Gage in June, "that we must avail ourselves of every resource, even to raise the Negros, in our cause." This practical alliance emerged most dramatically in Virginia. The royal governor in Williamsburg, Lord Dunmore, had hinted in May his intention of "proclaiming all the Negroes free, who should join him." By autumn, the patriots had forced him to take refuge on a vessel from His Majesty's Navy, and Dunmore was sailing the coastline, encouraging black Virginians to escape to British ships. In November he issued a proclamation emancipating any slaves who would join his forces, and black Virginians flocked to his banner. Within a month he had more than three hundred persons enrolled in his "Ethiopian Regiment," with the words "Liberty to Slaves" emblazoned across their uniforms.

Patriot leaders and Virginia planters expressed deep concern over the success of Dunmore's proclamation. Up and down the Chesapeake, and as far away as Georgia, enslaved blacks were making desperate efforts to elude their owners and come under the protective wing of the Royal Navy. On November 30, the *Virginia Gazette* spoke of "boatloads of slaves" struggling to reach British ships. When a contingent of blacks in Georgia gathered on Tybee Island near the mouth of the Savannah River, the local Committee of Safety secretly paid a band of Creek Indians to destroy them before they could reach British protection. Likewise, some of the South Carolina runaways who set up camp on Sullivan's Island near Charleston harbor were hunted down before they could board British ships.

Despite the high risk, hundreds of African Americans clamored safely aboard English vessels in the months after Lord Dunmore's proclamation. In late December 1775, George Washington expressed his fear of Dunmore's plan. The patriot commander wrote that if "that man is not crushed by spring, he will become the most formidable enemy America has; his strength will increase as a snow ball by rolling; and faster, if some expedient cannot be hit upon to convince the slaves and servants of the impotency of his designs." But during the spring of 1776, it was not General Washington who stopped the dramatic flow of black Virginians to join Lord Dunmore. Instead, an outbreak of smallpox in the crowded camps finally reduced the tide of hopeful refugees.

During the Revolutionary War that followed, numerous slaves took advantage of the continuing turmoil to seek their freedom, but most were disappointed. The new nation that was born out of the struggle over independence would fail to honor, in its Constitution, the stirring words of Thomas Jefferson's declaration that "all men are created equal." The vast majority of the country's half million African Americans were still living in the South and still bearing the yoke of slavery in 1776. It would take more than three long generations before the expectations for freedom raised by the American Revolution could be met through the bloodshed of the Civil War.

CHAPTER 3

Revolutionary Citizens

1776–1804

Daniel C. Littlefield

I n October 1772 a young Boston woman wrote a poem dedicated to William Legge, earl of Dartmouth, who lived in London. A man reputedly of humane character, the earl had recently been appointed by the British king as secretary of state for the colonies. He took charge during this troubled period in relations between Britain and its North American possessions. The young Boston woman hoped that the earl would respond favorably to the difficult issues that prevented harmony between the king and his colonial subjects. She flattered him as a friend of "Fair *Freedom*" who would end the "hated *faction*," or dissension, that the crisis created.

Ironically, the young woman who wrote so knowledgeably about the colonial struggle for liberty and who was so aware of the political affairs and personalities of the day was not free herself. Her bondage gave her an acute sensitivity to issues of slavery and freedom. As she wrote the earl:

> Should you, my lord, while you peruse my song,
> Wonder from whence *my love of Freedom sprung*,
> I, young in life, by *seeming cruel fate*
> Was snatched from Afric's fancy'd happy seat;
> Such, such my case. And can I then but pray
> Others may never feel *tyrannic sway*?

The poet's name was Phillis Wheatley, and she was brought from the West Coast of Africa, probably from the Senegambia region, to Boston, Massachusetts, in 1761. Her life spanned the era of America's revolutionary struggle with Great Britain, and her death in 1784 followed by one year Britain's recognition of America's independence. She wrote a poem lauding George Washington as well as one praising King George III, and she attracted the attention of revolutionary patriots such as Benjamin Franklin, Thomas Jefferson, Thomas Paine, John Hancock, and the American naval hero John Paul Jones. She was the first African American to publish a book of poetry and she gained international notice. Yet she was also a slave and composed most of her poetry while in that condition. Her color, enslavement, keen intelligence, and, quite likely, her gender all contributed to her fame. She was seen as unique because many people at that time did not think that Africans had intelligence or capability equal to that of Europeans. Many believed that Africans could not be educated, that they had no capacity for original or creative thought, and that they were best suited to servitude.

Phillis Wheatley began early on to disprove these notions. She was only seven or eight years old when she landed in Boston, but as John Wheatley, her purchaser, related, "Without any Assistance from School Education, and by only what she was taught in the Family, she, in sixteen Months Time from her Arrival, attained the English Language, to which she was an utter Stranger before, to such a Degree, as to read any, the most difficult Parts of the Sacred Writings, to the great Astonishment of all who heard her." Doubtless her owners quickly saw a chance to test the proposition that Africans were unable to learn and encouraged her to persist in educating herself. John Wheatley bought Phillis to aid his wife, Susannah, whom friends described as a woman of unusual refinement, sensitivity, and religiosity. She also had an interest in missionary activity, particularly among Africans and Native Americans. These characteristics help explain why Susannah encouraged Phillis to get an education. Besides studying Latin and English classics, she was tutored in astronomy, ancient and modern geography, and history. When one considers that she was a slave and also a woman in a period when most women and even more slaves received no such attention, her situation and accomplishments are remarkable. She was almost certainly one of the most highly educated young women in Boston at the time.

She was also well connected, for her mistress encouraged her religious interests and introduced her to leading advocates of the eighteenth-century evangelical Christian movement in America and Britain. Evangelical religion has been described as more a feeling and an attitude about religion than a strict religious system. Evangelicals refused to be bound by the rules of formal church organizations. They placed great emphasis on a personal knowledge of the Bible, a direct and emotional experience of God's grace, and the unity and equality of those saved by faith in the Holy Spirit. Consequently, they weakened existing distinctions between masters and slaves and undercut the traditional Christian toleration of slavery. Though not all evangelicals opposed slavery, the most radical among them did, particularly those of the Baptist and Methodist denominations that began a rapid expansion in England and America during Phillis's lifetime. They directed a particular appeal to the slaves.

The English noblewoman Salina Hastings, countess of Huntingdon, friend of Susannah Wheatley, and patron of Phillis, was a supporter of evangelical Methodism. Her personal chaplain, George Whitefield (whom Phillis celebrated in an elegy), was the leading figure in the Great Awakening religious revival movement (1739–45). It was characterized by highly emotional preaching, often delivered by itinerant ministers who sometimes preached in fields or tents as well as in church-es. It united black and white people in religious community and inspired some to reflect upon the blacks' secular condition, including speculations concerning their mental capabilities.

Phillis's achievements, therefore, had more than personal significance. She was embraced by abolitionists, many of whom were evangelicals, and offered as evi-dence that black people had the same possibilities as white people and deserved the same opportunities. After her *Poems on Various Subjects, Religious and Moral* was published in London in 1773, the Philadelphia physician and abolitionist Benjamin Rush extravagantly praised her "singular genius and accomplishments."

Her book, dedicated to the countess of Huntingdon, was printed a year after the famous Somerset decision of 1772, a court case that placed severe limits on slavery in England and caused considerable unease for her young master, Mrs. Wheatley's son Nathaniel, when they traveled there together in the summer of 1773. At the center of the case was James Somerset, an American slave taken to London by his Boston master in 1769. In England, Somerset escaped, only to be recaptured and as punishment threatened with relocation to the more rigor-ous slave environment of Jamaica. His plight came to the attention of Granville Sharp, an abolitionist committed to ending slavery in Britain. Chief Justice Lord Mansfield, who heard the case, was reluctant to make the decision for liberty toward which he felt the law leaned, because he feared the reactions of colonial planters if all the servants they had brought to England were suddenly declared free. He also feared the social and economic consequences of freeing all the slaves. He therefore delayed and attempted to get the case dismissed. When this tactic failed, he ordered Somerset's master to release him from service and established the precedent that in Britain slaves could not be compelled to serve. Although this case did not actually end slavery in Great Britain, as historians so often maintain, it did make the atmosphere uncongenial for slaveholders. Moreover, it brought the issue of slavery before the public and excited much sympathy for the slaves. Phillis Wheatley, however, did not take advantage of the situation. Instead, she cut short her stay and returned to Boston when her mistress, then ailing, request-ed her presence.

Her popular success in Britain notwithstanding, not everyone was impressed by Phillis's accomplishments. Despite his stirring affirmation in the Declaration of Independence that all men were created equal, Thomas Jefferson had severe reser-vations about blacks' abilities. Moreover, he readily discounted whatever evidence he found that discredited his opinion. Consequently, he dismissed Phillis Wheatley as being incompetent as a poet. "The compositions published under her name," he said, "are below the dignity of criticism."

A Jamaica planter, Edward Long, was even more harsh. He intended to parody Wheatley's verse and the uses to which she had been put by abolitionists when he wrote:

What woeful stuff this madrigal would be
In some starv'd, hackney sonneteer, or me!
But let a *Negroe* own the happy lines,
How the wit brightens! How the Style refines!
Before his sacred name flies ev'ry fault,
And each exalted stanza teems with thought!

Long clearly intended to suggest that the merits of Wheatley's poetry derived solely from the fact that she was black. Yet he exhibited a certain illogic because, while she may not have been, in his estimation, a genius, the common assertion was that blacks had not even a minimal competence.

The New World in which these commentators lived seemed to support such doubts, because by the middle of the eighteenth century, Africans were enslaved throughout the Americas. Abolitionist sentiment began to develop and have its first effects in Britain's American colonies. There were several reasons for this: First, British victories against France in the Seven Years' War (1756–63) extended Britain's possessions in the Caribbean and allowed for an increase in the supply of sugar reaching the mother country, temporarily forcing down its price. But the decline was not permanent because the British returned captured French sugar islands after the war, and the commodity's price in the British market, protected by restrictive regulations, recovered. However, increasing absentee ownership, rising slave prices, soil exhaustion in older islands, natural disasters, and slave unrest caused a rise in production costs. The outbreak of the American Revolution in the 1770s, which cut off the major source of island supplies, aggravated the situation. Planters, however, did not curb but rather expanded production, spurred by an economic boom in the 1790s. Jamaican planters, particularly, extended cultivation. Nevertheless, the French island of Saint Domingue produced more sugar, more cheaply, and undercut the British sugar price in Europe. The British simply could not compete because of the high production costs associated with their sugar industry. Some people began to question the whole process of British sugar production, and the most glaringly expensive factor in this production was slavery.

But economic stress does not adequately explain the British antislavery movement. Indeed, the movement achieved its first successes during a period when the sugar industry had, however briefly, regained its profitability. Moreover, similar crises among the Spanish or Portuguese had not led to the same questioning of human bondage. One historian explains the distinctive British reaction as being the result of a different historical background than that of the Iberian nations. Spain and Portugal had experienced slavery continuously from the time of the Roman Empire, and Iberians transported the institution to their colonies overseas as an ancient practice.

But slavery had died or was dying in northwestern Europe, and Englishmen readopted it in the sixteenth century mainly as a way to secure profits in tropical climes. They did not, however, approve of it at home. Where Iberians saw a familiar pattern of relationships because of their long slave tradition, Britons saw something new and relatively strange. Slavery was an institution for the colonies but not for Britain or the British. This does not mean that there were no slaves in Britain, for an estimated fourteen thousand resided there in the eighteenth century. But slaveholding was increasingly seen as an immoral choice, not part of British tradition.

One of the social, intellectual, and religious currents that forced people within the British Empire to look more closely at bonded labor was evangelical Protestantism. Millennialism (taken from the biblical prophecy in Revelations of Christ's one thousand-year reign on earth), which suggested the idea that man's sinful nature can be changed and that the world can be transformed into a heaven on earth, was an important feature of this outlook. It prompted much self-reflection. Millennialists equated slavery with sin and reform with virtue, and thus many of them became abolitionists. The ideas of the equality of all men before God and the necessity of free will for salvation were also sources of antislavery beliefs. Many Protestants considered free will to be essential to a conversion experience that emphasized personal commitment, and slavery permitted no free exercise of will.

Another intellectual concept that forced a reconsideration of slavery was the Enlightenment. Beginning in the late seventeenth century, this European philosophical movement developed around a number of concepts. The most important of these were a confidence in human reason as a guide to wisdom, a rejection of ignorance and superstition, a firm belief in the basic goodness of humankind, and a certainty that society, through reason, could be perfected. Eighteenth-century Enlightenment thought, particularly the idea of natural equality and the notion that society departed from that principle when it instituted slavery, supported abolition. These philosophical ideas intersected with religious ones: From both perspectives, slavery was seen as wrong and society could and ought to be reformed.

But it took economic change, which placed increasing emphasis on free labor and free trade, and a move away from the restrictive trading system derived from mercantilism, to make the arguments of abolitionists most effective. Mercantilism was an economic philosophy based on the concept that a nation's wealth depended on its supply of precious metals or other commodities, such as gold and silver (bullion) or jewels. These could be obtained through trade or conquest. A nation's colonies existed to aid the mother country in achieving wealth by supplying these commodities directly or by producing items that could be traded for them. Ideally, a colony that did not yield bullion directly produced raw materials that could be rendered into products that would bring in bullion. Slavery was not a necessary component of mercantilism except that it came to be considered the most effective and efficient means of raising the tropical products that created the wealth of eighteenth-century European empires.

The Scottish philosopher Adam Smith cast doubt on this relationship. In his *Theory of Moral Sentiments* (1759) and *The Wealth of Nations* (1775), he argued that slavery was inefficient as well as brutal and, in fact, not the most profitable system. "The experience of all ages and nations," Smith claimed, "demonstrates that the work done by slaves, though it appears to cost only their maintenance, is in the end the dearest of all." It encouraged idleness, Smith argued, and retarded progress. Neither enforced labor nor restricted trade brought the greatest material or social reward.

In North America, even before the revolutionary era, the beliefs of some Protestant sects led them to consider the injustice of slavery. As early as 1688 a Quaker group in Germantown, Pennsylvania, spoke out against the institution, and in 1693 Quakers published the first antislavery tract in America. Quakers were not only concerned about their personal salvation but had a commitment to social reform as well. Their antislavery sentiments increased in the eighteenth century as individual meetings, or congregations, took a stand against holding slaves. They were joined in their stance by members of other sects as a result of the Great Awakening.

Having ousted the French from the continent, the British government developed reorganization schemes designed to govern the empire more effectively and economically. These efforts ended a practice that had left colonials largely to their own affairs. In practical terms, the new policies brought much greater interference by the British Parliament in the colonists' daily lives—an intrusion the colonists resented. Most disturbing was Parliament's claim of the power to tax, formerly assumed by provincial legislatures. Americans viewed these innovations as disruptive of harmony, running counter to an ancient and valuable relationship, and corrosive of traditional liberties. What began as a struggle for traditional English rights (such as the principle that they could not be taxed without their consent), however, was extended under the influence of Enlightenment philosophy into a struggle for liberty as a natural (rather than an English) right. This struggle forced white Americans to consider the plight of blacks.

The Massachusetts patriot James Otis made this connection most clearly in 1764 when, in response to the Sugar Act, he declared that "the Colonists are by the law of nature free born, as indeed all men are, white or black." Skin color, hair texture, or other physical characteristics were not a logical basis on which to base enslavement. Or, as another revolutionary put it, "That all black persons should be slaves is as ridiculous as that law of a certain country that all red-haired persons should be hanged." He referred to *The Spirit of Laws* (1748), a book by the French Enlightenment philosopher Baron de Montesquieu that made fun of prejudice by describing a country where that was the custom.

But blacks were not satisfied to let others make their case for them. They, too, were affected by revolutionary ideology and were quite prepared to use it to argue for their own freedom. This was particularly the case for New England blacks, who, of all slaves, had the greatest opportunity to attain literacy. Thus in April 1773 four Massachusetts slaves addressed a letter to the Colonial House of Representatives stating that "the efforts made by the legislature of the province in their last sessions to free themselves from slavery, gave us, who are in that deplorable state, a high degree of satisfaction." They went on to suggest that they, too, desired freedom.

They adopted a peculiar strategy in pressing their case: "We are very sensible that it would be highly detrimental to our present masters, if we were allowed to demand all that of *right* belongs to us." But, they continued, "Even the *Spaniards,* who have not those sublime ideas of freedom that Englishmen have, are conscious that they have no right to all the services of . . . the *Africans,* who they have purchased." So they simply asked to be allowed one day a week to work for themselves to accumulate the money to buy their freedom. The House tabled the petition. When the blacks appealed to Governor Thomas Hutchinson, he said that he could do nothing for them.

After the Declaration of Independence was signed, petitions to the Massachusetts legislature from blacks became a little more aggressive. In New Hampshire blacks argued that "the God of nature gave them life and freedom, upon the terms of the most perfect equality with other men" and that "private and public tyranny and slavery are alike detestable to minds conscious of the equal dignity of human nature."

At the same time, free blacks moved against other aspects of discrimination. Although they were subject to taxation, free blacks in Massachusetts and elsewhere could not vote or hold office. Consequently, in February 1780 a group of blacks, under the leadership of a prominent local businessman, Paul Cuffe, and his brother John, took further advantage of revolutionary philosophy. They suggested to the legislature that "while we are not allowed the privilege of freemen of the state, having no vote or influence in the election with those that tax us, yet many of our own color, as is well known, have cheerfully entered the field of battle in defence of the common cause, and that as we conceive against a similar exertion of power in regard to taxation." In other words, they desired to extend to themselves the principle of no taxation without representation. Indeed, as part of the struggle, the Cuffes refused to pay taxes in 1778, 1779, and 1780. As a result, in December 1780 they were jailed. Three months later they admitted defeat and paid their back taxes, but they renewed their complaint.

Because blacks refused to let the argument die, it was difficult for New Englanders and other colonials to escape the logic of the revolution. Moreover, as the Cuffes noted, blacks were among the first to shed their blood in the common cause. Phillis Wheatley had a good chance to view the Boston Massacre on March 5, 1770—in which Crispus Attucks became celebrated as the first to die for colonial liberty—for it took place just down the street from the Wheatley mansion at King Street and Mackerel Lane, where she still lived.

Other blacks fought more personal battles. In April 1781, twenty-eight-year-old

The 29th Regiment have already left us, and the 14th Regiment are following them, fo that we expect the Town will foon be clear of all the Troops. The Wifdom and true Policy of his Majefty's Council and Col. Dalrymple theCommander appear in this Meafure. Two Regiments in the midft of this populous City ; and the Inhabitants juftly incenfed : Thofe of the neighbouring Towns actually under Arms upon the firftReport of the Maffacre, and the Signal only wanting to bring in a few Hours to the Gates of this City many Thoufands of our brave Brethren in the Country, deeply affected with our Diftreffes, and to whom we are greatly obliged on this Occafion—No one knows where this would have ended, and what important Confequences even to the whole Britifh Empire might have followed, which our Moderation & Loyalty upon fo trying anOccafion, and ourFaith in the Commander'sAffurances have happily prevented.

Laft Thurfday, agreeable to a general Requeft of the Inhabitants, and by the Confent of Parents and Friends, were carried to their *Grave* in Succeffion, the Bodies of *Samuel Gray, Samuel Maverick, James Caldwell,* and *Crifpus Attucks,* the unhappy Victims who fell in the bloody Maffacre of theMonday Evening preceeding !

On this Occafion moft of the Shops in Town were fhut, all the Bells were ordered to toll a folemn Peal, as were alfo thofe in the neighboring Towns of Charleftown Roxbury, &c. The Proceffion began to move between the Hours of 4 and 5 in the Afternoon ; two of the unfortunate Sufferers, viz. Meff. *JamesCaldwell* and *Crifpus Attucks,* who were Strangers, borne from Faneuil-Hall, attended by a numerous Train of Perfons of all Ranks ; and the other two, viz. Mr. *Samuel Gray,* from the Houfe of Mr. Benjamin Gray, (his Brother) on the North-fide the Exchange, and Mr. *Maverick,* from the Houfe of his diftreffed Mother Mrs. *Mary Maverick,* in Union-Street, each followed by their refpective Relations and Friends : The feveral Hearfes forming a Junction in King-Street, the Theatre of that inhuman Tragedy ! proceeded from thence thro' the Main-Street, lengthened by an immenfe Concourfe of People, fo numerous as to be obliged to follow in Ranks of fix, and brought up by a long Train of Carriages belonging to the principal Gentry of theTown. The Bodies were depofited in one Vault in the middle Burying-ground : The aggravated Circumftances of their Death, the Diftrefs and Sorrow vifible in every Countenance, together with the peculiar Solemnity with which the whole Funeral was conducted.

This account of the burial of the victims of the Boston Massacre appeared in the *Boston Gazette and Country Journal*. The coffin on the far right bears the initials of Crispus Attucks, the former slave who became a hero of the revolutionary era for his role in the incident.

Quok Walker left his master's service. He did so without permission and was sheltered by a neighbor, who employed him. His master discovered Walker, assaulted him with a whip handle, and charged the neighbor with enticing away his property. For his part, Walker brought suit against his master for assault and battery. The case came down to the issue of whether slavery was legally defensible, justifying the use of force. The master's lawyer argued that custom and usage of the country made slavery legal. Walker's lawyer argued, however, that custom and usage were unsustainable when they went against reason. The case eventually went to the Massachusetts Supreme Court. In coming to its decision in 1783, the court declared that since the state constitution of 1780 declared in its preamble that all men were born free and equal, slavery in the state was illegal. At the same time, it gave blacks who were taxed the right to vote. New Hampshire followed Massachusetts's lead when it decided that its Bill of Rights of 1783 forbade slavery, at least for those born after its adoption. Vermont was more forthright and prohibited slavery in its constitution of 1777.

While the judicial process worked its way in Massachusetts, Pennsylvania faced the problem head-on and became the first state to adopt a manumission, or freedom, law. As the home of Quakers, antislavery sentiment there was strong; many German immigrants, such as the Amish and Mennonites, also opposed the institution.

Perhaps no single person was more important in this process than Anthony Benezet. Born in France but forced to

Quaker leader Anthony Benezet actively supported the antislavery cause and sought to educate blacks in Philadelphia. He established integrated schools and published pamphlets attacking slavery and the slave trade.

flee because of religious persecution, he and his family eventually settled in Pennsylvania. Converting to the Quaker faith, he early became active in the anti-slavery cause. He published a number of pamphlets attacking slavery and the slave trade, dramatizing the evils of the trade and removing all doubts that it had any humanitarian features. Moreover, he studied the history of Africa to prove that Africans had cultures and civilizations comparable to those of other people in the world, and he argued that the chains of bondage alone were responsible for any failings they showed in America. He undertook to educate Philadelphia blacks, establishing integrated schools for that purpose. His writings had influence far beyond his locality. Thomas Clarkson, a leader in the British antislavery campaign, took his stance after reading Benezet's *A Short Account of that Part of Africa, Inhabited by the Negroes* (1762). John Wesley, founder of the Methodists, used Benezet's *Some Historical Account of Guinea* (1771) as the basis of sermons he preached in Britain against the slave trade. When Pennsylvania's manumission bill reached the Assembly, Benezet worked with the legislators to ensure passage.

As the first abolition law passed in America, Pennsylvania's 1780 statute was viewed as the perfect expression of American revolutionary philosophy. It provided for a gradual freeing of slaves over a period of years, yet it was not the most liberal such law to be passed. It merely came in advance of the rest, and along with Massachusetts and Vermont, Pennsylvania was one of the few states to end slavery before Britain's formal recognition of American independence.

But while blacks made use of revolutionary rhetoric to advance their freedom, and gave their blood in the colonial cause, they could not help but be reminded, even as they fought, that they were different. Thus, when blacks joined a crowd of Boston whites in an attack upon British soldiers in 1769, a Boston newspaper commented, "To behold Britons scourged by Negro drummers was a new and very disagreeable spectacle."

This consciousness of difference caused a group of slaves in the town of Thompson, Massachusetts, to end their request for freedom in 1773 with the statement: "We are willing to submit to such regulations and laws, as may be made relative to us, until we leave the province, which we determine to do as soon as we can, from our joynt labours procure money to transport ourselves to some part of the Coast of *Africa,* where we propose a settlement." Even before the end of the eighteenth century, then, there was the feeling among some blacks that a return to Africa was desirable. These emigrationists felt that because racial oppression in America was so great, black people could develop only if they returned to the land of their forefathers. They also thought that a return to Africa would help them to free their enslaved brethren in the New World by illustrating the competitiveness of tropical products grown with free labor. Finally, they believed that they could take with them to Africa the gifts of Christianity and civilization and serve as the means to uplift what common prejudice held to be a backward continent.

These ideas found resonance among the Christian evangelists of Phillis Wheatley's acquaintance. In 1773, one conceived a plan for educating two New England blacks, a free man named John Quamino and a slave, Bristol Yamma, and sending them to Africa as missionaries. The outbreak of the Revolutionary War doomed the project, yet not before Wheatley was asked to join the venture. She responded to the request with a statement that expressed the opinion of most American blacks, who, born and bred in the country, felt they had a right to consider it their own:

> Why do you hon'd Sir, wish those poor men so much trouble as to carry me [on] so long a voyage? Upon my arrival, how like a Barbarian shou'd I look to the Natives; I can promise that my tongue shall be quiet for a strong reason indeed, being an utter stranger to the Language. . . . Now to be Serious, This undertaking appears too hazardous and [I am] not sufficiently Eligible to go—And leave my British & American friends.

Wheatley's British and American friends would soon be at war, but the warfare provided other opportunities for blacks to achieve their freedom.

Battle Cry of Freedom

Eight months before the American Declaration of Independence was proclaimed in Philadelphia on July 4, 1776, a man named Lymus declared his own independence. He told his master in Charleston, South Carolina, as his master reported in the *South Carolina Gazette*, that he would "be free, that he w[ould] serve no Man, and that he w[ould] be conquered or governed by no Man."

In the year following the Declaration, two black men in Massachusetts advanced a different claim to liberty. They "ship'd on board the Armed Brigantine *Freedom*," as their friends related the story, "to fight ag[ains]t the Enemies of America." They thereby justified a claim to *personal* freedom. As their white compatriots announced, they "were volentieers [sic] in the business & ought to be considered in the same light as any other Sailors & by no means liable to be sold meerly because they are black." Somewhat earlier, a group of slaves in Boston devised still a different course. They petitioned the governor to propose, so Abigail Adams informed her husband John, that "they would fight for him provided he would arm them, and engage to liberate them if he conquered." The governor was General Thomas Gage, British commander in chief in America, and these slaves were clearly willing to fight on the British side if that would guarantee their emancipation. These people exemplify the claim of one noted African-American historian that black people in the revolution were more concerned about a principle than any one place or people—that principle being the natural right of human beings to their own person.

African Americans were motivated by the same desire for "life, liberty, and the pursuit of happiness" that animated other Americans. They were equally conscious of the natural rights philosophy of the Enlightenment and of the meaning of the phrases that Thomas Jefferson addressed to King George III. Thus black New Hampshire petitioners proclaimed: "Freedom is an inherent right of the human Species, not to be surrendered, but by Consent, for the sake of social Life." Abigail Adams expressed the same sentiments somewhat differently to her husband, John. "I wish most sincerely," she wrote, "there was not a slave in the province; it always appeared a most iniquitous scheme to me to fight ourselves for what we are daily robbing and plundering from those who have as good a right to freedom as we have."

When the fighting broke out, therefore, African Americans were among the first to rally to patriot banners. As they fought to free their country, they also fought to free themselves. Thus the slave of New Hampshire general John Sullivan, told by his master that they were going to join the patriot army to fight for liberty, responded "that it would be a great satisfaction to know that he was indeed going to fight for *his* liberty." Sullivan, impressed by the justice of his cause, freed him on the spot. Peter Salem, of Framingham, Massachusetts, was freed by his owners so that he could enlist. He fought in the battles of Lexington and Concord in April 1775 and helped to fire the "shot heard round the world" that heralded the beginning of America's military struggle. In June he fought at the Battle of Bunker Hill, where the colonials were forced to retreat after inflicting heavy losses on the British. Salem is credited with killing a British officer who led the final assault, and his musket is preserved at the Bunker Hill Monument.

Salem Poor, a free black, also fought at Bunker Hill. He came to the attention of fourteen officers who petitioned Congress to reward him for his bravery: "We declare that A Negro Man Called Salem Poor . . . behaved like an Experienced officer, as well as an Excellent Soldier." Although there is no record that Congress ever acknowledged him, he remained with the Continental army.

New England blacks were well situated to offer their services, for, despite laws prohibiting the practice, they had a history of duty in local militias. There simply were not enough white men willing or able to fill the ranks. African Americans served in twenty-five percent of Connecticut's militia companies and in noticeable numbers in other New England colonies. In spite of its relatively small black population, therefore, New England contributed more blacks to the Continental army than any other region. Rhode Island offered an all-black regiment, reported to be one of the few American regiments that enlisted for the entire war. Patriot general Philip Schuyler, on a military campaign in upstate New York, however, expressed a general objection to the presence of blacks. "Is it consistent with the Sons of Liberty," he asked, "to trust their all to be defended by slaves?"

Indeed, that was a question the colonials had to face as soon as the contending parties came to blows. In a country where slavery remained an important economic and social institution, few whites wanted the army to become a haven for runaway slaves. After the Continental army was formed in June 1775, commanding general Horatio Gates ordered that recruiters should not enlist "any stroller, negro, or vagabond," nor any deserter from the British army. He did not distinguish between slaves and free blacks. In September, the Continental Congress rejected a proposal of Edward Rutledge of South Carolina that blacks be totally excluded, but a council of generals in Cambridge, Massachusetts, adopted just such a policy the following month.

They took this position apparently in deference to George Washington, newly arrived commander in chief of the Continental army. Having scarcely ever been outside the confines of slaveholding Virginia and Maryland, he was appalled to find large numbers of blacks among the troops besieging the British in Boston in 1775. New England generals insisted that they made good soldiers, but Washington persuaded them that the use of African-American troops would hinder cooperation with southern colonies. Washington, however, did not have the same emotional dislike of blacks that affected Thomas Jefferson. Both from inclination and

VIRGINIA, *Dec.* 14, 1775.

By *the* REPRESENTATIVES *of the* PEOPLE *of the Colony and Dominion of* VIRGINIA, *assembled in* GENERAL CONVENTION.

A DECLARATION.

WHEREAS lord Dunmore, by his proclamation, dated on board the ship William, off Norfolk, the 7th day of November 1775, hath offered freedom to such able-bodied slaves as are willing to join him, and take up arms, against the good people of this colony, giving thereby encouragement to a general insurrection, which may induce a necessity of inflicting the severest punishments upon those unhappy people, already deluded by his base and insidious arts; and whereas, by an act of the General Assembly now in force in this colony, it is enacted, that all negro or other slaves, conspiring to rebel or make insurrection, shall suffer death, and be excluded all benefit of clergy: We think it proper to declare, that all slaves who have been, or shall be seduced, by his lordship's proclamation, or other arts, to desert their masters' service, and take up arms against the inhabitants of this colony, shall be liable to such punishment as shall hereafter be directed by the General Convention. And to the end that all such, who have taken this unlawful and wicked step, may return in safety to their duty, and escape the punishment due to their crimes, we hereby promise pardon to them, they surrendering themselves to col. William Woodford, or any other commander of our troops, and not appearing in arms after the publication hereof. And we do farther earnestly recommend it to all humane and benevolent persons in this colony to explain and make known this our offer of mercy to those unfortunate people.
EDMUND PENDLETON, president.

In response to Lord Dunmore's proclamation, Virginia's General Convention issued this statement threatening death to any slave caught trying to join the British side, while offering pardons to any slave who surrendered to the Continental army.

considerations of policy, Washington was convinced to listen when free blacks expressed their dissatisfaction at exclusion. He authorized their reenlistment and put the matter before Congress. Congress backed the decision but forbade any new black enlistments. That policy, however, was to change.

Among the considerations influencing Washington was the proclamation of the royal governor of Virginia, Lord Dunmore, offering freedom to slaves and indentured servants who joined the British troops. Although it applied only to the slaves of rebellious subjects and only to those able to join and fight, it nevertheless offered a clear choice that many accepted.

But neither Lord Dunmore's proclamation nor the Declaration of Independence caused any immediate change in the colonials' determination to keep slaves out of the war. States from New England to Georgia forbade blacks to enlist. Manpower shortages alone caused these prohibitions to be overlooked. Free blacks often took the place of whites when states drafted soldiers, and recruiting officers, sometimes paid by the head, were not particular about the inductees' color. When, beginning in 1777, Congress ordered the states to meet quotas to fill patriot ranks, the process of black recruitment picked up speed. African Americans were commonly enlisted in New England after 1777 and Rhode Island became the first state to authorize slave enlistment in 1778. Maryland took the same step in 1780, and New York in 1781. Virginia refused to follow Maryland's lead in enlisting slaves but did permit the service of free blacks. Nevertheless, some Virginia masters sent slaves to serve in their stead, promising freedom but frequently not making good on those promises after the war. In 1783, when it became aware of the situation, the state government freed those people.

Only the Lower South resisted the trend to enlist black soldiers. Greatly outnumbered by their slaves, planters who inhabited the coastal lowland regions of South Carolina and Georgia (often simply referred to as the low country) feared the consequences of permitting slaves to bear arms. They were more dependent than their neighbors on black labor and proved correspondingly less receptive to the logic of revolutionary reasoning. Yet even there it had effects.

No one better exemplified this fact than John Laurens, an aide to George Washington and son of South Carolina planter Henry Laurens, a former slave trader and president of the Continental Congress. Educated in Geneva, Switzerland, John had become influenced by antislavery sentiments. Early in the revolution he proposed recruiting slave soldiers in exchange for their freedom. He wrote his father in January 1778 asking that he be given his inheritance in able-bodied slaves, whom he would form into a battalion to be freed at the war's close. Henry asked Washington's opinion. John replied: "He is convinced that the numerous tribes of blacks in the southern part of the continent offer a resource to us which should not be neglected." The following year the Continental Congress gave its assent to the project and recommended the course to South Carolina and Georgia. But the Lower South would not be moved.

The issue of slave soldiers was controversial because it offered a threat to slavery itself. And the threat to slavery was important because it involved rights of property. The right to be secure in possession of their property was one of the things the colonists accused the British king of taking away from them when he taxed them without their consent. Thus when the Virginia legislature formally rejected the use of slaves as soldiers it was because, as one man reported, it was "considered unjust, sacrificing the property of a part of the community to the exoneration of the rest." Or, to put it another way, it was not fair to ask some people to give up their property in order to save the property of others.

The outbreak of fighting provided blacks some say in the matter. They had a choice of sides, and an estimated five thousand ultimately stood in Continental ranks. But the conflicted nature of their response was illustrated at the Battle of Great Bridge, fought on December 9, 1775, and described as the "Lexington of the South." This battle compelled Lord Dunmore to leave the soil of Virginia and operate thereafter offshore from naval vessels. Almost half of the British force of six hundred consisted of African Americans of Dunmore's "Ethiopian Regiment," who went into battle wearing sashes emblazoned with the words "Liberty to Slaves."

On the other side, a black spy for the Virginians tricked Dunmore into attack, and a free black from Portsmouth, William Flora, distinguished himself in the engagement against the British. Flora was "the last sentinel that came into the breast work," an officer remembered, and "he did not leave his post until he had fired several times. Billy had to cross a plank to get to the breast work, and had fairly passed over it when he was seen to turn back, and deliberately take up the plank after him, amidst a shower of musket balls." At least thirty of the blacks on the British side were captured.

Although Dunmore was forced away, the specter of his proclamation hung over the region, and periodic raids conducted by the British produced numerous slave defections. Thomas Jefferson had a reputation as a kind master, but when redcoats visited his estate in 1781, thirty of his slaves left with them. Robert "Councillor" Carter (so called because of his position on the governor's council from 1758 to 1772, where he had advisory and legislative functions), another kindly patriarch, was unusual in that he had accepted the Baptist faith and was united with his servants in a religious community. He made a special plea to his slaves to stay. But when royal troops arrived at one of his outlying farms, the lure of personal freedom proved too great. Jefferson estimated that about 25,000 Virginia slaves left their owners during the war, and many had to endure considerable danger and hardship to do so. Yet they were willing to pay the cost. As a correspondent to a Pennsylvania newspaper suggested, "the defection of the Negroes, [even] of the most indulgent masters . . . shewed what little dependence ought to be placed on persons deprived of their natural liberty."

Conflict between families and neighbors was more frequent in the Lower South than in the Chesapeake, and it created a violent atmosphere in which slaves had to tread lightly. British invasion provoked a bitter struggle between supporters and opponents of the crown. Indeed, several Georgia and South Carolina planters moved their families and slaves to more peaceful Virginia after the redcoats came at the end of the 1770s. As in Virginia, blacks were cautiously welcoming. A slave guide helped British forces in Georgia to outflank and defeat patriot forces in 1779, and when royal troops landed along the Carolina coast in 1780 they likewise had to depend on slave knowledge of the terrain. Many landowners abandoned their farms and plantations, leaving servants and white women and children to fend for themselves.

The British recruited blacks as guides or spies, as laborers to perform the heavy and exhausting work of building roads and fortifications, and some to serve as soldiers. Perhaps as many as twenty thousand African Americans served with the British in one capacity or another, and five thousand to six thousand left with them when they evacuated Charleston in 1782. A large number of slaves—maybe most (like many whites)—took no side but pursued their well-being as best they could in a situation of military uncertainty and social upheaval. Some fled to Charleston or Savannah and tried to pass as free people. Some continued to run plantations, with or without a white man's presence, assuming greater independence in the process. These were, after all, their homes, and the only places—outside of one of the contending armies—where they had any chance to secure a livelihood. In a period of chronic shortages of food, clothing, and other supplies, their old homesteads were sometimes the safest place to be. Of course, no guarantee existed even there, for marauding forces of one side or the other regularly confiscated whatever they needed and frequently destroyed the rest.

The remaining alternative for blacks (as for whites) was to migrate to some region away from the fighting. Some did so, retreating into the wilderness to form independent communities of their own. Some formed or became members of roving bands, occasionally interracial, that added to the disorder. They roamed the countryside, taking what they could for their own benefit. Some joined patriot fighting units such as that of South Carolina's "Swamp Fox" Francis Marion, who bedeviled the British with lightning raids and then melted away into Carolina's forests, marshes, or swamps. No slave was safe roaming about, however; capture could mean being sold, punished, or executed. It took considerable courage, therefore, even to run to the invader. In view of all the upheaval, some blacks welcomed the return of landowners and peace.

But warfare weakened slavery and provided bondsmen with at least a few options. They were limited because neither Britons nor white Americans were prepared to allow open black rebellion. Neither Britons nor white Americans could envision or accept a black republic. The only practical choices were to seek as much freedom as possible within the framework of revolutionary ideology in America or to trust the word of the British when they promised an eventual emancipation, there or elsewhere. Those who stayed on plantations accepted the realities of their condition but extended the boundaries of their servitude considerably, often acting virtually as free men.

Despite the planters' nightmares, war and revolution provoked no formal slave insurrection. About one-quarter of South Carolina slaves fled, however, and there was even more movement in Georgia. There, in response to British invasion, more than a third of the slave population walked away. No previous event in North American slavery equaled the slave exodus from Georgia, either in its size or consequences for undermining the institution. In the South as a whole, slave flight during the Revolution was of such an extent and character that it can almost be viewed as a kind of slave revolt.

While slaveholding colonials were zealous about guarding their claims to bondsmen they already possessed, they were less secure about arguing for the right to buy and sell them. They were particularly squeamish about the purchase of those newly brought from Africa. If the works of Anthony Benezet did anything, they dramatized the horrifying conditions under which the overseas slave trade was conducted. In those circumstances, the human rights of the captive were magnified and the property rights of the slave catcher or of the prospective buyer were greatly diminished.

Virginians had no difficulty, therefore, in attacking the slave trade. The Virginia constitution of 1776 accused the British king of an "inhuman use of his negative" in preventing the colony from excluding slaves, and Thomas Jefferson made the same charge in the Declaration of Independence. King George, Jefferson wrote, had "waged cruel war against human nature itself, violating its most sacred rights of life and liberty in the person of a distant people who never offended him, captivating and carrying them into slavery in another hemisphere, or to incur miserable death in their transportation thither." Never mind that the king had never forced any Virginian to buy slaves, nor that the prohibitive duties or taxes that Virginians and other colonists had placed on slaves before the Revolution (which is what Jefferson referred to) had been assessed for economic and social rather than humanitarian reasons. The fact is that the Atlantic slave trade was a horror difficult to ignore in a period of heightened humanitarian sensitivity.

For a combination of reasons, then, Americans moved against the slave trade. In New England, where slavery was relatively less important, legislatures began to terminate the trade with the first stirrings of revolutionary ardor. Rhode Island made the connection plain with a comment in its abolition law that "those who are desirous of enjoying all the advantages of liberty themselves, should be willing to extend personal liberty to others." When the Continental Congress decided in October 1774 to prohibit the import of slaves, however, it did so as part of a non-importation agreement designed to bring economic pressure against British merchants rather than because the trade was morally objectionable. Colonials intended these merchants to put pressure on Parliament to change its policies. When Virginia, North Carolina, and Georgia prohibited the trade, it had more to do with economic considerations and political pressure against the British government than with humanity. Nevertheless, the Congress reaffirmed its prohibition in 1776 and no state reopened the trade thereafter, except those in the Lower South. By their activities, therefore, blacks forced their masters to see some of the contradictions in their fight against England and laid the groundwork for a new birth of freedom.

Blacks and the British

As Americans wrestled with the question of what to do about the slaves, the British, unhampered by any inconvenient declaration of human equality, did likewise. Their West Indian empire as well as the southern portion of the North American colonies, which they still claimed, were based on slave labor. They had little interest in encouraging a social revolution that, if successful on the continent, might affect their holdings in the Caribbean. Moreover, they shrank from the prospect of being part of a bloody slave insurrection. Finally, they, too, generally accepted principles of white superiority that prevented them from considering a workable alliance with African Americans on terms approaching equality. It was clear, however, that blacks would have to be taken into account in a conflict in which they were an inevitable part.

An initial strategy was to use the black presence as a threat against the colonials. Thus General Gage warned South Carolinians that if they continued their opposition to Great Britain "it may happen that your Rice and Indigo will be brought to market by negroes instead of white people." This was not a pleasing prospect for either Britons or Americans, and proposals for emancipating southern slaves were not favorably received in Parliament. Lord Dunmore's proclamation and various other proposals to arm and free slaves caused public debate in England, for they were viewed as a shameful departure from a tradition opposed to using slaves against free people. Edmund Burke, a member of Parliament who supported the Americans, even considered such a policy hypocritical. Why, he wondered, should blacks accept "an offer of freedom from that very nation which has sold them to their present masters?" Doubts about the slaves' level of "civilization," an unwillingness to take the slaves of loyalists, and a fear of driving Americans to extremes beyond hope of reconciliation, all argued against a slave alliance. In both Virginia and North Carolina, royal governors who sought to use slaves spurred colonials to rage and brought royal forces to defeat.

Unfortunately for the British and their American opponents, African Americans were not prepared to stand idly by while others decided their fate. If they were to be pawns in a game of chicken or chess, they would not be passive ones. They forced the hands of both Lord Dunmore and George Washington, and the use of blacks by one side reinforced the use of blacks by the other. But it was the shift of warfare to the South, particularly the Lower South, where blacks frequently outnumbered whites in the general population, that sealed the British decision to utilize blacks, and changed their outlook toward the employment of black troops in other regions.

When Sir Henry Clinton, who replaced Gage as commander in chief of British forces in America, prepared to invade South Carolina in 1779, he began with the Philipsburg Proclamation. It was issued from his headquarters, Philipsburg Manor on the Hudson River in New York, on June 30. He declared that blacks taken in service with the patriots would be sold for the benefit of the crown, but that those who ran away to the British would be protected.

A policy provoked by military considerations rather than by humanitarian motives, it nevertheless chipped away at the foundations of slavery. It challenged blacks to take the British side. It did not formally offer them freedom but promised self-determination that was little short of it. Moreover, those who signed on as "pioneers," or laborers, to perform the drudgery of cleaning camp, building or repairing roads or bridges, constructing fortifications, or simply being on hand to take care of whatever undesirable tasks came up, were promised manumission in return for their devotion to duty. The same gift was held out to those who worked under British direction on agricultural estates or public works, or to the few enrolled as soldiers. African Americans took the bait in significant numbers.

Service with the British was not always to their liking, however. A policy prompted by military necessity was guided by military reasoning, and neither humanity nor fair play stood in the way of decisions that treated blacks harshly. They received fewer and inferior rations than white soldiers. They were not as well clothed. Their housing was inadequate and overcrowded. They were often overworked. They were consequently highly susceptible to disease, particularly various smallpox epidemics that afflicted the low country. Large numbers of them died. Nor were they exempt from sale for the use of the army when circumstances suggested that course.

Since the British army sought to maintain social order in regions it conquered, it had no philosophical objection to suppressing slave rebellions, particularly those directed against loyal subjects. It pledged to return the slaves of those whites who had remained loyal to the crown or to replace them with those of patriots. The degree to which slaves could view the British army as an army of liberation, therefore, was very limited indeed. No wonder it did not evoke wholesale desertions from the colonials.

Nonetheless the pull of freedom was great and the chance of leaving bondage improved as the British moved toward defeat. Manpower shortages and a demonstrated black resistance to tropical diseases prompted General Alexander Leslie to recruit black troops seriously beginning in 1779. The successful use of blacks in South Carolina caught the attention of other British officers and served as the precedent for the use of black soldiers in the West Indies. Shortly before the British left the Carolina coast, Jamaica's governor enrolled a battalion of troops from among the free black and colored, or mixed race, people of Charleston. They formed the Black Carolina Corps, which served in Jamaica and elsewhere, and they took with them American ideas about the rights of man. By the 1790s, Britain utilized black troops extensively to support its Caribbean empire.

When the British left the United States at the end of the war, the question of what to do about blacks who had sought their protection proved a source of controversy. Planters wanted their human property returned, but the new British commander in chief, Sir Guy Carleton, felt that the commitments made in previous proclamations of freedom to slaves who joined them ought to be honored.

The old slave dealer Henry Laurens, despite periodic expressions of sympathy for the Africans—and notwithstanding his son's championship of slave battalions—remained keenly aware of the property interests involved. He inserted a provision in the treaty ending the war, the Treaty of Paris of 1783, that obliged the British to return fugitive slaves. Sir Guy thought that would be dishonorable. He interpreted the clause to mean that he should shelter no more fugitives and gave orders to turn back any who had newly come in. Only those who had been with the army for a year or more would receive his protection. But those already with the army were, in his opinion, already free and no longer to be considered property. Or if they were, that issue would have to be solved by some kind of money transaction, for he was not prepared to violate the word of British officers by returning them. Nor could he believe that had been the intention of the government. British ministers, he said, could not possibly have agreed to such a "notorious breach of the public faith towards people of any complection." If the royal army's relationship with blacks had not always been the most admirable, at least at the end one general took the high ground and saved many blacks from a return to servitude.

George Washington stuck with the American position that the British ought to return fugitive slaves to their former owners. Yet compared to others who insisted firmly on the return of all slaves, Washington was unusually sensitive in this regard. He seemed resigned to the inevitable. "[S]everal of my own are with the Enemy," he reflected, "but I scarce ever bestowed a thought on them; they have so many doors through which they can escape from New York, that scarce any thing but an inclination to return . . . will restore many." He thereby indicated a property awareness strongly modified by a revolutionary spirit that was rapidly diminishing in the wake of American victory. If Thomas Jefferson most clearly expressed the ideals of the revolution, Washington, of all the slaveholding leaders of the revolution, came closest to practicing these ideals insofar as blacks are concerned. He certainly desired the return of property, but he was prepared to accept a black man's rejection of that status. In contrast to Jefferson, he provided in his will for the freeing of many of his slaves.

Boston King exemplifies the reasons many slaves left for the British side and also why many others did not. He was born in South Carolina, and as a child he performed many of the ordinary tasks common to plantation life, such as running errands and minding cattle. After an apprenticeship to a carpenter, he became a skilled laborer. He also had an uncommon experience. At one point he worked around racehorses, which permitted him a degree of travel. The job occasioned some hardship because the head groom was unkind and once made him go without shoes through the winter because he happened to lose a boot. His mentor in carpentry was also mean and mistreated him until his owner, Richard Waring, threatened to withdraw him from service.

Although King had an easygoing master, his experiences with other white folk made him wary of slaveholders' kindness and conditioned him to be receptive to British offers of freedom. He accompanied his master outside of Charleston—or Charles Town as it was then known—during the redcoats' occupation. But, he wrote in his memoirs, having obtained leave one day to see my parents, who lived about twelve miles off, and it being late before I could go, I was obliged to borrow [a horse]; but a servant of my master's took the horse to go a little journey, and stayed two or three days longer than he ought. This involved me in the greatest perplexity, and I expected the severest punishment, because the gentleman to whom the horse belonged was a very bad man, and knew not how to show mercy. To escape his cruelty I determined to go to Charles-Town, and throw myself into the hand of the English . . . altho' I was most grieved at first, to be obliged to leave my friends, and remain among strangers."

Boston King eventually followed the British to New York City and there married Violet, a fugitive from North Carolina. Recaptured by the Americans, he was treated well but "sorely distressed at the thought of being again reduced to slavery, and separated from my wife and family." He managed to escape and return to his English protectors. Unlike white Americans, Boston King was not filled with joy at the end of the war, "for a report prevailed at New-York that all the slaves, in number two thousand, were to be delivered up to their masters, altho some of them had been three or four years among the English. This dreadful rumour filled us with inexpressible anguish and terror, especially when we saw our old masters coming from Virginia, North-Carolina, and other parts, and seizing upon their slaves in the streets of New-York, or even dragging them out of their beds. Many of the slaves had very cruel masters, so that the thoughts of returning home with them embittered life to us." King and other slaves were therefore highly appreciative of the position taken by British general Sir Guy Carleton. King and his wife received certificates of freedom and left with other loyalists for Nova Scotia.

Large numbers of blacks accompanied British forces when they departed the coastal cities of Savannah, Charleston, Philadelphia, Boston, and New York at various times during the war and especially during the final evacuations. Besides Nova Scotia and the West Indies, London was also a destination for several hundred North American blacks. In London, which had a significant black population in the eighteenth century, these new arrivals attracted the attention of antislavery activists and fueled a concern about the treatment of blacks in England and the British Empire. The Somerset case of 1772 had established that English law did not recognize slavery in the kingdom itself, but it had not applied to the colonies.

Blacks on the streets of London, however, could not be ignored, particularly since so many were destitute and reduced to begging. For unlike white loyalists, who were frequently compensated for their losses and supported until they were reestablished in Britain and elsewhere, African Americans were given little assistance. The British government assumed that since they had nothing to begin with, former slaves should be thankful merely for their freedom.

In the absence of governmental concern, a group of humanitarian businessmen formed the Black Poor Committee in 1786 to provide temporary relief. They also persuaded the Lords of the Treasury to grant aid to the most needy, although, as it turned out, this was not enough for bare subsistence. At this point Henry Smeathman, an amateur botanist who had spent some time on the coast of Africa, offered to rid the committee and the government of their unwanted charges by settling them in Sierra Leone, on the west coast of Africa. Abolitionist Granville Sharp became involved with the scheme and even drew up a plan of government. In spite of Sharp's involvement, the initial idea seems to have been to get blacks out of England over all other considerations. The humanitarian and religious reasons usually associated with the settlement of Sierra Leone were not much in evidence when the colony was first proposed.

Nevertheless, once the scheme was advanced, it became the focus of antislavery groups as a possible means of attacking the slave system by introducing free labor into Africa. Quakers had begun petitioning Parliament against the slave trade and formed the majority of the Society for Abolition of the Slave Trade, founded in 1787, in which they were allied with other evangelicals. Their activities made the slave trade a public issue by 1787, at the time the Sierra Leone expedition was getting under way.

Despite Sharp's continued activity, the men around whom the movement focused were Thomas Clarkson and William Wilberforce. Clarkson's interest resulted from his decision in 1785 to enter a contest sponsored by Cambridge University. It offered a prize for the best essay on the question, "Is it lawful to make slaves of others against their will?" As he knew nothing about slavery or the slave trade, he read, among other things, Anthony Benezet's *Short Account of Africa* and set to work. He won the prize and a short time later received what he considered to be a divine mission to devote his life to abolition. He joined with Granville Sharp and others in the Society for the Abolition of the Slave Trade.

The role of Clarkson was primarily as researcher and writer. He was not a very good speaker, had little sense of humor, was somewhat petulant, and showed little inclination to compromise. Still, he had an immense capacity for work. He visited Liverpool, Bristol, and other slaving ports to gather data for use against the trade. He began a collection of horror instruments, such as thumbscrews, handcuffs, leg shackles, and mouth openers (which were used to force-feed slaves who sought to starve themselves to death) to illustrate the cruelty of the trade. He realized his limitations, though, and knew that, lacking oratorical skills, he was unlikely to become a captivating national leader. Someone would have to be found who had a gift for public speaking, preferably someone wealthy and well connected whom the slaving interests could not buy or intimidate. Such a man was William Wilberforce.

Born in Hull, England, Wilberforce was the son of a wealthy merchant. He was physically frail but brilliant and charming. His grandfather bequeathed him a fortune and he grew up addicted to the good life. He frequented the best clubs, kept company with prominent people, and took to gambling and heavy drinking. However, he was also an eloquent speaker as well as an amiable companion, and when he tired of dissipation he decided to enter Parliament. But Parliament bored him, too. He took a tour of Europe with a religious friend who converted him to evangelical Christianity and gave his life more meaning. He intended to resign from Parliament and find more useful employment until his friend Prime Minister William Pitt suggested that he involve himself in the abolitionist cause. A few parliamentary speeches brought him to the attention of the Society for the Abolition of the Slave Trade and he agreed to become its spokesman. He and Clarkson became close friends.

The two were dedicated to a common goal and complemented each other because each had qualities the other lacked. Together they mapped out a strategy. They decided to concentrate on the misfortunes suffered by English sailors engaged in the trade rather than on the Africans they enslaved, because they felt the English public would more likely be moved by the former. They also agreed to limit their attack to the trade and not malign slavery itself so as to avoid alarming West Indian planters. They assured planters that their slave property would be more valuable and insurrections less likely if the trade were abolished.

The first of these conclusions they derived from the fairly obvious relationship between supply and demand: If the supply ceased and the demand remained constant, the value of bondsmen already on, or capable to be put on, the market would rise. The second conclusion was put forward because newly imported Africans were frequently thought to be responsible for slave rebellions. But Wilberforce and Clarkson also felt that they could undermine the argument for slavery if a free labor colony in Africa, raising competing tropical products, proved successful. Such a colony would benefit English industrialists by furnishing raw materials for English manufacturers and providing a market for English goods. Moreover, such a colony would be only the starting point for opening a much larger African market, one that would absorb much more of Britain's production than its West Indian colonies. An African market would provide more work for English workingmen and more wealth for the wealthy. In other words, the abolitionists hoped to convince the English public and English business interests that they had more to gain than to lose by ending the slave trade and, ultimately, slavery.

A total of 459 people left Portsmouth, England, for the African coast on February 23, 1787, to found the colony of Sierra Leone. Most were black, but almost a quarter were white, most of them white women married to black men. At least half of the emigrants were former slaves from North America. Olaudah Equiano had been appointed by the navy commissioners as commissary for the voyage. He was responsible for the settlers' supplies. He complained, however, that preparations were inadequate. Moreover, he charged the white man who supervised the venture with incompetence, dishonesty, and racism. The supervisor misappropriated funds for his own use, Equiano said, and treated blacks "the same as they do in the West Indies." Although Equiano's charges had merit, he was recalled, and white men were left in control.

The voyage, therefore, did not have an auspicious beginning and the settlement came close to failure. The settlers came at the wrong time of year for building and brought the wrong kind of seeds for planting. They quickly succumbed to disease. By September almost half the original colonists were dead and only a supply ship sent by Granville Sharp the following year saved the remainder.

Abolitionists now began to take a serious interest in the African enterprise, for

Olaudah Equiano was taken from his African home as a child and sold into slavery in the Americas. The extraordinary details of his life, described in his autobiography, captivated readers in England and in America.

it was clear that its failure would harm their cause. Among other things, it would support the pro-slavery argument that blacks could not rule themselves and would work only under the threat of force; it would also ruin the vision of a free-labor society in Africa as a market for British manufactured goods. Thomas Clarkson, Granville Sharp, and William Wilberforce, therefore, were appointed as three of the directors of a new enterprise, the Sierra Leone Company.

What gave the colony a new lease on life was the arrival of immigrants from Nova Scotia, Canada. African-American migrants to that region had found harsh winters, rocky and infertile land, starvation, discrimination, and political limitations. Hardship faced both white and black refugees, but the blacks came with less of everything needed for their survival and were given less upon their arrival. In the meantime, Boston King recalled: "Many of the poor people were compelled to sell their best gowns for five pounds of flour, in order to support life. When they had parted with all their clothes, even to their blankets, several of them fell down dead in the streets through hunger. Some killed and eat [sic] their dogs and cats; and poverty and distress prevailed on every side."

John Clarkson, brother of Thomas, accompanied Thomas Peters, who had been a leader of the Black Pioneers, a British military unit formed in 1776, back to Canada, and in January 1792 they left Nova Scotia with almost 1,200 passengers for the Province of Freedom, as Sierra Leone was called. One of these was Henry Washington, who had run away from the American commander-in-chief in 1776. He proved to be a successful farmer in Sierra Leone until he was banished for involvement in a dispute over issues of taxation and representation in the African colony. His quarrel offers clear evidence that the settlers had not forgotten their American revolutionary experience.

Already the fight against slavery and the slave trade was beginning to have some impact. Britain was now the leading slave-trading nation, with the French not far behind. Prime Minister William Pitt attempted to negotiate an agreement with the French in 1787 for mutual abolition of the slave trade, but that attempt failed. Among other reasons, the French were not anxious to hamper the prosperity of their thriving sugar colony in Saint Domingue, in the Caribbean, which was heavily dependent on slaves.

The British Parliament nevertheless passed a law in 1788 to limit the number of slaves its own vessels could carry relative to their size. This law was designed to make the slave trade somewhat more humane by providing the captives more room and comfort. In 1789 Wilberforce introduced a motion in Parliament to abolish the British trade and began a series of hearings into the issue. Meanwhile, Clarkson set off for the continent to make contact with the Society of the Friends of the Blacks in France, formed in 1788 for the same purpose. He, like Pitt, hoped to coordinate the abolitionist activities of the two nations so that their opponents could not use a failure in one nation as an excuse for failure in the other. The outbreak of the French Revolution in 1789 and the subsequent slave rebellion in Saint Domingue made the slave trade's abolition impossible in the 1790s. Nevertheless a start had been made and African Americans had had something to do with it.

The influence of African Americans on this worldwide movement to end slavery operated at various levels. The American Revolutionary War provided African Americans a chance to fight for their freedom by playing one force against another. No other group more clearly saw the contradiction between revolutionary ideals and American practice. Occasionally, they succeeded in convincing their white compatriots to live up to their stated ideals of the natural equality of all people, or at least to recognize their inconsistency when they did not. Of course, the war also provided blacks an alternative course to liberty. Those who left the country took revolutionary notions with them—to Africa, to the West Indies, and elsewhere.

The war also cut off West Indian planters from supporters in North America and left them to fight the rising tide of abolitionism within the British Empire unaided. This was true not solely in political terms but in economic and social terms as well. They lost easy access to American supplies and to the American market for their molasses. They therefore became more dependent on the mother country and more vulnerable to imperial pressure. African-American immigrants into Britain forced the issue of slavery and caused people there to take a stand. They therefore helped to breathe new life into British abolitionism, contributing to the British attack on the slave trade and eventually on slavery itself. In their American homeland, however, the revolution had only limited success.

Slavery and Freedom in the New Nation

Revolution and war in America, based on principles of natural rights and human equality, created an environment destructive to slavery. Yet there were definite limits to the effectiveness of these forces. Among the revolutionary generation there was no clear line drawn between human rights and property rights; no feeling that the one ought to come before the other.

Thus Pennsylvania's chief justice, denying a slave woman's claim to emancipation in 1815, wrote that "I know that freedom is to be favoured, but we have no right to favour it at the expense of property." Significantly, this case came from one of the nation's most liberal states. The judge's statement accurately captures the spirit of the earlier age. Rather than being banned by the state on the grounds of immorality, slavery was seen as something that had to be abolished voluntarily, usually with some form of compensation to the former slaveowners. This was not a direct compensation from the government. Most people thought that would be too great a public expense. Indeed, some radicals felt that, in a moral sense, if such a payment were to be made it ought to go to the bondsman in return for his unrequited toil rather than to his master.

Instead, the gradual emancipation laws enacted in most northern states provided for freedom for children of existing adult slaves born after a certain date, but not to those slaves themselves. In addition, the children were bound to serve their parents' master until sometime in their twenties, depending on the state. Slave owners thus continued to benefit from slave labor for some years after these acts were passed. Nevertheless, in the northern states, where the institution was not economically crucial nor its abolition regarded as too socially disruptive, slavery gradually ended.

By 1784 the new nation was already well along the way toward a division between a northern region of free states and a southern one of slave states. Yet that vision is most clear in hindsight. A person who lived at the time may not have considered that result a foregone conclusion. For one thing, slavery was still fairly strongly entrenched in New York and New Jersey. Proposals to end the institution there in 1785 and 1786, respectively, failed. Indeed, slavery expanded rapidly in New York during the 1790s, particularly in New York City. The surrounding rural population, which was largely Dutch, remained strongly wedded to bound labor.

In Virginia, by contrast, there was widespread antislavery sentiment and the legislature passed a law in 1782 making it easy for individuals to follow their conscience and free their slaves. Moreover, Delaware and Maryland, like New York and New Jersey, also debated ending slavery, in roughly the same period and with the same results; the measures failed. But unlike New York and New Jersey, they followed Virginia's example and made manumission easier than it had been, Delaware in 1787 and Maryland in 1790.

North Carolina had some difficulty making up its mind and adopted various pieces of contradictory legislation, but in all these states the free black population expanded considerably. North Carolina Quakers were particularly active in conveying the enslaved to freedom. They took advantage of every legal opportunity that was offered, including ensuring that slaves promised freedom in return for fighting were not reenslaved. They also bought bondsmen and let them pay off the debt and live as free people in all but name.

Yet there were distinct differences between the situation in New York and New Jersey and in the states south of Pennsylvania. African Americans were never more than about ten percent of the population of these Middle Atlantic states. They made up almost a third of Virginia and Maryland, and nearly as large a proportion in Delaware and North Carolina. Moreover, they were an important economic asset in the South. This was true equally in terms of their labor on farms and plantations, where they were a much higher percentage of the labor force than in the North, and in their value as property. If they were freed, their labor could continue, of course, on a different basis. They could be paid instead of forced to work. But such a transformation still required a radical social and economic reorganization. Equally important, it required a mental restructuring.

Complicating the social issue was the question of race. Many white people did not think that white and black people could live together in peace—or, if they did so, only if one race was subordinate to the other. A prominent spokesman for this view was Thomas Jefferson. "Nothing is more certainly written in the book of fate than that these [black] people are to be free," he wrote on one occasion. "Nor is it less certain that the two races, equally free, cannot live in the same government."

He felt that peaceful relations would be prevented by prejudices that white people held against blacks and by the memories that black people had of the past injustices suffered from whites. Nor could he ever get over his feeling that black people were inferior to white people. Unlike some people, who felt that the environment of slavery was responsible for whatever shortcomings blacks exhibited, Jefferson struggled unsuccessfully against the suspicion that Africans were inferior by nature. This did not mean, however, that he intended to exclude African

This section from Jefferson's handwritten draft of the Declaration of Independence contains a passage condemning the slave trade. This clause was omitted because of objections from Georgia and South Carolina planters who needed slaves, and from New England shippers who sometimes engaged in slave trading.

Americans from the inalienable rights he declared all men to have. His charge in the Declaration of Independence that King George III had "waged cruel war against human nature itself" in his pursuit of the slave trade, and that the king had thereby violated Africans' "most sacred rights of life and liberty," indicates that Jefferson regarded Africans and African Americans as full members of the human community. Moreover, to underline the point, he would later say that "whatever be their [the blacks'] degree of talent it is no measure of their rights. Because Sir Isaac Newton was superior to others in understanding, he was not therefore lord of the person or property of others." But his reasoning could not withstand his emotion, and his was a perspective widely shared in Virginia and elsewhere in the country. When Jefferson spoke of abolition, therefore, he also talked of removing blacks from the continent.

There were elements of this outlook in the Middle Atlantic states, but because the black population there was smaller, opposition to emancipation focused

around the issues of property and compensation rather than on the social consequences of freeing blacks. Here the relationship between human rights and property rights could be more easily discussed. The problem surfaced everywhere, but
it could be more easily separated from other issues in the North than in the South.
Moreover, in New York and New Jersey, where slavery was generally more important than in New England, the discussion had more resonance. It affected more
people more closely. Everywhere the issue arose it involved the well-being of people. Part of this equation included money and wealth and comfort. Another part
included public and private safety and peace of mind. The various factors had to
be weighed practically as well as philosophically.

When New York's manumission law was finally passed, a legislator, blaming
opposition mainly on the Dutch, commented they "raved and swore . . . that we
were robbing them of their property. We told them they had none, and could hold
none in human flesh . . . and we passed the law."

Nevertheless, the freeing of slaves in New York and other Middle Atlantic states
took a long time to happen. Fifteen years after the end of the Revolutionary War
and fourteen years after the final acts of liberation in New England, New York
agreed to manumission. New Jersey did not do so until twenty years after the war.
In the 1790s, while slavery was dead or dying in Philadelphia, it was still growing
in New York City.

Slavery's usefulness and profitability in the 1780s and 1790s caused many to
adopt it to their advantage. But also, in view of the undoubted antislavery sentiment of the time, many Northerners disassociated their institution from the horrors that were assumed to characterize slavery on Southern or Caribbean plantations. Slaves were "better off than the generality of the white poor," one New Jersey
man argued, "who are obliged . . . to work harder than the slaves in general in this
state." In this way slave owners could salve their consciences and at the same time
attack slavery in the abstract. They could even work toward ending it locally,
though they did so with no apparent urgency.

Several things countered this comfortable middle position among those
inclined toward abolition in New York and meant that they would soon have to
choose sides. One was the increasing numbers of free blacks, whose presence and
activities weakened the institution. They served the slaves as examples of the possible. They were joined in their subversion by slaves themselves, who had a unique
history in this region of being able to negotiate the conditions of their servitude.
Black servitors had long been permitted to search for a new master if, for example,
their current situation or location displeased them. A slaveholder's move from city
to countryside might well prompt his servant to ask for permission to look for a
new owner, so as to avoid exile to a rural location far from friends and family. Many
did not stop at trying to better their terms of servitude, however; in a revolutionary age, bondsmen sought also to arrange their freedom. Their increased desire for
personal liberty marred any assumption that they were satisfied with bondage.

The immigration of refugees from the slave uprising in Saint Domingue was another factor disturbing the presumption of a benign servitude. White refugees frequently brought slaves with them and their severe treatment of them, conditioned by the harsher environment of the West Indies, strikingly illustrated the disadvantages of slave life wherever it existed. It was difficult to maintain the myth of a mild slavery when some were so obviously, and sometimes publicly, mistreated. For their part, Saint Dominguan slaves contributed significantly to slave unrest, further corroding the feeling of ease. Finally there were the activities of kidnappers who stole free blacks and sold them outside the state. They exhibited the crass economic nature of the institution, the unpleasant underbelly that was better left unexposed.

The New York Manumission Society arose as an answer to the problem of slavery in New York State. Formed in January 1785 in response to "violent attempts lately made to seize and export for sale several free Negroes," the society also aimed to promote eventual abolition. Its moral outrage was strictly limited, however. It did not engage in a scathing critique of slavery or slaveholders as they existed in New York, nor did it exclude slaveholders from membership. John Jay, the society's first president, owned slaves. He explained his apparent inconsistency: "I purchase slaves and manumit them when their faithful services shall have afforded a reasonable retribution." Whether his was an act of charity or hypocrisy, the fact that he and other slaveholders joined an antislavery society was indicative of the trend of the times. Even though they sometimes seemed to devote more effort to humanizing slavery than to getting rid of it, they nevertheless introduced gradual emancipation legislation and other measures to free and protect blacks. But if even some slaveholders could envision and work toward emancipation, one could reasonably foresee its doom. The ending of slavery in New York was drawn out and complicated. Its last manumission law, adopted in 1817, granted freedom to slaves born before July 4, 1799, to be effective July 4, 1827. But most slaves came to an agreement that provided their freedom considerably earlier than that date. New Jersey moved more slowly, adopting comparable legislation in 1804 and 1846. It still had a few slaves at the time of the Civil War.

If abolition came slowly in the Middle Atlantic, it was indefinitely delayed farther south. The Upper South, the region north of South Carolina, was as much affected by the ideology of the Revolution as any area of the country. George Washington, Thomas Jefferson, and many other prominent leaders of America's struggle against Great Britain were Virginians. Nearly all of them expressed reservations about slavery. Many, including Washington and Jefferson, expressed a desire to see it end.

Besides, there were more reasons than philosophy to support that position. Evangelical Methodists and Baptists, quite active in the Chesapeake in the 1780s, carried out widespread religious revivals. They added Christian egalitarianism, or the belief that all men are equal in the sight of God, to the secular claims of equality advanced in the Revolution. Moreover, they were effective. Virginia's Robert Carter, one of the richest and most successful planters in the country, freed five hundred slaves beginning in 1791, at least partly from religious conviction. "I have for some time past," he wrote in his deed of manumission, "been convinced that to retain them in Slavery is contrary to the true Principles of Religion and Justice, and that therefor[e] it was my Duty to manumit them."

Finally, there were economic considerations. Many planters in Virginia, Maryland, and Delaware began to shift from tobacco to cereal crops, such as wheat, oats, barley, and corn, beginning in the mid-eighteenth century. They made this shift because of a fall in tobacco prices at the same time that the worldwide demand for food crops increased. They also moved to grains because tobacco so rapidly exhausts the soil. These new products did not require as much slave labor and many planters felt that they had a surplus of slaves. They were prepared to consider alternatives like the labor of free blacks. So for many reasons people in the Upper South could seriously consider manumission, and some moved from thought to action. Yet Southern revolutionaries ultimately contented themselves with making manumission a matter of personal conscience. Proposals for total abolition were considered but dismissed.

A major objection, as we have seen, had to do with race. One Southerner, still sensitive to the issue of bondage, tried in 1797 to put the best face on an obvious Revolutionary failure. "On inquiry," he explained, "it would not be found the fault of the southern states that slavery was tolerated, but their misfortune; but to liberate their slaves would be to act like madmen; it would be to injure all parts of the United States." He implied that Southerners were self-sacrificing statesmen for their willingness to keep black people in chains and under control, and he meant thereby to make slaveholding a patriotic duty. But by that time the economy had changed again. Slaveholders in the Upper South could now find a ready market for their slaves in the expanding cotton regions of the southwest. The momentum toward the abolition of slavery in the Upper South began to slip away.

The Lower South states of South Carolina and Georgia were largely exempt from the tenderness of conscience that afflicted the Upper South. They had a plantation economy that was starved for bound black labor. While the loss of slaves during the war had inconvenienced Virginia planters, it had devastated those in the Lower South, whose prime concern was how soon the slave trade could resume. Moreover, slaves were a much higher percentage of their population; therefore the social and economic effects of the abolition of slavery were more significant. The relatively liberal period that flowered in the Upper South, therefore, had no counterpart in the Lower South. Some emancipations occurred, but these were prompted more by blood ties than abstract philosophy. Lower South planters were more likely to free their sons and daughters by slave mistresses than anyone else, so the free colored population that grew here was lighter-skinned than that in the Chesapeake, where manumissions were more often motivated by conscience.

Abolitionist pressure could in some instances be more effectively brought to bear at the national level, but the government formed under the Articles of Confederation (which were finally adopted in 1781) did not have much power. Having rejected a strong centralized government in Europe, few Americans were disposed to create a new one in their midst. The new states were jealous of their prerogatives and reluctant to surrender any more than necessary to what amounted to little more than a wartime alliance against England. Consequently, most activities that affected African Americans occurred at the state and local levels.

There was one crucial exception to this rule, and it had to do with territories to the west, where Americans expected their growing population would settle. Indeed, a struggle over the status of these lands kept the Articles from going into effect for years. Maryland, a small state, wanted the issue solved in such a way as to guarantee equal access to the West for the citizens of all the states, rather than trying to sort out conflicting and overlapping claims. Only when Maryland secured agreement that western territories would be considered the common property of all the states would it assent to the compact. Congress, under the Articles, therefore had to consider some plan for orderly settlement.

Thomas Jefferson offered a solution in his proposal for the Land Ordinance of 1784. Under his proposed law, slavery would have been prohibited in all western lands after 1800. This would have meant that all territory west of the Alleghenies, north and south, would have prohibited slavery at the beginning of the nineteenth century. But the proposal would have allowed a sixteen-year period for slavery to become entrenched before the law took effect. Some historians think that had that happened, the prohibition would have been repealed and slavery would have been allowed in all these western territories.

In any case, it failed by one vote. The measure that was adopted, the Northwest Ordinance of 1787, forbade slavery only in the area east of the Mississippi and north of the Ohio River, which was called the Northwest Territory. The ordinance did not free slaves already there, and it provided that any fugitive slaves who fled there should be returned to their masters. Slavery continued to exist in Indiana until 1818 and in Illinois until the 1840s. Nonetheless, an important principle had been established and slavery's spread had been curbed.

In making the Constitution of 1789, however, the Founders did not find revolutionary idealism all that useful. They had to reconcile many differences to form a strong nation, and to come to a compromise between the conflicting principles of freedom and property. In effect, this meant that blacks had to be compromised. This was not difficult for the framers of the Constitution because at the time of the Constitutional Convention in 1787 most states were slave states. Only in Pennsylvania and New England was slavery on the road to extinction. This did not mean that there could be no sectional division between North and South over this issue, because slavery was not nearly as important in northern places where it remained, nor did Northerners generally associate their practice with the southern one. Most

Northerners expected its eventual end in their localities. In a real sense, slavery was already the South's "peculiar institution."

The process of compromise began as early as 1783, when Congress had to decide on a basis for raising national revenue. The states with the largest slave populations, Virginia and South Carolina, wanted land values to be the standard. Other states wanted to use population. Congress eventually settled on population but adopted a formula whereby a slave would count as three-fifths of a free person in the calculation. The measure never became part of the Articles of Confederation because it was not unanimously adopted by the individual states. Nonetheless, Congress had devised a workable formula and it was revived when delegates met at the Constitutional Convention in Philadelphia in 1787.

One of the first problems that had to be overcome at that convention involved representation in Congress. Edmund Randolph's Virginia Plan proposed altering the practice under the Articles whereby each state had one vote. Randolph proposed that a state's power in the national legislature be determined by its population. That proposal sparked sharp disagreement among the delegates, one usually described as along the lines of small states versus large ones. Yet the division was also between slave and free states, because obviously a state with a large slave population might turn into a small state if slaves were excluded. Southerners feared that in such a national union they would be consistently outvoted by the larger free population of the North.

Many Northerners felt, however, that to count slaves equally with free people, or to count them at all, was ridiculous. Elbridge Gerry of Massachusetts, in protesting the three-fifths compromise eventually adopted (in which all slaves were counted as three-fifths of a free person to determine the number of representatives each state would be allowed in the House of Representatives), declared, "blacks are property, and are used to the southward as horses and cattle to the northward; and why should their representation be increased to the southward on account of the number of slaves, than horses or oxen to the north?" He did not argue the morality of keeping blacks as chattels in the same light as horses or oxen, nor did he dispute the assumption that there could be property in humankind. Yet such a criticism was implied, for no one would have suggested the representation of horses and oxen. Slave property was clearly of a different character than horses and oxen, at least in some respects. From the revolutionary perspective, that difference derived from the fact that they were human beings and as such deserved to be masters of their own destinies, but that attitude was of no use in an attempt to build a nation in association with those who insisted on the character of slaves as chattels. The revolutionaries had a choice: They could build two nations, based on opposing principles, or one nation, papering over contradictions and inconsistencies. They chose the latter course.

Northern delegates agreed to accept the principle that slaves would be counted for purposes of representation in Congress, and the South granted that they would not be counted as whole people. The sections settled upon the precedent-setting three-fifths compromise. Once that initial concession was made, other clauses respecting slave property could follow more easily. These included a fugitive slave provision, requiring runaway slaves to be returned to those who claimed them, and an agreement not to terminate the slave trade for twenty years. Northerners remained sensitive to the issue, however, and insisted that the word "slave" not appear in the Constitution. Slaves were instead referred to as "persons held to service or labor." Northerners even objected to placing the word "legal" before service, fearing that would suggest that black bondage was somehow legitimate, and disliked "servitude" as well as "slavery." Thus they could argue that they were being true to revolutionary principles at the same time that they denied them in practice.

The fact that the two sections were trying to reconcile opposites was no secret. This can be clearly seen in the way that Southerners defended, and felt that they had to defend, the new national compact in their arguments to convince their constituents to ratify it. Nor, in this instance, was there any difference between Upper and Lower South. "We have a security that the general government can never emancipate" the slaves, General Charles Cotesworth Pinckney of South Carolina argued, "for no such authority is granted; and it is admitted, on all hands, that the general government has no powers but what are expressly granted by the Constitution." He concluded, "In short, considering all circumstances, we have made the best terms for the security of this species of property it was in our power to make."

Moreover, the two foremost Virginians (George Washington and Thomas Jefferson), both of whom had expressed antislavery sentiments, decided that their political careers would be more secure if they ceased making public statements that might negatively affect their standing and influence. Consequently, when two British evangelists visited Washington in 1785 and asked him to sign a petition favoring emancipation, he refused. He said that it would not be appropriate. He indicated, however, that if the Virginia assembly agreed to consider the petition, he would give his opinion of it. The assembly refused and Washington remained silent.

Jefferson took no more public actions on emancipation, or at least no more favorable ones, after he drafted the Land Ordinance of 1784. His official actions thereafter were all supportive of slavery. He resisted publication of his *Notes on Virginia* (originally written as private answers to questions from a French friend) because in it he had expressed mild antislavery sentiments. His fears appeared to be justified. A South Carolinian wrote to tell him of "the general alarm" that a particular "passage in your Notes occasioned amongst us. It is not easy to get rid of old prejudices, and the word 'emancipation' operates like an apparition upon a South Carolina planter."

There was every reason for politicians to be careful when it came to slavery, for there was widespread Southern support for it. Simultaneously, Southerners were equally attached to liberty. But if Northerners had followed the logic of revolutionary ideology to the conclusion that there could be no right of property in men, Southerners had rejected that deduction. "By Liberty in general," a Charleston minister declaimed, "I understand [not just civil liberty but] the Right every man has to pursue the natural, reasonable and religious dictates of his own mind; to enjoy the fruits of his own labour," and "to live upon one's own terms." It meant to be able to dispose absolutely of one's "property, as may best contribute to the support, ease, and advantage of himself and his family," and that would include property in slaves. He and other Southerners were quite willing, therefore, to deny Enlightenment principles and qualify revolutionary declarations. Consequently, when Charles Cotesworth Pinckney recommended the Constitution to his constituents, despite its failure to include a bill of rights, he explained, "such bills generally begin with declaring that all men are by nature born free. Now, we should make that declaration with a very bad grace when a large part of our property consists in men who are actually born slaves."

Alternatively, Southerners defended themselves by disputing the assumption that blacks were fully men. It was true, as a South Carolinian wrote, that blacks had "human Forms," but, as another continued the argument, they were "beings of an inferior rank, and little exalted above brute creatures." They were thus fit objects as property. It followed that even as free people their defect of color, with all that it entailed, excluded them from citizenship. The revolution had been "a *family quarrel among equals*" in which "the Negroes had no concern."

Even in the North, where slavery was abolished, there was opposition to blacks as citizens equal to all others. This can be seen most clearly if one looks at the emancipation laws and controversies surrounding them. The Pennsylvania law (1780), the first to be passed, was also the most severe when compared to the emancipation acts of other Northern states passed between 1780 and 1804—this in a region dominated by Quakers and pretending to great liberality. No slave was immediately freed by it, and children born after March 1, 1780, had to serve until they were twenty-eight years old before their freedom was recognized. This represented a tightening of an earlier draft of the law that freed females at eighteen and males at twenty-one.

In Massachusetts, where there were fewer blacks than in Pennsylvania, the uneasy feelings directed toward blacks were somewhat greater. The first state constitution, passed by the legislature in 1778 but rejected by the people, denied African Americans the right to vote; Pennsylvania's did not. The constitution of 1780 that Massachusetts finally adopted removed that prohibition, but blacks were strictly limited in their possibilities of employment and singled out in newspaper editorials for their supposed inability to work. Nor could they attend the schools that their taxes supported.

These and other prejudicial actions on the part of white citizens in Massachusetts, Pennsylvania, and elsewhere forced black people even more than whites to reflect on the relationship between freedom, revolutionary principles, slavery, and race. Even many of their supporters did not expect African Americans to prosper, and their enemies occasionally sought to stand in their way.

Yet bad as the situation was, this antipathy between black and white people was not as great as it would later become. Indeed, one student of Northern working-class people in New York found them to be refreshingly free of the racial stereotypes that common white folks were supposed to have. Although jokes about black people were common, they suggested a sympathy for and an identification with blacks. Both blacks and working-class whites were pictured as underdogs. Even so, there was enough of an edge to the jokes and sufficient force behind some of the actions to convince a small group of blacks that they should seek their fortune elsewhere.

One of the first black organizations to advance this aim was the Free African Union Society. Founded in 1780 in Newport, Rhode Island, it was a benevolent and moral improvement society as well as an agency of black emigration. It, like white abolitionists, was concerned with the plight of blacks. Thus it encouraged its members to refrain from idleness and drunkenness, tried to ensure that they made their marriages legal, and promoted investment in real estate. The society provided death benefits for the wives and children of deceased members and furnished loans for those in need. It also had a religious mission and held weekly services. Most importantly, the society tried to convoke a consensus that a return to Africa was the best course of action.

In January 1787, the Free African Union Society decided that it would establish its own settlement in Africa. About seventy people agreed to participate in the venture. Although many were African-born, they did not wish to merge with the indigenous people but rather to found a new country of their own. They wanted to get clear title to land somewhere on the continent in order to avoid conflicts with local people.

To this end, they sought out a rather flamboyant antislavery Quaker, William Thornton of Antigua, who was visiting the United States. A wealthy man, he was also a philanthropist who had developed a scheme to free his own slaves and set them up on a self-sustaining plantation in the West Indies. When island authorities discouraged that plan as a threat to slavery, he envisioned colonizing his blacks somewhere in Africa. Advised that free Christian African Americans also wanted to emigrate, Thornton revised his plans. He believed that the literate blacks in New England would perfectly complement agriculturally sophisticated West Indian blacks, who together could secure the colony's survival. One group would bring morality and industry and the other technical expertise. In Africa they would grow tropical products, repay the cost of their passage, and show slaveholders how the institution might be brought profitably to an end. They would establish a trade in products grown as free men, the value of which would rapidly surpass that of slave-grown crops.

Though the plan was laudable, the details were not. The Free African Union Society soon made it clear to Thornton that its members had no interest in becoming part of any venture in which they would be subservient to whites. They wanted to go someplace where they would be their own rulers. Nor were they willing to let Thornton act as their agent. They did feel, though, that if he was a truly charitable person, he might be willing to finance an advance group of Newport blacks to search for a suitable location. They also made contact with seventy-five blacks in Boston who had recently petitioned the Massachusetts legislature to provide assistance for their removal to Africa.

The petitioners there were led by Prince Hall, founder of the first African-American lodge of Freemasons. The Masons were a fraternal organization of men who met to exchange news and ideas and occasionally to conduct religious services or discussions. They sought to overcome social and religious divisions among men and to create greater understanding based on Enlightenment principles. Hall described the "true spirit of Masonry" as "love to God and universal love to all mankind." In 1775 he and fourteen other blacks joined a lodge attached to a British regiment stationed in Boston. When the British left, they permitted the blacks to continue to meet as the African Lodge No. 1. Local Masons refused to recognize them, however, and they applied to England for a charter. Granted in 1784, the charter finally arrived in 1787. By that time, however, they were disillusioned—as individuals, if not as Masons—because, as they told Massachusetts's General Court, despite their freedom "we yet find ourselves, in many respects, in very disagreeable and disadvantageous circumstances; most of which must attend us, so long as we and our children live in America."

Having found kindred spirits in Boston, the Free African Union Society finally communicated with Granville Sharp in London, who was becoming involved with the settlement of Sierra Leone. But Sharp was not enthusiastic about American blacks coming over, especially if they insisted on acting independently. He made clear that if they came to Sierra Leone, they would have to act like English subjects and be bound by the common laws of England. The vision came to nought. Massachusetts was unwilling to put up any money to aid black emigration and Thornton, for all his planning, did not come through either. The blacks lacked the financial wherewithal to do it on their own.

Still, New England blacks would not give up. In 1789 the Free African Union Society addressed an appeal to compatriots in nearby Providence, Rhode Island, proposing a new plan of emigration. In this document they advanced an early black nationalistic concept of uniting blacks in Africa, the West Indies, and the United States. Because they were "attended with many disadvantages and evils with respect to living" in the new American nation, they sought a nationhood of their own. They suggested a return to "the natives in Africa from whom we sprang, [they] being in heathenish darkness and sunk down in barbarity"—to whom African Americans would bring light. The success of the project would benefit

Africans everywhere, for Africa's lack of civilization, as they saw it from a western point of view, was a source of shame. That lack was used to justify enslavement and the slave trade. If Africa were redeemed, the slave trade would cease, Africans overseas would be able to take pride in their homeland, the black man's humanity would be vindicated, and the link between blackness and slavery would be dissolved.

The Boston group invited the Providence blacks to join them in a united society that would meet every three months "to consider what can be done for our good, and for the good of all Affricans." "Now is the time," the Providence group would say in advancing yet another emigration plan in 1794, "if ever for us to try to Distinguish ourselves as the More remote we are situated from the white people the more we will be respected."

It is interesting to compare the plans developed by blacks (called "emigrationist") and those envisioned by whites (referred to as "colonizationist"). People like Jefferson who wanted blacks to depart were primarily concerned about the future and well-being of white people. Jefferson was not much interested in what happened to blacks, and his emancipation plans for Virginia would have compelled them to leave whether they wanted to or not.

People like Thornton, by contrast, had a religious and moral concern. They were interested in illustrating that blacks could progress in economic terms, both in America and Africa, because such advances would justify their struggles for black emancipation, validate their faith in the essential unity of humankind, and contribute to an end to black servitude worldwide. But they also adopted an attitude of paternalism: they doubted the ability of blacks and were sure that black people could make progress only under white direction. African Americans, believing as much in their capability as their equality, thought they could and had to develop themselves largely on their own. They could welcome white help but objected to white domination. They were cultural hybrids and appreciated their American identity. Having adopted western values, they intended to westernize Africa, but they also wanted to cultivate a pride in being black. Only a great black nation would prove without doubt that blacks were not born to be slaves. But, because of lack of financing from white Americans and those African Americans who did have money, these early emigrationist movements all failed. For this reason, revolution in Haiti, which was developing even as these projects vanished, was an event of crucial significance.

Despite the movements to return to Africa, the period before the turn of the nineteenth century was one of hopefulness. In half the nation slavery had ended. This occurred not because it was unprofitable, or because there had been no opposition, or because the climate was uncongenial. It had happened largely as a result of war and revolution. And the revolution was not just political but social as well, a revolution in thinking as well as in acting that caused a part of the nation to confront prejudice and injustice and put them partially to rout. It was true that slavery had never been as important in the places where it ended as in those where it remained, that people who opposed it often had practical reasons as well as philosophical reasons for doing it, that many of those who favored freedom often had little confidence in the capacity of blacks to handle it. But a start had been made, and African Americans moved swiftly to take advantage of their opportunities.

Richard Allen and the Promise of Freedom

On April 12, 1787, Absalom Jones and Richard Allen, "two men of the African race," as they described themselves in their Preamble and Articles of Association, "who, for their religious life and conversation have obtained a good report among men," met together with others in Philadelphia to form "some kind of religious society." Their Free African Society derived from "a love to the people of their complexion whom they beheld with sorrow, because of their irreligious and uncivilized state."

Jones and Allen's Free African Society was a mutual aid and moral improvement group that also had a religious bent. It was nonsectarian, in an attempt to attract African Americans of various Christian denominations, though it was closely associated with the Quakers. The society's rules specified that the clerk or treasurer should always be a Quaker, and eventually, meetings began with a period of silence in the Quaker fashion. The organization prohibited drunkenness among its members and provided death benefits.

Although it, like Newport's Free African Union Society, had been formed in the face of discrimination, and its assessment of the condition and immediate prospects of blacks in America was largely the same, its prescription was not. The Philadelphia group had none of the sense of mission or adventure evidenced in Newport. Or, rather, their sense of mission was distinctly different. They thought the solution to blacks' misfortune was self-improvement (with which New England blacks agreed), but otherwise they would depend on divine deliverance achieved through prayer and fasting. They rejected Newport's call for emigration. "This land," Richard Allen would later say about America, "which we have watered with our *tears* and *our blood* is now our *mother country.*"

The different reactions of two African-American organizations who had basically the same diagnosis of the plight of black people in the United States is evidence of the "double consciousness" that the esteemed black scholar W. E. B. Du Bois wrote about at the turn of the twentieth century. The African American, he suggested, "ever feels his twoness—an American, a Negro; two souls, two thoughts, two unreconciled strivings; two warring ideals in one dark body, whose dogged strength alone keeps it from being torn asunder." The people in these organizations memorialized their background by calling themselves African. They acknowledged their American identity by clinging to and seeking to spread various forms of Christianity. They adopted religious and cultural ideas of morality, hard work, thrift, and accumulation of wealth, and favored individual initiative together with group solidarity.

Within this common outlook, whether one stressed the African side of the equation and embraced black nationalism and a return to Africa, or seized upon America and more limited forms of separatism, depended to a great extent upon circumstances and personal inclination. In periods and locales where there seemed to be a chance for black progress in America, fewer were attracted to emigration; when and where the situation appeared less hopeful, more were inclined to leave. A firm religious belief and a conviction that, as Philadelphia responded to Newport, "the race is not to the swift, nor the battle to the strong," motivated some blacks to cling to their American identity, no matter what.

This attitude can be clearly seen in the lives of Richard Allen and Absalom Jones. Jones stayed in Philadelphia throughout the British occupation and remained with his master even after the English left. Allen also failed to run away, to either British or American forces. Both chose to take their chances under existing conditions and trust the promise of America. They had several reasons to do so.

Born a slave in Sussex County, Delaware, in 1747, Jones was at a young age removed from the fields and made a house boy. In that situation he was able to obtain some learning. From money earned around the house, he "soon bought . . . a primer," he related in an autobiographical sketch, "and begged to be taught by any body that I found able and willing to give me the least instruction." When his master left Delaware for Pennsylvania in 1762, he sold Absalom's mother and brothers and sisters, having no need for a large slave family in Philadelphia. But he took the fifteen-year-old Absalom with him. Whatever distress the separation from family caused, the move nevertheless permitted Absalom to pursue an education. Philadelphia was the scene of much Quaker abolitionist sentiment, and people like Anthony Benezet had made some provision for black education. Despite having to work in his master's shop throughout the day, obliged "to store, pack up and carry out goods," a clerk taught him to write, and he secured his master's permission to attend school at night.

When he was twenty-three, he married Mary, a neighbor's slave, and they determined to get their freedom. It made sense to secure Mary's first because that would allow their children to be born free, since children legally followed the condition of the mother. Absalom drew up a plea for his wife's freedom and carried it to prominent Quakers, some of whom lent, and others donated, the required cash. Working at night for wages, he and his wife repaid their loans. And while he beseeched his master to permit him to purchase himself, the couple saved enough money to buy a large house in a substantial neighborhood in January 1779, a few months after the British evacuated the city. Absalom owned property, therefore, while still a slave. Several more years passed before his master consented (in 1784) to his self-purchase. Bearing no animosity and receiving none in return, he continued to work in the store. When Richard Allen arrived in Philadelphia in 1786, Jones was a prominent black member of the largely white St. George's Methodist Church.

Richard Allen was born a slave in Philadelphia in 1760, but his master maintained a plantation in Delaware where Allen may have been raised. He was sold to a small slaveholder who worked a farm outside of Dover, Delaware, and his owner, a fair man, permitted him to join the local Methodist Society and attend classes after he was converted by itinerant preachers in the 1770s. His conversion may have been spurred by the sale of his parents and younger brothers and sisters shortly before his turn to religion. His conversion was no less sincere for that fact, and when neighbors criticized his master for permitting his slaves to attend frequent religious meetings, Allen and a remaining brother "held a council together ... so that it should not be said that religion made us worse servants; we would work night and day to get our crops forward."

This diligence enabled Allen's owner to confound his critics, and, as Allen reported in his autobiography, he "often boasted of his slaves for their honesty and industry." Perhaps the example of his slaves as well as the teachings of itinerant Methodists moved him, too, to religion. But Methodism at this point was opposed to slavery, and a minister told him that his slaves would keep him out of heaven. In 1780, therefore, he encouraged Allen and his brother to purchase their freedom.

Allen then became a traveling preacher himself, taking the Methodist gospel as far afield as New York and South Carolina and into the backcountry. He supported himself by doing odd jobs and he preached to white and black audiences alike. In Radnor, Pennsylvania, twelve miles outside Philadelphia, where he had "walked until my feet became so sore and blistered ... that I scarcely could bear them to the ground," he was forced to rest. Taken in and cared for by strangers, he repaid them by preaching. The townspeople took to him and persuaded him to tarry. "There were but few colored people in the neighborhood," he recalled; "most of my congregation was white. Some said, 'this man must be a man of God; I never heard such preaching before.'"

From there, in 1786, Allen received a call from St. George's to preach to the black congregants at 5:00 a.m. in order not to disturb white services. His ministry caught on. He soon had a group of blacks meeting separately for prayer meetings, among whom was Absalom Jones. Allen felt cramped within the confines of his relationship with St. George's, however, and proposed founding a separate black congregation. Other blacks agreed, but the white clergy was opposed. The minister, according to Allen, "used very insulting language to us to prevent us from going on," and tried to bar their meetings altogether. It was at this point that Allen and Jones organized the Free African Society as a nonsectarian organization. They conceived a plan to build an independent African-American community church that could attract black people without regard to denomination.

When the African Church of Philadelphia was formally proposed in 1791, its plan of church government was described as "so general as to embrace all, and yet so orthodox in cardinal points as to offend none." The group's justification for going its separate way was that a black church was more likely to attract black people than a white one. They reasoned that "men are more influenced by their moral equals than by their superiors ... and ... are more easily governed by persons chosen by themselves for that purpose, than by persons who are placed over them by accidental circumstances." In this phrase, directed at wealthy white people from whom they hoped to gain financial support, they combined democratic principles with strategic modesty and self-effacement. At the same time, they boldly declared their independence of paternalism and their rejection of discrimination within white denominations. White religious leaders, Methodist, Episcopalian, and Quaker, were virtually unanimous in opposition to the plan, revealing a clear unwillingness to relinquish their direction of black religious life. Moreover, they stood to lose their African-American congregants, who, whatever their humble status, sometimes made significant contributions to church affairs.

Not long after this effort was set in motion, an event occurred that is often said to have prompted the move toward black religious separation. Jones and Allen still worshiped at St. George's Methodist Church. Blacks, like other members, contributed to the church's expansion, but when the addition was completed, blacks were asked to retire to newly installed galleries. Even so, when Jones and Allen arrived for services one Sunday morning and knelt to pray above the seats where they formerly sat, they were approached by a trustee and asked to move. Jones requested him to wait until the prayer ended but the trustee said, "No, you must get up now, or I will call for aid and force you away." Jones again asked for a delay, but the trustee motioned for another to come to his aid. Just as the two were about to act the prayer ended and the blacks got up and walked out in a body. "They were," said Allen, "no more plagued with us in the church." This affair occurred in 1792, after plans for the African church were already in motion. Nevertheless, it reinforced the need for African Americans to form their own religious community.

Several years passed before the African church came into being. The disapproval of white religious leaders slowed donations, though such prominent people as George Washington, Thomas Jefferson, and Granville Sharp, in England, sent small contributions. Newport's Free African Union Society also made a donation. Blacks engaged in various efforts to raise money—but they were hindered in early 1793 by an influx of refugees from Saint Domingue and later in the year by a yellow fever epidemic. The latter furnished them an opportunity to show their public spirit by volunteering to nurse the ill and bury the dead, while many of the white people fled. The reception of Saint Domingue's white refugees, however, provided evidence of the black community's relative standing among the whites. Philadelphia's white citizens raised twelve thousand dollars in a few days for displaced slave owners, but the church for former slaves, costing less than a third as much, was delayed for several years for lack of money.

In July 1794 the African church opened its doors. Its members had decided to affiliate with the Episcopal church, feeling that some denominational connection was important for the security of the congregation. Only Jones and Allen voted for the Methodists. Calling itself the African Episcopal Church of St. Thomas, the congregation chose Absalom Jones as minister. The members sought to guarantee their local control by providing that only African Americans could be elected to church offices, except the minister and assistant minister, and that the congregation chose all church officers, including the minister and his assistant. They would permit themselves the possibility of choosing a white minister if they ever so desired, but they wanted the church to remain firmly in black hands. They would not surrender the revolutionary principle of self-government.

There were several reasons why blacks such as Jones and Allen were attracted to Methodism. As a new evangelical denomination, it had few ties with colonial slavery, and its founder, John Wesley, adopted an antislavery stance. Their religious egalitarianism reinforced revolutionary principles of equality, but, ironically, the fact that many Methodists were loyal to the British during the Revolution set them apart from patriotic groups, which were often proslavery. To many African Americans, Methodists represented a strain of British antislavery in opposition to an increasingly pro-slavery American nation.

The itinerant nature of Methodist evangelicals increased their appeal to blacks (and poor white people), for they went out onto the roads and highways, into the fields and byways, to spread their message of salvation. They usually spoke in a direct, simple, emotional style and appealed to the heart rather than the intellect. Their methods had much in common with a traditional African religious outlook.

The emotional attraction is important because it is perhaps the one aspect of Methodism that made it more appealing than Quakerism, which shared many of Methodism's other attributes. Although Quakers held slaves, they were also among the earliest to express opposition to the practice and perhaps the first to act against it. They dominated early antislavery societies in Britain and America and were often loyal supporters of the English as well as pacifists during the years of revolutionary struggle. Their loyalism, however, seemed to discredit them more than it did the Methodists—perhaps because the Quakers were a more powerful group in colonial America—and it lessened the effectiveness of their antislavery efforts in the immediate postrevolutionary era. By contrast, the Methodists were less rigid about their abolitionst message and modified it in order to accommodate slaveholders in areas where slavery was legal. Despite their willingness to get along with slaveholders, the Methodists had an emotional appeal for blacks that the Quakers could not match.

Nevertheless, the African church affiliated with the Episcopalians. This probably had to do with what they perceived as Methodist shortcomings, for the Methodists, like other white people, often viewed blacks as childlike creatures who needed firm regulation. Blacks, they said, could not be trusted on their own. There was also at least occasional jealousy at the competition blacks offered. Thus one chronicler related that Richard Allen was encouraged to get off the circuit and remain in Philadelphia because a prominent white Methodist itinerant minister compared unfavorably.

By contrast, a black Methodist in New York, George White, was forced to preach outside the city for years because of the refusal of white Methodists in the urban area to accept him as an equal. These prejudicial attitudes encouraged black Methodists in New York City, led by James Varick, to leave the parent organization in 1796. They founded what later became the African Methodist Episcopal Zion church, with Varick as its first bishop. Similar experiences in Baltimore and other cities provoked similar actions. Not merely prejudice but blacks' own religious and social outlooks encouraged black separatism. For blacks, slavery was a sin and America could never be a truly Christian nation so long as it condoned slavery. They could not, as their fellow white Baptist and Methodist believers did, relegate it to politics nor consider it beyond the scope of religion.

Despite the problems, Allen remained committed to Methodism. He refused to accept leadership of the African church once it allied with Episcopalians, allowing the position to go to Jones instead. Allen persisted in building his own Methodist church. Established in the same year, a few blocks away from the black Episcopalians, it became the foundation of an independent black denomination, the African Methodist Episcopal church. "Mother Bethel," as Allen's Bethel African Methodist congregation was called, also attempted to safeguard its rights of local autonomy. It was a fight over that issue, and over ownership of the congregation's property, that prompted African Americans to leave the white-dominated Methodist organization and form their own denomination in 1816.

Once the black churches were established, they became the centers of black settlement in Philadelphia. The surrounding neighborhoods did not become black ghettos, because blacks were frequently interspersed with working-class whites and were not in the majority. But community activities among blacks were of necessity stronger than among their white companions because they had few alternative sources of support. Nor could they move out of the neighborhood as easily.

Blacks also lived in other sections of the city and their numbers gave them a sense of possibilities. Philadelphia at the time had the largest free black population in the United States and developed the most thriving free black community. It had grown to two thousand by 1790. At the same date, New York City, with as many blacks, was largely a slave city; indeed it possessed more bondspeople than any other American city except Charleston, South Carolina. Boston listed no slaves by that date but had a smaller black population. Because of its size and influence, Philadelphia is a good place to view the situation of blacks in the years immediately following the revolution. The stages of community and religious development there were paralleled in other Northern cities.

It was a relatively successful community, despite a postwar depression that

This watercolor from the early nineteenth century offers a stereotypical view of blacks attending a church service in Philadelphia.

affected large segments of the city. Newly freed blacks flocked to Philadelphia from rural Pennsylvania and neighboring areas of Delaware, Maryland, New Jersey, and even southern New England. They sought gainful employment and economic independence. Men were drawn to seafaring, serving on merchant ships or working around the docks. By the beginning of the nineteenth century, about twenty percent of Philadelphia's merchant seamen were black. Women, who outnumbered men, reversing a disproportion in favor of men during slavery, worked primarily as domestics. Although most blacks worked as common laborers of one sort or another, some set up small business enterprises or engaged in professional activities. The 1795 city directory listed black grocers, fruiterers, shopkeepers, and milkmen, among others. There were also a few artisans practicing shipbuilding, metal- and leather-working, and other crafts.

The black situation was not idyllic, however, for many worked as servants in white households, much as they had in slavery. This meant, as in slavery, a fractured family life, because few white owners or employers were prepared to keep a whole black family together under one roof. They might be spread throughout the city, or even outside it. Many black youths were indentured—bound by contract to serve others for a specified number of years. This was a practice common with white children as well, but white females normally served until age eighteen and white males until twenty-one, whereas blacks usually served until twenty-eight. These were their most productive years in a lifespan that did not usually extend much past forty.

One of the first tasks of freed blacks, therefore, was to claim an independent residence. In view of their economic circumstances, this was not always easy, and the move out of white households and into stable two-parent family groupings proceeded by stages. Along the way, blacks sometimes formed extended families, locating several generations under one roof, or made other creative household arrangements in order to remove themselves sooner from the constraints of life in white homes. In Boston, where slavery ended soonest, a majority of blacks lived in two-parent households as early as 1790, and the percentage increased in the nineteenth century. This was also true in New York City at the same date, but its proportion decreased in the following decades as a result of the expansion of slavery in the city in the 1790s. In Philadelphia, where the emancipation process was slower than in Boston, close to half of blacks lived in two-parent households in 1790 and the process of independent family formation speeded up thereafter. Blacks moved rapidly after slavery to secure a degree of social and cultural independence based on strong families and their own religious outlook.

Perhaps Philadelphia blacks developed confidence in America, despite discrimination, because of their large and growing community and because of significant support from whites. Their most dedicated supporter, Anthony Benezet, died in 1784. But his place was taken somewhat by the physician Benjamin Rush, who gave active backing to the African church project and to other issues of concern to blacks. In addition, the Pennsylvania Society for the Abolition of Slavery was revived in 1784. It found renewed work in preventing the sale or kidnapping of bondspeople to the South, in monitoring other evasions of the manumission law, and in aiding blacks to get employment. The aged Benjamin Franklin lent his prestige by becoming president of the society.

The smaller black population in New England, not quite submerged in a sea of whites, apparently lacked similar support and showed signs of having greater disappointment in their white neighbors. Certainly the nature of repressive laws there suggests that conclusion. The experience of Phillis Wheatley also supports it. Despite her celebrity status, she was never able to raise a sufficient number of subscriptions in Boston to permit publication of a second volume of her work. She was reduced, instead, to labor outside her home, doing the kind of difficult domestic work in freedom that she was spared in slavery.

The domestic chores of housecleaning, washing, sewing, and cooking, the common lot of black women of the era, were strenuous tasks in the eighteenth century, and overtaxing to someone of Wheatley's delicate physique. She was probably also undernourished, for her marriage to free black John Peters in 1778 was not entirely successful. He was apparently overproud and unable to provide for her as well as she could have wished. She was reported at one stage to be living in abject poverty. None of her three children survived. She was only thirty-one years old when she died at the end of 1784.

While Northern blacks moved toward greater self-definition, southern blacks did the same. They operated under greater restraints than simple racism, however, for most were still enslaved. Although the religious revivals of the Great Awakening left the mass of slaves unaffected, they appealed to blacks nevertheless. African Americans responded particularly to the doctrine resolved by a Baptist committee in 1789 that slavery was "a violent deprivation of the rights of nature, and inconsistent with a republican government." By the 1770s, a number of blacks had been converted by Baptist or Methodist preachers and felt the call to go out on their own. If they were slaves, they sometimes left without permission, as runaway ads in newspapers testify. Such men were involved in the first black Baptist church in America developed independently of a white one, in Silver Bluff, South Carolina, between 1773 and 1775. From this region, including nearby Savannah, Georgia, came a band of black Baptists who went on to found separate black churches in various parts of the world.

George Liele has been described as the Southern (and Baptist) counterpart of Richard Allen and as the energy behind the early black churches in Georgia and South Carolina. Born in Virginia, he accompanied his master to Savannah, Georgia. His master was a loyalist who freed Liele before his death in British service in 1778. Liele, meanwhile, preached to slaves on plantations along the Savannah River and moved into the city of Savannah after his master's demise. There he continued to preach to slaves and he brought the future preacher Andrew Bryan to the faith. Liele left with the British, however, unsure of his free status without their protection, and introduced the Baptist church to Jamaica.

Still a slave, Andrew Bryan refused to depart with the others who cast their lot with the English; he ministered to a small congregation in Savannah instead. In the period of unrest at the end of the war, however, they were persecuted by anxious whites and Bryan had to suffer for his faith. He and his brother "were twice imprisoned, and about fifty were severely whipped, particularly *Andrew, who was cut, and bled abundantly,*" a fellow minister revealed in a letter. In 1788 Bryan was formally licensed to preach, eventually gained his freedom, and by the turn of the century was able to report that the First African Baptist Church of Savannah met "with the approbation and encouragement of many of the white people." The response to his message was so great that two other black Baptist churches soon formed in the city. In 1793, meanwhile, the Silver Bluff church, having outgrown its location, moved twelve miles away to Augusta, Georgia, to form the First African Baptist Church under one of the original founders, Jesse Galpin.

Slaves who preached, and the bound congregations to whom they ministered, had to operate within limitations set by their masters. Like the Methodists, many early Baptist congregations were integrated, even though blacks were normally restricted to a section of their own in the back or balcony. In rural areas, slaves often accompanied their masters to church. Blacks could preach to whites, and vice versa, but blacks usually preached to their own. Though many black churches came into being as a result of independent black activity, others were offshoots of white congregations. Unlike in the North, the move had to be one with which white people agreed, for the activities of enslaved blacks were strictly controlled. Frequently the move to separate came from white people, once the black membership became too large. Blacks might continue to operate on their own, much as they had before, under either a black or white minister, though most preferred a person of their own color, for the message in its subtleties and the preaching style would differ. They would remain under the watchful eye of whites in any case.

Baptist principles of congregational independence made this arrangement easier. Unlike the Methodists, Baptist churches were less subject to the control of a national church organization. They seemed more willing to accept black preachers and allowed more individual freedom. Although they possessed the same beliefs in the equality of all persons as the Methodists did, their lack of structure before the nineteenth century permitted individuals to accommodate a proslavery message earlier than the Methodists, without it having the same import. While Methodist convocations adopted antislavery policies several times in the 1780s, they had to back off because of popular opposition. Baptist declarations of that kind had not the same organizational support because the congregations were not so tightly bound together or used to taking orders from a national authority. There was no organizational decision on the matter. This permitted individual congregations to adjust to local sentiment without compromising a national decision or obligating other localities. In any case, blacks were early attracted to the denomination, which seemed to have the greatest appeal.

Things changed in the nineteenth century, when the Baptists, too, desired greater conformity among their members, and, under pressure from secular authorities, withdrew the freedom granted Southern black Baptists. In the meantime, blacks often had significant leeway in choosing their ministers, church officers, and even in sending representatives to regional Baptist associations. The transition can be seen, particularly in the hardening of racial lines, in two decisions of the Baptist Association of Portsmouth, Virginia. In 1794 the association answered the question "Is it agreeable to the Word of God to send a free black man a delegate to the Ass'n?" in the affirmative: "We can see nothing wrong in this. A church may send any one it chooses." In 1828, it decided that "whereas the constitution of independent and colored churches, in this state, and their representation in this body, involves a point of great delicacy," black churches could only be represented by whites.

Southern (and Northern) black Methodists had to fight to obtain the sort of independence enjoyed by Southern black Baptists. The Methodists' personal slights pushed them toward it, however, and blacks in Baltimore, under Daniel Coker, in

Wilmington, Delaware, under Peter Spencer, and in other locations departed congregations dominated by white Methodists and eventually joined with Richard Allen to form the African Methodist denomination or made other provisions. A harbinger of more repressive times can be found in the special edition of the Church's *Discipline* for Southern states in 1804 and 1808 (containing religious doctrines and beliefs), which omitted any reference to resolutions on slavery. Even Methodist Bishop Francis Asbury, an early leader of the church who abhorred slavery, eventually gave way before pro-slavery forces and wrote in his journal that it was more important to save the African's soul than to free his body. But not many African Americans were prepared to accept that priority. Increasingly, in the nineteenth century, they decided to worship apart from their white brethren.

That was true, of course, when they engaged in Christian worship at all. For important as Christianity was in fostering a will toward independence among blacks, in providing a gauge and a focus for greater self-assertion and self-reliance, in providing solace during times of deprivation, the likelihood is that most blacks were barely touched by it. One historian argues, in fact, that the slaves' religious practices were overwhelmingly more African than Christian. If slave preachers could not relate to those in a plantation community who knew little or nothing about Christianity, he suggests, they could not minister to most of their people. He and other historians push this argument into the nineteenth century. But it has particular relevance for the eighteenth century, and especially in the postrevolutionary period, for the number of Africans imported into South Carolina and Georgia exceeded 100,000 before the overseas slave trade finally ended in 1808. These imports brought renewed contact with Africa. But coastal South Carolina and Georgia had maintained a greater African presence than the Chesapeake had anyway, and African-American Christianity, there and elsewhere, was greatly influenced by African beliefs and attitudes. Most prominent is the "ring shout," a counterclockwise circular dance motion accompanied by singing and hand-clapping, which is a basic feature of low country Christianity in South Carolina and Georgia and is argued by several scholars to be essentially African. Yet Christianity developed an increasing appeal to African Americans in the period just before and after the Revolution and its influence was to grow.

Paul Cuffee and the Failure of Freedom

Despite the religious and, in the Upper South, secular feeling of generosity on the part of whites that made life more tolerable for southern blacks in the decade after the American revolution, planters renewed their commitment to black bondage. In most cases, indeed, it scarcely slackened. Although the Lower South was not as affected by the abolitionist trend of the times as regions farther north, it was not completely exempt either. The military proposals of John Laurens, to arm slaves and free them at the war's conclusion, were just one example. A few

This 1812 engraving shows Captain Paul Cuffe, a New England merchant-sailor who developed trading interests in Africa and transported black colonists there in 1815.

slaveowners were even moved to manumission. South Carolinian John Peronneau freed his slave Romeo in 1781 "in consequence of my aversion to and abhorrence of Slavery which natural Religion and common sense do equally condemn."

But most Southern whites did not go that far. A Georgia planter readily admitted that racial slavery was "subversive of every idea of moral as well as political justice." He was not prepared to concede that emancipation was the answer, however; rather, he believed that American slaves were better off than European peasants. One historian of South Carolina argues, in fact, that low country planters felt a need to justify slavery even before the revolution, and that this need developed out of an increased recognition of their slaves' humanity. This realization arose partly from the slaves' development of a creole, or American, culture in the second half of the eighteenth century. Creole originally referred to Europeans born in the New World but now extends to other peoples and things brought to life in the Americas, including culture—for example, language, religion, and new tastes in food. Despite the continued importance of the slave trade to low country planters, by 1760 less than half of South Carolina's slave population was African-born. Creole slaves were closer to their masters in culture and, unlike Africans, were better able to impress upon European-centered white people that they were human beings.

In both regions of the South, a relatively stable, family-based creole slave society had developed by 1770. In both regions, the slave population had begun to reproduce itself naturally, a clear advantage for planters who maintained family units on their estates. Natural reproduction was greater and more important in the larger and older slave society in the Chesapeake, but its value was also acknowledged farther south. War disrupted this not quite idyllic setting. Slaves were moved and families and communities torn asunder. This process continued in the war's aftermath and was accelerated by economic change.

Cotton was the crop that dominated the plantation economy of the nineteenth-century South—the South of myth and legend. Eli Whitney's improved cotton gin of 1793, which more easily separated the seeds from the strands of cotton, and is often blamed for perpetuating slavery in a region that expected rapidly to eradicate it, has been unfairly charged. The regions into which cotton expanded so quickly had been preparing for years, and frontier planters needed only the right circumstances to seize their expected promise. But Eli Whitney did make that expansion more certain. Slaves who could clean one pound of cotton in a day without Whitney's invention could prepare fifty pounds with it. The economic possibilities were obvious; production that had formerly been confined to home use could now be grown for commercial export.

In the Lower South, slaves produced cotton independently during the unrest and disorder of revolution and planters made concessions to ensure that they remained on the plantation. Both needed a domestic source of cloth, because imports of all kinds were cut off by British military activity. There was likewise more production of food crops for local consumption than before the war. For planters, the production of cotton and the wearing of local homespun woven from it became a patriotic duty, symbolic of their ability to do without British finery.

But slaves who did not leave the plantation had a personal interest in this cultivation, too, for their well-being, perhaps even more than their masters', depended upon it. Many simply produced food and cloth for their own use. Planters were happy to leave them to their own devices, so long as they remained on the land. If slaves could extract greater leeway from their owners to grow something they needed anyway, so much the better. But, as one historian keenly advises, there was a depressing irony in this situation of wartime independence. The crop that provided slaves a temporary liberation from the master's stern gaze during the Revolution formed the links of a chain that more tightly bound their children and grandchildren.

Low country planters continued to grow rice, both during and after the revolution, but the industry was undergoing a transition to a new method of cultivation using the tidal flow from rivers. This process required an initial output of tremendous labor to construct embankments, dig ditches, and build "trunks" or sluices to control the flow of water onto the rice fields. It saved labor in cultivation, particularly in terms of weeding, but required considerable maintenance.

Indigo, which had supplemented rice cultivation in the colonial period, was replaced after the Revolution by cotton. As with indigo, slaves attended to cotton during the periods when the rice fields needed less attention. A long-staple variety, called sea island cotton, suitable to warm, moist conditions, grew along the Georgia–South Carolina seacoast and on islands off the coast. Short-staple varieties spread inland into the piedmont and backcountry of South Carolina and Georgia, across the dark, fertile soils of Florida, Mississippi, Alabama, and Louisiana, and up over the Appalachians and Alleghenies into Kentucky and Tennessee. They penetrated the Virginia frontier and various locations in the Chesapeake. It was the spread of these short-staple varieties that Whitney's gin aided, for the seed separated more easily from long-staple cotton.

The spread of cotton affected African-American communities all along the eastern seaboard. The greater freedom that war had brought to slaves in most regions continued for some time thereafter, though more in some places than others. In the Chesapeake Bay area, slaves experienced more mobility, greater access to freedom, and more opportunity for employment and self-improvement once freedom came. Some planters, particularly in Maryland, freed their slaves and set them up as tenants. Other recently freed blacks began a slow process of setting themselves up independently.

However, as the Chesapeake area's major crop, tobacco, decreased in price, many slaveholders decided to sell their slaves to buyers in the booming markets of the southwest, or else move there themselves with their slaves. Between 1790 and 1810, 100,000 slaves were moved from the Chesapeake Bay area into newly opening cotton lands in the West and Southwest. Communities were ruptured and families dissolved as slaves accompanied masters toward a white man's opportunity. In their new locales, they had to begin the painful process of reconstructing family and community in a situation not as advantageous as the ones they had left. In the new regions there were more farms than plantations, few slaves on each unit, long distances between individual landholdings, hard labor in clearing fresh land, and little chance of finding a mate. The erosion of slavery continued in Maryland but, because of cotton, many blacks born there would not stay to see it. They went west to make their masters' fortune.

The frontier clamor for cotton slaves was also met by recourse to the slave trade. At least 100,000 slaves were imported from Africa between 1783 and 1807, and directed to developing cotton regions. This trade entered through Savannah in the 1790s, since South Carolina had suppressed the commerce. In view of the looming constitutional prohibition of the trade, which would take effect in 1808, however, South Carolina belatedly responded to inland settlers and reopened its ports in 1803. Slavers then shifted to Charleston and landed almost ten thousand Africans a year until the final termination of the trade.

Nearly half of these slaves came from the Congo-Angola region of Central Africa, reinforcing a strain of African culture that had predominated in the first decades of the eighteenth century. People from this region had led the largest slave revolt in colonial British North America and had a reputation for possessing an aptitude for mechanical skills. Another quarter left the Senegambia area of West Africa, fortifying a cultural tradition that had been influential throughout the period. People from this region contributed to the development of South Carolina's rice industry. These new imports were going mostly to different regions than their country people who preceded them, so the cultural effect may not have been as profound as it could have been. Indeed, these Africans were moving where they most likely encountered creole slaves from the Chesapeake. Culturally different, the two groups would have had to forge a common identity as they formed a new community.

Some blacks, who had developed maroon, or runaway, communities during the war refused to give up their freedom after it, and they continued to enjoy greater liberty than a slave society could possibly permit. Thus the *Charleston Morning Post* reported in October 1786 that a group of around one hundred African Americans had established an independent settlement on an island in the Savannah River, about eighteen miles from the coast. From there they conducted periodic foraging expeditions against neighboring plantations to supplement the supplies they grew. Aside from the threat to landowners in the vicinity, their message of self-assertion was not one that planters desired to see spread. Militia forces attacked the settlement, forced the blacks to retreat, and destroyed their homes, fields, and supplies.

Most African Americans, enslaved and free, found other ways to assert their autonomy. This is easiest seen in how they named themselves. Northern blacks who won their freedom frequently took a new name. The names their owners chose from Greek or Roman history or mythology, such as Caesar, Cato, Diana, or Daphne, or from European places such as London or Hanover, were gradually replaced by English or biblical names such as James, John, Elizabeth, or Sarah. Parents with these older names did not pass them along to their children. Commonly, they rejected their previous names themselves, choosing new ones soon after emancipation. The use even of African names diminished, indicating blacks' increasing American identification.

They also took surnames, seldom memorializing past masters. Neither Richard Allen nor Absalom Jones took the names of their former owners. Those who remained in bondage in Southern states claimed the right to name their offspring. They often called their children after relatives, particularly their fathers, from whom sons and daughters might be separated. Accordingly, Thomas Jefferson's slave woman Molly, wife of Phill Waggoner, named their first two children Phill and Phyllis. If their masters insisted on calling them one thing, they might still be known as something else in the quarters, among the common folk with whom they lived and worked. There was more than one way to insist upon their humanity.

While blacks struggled to define themselves, the nation also groped toward an identity. Free blacks in Southern slave society, even more than those in free-labor Northern ones, faced an uncertain situation in a nation in flux. Racial lines were drawn, but not as inflexibly as they would become. For instance, the situation of free colored people in Charleston, often of mixed blood and tied by interest and inclination to the planter class, was not the same as that of free blacks in the Chesapeake area, who were offered little protection by prominent whites and thus fended for themselves. The status of free blacks and coloreds, or mixed-race people, in New Orleans, when it became part of the United States in 1803, was different still. In 1790 Charleston's colored elite formed the Brown Fellowship Society, a mutual benefit organization similar to those formed by Northern blacks. However, it excluded people with darker skins. New Orleans had similar associations. The various regions of the nation and the variants of black culture would move toward greater uniformity in the nineteenth century. But it would be a mistake to read the present back into the past and to assume that race relations in the eighteenth century were always worse than in the twentieth. The careers of two men, both born free, one (Benjamin Banneker) in a slave society, the other (Paul Cuffe) in one of the earliest free societies that had once tolerated slavery, demonstrate the unformed and still flexible nature of the national atmosphere.

Born in 1731, Benjamin Banneker was the grandson of European and African immigrants, an Englishwoman named Molly Welsh and the African man she bought, freed, and married, called Bannaka. Interracial marriages were illegal in the Maryland of Molly Welsh's day, and she faced the enduring threat of punishment for her transgression. Yet in her life among her husband's people in the countryside outside Baltimore she apparently was not bothered.

Benjamin, whose mother was Molly's daughter and whose father was also a freed slave, grew up in a peaceful setting. He attended a one-room schoolhouse with several white and one or two colored youngsters, taught by a Quaker schoolmaster. The school was open only in the winter, and the rest of the year he had to help his family with the farmwork—raising tobacco and corn, caring for a few cattle and chickens, working in his mother's vegetable garden or his father's orchard, hunting and fishing in nearby woods and streams, and performing other chores that any farmboy who lived in a wilderness environment might have to do. He was more lucky than most, for his parents owned the land they worked and his name was on the deed. He would inherit it. Despite the necessity for physical labor, at an early age he developed an interest in mathematics and, in view of the limitations of his schooling, was largely self-taught.

He first came to local fame when in 1753, at twenty-two years of age, he built a clock. Modeled after a watch he had borrowed, it was painstakingly constructed nearly all of wood, and illustrated an unusual mechanical genius. It operated until his death more than fifty years later.

Late in life he added to his interest in horology, the science and art of measuring time and making timepieces, an interest in astronomy. He borrowed books and instruments from a neighbor and mastered a new science. He went on to publish several popular almanacs and was appointed by Secretary of State Thomas Jefferson to help survey the federal territory for the new national capital at Washington, D.C. He worked with Andrew Ellicott, the chief surveyor, from February to April 1791. He had never before been away from his birthplace. Excited about the project though he was, he was then an old man of sixty years and unaccustomed to

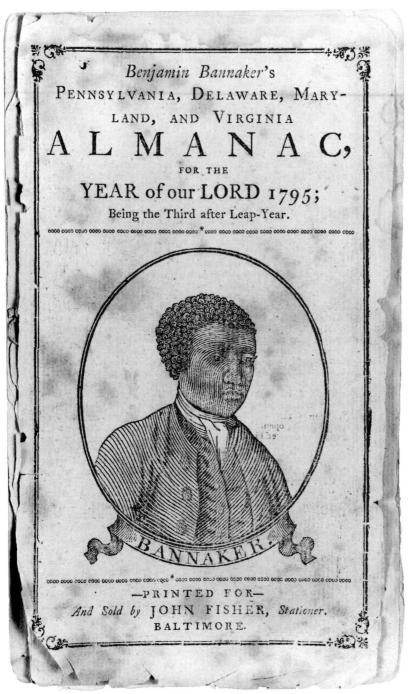

Benjamin Bannaker's

PENNSYLVANIA, DELAWARE, MARY-
LAND, AND VIRGINIA

ALMANAC,

FOR THE

YEAR of our LORD 1795;

Being the Third after Leap-Year.

BANNAKER.

—PRINTED FOR—

And Sold by JOHN FISHER, *Stationer.*

BALTIMORE.

The title page from Banneker's *Almanac*—on which his name was misspelled—from 1795. He sent a manuscript copy of his first almanac to Thomas Jefferson in 1791 in an attempt to discredit ideas about black inferiority.

the rugged discomfort of wilderness surveying. He was not unhappy to return to his farm when Ellicott secured other aid.

Born free, an owner of land, with a rudimentary education and gifted with uncommon mathematical and mechanical skill, Banneker experienced relatively little discrimination as far as we know. Nor was he much touched by the Revolutionary struggle. The region in which he lived largely escaped military conflict. His was not the typical eighteenth-century Maryland black experience any more than Phillis Wheatley represented the typical New England slave. This does not mean that he had no knowledge of America's racial divide, for he surely knew that the attention he received derived partly from his color and the assumptions people made about it. Moreover, when white engineers in the District of Columbia "overlooked" his color, as an early commentator described the scene, and invited him to eat with them, "his characteristic modesty" prompted him to decline the offer. He dined in the same tent but at a separate table. This surely tells much about developing racial customs.

Banneker, like Wheatley, was caught up in the abolitionist crusade through the continuing controversy over blacks' intellectual capacities. Accordingly, the *Georgetown Weekly Ledger* described him soon after his arrival in the Federal District as "an Ethiopian, whose abilities, as a surveyor, and an astronomer, clearly prove that Mr. Jefferson's concluding that race of men were void of mental endowments, was without foundation." If Wheatley was the rage of the pre–Revolutionary antislavery set, Banneker became almost as important for the post–Revolutionary generation. In some ways he was more important, for his achievements were scientific rather than literary. Of the latter there were several cases, but examples of the former were rare indeed. If blacks were to gain full rights of citizenship, it was clearly important that they exhibit a broad intellectual competence. With the coming of freedom to the North and the continuing struggle against the Atlantic traffic in slaves, postwar abolitionists sought as much evidence of black talent as they could muster.

Blacks also demonstrated organizational ability, or capabilities in financial management, but these were seldom brought forward for discussion in considering their intellect. Consequently, the business success of Paul Cuffe—a New England shipping entrepreneur—was not something that abolitionists immediately valued in championing blacks' mental equality. Indeed, if that were his only claim to fame, important though it was, he might be passed over quickly. Yet his career is a measure of what skill mixed with luck could bring about for a black man in early America and is an answer to American racism of that era. It is also a cautionary tale of how and why a black man of the time could become disillusioned with America's promise.

When Cuffe came to the attention of the Delaware Society for the Abolition of Slavery as a result of business connections, the society published a short biographical tract. The purpose of this pamphlet, which was published in 1807, was to prove that:

with suitable culture and a fair opening for the exertion of talents, the NEGRO possesses a portion of intellect and energy by which he is enabled to form great designs, to adopt means to the end in the prosecution of them, to combat danger, to surmount difficulties; and thus to evince that, with equal advantages of education and circumstances, the Negro–race might fairly be compared with their white brethren on any part of the globe.

The society wanted Cuffe to work with Quaker-dominated international anti-slavery interests in securing black settlements in Africa and it was important for them to show that black people were capable of enterprise. People concerned in the Sierra Leone venture took especial note.

Cuffe's father, Kofi, lived in the Asante kingdom among Akan-speaking peoples on the western coast of Africa. He came to America as part of the slave traffic in 1728 when he was eleven or twelve years old. To his good fortune, he was purchased by a Quaker family, one that evidently had antislavery leanings, and his owner, John Slocum, freed him in 1740. In 1746 he married Ruth Moses, a Wampanoag, and eventually bought a farm on the Massachusetts coast near Martha's Vineyard. Paul was born in 1759, the seventh child and youngest son of ten children. As a farm boy, he, like Banneker, was brought up to hard work and his education was limited. He was largely self-taught but extremely shrewd. His natural charm and native intelligence made up for what he lacked in formal education.

Cuffe was thirteen years old when his father died, and he assumed part of the responsibility of supporting his mother and younger sisters. He did not see his future in farming, however, and like many New Englanders turned to the sea. His skill as a seaman together with his daring as an entrepreneur led eventually to his acquisition of a respectable fleet of ships. Some of these he built himself in his own shipyard. He achieved wealth and popularity and was the most successful black businessman in America at the turn of the nineteenth century.

Unlike Banneker, who spent most of his life near his birthplace and was consequently somewhat shielded from racial discrimination, Cuffe traveled widely, which brought him face to face with it. This was particularly the case since he frequently traveled to plantation regions. Many slave societies regarded free blacks with suspicion and unease, none more so than the United States. The divide between slave and free states, however, did not necessarily mark a division in the treatment of free blacks, and Cuffe occasionally experienced racial slights in restaurants or on public transportation in the North as well as the South. Both Maryland and Massachusetts had laws against interracial marriages in the latter half of the 1780s (though Pennsylvania did not). Both Maryland and Massachusetts had repressive legislation aimed at unfamiliar free blacks in the 1790s, though neither state may have strongly enforced it. Repressive laws, whether enforced or not, and racial discrimination, whether constant or not, created an environment that reminded Cuffe of his racial status.

Because of his mother and his wife, Cuffe remained aware of both his African and Native American heritages. In his protests against discriminatory taxation laws applied against him and his family in the 1770s and 1780s, therefore, he was prepared to use whatever facet of his background that seemed the most favorable. In one petition he said that "we being chiefly of the African extraction" were subject to taxation without representation. In another he said that he and his brother were "Indian men and by law not subject of taxation." Increasingly, however, he identified himself with Africans, and as the nineteenth century dawned and racial attitudes hardened, his own attitudes hardened as well.

An acquaintance described Cuffe in 1806 as "averse to all mixtures," despite his own marriage across racial and ethnic lines. When his wealth and accomplishments brought white friends to his home, he served them at separate tables. He, like Banneker, "reluctantly partook of vituals with persons of other colors." The fact that this attitude developed as a result of unequal treatment is indicated by his observation to the acquaintance that "he would willingly consent to be skinned if his black could be replaced by white." He was increasingly drawn to the conclusion that black people might be better off in Africa, and he became a leading figure in nineteenth-century emigrationist projects. Although he carried a group of black people there in 1815, he never actually committed to moving to Africa himself. Certainly his wife had no interest in going, and perhaps his children did not either. Besides, whether they went there or not, many black Americans by that time looked with interest at the prospect of black nation-building much closer to home.

Haiti and the Image of Freedom

Prince Hall, the founder of African-American freemasonry, addressed his African Lodge in Cambridge, Massachusetts, in June 1797 concerning racial harassment directed at black Americans in public places in Boston. Ten years had passed since the arrival of the charter from England granting them formal recognition as a lodge, and various proposals for blacks to leave America to escape discrimination had failed. But the negative attitudes that had prevented black Masons from gaining a local charter, and caused some blacks to want to leave their homeland for an uncertain future overseas, were alive and well.

Indeed, in many areas of the United States they were stronger. The revolutionary current favorable to black freedom in the South had reversed itself and abolition had not yet succeeded in New York and New Jersey. Hall advised his brethren to be mindful of "these numerous sons and daughters of distress" yet enslaved and who, of all the downtrodden peoples on the earth, deserved their particular consideration. He also charged them to have patience and forbearance in face of the "daily insults we meet with in the streets of Boston," especially on "public days of recreation." He went on to describe vividly how envious white working men and women, some not long out of servitude themselves (for some had come indentured) and doubtless encouraged by alcoholic beverages imbibed to enliven the holiday, "shamefully abused" blacks who ventured upon the parks or public squares. "[A]t such times," he lamented, ". . . we may truly be said to carry our lives in our hands. . . . Helpless women have [had] their clothes torn from their backs." Nevertheless, Hall had hopes for change. He cast his eyes with expectation to the Caribbean where, a few years earlier, in response to revolution in France, enslaved men and women in the French Empire had staked their own claim to freedom. "[S]ix years ago, in the French West Indies," Hall related, "Nothing but the snap of the whip was heard, from morning to evening. . . . But, blessed be God, the scene is changed. They now confess that God hath no respect of persons."

At the time that Hall spoke, slavery had been abolished in the French colonies in the Caribbean, the most important of which were Saint Domingue, Guadaloupe, and Martinique. Moreover, under the French revolutionary slogan of "Liberty, Equality, and Fraternity," revolutionary patriots were attempting to construct interracial societies consistent with their beliefs. In Saint Domingue this process went farther and lasted longer than anyplace else. In 1797 the black liberator Toussaint L'Ouverture was well on the way to establishing his leadership over the colony. He had already made clear his disposition to build a society where people of all colors could live in peace and prosperity. Although his vision of interracial cooperation was ultimately to fade amid bloody strife, he led the only successful slave revolution in the history of the world. And the banner of black freedom he raised was to stand as a beacon to black men and women throughout the Americas. Its example would spur unrest and insurrection from Brazil to the United States. Its triumph would provide lingering inspiration.

Never before, not even in the ancient world, had slaves ever overthrown and restructured an entire slave society. The United States was the first nation in the Americas to achieve its independence, but Haiti was the second. And though the United States was the first to declare that all men were created equal, Haiti was the first to make that declaration a fact.

The Haitian Revolution was the third in a series of democratic revolutions that changed the way people in the Western world viewed government, society, politics, and individual freedom. The era is often called the Age of Revolution. Each was more radical and far-reaching than the previous one, and each expanded the limits of ideas expressed in the Enlightenment.

The American Revolution was the first of the three. It was conceived as a political rather than a social revolution (that is, it sought to change the government rather than the everyday lives of the people), although it laid the basis of a social revolution. Moreover, it had some immediate social consequences, including the Northern abolition of slavery.

The French Revolution was the second uprising in the Western world. It was a social as well as a political revolution, for it accomplished not just the displacement but the overturning and destruction of the French monarchy and much of the nobility and a reordering of French government and society. The most radical of its participants sought the absolute ruin of the former ruling classes. The shock waves of revolution in France extended to the colony on Saint Domingue. There it established principles of individual liberty beyond the dreams even of most of the revolutionary generation in North America, and of many in France itself.

The struggle in Saint Domingue was more bloody than even the French Revolution, because added to the conflicting outlooks and tangle of local interests was the complicating factor of race. Saint Domingue society was divided into three classes, consisting of whites, free people of color, and slaves. As in North America, and partly under American revolutionary influence, white colonists wanted less restrictive trade regulations. They particularly wanted greater leeway to exchange their goods with New Englanders, on whom they depended for many of their supplies. They also wanted greater say in how they were governed. Revolution in France provided an opportunity to press these aims, but it also posed a threat. As much as they wanted greater freedom for themselves, they desired no change in island social structure, and in this regard, the most radical principles of the revolution stood against them. The first article of the French Declaration of the Rights of Man proclaims that "men are born and remain free and equal in their rights." This is a dangerous principle in a society based on the labor of slaves. Moreover, Saint Domingue's free people of color were subject to severe social and political discrimination and they wanted greater freedom of their own. They saw no problem with maintaining slavery so long as all free people, regardless of color, participated in the government.

The free people of color were supported in France by the Society of the Friends of the Blacks. Too many people in France and the West Indies had too great a stake in slavery and the slave trade for the Friends of the Blacks to stand much chance of succeeding immediately in abolishing these evils. They contented themselves with championing the claims to equality of colonial free people of color. Both they and their opponents saw this as the first step toward a more radical social reconstruction of the colonies. Whites in Saint Domingue therefore rejected the National Assembly's recommendation that a limited number of free coloreds be granted citizenship rights. Consequently, in 1790 the free colored people revolted. The free colored revolt was ruthlessly put down, but the whites also divided among themselves, some favoring a greater degree of local self-rule and separation from France than others. Besides, in the colony, as in France, a few people still preferred royal authority to government reform of any kind. These disputes also led to violence. The divisions among the free classes over the meaning of the revolution provided an opening for the slaves.

The slaves needed no formal declarations, either from Europe or America, to justify their claim to liberty. They greatly outnumbered the white people—indeed, all classes of free people—in Saint Domingue. The vast majority of Saint Dominguan slaves were African-born, had experienced freedom before their captivity, and knew that their subjugation rested on no firmer basis than superior arms.

Encouraged by the rumor that the king and National Assembly had decreed three days a week for them to work for themselves and the abolition of whippings, they rose up on August 22, 1791. They would not finally lay down their arms until they proclaimed Haiti an independent nation on January 1, 1804.

The man who soon came to dominate the revolution was Toussaint L'Ouverture. Born in 1744, he was forty-seven at the start of the rebellion. Of mild disposition, he had been fortunate in his master and had not suffered the severe mistreatment of some slaves. Indeed, by the time of the outbreak, he was free in all but name; aside from the duties of coachman, he lived pretty much on his own, with his wife and three boys. He was and remained a devout Catholic. He was also literate, enjoyed reading, and in letters of state composed later made frequent reference to ancient history and philosophy.

His fortunate experience was unusual for a region where the face of slavery was particularly harsh, and provided him with a distinctive outlook toward interracial cooperation that set him apart from most people on the island. As a military leader, he was beloved of his men, a strict disciplinarian but willing to share their hardships and to lead by example. Extremely brave in battle, he was wounded seventeen times. He was once struck in the mouth by a spent cannon ball but only suffered the loss of some teeth. He had a talent for organization and a genius for warfare. By 1795 he was the colony's leading general and by 1798, with the expulsion of interfering British forces, its effective leader. He defeated French, Spanish, British, and opposing local forces in their turn. He had two abiding aims: to maintain black freedom and to rebuild the island's economy. The first he could do by force of arms; the second with white expertise and cooperation and the controlled labor of free black peasants.

The United States and Great Britain viewed events in Saint Domingue with alarm. Both had slave regions to preserve from the contagion of liberty. The British attempt at conquest as part of its war against France came to naught and when they evacuated, they came to a trade arrangement with Toussaint under which they agreed to supply him in return for his promise not to spread revolution to their territories. The United States was also party to the agreement. President John Adams and the Federalist party he represented had always been pro-British in the wars between Britain and France that broke out in the wake of the French Revolution. In addition, there had always been strong commercial relations between the French West Indies and New England that continued during the slave rebellion. In the last two years before 1800 the United States and France had engaged in an unofficial naval war that prompted a momentary interruption of commerce with French colonies; but that conflict was soon settled and, in any case, the United States was unwilling to allow the British to monopolize Saint Domingue's trade.

The election of President Thomas Jefferson in 1800 changed the situation. Jefferson was a slaveholder and highly sensitive to the consequences of slave rebelliousness. Moreover, the Democratic-Republican party he led had taken the French

This picture of "Free Natives of Dominica" offers a glimpse of how some of the wealthy free people of color in St. Domingue may have looked before the Haitian Revolution.

side of the European conflict. Napoleon Bonaparte, who had come to power in France, and would soon destroy the First French Republic, wanted to end black rule in Saint Domingue. Having temporarily made peace with England in 1801, he had little difficulty convincing that nation and the United States that the eradication of black government was in their best interests. Jefferson was not convinced that Napoleon would succeed in his mission, however, and delayed withdrawing American material support from Toussaint. His decision was further slowed by the news or rumor that Louisiana, recently a colony of Spain, had been transferred to France. Jefferson, like many Americans, looked forward to American expansion into the Louisiana Territory and was convinced that no nation who held that region could long be friends with the United States. He would hedge his bets until he was sure of French intentions. Not until after France agreed to sell Louisiana to the United States in 1803 did Jefferson cease to trade with Saint Domingue.

Part of the reason for Napoleon's decision to sell had to do with the outbreak of war with Britain again and his failure, as Jefferson suspected, to succeed in his conquest of Saint Domingue. Napoleon wanted to rebuild the French Empire, which, under his plan, included restoring slavery. Saint Domingue, once the jewel of French Caribbean possessions, would be restored to its original splendor, and French Louisiana would replace the United States as a supplier of foodstuffs not grown on the island. But he calculated without taking into account the blacks' attachment to their hard-won freedom.

Although he was virtually an independent ruler, Toussaint posed as a defender of the French Republic. The National Convention's law of February 1794 that abolished slavery also made the former slaves French citizens. Toussaint was always careful in his dealings with France to operate as if under the authority of the Republic. He had even resisted British and American pressure to declare Saint Domingue independent in 1798–99 when both nations, one officially, the other unofficially, were at war with France. Conditions changed when France made peace with these English-speaking nations. Under Napoleon's leadership, France now felt strong enough to reassert its control.

Napoleon sent his brother-in-law Charles Leclerc with sixteen thousand troops in 1802 to "rid us of these gilded Africans," as he ordered, referring to Toussaint and his black generals. Once he reasserted French authority, Napoleon planned to remove and banish all black or mulatto officers over the rank of captain in order to put his colonial plan into operation more safely. He thought the colony, deprived of leadership, would keep quiet. Hoping to prevent fanatical resistance at the outset, however, he resorted to deceit and denied any intention of bringing back slavery. Toussaint was not convinced, and he and his most trusted generals Henri Christophe and Jean Jacques Dessalines resisted.

So long as he posed as a champion of the French promise of liberty, Leclerc had some success. Christophe and Dessalines defected to the French and Toussaint agreed to lay down his arms. But not all rebels surrendered and the colony was still unpacified.

In April 1802 Napoleon reopened the slave trade and nullified the decree abolishing slavery. In June he ordered Leclerc to restore slavery at his discretion. Guadaloupe's governor acted before Leclerc, and the arrival of news that slavery had been restored in Guadaloupe and Leclerc's tentative moves in that direction in Saint Domingue aroused the suspicions of more blacks about their future, and more left to join rebel bands. At the same time, Dessalines, in particular, began to play both ends against the middle and lent the rebels secret support. The betrayal of Toussaint, whom the French lured to a June meeting on the promise of protection and then arrested and sent to France, caused outrage. He was to die in prison the next year (April 7, 1803) of suffering from frigid temperatures, bad treatment, and little food. Finally, the increasing brutality of the French spurred resistance. Leclerc decided, in fact, that French control of the island would never be secure until he had destroyed all black men and women over twelve years of age.

But Leclerc, like many of his men, died of yellow fever and was succeeded in November by Count Rochambeau. He was not the best choice. For as Leclerc warned Napoleon, "Rochambeau [is] a brave soldier and a good fighter, [but he] has not an ounce of tact or policy. Furthermore, he has no moral character and is easily led." It was Rochambeau who stood with Washington at the Battle of Yorktown to receive the British surrender. The hero of white revolutionaries in America, however, was the scourge of black revolutionaries in Haiti, and if Dessalines eventually chose to ensure Haiti's future by exterminating the whites, Rochambeau led the way when he tried to ensure France's future there by exterminating the blacks.

By August 1802 the black generals who had gone over to the French began to desert. In November they held a conference, supported independence, and recognized Dessalines as leader of the resistance. According to legend, Dessalines took the French flag, ripped out the white band, and left a flag of blue and red as the national banner. In 1804, after more months of struggle, the French evacuated and the Republic of Haiti, a name derived from a Native American word for a mountainous place, was proclaimed.

From Venezuela to Virginia slaves were encouraged anew to reclaim their natural rights. The Spanish governor of Cuba informed his superiors in 1794, at the height of Jacobin radicalism, that "the rumor is too widespread that the French desire that there be no slaves" and were determined to free them. In 1795 slaves mounted uprisings under French revolutionary influence, reminiscent of Saint Domingue, in Dutch Curaçao; Coro, Venezuela; and Pointe Coupee, Louisiana.

In the United States plots and rebellions or rumors of plots and rebellions occurred along the eastern seaboard during the 1790s and later. Whites in Charleston, South Carolina, blamed a series of fires in the city on a group of "French Negroes" who "intended to make a St. Domingo business of it." The most serious

An 1805 account of the Haitian Revolution included this gruesome illustration with the caption: "Revenge taken by the black army for the cruelties practised on them by the French."

threat occurred in Richmond, Virgininia, where, in 1800, the slave Gabriel planned a large-scale uprising. Born on a plantation outside the city in 1776, Gabriel was raised as a blacksmith and taught to read. He grew up in a period of revolutionary ferment and could not avoid being influenced by talk about the rights of man. As a skilled worker he was often hired out and spent much time among working-class people where blacks and whites mixed freely. He, like others, learned about the events in Saint Domingue and that was clearly one source of stimulation. He planned not a war against the whites but a war against the merchants. He expected working-class whites as well as slaves to join his rebellion and warned his followers to spare all "Quakers, the Methodists, and Frenchmen" because of "their being friendly to liberty." He planned to take Richmond and set up a new social and political order, though precisely what kind he did not say. However, he clearly envisioned personal freedom and racial and social equality.

Gabriel's conspiracy was widespread, including people in ten counties, a few whites among them. He estimated "his associates to the number of five–six hundred." While not all of these were people he could count on, at least 150 gathered for word of the outbreak. Torrential rains prevented the plan from going into effect on the night it was scheduled and the plot was discovered before it could be reorganized. Gabriel and scores of slaves were hanged and others were sold out of the state. But the governor of Virginia, James Monroe, and the vice president of the United States, Thomas Jefferson, could take little comfort in hanging revolutionaries, even black ones. "The other states and the world at large will forever condemn us," Jefferson wrote Monroe, "if we indulge a principle of revenge, or go one step beyond absolute necessity. They cannot lose sight of the rights of the two parties, and the object of the unsuccessful one."

Free blacks as well as slaves were attracted by French principles and the Haitian example of equality. Free African Americans lived in a country that boasted of its freedoms but increasingly denied them to former slaves. By the date of Haiti's independence in 1804, slavery was finally on the road to extinction in all the Northern states. At the same time, probably a larger number of slaves had been freed in the South by a master's personal act of conscience than by Northern legislative acts of emancipation. But also by that date racial lines had hardened.

In Virginia, for example, the legislature had once supported education for free blacks; in 1806 it reversed that decision and also denied them the right to carry firearms. Maryland's constitution of 1776 had made the possession of property rather than white skin the requirement for voting. In 1783 the state decided that no blacks freed after that date could vote, hold office, or testify against white people in a court of law, nor could any of their descendants. In 1810 it limited the vote to white men. In Philadelphia it had been customary for many years for black and white people to gather before Independence Hall on the Fourth of July to celebrate the birth of a new nation dedicated to freedom and opportunity. In 1805 the white people drove the black people away. Thereafter blacks approached the festival only at the risk of their lives. Throughout the nation similar events heralded a new birth of intolerance. American democracy, they said, would be limited to white people. In these circumstances Haiti stood out as a beacon of liberty to oppressed people of color all over the New World.

CHAPTER 4

Let My People Go

1804–1860

Deborah Gray White

On August 30 in the year 1800, a chilling fear spread among the white people of Henrico County, Virginia. Within a few days the fear had gripped the minds of most white Virginians. Within weeks, slaveholders as far west and south as what was then the Mississippi Territory were cautioning each other to beware of suspicious behavior on the part of blacks. On their tongues was the name Gabriel Prosser; in their minds were thoughts of what might have happened if Prosser had succeeded in leading Virginia slaves in revolt against slavery.

Prosser, his wife, Nanny, and his two brothers, Martin and Solomon, were a slaveholder's nightmare. Born into slavery, they declared themselves fit for freedom. They decided not only that they would be free but that all slaves should be free. Together they plotted to lead the slaves of the Richmond area in revolt against the city. Their plan was to capture the arsenal and, once supplied with weapons, to take over Richmond and then other cities in the state. Virginia, it was planned, would become a free state, a black state, a homeland for those unfit for slavery.

But Prosser never got a chance to put his plan into action. On the night of the scheduled attack on Richmond, a terrible storm washed out the bridges and roads to the city. Prosser had to postpone his rebellion, and the delay gave someone time to betray him and expose the plan. All who conspired in the revolt were captured and put to death. Gabriel was among the last to be captured, tried, and hanged.

He was, however, one of the first people in the nineteenth century to struggle in the name of freedom. And this is really the theme of this period of African-American history: the fight against slavery, the struggle to be free American citizens, and resistance, despite incredible odds, to maintain human dignity in the face of overwhelming inhumanity. The chance that the African Americans would succeed was small. The odds against it being a bloodless struggle were overwhelming. And those odds increased when cotton became this country's principal export crop, after Eli Whitney's cotton gin made the production of hearty short-staple cotton profitable.

169

By making cotton a profitable crop for Southern farmers, the cotton gin increased the demand for slaves and changed the course of history for black Americans.

Short-staple cotton was in demand throughout the world, especially in England, where textile manufacturers never seemed to get enough. It was not long before cotton became the principal cash crop of the South and of the nation. In 1790 the South produced only 3,135 bales of cotton. By 1800 this figure had grown to 73,145 bales; by 1820 output amounted to 334,378 bales, accounting for more than half of the nation's agricultural exports. On the eve of the Civil War, production peaked at

4.8 million bales. If ever circumstances conspired against a people, it was the coming together of the cotton gin, short-staple cotton, fertile lands, and world demand. Once this happened, slaves who might have been set free by debt and conscience-ridden Chesapeake planters were instead sold to the planters of the cotton-growing states of the Lower South. Cotton sealed the fate of slaves and slavery.

It seemed as though Gabriel Prosser knew this. Like so many other blacks, he probably saw slaveholders close down their Virginia tobacco farms and plantations and head with their slaves south and west toward the fertile black soil of the soon-to-be cotton belt. Like others, he no doubt winced at the sight of chained slaves heading out of the declining economies of Virginia, Maryland, and South Carolina to the booming areas of Alabama, Mississippi, Louisiana, Arkansas, and Texas. In 1800 these areas were not even states. Texas, in fact, was still part of Mexico. These places were not uninhabited, but were home to five Native American tribes, the Creeks, Choctaws, Seminoles, Chickasaws, and Cherokees. No matter, though. The certain wealth that cotton brought ensured that these areas would soon be flooded with white settlers who would see to it that the land became theirs. They would turn the territories into states and in the process transform the very nature of slavery.

Essential to the transformation was the domestic slave trade. Before 1800 a slave stood some chance of obtaining his or her freedom, either through self-purchase, meritorious service, or simply through the good will of a master or mistress; after 1800 the increased profitability of slavery made manumission for an individual slave less likely. Once cotton gave slavery a new lease on life, slaves who were of no use in the Upper South were not set free, but sold to the Lower South. This meant that a good many of the slaves born in Virginia, Maryland, or South Carolina were likely to die in Mississippi, Alabama, or Louisiana. The domestic trade established the means of getting them there. At the same time that slaves lived in fear of having their families torn apart and being "sold down the river," domestic slave traders calculated just how much able-bodied field hands, especially those between the ages of fifteen and twenty-five, sold for in the new markets.

The sale and transportation of black people within the United States thus became big business. What had once taken place mostly on the African continent—the theft of people, the rending of families—now took place with vulgar regularity before the eyes and ears of American whites and blacks. From Virginia alone, an estimated 300,000 slaves were transported south for sale between 1830 and 1860. As the slave pens sprung up, so too did the sights and sounds of human misery. Within view of the nation's capitol were slave pens that were, as kidnapped slave Solomon Northup described them, constructed so that "the outside world could never see the human cattle that were herded there." Within the walls of the pens, in open-air dirt yards, and on the auction blocks, slave husbands and wives were separated from each other, parents were parted from their children, and infants were torn from their mothers' breasts. Free blacks, too, feared the trade, for like Northup they could be, and were, stolen by unscrupulous traders anxious to make money by any means. Blacks, who once had hoped that the constitutional provision for the ending of the slave trade in 1808 would put slavery on the road to extinction, now knew that slavery was not about to die.

Free black men and women, like Philadelphia sailmaker James Forten or abolitionist Maria Stewart, were always an anomaly in a society where dark skin color was a badge of bondage, but they became even more insecure with the transformation of slavery. First and foremost, the newly revitalized institution of slavery decreased their numbers. This meant that the free black population would always remain small, with limited ability to affect the course of slavery. Free blacks always had to protect themselves against kidnappers. Those who made up the small communities of southern free blacks had to keep their free papers close or else be mistaken for slaves. In both the North and South free blacks found it beneficial to have white friends who could testify on their behalf should they be mistaken as slaves. The long and the short of it was that the transformation of slavery put free blacks at risk.

What it did to those in bondage was much worse. Their loss was very personal, because throughout the Upper South their families were torn apart. Whites who migrated to the Lower South went in family groups. Those who did not were usually single men who chose to seek their fortune in the new area. Slaves had no choice. They were taken or sold against their will, forced to leave family, friends, and all that was familiar. Lost to each other forever, family members separated by hundreds of miles suffered tremendous grief.

By the time cotton production began to soar in the states of the Lower South, Virginia, Maryland, North Carolina, and South Carolina were considered "old" states. The land had long been cleared of brush and trees, farms and plantations had already been built, fields had been readied for crops, roads made transportation and communication easy, cities made commercial and cultural exchange possible.

The Lower South was not so "civilized." All the work that had been done in the Upper South had to be repeated here. It was the new frontier, and as on all frontiers the work was more backbreaking. To Adeline Cunningham, an ex-slave from Texas, everything was hard. As she put it: "Dey was rough people and dey treat ev'ry body rough." Evidence of rough treatment could be found in the slaves' birth and death rates. Compared with African Americans in other regions in the United States, blacks in the Lower South did not live as long nor have as many children.

And yet, for all of the terrible changes that took place in the first few decades of the nineteenth century, the overall condition of the average slave actually improved. This is one of the great paradoxes of the history of bondage in America. As slavery became more entrenched, as more families were separated and freedom became less attainable, it actually got better in terms of physical treatment. In the nineteenth century there were far less brandings that marked slaves as personal property. Limb amputations for theft and running away were curtailed and disabling whippings and murder occurred less frequently. Work was still backbreaking and endless, punishment was still certain, but more attention was paid to diet, slaves were given more personal time, and marital life was encouraged.

The reasons for these seemingly contrary occurrences are easy to understand. They were the consequence of the closing of the international slave trade at the very time that cotton made slavery profitable. Once it was no longer possible to bring slaves from Africa, slaveholders were forced to treat the slaves they had better. They needed slaves for work, and so they needed to keep the slaves they had healthy and productive—and they needed those slaves to reproduce.

This need resulted in better material conditions for African Americans held in bondage. Even given the severe conditions on the frontier, in comparison with Africans held in slavery in Brazil, Cuba, and Puerto Rico, American slaves lived longer. Of critical importance was the high birthrate in the United States. The better living conditions that caused the higher fertility rates developed out of white greed and intense disregard for African-American humanity—negative qualities, but ones that helped the African-American community grow. Only here was the ratio of slave men to women relatively equal, and only here did families develop. Only here did this result in the creation of what has been termed "the slave community."

The lives of black Americans, however, compared to that of other Americans, was hard, intolerable, and unprotected. Everything about slavery went against every principle upon which the nation was founded. In slavery there was no liberty, no equality, no democracy. It therefore needed justification. A reason had to be found to explain why slavery existed in the nation that was the most free in the world. A reason was needed to excuse the South and ease the conscience of the individual slaveholder.

In the pro-slavery argument was every excuse upon which the South built its institution. At its center was denial of the worth of the African American. Blacks, the argument went, were not prepared for freedom. They were childlike, in need of direction. They were lazy people who would not work unless forced to. They were cursed by God, and slavery was God's punishment. They were, some insisted, so unlike whites that they were a different species. In short, the pro-slavery argument turned slavery into something that at its worst was a necessary evil, and at its best a positive good.

Slavery was good for the South, good for black people, and good for the nation, or so the argument went. William Harper, chancellor of the University of South Carolina, declared that blacks "are undergoing the very best education which it is possible to give. They are in the course of being taught habits of regular and patient industry, and this is the first lesson that is required."

Like Harper, pro-slavery writers generally overlooked or denied the brutality of slavery. Most insisted that cruelty occurred only in the rarest of instances. Most

THE NEGRO IN HIS OWN COUNTRY.

THE NEGRO IN AMERICA.

Two engravings from the *Bible Defence of Slavery* (1853). Many Southern slave owners believed that blacks benefited from slavery.

also believed that their slaves lived better than the average industrial worker, including those in the northern United States. Factory owners, it was argued, cared nothing for their laborers. In contrast to Northern and European "wage slaves" who were worked until they were of no use to the company, after which they were fired to fend for themselves, southern slaves received free food, clothing, housing, and medical care for life. A typical opinion on this matter was expressed by

Virginia Baptist minister Thorton Springfellow. Like most slaveholders, he believed that the slaves' "condition . . . is now better than that of any equal number of laborers on earth, and is daily improving."

Obviously, Gabriel Prosser and his followers thought differently. To them slavery was not a kind and caring institution but a malicious one that robbed them of their freedom. Their feelings were shared by both free and enslaved African Americans, all of whom struggled in one way or another against slavery, all of whom at one time or another raised the plaintive cry: "Let my people go."

What Slavery Was

In the South, before the Civil War, the year began the same way as it ended—with work in cotton. During January and February slaves finished ginning and pressing cotton, and hauled it in wagons to the point of shipment. In March and April they were ready to start planting again. It took at least three slaves to plant a row of cotton. One slave drove a mule and plowed through the dirt to break the land into a row. A young slave came behind dropping the seed into the ground, followed by another slave with another mule-drawn plow, covering up the seed. Between April and August, the cotton was plowed and hoed by slaves, first to make sure that there was only one stalk of cotton to what was called a hill, then to keep the land free of weeds and grass. In late August, slaves began the cotton-picking season. Unmercifully long, it lasted through January of the next year.

Slaves who cultivated rice, tobacco, hemp, or sugar had a similar year-round routine, and like those who worked in cotton, their work did not end with the sale of the crop. There were hogs to kill, and then the meat had to be cut and salted. New land was cleared. Ditches were dug, cleaned, and repaired. Fences were built and under constant repair, wood was cut and hauled, and vegetable gardens were cultivated. On top of all this was the cultivation of corn, a crop that needed extensive hoeing, plowing, and harvesting just like the cash crop.

The slaves' day did not end when fieldwork was done. At night men cut wood while women prepared meals, spun thread, wove cloth, and made clothes. On Saturday afternoons men often trapped while women washed clothes, made candles and soap, and helped the men tend the garden plots where they grew the few vegetables they ate.

Slaves whose chores were in the master's house worked as much as field hands. Besides taking care of their own families, and doing their cooking, cleaning, sewing, and washing, they did all of the domestic tasks, day and night, for the slave master's family.

For the slave this added up to endless work. But that is what slavery was, a system of forced labor in which the African American worked without pay for someone else's profit. Everything else derived from slavery was secondary to this central point. For instance, this system of forced labor provided slaveholders with the wealth and prestige that they needed to dominate southern politics and social relations. Further, slavery organized the races not only to separate blacks and whites, but to give all whites status simply because they were white, and to deny status to all blacks simply because they were black. An example of how inhumane one group of people could be to another, slavery was also one of the main causes of the Civil War, the bloodiest conflict ever fought on American soil.

As a system of labor that exploited black work, slavery usually benefited a white man, but sometimes the slave master was a white woman, a Native American, or rarely, a black man or woman. Ultimately, the nation prospered from this exploitation, because as the South grew rich off the cultivation of cash crops, so did the country as a whole. The losers were the African Americans whose lives were organized around endless work; the rewards always went to someone else.

Wherever one went in the South between 1800 and 1860 one could expect to see slaves doing some kind of work. They worked as lumberjacks and turpentine producers in the forests of the Carolinas and Georgia. In Virginia and Kentucky, slaves worked in the gold, coal, and salt mines. On the Mississippi River steamboats they worked as deckhands and boiler stokers. In Georgia and Louisiana they worked as textile laborers. Slave labor was so profitable that in 1847 the owners of the Tredegar Iron Works in Richmond, Virginia, shifted from using white laborers to slave labor. In addition to serving as factory laborers, slaves also made up a significant portion of the South's skilled artisans—carpenters, coopers, blacksmiths, silversmiths, and the like.

However, most of the four million African Americans who were enslaved in 1860 worked in the fields of the farms and plantations of the South. They worked on an average day fourteen hours in the summer and ten hours in the winter. During harvest time slaves often worked eighteen-hour days in sun that was piercing, heat that was sweltering.

Needless to say, their work was backbreaking. The average slave worked in cotton production, and during harvest season was expected to pick about 130 to 150 pounds of cotton per day. Work in sugar and rice was equally hard, if not harder. Both crops demanded constant cultivation and the digging of drainage ditches in snake-infested fields. At harvest time on the sugar plantations, slaves had to cut, strip, and carry cane to the sugar house for boiling. This was extremely strenuous work. Rice cultivation was even more miserable. Since rice is grown under water, slaves spent long hours standing in water up to their knees.

With so much wealth riding on it, slave work was hardly done haphazardly. On the contrary, it was carefully organized so that slaves worked either in gangs or according to tasks. Slave work gangs usually did as much work as the fastest worker could do. The task system provided greater flexibility, and although assignments were as taxing as those done by gangs, when a slave or a group of slaves finished the assigned task, they could quit work for the day. Unlike the gang system, in which men and women usually worked in separate groups, tasks were often assigned to a family.

A white woman whips a slave, probably a house servant. For slaves, violent attacks could come from any direction, and at any time.

Slaves who worked in the house had a totally different regimen, one that was physically easier but mentally taxing. Women predominated in the house, and like male slave artisans, they did work that allowed for more creativity and self-direction than the work done by field hands. Working indoors, they cooked, cleaned, did laundry, sewed, and cared for infants. Although they could count on better food and clothing than their counterparts in the field, they were under closer supervision, were on call both day and night, and were more often involved in personality conflicts with the white family. As put by one house servant, "We were constantly exposed to the whims and passions of every member of the family." This meant everything from assignment to petty jobs to insults, spontaneous angry whippings, and sexual assaults.

Although house servants were under the closest surveillance, compared to slaves in other parts of the Americas all slaves in the United States were relatively closely supervised. Unlike in Caribbean slave societies or in Latin America, slaves, slaveholders, and overseers in the United States lived in very close proximity to each other. In Jamaica, for instance, one-third of all slaves lived on estates with two hundred slaves or more, and three-quarters of all slaves lived on holdings of at least fifty. Such large numbers of bondsmen made close supervision of slave life and work impossible.

In the United States, by contrast, such large plantations were rare. Only one-quarter of all slaves lived on plantations with more than fifty slaves. Since most lived on holdings of ten to forty-nine slaves, and about one-quarter lived on very small holdings of one to nine slaves, slave work and life was constantly monitored and supervised so that masters could reap every bit of profit they thought they were entitled to.

Of course, slave masters like to think that slaves were happiest when they were at work. Some even made this claim as part of the pro-slavery argument. But most slaveholders understood that it was the threat of physical punishment that kept slaves hard at their jobs. In fact, the submission of most slaves was never perfect, and they could seldom do as much work as fast as the owners demanded. This is one reason why slaves were whipped: to get them to work harder, faster. This was certainly the case on Edwin Eppes's Louisiana plantation, where the end of the cotton-picking day brought fear instead of relief. At sundown the cotton was weighed, and no matter how much cotton they had picked, the slaves carried their cotton to the gin house in fear. As told by kidnapped slave Solomon Northup, "If it falls short in weight—if he has not performed the full task appointed him, he knows that he must suffer. And if he has exceeded it by ten or twenty pounds, in all probability his master will measure the next day's task accordingly. So whether he has too little or too much, his approach to the gin-house is always with fear and trembling. . . . After weighing, follow the whippings."

On antebellum southern plantations whipping and work went hand in hand. For instance, on one Alabama estate, women who had just given birth to infants and were still confined to the slave cabins had to spin thread. According to an ex-slave named Cato, "If they did not spin seven or eight cuts a day they got a whipping."

Overseers' and drivers' reports tell the same gruesome story. These black and white men who worked for slaveholders had the prime responsibility for the production of the crop. White overseers attended to the overall day-to-day and season-to-season strategy of plantation work, and black drivers were on-the-spot disciplinarians who made sure the work got done. Charged with managing slaves to ensure that the plantation turned a profit, and faced with the loss of their position if it did not, both overseer and driver used any means necessary to make slaves work as hard as possible. This was especially true on plantations where the owners were absent. Without the supervision of slaveholders, who were obviously more interested than their managers in protecting their investment in the slaves, over-seers and drivers could and often did use as much force as they wanted. This disturbed those who were vigorous supporters of slavery. Pro-slavery southerner Daniel R. Hundley admired and defended the South's institutions. Nevertheless, he admitted that "the overseers on many southern plantations are cruel and unmercifully severe."

Even those overseers and drivers not considered especially brutal revealed the inherent violence of the system. For instance, in one of his weekly reports Robert Allston's overseer casually noted that he had "flogged for hoeing corn bad Fanny twelve lashes, Sylvia twelve, Monday twelve, Phoebee twelve, Susanna twelve, Salina twelve, Celia twelve, Iris twelve." George Skipwith, a black driver for John Hartwell Cocke, a Virginia planter, was equally liberal with the whip. In 1847 he reported to his master that several slaves who worked under him "at a reasonable days work" should have plowed seven acres apiece but had only done one and a half. Therefore, without a thought of the unreasonableness of his demands, and without sympathy for those of his own race, Skipwith reported, "I gave then ten lick a peace upon their skins [and] I gave Julyann eight or ten licks for misplacing her hoe."

That Skipwith was black and that he wielded the whip as readily as any white man should come as no surprise. It was to the slaveholders' advantage to allow blacks a measure of supervision over some of the day-to-day work. Not only could overseers not be everywhere at once, but their tenure on a particular plantation was often short-term. In contrast, as a slave, and a valued one at that, the driver's service was perpetual, and because it was, he provided continuity that made for the smooth running of the plantation. Since drivers lived with the slaves, their supervisory role extended into the after-work hours, which were spent away from white overseers. In fact, it was this familiarity with the slaves that made the drivers so necessary. Although it was illegal, some masters never even hired white overseers, but relied on the driver, a man who usually knew as much, if not more, about the daily management of a plantation.

Like overseers, drivers came with all kinds of temperaments and skills. Some were particularly cruel and mean. They raped women and used their power to prey on their fellow bondsmen. Such was the driver remembered by Jane Johnson, a former South Carolina slave. According to her, the driver was "de meanest man, white or black." Other drivers, though, used skillful methods of leadership to get their way. They used the whip only when necessary. They mediated disputes between slaves and acted as their representative to the master. They earned the respect of their fellow slaves and therefore their compliance. Such was the driver remembered by West Turner of Virginia. This driver whipped hard only when the master was looking. At other times "he never would beat dem slaves," but tie them up and pretend to beat them.

However they accomplished their jobs, drivers were part and parcel of the system that not only got maximum work out of the slave but also ensured "perfect submission." Indeed, slaveholders could command a slave's labor only if they could minimize the slave's resistance to their authority. Resistance, no matter how slight, was rightfully perceived as a reflection of independence. Since independence was clearly incompatible with slavery, all behavior on the part of the slave that suggested even a hint of self-determination had to be squelched. Dependence had to be instilled. Slaves who showed too much self-direction were deemed rebellious and judged dangerous. Punishment, therefore, served the purpose of making slaves work, but it also functioned to awe the slave with a sense of the master's power. And power is what the master used to make the slave stand in fear.

The slaveholder and his family demonstrated their power in a variety of ways. To begin with, they always made the slave show deference, not just to them but to all white people. Slaves had to bow in the presence of whites, they had to give way to whites walking in their path, and they were subject to whippings given by white children. When they approached the overseer or the master they had to show humility. On Charles Ball's plantation the slaves, according to one of Ball's former slaves, "were always obliged to approach the door of the mansion, in the most humble and supplicating manner, with our hats in our hands, and the most subdued and beseeching language in our mouths."

Hand in hand with humility went cheerfulness. Slaveholders feared the rebelliousness of slaves who showed dissatisfaction, and therefore did not tolerate sullen or sorrowful moods. Former slave Henry Watson noted that "the slaveholder watches every move of the slave, and if he is downcast or sad,—in fact, if they are in any mood but laughing and singing, and manifesting symptoms of perfect content at heart,—they are said to have the devil in them."

The power to make slaves work and to show deference and false happiness was granted to slaveholders by state and city legislatures through statutes called slave codes. Historians debate the protections afforded blacks by slave laws, but it is clear that throughout the South the legal system was designed to protect the interests of white slave owners. Slavery differed as one went from one region of the South to another, from one crop to another, even from one master to another. What gave the system its uniformity, however, was the consistency of social thought on the matter of slaveholder power. Manifested throughout the South in the slave codes, the white South's thinking about slavery left the enslaved no legal means to challenge actions committed against them in violation of the law.

The Louisiana slave code was typical of other state and city codes. The very first provision stated that the slave "owes to his master, and to his family, a respect without bounds, and an absolute obedience." The code defined slaves as property that could be "seized and sold as real estate." Most of the provisions stated what slaves were prohibited from doing. For instance, slaves could not travel without a pass, nor assemble in groups. They were prohibited from buying and selling any kind of goods and they could not carry arms, nor ride horses without the permission of their master. Besides dictating the behavior of blacks, the codes also restricted the actions of whites. Whites could not sell to, or buy anything from, slaves. Whites could not teach slaves to read or write, and a slaveholder could not free a slave without posting a thousand dollar bond guaranteeing that the freed slave would leave the state. The code also made death the penalty a slave suffered if he or she willfully harmed the master, mistress, their children, or the overseer. If a slave set fire to the crop or any part of the owner's property, if a slave raped any white female or assaulted any white person in an attempt to escape from slavery, the code also made death the punishment.

Whether or not the slave codes were enforced, the stories told by ex-slaves reveal this system of forced labor to be just as cruel and inhumane as the statutes suggest it was. Even the "kindest" masters kept their slaves illiterate, broke up families through sale, gave them too much work, and fed their slaves a diet that lacked fresh meat, dairy products, and vegetables. Throughout the South slave children were denied proper physical care and emotional support, and adult slaves were stripped naked and whipped in front of family and friends for the slightest infractions. Sadly, too, the presence of thousands of mulatto children gave undeniable testimony to the frequency of the sexual abuse of black women.

And yet, African Americans survived this barbarity better than any enslaved black people in the Western Hemisphere. Survival was a tribute to the North American slave's ability to adapt and resist, and to create communities that nourished the strength it took to resist some of the most inhumane aspects of the system.

Slave Communities

In the slave quarters, far removed from the eyes and ears of the slave master and his family, slave parents told their children the now-classic story of Br'er Rabbit, the Wolf, and Tar Baby. The story begins when the strong and powerful Wolf creates a sticky doll, or Tar Baby, to trap Rabbit, who is inquisitive and sly. While walking through the woods one day, Rabbit comes upon Tar Baby sitting by the side of the road, where it has been placed by Wolf. Being a friendly sort, Rabbit greets it with a "Hello, howdy do." When Tar Baby does not reply, the angry Rabbit hits the baby doll. First one hand gets stuck, then the other. Losing his temper even further, Rabbit kicks Tar Baby and butts it with his head, only to get his entire body stuck to Tar Baby.

When Wolf arrives to collect Rabbit, he decides to kill him by burning him in the brush. Instead of cringing in fear, Rabbit's clever response is to pretend that he wants to feel the warmth of fire on his coat. Wolf falls for Rabbit's deception and decides that the thorny briar patch might be a more suitable punishment. Rabbit, however, knows that if he gets thrown in the briar patch he can work his way loose from Tar Baby and escape. He therefore pretends to cringe at Wolf's threat: "Mercy, mercy, whatever you do, please don't throw me in the briar patch." Wolf falls for Rabbit's feigned terror and throws him in the briar patch, whereupon Rabbit makes a quick escape.

In the assortment of tales told by adult slaves to the young was another about a very talkative slave. In this tale, the slave comes across a frog who can speak. Amazed at such a wonder, the slave runs and tells his master of this miracle. The master does not believe the slave and threatens to punish him if he is lying. When the frog refuses to talk for the master, the slave is beaten severely. Only when the master leaves does the frog speak, saying, "A tol' yuh 'de othah day, yuh talk too much."

These are only two of the hundreds of tales that were told in the slave quarters, but if we use these tales to represent plantation life, they tell us a great deal about the relationship between slaves and masters. One thing they tell us is that masters did not always have their way. Wolf had Rabbit in his control, at his mercy, but he was still unable to conquer him. Slaves learned from this. They learned that quick-wittedness was an essential survival trait, and that deception could give the weak some control over the strong, allowing the powerless to survive with a minimal amount of physical or emotional assault. The story also laid bare the concepts that might did not always make for right, and that rash behavior, like that indulged in by Rabbit, seldom yielded rewards. These were important lessons for the slave child. They were lessons about life—not a life that was distant and abstract, but one the slave had to live every day.

The same was true of the second story. Though simpler than the first, it taught young blacks important lessons about survival. First, it showed the slave's world to be unpredictable. Where else but in a world filled with uncertainty would a frog speak, and speak to a powerless slave, at that? In the slave's real world, masters, angry at God knows what, might lash out at a slave at any moment. A mistress might all of a sudden find fault with her housemaid and strike out with a fist or a foot. A year or two of bad harvests might lead to a slaveholder's financial ruin, forcing him to sell some of his slaves. This might separate parent from child, husband from wife, brother from sister.

What the slave learned from the story of the talking frog was that the best defense against unpredictability was silence, the key to secrecy. Silence kept masters ignorant of everything that went on behind their backs: the food slaves stole, the religious services held in secret, the escapes made by the boldest of slaves, the anger and hatred that blacks felt toward whites. Silence protected the slave quarters. It kept the slave family and the slave's religious life removed from white invasion. In other words, the story taught the slave child how to protect African-American plantation communities.

If masters could have survived without the slave community they no doubt would have. Work, not community, was what they wanted most from slaves. Relationships that gave the slave points of reference outside of their influence were not as important as those that put the slave under their control. They did not want bonded men and women to have too many roles that were independent of that assigned to them. Therefore, to the master, the fact that African Americans were parents, preachers, or anything other than laborers was immaterial. They demand-ed, and usually got, obedient workers.

And yet, because masters and slaves were locked in a cycle of mutual depen-dency that both understood, their demands aided the development of the slave community. Slaves knew that the laws of slavery gave the master the power of life and death; and that these laws in turn made them dependent on their master's good will. But they also knew that as long as slave owners relied on them for their wealth there were limits to the slaveholder's power. Masters understood this too. They had the power of life and death over the slave, but dead slaves could not cul-tivate crops, and injured or rebellious slaves could not work. In the end both mas-ter and slave settled on an arrangement that took into account this mutual depen-dence. Though complex in its workings, the relationship that developed was really quite simple. In general, as long as slaves did their work with diligence, deference, and obedience, masters allowed them some discretion over how they spent their non-work time.

The slave family was at the center of life on the plantation, but was viewed in different ways by the master and his enslaved workers. For the master, slave families provided a means of organizing the plantation. Rather than the barrack-style living that one found in the Caribbean and Latin America, slaves in the Amer-ican South lived in quarters with their families. These living arrangements made for less rebelliousness among the slaves, a fact that masters took advantage of.

Although slave owners used the slave family to maintain control over bonded men and women, their most obvious use for the family was to reproduce the slave population. This was especially so after the foreign slave trade became illegal in 1807. After that the only legal way for a master to increase his holdings in slaves was to purchase them from another slaveholder or a slave trader, or to encourage his own slaves to have children. The latter means was preferred because it was cheap-er, easier, and the most natural—natural because slaves had their own reasons for wanting to have children, and easier because it usually did not require forceful intervention by the master.

Families therefore were in the master's best interest and fertility statistics prove it. In each year between 1800 and the Civil War more than one-fifth of the black women between the ages of fifteen and forty-four years of age bore a child. On average female slaves had their first child at age nineteen, two years before the aver-age southern white woman had hers. Slave women continued having children at two-and-a-half-year intervals until they reached the age of thirty-nine or forty. It bears repeating that this level of fertility is what made North American slavery unique in the Western Hemisphere. In most other places slave owners relied heav-ily on purchasing new slaves from Africa.

To say that slave owners depended on natural increase is not to say that they did not try hard to manipulate family formation. In addition to the verbal prodding to encourage young women to reproduce, slave owners used more subtle techniques

Children were given chores at an early age. Here, women and children work and play in front of their cabins during a break.

as part of the management of their plantations. For example, most, though by no means all, pregnant and nursing women did less work and received more food than non-pregnant women. Frances Kemble reported that on her husband's Georgia and South Carolina rice plantations, when children were born "certain additions of clothing and an additional weekly ration were bestowed upon the family." If inducements such as these were not sufficient to secure the cooperation of the slave of childbearing age, the master always had recourse to punishment. According to ex-slave Berry Clay, "a barren women was separated from her husband and usually sold." And it was not uncommon for slaveholders to demand their money back for female slaves they had purchased who later proved incapable of giving birth.

Because most slaves themselves wanted a family life, they actively sought out their own mates and did what they could to make the family a stable unit. It was hard, of course. The slave master's power was disruptive. But it was the family that softened the impact of that power. The family was the buffer that stood between the master and the individual slave.

Only in the eyes of the law and the master were slave marriages not binding. For slaves who had chosen their own spouses, marriage vows were sacred. It did not matter that the ceremony was often a simple ritual, sometimes accompanied by the act of jumping over a broom to symbolize the beginning of domestic living together. For slaves, it was attended with reverence.

And for good reason. The family gave the slave a point of reference that did not begin and end with the master. It gave bonded men and women the role of parent. It gave their children the sibling role, which evolved into the roles of aunt and uncle. With the family, slaves became providers and protectors for their spouses and their children. If parents were lucky enough to survive into old age without being separated, and usually it was a mother surviving with a daughter, then the mother could count on her daughter's care. Clearly, family life happened within the constraints of slavery, but the little room left by the master's dependence on the slave allowed it to happen nevertheless.

Courtship patterns show how the slave community and the family absorbed so much of the pain and desperation of slavery. For instance, during the week the clothes of field workers were tattered and dirty, but on Sundays slaves wore their best clothing. This made a real difference in their otherwise dreary lives, especially the lives of slave women. On Sundays they wore dresses that had been packed all week in sweet-smelling flowers and herbs, dresses perfumed to attract the opposite sex. Ex-slave Gus Feaster had pleasant remembrances of the women who "took their hair down outen the strings," who charmed the men "wid honeysuckle and rose petals hid in dere bosoms," and who "dried chennyberries and painted dem and wo'em on a string around dere necks." If courtship allowed for feminine expression, it also gave men the opportunity to demonstrate masculinity in a domain not controlled by the master. When these courtship rituals resulted in marriage, the slave could count on an even greater variety of roles, not to mention a new kind of companionship. From each other, slave husbands and wives could count on compassion.

In what was, by necessity, an egalitarian marital relationship, both parents provided what extras they could for each other, their children, and other relatives. As parents, slaves also educated their children. Part of that education included teaching the children how to become good parents and providers when they grew older. Fathers took pride in teaching their sons how to trap wild turkeys and rabbits, how to run down and catch raccoons, how to build canoes out of great oak logs. Mothers taught their daughters how to quilt and sew, and hunt and fish, too. Both parents told their kids the animal stories that taught so many lessons about how to live in a cruel and uncertain world. And usually, at their own peril, both parents did what they could to show their children how to protect their own. A case in point involved the mother of Fannie Moore. With pride, Moore recalled that in the face of hatred from "de old overseer," her mother stood up for her children and would not let them be beaten. For that "she get more whippin . . . dan anythin' else."

Lest we err on the side of idealism, it should be remembered that for all the good the family could do for the slave it could also be a source of heartbreak and did in

HEWLETT & BRIGHT.

SALE OF

VALUABLE

SLAVES,

(On account of departure)

The Owner of the following named and valuable Slaves, being on the eve of departure for Europe, will cause the same to be offered for sale, at the NEW EXCHANGE, corner of St. Louis and Chartres streets, on *Saturday,* May 16, at Twelve o'Clock, *viz.*

1. **SARAH, a mulatress, aged 45** years, a good cook and accustomed to house work in general, is an excellent and faithful nurse for sick persons, and in every respect a first rate character.

2. **DENNIS, her son, a mulatto, aged 24 years, a first rate cook** and steward for a vessel, having been in that capacity for many years on board one of the Mobile packets; is strictly honest, temperate, and a first rate subject.

3. **CHOLE, a mulatress, aged 36 years,** she is, without exception, one of the most competent servants in the country, a first rate washer and ironer, does up lace, a good cook, and for a bachelor who wishes a house-keeper she would be invaluable; she is also a good ladies' maid, having travelled to the North in that capacity.

4. **FANNY, her daughter, a mulatress, aged 16** years, speaks French and English, is a superior hair-dresser, (pupil of Guilliac,) a good seamstress and ladies' maid, is smart, intelligent, and a first rate character.

5. **DANDRIDGE, a mulatoo, aged 26 years,** a first rate dining-room servant, a good painter and rough carpenter, and has but few equals for honesty and sobriety.

6. **NANCY, his wife, aged about 24 years,** a confidential house servant, good seamstress, mantuamaker and tailoress, a good cook, washer and ironer, etc.

7. **MARY ANN, her child, a creole, aged 7** years, speaks French and English, is smart, active and intelligent.

8. **FANNY or FRANCES, a mulatress, aged 22** years, is a first rate washer and ironer, good cook and house servant, and has an excellent character.

9. **EMMA, an orphan, aged 10 or 11 years,** speaks French and English, has been in the country 7 years, has been accustomed to waiting on table, sewing etc.; is intelligent and active.

10. **FRANK, a mulatto, aged about 32 years** speaks French and English, is a first rate hostler and coachman, understands perfectly well the management of horses, and is, in every respect, a first rate character, with the exception that he will occasionally drink, though not an habitual drunkard.

All the above named Slaves are acclimated and excellent subjects; they were purchased by their present vendor many years ago, and will, therefore, be severally warranted against all vices and maladies prescribed by law, save and except FRANK, who is fully guaranteed in every other respect but the one above mentioned.

TERMS:—One-half Cash, and the other half in notes at Six months, drawn and endorsed to the satisfaction of the Vendor, with special mortgage on the Slaves until final payment. The Acts of Sale to be passed before WILLIAM BOSWELL, *Notary Public,* at the expense of the Purchaser.

New-Orleans, May 13, 1835.

When the owner of these slaves moved to Europe, he auctioned off his slaves individually. Slave families lived with the constant fear that they could be torn apart or sold away from one another at any moment.

fact lessen resistance to the master. Few men who had romantic relationships with women escaped without wounded pride, enduring anger, and a diminished sense of manhood. Louis Hughes stood stark still, blood boiling, as his master choked his wife for talking back to the mistress. His wife was subsequently tied to a joist in a barn and beaten while he stood powerless to do anything for her. The family was also the scene of domestic violence. When Ellen Botts's mother showed up in the kitchen of a sugar plantation with a lump on her head it was because her hot-tempered husband had put it there. And for all that parents could do for their off-spring, they could not shield them from the painful realities of perpetual servitude, from the whip, or from the knowledge that whatever instructions they gave them, masters and mistresses had the ultimate authority.

And yet in the slave's view, the family, with all that could go wrong with it, was the most important unit on the plantation. So much so that when family members were separated by sale or death, unrelated members of the slave community filled in as kin. If a child was left motherless or fatherless an aunt or uncle or close friend "adopted" the child and became its mother or father. Older community members became grandparents to children who had none. When men from Upper South slave states like Virginia and North Carolina were sold to the new Lower South states of Mississippi, Alabama, and Arkansas they created brothers and sisters of slaves who, like themselves, had been separated from their real family. Always there was this familial bonding, always the search for an identity that made the slave more than a beast of burden.

The slave's sacred world, reflected in song, music, religion, and folk beliefs, was another space African Americans created apart from the realm of the slave master. Like the family, the sacred world put distance between the master and the slave. It prevented legal slavery from taking over the soul. Even more than the family, which could after all be split apart and affected in other ways by whites, the sacred world, the world that grew from the spirit, inhabited an untouchable sphere.

But as they did with the slave's family, slaveholders tried to control it and use it to their advantage. They especially tried to use religion as a means of social control. "You will find," wrote Thomas Affleck in his instructions to overseers, "that an hour devoted every Sabbath morning to [slaves'] moral and religious instruction would prove a great aid to you in bringing about a better state of things amongst the Negroes." From the slaveholder's point of view a better state of things meant more obedience, less stealing, more hard work. Slave testimony reveals that white preachers always stressed these points. Hannah Scott resented it: "All he say is 'bedience to de white folks, and we hears 'nough of dat without him tellin' us." The religion the masters ordered for the slave was not only meant to directly control the slave; it was also an attempt to make slavery safer and legitimate. It was no mere coincidence that masters began hiring preachers in great numbers around 1830, the same time that the pro-slavery argument was pushed with greater intensity. Both eased the sometimes troubled mind of the slave master. Religious instruction

A plantation owner and his family attend church services with their slaves. Slaveholders tried to use religion as a tool to more fully dominate the lives of their slaves.

gave slaveholders the means of imparting their own code of morality, while it also gave them a way to prove to themselves that they were really trying to uplift those they had declared barbaric heathens. The thought that religion could make slavery safer by making slaves less rebellious was an additional source of psychic comfort. For masters who feared that slave ownership dammed their own souls, the religious instruction they gave their slaves was the means by which they hoped to redeem themselves.

Masters made similar use of other aspects of the slave's sacred world. Slave song, for instance, was taken by them and their families as evidence of the slaves' happiness. On some plantations the slave's music even became the centerpiece of entertainment, with blacks asked to perform their spirituals and play their instruments before invited white guests. These performances lent the appearance of master and slave locked in harmonious bliss, each content with their status and rank, each satisfied with their particular "place."

Appearances, though, were deceiving, especially to the master. Slave religion, and the song that was an integral part of it, reflected a world the master could not see. They were the outward manifestation of a worldview possessed by black people. Together with folk beliefs and slave tales, religion and music demonstrated not that slaves were content, nor that slavery was safe. The sacred world of black people demonstrated the indomitable strength of the spirit.

Christianity is a prime example. It was given to slaves one way, but digested another. African Americans took at face value the idea that all men were equal in the sight of God. Because they did, they could not take seriously the white preacher's text "slaves obey your masters." If God was the all-powerful Master with no one, not even the slave master, above Him, and if all men and women were God's children, without regard to rank and station in life, then all God's children were equal, white and black alike. All, including the slave owner, had to answer to a higher authority.

Slaves believed that the slaveholder, not the slave, was the sinner, and the Bible gave them the evidence that they were right. Hadn't God sent Moses to deliver the Israelites out of bondage? Had he not punished the Egyptians for enslaving his chosen people? Had he not sent his son, Jesus, to redeem the world, and was not Jesus, like the slave, a humble sufferer, a servant? By identifying with the Israelites and with Jesus, the slave turned the master into the sinner and gave himself the inner strength that flowed from the belief in his own salvation in the next world. In his everyday world, this inner strength gave the slave enough psychic freedom to resist becoming completely subservient to white people.

The deliverance slaves prayed for was not just for the next world. They wanted to be free in this world, and many of the sacred songs contained elements of protest and messages of liberation. For example, when Frederick Douglass, and many of his fellow slaves, sang "O Canaan, sweet Canaan, / I am bound for the land of Canaan," they were singing not only about someday going to heaven, but about reaching the North. The North was also the implied destination in the song "Run to Jesus, shun the danger, / I don't expect to stay much longer here." In the same vein, when slaves sang "Steal Away to Jesus," they were just as likely to be announcing a secret worship service as they were to be talking about salvation. The service, under the direction of preachers African Americans themselves chose, gave slaves a sense of independence, a kind of freedom, and the courage to resist and escape slavery altogether.

Folk beliefs, another crucial part of the slaves' sacred world, also instilled this sense of freedom and resistance. Although most whites, and some slaves, generally found beliefs in fortune tellers, witches, magic signs, and conjurers to be at odds with Christianity, for most slaves there was no gap between the two. The same slave who believed fervently in Jesus Christ could also believe that the dead returned to the living in spiritual visitations, that children born with teeth or as twins came under an ominous sign, that conjuring caused insanity and other illness.

In slave folk religion signs were important. A screech owl's cry was a sign of death that could be countered by turning shoes upside down at a door, or turning one's pockets inside out; a black cat crossing one's path was bad luck unless one spit on the spot where the paths met. Many slaves believed that a cross-eyed person could bring on a spell unless one crossed one's fingers and spat on them.

Dreams were also taken seriously. A former South Carolina slave reported that he dreamed he saw his three uncles skinning a cow and cutting it open while women and children sat around crying. When he told his mother about the dream she told him that fresh meat in a dream was a sign of death. "Sure enough that very evening Uncle Peter Price died." According to the former slave, his dreams came true so often that the older people on his plantation used his dreams as a way of predicting the future.

And in a way predicting was what folk beliefs were all about. Slaves lived in a world over which they had little control. For them, life held so many uncertainties, so little that was predictable. Folk beliefs provided a way of imposing order on an unstable environment. Like Christianity, slave folk beliefs could not be controlled by whites and therefore became another source of strength.

Although all slaves could make use of this power, conjurers were the people believed to have a special gift for reading signs and dreams, at effecting change through the use of spells, herb mixtures, and charms. African in origin, conjuring survived white attempts to eliminate it. Most slaves feared conjurers as much as they feared the master because they believed that these men and women could bring about all manner of bad or good luck. They could make mean masters kind and kind masters mean, prevent or cause whippings, separations, illness, or death, ensure love and happiness or friction and hate. They were especially known for the evil they could do.

Rather than submit to the cures of white medical doctors brought in by masters, African Americans usually preferred to treat their own illnesses and make their own medicines. They had good reason. Because early nineteenth-century medicine was hardly an exact science, the medical practitioners' treatment was likely to be as successful as that applied by black root and herb doctors. Slaves looked to their own when they were sick or in need of spiritual guidance. Because they did, they strengthened their own community and gave men and women a chance to gain status in their own group.

Without their community to confirm and reinforce their families, religion, and folk beliefs, the individual slaves would have had only the master's definition of their existence. As it was, slave children did learn at an early age that they were among the world's weak and powerless. But through the slave tales they learned how to survive and circumvent the powerful. They belonged to a community that, though powerless, put psychological space between themselves and the whites around them.

Fit for Freedom

Sometime around 1833, Frederick Douglass looked out across the Chesapeake Bay with his mind bent on freedom. He asked himself, "O why was I born a man, of whom to make a brute!" The more he thought, the more he knew he wanted his freedom:

The Fugitive's Song was composed in 1845 as a tribute to Frederick Douglass, who had escaped from slavery in 1833 to become a revered abolitionist, newspaper editor, and lecturer.

> Why am I a slave? I will run away. I will not stand it. Get caught or get clear. I'll try it. . . . I have only one life to lose. I had as well be killed running as die standing. . . . It cannot be that I shall live and die a slave.

For all the millions of slaves who at one time or another had these thoughts, only about a thousand a year actually acted on them. This is because escape was incredibly difficult. Slaves like Douglass, who were in the Upper South, close to free states, stood the best chance of success. Those close to southern cities also had a good chance, for if they escaped to an urban area they could become lost in its hustle and bustle, as well as in its free black community. Slaves who accompanied their masters and mistresses on northern trips were also likely runaways, but like any slave they had to have the will to run. This will had to be more powerful than the fear of a brutal whipping or sale away from family and loved ones, more powerful even than the fear of death.

Douglass found he had the needed will when one day he refused to be whipped. His master had hired him out for a year to a man named Edward Covey, who was widely known for his ability to break the spirit of unruly slaves. Covey had almost succeeded in working and beating Douglass into the most abject obedience when Douglass by chance visited a conjurer, who gave him a root reputed to prevent whippings. As he was told to do, Douglass kept the root in his right pocket. The next time Covey tried to beat him he seized Covey around the throat, flung him to the ground, declared that he would no longer be treated as a brute, and fought off the other slaves Covey got to assist him. The fight continued for two hours, but in the end Douglass won out over Covey, and he was never again whipped by him or any other white man.

The victory Douglass won over Covey was small compared to the one he had won over his own fear. As he put it, "I felt as I never felt before. . . . My long crushed spirit rose, cowardice departed, bold defiance took its place; and I now resolved that, however long I might remain a slave in form, the day had passed forever when I could be a slave in fact." Four years later Douglass escaped from slavery and found his way to New York.

But the records of slavery show that few fled slavery as Douglass did. Fewer still participated in large-scale rebellions aimed at overthrowing the institution. There were, however, many slaves who took a stand against their servitude, who somehow managed to be slaves in form but not in fact. These were men and women who resisted the worst aspects of slavery. Some, like Douglass, refused to be whipped; some ran away for short periods of time. Some feigned ignorance of how to do a particular chore and others feigned illness rather than work to the limits that the master wanted. Still others used individual acts of violence to counter the authority of the master.

Unlike running away, this kind of resistance only separated the slave from the worst aspects of slavery. Its end was not liberty, just release from some of slavery's misery. However, like the slave family, slave Christianity, and folk religion, it nevertheless helped African Americans survive this most inhuman institution. Resistance of all types proved that black people were fit for freedom.

Whatever other circumstance came together in the life of a slave to make him or her commit an act of individual resistance, one thing is for sure: the slave who resisted did not stand in perpetual abject fear of their master, nor did the slave completely lose those qualities which made him or her a whole human being.

Slaves who stole extra food, for example, cared enough about their own well-being to defy the slaveholders' rationing system. Slaves who risked their lives in their struggle not to be whipped were making a personal statement about their self-esteem and individual honor. Women who kicked and clawed their sexual abusers made eloquent statements about their personal dignity. These individual acts of resistance were attempts to retain or take back some control over lives that were by law assigned to someone else.

Nowhere is this more apparent than the attempts by some slaves to get enough to eat. The usual fare on most farms and plantations from Virginia to Mississippi was salt pork and corn meal. When they could, slaves supplemented this with vegetables grown in their own gardens, and meat and fish they caught. Most slaves needed more and most stole what they needed. Many did not view stealing from the master as something sinful. Whether they stole clothing, money, crops, or food, slaves often justified their actions with the argument that not only had they worked for the goods, but they were simply moving them from one part of the master's property to another.

This thinking was especially obvious during the Civil War. Those who fled to Union troops taking their master's goods with them felt that the promised time of retribution had arrived. Southern mistress Adele Pettigru Allston probably made an accurate assessment of the slave's attitude when she complained: "The conduct of the negroes in robbing our house, store room, meat house, etc., and refusing to restore anything shows you they *think it right* to steal from us, to spoil us, as the Israelites did the Egyptians."

Many slaves did not wait until the Civil War to act this way. Besides stealing, they burned gin houses, barns, corncribs, and smokehouses. Some slaves used poison or outright physical force to kill their masters. Capture always meant certain death, but they did it nonetheless.

To guard against violence, especially that which could lead to large-scale rebellions, slaveholders created the slave patrols. These were groups of white males, usually of the lower classes, called together to look for runaways, to prevent slave gatherings, and generally ensure the safety of the white community. Since slaves were not allowed to travel the countryside without a pass from their master, a principal task of the patrols was to enforce the pass system. This they often did with excessive brutality, administering beatings on the authority given them by slaveholders who used the patrol system as a way of binding all whites together against all blacks.

Despite the patrol system slaves resisted. They used passes written by the few in their own group who could read and write. They sheltered runaways in their cabins, and they laid traps that tripped up patrollers' horses.

Some slaves just stood and fought. Some found the courage to escape, and many more found the will to try. Georgia slave John Brown ran away several times before he finally succeeded. One time he got as far as Tennessee; another time, thinking he was going north, he traveled almost all of the way on foot to New Orleans. Each time he was captured he was whipped, chained, and had bells attached to him. Over and over again he escaped until he finally reached Indiana. Aunt Cheyney of the Kilpatrick cotton plantation in Mississippi was not so fortunate, however. One of her master's mistresses, she had recently given birth to the fourth of her master's children when she ran away. Kilpatrick set his dogs on her trail. When they caught up with her he ordered them to attack. According to her friend Mary Reynolds, "The dogs tore her naked and et the breasts plumb off her body." This served as a punishment for Cheyney, but it was also Kilpatrick's way of warning all slaves, especially women, against running away.

However much African Americans were haunted by these kinds of horrors, there were still those who would not be stopped. The stories of escape reveal as much relentless perseverance as they do ingenuity. Henry "Box" Brown, for example, was carried for twenty-seven hours from Richmond to Philadelphia by Adams Express in a box three feet long and two feet deep. He literally mailed himself to freedom. The light-skinned Ellen Craft escaped by pretending to be a sickly white man traveling in the company of his slave. The slave in attendance was in fact her darker-skinned husband William. Together the two traveled by stagecoach, boat, and train from Georgia to Philadelphia. They stopped at some of the best hotels along the way, and Ellen even conversed with slaveholders about the trouble of runaway slaves.

The person who seemed to give the South the most runaway trouble, though, was Harriet Tubman. She was born a slave some time around 1821 on Maryland's Eastern Shore and lived in slavery for twenty-eight years. Like most slaves in this Upper South region, Tubman lived in dread of being sold to the Deep South. In 1849, when she learned that she was indeed going to be sold, she joined the thousands of others who took to the woods and stole themselves.

What made her unique is that she returned, not once but many times, to rescue others, including her sister, her sister's two children, and her parents. Given the identification of African Americans with the Israelites it should come as no surprise that Tubman was called "Moses." And given the way African Americans used their religion to speak about freedom, it is also not surprising that when Tubman said, "Tell my brothers to be always *watching unto prayer,* and *when the good ship Zion comes along, to be ready to step on board,*" this was her signal to leave, not for heaven, but for freedom. It is said that she returned nineteen times and rescued more than three hundred slaves. She was so good at what she did that Maryland planters offered a forty thousand dollar bounty for her capture.

Slaveholders wanted to catch Tubman about as much as they wanted to put an end to the Underground Railroad. This network of hiding places run by opponents of slavery provided the slaves fortunate enough to use it with food, shelter, money, clothing, and disguises. A black man, William Still, an officer of the Philadelphia Vigilance Committee, was the moving force behind the Underground Railroad. He wrote of Harriet Tubman that she was "a woman of no pretensions," and "in point of courage, shrewdness, and disinterested exertions to rescue her fellowman, she was without equal."

In general women had a harder time escaping than men because they were more reluctant to leave without their children. At the same time, it was the fear of losing them that often provided the incentive to flee. Escaping alone was difficult enough; escaping with children was close to impossible. There is no question that male runaways regretted leaving their wives and children behind, but women, it seems, suffered a special agony when faced with such a decision.

Truancy seems to have been the way many slave women reconciled their desire to flee with their need to stay. Men too practiced truancy, but women made the most likely truants because they nursed and were directly responsible for their children. Former slave Benjamin Johnson remembered that sometimes when women would not take a whipping they "would run away an' hide in de woods. Sometimes dey would come back after a short stay an' den dey would have to put de hounds on dere trail to bring dem back home."

Women's short-term flight was by no means a reflection of their lesser courage or greater accommodation to slavery. Truants faced punishment when they returned, punishment many braved over and over again. Moreover, truancy involved as much danger as running away. As Johnson's comment indicates, dogs hunted them down, and the woods and swamps they hid in held all kinds of dangers.

Rather than reflecting a lesser danger, or level of courage, what truancy mirrored was the different slave experiences of men and women, and therefore their different ways of resisting. For example, the division of labor on most farms and plantations conferred greater mobility on males than on female slaves. Few of the chores performed by female slaves took them off the plantation. Usually masters chose their male slaves to assist in the transportation of crops to market, and the transport of supplies and other materials to the plantation. More male than female slaves were artisans and craftsmen, and this made it more difficult to hire out a female slave than a male slave. Fewer female slaves therefore had a chance to vary their work experience. As a consequence, more men than women were able to test their survival skills under different circumstances.

Another factor affecting slave mobility was the "abroad marriage," a union between slaves who resided at different locations. When "abroad" spouses visited each other, usually once a week, it was most often the husband who traveled to the wife. All in all, it was female bondage, more than male bondage, that meant being tied to the immediate environment of the plantation or farm. For these reasons, female slaves much more than male slaves just "stayed put."

By and large, though, women did resist in subtle ways. For instance, they "played the fool" more than men. In other words, in order to avoid doing some onerous chore, they would smile humbly and pretend to misunderstand instructions given by the master, mistress, or overseer. The use of poison also suited women because they officiated as cooks and nurses on the plantation. As early as 1755 a Charleston slave woman was burned at the stake for poisoning her master, and in 1769 a special issue of the *South Carolina Gazette* carried the story of a slave woman who had poisoned her master's infant child. Since the slave's objective was not to get caught we will never really know just how many whites were ushered by slave women to an early grave.

We also will never know how many instances of illness were actually ruses to escape backbreaking labor. Women had an advantage over men in this realm because childbearing was a primary expectation that slave owners had of slave women. In an age where women's diseases were still shrouded in mystery, getting the maximum amount of work from women of childbearing age while remaining confident that no damage was done to their reproductive organs was a guessing game that few white slave owners wanted to play or could afford to lose. In deference to their "mysterious" conditions, women, especially those of childbearing age, were seldom designated as able-bodied workers. Unlike healthy young and middle-aged men who were considered full hands, women, depending on their stage of pregnancy and their frequency of nursing, were labeled three-quarter hands, half hands or quarter hands. Men could and did feign illness. But since women did, in fact, have more sickness because of menstruation and childbirth, they were more likely to get away with it.

Whether they also got away with birth control and abortion is something we will never know. Few nineteenth-century women, white or black, were ignorant of the ways and means of avoiding pregnancy. The decline in the birthrate among white Americans from 7.04 in 1800 to 3.56 by the eve of the twentieth century is evidence of the use of birth control, including abortion. For white women, particularly those of the urban middle classes, a small family had its benefits, not the least of which was the lower risk of dying in childbirth and the ability to spend more time with an individual child.

The slave woman, however, had no such benefit. In fact, though she, like other nineteenth-century women, approached pregnancy with fear and never had enough time to spend with any of her children, she risked sale if she remained childless. The risk notwithstanding, some women just refused to have children. How they managed to stay childless, what methods of birth control they used, and the frequency of abortion, remained secrets that were virtually exclusive to the female world of the slave quarters.

Though few slave women divulged these secrets, slaveholders were convinced that black women knew how to avoid pregnancy and also how to bring on a miscarriage. A Tennessee physician, Dr. John H. Morgan, wrote that slave women used the herbs of tansy and rue, the roots and seeds of the cotton plant, cedar berries, and camphor to bring about miscarriage, and Dr. E. M. Pendleton claimed that planters regularly complained of whole families of women who fail to have any children.

More serious were the infrequent cases of infanticide. Women who chose to kill children they had risked their life having were clearly desperate. Yet they struck out at the system where they knew it would hurt, where they knew they had real impact—in the increase of the slave population. That they hurt themselves more than they hurt the master can be assumed, for they were either prosecuted and hanged, or they suffered emotional distress forever.

If African Americans could have overthrown the system that forced such tragic decisions, they would have. But black people faced hopeless odds. Unlike other slaves in other nations in the Americas, black people in the United States were overwhelmingly outnumbered by whites and grouped in small numbers on plantations that were miles apart. Whites had the guns, the ammunition, the horses, the dogs, and the law. They had the resources to crush any revolt by slaves, and the slaves knew it. Resistance, therefore, was individual because it had to be; whites put down the few large-scale rebellions and planned revolts with a viciousness that served notice that revolt was futile.

In spite of the odds and the repression, rebellions did occur, and conspiracies abounded. Among the first was the largest—an uprising in 1811 of close to four hundred slaves in St. Charles and St. John the Baptist parishes in Louisiana. Led by a slave named Charles Deslondes, the slaves sent whites fleeing their plantations for safety in New Orleans. Further east, in 1817 and 1818 blacks joined the Seminole Indians in their fight to keep their Florida homelands. To defend themselves, units of blacks and Indians raided plantations in Georgia, killing whites and carrying off slaves. Again in 1835 blacks joined the Seminoles in their unsuccessful fight against the militias of Florida, Georgia, and Tennessee. Seminole lands had continued to be havens for runaway slaves, and by the 1830s President Andrew Jackson was determined to eliminate these independent communities and seize all Indian lands for white slaveholders. By that time, though, it was hard to call Seminole land Indian territory because blacks and Indians had intermarried to the extent that they were indistinguishable. Indeed, so many hundreds of blacks fought on the side of the Seminoles that United States general Thomas Jesup declared: "This, you may be assured, is a negro, not an Indian war."

General Jesup understood what all slaveholders knew—that resistance had always gone hand in hand with slavery. The century had begun with Gabriel Prosser's attempt to seize Richmond, and the year he died, 1800, was the year that Denmark Vesey bought his freedom from his master and began his life as a free man. That same year Nat Turner was born. Both men were to become the slaveholder's worst nightmare.

Vesey was a free African-American carpenter who worked hard enough to become not just self-supporting but relatively wealthy by the standards of the day. He was a proud, literate, free black man who hated slavery and hated to see his people bowing and scraping to whites. At age fifty-three he gathered around him trusted black men, both free and slave, and planned to capture the city of Charleston. His followers were church leaders and craftsmen. One of them, Gullah Jack, was a conjurer. For months they planned their attack on the arsenal at Charleston and on plantations surrounding the city. During this time they recruited slaves and free men who had the steady nerves to carry out the plan. Then, on a fateful day in 1822, they were betrayed. Betrayal meant capture, and capture meant death. Peter Poyas, one of Vesey's lieutenants, went to the galleys with the words of the spirituals on his lips. "Fear not," he told the blacks of Charleston, "the Lord God that delivered Daniel is able to deliver us."

Nat Turner believed himself to be the deliverer. He carried himself in the manner of a messiah. Proud and self-confident, literate and articulate, he saw visions of God's deliverance of black people from bondage. He felt himself to be the Moses who would lead his people out of bondage. Acting on that feeling, Turner led about seventy slaves in an assault on the whites of Southampton, Virginia. In one of the most clear-cut cases of slave rebellion that occurred in this country, Nat Turner went from one plantation to the next killing whites. His instructions to his fellow insurrectionists were followed to the letter. They spared no one. Age and sex made no difference.

In the end Nat Turner was caught. By the time his murder count reached around sixty, bands of white men caught up with his men and put down the revolt. Turner took to the woods and managed to evade capture until most of his men had been put to death. As had happened in the Prosser and Vesey conspiracies, the fear of insurrection spread across the South with alarming speed, and whites lashed out mercilessly at blacks, especially those in the vicinity of the rebellion. Anyone suspected of aiding Turner was put to death. All acts of disrespect were taken as a direct challenge to white authority, and slaves who did not act in the most humble manner were punished severely, even killed. Blacks were not allowed to hold religious services or gather in groups at all. All blacks, slave and free, were watched by patrols who had their numbers increased and firearms ready. The message was clear. America was home to the free and the brave, but only for those who were white.

Somewhere though, deep down, slaveholders understood that as long as slavery existed so too would resistance. This is one of the reasons why nineteenth-century slaveholders tried to improve the material conditions of the slaves. They thought that more food, better living quarters, and fewer whippings would make slaves less rebellious and more content and willing to bear all of slavery's burdens.

African Americans did bear slavery's burdens, but not without resistance. The continuing struggle against slavery created the psychic space black people needed to survive, and it proved to contemporary and future generations that though enslaved, African Americans were fit for freedom.

A Different Kind of Freedom

On April 8, 1816, April Ellison, a mulatto expert cotton gin maker, stood with his white master, William Ellison, before a magistrate and five freeholders of the Fairfield District of South Carolina. It was a solemn occasion. No doubt every word, every movement became indelibly etched in April's mind, because it was the day of his manumission, the day that he bought himself out of slavery. At that time, April was twenty-six years old. By the time he was thirty he had legally changed his name to William, had bought his wife, Matilda, and his daughter, Eliza Ann, out of slavery, and had freed them. He had moved out of the district of his slave youth and established himself as a free person of color in Stateburg, in the Sumpter District. And he had bought two adult male slaves to help him in his business. Two years later, in 1822, he bought an acre of land, and two years after this he petitioned and received permission from the white members of Holy Cross Episcopal Church to worship with them on the main floor of the vestry, away from the slaves and free blacks who were confined to the balcony.

Elizabeth Hobbs, an attractive mulatto, was born into slavery in 1818, a year after Frederick Douglass's birth. She was born in Virginia, but in her teenage years she was sold further south to a North Carolina master by whom she had a son. Repurchased by a member of the family that had sold her to begin with, she was taken to St. Louis, Missouri, where she met and married a black man named James Keckley. Though Keckley told her that he was free, he was in fact a slave, and their life together was a short one. Far more long-term in its consequences were Elizabeth Keckley's abilities as a seamstress, skills perfected at her mother's instruction when she was just a child. As a dressmaker in St. Louis, she was so good, and so popular, that her customers offered to lend her the money to buy herself and her son out of slavery. In 1855, when she was thirty-seven years old, Keckley and her son became free persons of color. After she learned to read and write and paid off her loan, she returned east, first to Baltimore then to Washington, D.C. In Washington, her clients were among the city's elite, the most notable being President Lincoln's wife, Mary Todd, to whom she became a companion and friend.

While Keckley was keeping the company of the First Lady, Sojourner Truth was aiding and nursing refugee slaves fleeing the carnage of the Civil War. At the war's beginning she was sixty-one years old and had in her lifetime been a housekeeper, a preacher, an abolitionist, and a public speaker for women's rights. A dark-skinned woman, she had been born Isabella Bomefree about 1799, and was freed in 1827 by New York State law. Unlike Keckley or Ellison, Truth never learned to read or write, nor did the South ever hold her as a slave. Nonetheless she was eloquent in her attacks against slavery, and more than anyone else of her time, she was steadfast in her public defense of black women.

The lives of William Ellison, Elizabeth Keckley, and Sojourner Truth tell us a lot

A certificate signed by an Illinois county clerk was granted to a free black woman to certify her claim to freedom. Free blacks always had to keep such documents close by to avoid being sold into slavery by unscrupulous slave traders.

about the lives of all blacks who were free during the time of slavery. More than anything else, their lives, and those of all free African Americans, reveal that black freedom and white freedom were always very different.

The reason for the different realities of black and white freedom was white prejudice. It was strong in the South, where ninety percent of all blacks were slaves and a dark skin was a presumption of bondage. It was equally strong in the North and West where there was an abiding sentiment against both blacks and slavery. What

Fanny Kemble, a well-traveled white woman, said of free blacks in the North held true all over the country. "They are not slaves indeed, but they are pariahs, debarred from every fellowship save with their own despised race. . . . All hands are extended to thrust them out, all fingers point at their dusky skin, all tongues . . . have learned to turn the very name of their race into an insult and a reproach."

That some African Americans had a heritage of freedom that predated the American Revolution was of far less significance to whites than the fact that they were black. As the nineteenth century progressed and the country moved closer and closer to the Civil War, a dark skin carried the presumption of slavery in both the North and the South. More and more, free blacks had to prove that they were not slaves. This was a burden that no white person carried, because white skin color carried with it the presumption of freedom.

After the American Revolution, the free black population numbered 59,000 in 1790 and grew to 488,000 by the eve of the Civil War. These numbers were increased by blacks born of free mothers, including those of white women with black partners, and free mulatto immigrants from the West Indies, especially those who fled Haiti after the 1790 slave revolt led by Toussaint L'Ouverture. Every year natural increase added to their numbers.

When newly freed blacks chose their new names, they sometimes picked those that reflected their complexion. There were thus many Browns and Blacks among the freed population. Sometimes the name reflected their occupation. For example, the literal meaning of Sojourner Truth is traveling preacher. Indeed, Truth's oratorical skills were renowned and she used them in the cause of Christianity as well as abolitionism and women's rights. Henry Mason, for example, was a bricklayer, Charles Green was a gardener, and Thomas Smith could have been a blacksmith or a silversmith. Other former slaves chose the names of liberty. There were names like Justice, and many chose the name Freeman as a mark of their new identity.

In addition to signifying a new identity, the name chosen by these free men and women reflected their evaluation of their chances of success. Those who took the name of their craft, for instance, probably felt good about prospering economically. The few like William Ellison, who took their master's name, no doubt saw advantages in their choices, too. In a world where a black skin was inhibiting, white men could ease the way to economic independence. Ellison knew this. His business making cotton gins was built as much on his own skills as on the Ellison name, a name associated with one of the wealthiest planters in a region where such wealthy planters had a need for his skill and product.

More than keeping his master's name, Ellison also kept his attachment to his master by staying fairly close to him, something most freed slaves avoided. Ellison's choice no doubt had a lot to do with the fact that his master was probably also his father. Though he did move about fifty miles to another town, this was far less of a move than that made by many freed people. Of course, runaways had to flee because their lives depended on it. But legally emancipated slaves also left the

A badge issued to a freed black living in Charleston, South Carolina. Both freed blacks and slaves were required to wear these identification badges.

area where they had been enslaved. Some just needed to test their mobility as a way of demonstrating their liberty. Others migrated to areas where they knew they had friends and family. Still others left for only a short while, returning *because* of the familiarity they had with the area and the people. Above all, they tried to get out from under their former master's supervision. The best way to do that was to move.

And yet, for black Americans freedom did not mean total liberty. Those who moved to rural areas found it difficult to make freedom work for them. In the South, rural free blacks who were not attached to plantations as carpenters, blacksmiths, coopers, and the like, rented land, equipment, and supplies and tried to eke out a living by growing and selling their crops. Very few were successful. White landowners charged exorbitant rates for the rental of land and just one mediocre harvest could put a free black family far into debt. African Americans in this situation were forced to go to prison or, to meet their debts, sign over their future crops to the landowner. In either case they became peons, people tied to the land. They either had to work forever for the person whose land they rented or be imprisoned. If they went to jail they were subsequently hired out and forced to work for the person the authorities had sold their labor to, to persons willing to pay their debts. Either way many rural free blacks found themselves in virtual servitude.

Faced with the choice of renting land under such unfavorable circumstances or signing labor contracts, most rural free blacks opted for the latter. But this too put them in slavelike circumstances. Most contracts specified that free Negroes work according to the same rules governing slave hands. Thus when Aaron Griggs hired himself to a Louisiana planter he pledged "to work as one of the hands of the plantation." He pledged also not to leave the plantation during his term of service, "to go out to the fields at the same hours with the people of the plantation & to work with the plantation overseer." In all likelihood Griggs got the same amount of food and clothing as the slaves, but since he had to pay for them at prices set by his employer he found himself at the end of the year in debt to the very person who he had worked for like a slave.

Free blacks who succeeded in the rural South were the rare exception. William Ellison falls into this category. His skill as a ginmaker made him indispensable to white planters. He was therefore able to make freedom work for him. But Ellison also had other advantages. He was light skinned, and whites, especially those in the Lower South, showed a definite tolerance for blacks who were close to them in skin color.

It was not just a matter of standards of beauty. A light color signified a birth connection to a white person. Although there were enough whites who believed that one drop of Negro blood made one a Negro, there were also many white men who had fathered mulattoes, and some white women who had given birth to them. These white parents were often reluctant to leave their children totally exposed to racist hostility. They thus protected them by providing for some education or training in a trade. The industriousness of these free persons of color made some white South Carolinians feel safe in their presence. As a group of white men who signed an 1822 Charleston petition put it, mulattoes were "a barrier between our own color and that of the black."

For sure, Ellison made the most of this sentiment. Records show, for instance, that he was probably the son either of his master or of his master's father. It was this blood connection that saved him from becoming an ordinary field hand on the cotton plantations owned by his relatives. That he took the name of his masters, and identified with them in every way, even to the extent of holding slaves, is quite understandable.

Since most free blacks lacked Ellison's advantages, they had to find other ways of surviving. In both the North and the South the cities held more opportunities for African Americans than rural areas did. This is where most of the unskilled jobs were, and since, unlike Keckley or Ellison, most free African Americans were unskilled laborers, the city was the place to find work.

It was also a place to find other free blacks and begin the task of making new friends and building a new life. In the cities free blacks had more choices than they had in rural areas. There they could join a black church and worship the way they wanted. They could send their children to a school set up by that church or the school established by the benevolent society that they might also belong to. In the city they could hold celebrations. They could go to the grog shops or bars, or attend a show, or even bury their dead in a service under their own direction. They could do so, moreover, away from the constant supervising eyes of white slaveholders.

Small wonder then that by 1860, on the eve of the Civil War, free blacks could be described as the most urban of all of America's people. In the South more than a third of the free black population dwelled in cities or towns, although only fifteen percent of the whites and about five percent of the slaves lived in cities. In the North, Boston, New York, Cincinnati, and Philadelphia held the bulk of the free black population.

Opportunities prevailed in antebellum urban America but not without struggle. As in rural areas, blacks faced obstacles. Everywhere they turned they encountered white suspicion, competition, and hostility. Opposition to them was so fierce, and their freedom was so restricted, that like free rural African Americans it is more apt to describe their condition not as free but as quasi-free.

Most cities and states, in fact, tried hard to limit the size of the free black population, and where possible, to eliminate it. This effort began early in the 1800s and could be traced to the waning of the revolutionary fervor over liberty, the rise of cotton, and the resulting demand for slaves. Specifically, as the nation settled into its growing-up stage, and as its economy became more and more fueled by the money made from cotton production, anything that threatened slavery, the institution upon which cotton production was based, was perceived as dangerous.

By white standards, therefore, free blacks were dangerous. They threatened to disrupt the existing order because they contradicted the pro-slavery argument that Negroes could not survive without white supervision. They also threatened slavery because they had a vested interest in slavery's elimination. Not only did most have bitter memories of their time in slavery, but most had relatives or friends still in bondage. Moreover, as long as slavery existed, and as long as most blacks were slaves, all blacks were presumed slave, even free blacks. Free African Americans therefore had every reason to want—and work toward—slavery's elimination.

Antebellum whites had a totally different mindset. In the North, South, and West, whites who were skilled artisans and common workers feared free African Americans. Thanks to the 1820 Missouri Compromise, slavery was outlawed north of the 36th parallel. Northern and western white laborers, therefore, did not have to compete against slave labor, a competition they could never win because they could not sell their labor as cheaply as the slave who, of course, worked for nothing. The free black, though, was a formidable competitor because discrimination forced African Americans to sell their labor for less than it was worth. It was in the white laborer's interest, therefore, to eliminate all black competition however he could.

One way he did this was by refusing to work alongside blacks. Frederick Douglass ran into this problem when, as a fugitive from slavery, he moved to New Bedford, Massachusetts, and sought work as a caulker. Employers would not hire him because they risked losing all their white employees. As Douglass explained, "I was told by an antislavery ship builder there, who had a vessel on the stocks to be caulked, that if he should even venture to send me on that ship, every white man would leave him, and he could not get her ready for sea. Go where I would, I could not get employment at my trade." Ex-slave carpenter Henry Boyd had a similar experience in Cincinnati. After days of unsuccessful job hunting, he finally found an Englishman who would hire him. When he entered the shop, though, "the workmen threw down their tools, and declared that he should leave or they would. 'They would never work with a nigger.'"

Laws restricting the movement and rights of free blacks were as effective as such impromptu attempts to limit the freedom of African Americans. In the South free blacks were forced to carry certificates of freedom on their person. If caught without one there was the danger of being claimed as a slave. In many places free blacks had to register with the police or court authorities. South Carolina, for instance, required free people of color between the ages of sixteen and sixty to pay a $2 tax each year. The tax enabled whites to know who was free and where free blacks lived. Like other Southern states, South Carolina also prohibited the migration of free blacks into the state, as well as the emancipation of slaves. These laws aimed to reduce the number of free blacks, and they did so very effectively.

A host of other laws were passed to curtail the rights of Southern free blacks. When free African Americans met in any numbers, even in church, they were required to have a white person in attendance. Southern laws also set curfews for black gatherings. Blacks were widely excluded from public parks and burial grounds, relegated to the balconies of theaters and opera houses, and barred from hotels and restaurants. Of all the Southern states only Maryland, Tennessee, and North Carolina gave free blacks the vote, but by 1835 all had repealed this right. To add insult to injury, no Southern court allowed them to serve on juries or give testimony in court against whites. And, if convicted of any crime, the punishment meted out to them was always more severe than that given to whites convicted of the same crime. Free blacks faced public whippings and, most ominous of all, enslavement, a fate whites never suffered.

Conditions in the non-slaveholding states were slightly better but got worse as one traveled from the Northeast to the Northwest. Slavery had been outlawed in the states of Ohio, Indiana, Illinois, Wisconsin, and Michigan by the Northwest Ordinance of 1787, but whites there were still prejudiced against blacks. As in the South, skilled laborers were especially fearful of black competition. To discourage black migration, Northwestern and Western states alike passed black codes that resembled the restrictive laws of slavery. Like Southern states they also required blacks to register their certificates of freedom at a county clerk's office, but here free blacks had to pay a bond of $500 or $1,000 guaranteeing that they would not disturb the peace or become a public charge. Illinois, Indiana, and Oregon actually excluded black migrants altogether.

Conditions for free blacks were probably the best in the Northeast, but even in these states restrictions were intolerable. Most qualified black voters lost the vote and social custom kept them off juries. What the law did not do, mob violence did. Blacks in Philadelphia suffered the fury of the mob as early as 1805, when dozens of white citizens turned on those gathered for a Fourth of July ceremony and drove them away from the festivities with a torrent of curses. During the 1830s and 1840s, riots occurred again in Philadelphia, and also in New York, Pittsburgh, Cincinnati, and Providence. In each case white mobs burned and looted black churches, meeting halls, and homes, and beat, stoned, and even murdered black citizens.

To survive, most African Americans found a way to work around white prejudice. Nowhere in the United States was this easy. In the Northeast, employment opportunities in the emerging industries went almost entirely to whites who used every means, including violence, to keep their economic advantage. Blacks could find jobs only at the bottom of the job ladder as common laborers. They loaded ships, dug wells, graves, and house foundations, and toiled as sweepers, porters, ashmen, chimney sweeps, and bootblacks.

Paradoxically, economic opportunities increased for free blacks the further south one went into slave country. Not only were there fewer skilled and unskilled white immigrant laborers in the South, but white employers were accustomed to hiring blacks to do work that white men would not do. Free blacks, therefore, were able to eke out a living even though they faced competition from both slaves and native-born whites. For example, nowhere in the South would white men cut hair. Free blacks therefore acquired a monopoly on the barbering trade. In Charleston, skilled white carpenters, tailors, and millwrights were scarce, leaving these occupations to be filled by free blacks. Blacks also found employment in Southern industries, usually in the least-skilled positions. In Richmond, for instance, half the employed Negro men labored in tobacco factories, paper mills, and iron foundries.

Free black urban women did not have as many opportunities as their male counterparts. Elizabeth Keckley was exceptional. Both North and South, few blacks owned their own businesses or commanded their own time. Most worked in the service trades as laundresses, cooks, and maids. Even in this kind of work they faced competition from native-born white women of the poorer classes, and as the period progressed, from immigrant women, especially those from Ireland. Like free black men, though, they worked longer hours than the average white person, and longer hours than the average white woman, who often did not work at all. With some luck they managed to survive on their own.

Whether male or female, surviving in the city and surviving well meant being blessed with some amount of luck. Luck had different meanings for whites and free blacks. For the latter luck meant having a trade that was not taken over by white laborers. Luck also meant being able to support one's children so that officials could not force them into legal apprenticeships. Thousands of black parents in both the North and South had their children taken away and forced into eighteen or twenty years of service because state or city officials deemed them unable or unfit to care for them. In Philadelphia, apprenticeship periods for blacks were sometimes as long as twenty-eight years. Once in an apprenticeship black children seldom received the education or the training in a trade that white children received.

In light of all the restrictions on free blacks and the discrimination and prejudice they faced, it is worth remembering that they were not slaves. Although they were only semi-free, they were not in bondage. This status had real significance, significance a slave could appreciate. For, after all, free blacks could legally rename themselves. They could marry legally, and free women gave birth to free children. They had more opportunities to learn to read and write. For instance, although only one of Sojourner Truth's five children obtained any education, at least two of her grandchildren obtained literacy during the days of slavery. William Ellison's children were more fortunate than Truth's. He sent them to Philadelphia to be educated at the Lombard Street Primary School, a school run by Margaretta Forten, a free black teacher.

Free blacks could also make their lives meaningful in ways slaves could not. Throughout the country free African Americans had more control over their religious practices. Shortly after Sojourner Truth was freed, she joined a Methodist congregation in Ulster, New York. Like thousands of free blacks, Truth found the more participatory, unconstrained emotional services of the Methodists more to her liking than the quiet, solemn services of other denominations.

For free blacks, though, it was not enough to be accepted in a white congregation. Whites, however, protested independent black organizing, such as that conducted by Absalom Jones's Free African Society in Philadelphia. Especially in the South blacks encountered strenuous white resistance to black churches.

In the end, however, white prejudice worked *for* African Americans. In the South, where laws prohibited black assembly, whites nevertheless shunned integrated worship with free African Americans. Yet, adopting the same reasoning they employed regarding slaves, whites believed that Christianity would make free blacks more controllable and less dangerous. Therefore, even though black churches were often raided and shut down by suspicious whites, between 1800 and 1860, and especially after 1840, independent African-American churches grew and thrived.

To the extent that the churches survived and prospered, so too did African-American communities. Like slaves, free blacks identified with the Jews of the Old Testament and believed that God would deliver them in this world and the next.

For free blacks, however, the church was a structure—an institution—in a way it was not for the slave. Besides being the one corner of the world where blacks went unhindered by whites, the church was the center of black life. Most black schools were founded by the black church. Most self-help activities were conducted through the church, and most positions of leadership in the community were held in the church. Not surprisingly, it was often the church's struggle for survival against white efforts to shut its doors that lent unity and solidarity to many African-American communities.

So much was dependent on the survival of the black church. Black schools offer a good example. In antebellum America in both the North and the South adult education was almost nonexistent, and black children were either given substandard education or were barred from public and private schools altogether. It was usually the church that took up this burden. In the North and the upper and border Southern states, African churches ran Sunday schools where children were encouraged to read the Bible. Most churches in these areas had day schools that children attended for free or for a small fee.

In addition to the church, benevolent societies were a unifying element in free African-American society. One of the first was founded in Boston by Prince Hall, who before the American Revolution was granted a charter from England to establish a Masonic lodge. In 1797 Hall presided over the installation of the first officers in Philadelphia's African Lodge of Pennsylvania. By 1815 there were four lodges in Philadelphia that had pooled their resources to build a black Masonic Hall.

Like benevolent societies in other cities in both North and South, these organizations provided services to their members as well as to the larger black community. For example, they provided disabled members with "sick dues" to assure them an income when they could not work, and they also gave elderly members money to live on. They organized the burial of their members, providing plots, headstones, and ceremonies for the departed. Some of the associations ran schools for orphan children and provided for companionship for the sick and disabled. Some workingmen's associations tried to secure better wages and job security, and still others functioned like Baltimore's Society for Relief in Case of Seizure, an organization that guarded against the kidnapping of free blacks into slavery.

These benevolent societies not only provide an excellent example of African-American self-help but also give us insight into the social organization of most African-American communities. In 1790 the Brown Fellowship Society of Charleston, South Carolina, was formed by five free men of color. Membership was limited to fifty persons, who had to pay an initial membership fee of fifty dollars plus monthly dues. The fellowship used this money to provide for the funeral and burial expenses of its members and monthly stipends for the widows and orphans of members. The society also provided for the care of some of the poor among Charleston's free black population. Another society, also of Charleston, the Friendly Moralist Society, founded in 1838, functioned similarly. Yet another Charleston organization, the Humane Brotherhood, was formed in 1843, and it too provided sick benefits, burial expenses, and a fixed yearly income for widows and orphans of deceased members.

What makes these associations interesting is their organization around wealth and complexion. Obviously any free black who could afford the membership dues of these societies belonged to the exceptional class of free African Americans—people who, like William Ellison, had distinguished themselves from the masses of illiterate and unskilled free blacks. They owned property, were educated, and could provide for the education of their children, even if it meant sending them out of the state or even out of the country.

In every city, whether New York or New Orleans, there were classes of African Americans who were distinguished this way. They were the elite who succeeded despite all the obstacles placed in their way. In city after city they formed musical and literary societies. They preached a gospel of moral purity, and their social events were reported in black newspapers such as *Freedom's Journal,* first published by John Russwurm and Samuel Cornish in 1827 in New York City. They held themselves up to blacks and whites alike as the moral guardians of the race, the standard of excellence that all blacks could achieve if white prejudice disappeared.

These societies in Charleston were also notable because they were organized around color. Specifically, the Brown Fellowship and Friendly Moralist societies were exclusively for mulattoes, while the Humane Brotherhood was limited to no more than thirty-five "respectable Free Dark Men." This division of benevolent societies along color lines could be found everywhere in the United States, but it was especially pronounced in the Lower South, from South Carolina to Louisiana. It was in these states, where slavery was most entrenched, that the free black population was the smallest and most restricted. Manumissions, even during the revolution, were never numerous, and slaves who were emancipated were very likely blood relatives of their master. In these states, mulattoes, usually called free people of color, were presumed by authorities to be free, and dark-skinned blacks, even those who were free, were presumed to be slaves.

In practical terms this meant that mulattoes had a better chance of surviving and succeeding than dark-complexioned blacks did. Often it was because their white relative gave them some advantage over other African Americans. In William Ellison's case it was an education and training as a cotton gin maker; for others it included a ticket out of the South. The fact that whites were not as threatened by mulattoes as they were by the darker-skinned worked in the former's favor as well. Upper-class African-American society therefore was generally lighter than the poor, working, and middle classes.

And yet, the existence of the dark-skinned, upper-class Humane Brotherhood is evidence that wealth and good fortune were not always synonymous with a light skin. At the same time that many dark-skinned blacks excelled, southern plantations held many mulattoes in slavery. Some were so white that their African heritage was not obvious. For African-American women, light skin could bring dubious advantages. White men often found them desirable and this sometimes had its end in freedom for the mulatto woman, but more often than not, the result could be a lifetime of sexual exploitation. Mulatto women probably saw more house service than did their darker sisters, but house service was not always a blessing.

A light skin could help with success, but other factors such as literacy, a trade or profession, and white connections helped structure free black antebellum society. And structured it was. Differences in wealth, literacy, complexion, and occupation made for different social connections and classes within black society. It was not unusual for wealthier African Americans to attend a different church from those of the middle and lower classes. Usually the wealthier the free black, the less emotional his religious denomination. Methodists and Baptists attracted the African-American masses, and those with skills, literacy, and wealth usually joined or formed their own more reserved Episcopal or Presbyterian church.

Despite the differences, though, despite their varied occupations and chances for success, freedom for African Americans was always and everywhere limited. White freedom and black freedom were never the same, and although there were many things to divide blacks from each other, their partial freedom brought them all together. As the nation moved closer to the Civil War, the more similar all black life became. In the South, where by 1860 the color line was drawn fast and tight, all free African Americans—the light skinned and the dark, the skilled and the unskilled, the literate and the illiterate, the Episcopalian and the Baptist—faced the same hostile whites. As they raised their voices in protest in the years immediately preceding the Civil War they struck a chord of unity—unity with each other, and unity with the slave.

Let My People Go

In 1847 the first edition of Frederick Douglass's newspaper, the *North Star,* rolled off the presses. It was not the first African-American newspaper nor would it be the last. And like the names of many other African-American publications, *North Star* signified black aspirations, because the North Star, the light that guided so many runaways out of the South, symbolized freedom.

In his dedication Douglass tied the fate of all blacks together, the free and enslaved, those north and those south. "We are one," he declared, "our cause is one" and "we must help each other." Douglass went on to declare the unity of the free black with the slave. "What you suffer, we suffer; what you endure, we endure. We are indissolubly united, and must fall or flourish together."

Douglass's words were prophetic, but it did not take a prophet to see the wisdom of his remarks. The nation was just thirteen years from the Civil War. Already the ferment was rising. The American Antislavery Society was fourteen years old. Founded by blacks and whites, the society held religious revival-style meetings where abolitionists made stirring speeches condemning slavery as a moral wrong. They urged their listeners to put pressure on state legislatures to end slavery. The abolitionist movement spawned the Liberty party, and in 1840 and 1844 it ran antislavery Presidential candidates. Although the Liberty party did not attract a significant following, it did plant the seed of fear of "slave power." The admittance of Texas into the Union as a slave state in 1845 and the promised addition of slave states from the territories taken by the United States as a result of the Mexican War in 1846 did in fact convince many Northerners that slaveholders would use their political and economic power to make slavery legal everywhere. More and more, Northern whites wondered whether slavery would or could be confined only to the South; more and more they wondered about the fate of white laborers in a slave labor economy.

Blacks, too, pondered their fate. But for them, the issues were different. Most important, the concerns of African Americans did not divide them as much as the debate over slavery divided whites. They had much to gain from white conflict over slavery, and they understood that they would not benefit at all if they were not united. And for the most part they spoke with one voice. Free blacks, those who could speak out against injustice, all wanted freedom for the enslaved and justice for the free. All wanted blacks to have the rights that were accorded by the Consti-

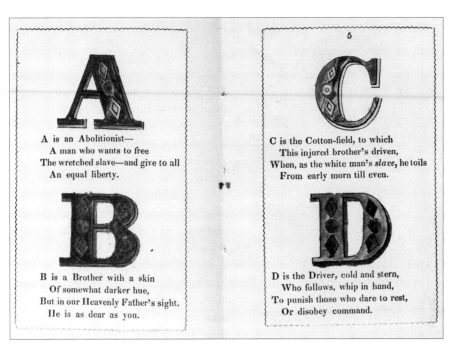

The Anti-Slavery Alphabet, published in 1847 for an anti-slavery fair in Philadelphia, used simple rhymes to expose children to the horrors of slavery.

tution to all Americans. They differed, however, on the means to achieve these ends. The story of black protest in the years before the Civil War is one of unity on the large issues of rights and debate about the way to achieve them.

Black protest against slavery began long before the 1833 formation of the predominantly white American Antislavery Society. During the revolution the Continental Congress was bombarded with petitions from Northern slaves who used the "all men are created equal" clause of the Declaration of Independence to claim their freedom. Protest against slavery continued through the Confederation period, and at the beginning of the nineteenth century the African Methodist Episcopal minister Absalom Jones walked the streets of Philadelphia carrying a petition that protested the renewal of the slave trade in Maryland, the birthplace of many Philadelphia blacks. In their churches and benevolent societies African Americans raised money to help runaways, wrote petitions protesting slavery, and spoke against black bondage whenever and wherever the opportunity arose.

On a more subtle level, blacks celebrated New Year's Day as their Independence Day. As Frederick Douglass noted, to the slave the national Fourth of July celebration was a day that revealed "the gross injustice and cruelty to which he is the constant victim." To the slave, the shouts of liberty and equality, the prayers, hymns, sermons, and thanksgivings were "hollow mockery ... mere bombast, fraud, deception, impiety, and hypocrisy—a thin veil to cover up crimes which would disgrace a nation of savages." New Year's Day, in contrast, had real meaning for African Americans. It was the anniversary of Haitian independence in 1804 and the end of the foreign slave trade with the United States in 1808.

As each New Year's Day passed, free blacks increasingly condemned the federal government for its perpetuation of slavery. They did not have to go much further than the Constitution to find a federal document worthy of condemnation. The Constitution allowed the foreign slave trade to persist for twenty years after its signing. For purposes of representation, it counted enslaved African Americans as three-fifths of a person. It also promised to put down slave insurrections and to track down fugitives from slavery and return them to their owners. This last provision, which put the federal government in the business of slave catching, was reinforced by a fugitive slave law in 1793 and by a particularly harsh one in 1850. African Americans vigorously opposed these laws, but between 1836 and 1844 the House of Representatives adopted a "gag rule" against all antislavery petitions. Under this rule all abolitionist petitions were automatically tabled so that they could not even be discussed on the floor of the House.

Still blacks protested. They took particular aim at the program of the American Colonization Society. Founded in 1816, this society counted some of America's most notable citizens among its members. Presidents James Madison and Andrew Jackson, Senator Daniel Webster, and Francis Scott Key, author of "The Star-Spangled Banner," all argued that blacks should be returned to Africa because it was the only natural home of black people. Central to their argument was their belief that blacks would never be accepted in America. According to national leader and Presidential hopeful Henry Clay, the "Great Compromiser," blacks would ever inhabit "the lowest strata of social gradation." In his opinion blacks were "aliens— political-moral-social aliens, strangers, though native." Africa, on the other hand, held hope for blacks. It was a place where they would not be degraded and debased. Moreover, advocates of colonization believed that American Negroes, having come under the civilizing influence of Christianity and having observed the benefits of democracy and capitalism, would redeem Africa. They argued that African Americans would transform Africa into prosperous mini-American black republics. Colonization would open up new commercial routes between Africa and America. In short, what blacks could not do here in America, they could and would do in Africa. In their minds, the end result of colonization would benefit both blacks and whites, America and Africa.

Colonizationists tried to recruit well-known, successful blacks to lead the exodus to Africa. The most common strategy was to lure influential black leaders with the prospect of power, wealth, and prestige. For example, they offered James Forten, a wealthy sailmaker, commercial advantages if he would lead blacks back to West Africa. He refused, but it did not stop colonizationists from sensationalizing the advantages of going to Africa.

All but a few declined the opportunity to return. Those who did leave settled on land near the British colony of Sierra Leone. Located on land purchased by the American Colonization Society in 1822, the colony was named Liberia, the "land of freedom." Settlers hoped that this small country would fulfill the promise of its name and provide the liberty that America withheld. Certainly this was the hope of two of its most renowned settlers, the black sea captain and shipowner Paul Cuffee and John Russwurm, an educator and the editor of *Freedom's Journal.* Both men endorsed colonization because they felt America would never treat its black citizens fairly. "If the slaves of our country with one accord were delivered from bondage," Russwurm asked, "can they be elevated to an equality with the whites? Can they while in this country be divested of the odium of inferior and degraded caste?" Russwurm's answer to his own question was "No!" For him and his small following, Liberia would provide the liberty denied by America.

But only a few people were willing to follow him. News of the troubled relationships that the settlers had with surrounding African tribes and the difficulty American blacks had with African diseases thwarted settlement. However, the most important reason why African Americans refused to return to Africa was their feeling that America was their country. Africa was indeed their *ancestral* homeland, but America was their birthplace and from it they drew their identity. They had fought and died in America's wars, had cleared this country's land and swamps, had helped build up its towns. The world, not just America, grew rich off the cotton, rice, and sugar grown by black people. They believed they had proved themselves productive, self-sufficient citizens, more so than even the slaveholder who had fewer skills, and who lived off the labor of others. To be asked to leave after such sacrifice to America was sheer injustice.

Many African Americans also believed that this push by whites exposed unadulterated white racism. African Americans asked that they be allowed to live free in this land that was the beacon of liberty. They protested the colonizationists' claim that blacks were incapable of living in freedom. They challenged America to stand by its principles of democracy and liberty.

Free blacks understood that it was their organized opposition to slavery that was threatening. Prominent among the leaders and members of colonization societies were slaveholders, none of whom supported the emancipation of slaves and their return to Africa, but all of whom argued that blacks were unprepared for freedom. In the opinion of most African-American leaders, colonization was a scheme to protect slavery and preserve freedom for whites only. Their fight against colonization, therefore, was a fight for themselves but also for their brothers and sisters in slavery. As they saw things, they were the slave's best hope, and the slave was their best ally in the cause of black rights.

Not that they did not want to forge alliances with white Americans, too. These were more problematic, however. For one thing, most prominent African-

American leaders were dismayed by the widespread support given to colonization societies. Before the 1830s men like William Lloyd Garrison, Gerrit Smith, Arthur and Lewis Tappan, and Benjamin Lundy—whites who actively opposed slavery—also supported colonization. They did not see how colonization helped preserve slavery, or how the scheme exposed free blacks to the rage of anti-black mobs.

Such a mob let loose its venom in Cincinnati in 1829. Tension in the city had been growing throughout the 1820s. As the free black population increased and competed for jobs, whites demanded their expulsion. They were encouraged by the leaders of the Cincinnati Colonization Society. Since its founding in 1826, it had prompted ministers and local newspapers to agitate against the city's blacks. Its propaganda provided the justification for driving them from the city. In the summer of 1829 city officials tried to push African Americans out by enforcing the Ohio Black Laws, which required blacks to post bonds guaranteeing "good behavior." Before black leaders could get a reprieve from the city legislature, white mobs attacked defenseless blacks. More than half the black population fled to Canada and other parts of the United States.

Although this and similar incidents convinced some sympathetic whites that colonization was inherently evil, it did not alter their prejudice toward blacks. This was another reason that African-American leaders found alliances with whites problematic. For example, even though black abolitionists like Peter Williams and William Watkins coaxed white men like William Lloyd Garrison and Gerrit Smith away from colonization, when Garrison and a small group of white friends met to organize the New England Antislavery Society in 1832, they invited blacks to join them only after all their plans had been formulated. Similarly, only three blacks were among the sixty-two signers of the American Antislavery Society's Declaration of Sentiments. Though it had twenty-six vice presidents and a nine-member executive committee, the society had no black officers.

African-American leaders were further disturbed by the limited perspectives and goals of white abolitionists. As free blacks they spoke against slavery as well as blanket discrimination against all blacks. White abolitionists, they found, were not much concerned with racism. Many black abolitionists shared the reaction of Theodore Wright, who criticized the "constitutions of abolition societies, where nothing was said about the improvement of the man of color!" Speaking before the New York Antislavery Society in 1837, Wright complained that "they have overlooked the giant sin of prejudice. They have passed by this foul monster, which is at once the parent and offspring of slavery."

Black abolitionists further noted that many white abolitionists refused to admit black children to their schools, would not hire black workers for anything but menial jobs, and even failed to hire blacks to work in antislavery offices. They also observed that in the early stages of their efforts, white abolitionists did not hire black lecturers, and when they eventually did they tried to control every aspect of their language and message.

A case in point involved Frederick Douglass. When Douglass first began lecturing in 1841 he related the trials of his slavery and the terrors of the institution. Garrison and others were pleased. They encouraged Douglass to repeat his performance over and over. As Douglass matured as a speaker, and as he pondered the meaning of freedom for himself and the nation, he grew more philosophical and learned in his talks. White abolitionists found Douglass the philosopher to be less "authentic" than Douglass the ex-slave. They did not want him to grow. Instead they repeatedly criticized him for appearing too smart. At one point he was told, "People won't believe you ever were a slave, Frederick, if you keep on this way. . . . Better have a *little* of the plantation manner of speech than not."

But Douglass, like other African-American leaders, listened to his own voice, and his own people, and in a very short time went his own way. Blacks continued to build their own movement, and central to it was the black press. Newspapers founded by leading personalities reminded black Americans of their role in the development of the American nation. There was no lack of articles on the role black soldiers played in the American Revolution and the War of 1812.

At the same time that newspapers confirmed the black's identity as an American, they also grounded that identity in the common black experience. Thus in their reporting of slave resistance, the terrors of slavery, and the free black communities' assistance to fugitive slaves, newspapers made it difficult for free blacks to forget their relatively privileged status in relation to the slave. Just as important, these accounts helped cement the bond between slave and free.

Newspapers with such names as *The Colored American,* the *Weekly Advocate,* the *New Era,* and the *Weekly Anglo-African* helped unify African Americans by keeping them informed of happenings in their own community and the nation. Articles and advertisements covering their various concerts, lectures, church events, educational opportunities, and school programs were regular features of black newspapers. By reporting national events from a black perspective and accepting editorials from ordinary African Americans, these newspapers allowed blacks to express their ideas on a variety of subjects and vent frustrations that had no other outlet. Since only a small percentage of the African-American population was literate, and these privileged few had to read or otherwise communicate the newspaper's contents to those who could not read, newspapers helped forge the bonds of community. They bridged the gap between the educated and the illiterate.

Through their own newspapers and a few edited by white abolitionists, ordinary African Americans learned of the protest activity of their leaders—men and women such as Douglass, Martin Delany, Henry Highland Garnet, William Wells Brown, William Whipper, and Maria Stewart. The question was how blacks should obtain their freedom. The decision was not an easy one. Would armed rebellion succeed? From their relatively safe surroundings, should they encourage the slaves to risk everything in a break for freedom? How far should free blacks go in opposing the fugitive slave laws? Should they hold off slave catchers with guns or would civil disobedience be enough? How would they achieve their rights of full citizenship?

Answers to these questions came from many quarters. In his speeches and in a pamphlet entitled *Walker's Appeal . . . to the Colored Citizens of the World But in Particular and Very Expressly to those of the United States of America,* David Walker urged African Americans to meet the slaveholders' violence with violence of their own. He blamed the oppression of blacks on white greed for money and power. In the by-now-typical African-American tradition of blending the secular with the sacred, of using religion to help solve life's problems, Walker urged black people to rise up and wage a holy war against whites, who had by their sin against African Americans sinned against God. "They want us for their slaves," he wrote. They "think nothing of murdering us in order to subject us to that wretched condition." In his justification of armed resistance, Walker wrote, "It is no more harm for you to kill a man who is trying to kill you, than it is for you to take a drink of water when thirsty: in fact the man who will stand still and let another man murder him is worse than an infidel."

No doubt many African Americans felt the same way Walker did, but most spoke with more moderate voices. Although they did not lose sight of the role played by whites in black oppression, many leaders urged African Americans to take an active role in liberation by uplifting themselves. Maria Stewart, one of the few African-American female public lecturers, urged blacks to give up drinking and invest in schools and seminaries. An admirer and follower of Walker, Stewart nevertheless believed that "nothing would raise our respectability, add to our peace and happiness, and reflect so much honor upon us, as to be ourselves the promoters of temperance, and the supporters . . . of useful and scientific knowledge." An advocate of female education during a time when it was thought that women best served the race by serving their husbands, brothers, and fathers, Stewart argued that the race needed both men and women in public roles. "Daughters of Africa" needed to unite. They could raise money to build schools to educate black youth, they could own stores that would service their community, they could educate themselves and through them the race would be uplifted.

As despairing as Stewart sometimes was when she looked at the plight of African Americans, she, like many others, was still more optimistic about the future than David Walker was. The goal of uplift was, after all, eventual integration into American life. Blacks were behind not because of natural inferiority but because of prejudice and slavery. Once these impediments were abolished, education and opportunity would remedy the situation.

Throughout the 1830s and 1840s Frederick Douglass shared Stewart's optimism. He did not support armed resistance or programs to go back to Africa. He believed that through constant preaching, political lobbying, and hard struggle blacks would eventually find liberty in America. "You must be a man here," he insisted, "and force your way to intelligence, wealth and respectability. If you can't do that here, you can't do it there."

But there were many who disagreed. Martin Delany, a Harvard-educated physician, was the most articulate spokesman against the views Douglass and others expressed. "No people can be free who themselves do not constitute an essential part of the *ruling* element of the country in which they live." These words, published in his 1852 book entitled *The Condition, Elevation, Emigration, and Destiny of the Colored People of the United States,* were part of his argument for emigrating from the eastern United States to Central or South America or to some nonsettled area in the American West. He did not share with Douglass the belief that America would allow blacks to become citizens. Much like Native Americans, blacks, he wrote, were "a nation within a nation." Blacks and whites shared a common country. But whites were an oppressor nation and blacks the oppressed nation. Black people, he claimed, loved America, but because that love was met with only belittlement and degradation, black people were "politically not of them, but aliens to the laws and privileges of the country." Thus separated, African Americans had a duty to establish a black society where they would be free to enjoy the privileges of citizenship.

These, then, were the lines of protest in African-American communities before 1850. Despite their different levels of optimism and different strategies of resistance, antebellum black leaders were united in their good feelings about themselves. Never did they give in to self-hatred, nor did they ever believe the pro-slavery arguments that held that they were naturally inferior to whites. Before America they stood tall and proud.

It was this black pride that eventually drove all black abolitionist leaders to advocate some degree of black separatism. In their minds, blacks, as a people, had to do for themselves; self-improvement had to be based on self-reliance. Said Phillip A. Bell, in the *Weekly Advocate,* whites may make "OUR CAUSE" their cause all they want, but their efforts will be unavailing "without our thinking and acting, as a body, for ourselves."

In thinking and acting for themselves blacks met during the 1830s through the 1850s in black-only national conventions. Northern cities such as Albany, Rochester, Cincinnati, Philadelphia, Buffalo, and Cleveland were the sites of some of the meetings where the means of uplift and strategies of resistance were debated. Although those who attended these conventions realized that some might think that all-black meetings worked against the goal of integration of blacks into the American mainstream, most concluded that racial solidarity was necessary to secure their status as full-fledged Americans. Separatism, whether in conventions, schools, or churches, was not the end in itself, but the means to the end.

For all of their work, it was, in the end, not black or even white abolitionists who struck the fatal blow against slavery. The institution proved so entrenched that it took a civil war to end it. Black protesters, however, could be proud of the work they did in unifying the spirits of free blacks and in forging the bond between free and enslaved African Americans. In so doing, they laid the intellectual foundation on which the protest of future generations of blacks and whites was built.

From Desperation to Hope

At the end of 1850 African Americans did not know that the nation was just a decade away from civil war, that slavery would be its cause, or that the war would end slavery for good. They could not know that it would be the bloodiest war ever fought on America's soil or that their citizenship and voting rights would hang in the balance.

However, black people could not help but sense that something out of the ordinary was happening. Slavery was at the heart of heated discussions about the nation's future, and the Compromise of 1850, meant to quell anxiety about the slavery question, actually fanned its flames. The Compromise brought California into the nation as a free state, eliminated the slave trade in the District of Columbia, and organized the territories of Utah and Mexico. Its most obnoxious part was the Fugitive Slave Law. Under its harsh provisions, the law forced blacks accused of being fugitives to prove their free status, not to a jury, but to a special commissioner who was paid more (ten dollars) for returning a slave to his owner than for setting him or her free (five dollars). The law also compelled Northerners to hunt down and turn in runaway slaves.

As slave hunters known as "kidnappers" flooded the North seizing fugitives, blacks had to decide what to do. They had always resisted fugitive slave laws, but by putting a bounty on every runaway's head, and making every white person a potential slave catcher, this latest fugitive law made resistance more risky and life for free blacks terribly insecure—so insecure that many free blacks took one last stride toward freedom by fleeing across the Canadian border.

The vast majority who remained faced a nation racked with conflict that did not lessen. Abraham Lincoln's election to the Presidency in 1860 brought some hope that liberation was on the horizon. Mostly though, there was despair over the way the decade had proceeded and wretched bitterness over the country's betrayal of blacks.

Ironically, the 1850s was a decade of prosperity. Not only whites but blacks, too, did relatively well. This was indicated by the steady increase in black land and property ownership all over the country. In Nashville, for example, in 1860 there were twenty-six free blacks who were worth more than a thousand dollars who had owned no property ten years earlier. Charleston had always had a wealthy colored elite, but during the 1850s as many as seventy-five whites rented their homes from freemen. In Baltimore free blacks monopolized the caulking trade, and throughout the Upper South free black agricultural laborers took advantage of the movement of slaves south by demanding and receiving higher wages.

Economic success generated confidence. This confidence was visible in the new churches being built by larger and wealthier black congregations in the North and the South. It was also shown by the increased audacity of free blacks. In Petersburg, Virginia, for example, whites complained that blacks were slow to give way to whites on walkways.

Blacks also exuded more confidence in the way they responded to oppression. In Richmond, for instance, free blacks petitioned the city council to repeal the city's repressive Black Code, and in New York City there was the stunning behavior of Elizabeth Jennings. On a Sunday morning in 1854 she was pulled out of a horse-drawn trolley car and wrestled to the ground by a white conductor and driver who sought to keep her from sitting in the white section. With the same conviction and audacity shown by the free blacks of Richmond, Jennings took her case to court. Her victory there broke the back of segregation on public conveyances in New York.

All over the country blacks tried to do the same to the Fugitive Slave Law. Twice in Boston, blacks and whites stormed a courthouse in failed attempts to rescue Thomas Sims in 1851 and Anthony Burns in 1854. Others, such as Elijah Anderson, John Mason, and of course, Harriet Tubman, continued to risk life and limb going into the South and delivering African Americans from slavery. Frederick Douglass also risked harm by his resistance to the law. Though very much in the public eye, he, like countless others, raised money for fugitives, hid them in his Rochester home, and helped hundreds escape to Canada.

And, like others, he had to struggle with the meaning of the Fugitive Slave Law. In Rochester, New York, in 1853 Douglass and other black abolitionists held one of their largest conventions to try to decide what to do about resisting the law. Reluctant though they were to call for the creation of separate black institutions, they felt the Fugitive Slave Law left them no choice. America seemed determined to cast them aside and destroy their rights as citizens. Somehow, they had to salvage them. In their attempt to do this, black abolitionists called for the creation of a national council to oversee black improvement and a manual labor school for the education of black children in science, literature, and the mechanical arts. They did this, they said, not to "build ourselves up as a distinct and separate class in this country but as a means to . . . equality in political rights, and in civil rights, and in civil and social privileges with the rest of the American people."

Although black abolitionists as a group took larger strides toward separatism, some individuals spoke out in favor of armed resistance. Douglass was among them. He not only increased his aid to fugitive slaves but he became decidedly more militant: "The only way to make the Fugitive Slave Law a dead letter is to make a half dozen or more dead kidnappers."

For Martin Delany, Douglass's response fell short of a remedy. It was not enough to challenge the individual kidnapper when the source of the problem was the prejudice that permeated all American institutions, including the government.

Shoot one kidnapper, and another would take his place. The law was a reflection of government policy, and in Delany's opinion even the call for separate black institutions did not go far enough to counter white racism. When Delany pondered institutional discrimination and the Fugitive Slave Law, he concluded that "a people capable of originating and sustaining such a law as this are not people to whom we are willing to entrust our liberty at discretion." His advice was to "go to whatever parts of Central and South America" and "make common cause with the people." For Delany, emigration was still the only answer.

Delany found support at conventions held in Maryland in 1852 and Cleveland in 1854. Unlike the delegates to the Rochester convention, those who attended the Cleveland meeting were not reluctant supporters of black separatism, nor did they see the point in arguing for separation as a means to American citizenship. As Delany put it, it was time for black people to look outside of America, to grab hold of those places in the world where chance was in their favor and where the rights and power of the colored race could be established.

Although more blacks than ever took up this position in the 1850s, most African Americans remained hopeful of change within the United States. They could not abandon the land of their birth, give up the dream for which their forefathers had sacrificed so much, nor leave their enslaved brethren with no black advocates for freedom. Delegates to the Baltimore convention found this out when the meeting they called to discuss emigration was broken up by angry black crowds who wanted no part of Africa, Haiti, Mexico, or Canada. They did not disagree with the delegates' demand to be treated like men. Nor did they take issue with the convention's general sentiment that in Maryland swine were treated better than free Negroes. Clearly though, they, like most free blacks, wanted to make their stand here in America.

In the first few years of the decade it seemed that they had support. In fact, white Northerners did grow more sympathetic. This was in part because the Fugitive Slave Law brought the issue of slavery to their doorstep. Whites who witnessed slaves being dragged unwillingly back South found it difficult to remain detached from the issue. They could no longer treat it as something that just happened "down there."

And what was happening "down there" was made even more real by the publication in magazine installments, and then as a book in 1852, of Harriet Beecher Stowe's *Uncle Tom's Cabin*. In a brilliant manipulation of public sentiment, Stowe raised public consciousness about the evils of slavery. She did this by making her slaves people with whom almost all whites could identify. There were few Northern mothers who did not hail Eliza's courageous escape across the floes of the Ohio River, or cry over Little Eva's death. Only the meanest could side with the wicked Yankee slaveholder Simon Legree, and all could see the Christlike goodness of the beloved Uncle Tom. So large and so stirred was the northern readership that when Lincoln met Stowe in 1863 he is supposed to have said, "So you're the little woman who wrote the book that made this great war!"

If African Americans had reason to be buoyed by this new awareness on the part of the Northern public, they surely had reason to be wary of the response it drew from Southerners. Already unnerved by the steady economic progress and increasing boldness of free blacks, Southern whites' anxiety only increased in the face of Northern antislavery activity. In particular, slaveholders were sure that free blacks and increased antislavery activity had something to do with the increase in the number of runaway slaves and incidents of overt resistance.

And to Southerners it seemed as though every day brought news of some other violent incident involving slaves. It was said that overseers in the Mississippi Valley so feared for their lives that they were never caught without their guns. In Tennessee four slaves were put to death for attempting to attack the iron mills where they worked.

Some blacks in Texas also seemed ready. From that state came news of an alleged plot that was to bring blacks and Mexicans together in an attempt to rid the state of its white population. Although whites killed five blacks suspected of fomenting the insurrection, they could not quell black discontent, nor white fear of it.

They tried to, though. Because they felt that the ever-growing free black population was inciting slaves to flee and rebel, Southerners tried to get rid of them. With the exception of Delaware and North Carolina, every Upper South state instituted a colonization plan. Virginia's was typical. In 1850 it appropriated thirty thousand dollars annually for five years to send free blacks and emancipated slaves to the West African nation of Liberia. A tax placed on free blacks added an additional ten thousand dollars. Maryland passed a similar law in 1852, Tennessee in 1853, and Missouri and Kentucky in 1855.

These plans failed for two reasons. To begin with, not enough money was appropriated for such a massive removal of people. But even had there been enough funds, there were few people who wanted to go. African Americans were already opposed to the emigration plans proposed by their own leaders. They were hardly more disposed to leaving under a program arranged by their oppressors. John Rapier said what most blacks believed: "They [colonizationists] would not care if all the free negroes in the United States was at the Botom of the Sea so they was out of the United States."

Not only was Rapier right, he caught what was fast becoming the temper of the nation. Everywhere, not just in the South, anti-black sentiment was rising. Indiana offers a good example of this mood. In 1851 state legislators rewrote the state constitution with provisions that deprived blacks of the rights to vote, attend white schools, and make contracts. African Americans who could not post a five hundred dollar bond were expelled from the state, and an 1852 law made it a crime for blacks to settle in Indiana.

If nothing else these state laws demonstrated that antislavery sentiment easily coexisted with hostility toward African Americans. Most white citizens did not want *any* blacks in their midst, slave or free. This sentiment found national expression in

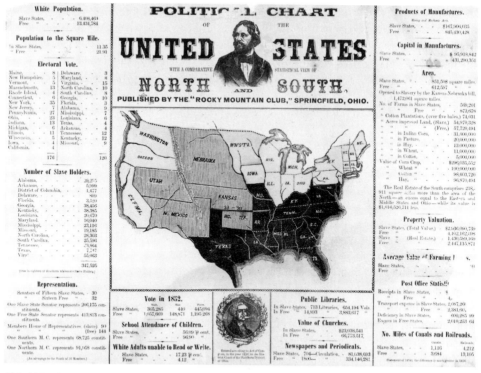

This 1856 chart of the United States shows the division between free and slave states. The chart also offers a statistical comparison between the North and the South, with figures for the number of public libraries, the number of children who attend school, and other categories.

the new Republican party, which was founded in 1854. The principal platform of this mostly Northern party was "no slavery in the territories." By this Republicans meant that they wanted to keep the new western territories as "free soil," meaning free of slavery. Slavery, they believed, retarded upward mobility and economic growth. From their point of view the South was stagnant and backward, while the North and Upper Midwest were energetic and progressive. Republicans promised not to oppose slavery where it already was. But inasmuch as America's democracy and its institutions depended on the ability of men to move and work in a free labor market, they argued that the future greatness of the American nation depended on the confinement of slavery and the expansion of free soil.

For African Americans the Republican party was both good and bad news. The good news was that many Republicans were abolitionists who opposed not just the expansion of slavery but also slavery where it existed. Senator William Seward of New York and Senators Charles Sumner of Massachusetts and George Julian of Ohio were ardent abolitionists who sought to divorce the federal government from the support of slavery by freeing slaves in the District of Columbia, repealing the Fugitive Slave Law, and eliminating the domestic slave trade.

There was good news too in even the limited goal of keeping slavery out of the territories. The rival party, the Democrats, had already gone on record as supporting popular sovereignty, the settler's right to decide whether slavery should exist in the territories. Its leading politician, Stephen A. Douglas, had pushed the Kansas-Nebraska Act through Congress early in 1854. This act allowed the people who settled in the newly organized Kansas and Nebraska regions to decide for themselves whether they wanted slavery. In allowing for the possibility of slavery in these territories the act overturned the 1820 Missouri Compromise, which had outlawed slavery in regions north of Missouri. The Republicans thus offered a much-needed counter to what was without a doubt a major threat from the power of the slave owners.

The bad news, though, was that the bulk of the party's support came from whites who were as much anti-black as they were antislavery. From the African American's point of view this made the party suspect. Republicans did not directly oppose slavery where it was, nor did they tackle issues like the domestic slave trade or the Fugitive Slave Law. Furthermore, the party's supporters and its prominent leader, Abraham Lincoln, did not favor equal rights for African Americans. In opposing the vote, jury service, and intermarriage, Republicans made clear their belief that whites were superior to blacks, and that the two races could not live together on terms of social and political equality.

The formation of the Republican party, therefore, left blacks with a lot to think about. They took heart that there was, for the first time, a political force opposing slavery, but they worried about the limits of that opposition and the extent to which the Republicans would go to keep blacks from exercising civil and political rights. That they were still without effective national allies in an increasingly hostile environment was a fact that did not escape them.

The depth of the nation's hostility to blacks was revealed by the Supreme Court's 1857 decision in *Scott* v. *Sandford* (the "Dred Scott case"), a ruling that sent shivers down the spine of black America. In 1846 Dred and Harriet Scott had filed suit in Missouri for their freedom. They argued that because their master had taken them into Minnesota, Wisconsin, and other territories where slavery had been outlawed by the Missouri Compromise, they were by right free. Chief Justice Roger B. Taney, writing for the court, disagreed. Dred and Harriet Scott were not free. Taney stated that blacks were "beings of an inferior order" and therefore "had no rights which white men were bound to respect." Justice Peter V. Daniel, of Virginia, added insult to injury by his claim that "the African Negro race" did not belong "to the family of nations" but rather was only a subject for "commerce or traffic," "slaves," "property."

If this part of the ruling fell like a dead weight on free blacks, the court's decision regarding the Missouri Compromise was a death sentence. In stating that the 1820 law was unconstitutional because Congress did not have the right to ban slavery in a territory, the court opened the entire country to slavery. If Congress could not ban slavery in the territories then it could not keep it out of northern states.

Slaveholders could take their slaves north, settle wherever they wanted, and according to the logic of the Dred Scott decision, there was nothing that could be done about it. When put together with the Fugitive Slave Law, the Dred Scott decision left nowhere for the fugitive to run. Questionable as the North was as a haven for free blacks, these two measures eliminated it as a haven of any sort.

Events in Kansas between 1854 and John Brown's raid at Harpers Ferry, Virginia, in 1859, literally left free blacks nationless. After the Kansas-Nebraska Act was passed both pro- and antislavery forces rushed into Kansas, each group attempting to make sure that the territory was settled according to its wishes. At stake was whether the territories would be slave or free. With both forces willing to die for their cause, violence was inevitable. As the forces clashed in guerrilla-style warfare, only the free blacks' future there was certain: slaveholders did not want them in their midst, and free-soilers wrote a constitution that forbade them from entering the state.

John Brown's raid only made the situation of free blacks more precarious. When the dust settled after the band of twenty-two men tried to take the federal arsenal at Harpers Ferry, free blacks were found to be among the conspirators. Slaveholders cringed when they thought about what might have happened had Brown's plan to seize and distribute weapons to slaves succeeded. They could and did hang John Brown for treason, but many thousands of free blacks who stood ready to take up Brown's mantle remained among the population. Having always viewed the free black as out of place in the South, white Southerners now saw an opportunity to eliminate this group for good.

Life for Southern free blacks had grown harder and more dangerous. States that had already made efforts to force them to leave through colonization renewed their efforts to eliminate them—this time through outright expulsion. Events in South Carolina, the home of William Ellison, were typical. On the urging of Charleston's white mechanics, city officials cracked down on free people of color. In October 1858 they began arresting those who had failed to pay the capitation (literally, "per head") tax, the tax free persons of color had to pay to attest to their freedom. In December of the following year, white Charlestonians formed a Committee of Safety to search out and arrest anyone with abolitionist sympathies. These included whites who ran black schools and blacks who received abolitionist newspapers or otherwise engaged in suspicious behavior. A similar committee was formed by Ellison's neighbors in Stateburg.

Meanwhile, as the state legislature debated reenslavement bills, South Carolina's newspapers carried articles assailing the free African American at every turn. One contributor asked why free blacks were allowed to attend balls, churches, and funerals in carriages; why they were allowed to assume the prerogatives and distinctions that "ought to be, among the landmarks separating the classes." "Shall they," he continued, "in silks and laces, promenade our principal thoroughfares, with the arrogance of equals."

If the white slaveholders who were the guardians of free blacks were willing to put up with such behavior, white workingmen made it clear that they were not. In the South Carolina state legislature their leaders introduced a bill that prohibited all free persons of color from "entering into contracts on any mechanical business on their own account." With a call to "MECHANICS, WORKING MEN AND ALL WHITE MEN WHO LIVE BY THE SWEAT OF THEIR BROW," white workers urged solidarity against free blacks.

Along with thousands of other free blacks throughout the South, most of whom were not nearly as wealthy, William Ellison and his family made plans to emigrate. Between 1858 and the election of Lincoln in 1860, the stream of free blacks heading out of the South became a river. As in South Carolina, every Southern legislature debated expulsion and reenslavement, and like Ellison, free blacks considered moving either north to Canada or south to Haiti or Central America. It did not matter that by the Civil War only Arkansas had actually expelled free blacks, ordering them to leave the state by January 1, 1860, or be enslaved. The fury with which expulsion and enslavement were being debated scared African Americans.

African-American leaders could not help but be disturbed. Everywhere they looked forces seemed arrayed against their people. Events in Kansas, the Dred Scott decision, the Fugitive Slave Law, expulsion and reenslavement bills all made for despair. The nation was moving toward dissolution with a certainty that was frightening. While free African Americans were being sacrificed, Southern calls for secession threatened to tighten the noose of slavery around blacks forever. So depressed was the ever-optimistic Frederick Douglass that he, like Ellison, began looking toward Haiti as a possible homeland for black people. Martin Delany, who had by Lincoln's election already moved himself, his wife, and his five children to Canada, traveled to West Africa in search of a place for his people to settle.

Amazingly, but understandably, the same events that caused so much despair for free blacks and their leaders seemed to inspire slaves. As they had done during the American Revolution and the War of 1812, slaves turned the nation's turmoil to their advantage. That they were at the center of the nation's divisions did not escape them, because by 1860 the future of slavery was on everyone's mind and lips. The slaves' knowledge was manifested by acts meant to subvert the system. From Austin, Texas, came reports of slaves' attempts to repeat "the horrors enacted at Harpers Ferry." In Montgomery, Alabama, it was reported that Negroes had plotted to divide up the estates, mules, lands, and household furniture of their white masters. The more conversations they overheard, the more newspaper articles that literate blacks read, the clearer it became that there were forces beyond the South lining up against slavery.

What was not clear though was the nature and the strength of these forces. The Republicans opposed slavery in the territories, but they also opposed black rights. Abraham Lincoln wavered when it came to African Americans. At one point he spoke in favor of black rights. Blacks, he said are "my equal and . . . the equal of every living man." The Negro man, he declared, is "entitled to all the natural rights . . . in the Declaration of Independence" and had the right also to "put into his mouth the bread that his own hands have earned." At another point, though, Lincoln spoke words that were more in line with most of his generation. He claimed that he was against "the social and political equality of the white and black races," that he did not "favor making voters or jurors of negroes, nor of qualifying them to hold office, nor to intermarry with white people." Since, he said, there was a "physical difference between the white and black races which . . . will for ever forbid the two races living together on terms of social and political equality," Lincoln went on record as favoring whites over blacks. "There must be," he said during his campaign for the Senate in 1858, "the position of superior and inferior, and I as much as any other man am in favor of having the superior position assigned to the white race."

Expressions such as these inspired increasing despair. To Southerners, Abraham Lincoln was the devil incarnate, ready and willing to snatch their slaves from them at whatever cost. Upon his election to the Presidency, legislatures of states in the South seceded from the United States by declaring that the states were no longer part of the Union. First, South Carolina seceded on December 20, 1864, followed by Mississippi, Florida, Alabama, Georgia, Louisiana, Texas, Virginia, North Carolina, Arkansas, and Tennessee. These eleven states joined together to form the Confederate States of America. They elected their own President, Jefferson Davis, and after initial debate established a capital in Richmond, Virginia.

Like Douglass, blacks wanted "the complete and universal *abolition* of the whole slave system," as well as equal suffrage and other rights for free blacks. In early 1861 Lincoln was still promising not to touch slavery where it was and not to repeal the Fugitive Slave Law. Small wonder then that African Americans hardly celebrated his inauguration.

The firing on Fort Sumter, South Carolina, on April 12, 1861 did, however, bring celebration. These first shots of the Civil War stirred real hope that slavery would soon end. It all happened so suddenly, soon after the officer in charge of the fort, Major Robert Anderson, informed Lincoln that he needed men, arms, and supplies to maintain the federal presence in Charleston harbor. Lincoln's dilemma was obvious. If he did nothing, he would appear weak and Sumter would fall to the Confederacy, as had other federal forts, custom houses, and post offices. On the other hand, if he sent forces this would no doubt be taken by the Confederacy as an act of war. Lincoln's choice—to send supplies but no troops or arms—shifted the burden of war to the Confederacy, which itself stood to lose credibility as a sovereign nation if it allowed Lincoln to maintain the fort within its borders. It was hardly their intention, but the shots Confederate generals fired on the ships sent to resupply Anderson were shots that put slavery on the road to extinction.

CHAPTER 5

Breaking the Chains

1860–1880

Noralee Frankel

I n 1898, years after the Civil War, Alfred Thomas, an African American soldier in the Union army, explained his decision to enlist. He was a slave in Mississippi when he first encountered the Yankees. After the Union soldiers rescued a slave from the plantation where Thomas lived, he and his companions became convinced that they should escape slavery themselves by going with the Union soldiers. As he recalled, "Well we had been hearing the guns at Natchez and all over the country and everybody was scared and kept hearing people say the negroes would be free and we heard of colored people running off to the Yankees...." Alfred Thomas was one of 180,000 African Americans who served in the Union army during the Civil War. There were also some 29,000 African Americans who fought in the Union navy. African Americans participated in fifty-two military engagements, and 37,000 died.

As the United States became increasingly polarized over slavery in the 1850s, the North and South became suspicious of each other's political power. Slavery was tied to the fight over states' rights—the doctrine that all rights not reserved to the federal government by the U.S. Constitution are granted to the states. Disputes between the supporters of slavery and the proponents of free labor were responsible for many of the political, economic, cultural, and ideological differences that divided the country during the war.

After Fort Sumter surrendered to the Confederacy on April 14, 1861, the southern states proceeded to organize an army under the leadership of Robert E. Lee. A West Point graduate and trained officer, Lee had turned down President Lincoln's offer to command the Union troops. Failing to obtain Lee, Lincoln named George McClellan general of the Union forces. But Lincoln grew frustrated by McClellan's cautiousness and failure to pursue the enemy. He replaced McClellan with a succession of generals to head the Union forces but found them all unsatisfactory. Lincoln finally selected General Ulysses S. Grant to head the Union's forces because he had proved to be an aggressive, tenacious fighter. Grant's fearlessness ultimately resulted in far greater casualties than would have occurred under McClellan, but under Grant's leadership the Union army won the war.

For the first two years of the war, Lincoln justified the fighting only as necessary to save the United States from becoming two separate countries. Not wanting to antagonize the border states like Kentucky and Missouri, which were slave states that had stayed in the Union, Lincoln refused to deal with the slave issue in any systematic manner. As the war progressed, however, African Americans and white abolitionists pushed Lincoln to change his mind and add the elimination of slavery to the reasons the Union was fighting the Civil War.

Free African Americans as well as slaves were convinced much earlier than Lincoln that a Northern victory would end slavery, even though the stated purpose of the war was to save the Union. As Frederick Douglass explained, "The American people and the Government at Washington may refuse to recognize it for a time but the 'inexorable logic of events' will force it upon them in the end; that the war now being waged in this land is a war for and against slavery." One African American complained, "Our union friends says the[y] are not fighting to free the negroes . . . we are fighting for the union . . . very well let the white fight for what the[y] want and we negroes fight for what we want . . . liberty must take the day."

During the war, some slaves remained on the plantation while others, often seeking liberty, escaped to the Union lines. Some planters fled to Texas and other states to keep their slaves away from the Union army. These flights made slave escapes almost impossible. When the soldiers were nearby, male slaves could escape but elderly slaves and women with small children often found it difficult to run to Union lines. As slaves fled, the work of those who remained on the plantation expanded. As one man recalled, during the war, slave owners made slave children "do a man's work."

Raids on a plantation by soldiers—of both armies—increased the difficulty of the slaves' work. Soldiers also raided the slaves' quarters, taking their few possessions. Deprivations caused by the war affected both the Southern whites and the African Americans on plantations.

Harsh treatment by Union soldiers made some slaves wary of them. Moreover, if slaves helped the Northern soldiers, they could be punished by their masters once the soldiers left. Some slaves therefore failed to cooperate, to protect themselves. Once when a Union soldier confronted a slave woman and demanded to know where the silverware was hidden, she told him that her owners were too cheap to buy anything that nice. (She had earlier helped bury the silver near the very spot where she was speaking to the soldier.) However, many other slaves did not protect their masters' property from soldiers.

The taking of food by Union soldiers and their destruction of plantation property confused some slaves, especially children. They developed an ambivalence toward the Union soldiers, unable to decide if the Yankees were their liberators or merely new enslavers. Even before having contact with them, slave children were predisposed to be afraid of Yankee soldiers because they had heard Southern whites refer to them as devils and monsters. Some slave children interpreted these words literally. Mollie Williams later recalled, "Us all thought de Yankees was some kin' of debils an' we was skeered to death of 'em."

Fear of the Union soldiers did not mean, however, that the slaves who remained on the plantations supported slavery or continued to work and act as they had under slavery. The Civil War and the general turmoil it brought destroyed the customary white authority on most plantations and small farms. As a result, slaves often refused to do certain kinds of work and argued over matters of discipline and the management of the plantation. Even before emancipation, they began to assert their rights as freed people. Before the close of the war, one slave owner greeted one of his workers with "Howdy, Uncle," but the slave responded with a demand for proper respect: "Call me Mister." On a minority of plantations, the freed slaves became violent, burning property and looting from their previous owners. Because of the war, some owners simply abandoned their plantations. The slaves who stayed behind divided the land and property among themselves. They planted food crops and sometimes cotton to sell.

Other slaves left their plantations to escape slavery. In the South, all through the war thousands of slaves freed themselves by running to the Union lines. As one military chaplain described it, "Blacks illustrated what the history of the world has rarely seen—a slave population . . . leaving its bondage of centuries . . . individually or in families. . . . Their comings were like the arrivals of cities." Leaving one's family to seek freedom behind the Yankee lines was difficult, both emotionally and physically. When his father escaped, Levi McLaurin's son recalled, "I was present when he left and I told him goodbye. He said he would be back after us all." The son "saw men put dogs on his tracks and heard dogs running after my father." Another male slave joined McLaurin but turned back after three miles "because I could not leave my family."

If freed people running toward the Union lines were caught by their masters, they were whipped or even killed. One newly freed man, John Boston, escaped to a regiment from Brooklyn that was stationed in Virginia. Missing his still-enslaved wife, he wrote her: "My Dear wife It is with grate joy I take this time to let you know Where I am[.] i am now in Safety in the 14th Regiment of Brooklyn[.] this Day i can Adress you thank god as a free man[.] I had a little trouble in giting away." He added, "I trust the time Will Come When We Shal meet again[.] And if We dont met on earth We will Meet in heaven."

As the war progressed, more women, particularly if they did not have small children, accompanied the men. Former slave woman Maggie Dixon recalled that when "the Union cavalry came past our plantation, told us to quit work, and follow them, we were all too glad to do so." Slaves were especially eager to leave the plantations after soldiers destroyed the food supplies there.

At the beginning of the war, the federal government had no policy regarding the

In this cartoon, slaves abandon their master and run to Fort Monroe. General Benjamin Butler, who was in command of that Virginia fort, had declared such runaways "contraband" and had allowed them to stay with the Union forces.

treatment of escaping slaves. However, the sheer number of fleeing slaves soon pushed Congress and the Union army into forming a plan to deal with the slaves' aspirations for freedom. As soon as the Union army approached, slaves from neighboring plantations ran to its lines, hoping for their freedom. But to the slaves' disappointment, Northern soldiers in the early part of the war returned runaway slaves to their masters. Not all the Yankee generals agreed with this policy. In May 1861, General Benjamin Butler, stationed in Virginia, declared the runaway slaves "contraband," or property taken during war, and allowed them to stay with the army. Butler later explained, "I was always a friend of southern rights, but an enemy of southern wrongs." Butler's policy of freeing individual slaves who escaped to the Union army was tolerated by the federal government. Nevertheless, when other Union generals issued more sweeping orders freeing all the slaves in territories under their command, President Lincoln overrode them.

To help clarify the status of the slaves, in August 1861 Congress passed the first Confiscation Act, which kept slave owners from reenslaving runaways. Union soldiers occasionally continued to act as slave catchers and forced escaped slaves to go back to their masters. Finally, in March 1862, Congress passed a law forbidding Union soldiers from returning escaped slaves. Then in July 1862, Congress passed the second Confiscation Act, which more broadly freed the slaves of any master helping the Confederacy. Together, these measures began slowly to change the focus of the war toward a struggle for liberation by the slaves.

Throughout the war, the Union army had the practical problem of what to do with all the people fleeing to it. The army quickly put the men to work as drivers, cooks, blacksmiths, and construction workers, but the women, children, and elderly were more difficult to employ. For the fleeing slaves, the military established areas called contraband camps, usually near Union encampments. These contraband camps were often overcrowded and unsanitary. Moreover, when the soldiers moved on to fight another battle, their departure jeopardized the safety of the freed people living in the camps. White Southerners sometimes raided the camps, killing or recapturing their former slaves. Still, African Americans often established lasting friendships while living in the camps.

The composition of the contraband camps changed after July 1862 when the federal government began to allow African-American men to serve in the Union army. Once the men left, the women, children, and men unable to serve remained. Afraid that civilian freed people were becoming too dependent on government aid in the camps, U.S. officials decided to put them to work. The military therefore removed slave women, children, and men unfit for military duty from the contraband camps and placed them on abandoned plantations. There they became part of the first major experiment with non-slave labor in the South. These plantations were run either by Northern white men or by Southern planters who had taken a loyalty oath. In many areas, the employers had to promise not to whip the freed workers or use physical punishments against them.

These free laborers were supposed to be paid, but often they received very low wages or no compensation at all. Their labor contracts also contained many restrictions. Some required, for instance, that the workers carry passes when they left the plantations, in a system reminiscent of slavery. Also, food and clothing were usually in short supply. Adult workers were charged for their food and that of their children. Compounding these problems, Confederates sometimes raided these plantations and reenslaved the workers.

By the end of 1862, the women typically stayed in contraband camps or on plantations as wage laborers on Union-controlled plantations, while African-American men served in the army. The North was slow to see the value of enlisting African Americans, whether slave or free. As soon as the war started in 1861, many white abolitionists and blacks lobbied for enlisting African-American men into the army. When African-American men in the North tried to enlist, army recruiters turned them away. As one man from Ohio wrote to the secretary of war, "We beg that you will receive one or more regiments (or companies) of the colored of the free States. . . . We are partly drilled and would wish to enter active service immediately. . . . To prove our attachment and our will to defend the government we only ask a trial." The federal government refused, however, because officials were afraid that white soldiers would not want to fight alongside blacks. As the war dragged on, however, fewer white men wanted to serve in a war with such high casualties. As voluntary enlistments dropped off, the federal government instituted a draft that proved highly unpopular with many Northern whites. In July 1863 whites rioted against the draft in New York City, blaming African Americans for the war, and rampaged against them. Rioters murdered blacks and burned down an African-American orphanage and a church. The administrator of the orphanage managed to remove all the children to safety before the building was torched, however.

In July 1862, the government decided to allow African Americans to join the Union army. Although some of those who served in all-black regiments were free Northern blacks, such as Frederick Douglass's sons, most African-American

The U.S. Colored Artillery practices gun drills. Forced to serve in segregated regiments, black men faced unfair treatment by the federal government. They were paid less than white soldiers, often used inferior weapons, and received inferior medical treatment.

soldiers were former Southern slaves. Many runaways chose to enlist, although some were given little choice by Union officers needing to make their quotas of recruits.

African-American soldiers faced many more obstacles than white men in trying to join the army. According to one report, when a group of African-American men in Kentucky enlisted in the Union army, "a mob of young men . . . followed these black men from town, seized them and whipped them most unmercifully with cow hides." Afterward "they declared that 'negro enlistments should not take place.'" On occasion white men beat, whipped, and even killed African Americans who tried to join the Union army.

Although the army paid white soldiers thirteen dollars a month, African-American soldiers received only ten dollars, with three dollars deducted for their clothing allowance. In protest, African-American soldiers in the 54th Massachusetts Infantry refused to accept any money until Congress guaranteed them equal pay, which it did in 1864. As one corporal in the 54th pointed out to President Lincoln: "We have done a Soldiers Duty. Why cant we have a Soldiers pay? . . . We feel as though, our Country spurned us, now we are sworn to serve her." Soldiers were also concerned about what receiving less money meant for their families.

African Americans served in segregated regiments, and the government refused to allow them to become officers. Blacks resisted these unfair policies. As one African-American sergeant wrote, "All we ask is to give us a chance, and a position higher than an orderly sergeant, the same as white soldiers, and then you will see that we lack for nothing." The government finally reversed itself and allowed African Americans to become officers.

African-American soldiers often worked not as fighters but as laborers, digging trenches, building forts, setting up camps, burying dead soldiers, cleaning, picking up garbage in camp, and other noncombat labor. In addition, African Americans used poorer quality weapons than whites while in the service. They also often received poorer medical attention. As one white doctor confessed, "Very few surgeons will do precisely the same for blacks as they would for whites."

Occasionally, women were able to accompany their men into the army, if they became army washerwomen and cooks. As army widow Elizabeth Kane explained, "I was with him [her husband] in the army. I washed for him during his entire service in the army. . . . The officers let me live in a tent with my husband." And when he was 10 years old, Robert Paul, whose father served in the infantry and whose mother worked as a laundrywoman for the army, explained that he "stayed with my father at the barracks a good deal" and "was well known by all the Company men." Black women following the army tried to stay close to their male family members, but the army felt that the presence of families undermined army discipline, so women and children were occasionally forced out of the barracks. African-American soldiers resented that white officers kept their wives in their own barracks but often forbid African-American women from living with their men.

When they remained on their old plantations, wives of the African-American soldiers faced retaliation from their slave owners. As one wife expressed to her husband in a letter: "You do not know how bad I am treated. They are treating me worse and worse every day. Our child cries for you." The letter ended hopefully, though, with "do the best you can and do not fret too much for me for it wont be long before I will be free and then all we make will be ours." Receiving such letters caused mixed reactions. Some soldiers wanted to leave the army and rescue their families; others became more motivated to stay and fight for freedom.

Many Northern whites believed that slavery produced men too docile and cowardly to fight. Because of such prejudices some whites doubted that blacks had the competence to fight in an orderly military fashion. Once former slaves had fought as Union soldiers, however, the doubters quickly changed their minds. As one white newspaper reporter raved, "It is useless to talk any more about negro courage. The men fought like tigers, each and every one of them." Whites were surprised when African-American regiments fought bravely at Port Hudson and Milliken's Bend, Louisiana; Fort Wagner, South Carolina; and the Battle of the

Crater, near Petersburg, Virginia. At Port Hudson in May and at Fort Wagner in September 1863, African-American troops battled fiercely against tremendous Confederate advantages. Union deaths from the battles ran as high as forty percent. The battle at Milliken's Bend took place just ten days after the one at Port Hudson. At first the Confederates seemed certain of victory. Outnumbered, the African Americans fought with bayonets in hand-to-hand combat against the Confederate charge. The Confederates could not defeat them. After initially falling back, the black troops held their line and the Confederates finally retreated.

At Big Black River in Mississippi (May 1863), under fire from Confederate soldiers, the African-American soldiers burned a railroad bridge the Confederates needed to bring in supplies. The soldiers also destroyed a section of railroad track. One general described the African-American soldiers: "Of this fight I can only say that men could not have behaved more bravely. I have seen white troops fight in twenty-seven battles and I never saw any fight better." Military strategists utilized African-American soldiers as an element of surprise in the opening charge against Confederate soldiers. Such maneuvers proved effective.

The Confederate government tried to counteract this development by threatening to refuse to grant black troops the status of prisoners of war if captured. It announced that captured African-American soldiers would be resold into slavery or perhaps even killed. This policy was calculated to increase the risk to African-American soldiers if they enlisted in the Union army. One general recalled that in one fight "such of the Colored Soldiers as fell into the hands of the Enemy during the battle were brutally murdered." Nevertheless, the Confederate government's refusal to recognize the rights of African-American prisoners did not deter the soldiers. One answered his commander's warning that "it may be slavery or Death to some of you today" by saying "Lieutenant, I am ready to die for Liberty." In July 1863, President Lincoln announced that he would not exchange Confederate soldiers for Union prisoners if African-American men were not treated the same as white prisoners of war.

Although some Confederate soldiers treated African Americans as legitimate prisoners of war, others were far more brutal. In April 1864, for instance, Confederate soldiers killed unarmed African Americans trying to surrender at Fort Pillow, Tennessee. This massacre became a symbol of Confederate brutality against African-American troops. One black New Yorker wrote to President Lincoln: "If the murder of the colored troops at Fort Pillow is not followed by prompt action on the part of our government, it may as well disband all its colored troops for no soldiers whom the government will not protect can be depended upon."

In spite of their own and their families' hardships, African Americans were proud of their wartime contributions. As one African-American soldier explained, "This was the biggest thing that ever happened in my life. I felt like a man with a uniform on and a gun in my hand." These soldiers fought for freedom for themselves and their families. "If roasting on a bed of coals of fire would do away with the curse of slavery, I would be wiling to be the sacrifice."

African-American men made up almost a quarter of the navy during the Civil War. One reason is that sailors did not have to contend with as much discrimination as soldiers. For example, the Confederate policy of not exchanging African-American soldiers for whites did not apply to sailors. And because the ships of the time were too small to set up racially segregated facilities, blacks and whites worked, ate, and bunked in the same quarters. Particularly toward the end of the war, few ships sailed without African-American crew members. They even made up the majority of the crew on a few ships.

Besides serving as soldiers, former slaves also acted as spies for the Union army. They were able to maneuver in and out of Confederate lines with more ease than Northern white men could. Southerners rarely suspected African Americans of carrying out covert activities. For instance, Harriet Tubman spied during the war for the Union. She went to South Carolina, where for three years she gathered information for the military by talking to slaves living in Confederate-held areas.

Slaves contributed, often unwillingly, to the Confederate war effort. They frequently accompanied their masters into Confederate army camps to serve as personal servants. The Confederate government used slave labor to build fortifications: they cut wood, dug foundations, and did carpentry work. Slave men also moved supplies. The army paid the masters for their slaves' services. A few African-American soldiers did serve in the Confederate army. In New Orleans, free African Americans formed two regiments, not in defense of slavery but to defend their homes against Yankee attack. Once the North took control of New Orleans, however, many of these African-American Confederate soldiers went over to the Union army, revealing the tenuousness of their commitment to the Confederacy. In March 1865, a month before the Civil War ended, the Confederacy, in desperation, finally allowed African-American soldiers to fight in return for their freedom.

When the North's African-American soldiers marched into Richmond, Virginia, as the capital of the Confederacy surrendered, white Southerners must have recognized that the war had destroyed slavery forever. Thousands of slaves had freed themselves by crossing over the Union lines. African-American soldiers served their country proudly in the Civil War, and many died for the honor. For their part, African-American women and children, crowded into contraband camps, endured the war as best they could. Many also worked on plantations and became part of the Northern plan of freed labor that started during the war. The military policies regarding such labor influenced the working relationships between the freed people and their former owners during the period of Reconstruction that followed the war. The Civil War brought freedom to the nation's slaves, but just what this freedom would mean for the formerly enslaved people was unclear.

Freedom: "Take Your Freedom, My Brothes and Sisters"

After President Lincoln issued the Emancipation Proclamation in September 1862, Union soldiers went to the plantations and announced the slaves' freedom. The newly freed people, who had long yearned for freedom, greeted the news with great excitement and much celebration. Interviewed during the 1930s, Harry Bridges vividly recalled the day when three federal cavalrymen rode onto Major Sartin's plantation in Mississippi, where as a boy, Bridges had been enslaved. While looking for Sartin, they chanced upon a group of slave women hoeing cotton. Going before the women, a slave man was helping loosen the soil by plowing. As Bridges described it, "The Yankees stopped their horses and the leader called to the old negro at the plow and asked for the owner of the place. . . . The soldiers then inquired of him who the negroes were working for and if they had been told that they were free." When the women overheard the soldiers, "knowing a change had taken place" they "rushed to the quarters telling the news to the other women and children." Sartin had refused to tell his slaves that they were free, but the Union soldiers "told them of their freedom. One negro woman who was unable to believe the news asked if they might leave the plantation at the moment to go where they wished and of course she was answered in the affirmative much to her surprise."

The freeing of Major Sartin's slaves illustrates two important themes of the Reconstruction period. The first is that former slave owners and Southern whites generally resisted treating African Americans as free and no longer slaves. When they finally did reconcile themselves to the end of slavery, former owners never believed that African Americans were equal to and should be granted the same rights as whites. The second is that freed people had to define freedom for themselves, like the woman described above. Typical definitions of freedom often included living where one wanted and receiving payment for one's labor. One woman recalled in the 1930s that the freed people had expressed the desire to "do like dey please wid no boss over dem, an' den dey wanted to go places an' have no patroller ketch dem."

Gradually, the federal government began to plan for the former slaves becoming free. In September 1862, after the Union forces won at Antietam, Maryland, President Lincoln issued his Emancipation Proclamation, declaring freedom for the enslaved people in the Confederacy effective January 1, 1863. Lincoln deliberated for quite a while before changing the focus of the Civil War from a war to save the Union to one to end slavery. Although he personally opposed slavery, he had acted cautiously because of political considerations, fearing opposition from such loyal slave states as Maryland and Missouri. He favored gradual, compensated emancipation, with slave masters receiving payment if they voluntarily freed their slaves. Lincoln slowly began to agree with those who thought that the fastest way to break the South's resistance and end the war would be to free the slaves. He also wanted to preempt the possibility of Great Britain's entering the war on the side of the South, because England depended on the South's cotton. He believed that the antislavery sentiment in Great Britain would keep that country out of the Civil War if a Northern victory were to free the slaves.

Of course, thousands of former slaves had already freed themselves by taking refuge among the Union soldiers, and thousands more would follow them. Where African Americans were already free, they celebrated January 1, 1863, as Emancipation Day. In Washington, D.C., for instance, one freedwoman changed the lyrics of the song "Go Down, Moses" to "Go down, Abraham, away down in Dixie's land, Tell Jeff Davis to let my people go." Although the Emancipation Proclamation did not free slaves throughout the nation (specifically in the border states), it did declare freedom for those slaves in Confederate-held territory and it did allow Union solders in the future to liberate slaves, like Major Sartin's, wherever they found them.

As soon as the Civil War began, slaves—believing that the war would free them—traded information about the progress of the war and Union troop movements. As the noted African-American educator Booker T. Washington recalled, "Though I was a mere child during the preparations for the Civil War and during the war itself, I now recall the many late-at-night whispered discussions that I heard my mother and other slaves on the plantation indulge in." Washington added, "These discussions showed that they understood the situation, and that they kept themselves informed of events by what was termed the 'grapevine telegraph.'"

With emancipation, discussion among African Americans intensified as to their vision of life as freed men and women. In 1865, just before the Civil War ended, twenty African-American ministers met in Savannah, Georgia, with Secretary of War Edwin Stanton and Union general William Tecumseh Sherman to consider the future of the newly freed people. When the ministers were asked about the meaning of freedom, one responded that "freedom, as I understand it, . . . is taking us from under the yoke of bondage, and placing us where we could reap the fruit of our labor, take care of ourselves and assist the Government in maintaining our freedom." When asked how the government could best assist freed people, one minister answered, "The way we can best take care of ourselves is to have land, and turn it and till it by our own labor."

The primary desire for independence expressed by the ministers was echoed by many freed people. "I had a kind master," one former slave explained, "but I didn't know but any time I might be sold away off, and when I found I could get my freedom, I was very glad; and I wouldn't go again, because now I am for myself." Freed people held definite opinions about what freedom meant. For all, from the youngest to the oldest, it meant being allowed to live with their families without the threat of any of them being sold.

Former slaves, like the ministers who met with Secretary Stanton, also interpreted freedom as being able to live where they chose, to own land, and to be paid for their labor. Freedom also meant being able to travel freely.

Jourdon Anderson, a runaway slave during the Civil War, understood that freedom involved mobility and separating oneself from one's master. After Anderson escaped to Ohio in 1865, his former master requested his return to Tennessee, promising Anderson and his wife, Mandy, their freedom and compensation for their labor. Anderson's remarkable letter to his former owner explained his concept of emancipation, which included decent wages, proper respect, education for his children, and a place of worship of his choosing. Addressing his former master as an equal, Anderson described his new life in Ohio: "I get twenty-five dollars a month, with victuals and clothing; have a comfortable home for Mandy (the folks here call her Mrs. Anderson) and the children, Milly, Jane and Grundy, go to school and are learning well."

Freed people characteristically defined freedom as the ability to make choices about how they would look and act. As one said, former slaves "wanted to make money like de white folks an' do deir own buyin.'" They did not want to dress as they had during slavery, particularly on special occasions. Freed women typically bought new cloth for dresses to wear to church or on holidays because new clothes symbolized their new status. No longer slaves, they could chose their own apparel.

Freed people regarded the use of surnames as a sign of respect, as had Jourdon Anderson in Ohio. Whites had never called slaves by their surnames but demanded this courtesy from blacks. After the war, freed people began to choose their own last names. Even though some enslaved people had used last names, many had not. Sometimes freed people adopted the last name of their master at the time of the war or chose one of an earlier master. As one man explained, taking a master's surname "was done more because it was the logical thing to do and the easiest way to be identified than it was through affection for the master." This man chose, however, not to use his master's name. "I made up my mind I'd find me a different one. One of my grandfathers in Africa was called Jeaceo, and so I decided to be Jackson." When an army officer asked one soldier, "Do you want to be called by your old master's name?" he responded tersely, "No, sur, I don't. I'se had nuff o' ole massa."

Above all, freedom equaled autonomy, the ability to make decisions for oneself and in the best interests of one's family and community. Ultimately, it involved not having to take orders from a white master. As one former domestic slave, whose owner used to ring a bell when she wanted her, insisted, "answering bells is played out." African Americans also wanted to drop slavish mannerisms toward whites. They wanted the right to refuse to yield the right-of-way to whites when they met on the street or paths, to refuse to remove or tip their hats to white men who never reciprocated, and to be called by their surnames like an adult, not by their first names without a title, like a child. Grown African-American men resented being referred to as "boy" by whites. And freed people's expectations of freedom were interrelated: the ability to travel allowed both for slave families who had been separated to reunite and for those needing employment to move to new jobs.

Part of the quest for autonomy involved the desire of the freed people to own land and become economically independent rather than continue to work for whites. Francis L. Cardozo, an African-American minister, educator, and politician, spoke in favor of land redistribution at the South Carolina constitutional convention after the Civil War. He argued that "in the North ... every man has his own farm and is free and independent" and demanded, "Let the lands of the South be similarly divided.... We will never have true freedom until we abolish the system of agriculture which existed in the Southern States." Freed people argued that they deserved land because during slavery they had worked without compensation to make their owners wealthy. When asked by his former master to come work for him, Jourdon Anderson astutely suggested that his former master show good faith by giving Anderson and his wife "back pay" as slaves. "This will make us forget and forgive old scores, and rely on your justice and friendship in the future. I served you faithfully for thirty-two years and Mandy twenty years. At twenty-five dollars a month for me, and two dollars a week for Mandy, our earnings would amount to $11,680." Anderson even suggested that his former owner keep the interest on the unpaid money to pay for the clothing and medical care that Anderson and his family had received as slaves. Of course, Anderson did not really expect his former master to pay him back wages. Rather, he was pointing out the inequality of slavery as opposed to being a free person.

Freed people initially had reason to believe they would receive land from the federal government. In a few areas, the government divided up plantations deserted by slave owners who had escaped the Union soldiers. The government experimented with dividing land off the coast of South Carolina and at Davis Bend, Mississippi. Davis Bend was part of the plantations of Confederate president Jefferson Davis and his brother Joseph. Some freed people did receive small plots, although the government sold or rented the vast majority of the land to white Northerners or Southerners loyal to the Union.

Concerned about the number of escaping slaves during the war, General William Tecumseh Sherman, on January 16, 1865, ordered parts of South Carolina near the coast and on the Sea Islands to be cultivated by freed slaves. According to Sherman's Special Order No. 15, the military would give each family forty acres. Sherman also encouraged the army to lend the families army mules for plowing. He wanted freed families to become self-sufficient so that they would not depend on army supplies. In Georgia, freed people also established their own farms on land seized by the military. They worked hard to raise crops on these plots of land, did quite well, and also set up a limited local government in some areas. At the time, some military officers were so pleased by the results that they promised the land to the freed people, although such commitments were not honored after the war.

In March 1865, to encourage land ownership, Congress passed legislation stating that to "every male citizen, whether refugee or freedman, there shall be assigned not more than forty acres of land." However, this legislation was never put into effect because President Andrew Johnson vetoed the bill. In 1865, Johnson returned the plantations to the former owners once they promised loyalty to the U.S. government. Many years later, former slaves continued to express a sense of betrayal. More than sixty years after the war ended, Sally Dixon recalled, "We was told when we got freed we was going to get forty acres of land and a mule. 'Stead of that, we didn't get nothing."

Although the federal government did not give land to freed people, Congress did pass other laws to aid the former slaves. In the Senate, Charles Sumner of Massachusetts sponsored civil rights legislation and laws to aid the newly freed slaves, including provisions for having the federal government help establish schools. Before the Civil War, Sumner had been such a vocal critic of slavery and proslavery senators that he infuriated Representative Preston Brooks of South Carolina, who severely beat Sumner with a cane while he sat at his Senate desk. Sumner never fully recovered from the beating.

While Senator Sumner led the fight for freedmen's equity in the Senate, Thaddeus Stevens championed the cause of civil rights for African Americans in the House of Representatives. As a lawyer in Pennsylvania, Stevens had defended runaway slaves, arguing against their return. As a congressman, he bitterly opposed the Fugitive Slave Act that was passed as part of the Compromise of 1850. This act gave Southern whites the right to reenslave escaped slaves who had run away to the free states in the North. In spite of severe heart trouble, until his death in 1868 Stevens chaired the important Ways and Means Committee, which controls budgetary issues. With Sumner, Stevens was a member of the Joint Committee on Reconstruction that shaped Congressional Reconstruction policy regarding the South.

Under the leadership of men like Sumner and Stevens, the Republican-controlled Congress passed three amendments to the Constitution concerning the newly freed people. These changes were accepted with the necessary two-thirds congressional majorities, after which three-fourths of the state legislatures voted for the amendments. They then became part of the Constitution. The 13th Amendment, abolishing slavery in the United States, was adopted by the states in 1865. The 14th Amendment, granting citizenship to freed people, was added to the Constitution in 1868. This right had been denied to slaves in an 1857 Supreme Court decision. The 15th Amendment guaranteed the right of African-American men—but not women—to vote. It was adopted in 1870. The 14th and 15th Amendments also allowed African-American men to vote for new state constitutions and state legislatures during the period known as Congressional Reconstruction, from roughly 1867 to 1869, when Congress implemented its plan for rebuilding the South. Congressional Reconstruction differed from Presidential Reconstruction, which had occurred from 1865 to 1867, by supporting the political rights of freedmen. During this era, African-American men ran for office, and won, while white Southern men who had supported the Confederacy were either temporarily disenfranchised or refused to vote, to protest the suffrage granted to African-American men.

TO THE
Freedmen.
WENDELL PHILLIPS
ON LEARNING TO READ AND WRITE.

BOSTON, July 16, 1865.

My Dear Friend:

You ask me what the North thinks about letting the Negro vote. My answer is, *two-thirds* of the North are willing he should vote, and *one* of these *thirds* is determined he *shall* vote, and will not rest till he does. But the opposition is very strong, and I fear we may see it put off for many a year.

Possibly there may be an agreement made, that those who can read and write shall vote, and no others.

Urge, therefore, every colored man *at once* to learn to read and write. His right to vote may very likely depend on that. Let him lose no time, but learn to read and write *at once*.

Yours truly,

Mr. JAMES REDPATH.   WENDELL PHILLIPS.

This public letter from reformer Wendell Phillips urges blacks to educate themselves so they can assume the duties of citizenship.

Besides passing these three amendments, Congress overrode President Johnson's veto to establish the Bureau of Refugees, Freedmen, and Abandoned Lands, known as the Freedmen's Bureau. Its mission was to help freed people make the transition from slavery to freedom. The bureau gave out food to both Southern whites and African Americans if they needed it. It also provided an opportunity for former slaves to legalize their marriages, by issuing marriage licenses. Once the freed people realized they would not obtain land, bureau agents helped negotiate labor contracts between the freed people and their new employers and settle labor disputes. Establishing schools and hospitals was another part of the Freedmen's Bureau's work, particularly as it became clear that white Southerners wanted facilities that excluded African Americans.

Understaffed and underfunded, the Freedmen's Bureau did not always work the way Congress intended. Sometimes its employees living in the South were overly sympathetic to white employers and prejudiced against African Americans. Also, freed people found it hard to take time off from work to walk to the bureau in the closest town and make a claim against an employer.

Besides passing legislation to set up the Freedmen's Bureau, Congress tried to protect freed people's rights through other laws. Congress passed the Civil Rights Act of 1866 to overturn the discriminatory Black Codes that Southern states had passed after 1865 to limit the rights of African Americans. Although President Johnson demanded that the Southern states abolish slavery by ratifying the 13th Amendment, he encouraged Southern state legislatures to reject the concepts of African-American suffrage and equality.

Immediately after the Civil War, during what is referred to as Presidential Reconstruction, Southern state legislatures under the control of whites sympathetic to the Confederacy passed laws that applied only to African Americans. These laws, passed from 1865 to 1866, attempted to thwart African Americans' visions of freedom and their quest for individual and community independence. These Black Codes bestowed certain legal rights on former slaves, such as the right to enter into contracts legally. As a result, freed people gained the right to marry and acquire personal property.

More significantly, however, the Black Codes limited various aspects of African Americans' lives. Most states passed vagrancy laws, which meant that African Americans had to prove they were employed by whites or risk arrest. To further ensure that African Americans were available for employment by whites, the states passed strict rules enforcing year-long labor contracts so that workers could not change employers for at least a full year, even for higher wages. In Florida, employees who broke their contracts could suffer physical punishment or be required to provide a full year's labor without pay. Mississippi passed some of the most repressive laws, such as legislation prohibiting African Americans from possessing guns and leasing or renting land in rural areas. Some Black Codes also allowed former masters or other whites to apprentice or have the children of former slaves work for them if the courts ruled that the children's parents were destitute. Thus, former slave owners could keep African-American boys until they reached twenty-one and girls until they turned eighteen without paying them or their parents anything for their labor. The Black Codes also forbade interracial marriage and prohibited African Americans from serving on juries. Although the Black Codes allowed African Americans to be witnesses in court, they could not testify against a white person.

Along with the passage of the Black Codes, white vigilante groups sprang up throughout the South to terrorize African Americans and keep them from exercising their vision as free people. The best-known such organization was the Ku Klux Klan, which was formed in Tennessee in 1866. An early leader of the Klan was Nathan Bedford Forrest, a Confederate soldier and former slave owner whose men were responsible for butchering African-American men at Fort Pillow, Tennessee, during the Civil War. The Klan and other groups targeted whites and African-American men and their families who were active in the Republican party as well as white and African-American schoolteachers. They also attacked black landowners and African Americans refusing to behave in a manner subservient to whites.

Through their dealings with Southern whites, African Americans learned that freedom could not be easily attained but would involve struggle. Freed people adopted a variety of methods to try to ensure what they considered freedom. When possible, they made complaints to the Freedmen's Bureau regarding white injustices. On plantations they joined together to demand better wages and working conditions. Within their communities they established their own churches and schools. With the passage of the 14th Amendment to the Constitution, African-American men, along with women and children, marched to polling places. There, the men cast their votes for Republican candidates to help ensure civil rights for themselves and their communities.

Politics: "Slavery Is Not Abolished until the Black Man has the Ballot"

As a young child, Robert Smalls was a well-treated house servant. When he was twelve, his master hired him out as an urban slave. He worked on the docks at Charleston, South Carolina, and learned sailmaking. Then in May, 1862, in his twenties, Smalls and his wife, Hannah, decided to escape slavery by stealing a Confederate boat and sailing it to freedom. The one they took was a boat Smalls worked on, which had a slave crew and three white officers. There were sixteen people, including Smalls's family, on the ship early one morning while the white crew members were still sleeping onshore. With a straw hat hiding his face, Smalls guided the boat past the Confederate posts, correctly signaling the Confederate codes. Some Confederates thought the boat was out patroling very early, but they allowed it through the checkpoints. After passing the last point, Smalls dropped the Confederate flag and raised a white bed sheet as a sign of surrender. Then he sailed to Charleston, which the Union forces controlled, and turned over the boat to the

Union soldiers. Smalls not only won his freedom but the U.S. Congress paid him a reward for providing the Union army with a working Confederate war vessel.

Robert Smalls went on to serve as a second lieutenant in the Union navy. In 1864, while in Philadelphia, he was thrown off a streetcar. The protests that resulted from this incident led the streetcar companies to integrate their cars. After the war, Smalls continued his political activism. As he grew more successful, Smalls compensated as a free adult for his lack of formal education during slavery. From five to seven o'clock each morning, he studied on his own and, for the next two hours, had private lessons. To improve his reading ability, he subscribed to a newspaper. He became a delegate to the South Carolina constitutional convention. In 1870, he won a seat in the South Carolina senate and served as a U.S. congressman. Smalls became one of the most influential politicians in South Carolina during Reconstruction, supporting public education and voting rights for African-American men.

During Reconstruction, for the first time, African Americans in the South held office in local and state governments and even became lawmakers in the U.S. Congress. Some of these lawmakers had been free before the war, but others, like Smalls, were formerly enslaved. Guaranteeing and protecting the right of African-American male suffrage was important to these leaders, as it was to Smalls. In the face of intense—even violent—opposition, they served in public office.

Before the end of the Civil War, African Americans participated in meetings, organizations, and conventions to voice their political concerns and aspirations. In 1864, African Americans met in Syracuse, New York, to form the National Equal Rights League. The League encouraged the formation of state branches. African Americans in New Orleans formed their own chapter. Calling for African-American male suffrage, the League championed other civil rights issues and demanded, for example, that African Americans be permitted to sit wherever they wanted on streetcars rather than being relegated to the dirtiest, most crowded cars or having to stay on the platform outside.

During Reconstruction, African Americans throughout the country participated in civil rights groups called Union Leagues. Many of the leagues were racially segregated, but some included both African American and white Republicans, working together to oppose the former Confederates, who were Democrats. Union Leagues often supported reforms on the local level such as protesting all-white juries and raising money to build schools and churches. Committed to the issue of workers' rights, the leagues provided advice on negotiating for better wages and even organized strikes in Alabama and South Carolina. To keep mobs of whites from interrupting their meetings, the league often encouraged African-American men to arm themselves when attending. On some of these occasions, black women kept guard over stacks of weapons.

During and after the war, African Americans organized state conventions to advance the political and economic issues of significance to them. These conventions demanded such rights as being allowed to serve on a jury, gain an education, and carry guns. "We claim exactly the same rights, privileges and immunities as are enjoyed by white men—we ask nothing more and will be content with nothing less," declared a statement from the 1865 Alabama convention. It continued: "The law no longer knows white nor black, but simply men, and consequently we are entitled to ride in public conveyances, hold office, sit on juries and do everything else which we have in the past been prevented from doing solely on the ground of color." At the South Carolina convention, William B. Nash, who later became a state senator, summed up several of these demands: "We ask that the three great agents of civilized society—the school, the pulpit, the press—be as secure in South Carolina as in Massachusetts, or in Vermont. We ask that equal suffrage be conferred upon us, in common with the white men of this state." At first it was the African Americans who had been free before the war who controlled the convention agendas, but increasingly freedmen became active.

Immediately after the war, Southern and Northern blacks began to agitate for voting privileges for African-American men. Frederick Douglass argued that "slavery is not abolished until the black man has the ballot." African-American men petitioned the government to grant them the right to vote, arguing that "if we are called on to do military duty against the rebel armies in the field, why should we be denied the privilege of voting against rebel citizens at the ballot-box?"

Tying the vote to military service automatically excluded African-American women from being considered for suffrage. Neither political party endorsed woman suffrage, and the issue lost in several state referenda across the country. Failure to receive the vote did not keep African-American women from other kinds of political activity, however, such as declaring their loyalty to the Republican party through wearing campaign buttons, attending meetings, and marching with their men to the voting places.

President Lincoln favored limited African-American male suffrage, for "the very intelligent, and [for] those who serve our cause as soldiers," but he did not make the advocacy of black male suffrage part of his plan for the South. When he became confident that the North would win the Civil War, he began to work out measures to deal with the Southern states involved in the rebellion. Under Lincoln's policy, men highly placed in the Confederate army or government would not immediately regain their right to vote, but most Southern men would not be punished if they promised to support the U.S. government and accept the end of slavery. Lincoln's plan allowed that after ten percent of a state's 1860 voting population declared its loyalty to the Union, the state could establish a new government. Only three Confederate states agreed to Lincoln's policy: Louisiana, Arkansas, and Tennessee. Because Lincoln developed this plan during the war, it remains unclear how he would have dealt with the South once the war ended.

Members of Congress reviewing Lincoln's plan felt it was too conciliatory to Confederates and did not go far enough in protecting the newly freed slaves.

Congress exercised its prerogative not to allow representatives from Louisiana, Arkansas, or Tennessee to join the U.S. Congress. Additionally, Congress countered Lincoln's policies with the Wade-Davis Bill, which temporarily placed the former Confederate states under military control. Rather than automatically having these states represented in Congress, as in Lincoln's plan, this bill had the President appoint governors to oversee the transition within the former Confederate states. Under these governors, a majority of the voting population (as opposed to Lincoln's ten percent) had to swear loyalty, after which each state was required to pass a new state constitution outlawing slavery. Like Lincoln's plan, in this one high-ranking Confederate government and military men could not vote. In addition, only men who swore that they had not supported the Confederacy or fought against the Union could vote for delegates to write the new state constitutions. This test of loyalty was referred to as the "ironclad oath." The Wade-Davis Bill also provided freed people with limited civil rights. Because Lincoln refused to sign the Wade-Davis bill, it never became law.

Lincoln and Congress were never able to work out a compromise for reconstructing the South. On April 14, 1865, while enjoying a play with his wife at Ford's Theatre, in Washington, a proslavery actor named John Wilkes Booth shot the President in the head with a pistol. Booth himself fell onstage, breaking his left leg. Some members of the audience thought he yelled in Latin, "Thus be it ever to tyrants." Booth limped outside and rode away. Early the next day, President Lincoln died. On April 26 a soldier who was trying to capture Booth shot and killed him.

Upon Lincoln's death, Vice President Andrew Johnson assumed the Presidency. Johnson, a former slave owner, had remained loyal to the Union. He was a compromise candidate for Vice President, chosen to appease the border states and slave owners not in rebellion. Johnson's plan for Reconstruction, referred to as Presidential Reconstruction, was in effect from 1865 until 1867. It differed from Congress's later plan, referred to as Congressional Reconstruction. Johnson's proposals included making white Southerners from Confederate states take loyalty oaths to the Union and called for the writing of new Southern state constitutions. They specified the election of new state governments before a state's representatives to the U.S. Congress would be accepted. Johnson demanded that Southern whites owning more than twenty thousand dollars worth of property request a special Presidential pardon as a way of further humiliating them.

Unlike many members of Congress, Johnson showed little concern over the status of freed people, believing that they needed to be controlled by Southern whites. After presenting his plan for Reconstruction, Johnson vetoed a bill funding the Freedmen's Bureau and the Civil Rights Act of 1866. However, Congress obtained the two-thirds majority required to override a veto, and both bills became law. Johnson tried to undercut Congress's position by attempting to sabotage its efforts at Reconstruction of the South. The ongoing disagreements between Johnson and Congress over governmental policies regarding Reconstruction caused a widening rift between the executive and legislative branches of government. Congress passed a law that the President could not remove Presidential appointments approved by the Senate, but Johnson ignored it. Hostilities grew to the point where the Congress actually impeached the President, although in 1868 it voted not to remove him from office.

The Southern states were quick to accept many facets of Johnson's plan for Reconstruction because much of it was more agreeable to them than Congress's. In 1865-66, white men—many of whom were former Confederates and slave owners—were elected as delegates to rewrite the state constitutions and soon after became state legislators. Although the states' revised constitutions recognized the end of slavery, the state legislatures in most Southern states also passed the Black Codes, which restricted African Americans' civil rights.

Angered in part by the Black Codes, by white attacks against African Americans in race riots in Memphis and New Orleans in May and July 1866, and by the Southern states' unwillingness to accept civil rights for newly freed slaves, the U.S. Congress decided that a plan tougher than Johnson's was needed. For one thing, Congress refused to accept senators and representatives elected from the states that had adopted Johnson's Reconstruction plan. Then, in 1866, Congress passed the 14th Amendment to the U.S. Constitution, which granted citizenship to African Americans and ensured that they were counted in the population for representation purposes in the House of Representatives. Congress further declared that any man who had supported the Confederacy could not be elected to any state or federal office unless Congress approved. This provision incidentally helped promote the Republican party in the South because most of the men disenfranchised were Democrats. Although accepting the 14th Amendment was a prerequisite for congressional recognition of a state's representatives and senators, all the Southern state legislatures except Tennessee initially voted against the 14th Amendment. It ultimately passed in 1868.

In 1867, Congress acted on its own Reconstruction plan. Congress placed military commanders with federal troops in charge of the former Confederate states. Although the Southern states complained about having Union troops stationed in the South, by the end of 1866 only 38,000 remained, mostly in frontier areas.

Another part of Congressional Reconstruction was its requirement that the former Confederate states rewrite their constitutions to supersede those passed during Presidential Reconstruction. A state could then set up a state legislature and, if it ratified the 14th Amendment, be readmitted into the Union and have its representatives accepted in the U.S. Congress. To guarantee African-American men the right to vote, Congress also passed the 15th Amendment to the United States Constitution. It was ratified by the states in 1870.

The new state constitutions written during Congressional Reconstruction were often the most democratic ones passed in the South. They provided funds for public schools, railroad construction, and other improvements needed in part because of war damage. They supported services for the poor and physically disabled as well as the establishment of orphan asylums. The state constitutions also included such progressive measures as abolishing imprisonment for owing money and public whippings as punishment for crimes. Through the revised constitutions and new state laws, much of the racially discriminatory legislation passed under the Black Codes was eliminated.

The Republican-dominated Congress supported African-American male suffrage, in part because some members believed that blacks would achieve equity and justice only if they received suffrage. Congress also knew that freed people would be more likely to vote for the Republican rather than the Democratic party. African Americans supported the Republican party because Republicans endorsed equal rights and the end of slavery, whereas the Democrats had opposed the federal government's ending of slavery.

Congressional Reconstruction made available unprecedented political opportunities for African-American men in the South. Even Northern African Americans headed South to become community leaders and officeholders. On the local level, African Americans became increasingly active, electing men to positions as mayors, police chiefs, school commissioners, and state militia officers. They sat on juries and became policemen and tax collectors. Nineteen African Americans in Louisiana and fifteen in Mississippi became sheriffs. African-American coroners as well as racially integrated juries and sheriffs helped African Americans receive the justice denied to them as slaves. Local black leaders built coalitions with other African Americans to help influence state policies and aid in electing African Americans to offices at the state level.

African Americans voted in large numbers for state delegates to the new state constitutional conventions at a time when many white Democrats who had supported the Confederacy were refusing to vote. With these elections, African Americans became part of the constitutional delegations in the South. Whites, including both Northern Republicans who had moved to the South as well as Southern whites who had stayed loyal to the Union during the war, made up the majority of the delegates. Only in Louisiana and South Carolina were African Americans the majority in the delegations.

When state elections were held after the ratification of the new state constitutions, male voters of both races overwhelmingly elected Republicans, both white and African-American. Many black delegates to the state constitutional conventions later became state legislators. African Americans representatives advocated land redistribution, equal access to public schools, women's rights, a ten-hour workday rather than having laborers work from sunup to sundown, and prohibitions against family violence. They also argued for racially integrated restaurants, hotels, theaters, and transportation systems. Although African-American legislators disagreed among themselves on many of these issues, almost all wanted full political rights for African Americans.

The Mississippi legislature of 1874–75 includes several black representatives. At the time, Mississippi had more African-American officeholders than most other states.

Besides serving at the state and local levels, African Americans were also elected to national office. Sixteen African-American men served in the U.S. Congress during Reconstruction. In 1870, Hiram Revels from Mississippi became the first African-American U.S. senator. He took the Senate seat once held by Jefferson Davis, who had resigned to become President of the Confederacy. Before the war, Revels's parents, as free blacks, had lived in North Carolina. Revels attended college, became a minister at the African Methodist Episcopal Church in Baltimore, and was a chaplain for an African-American regiment stationed in Vicksburg, Mississippi. Revels also recruited black soldiers for the Union army.

Blanche Kelso Bruce also served as a U.S. senator. As a slave in Missouri, Bruce had become a printer. During the war, he ran a school for African-American children. Then he went to Mississippi, where he became a sheriff and a tax collector. After election to the Senate, he worked on such issues as Indian policy, improvements to the Mississippi River, and racial equity.

Joseph H. Rainey of South Carolina was the first African American to serve in the U.S. House of Representatives. Rainey had been a free African American before the Civil War and had worked in Charleston, South Carolina. Robert P. Elliot was a delegate to the South Carolina constitutional convention and served in the South Carolina House of Representatives, becoming speaker in 1874-76. He was also a U.S. congressman. In Alabama, three African Americans served as congressmen including James T. Rapier. Rapier supported expanding public funds for education rather than relying solely on private schools, and he helped freed people obtain land in the West.

Alonzo J. Ransier, born in England, was another South Carolina congressman. Free before the war, he worked as a clerk for a shipping office. John R. Lynch, the son of a slave woman and a white man, became free during the Civil War. After serving as justice of the peace, he was elected as a representative to the Mississippi legislature and served two terms in the U.S. House of Representatives. He advocated voting rights for African-American men.

In the South during Reconstruction, most of the highest state offices were held by whites. Only Louisiana had an African-American governor, Pinckney B. S. Pinchback. He supported African-American male suffrage, education for freed people, and integrated accommodations on trains and boats. Mississippi and South Carolina both had African-American lieutenant governors. In Louisiana and South Carolina, African Americans served as state treasurers. African Americans became secretary of state in Florida, Mississippi, and South Carolina. Arkansas, Florida, Louisiana, and Mississippi had African-American superintendents of education during Reconstruction. In some states, these officials oversaw the development of the first state public school systems for whites as well as blacks.

The African-American lawmakers serving at the state level came from a variety of backgrounds. Some, like James Lynch of Mississippi, were free Northern African Americans before Reconstruction. Educated in Pennsylvania, he went to Mississippi after the war to work for the Methodist Episcopal Church. During the war, Lynch served as a cook in the army. As he wrote in his diary, "I have convictions of duty to my race as deep as my own soul. . . . They impel me to go [to] a Southern state, and unite my destiny with that of my people." Lynch campaigned for the Republican party, organized a Loyal League to support it, and became secretary of state in Mississippi. On July 4, 1865, speaking to freed people in Augusta, Georgia, Lynch argued that "all that my race asks of the white man is justice." Francis L. Cardozo worked as a carpenter, saved his earnings, and went to Europe for an education. A minister, he traveled in the South to train African-American teachers. Cardozo, a delegate to the South Carolina state constitutional convention, later became the first African-American secretary of state.

More than six hundred African-American men were elected to state legislatures in the South, although whites continued to chair most of the important committees. Except in Louisiana and South Carolina, most of the black legislators were former slaves.

During Reconstruction, resistance was fierce to African-American lawmakers and Northern-born as well as Southern white Republicans who dominated Southern legislatures. Whites formed secret organizations such as the Ku Klux Klan and White Camelia. Well-armed groups like the Red Shirts, rifle clubs, and white leagues like the Klan tried to keep African-American men from voting and killed or drove out African-American politicians from their homes, even sometimes out of the South. As historian Eric Foner has explained, "In effect, the Klan was a military force serving the interest of the Democratic party, the planter class, and all those who desired the restoration of white supremacy." One freedman recalled that Klansmen assaulted African Americans and once "ravished a young girl who was visiting my wife." He explained, "The cause of this treatment, they said, was that we voted the radical [Republican] ticket."

Ku Klux Klan violence devastated the Loyal League and made holding mass political meetings increasingly difficult for African Americans. One African-American minister recalled being terrorized by the Klan: "The republican paper was then coming to me from Charleston. It came to my name. They said I must stop it, quit preaching, and put a card in the newspaper renouncing republicanism, and they would not kill me; but if I did not they would come back the next week and kill me." In his testimony to Congress, one African-American justice of the peace in Tennessee stated that Klansmen assaulted him "because I had the impudence to run against a white man for office, and beat him." An attempted murder of an African-American politician in Alabama was justified by whites, according to testimony about Klan activities, on the grounds that he "was going around instructing and enlightening negroes how to act and how to work for their rights, and to make contracts to get their rights." The Klan sent a message to a black Georgia congressman expressing its contempt: "For we swear by the powers of both *Light and Darkness* that no Negro shall enter the Legislative Halls of the

South." Even faced with such opposition, African Americans continued to serve at the national, state, and local levels. Georgia state senator Aaron Bradley, along with other African Americans, fought against the Klan. He wrote a public notice to the "KKK and all Bad Men" that stated, "If you strike a blow the man or men will be followed, and house in which he or they shall take shelter, will be burned to the ground."

African Americans resisted white vigilantism, but they could not fight the combined legal and illegal methods whites used to disenfranchise black voters. In Alabama, African Americans told Klansmen that "they were willing to go out into an open field and 'fight it out.'" But such courageous stands could not effectively protect white and African-American Republicans. Resistance to the Klan and other white violence was dangerous because local whites often did not support African Americans' attempts to retaliate against the Klan. Also, the Klan often possessed superior weapons. African Americans correctly feared that armed confrontation with Klan members and other white vigilantes would increase the likelihood that whites would retaliate and spread the violence against African Americans. During 1870 and 1871, the United States passed Enforcement Acts, which expanded the use of federal courts against election fraud, and in 1871, the Ku Klux Klan Act gave the federal government the right to use federal courts as well as troops against groups conspiring to keep people from voting, sitting on juries, or holding public office. When troops were used in South Carolina, violence declined for a short time in the South.

Nonviolent means were also used to keep African Americans from participating in government. In Georgia in 1868, the state legislature refused to allow duly elected African-American members to attend state congressional sessions, on the grounds that because of their race, the African Americans did not possess the right to serve as lawmakers. The black legislators were finally seated by order of the U.S. Congress. Many white Republicans involved in political coalitions with African Americans preferred that the blacks not hold office but simply elect white Republicans to represent them. The majority of Southern whites never fully accepted the idea of African-American male suffrage, and many secretly hoped to subvert it once the federal government removed its troops from the region.

After a lull during the election of 1872 because of federal intervention, violence flared again. In Mississippi, an African-American sheriff pleaded in a letter to the governor for federal troops to protect African-American officeholders and voters. He observed, "A perfect state of terror reigns supreme throughout the county." During the election of 1875, when violent white mobs tried to keep African-American men from voting, one black policeman told his former master, "We are gwine to have this election; we mean to get it by fair means if we can, but we are bound to have it anyhow." Besides violence aimed at keeping African-American men from voting, Southern whites also refused to rent them land or give them credit or jobs if they supported the Republican party. As one African-American lawmaker recalled, "I always had plenty of work before I went into politics, but I never got a job since." He conjectured that whites refused to hire him "because they think they will break me down and keep [me] from interfering with politics."

During the 1870s, Northern commitment to Reconstruction began to wane. Republicans split over issues such as corruption, tariffs, and free trade. Corruption in government, including bribery of officials, was a problem nationwide after the war. Economic growth and particularly the expansion of the railroads were accompanied by attempts to sway politicians, whether by lawful or unlawful methods. While corruption and graft were much greater in the North than the South, Reconstruction was often blamed for the dishonesty in government. White Southern politicians received much more in illegal payments and railroad stocks than the African-American lawmakers, but some black lawmakers were also found to have accepted bribes. Railroad companies handed out money or stock to gain state legislators' support for their projects, inducing politicians to vote for projects in which they had an economic interest. U.S. Congressman Robert Smalls of South Carolina, along with others, was convicted of taking a bribe, although he was later pardoned.

In the North, whites wearied of the turmoil of Reconstruction. Many began to believe that peace would occur only if the Southern whites, particularly the planters, controlled Southern state governments and African Americans, even though this meant that white domination would subvert the ideal of equal rights. After 1872, the federal government became increasingly unwilling to use federal troops to stop violence against African-American voters and lawmakers. In that same year, Congress gave back the right to vote to most Confederate supporters. As a result of whites voting once more, the desertion of some Southern whites from the Republican party, and the disenfranchisement of some African-American male voters through violence and other means, more Democrats were elected and took control of state governments in the South. As one African-American politician noted, "The whole South—every state in the South—had got into the hands of the very men that held us as slaves." These men favored a white supremacist government and society, with African Americans subservient to whites in their political, economic, and social relationships. These white legislators enacted various methods of keeping blacks from voting. Along with moving polling places into white areas and providing fewer ones where African Americans lived, they also passed poll taxes and established property qualifications for voting. Poor African Americans who could not afford to pay the poll tax could not vote. As a result, fewer African American lawmakers were elected. White officials also increasingly barred blacks from serving on juries.

In 1876, the federal government withdrew even its marginal support for Reconstruction. In the Presidential election of that year, the Democratic candidate,

Samuel J. Tilden, won the popular vote over the Republican nominee, Rutherford B. Hayes. Because in some states, particularly in the South, the votes were contested with both parties declaring victory, Tilden did not gain the needed electoral college votes. In 1877 Congress worked out a compromise through a special election commission that decided in favor of Hayes by one vote. Meanwhile, Republican and Democratic leaders informally decided that if Southern congressmen would accept Hayes, he would withdraw federal troops from the South. Such a policy, which Hayes had favored even before the election, would allow white Southerners to disenfranchise Southern black men without federal interference. Southern Democrats also wanted more control over federal jobs in the South and federal help in financing road construction, bridge repair, and other such improvements.

The African-American men who held office during Reconstruction provided Southern blacks with more legal equity than they had previously received as slaves or would gain under legislatures controlled by the Democrats after Reconstruction. The new constitutions passed during Reconstruction instituted many reforms within the South. The political failure of Reconstruction, during and after the Reconstruction era, was that these achievements were often undermined.

Labor: "I Mean to Own My Own Manhood"

Major Martin Delaney, one of the few African Americans to become an officer in the U.S. Army during the Civil War, went to South Carolina as a Freedmen's Bureau agent in 1865. He delivered a speech encouraging freed people to refuse to accept poor working conditions. First he reminded them of the wealth produced by slaves: "People say that you are too lazy to work, that you have not the intelligence to get on yourselves.... You men and women, every one of you around me, made thousands and thousands of dollars. Only you were the means for your master to lead the idle and inglorious life, and to give his children the education which he denied to you for fear you may awake to conscience." Then Delaney denounced the inequity of free (non-slave) labor: "Now I look around me and I notice a man, bare footed covered with rags and dirt. Now I ask, what is that man doing, for whom is he working. I hear that he worked for thirty cents a day. I tell you that must not be. That would be cursed slavery over again." Delaney's speech raised significant issues for freed people such as low wages and the failure of African Americans to receive just compensation for their servitude. He also stressed that even with freedom, few blacks were reaching the degree of economic independence from whites that they desired.

Most blacks failed to achieve the level of economic well-being that Major Delaney and the freed people hoped for immediately after the war. During Reconstruction, a small minority of African Americans became landowners with small family farms. In South Carolina, for instance, the state government helped some gain small homesteads. But those who became landowners were the exception. By the end of Reconstruction, most African Americans in the South still worked at agricultural labor for white employers, doing the same kind of work they had done as slaves—but now they expected to be paid for it.

Freed people expected free labor, in contrast to slavery, to mean fewer work hours and more control over their work. Freedom meant no more overseers, no more beatings. Workers now expected to be able to leave their employers at will, for better wages or improved working conditions. The former slave masters, however, often disagreed with this definition of free labor. They expected their laborers to go on working from sunup to sundown as before, with one payment at the end of the year, and under many of the same restrictions as under slavery. The agricultural and domestic work environment thus set the scene for struggles between freed people and their employers over their conflicting definitions of free labor.

As 1865 ended, freed people were becoming reluctant to work for white employers because at that time they expected to receive their own land from the federal government. As one man argued, "Gib us our own land and we take care of ourselves; but widout land, de ole massas can hire us or starve us as dey please." And after refusing to work for twenty-five cents a day for his former owner, another worker declared, "I mean to own my own manhood, and I'm goin' on to my own land, just as soon as when I git dis crop in, an' I don't desire for to many change until den. . . . I'm not goin' to work for any man for any such price." Freed people argued that they deserved the land because they had never been paid for their labor as slaves.

Regardless, President Johnson returned to the former slave owners the land the freed people had gained during the war. Most white Northerners agreed with Johnson's decision to advocate wage labor rather than land ownership for former slaves. They believed that land confiscation was too radical a practice for the federal government to promote. Agents from the Freedmen's Bureau therefore traveled throughout the South explaining that the government was not, in fact, going to distribute land. These agents also insisted on having labor contracts between employers and freed people in order to provide fair wages and working conditions for employees and give planters a reliable labor force. Such contracts were agreements between workers and employers indicating wages to be paid and the kind of work to be performed. Other clauses were often included as well, such as statements on deportment. In one case, workers were "required to be orderly industrious people and observe the rules of the place." Contracts also restricted when workers could have guests, as in stipulations such as "no neighboring negroes will be allowed to remain in the quarters [housing for former slaves] longer than twelve hours, without reporting to [the employer]."

At first, African Americans resisted signing labor contracts because they wanted to hold out for owning their own land. They were afraid of "signing them-[selves] back to their masters" as one Freedmen's Bureau agent said. A freedman declared, "If I can't own de land, I'll hire or lease land, but I won't contract." Hoping for more economic independence from whites, some African Americans organized to protest these year-long labor contracts. Other freed people tried to exist on abandoned lands, as self-employed families, by planting crops, hunting, and fishing.

With or without labor contracts, freed people eventually began to work for white employers simply because they were poor and needed the work. And as part of the Black Codes, state governments passed vagrancy laws that punished African Americans by jailing them if they were not employed by a white person. Even when pressured into working for wages, freed people resisted as much as they could. Workers turned the yearly signing of labor contracts into negotiating sessions in which they discussed working arrangements. They held out as long as possible to work out the best deals. Immediately after the war, labor shortages developed in the South that not only kept wages competitive but also allowed laborers to gain extra concessions, such as the right to keep their own garden patch and to have more say in managing the plantation.

The majority of the freed men and women worked in the fields growing cotton, rice, and other crops. Planters continued to need agricultural workers, but few postwar Southern households employed as many house servants as they had previously. Former slave owners hired some freedwomen as maids and cooks, but the contracts show that they also performed other work related to food production.

Wages for agricultural workers varied. Monthly wages ranged from ten dollars to twenty dollars for men and eight dollars to ten dollars for women and children older than twelve. These wages did not buy very much. For example, one freedwoman bought a bar of soap for fifty cents from a store located on the plantation where she was working. This purchase alone probably represented five percent of her monthly income. Often the sugar plantations paid the highest wages because the owners were paid better prices for this crop than others. Some planters calculated a monthly wage and would agree to pay with cash only when they sold the crops. Other farmers paid by giving workers a share of the crop, which the employer usually sold after harvesting. He would then divide the money between himself and the workers. Shares for the work force ranged from one-half to one-quarter of the crop. Occasionally, planters would give the workers' share of the crop directly to them and let them divide it among themselves. At first, planters used the same labor contract for many workers, whether they were related or not. Over time, however, contracts became narrower, with only one family per contract.

Initially, the former slave owners anticipated ruling their employees with the same authority masters had exercised over slaves. Despite their acceptance of the demise of slavery, they could not accept a free labor system in which African Americans would be able to exercise the same rights as whites, such as changing employment or working without physical coercion. As a result, employers sometimes reacted violently to any challenge to their dominance. As one Mississippi newspaper summarized the attitude of most former slave owners, "The true station of the negro is that of a servant. The wants and state of our country demand that he should remain a servant."

The freed people believed, however, that they were entitled to protest labor conditions they considered unfair. Workers and employers argued not only over wages but also about nonpayment of wages. The latter represented the largest number of complaints brought to the Freedmen's Bureau by freed people. As one argued, "I craves work, ma'am, if I gets a little pay, but if we don't gets pay, we don't care—don't care to work." To justify not paying workers their wages, planters typically used the defense that the laborers had bought items in the employer-owned stores on the plantations and had in this way already spent their wages. Employers also deducted stiff fines for missed work, as much as fifty cents or a dollar a day. This rate was often much higher than what employees were paid per day. Freed men and women complained that their employers routinely found trivial excuses to dismiss them after the harvest, to avoid paying them. Since they lived where they worked, when planters ordered laborers off the plantations, the workers lost their homes as well as their jobs.

The former slave owners' reluctance to accept the loss of restrictions on workers such as had existed under slavery was compounded by their own economic difficulties. They had, in fact, very little money to pay their workers with, in part because after the war the federal government declared the Confederate dollar worthless. Even before the war, much of the planters' wealth had depended on their slaves and land. The planters lost their slaves without compensation, and in parts of the South some of the land and property was ruined by the war. In general, land values declined after the war. On top of this, the years 1866 and 1867 witnessed agricultural disaster throughout many areas of the South. Bad weather and an invasion of army worms, which are particularly voracious caterpillars, contributed to crop failures. In 1867 and 1868 when cotton prices decreased from wartime highs (although not to the levels of prewar prices), interest rates rose as planters' ability to borrow tightened. Planters were often in debt to merchants for their supplies.

Planters often proved unable to pay their workers or were unwilling to share the very small profits they had achieved at the end of the year. Given these financial woes, planters wanted a docile labor force willing to work for low wages. Employers were convinced that African Americans would not work without being compelled to through stringent vagrancy laws, restrictive labor contracts, and the threatened use of the whip. Whites saw work as labor for white employers, not African-American self-employment. They feared economically independent African Americans because they believed they would be harder to control.

As Democrats regained majorities in Southern state legislatures, they passed laws that helped planters assert authority over African-American workers. They enacted legislation that made it more difficult for workers to get paid by allowing planters to pay merchants and other creditors before paying their laborers. Furthermore, to keep African Americans more financially dependent on planters and merchants, laws were passed that limited their rights to hunt and fish. During Reconstruction, the Ku Klux Klan perpetrated violence against workers if it thought that they were not sufficiently subservient to whites. The Klan especially targeted African Americans who were self-employed and therefore not dependent on whites. As one freedman explained, the Klan "do not like to see the negro go ahead."

Besides difficulties over the payment of wages, conflicts erupted between freed people and planters over how work should be done and when. The former slave owners wanted their workers to labor in groups referred to as "gangs." After the war, planters hired men they referred to as agents or foremen to do the work of overseers. Workers resented these agents (even in the rare cases where they were African American) and refused to work in the field with them. One planter reported that his workers told him, "We won't be driven by nobody." Freed people insisted on working in smaller groups, often with family members, without continual white oversight.

In addition to resisting working in gangs under close supervision from whites, blacks also protested the use of violence, such as whipping, to discipline workers. Although labor contracts often forbade whippings, many white employers were convinced that blacks needed the threat of violence to make them work.

Workers protested their conditions in various tangible ways. Some joined together to resist violent behavior. In Mississippi, when one overseer tried to harm a field worker, the others turned on him so that he "had to run for [his] life," according to his testimony to the congressional Joint Committee on Reconstruction. One planter's wife wrote about a group of workers who reacted to abuse perpetrated by an employer's son by becoming "a howling, cursing mob with the women shrieking, 'Kill him!' and all brandishing pistols and guns." The son was quickly sent to a private school away from the plantation.

In July 1876, workers in the rice fields of South Carolina went out on strike because the planters had paid them with scrip that could be redeemed only in plantation stores. These stores often had higher prices than outside places. Feeling cheated, the workers wanted the freedom to make their own decisions about how and where to spend their wages. This strike ended in partial victory for the laborers. Although the strike organizers were jailed, the planters agreed to stop paying their workers only in scrip.

Freed African Americans now refused to perform labor not expressly negotiated in their contracts or not associated with the actual raising of the crops. For instance, some freed people resisted repairing fencing or feeding livestock. They demanded opportunities to make more decisions about the crop they were raising, particularly when they were working for a share of it. They wanted to decide early on with the planter how much of each crop to plant and when and where to sell it. Planters preferred waiting until the end of the year to pay them, however, to help ensure that the workers performed noncrop-related labor during the rest of the year.

Planters continued to believe, as Major Martin Delaney pointed out, that freed people did not work as hard as they might. But increasingly, they came to realize that giving laborers a share of the crop was a better incentive than contracting with them for cash. When signing labor contracts, freed people tried to negotiate for the form of payment they preferred. For example, freed people who never received the cash wages they were promised wanted a share of the crop, feeling more assured of such payment.

Disputes also developed over freed people's intention to work fewer hours than they had as slaves. They resisted working from sunup to sundown. They now began to demand Saturday as well as Sunday as days off. Besides working for their regular earnings, freed people cultivated gardens or sometimes rented a small plot of land to raise vegetables and other crops to sell on their own. Having fewer hours of field work provided new spare time for such activities. Freed people also came to expect to spend more time with their families, friends, and neighbors. Although planters opposed any changes from slave conditions, freed people expected the needs of their families to be considered in decisions on how much time freed-women and children should devote to outside employment. African Americans now wanted their children to go to school, not work in the fields.

Freedwomen's tasks for their families increased after the war. Under slavery, breakfast and dinner were often eaten in the fields. The master would typically designate an elderly black woman to look after all the children while their parents worked. With freedom, cooking and making clothes now often ceased to be communal activities. Besides doing the cooking, washing, sewing, and gardening, freedwomen took charge of caring for their own children. Pregnant and nursing mothers wanted to give up outside work. Mothers sometimes argued with their employers about giving their babies more attention instead of working in the fields. One planter complained in his journal, "Harriet and Amelia nursing over twelve months, disobeyed order to quit suckling [nursing]." A few planters even reacted violently against mothers who spent more time with their families than employers allowed. William Jenkins, the employer and former master of a freed-woman named Annette, once whipped her because she arrived late to work. When Jenkins ordered her to strip off her clothes for the beating, she pleaded, "Master William I had my children to tend to made me so late." Jenkins then gave her two hundred lashes with his rawhide whip. Clearly he had not yet made the transition from a slavery mentality to one of freedom.

Freedwomen's need to spend more time with their children without constant interference from white employers was only one of the factors that encouraged the growth of postwar sharecropping. Sharecropping spread at different rates in

Women wash clothes outdoors, under South Carolina pines, around 1880. Although they engaged in such communal activities, freedwomen tried to spend as much time as possible with their own families, caring for children and husbands.

different parts of the South. It was often preceded by other labor experiments, including monetary wage contracts and the practice of working in small groups referred to as squads. Sharecropping usually involved a planter's paying his workers a part of the crop, up to as much as half, for their labor. The planter generally provided the tools and seed.

Sharecropping developed because freed people did not receive land and because employers often failed to pay promised wages on a regular basis. For freed people, sharecropping also meant less direct supervision by white overseers and the ability to work in groups smaller than gangs. It allowed women to balance their time between field work and doing their own families' domestic tasks. Under sharecropping, freedmen could make more choices about how to use their family resources and labor. Freed people also tried to arrange their field work so that their children were able to attend school. The planters ultimately came to accept sharecropping, although they preferred the gang system of labor under the supervision of a white overseer.

Although sharecropping allowed freed people more independence than they had under slavery, it had severe drawbacks. Since sharecroppers bought their food, clothing, and other items from the plantation store, they often finished the year in debt or with very little profit. And as cotton prices fell, sharecropping increasingly became economically devastating for African Americans, poor whites, and the South as a whole. As one freedman summed it up, his people had received "freedom without giving us any chance to live to ourselves and we still had to depend on the southern white man for work, food, and clothing, and he held us through our necessity and want in a state of servitude but little better than slavery." As another wrote, "No man can work another man's land ... even for half and board and clothe himself and family and make any money. The consequence will be the freedmen will become poorer and poorer every year."

Many of the newly freed wanted to leave their plantations to seek out better economic opportunities and education for their children. However, when they migrated into either Southern or Northern cities following the war, they found the employment opportunities very limited. Often, the men found jobs as blacksmiths, bricklayers, or carpenters if they had done these jobs as slaves. They also found work as barbers and as waiters in restaurants and hotels. The Republican party helped some African Americans gain politically appointed jobs as postal clerks, mail carriers, deputy sheriffs, county clerks, and customs workers. A few blacks attempted to start their own businesses, but many of these failed in the wake of the depression of 1873. Freedwomen typically became domestics and washerwomen.

African-American men, like other Americans, looked to the West for better employment opportunities. Although they found more diverse types of employment in the West than in the North or South, they also faced discrimination. As African-American men moved West during Reconstruction, they joined cattle drives as cooks and cowboys and drove cattle in Kansas and Texas. According to his book, Nat Love, who drove cattle, earned the nickname Deadwood Dick by winning a roping contest in Deadwood, Arizona. Some African Americans became farmers in the West by taking advantage of the Homestead Act, which offered free land to those who agreed to cultivate it. Others went west as soldiers. In 1866 the U.S. Army formed African-American regiments of the 9th and 10th Cavalry and organized the 24th and 25th Infantry in 1869. The troops went west and southwest to protect the settlers moving out there. They also built roads, constructed telegraph lines, captured cattle rustlers, protected workers constructing the railroads, and guarded the mail. African-American men tried other kinds of employment in the West and Southwest, such as becoming railroad workers and miners, because these jobs paid more than field work. In San Francisco, where most African Americans were single males, men worked as sailors and railroad personnel. Black women in western cities were still primarily limited to domestic work; some found employment as laundresses.

In Charleston, workers shovel coal. Such unskilled labor was often the only choice for black men, who faced discrimination by white employers.

Some African-American men in the West became very successful. In 1865, blacks in San Francisco owned tobacco and soap factories as well as laundries and real estate offices. A few men formed mining companies, such as the Colored Citizens of California. African Americans also owned silver mines in Nevada, Montana, Colorado, and Utah. In 1870, Clara Brown, who cooked and washed for miners, became the first African-American member of the Colorado Pioneer Association. A few African-American entrepreneurs were quite successful, including the founders of the Cosmopolitan Coal & Wood Company.

Increasingly, after the war—in both the North and the West—black skilled workers like carpenters, blacksmiths, and barbers, who often had received their training during slavery, found that gaining employment was difficult. White employers did not want to hire them, partly because white workers, fearing the competition of blacks, often refused to work with them. On occasion, whites hired African Americans to replace better-paid whites or used African Americans as strikebreakers, which promoted racial hostility. In 1865, white workers in Baltimore drove off African-American carpenters and caulkers from their jobs. Another reason white employers did not hire blacks was that they preferred to rely on the labor of immigrants, who were considered easier to control. Skilled African-American workers were often therefore forced into unskilled labor, doing the lowest-paying, dirtiest, least skilled jobs. By 1870, most African Americans were unskilled laborers or service workers.

Lack of union support also increased the labor difficulties of skilled African Americans. Unions often refused to allow blacks to join, although a few did organize segregated locals, which separated white and African-American workers. Typical was the experience of Lewis Douglass, the son of Frederick Douglass. Lewis Douglass was prohibited from joining the Typographical Union in Washington, D.C., even though he had worked in his father's print shop and had excellent experience. The inability to join a union kept African-American youth from apprenticing themselves to skilled workers and learning a trade. In December 1869, the National Negro Labor Union was established to enable African Americans to join a union and fight for better wages and working conditions. The great majority of African-American workers, however, even those living in the cities, remained outside unions.

In cities as well as the countryside, white employers paid African-American workers less than whites. Tobacco factory workers in Richmond, Virginia, complained that "we the Tobacco mechanicks of this city and Manchester is worked to great disadvantage.... They say we will starve through laziness that is not so. But it is true we will starve at our present wages." Collective action by African-American workers such as washerwomen and day laborers to protest their low wages and poor working conditions was not uncommon. African-American urban workers organized strikes, but they often failed to achieve either higher wages or better working conditions.

During Reconstruction, African Americans were ultimately unable to fulfill their dreams of economic independence. Poor agricultural conditions, labor restrictions, legal and illegal discrimination, failure to obtain land, and the worsening economic times during the depression of 1873 guaranteed poverty for the majority of Southern African Americans. The economic plight of the nation's freed people represented one of Reconstruction's biggest failures.

Family: "My Name Was Peggie One of the Children of Prince and Rose"

Freedwoman Maria Clark recalled in some detail her relationship with her husband, specifically how it began during slavery and survived the war: "I had been with my young mistress about three years when I married Henry Clark in 1859, I fix the date by knowing it was about two years before the late war broke out. My Master performed the marriage ceremony, he did not give me or my husband papers to show for our marriage, but gave us a great treat for all the slaves on the plantation." The couple "remained on the Clark Plantation in Hinds County [Mississippi] thru [the] battle of Vicksburg end[ing] in 1863, which was the first time we knew we were free, all the slaves in the surrounding county was gathered into a camp on a plantation about five miles from Vicksburg."

Henry and Maria Clark stayed in the contraband camp until Henry and many of the other men were enlisted in the Union army. Maria then followed her husband into the army to cook for the soldiers. "When the troops moved off many of us were sent upon the Paw Paw Island where I rented ground to make my living in his absence. I received news that he was very sick in [a] Hospital at Memphis, Tenn. As soon as I could raise money I went there with the determination to take care of him, when I arrived there I found him some better." Clark was discharged soon after his wife arrived and she took him home, although he was "very weak and complained of great suffering. While on the journey, when the boat struck the landing at Paw Paw Island we met several of our friends, who were acquainted with him before he entered the service they assisted me in getting him from the boat." Clark died six months later.

As Maria Clark's narrative shows, slavery did not destroy all African-American families. Some slave couples remained devoted to each other in spite of hardship, even though slave marriages were not legal. Such marriages provided the foundation for many African-American families after the war.

Even though couples could not legally marry during slavery, slave families sustained each other through its day-to-day rigors. Slave couples participated in marriage ceremonies, often with permission of the masters, who sometimes allowed slave weddings to be held on holidays such as the Fourth of July. But the three-day Christmas holiday, which most masters gave as time off from work, was the favorite time to get married. The weddings of house slaves were often quite elaborate, with food and dancing. When a slave named Susan Drane married fellow slave Charles Hooven, a white preacher conducted the ceremony in the owner's parlor. The event was attended by the master's family "and a number of invited guests. They had a grand supper upon the occasion." At some ceremonies the master read from the Bible.

Some slaves did not have a wedding ceremony. One formerly enslaved father remembered that when his daughter married a man from another plantation, "I gave my consent and both the owners agreeing, he came on a certain night and they went to bed together and after that time he visited and cohabitated with her as his wife." He added that "there was no formal ceremony, but they considered themselves husband and wife and were so regarded by others." The father recalled that he had been married the same way as his daughter.

Slavery constantly threatened such marriages. The marriage registers of freed people kept by the Freedmen's Bureau have provided an indication of how long slave marriages generally lasted. One historian has determined that approximately eighteen percent of slave marriages ended involuntarily. Others have calculated that almost thirty-nine percent of slave marriages were "broken by the master."

Emancipation brought legalized marriage to the formerly enslaved couples. During the Civil War, African-American couples kept Union army chaplains busy performing marriage ceremonies. Lucinda Westbrooks recalled being "married by a white man preacher Miller—who came there with the first Yankees and went around marrying the soldiers. He married lots of other soldiers the same day." Chaplains often held soldiers' weddings for several couples at once. Freed people referred to legal marriages as marriages "under the flag." Army regulations promoted such marriages because the military allowed only legally married spouses to visit soldiers.

After the war, couples delighted in the festivities accompanying weddings, either for new couples or as second weddings for those who had been married during slavery. Freed people viewed their slave marriages as binding even after emancipation. However, the Freedmen's Bureau discounted slave marriages because they had not been legal and regarded these new weddings as celebrating first marriages.

African Americans' reasons for wanting to marry after the war varied. For many, marriages symbolized freedom because a master's permission was no longer required. Legalized marriage also meant that children now belonged to their mother and father and could not be sold. Furthermore, church membership often required legalized marriage. The First African Baptist Church of New Orleans, for one, passed such a policy after the abolition of slavery, declaring, "Any person wishing to become members of this church who may be living in a state of illegitimate marriage shall first procure a license and marry." As one woman recalled, "We got married by license, because the church we joined required every one to be married by license." Many freed people marrying after the Civil War sought out a church with an African-American congregation and preacher. As one Freedmen's Bureau official wrote in 1865, freed people "all manifest a disposition to marry in the church, and prefer a minister of the Gospel to unite them."

Former slaves acquired a second family during slavery if they were sold and then remarried. These circumstances, as well as other marital problems often made worse by poverty, caused abandonment by spouses. Desertion brought about particularly serious consequences for African-American women with children. In one case, Nathan Williams, after nine years of marriage to his wife, Louisa, left her and "married again leaving her with one child without means of support," according to a Freedmen's Bureau agent. Such abandonments could be emotionally painful for the spouse left behind. Once a Northerner inquired of a freedwoman, "You have no husband?" The woman responded, "I had one ... but he ran away one day with another woman. . . . Feel like it most killed me at first. I get over it now."

Marital disagreements occasionally led to domestic violence. When this happened, African-American women felt justified in leaving abusive husbands. One black woman named Amanda Fay had a slave husband who, according to her pension examiner, used to "whip her and treat her roughly," so "she quit him because he treated her badly, and; because she thought she had a perfect right to [do] so." Often, members of the extended family would intervene in marriages when violence became a pronounced problem.

While thousands of men and women married as slaves later remarried, some African Americans chose not to go through a formal marriage ceremony. Some refused to marry because a new marriage would jeopardize the woman's pension from the U.S. government. When Union soldiers died, whether during or after their service, their widows were entitled to a pension, or payment, from the government. These widows' pension (eight dollars a month for a private's wife) sometimes made women reluctant to remarry after a husband's death. The federal laws relating to the dispensation of pensions forbade women who remarried or lived with a man from claiming a military pension. Some widows believed they could hide the reality of their living with a man more easily than they could disguise remarriage because cohabitation did not create records such as a marriage certificate.

Such relationships after the war were just like marriages, except that they were not legalized. Couples lived together, with the woman adopting her man's surname. They cared about each other's well-being, and they were sexually intimate. After explaining that she and Thomas Toller had never married but had "lived together until he died," from 1866 to 1904, freedwoman Isabella Toller elaborated, "I had the name Carter and was called Isabella Toller and have not been called or known by any other name since." She noted that when their first child was born, "It was his child and he said it was and we agreed, he and I and my mother, that we would go together for all time." As soon as the pension office discovered these relationships, through intensive questioning of whites or African Americans who knew the women, they ceased paying pensions to them.

When a freedman did marry, he became the legal head of the family. During slavery, the slave masters had held all legal rights to slave families, including the power to sell family members. Even so, a slave father played a part in his family's life. When the master distributed blankets or clothing, for example, to the head of each slave family, the slave father rather than mother usually received them if the couple lived together on the same plantation. Slave men also held leadership positions on plantations as drivers, artisans, and preachers.

After slavery, the freedman, as husband and father, rather than the master assumed legal responsibility for his family, including guardianship of his children. When employers refused to pay their wives or drove their families off of plantations, husbands represented their family members before the Freedmen's Bureau agent or in court. Men tried to protect their spouses and children, particularly from beatings by employers. One freedman defended his shooting of a white man by arguing that the man had "abused [his] wife." Sometimes men signed labor contracts for the entire family and received the whole family's wages.

Increasingly, after the war, employers put labor contracts and accounts at the plantation store in the husband's name, even when other members of the family also worked there.

After the war, freedmen greatly expanded the economic responsibilities they assumed for their families. According to testimony from a pension examiner, one freedman began thinking about his new role while serving in the army: "He had a chance to marry in the service, but could not take care of a wife like he ought to in the army, and did not marry." Four years after the end of the war, once he found work, he did marry. One will left by a freedman showed the extent to which men thought of their wives' economic well-being. Although few freed people left such documents because they often lacked property and were illiterate, freedman Daniel Sanders dictated a will to his employer. He directed that "after my burial expenses are satisfied and all of my just debts are paid which is few I will all I have to go to my wife Leather as long as she lives, And then to be disposed of as she may see fit." Sanders also made provision for his wife's grandson. The Sanders estate "consist[ed] of one mule, one cow, and some debts due me."

Men and women performed different tasks for their families. Freedwomen took on more child care than they had during slavery. They also did such household work as cooking, washing clothes, and cleaning the houses or cabins. Although freed men and women considered the husband the main provider in the family, freedwomen also worked, either as field laborers or as domestic servants for white families. A freedwoman's contributions were important to the welfare of her family. Women sometimes raised vegetables or other crops for the family outside of any wage labor or a sharecropping arrangement. For example, in 1868, when Robert Shackleford signed a contract concerning yearly wages for himself and his sons, the employer also agreed "to let the wife of said Robert Shackleford have for cultivation a certain piece of land ... for her sole care and benefit" as well as land for a garden.

Purchase records from plantation stores reflect the differences in men's and women's family activities as well as distinctions in their dress. In January 1868, on the Oakwood plantation in Mississippi, men bought pants, caps, shirts, boots, and hunting and fishing gear like shot, fishing line, powder, hooks, and buckets. Women purchased material for clothes making like cotton plaid, but no pants or shirts. Men and women both bought whiskey, tobacco, lamp oil, and thread. Freedwomen wore dresses, or skirts and blouses for field labor, while African-American men wore pants and shirts. Women decorated their outfits by adding ribbons and, when they could afford it, enjoyed wearing jewelry, often buying earrings. They willingly spent part of their pay on their attire. Freedwoman Hattie Jefferson purchased a dress upon receiving her first wages for picking cotton. Women elaborately styled their hair by wrapping it with strips of cloth, particularly on special occasions. Wrapping hair and wearing decorative handkerchiefs were both African traditions.

Whites often ignored a freedman's place as head of a family. When husbands who had been separated from their families either by slavery or war returned, whites often resisted their efforts to reclaim their families. Employers did not want men reuniting with their families if it meant losing workers before harvest time.

Whites, particularly employers, refused to recognize either the right of freed people to form independent families or African-American women's right to choose their own sexual partners. Along with attempts to keep family members separated, white men sometimes sexually abused black women. On occasion, although less often than during slavery, whites sexually harassed and even raped African-American women. Particularly during the period of Presidential Reconstruction, local courts often refused to take African-American women's complaints against white men seriously because they believed these women to be less moral than white women. Whites argued that black women's innate seductive behavior provoked the attacks, a charge the freed men and women denied.

During the days of slavery, rapes of slave women by whites generally went unpunished, but state legislatures in the South in the antebellum period passed laws prohibiting interracial marriage. This was to further ensure the inferior status of African Americans and to keep the races legally separated. In the South, interracial relationships had been without legal standing before the war, and immediately after it, the state legislatures passed new laws as part of the Black Codes to reestablish these restrictions. White Southerners especially feared having African-American men marry white women because such unions destroyed any claims whites might make to racial superiority. Later, during Congressional Reconstruction, state legislatures made up of whites and blacks repealed such laws. After Reconstruction, as segregation grew, the Southern states reinstated them.

One significant threat to the African-American family during Presidential Reconstruction was the apprenticing by whites of African-American children. In this era, state legislatures controlled by white former Confederates passed laws allowing whites to keep African-American girls until age eighteen and boys until twenty-one without paying them or their parents for their labor. In order to remove African-American children from their parents' custody, whites were supposed to prove to the courts that the children's parents were incapable of caring for them.

In Mississippi, as in other states, the law gave former slave owners preference in taking the children. Given that the courts were sympathetic to former slave owners immediately after the war and given the freed people's prevailing poverty, whites could easily convince judges of the parents' inability to provide for their children even when it was not true. The parents of apprenticed children often went to the Freedmen's Bureau for help in getting their children back. African Americans resented the apprenticing of their children and the ongoing attempts by whites to break up their families. "I think very hard of the former owners," said one freed person, "for Trying to keep My blood when I kno that Slavery is

WHAT MISCEGENATION IS !

—AND—

WHAT WE ARE TO EXPECT

Now that Mr. Lincoln is Re-elected.

By L. SEAMAN, LL. D.

The title page of this racist pamphlet, published around 1865, graphically illustrates white fears of miscegenation, or interracial marriage. After the war, state legislatures in the South passed laws to prohibit marriages between blacks and whites.

dead." If a child's parents died, other relatives such as grandparents, aunts, uncles, brothers, and sisters would petition the Bureau to gain the release of the child from apprenticeship.

Such concern for family members, whether immediate or extended family, began when children were small. After the war, freedwomen came to depend on their older children to assist in providing care for younger siblings. This was often necessary because women had to work in the fields for wages or a share of the crop even when they preferred to be with their children. Children only a couple of years older helped watch over sisters and brothers. Freedwoman Sarah Robinson recalled, "When I got big enough I 'toted' my brother about." At twelve, Rose Dowan cared for children from the time "they [were] borned and nursed them from that time up until they was large enough to care for themselves."

Knowledge of their lineage was important to African Americans so that their children would know their people. Children learned about their fathers even if they had died or were separated from their mothers when the children were young. Before and after the war, on many of the larger plantations, extended kin lived with their families. In addition, stepfamilies, like extended families, were often relied on as part of the family network.

After the war, women relied on relatives when they did not have a husband. Widows received help from their parents or brothers and sisters when they asked. After the death of her husband, a soldier during the war, freedwoman Helen Thomas Shaw lived with her mother and father. She recalled that "her father helped support me till he died."

Being part of an extended family meant that people cared for their elderly relatives when they were able to. Aged former slaves discovered that finding jobs after the war was difficult. Employers hired only the most physically fit men and women to do agricultural labor. Worn out from slavery, the elderly were forced to depend on their children and other family members to provide for them. Freed people tried to support their parents, but given their own poverty, found it difficult. Immediately after the war, when freed people needed help, they turned to the Freedmen's Bureau. The Bureau was reluctant to incur the cost of providing for aging former slaves, but it did build hospitals for the freed people. When necessary, it transported the destitute or sick to medical facilities.

Local governments, particularly those under Democratic control, resisted taking responsibility for older former slaves unable to work. Even though African Americans paid taxes, local municipalities refused to provide services for blacks in need. During Presidential Reconstruction, local governments passed specific "pauper" taxes, which only African Americans had to pay, but whites still continued to claim that they could not provide assistance to African Americans. However, during Congressional Reconstruction, more hospitals and orphanages were built, due in part to the lobbying by African-American lawmakers.

Families of freed people in the South showed both continuity and change from the days of slavery. As with slave families, the extended family continued to play an important part in people's lives. Unfortunately, white denigration of the male role in the black family and whites' sexual abuse of African-American women carried over from slavery. The practice of whites' apprenticing freed people's children also affected family unity. These issues all stemmed from attempts by white Southerners to establish their racial domination after the war. Even though whites did not fully recognize freed people's right to make decisions for their own families, African Americans were able to exercise much more control over their family life than they had been able to as slaves. Men became the legal heads of their households, and men and women alike were able to raise their children without constant white intervention. Racial oppression failed to extinguish the strength of African-American families during Reconstruction.

Community: "It Was a Whole Race Trying to Go to School"

During the Civil War, the Reverend William H. Hunter, a chaplain in the U.S. Army, returned to North Carolina, where he had been a slave, and preached the following sermon.

> A few short years ago I left North Carolina a slave. I now return a man. I have the honor to be a regular minister of the Gospel in the Methodist Episcopal Church of the United States and also a regularly commissioned chaplain in the American Army. . . . I am proud to inform you that just three weeks ago today, as black a man as you ever saw, preached in the city of Washington to the Congress of the United States; and that a short time ago another colored man was admitted to the bar of the Supreme Court of the United States as a lawyer. One week ago you were all slaves; now you are all free.

Hunter, like many freed people, saw the Civil War in religious terms: "Thank God the armies of the Lord and of Gideon has triumphed and the Rebels have been driven back in confusion and scattered like chaff before the wind."

The political nature of Hunter's sermon is representative of others during Reconstruction, for community activities within the church served as a power base for African-American leadership. Throughout the country, barriers against African Americans' full participation in U.S. society began to fall during Reconstruction, as blacks struggled during and after the war to achieve equal rights in both the South and the North. They also formed their own organizations such as churches, schools, and social clubs.

These new institutions took the place of the slave communities that were then breaking up on the plantations. As sharecropping developed, freed people gradually moved out of their old slave quarters—rows of cabins, often attached to each other—and into individual cabins built on the land on which they worked.

African Americans could use forms like this one to record their family history and list the networks of relatives that many families depended on. It includes, at bottom, a sentimental depiction of what life was like for blacks during slavery and after the war.

Workers usually rented these places. While no longer in the close living quarters of slavery, freed people continued to socialize. Weekends, particularly Saturday night and Sunday, and holidays were a perfect time to get together. Friends and neighbors gathered at church services, weddings, and funerals.

Such closeness did not mean the absence of tension among African Americans, however. Most complaints brought to the Freedmen's Bureau were about white employers not paying their workers, but occasionally freed people brought grievances against one another. Occasionally, an African-American employer did not pay his employees, or lack of fencing sometimes caused friction when a mule or cow invaded a neighbor's garden.

Conflict between individuals did not keep freed people from working toward common goals, such as education for themselves and their children. Education fulfilled practical needs, such as being able to read labor contracts, and it increased the possibility of the next generation's upward mobility. As one freedman said, "I wishes the Children all in School. it is better for them then to be their Serveing a mistes." Being educated was also a way to counter the racist myth that African Americans were innately intellectually inferior to whites.

During the war, many freed people received their first formal lessons from Northern teachers who visited army and contraband camps. One teacher commented on soldiers stationed in Vicksburg: "I have taught in the North . . . and have never seen such zeal on the part of pupils, nor such advancement as I see here." Education was as important to black soldiers as their freedom. One soldier proudly declared, "A large portion of the regiment have been going to school during the winter months. Surely this is a mighty and progressive age in which we live."

Groups such as the American Missionary Association arranged for teachers to travel south to instruct both soldiers and civilians. Charlotte Forten, an African American from Philadelphia whose relatives were prominent abolitionists, taught former slave children during the war on the Sea Islands off the coast of South Carolina. She wrote in her journal: "I enjoyed it much. The children are well-behaved and eager to learn. It will be a happiness to teach them." Besides instructing her students in the fundamentals of reading and writing, she taught history, such as the overthrow of French rule in Haiti led by Toussaint L'Ouverture. Forten "talked to the children a little while to-day about the noble Toussaint. They listened very attentively. It is well that they sh'ld know what one of their own color c'ld do for his race. I long to inspire them with courage and ambition (of a noble sort) and high purpose."

Northern teachers set up makeshift schools on plantations that were under Union control. Southern planters and the Northerners leasing plantations were unenthusiastic about any educational efforts, fearing they would interfere with their disciplining of the labor force. During and after the war, freed people established their own schools. Sometimes they received help from the Freedmen's

The main building of Howard University in Washington, D.C., in 1870. Founded only three years earlier, Howard was one of several black colleges established after the war that provided professional training in medicine and other fields.

Bureau or Northern societies set up to aid the newly freed slaves, but they also opened schools without outside assistance.

Along with primary schools, during Reconstruction institutions of higher education for African Americans were also founded. Among these were Howard University, Fisk University, Atlanta University, Clark University, Alcorn State University, Bethune-Cookman College, Hampton Institute, and Richmond Theological Seminary. Many of these institutions were founded as teachers' colleges to train African Americans as educators, although they also taught other job skills.

After the war, the Freedmen's Bureau established 740 schools with more than one thousand white and African-American teachers. More significantly, during Congressional Reconstruction, under pressure from blacks, Southern states developed school systems financed by public rather than private funds. Throughout the South, schools of whatever sort were segregated, although African Americans made attempts to integrate them.

While children attended schools during the day, adults went to night school after a full day of work. As the African American educator Booker T. Washington explained, "Few people who were not right in the midst of the scenes can form any exact idea of the intense desire which the people of my race showed for education. It was a whole race trying to go to school. Few were too young, and none too old, to make the attempt to learn." At one school in Atlanta, for example, children attended school until two o'clock in the afternoon, followed by adults; evening classes were held until ten o'clock at night. "The parents are delighted with the idea of their children learning to read, and many take great pleasure in visiting the schools," one educator reported, "and asking the teacher to pay 'ticular pains to our children, as we wish them to get all the learning they can, 'caus you know Miss, I's got no learning myself consequently I know how much I loses without it."

Many Southern whites remained distinctly hostile to formal education for African Americans. Resentful about being taxed to pay for their education, whites were afraid that once blacks gained an education, they would fight white supremacy with even greater determination. Planters typically preferred African-American children to work in the fields rather than attend school. They feared that once their laborers gained an education, they would refuse field work and domestic service in favor of higher-paying jobs with better working conditions.

Because white Southerners refused to rent rooms to Northern teachers of African-American students, the teachers often had trouble finding places to live. Local whites, including the members of the Ku Klux Klan, sometimes threatened teachers, forcing them to leave. Also, whites often resisted former slaves' attempts to buy land to build schools. Occasionally, they took the extreme measure of burning down African-American schools, or they destroyed books. Other, more moderate whites encouraged the establishment of segregated schools to avoid the possibility of integration.

The desire for education for their children and more autonomy in the workplace caused thousands of rural African Americans to leave their plantations and go north and west or into Southern cities. Oppressive economic, social, and political conditions in the South caused thousands of African Americans to go west, particularly in the late Reconstruction period. The West seemed to promise fewer racial restrictions and more opportunities, although before the war, many western territories had restricted the settlement of free African Americans. In the Wyoming territories, however, African-American men were allowed to vote.

During Reconstruction, African Americans achieved some measure of equality, aided by a coalition of white Republicans. In the North and West, blacks utilized the civil rights acts passed by Congress to end discrimination and gain access to public facilities. In the West, even though their numbers were small, African Americans agitated for equality during Reconstruction. Under the influence of the dominant Republican party, legalized discrimination diminished in the West. Minnesota and Iowa granted suffrage to African-American men even before the ratification of the 15th Amendment. In 1865, Illinois and Ohio repealed many of their discriminatory laws, including those prohibiting blacks from serving on juries. In California, African Americans began a petition drive to support the right of black men to testify in court, which was granted in 1863. Several western states started to desegregate their streetcars. In San Francisco, as elsewhere, transportation was desegregated, but some public facilities were segregated and restricted seating to separate areas.

African-American political involvement grew noticeably after the 15th Amendment was ratified. In the West, as in the South, blacks were overwhelmingly Republican. In Detroit, men formed the Lincoln Sixth Ward Republican Club, and blacks later ran for public office there with only limited success. In Colorado, African-American men served as delegates to Republican conventions.

African-American communities grew in the West, despite their small populations. California contained the largest number of African Americans in the Far West—more than four thousand. In the Midwest, more than seventeen thousand blacks lived in Kansas, far more than in any other western state. There were some six hundred African-American ministers in the West, about two hundred in Kansas alone. In 1864 an African Methodist church was formed in Carson City, Nevada, even though the entire population of blacks in the whole state was only 367. Fraternal and social clubs and newspapers were all started, and San Francisco had two African-American newspaper editors.

Reconstruction also had an impact on the Northern African-American population as well as on blacks in the South and West. African Americans made up less than two percent of the population in the North, but they had long agitated there for equal rights. In Massachusetts, African Americans integrated various public places for the first time. In 1867, Philadelphia allowed African Americans to sit with whites on streetcars. However, only with the passage of the 15th Amendment could African-American men vote throughout the North. And once they were able to vote, their small proportion in the overall population made it difficult for them to achieve significant political power. As a result, very few Northern African-American men were elected to office.

As opposed to the South, where only New Orleans allowed white and African-American children to attend school together, several states in the West and North desegregated their public school systems. Rhode Island in 1866 and Connecticut in 1868 allowed white and African-American children to go to school together. In many large cities, such as Chicago, black children were educated alongside whites. Michigan desegregated its schools in 1867, although the Detroit school board did not comply until 1871. African-American parents protested that the board had earlier ignored the desegregation ruling, and their activism helped persuade it to end the practice of having separate schools. In the 1870s, Nevada and Oregon allowed integrated schools, and in San Francisco, blacks met and passed resolutions opposing separate schools. The state courts there ruled that schools could be separate but

Students from an integrated school in New Orleans. Although some western and northern cities allowed integrated schools after the war, in the South only New Orleans approved such an arrangement.

they must have equal facilities. In 1875, the segregated schools were abolished in San Francisco. The measure passed in part as a response to the declining economy of the 1870s, which made maintaining separate school systems more difficult.

In the North, African Americans gained access to state-funded colleges that had previously denied them admission. Discrimination continued to be a problem there, however. In Cincinnati, one African American pointed out that racism "hampers me in every relation of life, in business, in politics, in religion, as a father or as a husband."

Along with moving to the North and West, African Americans also settled in Southern cities in an attempt to find freedom. In the five-year period after the war, the African-American population doubled in several Southern cities. Violence on the plantations was part of what motivated blacks to move to the cities. As one African-American state representative pointed out, "People who get scared at others being beaten go to the cities." In the cities, African Americans joined newly established churches, voluntary associations such as burial societies (which insured funds for funerals), savings and loan associations, and clubs—both social and political—established by and for African Americans. Lodges such as the Colored Masons and Colored Odd Fellows were founded. Blacks also formed their own volunteer fire companies such as the Victor Engine Company and the Bucket and Ladder Company in Raleigh, North Carolina, in part because Southern whites refused to integrate those already in existence. The state militia also developed all-black units. In Southern cities, African Americans lived in areas that became increasingly segregated from whites, in substandard housing, often at the edge of town.

Southern cities did not offer an escape from unequal treatment. Occasional outbreaks of violence, including rioting against African Americans in Memphis and New Orleans in 1866, made blacks wary. Public facilities were usually segregated, with African Americans rarely receiving the same level of service or accommodations as whites. Theaters allowed African Americans to attend, but let them sit only in certain sections, often those with the least desirable seats. Some places, such as the New Orleans Opera House, that did not racially segregate people often openly refused admittance to African Americans. In many cities—including Charleston, New Orleans, Richmond, Mobile, Nashville, Louisville, and Savannah—African Americans organized campaigns to integrate streetcars but had limited success. Often, they had to settle for segregated cars.

Both in the cities and in rural areas after the war, freed people established their own places to worship. Those who as slaves had gone with their masters to church services and listened to white preachers exhort them to be obedient to their masters now organized churches independent and separate from those of whites. To this effort, blacks throughout the South gave their money. For example, in Charleston, South Carolina, by 1866 African Americans had established eleven churches. White churches became increasingly segregated as whites refused to integrate their facilities or allow blacks to hold leadership roles. In rural areas, freed people attended church services in cabins or held outside prayer meetings away from their former masters and other whites. Most blacks gravitated to African-American controlled Baptist churches, but others joined the African Methodist Episcopal Church. In certain parts of the South, particularly in New Orleans, African Americans practiced Catholicism.

Churches forged vital links within the freed African American community. Particularly in the cities, attendance was so great that churches often offered three, rather than the normal two, services on Sunday. Services sometimes lasted two hours, during which ministers read letters from former slaves wanting to know about family members separated during slavery. Church buildings also provided school classrooms and places for meetings and lectures. And social life often centered around the church.

Entire religious communities encouraged and celebrated the individual's salvation, which brought a person into the religious congregation. "Saw a wonderful sight to-day, 150 people were baptized in the creek near the church," remarked Charlotte Forten. "They looked very picturesque—many of them in white aprons, and bright dresses and handkerchiefs. And as they, in procession, marched down to the water, they sang beautifully. The most perfect order and quiet prevailed throughout."

Religion also played a role in encouraging education. Because many freed people held deeply felt religious convictions, wanting to read the Bible provided them with another strong incentive to learn to read.

During Reconstruction, freed people used the church—the African-American institution least controlled by whites—to promote political participation. Ministers freely mixed religion with political activism. As one religious leader in Florida explained, "A man in this State cannot do his whole duty as a minister except he looks out for political interests of his people." During Reconstruction, more than one hundred ministers served in Southern state legislatures. Involvement with the church for both the clergy and lay officials as with organizing schools and burial and fraternal societies gave African-American men experience as leaders within their own institutions and helped train them to become effective politicians.

As with religion, whole communities of African Americans participated in political events. Loyal Leagues, formed to support the Republican party, held social gatherings including dances. In at least one Mississippi community, freed people gathered at the church and walked together to local polling places. Women and children marched with the men voters in these parades.

Politics was important to the entire community of African Americans. Freed people often thought of the vote as belonging to the community of freed people rather than to just one person. African-American women, like the men, hoped that having black men vote would ensure a redistribution of land, better schools, equal opportunity for jobs, and equal access to public facilities. African-American men voted overwhelmingly for the Republican party, sometimes with a turnout as high as ninety percent, and African-American women supported their men's decisions. As one Northern teacher described the scene at a polling place, "The colored women formed a line of one hundred or more, and ran up and down near the line of voters, saying . . . 'Now Jack, ef you don' vote for Lincum's men I'll leave ye.'" Planters complained that their field laborers left work to attend political rallies. In Richmond, Virginia, during the Republican state convention, the owners of tobacco factories had to shut down because so many of their African American workers had gone to the convention.

During Reconstruction, the old, tightly knit slave communities on the larger plantations began to disperse, especially with the spread of family sharecropping and the building of separate cabins. After the war, a sense of having shared interests and goals strengthened collective efforts in education, religion, and politics, widening freed people's vision of the meaning of community. Despite fierce white opposition that included violence, African Americans persevered to establish their own churches and schools.

Resisting intense hostility, African Americans participated in America's political life through meetings, conventions, protests for the integration of public facilities, and voting. Even with the ultimate failure of Reconstruction and the return of Democratic party rule, the new autonomy compared favorably to slavery, and African-American families, churches, and schools endured to provide a lasting legacy.

CHAPTER 6

Though Justice Sleeps

1880–1900

Barbara Bair

I n his 1884 book *Black and White*, African-American journalist and activist T. Thomas Fortune analyzed the denial of justice to African Americans and the process of disenfranchisement that characterized the post-Reconstruction era. He observed that the exclusion of African Americans from land ownership and voting were the twin roots of the "great social wrong which has turned the beautiful roses of freedom into thorns to prick the hands of the black men of the South." Despite the promises of freedom, including legal emancipation from slavery and postwar talk of righting economic inequities and providing opportunities, the majority of African Americans faced landlessness, underemployment, and lack of access to political rights or protections. Land, as a symbol of freedom and citizenship, and as a means of independent livelihood, was at the crux of African-American desire in the last two decades of the 19th century.

During this period, nine out of ten of the 6.5 million African Americans in the United States made their homes in the South. Eighty percent of these black Southerners lived in rural areas, and most of them were farmers or agricultural laborers. Some were landowners and had their own small farms, but most were tenants. They rented the land where they worked for cash or a share of the crops they raised. Others worked for hire.

It was very difficult for tenant farmers working under sharecropping arrangements to get ahead financially, and having enough to eat and adequate clothing were always worries. Most faced each new year owing money from years before to the white people from whom they rented land and to the merchant who ran the store where they purchased their goods. "We make as much cotton and sugar as we did when we were slaves," one black tenant farmer in Texas observed, "and it does us as little good now as it did then." Laborers who questioned the high prices charged to them, which would invariably be set at a rate that would encompass or exceed the value of their entire year's crop, had little legal recourse. As one black Mississippian testified to the Senate, "Colored men soon learn that it is better to pay any account, however unjust, than to refuse, for he stands no possible chance of getting justice before the law."

Many African-American sharecroppers and farmers sought greater justice by moving to different land. When their contracts were up at one place, they would often pack their belongings and enter into a new arrangement on another tract of acreage, hoping to improve over their last year's experience. One Alabama share-cropper reported the frustration she felt when she went out in the moonlight to plant rosebushes to beautify the plot of land she was renting, never knowing whose yard it would be the next year. Some moved even further than from one plot in the neighborhood to another. They migrated from the South to form new black towns in the West, or dreamed of a life of justice and independence in an all-black Africa.

Leaving, for families already in debt and under white economic control, was no easy matter. It was hard to do without much money, and it could be dangerous. White Southerners did not want black laborers to leave, because their low-paid work made white economic gains possible. Despite the risks involved, thousands of laborers and middle-class people desirous of greater opportunities left for Kansas, Oklahoma, and other areas outside the South. "The word it has been spoken; the message has been sent," wrote Sojourner Truth in verse she composed about the migrations: "The prison doors have opened, and out the prisoners went." For Truth and other older activists who had worked hard to bring about the end of slavery, the post-Reconstruction treks to new lands were seen as one more step in the march toward real emancipation. For other leaders, such as Frederick Douglass, the migrations were a mistake. Douglass felt that African Americans should remain where they were, confront violence, and take a stand for equal rights. This was difficult to do, and while many African Americans did work and speak out to change conditions in the regions where they lived, others, partic-ularly the poor, who lived under harsh circumstances, longed to escape rather than place their hopes in reforming political and economic systems that were so weighed against them.

Some black leaders argued that the federal government should make public lands available to black settlement as compensation for the centuries that Ameri-cans of African descent had spent in slavery. In 1887 William H. Thomas wrote in the African Methodist Episcopal *Church Review* that he saw the involvement of the government in the distribution of land as an issue of morality and legal principle, mandated by the "equity of justice between man and man, and government and citizen." If slavery was wrong, Thomas argued, then "Negroes were illegally held to service; some measure of compensation, therefore, is due them, not only from individuals who were the nominal owners, but from the National Government which was the prime factor in their enslavement and maintenance in bondage. . . . No measure of compensation would work such beneficial results to the free peo-ple," Thomas concluded, "as the ownership of land." Thomas, like many others who had come before and would follow him, proposed the creation of a separate black territory or state within the United States. In Thomas's vision, the government would buy expanses of land in Southern states and divide their acreage into small homesteads that would be made available for black settlement.

The longing for land and political control that beckoned laborers and middle-class investors west also made them think of Africa. Henry Adams and Benjamin Singleton were among the African-American activists who advocated mass black emigration from the South in the late 1870s and 1880s. These advocates contacted organizations founded to provide passage to African Americans who wanted to move to West Africa, including the long-established (and white-dominated) American Colonization Society and several newer enterprises such as the black-administered Liberian Exodus Joint Stock Steamship Company. Gathering support from tens of thousands of rural black Southerners, Adams and other organizers like him viewed Liberia as a potential home for working people with agricultural skills.

Other African Americans, especially middle-class leaders, saw West Africa not so much as a place to escape from white violence or as a land of opportunity for workers with few resources, but as a place where educated blacks of African and African-American origin could develop their own business enterprises and political structures. In the mid-1880s and 1890s, grassroots groups like Benjamin Singleton's United Transatlantic Society, based in Tennessee and Kansas, continued to advocate migration to Africa as a means of racial unity and progress at the same time that they encouraged Southern blacks to move westward.

Bishop Henry McNeal Turner, a leader of the African Methodist Episcopal Church and an advocate of black emigration, had traveled to Liberia and wrote and spoke of its promise. Organizers for the American Colonization Society also toured through the South, speaking at churches and community centers about African heritage and black nationhood in Africa. When African Americans read Turner's letters about Liberia that were published in church newspapers in 1891, they responded. They formed local clubs to encourage emigration, and many wrote to inquire about securing passage or came East in hope of boarding a transatlantic steamer, but the colonization society did not have enough boats to carry them or the funding to promise future voyages. These disappointed travelers became temporary urban refugees. They either returned West or made homes in the city.

While the influence of the colonization society declined as a result of its financial hardships and administrative reorganization after 1892, several independent movements were formed in the 1890s. Emigration remained an important topic of discussion among lower- and working-class African Americans.

Small groups of emigrants successfully left for Africa, but the overwhelming majority of African Americans remained in the United States. Many who wanted to go to Africa could not afford to pay for the passage. If they decided to leave the South, they looked instead for places relatively close to home to secure land and contribute their labor. Since the late 1870s, black people from Kentucky, Missouri, and Tennessee had been establishing new lives in Kansas and in small settlements

For a fee of five dollars, black settlers of Nicodemus, Kansas, were granted this certificate entitling them to any vacant lot in the town. The chance to own their own land was a powerful lure for many African Americans.

on the Western prairies. Just as national proponents of African repatriation visited churches and schools to teach African Americans about Africa and the possibility of going there, so promoters of migration clubs who wanted to encourage relocation to the West organized through existing black social institutions.

The motivation for going to other states was similar to the idea of going to Africa. "We as a people are oppressed and disfranchised," one westward migrant wrote in a letter in 1891. "We are still working hard and our rights taken from us. [T]imes are hard and getting harder every year. We as a people believe that Affrica is the place but to get from under bondage are thinking of Oklahoma as this is our nearest place of safety."

In 1889–90 portions of what was called the Unassigned Lands in Indian Territory and all of Oklahoma Territory (areas that in 1907 would become parts of the state of Oklahoma) were opened to settlement by non-Indian peoples. Indian Territory had been the home of relocated Indian peoples since federal policy had forcibly moved Native Americans from their traditional homelands in the East in the 1830s. Many blacks and people of mixed race living in the region were former slaves, or the descendants of those who had been held in bondage by Cherokee, Creek, or other Indian peoples for generations. Many of these freedmen and their families were themselves citizens of the Indian nations. In the early 1890s, African

Americans from neighboring Arkansas and other Southern states were attracted to the land grants available in the areas newly opened to settlement by outsiders. More than seven thousand of them moved. They did so with the hope not only for property, but for political independence.

Several all-black towns were established in the territories. These were places where African Americans could form their own municipal governments and protect one another from white incursions and violence. Langston City was one such town. It had its own newspaper, and when black residents across the South read about the plans for the town, they joined dozens of Oklahoma booster clubs that advertised opportunities and promoted migration. A few hundred came to Langston. In 1897 Langston University (also called the Agricultural and Normal University), a college where black teachers were trained, was established in Langston by the territorial legislature. The town's primary promoter, Edward (also Edwin) P. McCabe encouraged emigrants to become involved in Republican party politics and to start businesses. McCabe had earlier helped settle the black town of Nicodemus, Kansas, which was named for an African prince who was brought to the American colonies as a slave and later purchased his own freedom. He hoped enough black people would respond to the Oklahoma Territory land rush that voting majorities of blacks would be created in the territory's local districts. African Americans who came would own land and businesses, and would be able to govern themselves.

Most newly arrived residents in the West and Midwest lived in simple dugouts and took up subsistence farming, much like the African Americans who were already living in the region. A more prosperous middle class also emerged, and these people operated hotels, blacksmith shops, barbershops, saloons, and other service-oriented establishments. Other blacks became deputy marshals or worked on ranches as cowboys and wranglers. Black churches, women's groups, and fraternal orders were founded. By 1900, more than 55,000 African Americans were living in Oklahoma and Indian territories, and between 1890 and 1910, twenty-five black communities were founded in the Oklahoma region.

Efforts at westward migration and the formation of black towns, like transatlantic emigration to West Africa, were plagued by the relative poverty of the majority of black workers and subsistence farmers. Neither the emigration clubs nor African colonization organizations and companies had funds for long-term investment. Middle-class organizers and developers involved in the black-towns movement and in Liberian colonization schemes tried hard to attract settlers who had the financial capital to start or support businesses, purchase land, and establish long-lasting schools, churches, and civic and social associations. Accomplishing these things was difficult to do for those with little money. Colonists in Africa faced prolonged rainy seasons and types of illnesses and fevers they were not used to, and they often arrived in Africa to find that provisions and resources that had been promised to them were scarce.

Blacks who participated in the westward exoduses purchased more than twenty-thousand acres of land in Kansas in the early 1880s, but at the same time thousands of individuals arrived after difficult journeys, impoverished, undernourished, and in need of help. For them, basics like seed, clothing, and farming implements were hard to buy. Many took jobs on the railroads or in towns instead of establishing their own small farms as they had hoped to do. Crop failures and droughts made conditions worse. The economic depression of 1893–94 drove down cotton prices and raised interest rates, burying tenant farmers in deeper debt within the credit system, and made cash and jobs even more scarce than before.

Still, there were successes. The presence of a nearby railroad line could make a big difference in a black town's ability to last over time. Mound Bayou, Mississippi, had a railroad depot. Mound Bayou was a town with a majority black population that, like sites further to the west, was founded on the principles of racial pride and economic opportunity. Black citizens there were able to steadily increase the number of acres of land under tillage in surrounding farms. They established several commercial businesses, such as cotton gins and sawmills, whose success was linked to the availability of rail transportation that quickly moved products created or processed by the businesses to the market. In the 1890s, the residents of Mound Bayou replaced dugouts and log cabins with wood houses and built five new churches and a school building. Black people were elected as city aldermen and held office as mayor.

In the 1890s the Langston City, Oklahoma, *Herald* newspaper emphasized the desire of town leaders and promoters to attract middle-class people to their town. Ads called for shoemakers and other artisans, and invited those who could begin new businesses such as a lumberyard and a harness shop. Several grocery stores already existed, as did saloons, blacksmiths, barbershops, feed stores, mills, yeast and soap factories, a bank, hotels, and an opera house. The newspaper's editors also promised black readers that political liberty and justice would be by-products of life in Langston.

But in the same period when this promise was being made, African Americans saw their political rights increasingly under attack. By the 1890s, Jim Crow laws segregated people of different races in public places such as schools, restaurants, and theaters. They also applied different rules that affected blacks' and whites' ability to do things like vote, secure loans, or chose a place to live. The term "Jim Crow" was an old pejorative way of referring to black people. It had been in popular use since the 1830s. The Jim Crow laws made areas of the West and Midwest, which at first had seemed attractive, difficult places for blacks to fulfill their dreams of independent lives free of white control or repression. Despite injustices, people made good lives for themselves and their neighbors. They worked hard, raised families, and looked after one another in their communities. African Americans also had a large presence in the West serving in the U.S. military and working in ranching and the cattle industry. Many experienced black cowboys were born in the West or had served in U.S. Army infantry and cavalry regiments stationed in Western states.

Black cowboys in Texas around 1890. During the last part of the nineteenth century black cow-boys played a large role in the development of the Western economy, participating in cattle drives and working on ranches.

With the coming of the railroads and the fencing of the land, the massive trail drives in which African-American cowboys had traditionally found employment gave way to the shipment of cattle by train. In the last part of the nineteenth century, the proportion of cowboys who were black varied from twenty-five to sixty percent in different areas of the West. Many of them worked in Texas and Indian Territory. By the late 1880s and early 1890s, these hands worked for hire on individual ranches, sometimes farming their own homesteads on the side and raising small herds. Other highly skilled cowboys entered the roping contest circuit, turning the work they did on the range into performance art. They competed for prize money as horseback riders and ropers in small town exhibitions, large regional expositions, and state and county fairs. Their presence on the roping circuits set the stage for the later achievements of men like Bill Pickett, a black cowboy at the Miller 101 Ranch who became famous for his performances in rodeo and Wild West shows.

Unlike men who made their living in the cattle industry and its offshoots, women in the West were employed primarily in farming family plots. And many were employed in the service economy, working as cooks, cleaners, and laundresses in households and boardinghouses or hotels, raising other people's children, or for a few, working in black-owned stores.

For most black women who remained in the South, the kinds of domestic chores and farmwork that they did had not changed much since emancipation. They worked long hours scrubbing floors, cooking and preparing food, sewing, washing, mending, and doing dishes. They cared for their children, and they planted, chopped, and picked cotton and helped with wheat, corn, and tobacco crops. They also grew small gardens or sometimes kept a cow in order to add greens, butter, and milk to the regular family diet of cornmeal, salt pork, and molasses. They often would try to do what they could to earn a little cash: raise chickens and sell the eggs, pick wild berries for market, or take in extra laundry.

Most African-American households were headed by a husband and a wife, and on average they had four or five members living under one roof. Men usually were married by the time they were twenty-five years old, and women by age twenty. Hard manual labor, poverty, and poor nutrition among the majority of African Americans who worked as sharecroppers were reflected in low fertility rates, high child mortality rates, and an average life expectancy for black men and women of just thirty-three years. Many families lived near other kin, and as women and men grew older they often took into their households other relatives and boarders from outside their immediate family. In addition to caring for her family, a woman living in the rural South would also be involved in working with other women in her neighborhood.

Some African-American families left agricultural life behind completely. Moving to the city, like migration west and repatriation to Africa, was one of the forms of movement that African Americans engaged in as they searched for a better life. While tenant farmers or sharecroppers would often move from one plot of rented land to another, country people also moved from farms to small towns and from towns to cities. In the 1880s and 1890s, although four-fifths of African Americans still lived in rural areas, the concentration of black populations in the urban parts of the South and of black workers in industries continually increased. For them, it was not land but work that was the focus of their search for equality and rights.

Labor: "Let Us Put Our Shoulders to the Wheel"

In a letter published in the *United Mine Workers Journal* on July 14, 1892, African-American union organizer Richard L. Davis talked about the rights of working people and addressed some thoughts to those who saw solutions for blacks in migration or back-to-Africa movements. "The negro has a right in this country," Davis wrote, "They are here and to stay."

One of the places that African Americans were staying was in the cities of the South. Some black urban residents had been in the cities since before the Civil War, when they worked either as slaves or as free men and women. Others came or were born there in the last decades of the 1800s, when the numbers of black people in large Southern urban centers grew. In 1880, for example, the U.S. census showed 16,337 black people living in Nashville, Tennessee. They made up thirty-eight percent of the total population of the city. By the time of the next U.S. census, in 1890, there were 29,395 blacks in Nashville, comprising thirty-nine percent of the city's population. While African-American citizens were still a minority in Nashville in 1890, they made up more than half the populations of other cities, including Montgomery, Alabama, and Raleigh, North Carolina.

Although in this period only a small percentage of the black population of the United States lived in Northern states, of those who did, most lived in cities. In the great migration movements of the 1900s, many black people moved to major industrial urban centers like Chicago, Detroit, and New York, but in the 1880s and 1890s, Philadelphia had the largest number of black residents of any of the Northern cities. In 1880, 32,000 African Americans were living in Philadelphia, and by 1900, 63,000 black people made their homes there and accounted for four percent of the city's population as a whole. Proportionately small but significant black populations also lived in the Southern-Northern border city of Washington, D.C., in Baltimore, Maryland, the New England city of Boston, and other urban areas of the North.

For African Americans in the cities, North and South, employment helped determine the way marriages and families were organized. Racism limited black people to a small number of occupations, mostly very poorly paid. Severe racial discrimination also affected where African Americans could live within cities. These conditions made options regarding marriage and family for black people different than those of their white counterparts.

Life was very difficult for the white urban poor also, especially for recent immigrants from Europe who were impoverished and subjected to ethnic prejudice from native-born whites. But while employment options expanded for American-born whites and white-ethnic immigrants, especially in factory and industrial work, opportunities for African Americans in the cities became even more narrowly defined in the 1880s and 1890s.

Earlier in the century, most free black men and male slaves (and, after the Civil War, ex-slaves) who worked in the cities were manual laborers. A significant proportion of men also worked in skilled positions or as artisans and in construction trades such as carpentry and masonry. Richard R. Wright, who became a social scientist, recalled that when he was a young man in Savannah, Georgia, he could walk down the streets and see black carpenters, bricklayers, and wood sawyers at work. Much of the construction of the public works and transportation systems that made Southern cities function, their "railroads and streets . . . sewers and water works," Wright remembered, were "largely constructed by Negroes." Over time, however, black men were increasingly excluded from the trades and the variety of their presence in the city work world was diminished.

The racism that grew more overt in the last two decades of the 1800s meant greater segregation, restriction, and exclusion of black men from apprentice opportunities and from higher-paid skilled types of work. Some black men in the cities continued to work as artisans—as shoemakers, blacksmiths, coopers, bakers, and barbers. Indeed, one of the most famous shoemakers of the era was an African-American named Jan Matzeliger who lived in Lynn, Massachusetts. He revolutionized the shoemaking trade when he invented a machine that he patented in 1883. His lasting machine shaped and stitched the upper portion of a shoe to its sole, something that previously had to be done by hand.

Despite their skill and achievement, black artisans and small shopkeepers were increasingly segregated and saw white patronage disappear. They found their customers among the growing number of African Americans coming to the cities, many of whom were very poor. Although there were very successful black businessmen and -women who achieved wealth, it was difficult for most black artisans and shopkeepers to make enough money to achieve middle-class status. Most of the relatively small number of middle-class blacks who made up the elite of African Americans in the cities were professionals—teachers, doctors, or lawyers—or were employed in white-collar government work.

The majority of black men in the urban work force after 1880—about seventy-five percent—were confined to manual labor positions or jobs in personal service. The laborers were stevedores, sailors, hod carriers (who carried supplies like mortar or brick to bricklayers, stonemasons, and others at a construction work site), janitors, and the people who did the heavy labor rebuilding city streets or installing public works such as sewer lines. One-third of the African Americans in Philadelphia in the late 1890s worked as servants. They were house servants, valets, and coachmen, porters, hotel help, or waiters. Men made more money in personal service occupations than manual laborers or women in similar service jobs. Given the more strenuous alternatives for employment, they formed a kind of social elite who tended to look down upon those who made a living in ways that involved more dirt and brawn.

Women, too, were restricted in the types of jobs they were allowed to do. The majority of African-American women worked in household service or as laundresses or washerwomen. A few were dressmakers, hatmakers, seamstresses, typists, nurses, or teachers, but it was difficult to get these kinds of work because of white prejudice. White shopgirls or office workers would refuse to work beside black women, and white women would not patronize black women who had skills to offer in health care or fashion. Prostitution was also an urban occupation for women. Like live-in personal service, it was a way of making a living that made child rearing difficult.

One out of five African-American residents of cities, men and women combined, worked as domestic servants within white households. Though many went home at night from these jobs, significant numbers lived in the household where they worked, separated from their families. As cities grew, many African Americans found themselves living among networks of friends or kin but outside a formal nuclear family structure. Besides the nature of employment that took them away from their families, many city dwellers were single men and women who had come to the city from the country seeking work. People who were poorly paid in their jobs, or who could not find work, or were turned away because of prejudice, waited longer to marry. As a result, African Americans in the cities remained single later than those in the country and began having children when they were older. Among the poorest black urban residents—people who suffered most from the strains of overcrowded housing, poverty, and crime—relationships might not be formalized and family arrangements might not last. Because of work conditions that fueled the cycle of poverty, black families tended to be smaller in size in the city than in the country. In the Northern cities, many more black women than those in the rural South remained childless throughout their lives. Whereas all members of a sharecropping family, old and young, worked in the fields and contributed to the family income, in the city it was the individual adult, rather than the family unit, who was most involved in earning support.

A neighborhood survey conducted in 1896 in Philadelphia found that 57 percent of black women and 48.7 percent of men over the age of fifteen were single, widowed, or divorced. These figures included the 85 percent of women over the age of sixty who were either no longer or never married. Black women outnumbered black men in major Southern cities such as Atlanta, New Orleans, Mobile, Richmond, and Savannah. This was true in Philadelphia as well, where an 1896 survey of the black population of the Seventh Ward revealed that there were 1,150 females to every 1,000 males. Of those African Americans who established families, about eight out of ten, in Southern and Northern cities alike, lived in households that were headed by two parents. But about twice as many urban as rural black households were headed by a woman alone.

In 1896–97 the African-American scholar W. E. B. Du Bois interviewed hundreds of black residents about their families in a house-to-house study he conducted with the help of Isabel Eaton in Philadelphia. Their findings were published in a book called *The Philadelphia Negro*. In addition to noting "an abnormal excess of females" among the black people in Philadelphia, Du Bois reported that an African-American "woman has but three careers open to her in this city: domestic service, sewing, or married life." Staying home from work to make married life a woman's "career," although it might have been desired by working-class couples, was mostly just an option for the middle class. While white women of all classes viewed marriage as an alternative to employment, and most endeavored to stop working outside the home when they married, this was not true for black women. Many black women worked for pay throughout their life spans, in spite of marriage, child rearing, and old age.

Residential segregation meant that African Americans were excluded from living in the nicer sections of cities, which were occupied by whites, and were crowded into neighborhoods that had become defined as black. In Washington, D.C., blacks lived in brick or wooden-framed houses in alleyways, built in the middle of blocks behind more stately buildings fronting the main streets and occupied by whites.

In other cities, including Boston and Philadelphia, the backyards of existing buildings were filled with new tenements to accommodate the great need for housing. Theft, violence, and vice were part of black city life, and became more so in the 1890s as black young people who were reared by working parents with little means could often find no jobs for themselves and were welcomed into a developing criminal subculture. Illness also had its impact on black families. Becoming seriously ill was a constant threat for poor city dwellers, who lived in conditions of malnourishment, poor ventilation, and lack of heating in which infectious disease could flourish.

Pay for all African Americans was low. Black men were paid at lower rates than white men or women for equivalent work, and black women made less than black men. In Philadelphia in the late 1890s, according to the Du Bois study, a black man working as a cementer reported that he "receives $1.75 a day; white workmen get $2–$3."

At the same time that pay was lower, rent for African Americans was higher than that paid by whites for the same accommodations. Black Philadelphians living on one street in 1896 reported that African Americans paid "twelve to fourteen dollars and the whites nine and ten dollars. The houses are all alike."

Skin color made a difference in employment. Lighter-skinned women and men of mixed-race heritage were more likely than blacks to be middle-class or wealthy, to have inheritances, own property, have acquired skills through education, be involved in the leadership of organizations, and work in professional or entrepreneurial capacities. Clergy, teaching, medicine, and the law were the most common professional occupations among middle-class African Americans in the city. Still, because of the racial prejudice of whites, a majority of mulatto people were restricted to the same narrow range of occupations and opportunities as their darker-skinned sisters and brothers. The bottom level of urban employment was filled with literate and capable African-American men and women who had skills and abilities they were not allowed to use in the workforce and who were vastly overqualified for the work that they were hired to do.

African Americans did many things to counteract job discrimination and to overcome the isolation and family problems that were the social side effects of that form of prejudice. Social status among blacks in cities came from sources other than a person's occupation. As in the country, women who moved to towns and cities often took up residence near kin and friends, so that their household existed not in isolation but in a network of others. They also boarded in the homes of siblings, cousins, or acquaintances, or took in boarders themselves. Black benevolent societies, mutual aid associations, fraternal orders, and church auxiliaries also thrived in the cities, with women's groups very active among them. In places like Petersburg, Virginia, and Atlanta, Georgia, in the 1890s black women's volunteer groups such as the Ladies Union, the Ladies Working Club, the Daughters of Zion, the Sisters of Love, and the Sisters of Rebeccah provided help in the form of food, clothing, medical care, and assistance with funeral arrangements to working women and families in need. They also functioned as social clubs, bringing community activists and neighbors together for fun and friendship. Like these associations, black churches combined social welfare functions and opportunities for socializing. In addition to providing services such as food kitchens and informal employment bureaus, they were key centers for mass meetings and political debates, spiritual renewal, and shared expressions of faith.

The self-reliance and loyalties that were fostered by these group aspects of urban life were also reinforced by the choices that black men and women made about their labor. Although white employers in the cities wanted black women to supply the domestic labor that was necessary to maintain white households (much as white rural landlords wanted black sharecropper families to work the land for white profit), black women preferred the greater autonomy that they had working as independent laundresses instead of as household servants. As isolated live-in maids and cooks, they rarely saw their own children and were never far from their white employer's beck and call. By working in white households but living in their own homes, or taking in washing and ironing and staying at home, domestic workers and laundresses were able to give more time to their own families and social networks.

The Atlanta washerwomen's strike of 1881 is an example of the successful statement black working women could make by standing together. White city boosters in Atlanta organized an International Cotton Exposition to celebrate the New South's embrace of industrialism and Northern capital investment. The washerwomen, meanwhile, spread the word through church congregations that a mass meeting would be held at a certain church, and in July 1881 they met and formed a Washing Society. On July 19 they went out on strike, demanding higher wages to be paid to all members at a standard rate.

The white city council threatened to levy a business tax against the women workers, and landlords punished strikers who were their tenants by raising rents. The August 3, 1881, edition of the *Atlanta Constitution* reported that the strikers countered by announcing that they were willing to pay fees to the city "as a protection so we can control the washing for the city." They also told the council members to make up their minds soon: "We mean business this week or no washing." The influence of the initial mass meeting at the church continued to grow wider, as household workers, asking for higher wages, walked off their jobs and black male waiters at a prominent Atlanta hotel refused service to the dining room until their wages were raised.

In addition to doing service and trade work in the cities, African Americans worked in industries. Sometimes families that were primarily from the country would combine farming with seasonal industrial work. When men would go away for part of a year to work for wages, the women and young people in the family would remain behind to work the farm. Different sorts of wage work were available. In Florida in the 1890s, for example, more than 100,000 black men worked in the forestry industry, felling trees.

Sometimes the pattern of leaving and staying among men and women was reversed: for families who lived along the Atlantic coast, it was often the women, rather than the men, who would leave home to find seasonal work in seafood

While the majority of African-American women found employment as laundresses or in domestic service, a growing number were employed in industry, including those who removed stems and sorted leaves in tobacco processing plants.

processing plants. In rare instances, women would do jobs usually done by men, stepping in, for example, when a husband or brother was unable to work and filling his place in earning wages for the family in industry or manual labor.

Not all labor that African Americans did was voluntary. The convict lease system, in which prison officials collected fees from private employers who contracted with the state for work done by prisoners outside prison facilities, was a source of revenue for the penitentiaries and states that allowed the practice. It also provided industrialists with a steady labor supply otherwise unavailable in the South, where a majority of white as well as black workers were trained in agriculture rather than industry and were used to seasonal or part-time patterns of working.

The Black Codes made black people susceptible to arrest for petty crimes and, once imprisoned, made them available to be assigned to do forced labor. Under these laws, for example, black men who were homeless or unemployed could be arrested by whites and imprisoned on charges of vagrancy or loitering. Once convicted of a crime, they could be made to work under guard for the duration of their prison term rather than spend the time inside a penitentiary or jail.

The states of Alabama, Georgia, and Tennessee all had convict lease systems, and the brunt of the system was borne by African Americans. Eighty to ninety percent of all inmates in Alabama in the 1880s and 1890s were black. In Tennessee, more than sixty percent of the prison population was black, and black convicts made up more than seventy percent of those who were leased out to work in coal mines. Between October 1888 and September 1889, twenty-six convicts died from injuries suffered in the Dade Coal Company mine in Georgia. Others were flogged for rebelling, and two men were shot trying to escape.

In 1891 labor activists in eastern Tennessee challenged the policies of the Tennessee Coal and Iron Company, which was by that time one of the major employers of convict labor in the state. In July 1891 hundreds of miners held a mass meeting. After the gathering they began a series of actions in which they armed themselves and took control of convict camps, freeing the men who were held within them. In the first such action, they freed convicts who were being sent to work in the company's Briceville mine and put them on trains headed for Knoxville or Nashville. Most of the liberated prisoners were black. More than one hundred of them were able to escape, but most were eventually recaptured and returned to prison.

The free laborers were furious that the mining company planned to replace them with less expensive convict workers whose labor they could better control. One observer of the rebellion of the free laborers, H. H. Schwartz, reported in the *United Mine Workers Journal* that "whites and Negroes are standing shoulder to shoulder" in the actions. Their protest sparked surprise investigations of the mines, during which the investigators found many safety and health violations. It also forced the Tennessee State Legislature to hold a special session to reconsider use of the convict labor system. When the legislators decided to continue the system because of the money it made for the state and the contracting companies, the scattered protests became an organized uprising. Support for the Tennessee protestors spread among miners in Kentucky and Virginia. In August 1892 the convict camp at Tracy City, Tennessee, was burned to the ground by protesting miners, and the inmates set free. Hundreds of miners were imprisoned by state militia that had been called out to subdue the protesters, and Jake Witsen, a black miner who was a leader of the free laborers' actions, was shot to death by soldiers. Thousands of opponents of the convict lease system attended his funeral in respect for his leadership and to bring public notice to the injustice of his death. As a result, in 1893 the Tennessee legislature passed a bill abolishing convict leasing as of January 1896, which is when the Tennessee Iron and Coal Company's contract with the state ended.

Several of the activists who led the convict wars in eastern Tennessee were involved in the Knights of Labor or in the United Mine Workers of America. The United Mine Workers was formed in 1890 during a time when mining was expanding as an area of employment for African Americans. By the turn of the century, some ten to fifteen percent of the 400,000 people working in mines were African Americans. They worked mainly in areas bordering between the North and the

South (West Virginia, Kentucky, Tennessee) and in Alabama. In the 1890s some of them also went to work in mines further north—in places like Ohio, Illinois, or Pennsylvania—as did immigrants from eastern and southern Europe, who joined the Irish immigrants and native-born whites who had previously made up most of the workforces in the mines. Instead of organizing these different groups of miners separately, the United Mine Workers attempted to join members of different backgrounds into what were called "mixed" locals. African Americans were an important part of building the union, and by 1900 twenty thousand black miners belonged to it.

Richard L. Davis was a black organizer in Ohio. He was one of the founders of the United Mine Workers and became a national leader of the union. He was born in Virginia at the end of the Civil War and had begun working in a tobacco factory in Roanoke when he was eight years old. At age seventeen he became a coal miner and went to work first in West Virginia and then in Ohio, where he married and had a family. He and other workers in the town of Rendville, Ohio, faced long periods of unemployment in the mid-1890s, when an economic depression caused many of the mines in Ohio to shut down or operate on irregular schedules.

A powerful speaker, Davis was elected to the national executive board of the United Mine Workers in 1896 and again in 1897. He often used verses from the Bible and examples of things that his fellow workers knew well from church to explain the importance of standing together to try to win greater rights, and to look for justice in this world as well as in heaven. "I know that in former days you used to sing 'Give me Jesus, give me Jesus, you may have all the world, just give me Jesus,'" he told his audience of miners in a letter to the *United Mine Workers Journal* on April 18, 1892. "But the day has now come that we want a little money along with our Jesus, so we want to change that old song and ask for a little of the world as well. Don't you think so, friends?"

Davis was involved in the Knights of Labor as well as in the United Mine Workers. The Knights of Labor was organized in 1869 and reached the height of its influence in 1886, when more than 700,000 members belonged. The membership included between sixty thousand and ninety thousand black people, who, like Davis, joined through the locals in their communities. But unlike most traditional unions or the United Mine Workers, which focused on skilled workers or those in a particular trade, the Knights of Labor welcomed all kinds of laborers: farmers, field workers, women, men, black and white crafts workers, and those employed in all kinds of jobs in different industries.

African Americans like Davis were among the organizers who went into neighborhoods, churches, and workplaces to encourage other laborers to join. Many who became involved in the Knights of Labor did so for idealistic reasons. They believed, as Davis wrote in a letter to the mine workers' journal, in the "brotherhood of all mankind no matter what the color of his skin may be" and in the inherent equality of black and white people. Organizers like Davis who believed in these values established a tradition of interracial unionism among lumber workers in Florida, coal miners in Birmingham, Alabama, freight handlers in Galveston, Texas, and male and female tobacco workers in Richmond, Virginia.

Although many white members of the Knights opposed the organization of black workers, the Knights took steps to defy public practices that denied social equality to blacks. In October 1886, for example, they held a convention in Richmond, Virginia, at which a black delegate named Frank Ferrell, who was from New York, spoke to the assembly along with white dignitaries. He did so in defiance of local custom, which barred black people from sitting with whites in public places or from speaking to audiences made up primarily of whites.

Terence V. Powderly, the head of the Knights, believed that white and black workers doing the same kind of work should have equal wages. He also noted that one of the goals of the Knights was to provide education to working-class children, not just to those of the middle and upper classes. In a speech to an assembly in Richmond, Virginia, in January 1885, he explained that in the places where the Knights had become established the "colored men are advocating the holding of free night schools for the children of black and white. . . . The politicians have kept the white and black [working] men of the South apart, while crushing both. Our aim shall be to educate both and elevate them by bringing them together."

For many working-class African Americans, participation in Knights of Labor activities was one way of being treated with the kind of respect that was afforded mainly to middle-class people, and to the working class within their own churches and secret societies. This was especially true for the women. The African-American journalist Ida B. Wells reported on a meeting of the Knights of Labor that she attended in a piece published the January 22, 1887, issue of the *Cleveland Gazette.* "I noticed that everyone who came was welcomed and every woman from black to white was seated with courtesy usually extended to white ladies alone in this town," Wells observed.

The Knights of Labor also tried to use collective actions to better working conditions. In Louisiana the year after Frank Ferrell spoke in Richmond, some six thousand to ten thousand laborers, mostly black, walked off their jobs in the sugar-cane fields in support of a Knights of Labor strike for higher wages. Like the mine workers who participated in the convict wars in Tennessee, they faced white violence as a consequence of their demands, and several black strikers were killed when companies of state militia were sent in to end the strike.

African-American workers had success organizing in New Orleans, where in 1880 black and white dockworkers who pressed, moved, and shipped bales of cotton on the Mississippi River wharves formed a labor coalition called the Cotton Men's Executive Council. The council coordinated the goals of several dock unions, and covered common laborers as well as men working in the trades. Prior to the formation of the council, black cotton rollers, teamsters, coopers, wheelers, and freight handlers had already created their own separate benevolent or mutual aid associations similar to the Washing Society that black washerwomen had formed in Atlanta. They met together to set uniform wages for their specialties and to help each other in times of need. Demands of the unions involved in the council, which represented some fifteen thousand workers, centered around the need for higher wages. In September 1880 black unionists joined whites in their same industries in a series of strikes that brought wage increases for teamsters, loaders, and other dockworkers.

A year later the unionized waterfront workers struck again, asking for fair wages and for the employers to recognize the union as the representative of the workers. Black unionists kept order until the second week of the general dock strike, when a lone policeman attempted to arrest a black teamster on a city street. The teamster, James Hawkins, was a person that the September 1881 *Weekly Louisianian* described as a "law abiding, peaceful man." He proclaimed his innocence when approached by the policeman and resisted the arrest. The policeman's actions drew the ire of the local African-American women, who threw frying pans and utensils at him from their windows. In the resulting commotion, the police officer drew his gun and shot Hawkins twice, killing him.

Hawkins was murdered, as one of the *Weekly Louisianian* reports of the killing put it, "for no other cause than that a negro has no rights which a police officer is bound to respect." Hawkins's death galvanized the working-class neighborhood.

White unionists joined black dockworkers and their families at Hawkins's funeral, and they emerged determined to defy the powers that would deny them a better standard of living and their desire to have a say in the structure of their own work. They shut down work on the riverfront. Soon all parties involved in the strike met and negotiated a settlement. The strikers succeeded in winning the employers' agreement to standard wages on the docks for each category of labor and some protections for the unions in hiring. More important, they set a standard for biracial working-class unionism that lasted in New Orleans into the 1890s.

The closely related populist and agrarian movements of the 1890s were other ways in which black workers sought to organize both among themselves and, for greater strength, with white working people. Their goals were the defense of racial justice and economic equity in American society. Populism and small farmers' associations were part of a grassroots political movement whose supporters sought to form alliances between poor and working people, especially those who made their living in agriculture.

For example, black farmers in Lovejoy, Texas, formed the Colored Farmers' National Alliance and Cooperative Union in March 1888. Their membership expanded and they joined with white farmers' groups from the Midwest and South. By 1891 the alliance had more than one million members in twelve states. Like the Knights of Labor, the farmers' alliances supported the idea of workers' cooperatives, enterprises in which workers would pool their resources, exchange labor or contribute goods, and share profits. They also wanted to reform wage work to give working people better payment for their labor, and they organized boycotts of merchants who engaged in unfair practices. They sponsored consumer cooperative stores in Southern cities, helped members who were struggling to pay mortgages on their land, and worked to improve the education provided to rural black children.

While the farmers' alliances were being formed, the Populist or People's Party emerged as an independent political party in February 1892, when farmers, labor unionists, and reformers met in St. Louis to develop a program to challenge business interests and the low prices being paid for agricultural goods. Populists supported the rights of non-landowning laborers, including black tenant farmers and field workers, and wanted reform of the country's financial system.

In some areas, one of the party's strategies for change was to try to elect black officials to public office. These officials, it was hoped, would be committed to black civil and political rights, including an end to convict lease systems, the right of black people to serve on juries, and what one black delegate from the Colored Farmers' Alliance termed a "free vote and an honest count."

This strategy had some success in North Carolina, where ten black candidates were elected to the state legislature on Populist-Republican tickets in the 1890s, and many more gained county and municipal offices. Racism as well as class differences marred the progressive aspects of the Populist cause over time, as white small farmers who owned land saw their own interests diverge from those of black sharecroppers and tenant farmers who did not own property.

There were many successes in black-white working people's cooperation in farmers' alliances, populist political coalitions, the Knights of Labor, and among unionists. But one of the unresolved questions in black industrial workers' minds at the end of the 1800s was whether it was better to compete against free white labor for jobs or to join in coalition with white workers to collectively demand better wages and conditions. Skepticism about the genuineness of whites' desire for long-range cooperation was rampant. As John Lucus Dennis, a black worker at the Black Diamond Steel Works in Pittsburgh, put it in a letter to the *New York Freeman*: "Our experience as a race with these organizations has, on the whole, not been such as to give us either great satisfaction or confidence in white men's fidelity."

Mining and work in the cities were two areas where the dilemma between competition or attempted coalition continually played out. In the North, mine workers in the late 1800s were almost all white. Mine operators' use of Southern black workers as strikebreakers thus took on more directly racial meanings than it did in the South, where blacks found themselves on both the unemployed and free labor sides of such conflicts. In both the North and the South, industrialists used racial differences to divide the work force and prevent unionization. They paid black workers less money than white workers for the same labor, and they denied the higher-paid and higher-status positions in industries to blacks. Organized labor often followed these kinds of prejudiced policies. White union members often prevented blacks from becoming apprentices in trades or members of unions, and even unions that claimed biracial principles were dominated by white leadership and weakened by segregated practices, including the organization of separate locals for whites and blacks. African-American experience in unions varied a great deal from industry to industry and from one region or locale to another. It also varied in the same places over time: a successful action in which white and black union members rallied together could be an exceptional event. A long history of exclusion and discrimination might precede and/or follow the period of cooperation. Many black workers were alienated from the very idea of involvement in organized labor because of their association of labor activism with white working-class racism and with union opposition to black industrial employment. At least fifty strikes took place in American industries between 1880 and 1900 in which white workers opposed the hiring of blacks.

Blacks who worked in crafts like carpentry, woodworking, or bricklaying were among those who suffered from white policies of exclusion. This was one reason why the number of black artisans and crafts workers that had once seemed so prevalent in the cities declined, and black men were gradually moved more and more into unskilled areas of labor.

Nonunion white women spinners and weavers in textile factories often spurned working with newly hired black women. Workers who did not have a trade or do skilled work were often excluded from union eligibility of any kind, since craft unions—such as those that represented conductors, locomotive firemen, or engineers in the railway industry—did not accept unskilled or semiskilled workers into their membership.

Black workers also sometimes found themselves in a tug-of-war between industrialists and the unions. In 1890 a leaflet was circulated among black miners in Birmingham, Alabama, that stated "WANTED! COLORED coal-miners for Weir City, Kan., district, the paradise of colored people. . . . Special train will leave Birmingham the 13th. Transportation advanced. Get ready and go to the land of promise." When the black miners who responded to this call arrived in Kansas, they found the white workers at the mines on strike and manning a stockade barring the entrance to the work site. Some joined the strikers; others returned home to Alabama when the union paid their way. Still others seized the opportunity for employment at higher wages than they earned in Birmingham, but under conditions that hardly constituted a paradise for black people.

What was happening in the places where people worked mirrored the changes that had slowly been occurring on the political front since the end of the political Reconstruction that followed the Civil War. The exclusion from skilled and better-paying jobs and from union representation that African Americans were experiencing in the workplace coincided with the loss of rights to vote, to be elected to office, to live where one chose, or to receive the kind of education that black parents wanted for their children.

Justice: "They Have Promised Us Law . . . and Given Us Violence"

It was a spring day in May 1884. A young, well-dressed schoolteacher named Ida B. Wells refused to comply with a conductor's request that she move from the first-class "ladies'" section of a Chesapeake, Ohio, and Southwestern Railroad train to a second-class smoking car further back in the train. Ida B. Wells was twenty-one years old. She often took the ten-mile train trip between Memphis, Tennessee, where she lived, and the town of Woodstock, where she taught public school.

But this day was different. On this day the conductor who came to take her ticket tried to enforce a Jim Crow law that had been passed in Tennessee two years before, authorizing separate accommodations for black and white travelers. When the conductor asked her to change cars, Wells protested. Then the conductor tried to pull her from her seat. Soon the two of them were scuffling in the aisle of the ladies' car as he tried to force her off the train and she attempted to keep her seat. Two other railroad employees came running to aid the conductor, and Wells was dragged away, resisting, and removed from the train, which was stopped in a station at the time the incident took place. When Wells chose to resist the trainmen, she turned a corner in her life. She began what would become a lifetime of public activism in which she would use words and deeds to challenge the injustices the American legal system dealt to African Americans.

On that May day she did not stop with standing up for herself inside the train. When she got home after the incident, she sought out a lawyer and filed a lawsuit against the railroad. Legal victory was briefly hers. The judge who heard the case in the local circuit court in December 1884 ruled in her favor. Although he did not question the policy of segregation itself, he found that the smoking car did not constitute accommodations equal to those of the first-class passenger car, and that Wells, having paid for a first-class ticket, deserved first-class conditions of travel. The railroad appealed his judgment, however, and at the beginning of April 1887 the Tennessee Supreme Court reversed the lower court's ruling.

"I felt so disappointed," Ida B. Wells wrote in her diary on April 5, 1887, describing how she reacted to the news of the high court decision. She went on to explain what she had wanted to accomplish by filing the case. "I had hoped such great things from my suit for my people generally. I have firmly believed all along that the law was on our side and would, when we appealed to it, give us justice." She then voiced her disillusionment in discovering that this ideal was not supported. "I feel shorn of that belief and utterly discouraged," she confessed to her diary, "and just now, if it were possible, would gather my race in my arms and fly away with them." "O God," she continued, "is there no redress, no peace, no justice in this land for us?"

Ida B. Wells's act of defiance and her decision to bring the issue before the Tennessee courts made her a key part of the African-American challenge to a larger legal process that was occurring throughout the 1880s and 1890s. During this time American laws that had been created in the Reconstruction era to guarantee the extension of rights to former slaves were reinterpreted by state and federal courts. As a result, the standard of justice by which black and white citizens lived was altered for decades to come.

These changes in rights came in two important areas. One was in a series of laws and court rulings about the right of blacks to equal access to public places such as inns, restaurants, parks, and—perhaps most important—schools, as well as the ability to travel in the same way as whites on trains, ships, and streetcars. These legal actions raised questions about how the principle of equality should be understood, and also how that principle should be justly applied to society. Most specifically, they created a legal debate about racial integration versus segregation.

The second area where legislation and court cases changed the meaning of racial justice was in regard to political or citizenship rights. In the last decades of the nineteenth century, states began to pass measures that resulted in the loss of political participation by African Americans. The loss of Reconstruction-era protections of the right of African-American men to vote influenced other rights as well, including the ability of blacks to be elected to political office, participate in political parties, and serve on juries. This last loss was doubly harmful, because the exclusion of African Americans from juries interfered with the right of black defendants to have their cases heard by juries of their peers—to be judged, according to the law, by people like themselves.

The most terrible outcome of this erosion of rights was the denial of due process of law: people who committed crimes against African Americans failed to be arrested or prosecuted, and African Americans who were accused of wrongdoing were not assured a fair trial. In the years when statutes were going into effect limiting black people's social and political rights, violence was often directed at African-American citizens. Black men and women were hurt or killed without being tried for alleged misdoings, and the white people who committed atrocities against blacks were not penalized for them. Often the misdeeds for which African Americans were punished outside the law was the simple "crime" of success itself.

Ida B. Wells's case against the railroad fit squarely into the first area in which African-American rights were denied. Her refusal to give up her seat on the train and the lawsuit that stemmed from her action foreshadowed a similar protest that a man named Homer A. Plessy would begin aboard a train in Louisiana in 1890.

Plessy's case, which was heard by the U.S. Supreme Court in 1896, would set the legal precedent by which other similar cases would be judged and made it possible for states to continue to enforce racial segregation laws and practices. Jim Crow laws created between the 1870s and 1910 would remain in force for decades. They would not be overthrown until a successful legal campaign by a new generation of African-American activists led to the U.S. Supreme Court's 1954 ruling in *Brown* v. *Board of Education* and to the civil rights movement that followed it.

WHAT IS
AFRICA
TO ME?

When Countee Cullen asked "What is Africa to me?" in his 1925 poem "Heritage," Africa was still very much a mystery, even to the "New Negro" generation to whom the poem was addressed. Although Africa evoked feelings of home as well as dislocation, Cullen had to view Africa through the filter of European imperialism—a filter fraught with myths and stereotypes. Then in the 1950s and '60s things began to change. Africa was on the move, challenging colonialism, building newly independent modern nations. Africa, and thus the place of African Americans in the world, held an even more prominent place in the black imagination. Influenced by new political and cultural movements, African-American artists revisited the place of Africa in the black imagination, exploring feelings of community, cultural connection, and spirituality as well as loss and alienation.

The discovery of African "folk" art in the New World profoundly shaped the post-war generation of black artists in search of their roots. They learned that enslavement did not destroy Africans' cultural memory. Although masters frequently outlawed drums, African musical practices were passed down through other instruments. This guitar is one example of Africa's long tradition of stringed instruments, one that includes the Oud and the Kora, precursors of the American banjo. Indeed, in some cases the tunings used for these and other instruments prefigured the modern blues scale in the United States.

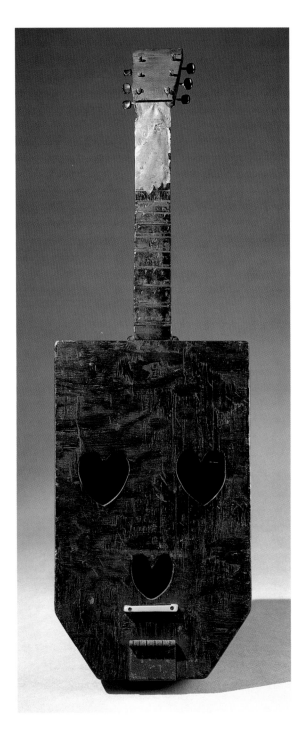

Guitar with Heart-Shaped Sound Holes. Unidentified African-American artist (undated), painted wood and mixed media, $34\frac{3}{4}$ x 11 x $3\frac{1}{2}$". National Museum of American Art/Hemphill Collection/Art Resource, NY

For Norman Lewis, abstract expressionism was one way to release black artists from the burden of realism, enabling them to explore black life through a color-blind universalism. *Harlem Courtyard* alludes to black urban life, jazz music, and the bustle of pedestrians. Although he denies the figural a place in his work, Lewis does not eschew his heritage: "Being Negro . . . is part of what I feel, but in expressing all of what I am artistically, I often find myself in a visionary world, to which 125th Street would prove limited . . . by comparison."

Harlem Courtyard Norman Lewis (1954), oil on canvas, 60 x 40". Private collection. Courtesy the Estate of Norman W. Lewis

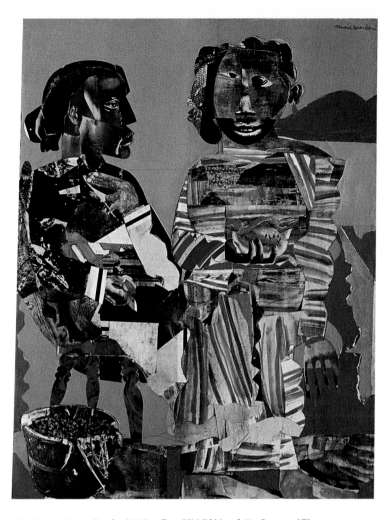

Melon Season Romare Bearden (1967), collage. ESM-Ed Meneely/Art Resource, NY

Romare Bearden's style of collaged frag-
ments is an improvisation, like jazz
music or the abstract expressionism of
Norman Lewis's *Harlem Courtyard*—"a
style in itself eloquent of the sharp
breaks, leaps in consciousness, distor-
tions, paradoxes, reversals . . . which
characterize much of Negro American
history," wrote Ralph Ellison. *Melon
Season* draws from Bearden's childhood
in Charlotte, North Carolina, while also
evoking images of an African pastoral
life. Though other artists might have
depicted in protest the racist marketing
image of blacks enjoying watermelon,
Bearden reappropriates it as a fond
memory of the majesty of everyday life.

Many of Betye Saar's autobiographical assemblages interrogate race and gender identity. In *Black Girl's Window* she depicts a girl—herself—peering into the world, beneath eight images of life centered around death. Above her head hovers an image representing her own part-white heritage, but her spiritual side is of Africa, her fate marked on her hands in symbols redolent of palmistry, voodoo, and shamanism. As we look through the window to the girl's soul, we canot help wondering if she feels trapped on the other side of the glass.

Black Girl's Window Betye Saar (1969), mixed media assemblage, $35\frac{1}{4}$ x 18 x $1\frac{1}{2}$". © Betye Saar. Courtesy of Michael Rosenfeld Gallery, NY

Masks similar to this one, made of beads, raffia, cloth, and gourds, have traditionally been worn in West African ceremonial dances. Ringgold's embrace of black feminism in the 1970s infuses this mask not only with a sense of its original purpose but also with powerful messages about the anonymity of black women fighting for a place in the art world and in society. By referring to the figures in the series as witches she also invokes the spirit of powerful women, past and present, whose challenge to male power has led to persecution and marginalization.

Women's Liberation Talking Mask, Witch Series No. 1 Faith Ringgold (1973), mixed media, 59 x 29½". © 1973 Faith Ringgold

Famous Moon King Jean-Michel Basquiat (1984), oil and acrylic on canvas, $70\frac{7}{8}$ x $102\frac{3}{4}$". © 1984 Estate of Jean-Michel Basquiat. Used by permission

Jean-Michel Basquiat represented a new generation of black artists who came of age after the black revolts of the 1960s and 1970s, during a period when Africa's importance began to fade. The former grafitti artist first exhibited his work in 1980 and almost overnight became the darling of the predominantly white, wealthy art world, despite the fact that his paintings explored the condition of black people and appropriated, often ridiculed, Western art traditions. Basquiat's hundreds of paintings and drawings utilized a range of symbols and figures to examine the many dimensions of identity, the centrality of black culture in the West, and the urban condition.

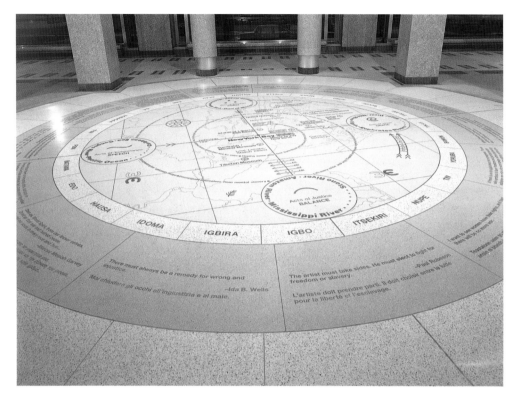

The New Ring Shout Houston Conwill, Joseph DePace, and Estella Conwill Majozo (1995), polished brass and terazzo floor, 40' diameter, 290 Broadway, New York, NY. Courtesy of the artists

The New Ring Shout marks the site of the eighteenth-century African Burial Ground in lower Manhattan. The cosmogram reflects the form and motion of the ring shout, a circle dance performed by slaves in the New World as a link with historical and spiritual ancestors, and a tie of community and hope. The cosmogram maps the movement of Africans to New York City, at the center of the circle, enclosed by a ring of names of African nations whose peoples were subjected to the slave trade. The unity and diversity of the rings speak of myriad possible stories united in a common heritage.

In filing her suit to protest the railroad's attempt to segregate its passenger cars by race, Wells became the first African American to challenge the U.S. Supreme Court ruling of 1883 that denied access to blacks to transportation, theaters, hotels, or other places regularly used by the public. That case had revolved around the meaning of the 14th Amendment to the U.S. Constitution, which guaranteed that no state could make discriminatory laws or "deprive any person of life, liberty, or property without due process of law, nor deny to any person within its jurisdiction the equal protection of the laws." The justices ruled that this amendment was not meant to be applied to what they called "private wrongs," or the experience of discrimination by individual persons on private property. (The justices included in their definition of such property privately owned theaters, trains, and hotels.)

African-American journalists and politicians were in the forefront of the public outcry against the legal decisions and state laws that endorsed segregation. The newspaper writers and editors who gathered at the Afro-American Press Convention of 1890 denounced the consignment of black people to second-class facilities aboard railroads. Black members of the state legislatures in Louisiana and Arkansas fought against the segregation bills that were introduced in their legislative bodies in 1890 and 1891. Resistance also continued among African-American citizens' groups in cities and towns around the nation.

In Atlanta, Georgia, in 1892 a group of black citizens organized a successful boycott of the city's streetcars after the city council ordered separate cars for white and black passengers. Similar public demonstrations and boycott actions took place in Augusta, Georgia, in 1898, and in Savannah, Georgia, in 1899.

Homer A. Plessy was one of the countless number of African-American activists in cities North and South. The case that carried his name, *Plessy* v. *Ferguson,* was heard in the courts as the result of organized local African-American opposition to the Louisiana Separate Car Act of 1890. The new Louisiana law required what was termed "equal but separate" accommodations for white and nonwhite passengers on railways, with seats to be assigned in segregated cars according to race. In practice, these separate-but-equal regulations actually resulted in segregated and unequal treatment, with whites receiving the best accommodations or services available and blacks given inferior accommodations. According to the Louisiana law, passengers who refused to comply with the rules of segregation could be removed from trains and were permitted no legal recourse.

African-American members of the American Citizens' Equal Rights Association in New Orleans reacted immediately to the threat of the separate cars bill. They filed a memorial with the Louisiana legislature on May 24, 1890, protesting that the measure violated the principle that all citizens are created equal before the law. The leaders of the protest action were Dr. Louis A. Martinet, a lawyer and physician who owned the *New Orleans Crusader,* and Rodolphe L. Desdunes, a customs clerk. Both men were prominent middle-class members of New Orleans's mixed-race creole community. They used the *Crusader* as a forum to attack the separate car act and called for cases to be brought to the courts that would test the constitutional-ity of the new legislation.

The first major test case was instigated by Homer A. Plessy, a thirty-four-year-old friend of the Desdunes family, who was also a light-skinned member of the elite New Orleans creole community. Plessy was arrested soon after he boarded the East Louisiana Railway on June 7, 1892, and sat down in the coach set aside for whites.

The results, as in Ida B. Wells's case, were not what the African-American activists who planned the test case had sought. Instead of upholding the rights of equity and federal protection guaranteed by the 14th Amendment, as the Citizens Committee activists had hoped, the court in effect dismantled the authority of the amendment's equal protection clause and instead ruled that separation of races on railways was valid. The court also ruled that the passage of separate-but-equal Jim Crow laws was an appropriate and reasonable exercise of state legislative authori-ty. The court thus provided the constitutional basis by which Southern states could enforce the practice of racial segregation.

It was not only the 14th Amendment but the 15th that came under fire by white supremacists in the 1880s and 1890s. The 15th Amendment to the U.S. Constitu-tion guaranteed that the "right of citizens of the United States to vote shall not be denied or abridged by the United States, or by any State, on account of race, color, or previous condition of servitude." Beginning with Mississippi in 1890, South Carolina in 1895, Louisiana in 1898, and North Carolina in 1900, and Alabama and Virginia shortly after the turn of the century, several states amended their consti-tutions with the intention of denying blacks the right to vote. In other states, the legislatures passed laws that were similarly designed to eliminate black voting. These included laws that required people to pass a literacy test, hold property, or reside on the same property for long periods of time in order to register to vote.

Literacy tests discriminated against all people who were not middle-class or wealthy and who thus did not have the benefit of education. But they had a par-ticularly devastating effect on former slaves who had been barred under bondage from learning to read. Residency and property requirements worked against the majority of African Americans in the South, too, because most of them worked as sharecroppers or tenant farmers. They neither owned property nor stayed on the same land from year to year. Poll taxes, or fees that had to be paid in order to be eligible to vote, were among the most effective means of excluding blacks from the ballot box, because African Americans made up a disproportionate number of the poor who could not afford to pay the taxes.

In many Southern states, grandfather clauses stated that anyone whose father or grandfather had been qualified to vote in 1867 did not have to pass literacy or citizenship tests or be subjected to other hurdles to registration. Since the 15th Amendment enfranchising black men was ratified by Congress in 1870, these clauses virtually excluded African Americans, while making it possible for poor whites who might otherwise not be able to pass the tests to vote without having to take them.

What was called the "white primary," or exclusion of blacks from participation in the Democratic party's primaries, also nullified the black vote. That was because the Democratic party so dominated the South by 1900 that whoever was designated as a Democratic candidate was virtually assured of victory in the subsequent election.

These white supremacist measures were effective in taking the vote away from African Americans. The changes they wrought were dramatic. The promises of citizenship for blacks that had been part of the rhetoric of the federal government during the Reconstruction period were undone by state actions and the failure of the federal government to counteract them. The federal government failed to act in part because of racism and in part because of a desire to heal the divisions between the national government and the power of the states, especially the Southern states, that were still ripe from the Civil War.

Passage of voter restriction laws had a very substantial effect. In Louisiana, where literacy, property, and poll-tax restrictions were enacted, there were 130,344 black registered voters in 1896 and African Americans made up the majority of voters in twenty-six parishes (districts). By 1900, after these laws were passed, there were only 5,320 black registrants and not one parish had a black majority. By 1904 the number of black registered voters had slipped to 1,342. In Alabama in 1900 there were only 3,000 registered African-American voters, out of a potential pool of almost 150,000 black men who were of voting age.

Corruption and intimidation had preceded the passage of these restrictive laws and helped whites control and limit the black vote. Black support for alternatives to the white supremacist platform of the Southern Democratic party was often suppressed by violence. In Virginia in 1883 there was a white backlash against the Liberal Readjuster party, a coalition of Radical Republicans who had supported black emancipation and postwar Reconstruction, lower-class white farmers, owners of small businesses, and black farmers, sharecroppers, and factory workers that had gained power in the elections of 1879 and voted in progressive reforms that benefited black people.

In Danville, Virginia, shortly before election day, November 6, 1883, a group of prominent white businessmen issued a circular in the town decrying the idea of black people in positions of authority and claiming that by gaining some political representation, African Americans had become less tractable workers in the white-owned tobacco industry. Blacks were warned not to be on the streets on election day. One conservative proclaimed that the white supremacists would win the election in Danville "votes or no votes" if they had to do it "with double barrel shotguns, breach loading shotguns and Smith and Wesson double-action." White vigilantes took control of the town, forcing campaigning by black and white members of the liberal reform coalition to end. On November 3, they killed three black citizens.

Elsewhere in Virginia, black residents of towns rallied successfully to ensure their ability to get to the polls. In Petersburg, Virginia, African-Americans organized a parade and guarded the polling places in the city precincts.

Mob violence and lynching were an effective tool by which conservative whites controlled all kinds of black behavior, not just the effort to exercise citizenship rights, hold political office, or vote. Lynchings most often happened in rural areas and small towns, but mob riots were the creatures of the cities. Violence or the threat of violence was random and widespread. When a black man named Baker was appointed postmaster in the small town of Lake City, South Carolina, in 1898, a white mob surrounded his house and post office in the night and set the building afire, with him and his family members inside. When Mr. and Mrs. Baker and their children attempted to run from the burning house, they were shot on the threshold, Mrs. Baker with her infant in her arms. In the same year that the Bakers died, whites went berserk in Wilmington, North Carolina, at election time and swept through the black district of the city, setting homes and businesses afire and killing and wounding African Americans whom they encountered.

Between 1882 and 1901 more than one hundred people were lynched each year, the great majority of them blacks living in Southern states. Almost two thousand lynchings of African Americans were officially reported in those two decades. Additional murders by lynching occurred, but they went unreported as such in local records and overall statistics.

Lynchings were attacks motivated by racism during which people were brutally murdered—sometimes in the night, but often in a public way with many witnesses. Lynchings often involved the hanging of victims, but lynch mobs also killed people in other ways. Some victims endured terrible atrocities, such as being dragged behind a wagon, beaten, seeing loved ones harmed, being tied up and burned or having parts of their bodies dismembered, and other forms of torture. These vicious attacks occurred outside any due process of law, and sometimes with the knowledge or participation of law enforcement officials. State and local courts did little to punish lynchers, and if attackers were identified, penalties for killing African Americans in this way were small and considered to be in a different legal category from other kinds of murders. African-American men were the most common targets of lynch mobs, but women were also hurt and killed. Men were the most common members of white mobs or vigilante groups, but white conservative women were among those who supported the practice and participated in it as spectators.

African-American activists were not silent in the face of the injustices of lynching. In 1899 black churches observed Friday, June 2, as a day of fasting and prayer in which parishioners gathered to pray for justice for African Americans in the courts and for freedom from violence. In this unified effort to demonstrate, as the *New York Tribune* described it, "ceasing to be longer silent," ministers were asked to make the following Sunday, June 4, the occasion for sermons on these topics. Refusing to ignore lynching, activists scanned local newspapers and records and compiled and published data on the names of individuals who had been killed and the dates on which they died. Middle-class leaders raised the issue at public meetings and addressed it in editorials. Frances Ellen Watkins Harper, a writer and African-American feminist, spoke out at a meeting of the National Council of Women held in Washington, D.C., in February 1891. "A government which has power to tax a man in peace, [and] draft him in war, should have power to defend his life in the hour of peril," she told her audience.

Antilynching crusader Ida B. Wells with Maurine, Betty, and Tom Moss Jr., the family of Memphis grocery store owner Thomas Moss, who was lynched in 1893.

Among all the prominent African-American lecturers and journalists who took a public stand against lynching and worked tirelessly to bring an end to the practice, the most important was Ida B. Wells. Just as her test of the constitutionality of racial segregation laws was sparked by her expulsion from the railroad passenger car, so her campaign against lynching began as the result of a specific incident. This time the incident of discrimination was not just a question of equality and dignity, but one of horror.

Three African-American small businessmen, Thomas Moss, Calvin McDowell, and Henry Stewart, owned and ran a very successful cooperative grocery store called the People's Grocery that was located in an African-American district of suburban Memphis known as the Curve. Moss and his wife, Betty, were the best friends of Ida B. Wells, and Wells was the godmother to their little girl, Maurine. Thomas Moss worked as a letter carrier by day and in the store by night, and he was very active in his church and his lodge. Because of his deep involvement in the community and its functions, everyone in the neighborhood knew him, and he was much beloved.

An economic rivalry soon developed between the People's Grocery and an older, less successful store that had been in the neighborhood longer and was owned by a white man named W. H. Barrett. Barrett had a deep resentment of Moss because of the success Moss and his partners had achieved in their business. That hatred deepened one day when a sidewalk quarrel broke out between black and white boys over a game of marbles. The African-American children bested the white children in the fight, whereupon the white parents, including Barrett, tried to take legal action against the black boys. The case was dismissed after the payment of small fines.

Tensions escalated, and the whites, still vengeful over the success of Thomas Moss's store, which had taken much of the business away from the white-owned grocery, organized a raid on the People's Grocery. They carried out the raid on a Saturday night, just as the store was closing. When they burst in, Moss was busy working on the store's accounts and McDowell was waiting on the last customers. Fearing that threats of violence would be carried out, friends of the partners had stationed themselves in the rear of the shop to guard the store. When the white men broke in through the back of the store, they were met by gunfire, and three of them were wounded.

The next morning there was a general raid of the black households and businesses near the Curve in order to locate the men who might have fired the shots that wounded the white vigilantes. Moss, McDowell, and Stewart were among those picked up and incarcerated in the jail. Black members of the Tennessee Rifles, a local militia that had an armory nearby, guarded the jail against white attacks for the first two nights. But when it was clear that the men who had been shot would recover, they felt that tensions had passed and ceased their watchfulness. On the third night, a mob of white men was given access to the jail. They dragged Thomas Moss and his partners from their cells, loaded them aboard a railroad boxcar, took them outside the city limits, and lynched them. According to an eyewitness newspaper report of the lynching, McDowell tried to struggle with the lynchers and was mutilated before he was killed. Thomas Moss pleaded with his abductors to spare his life on behalf of his wife and children, including his young daughter Maurine and the unborn baby his wife was carrying. His plea was ignored, and when asked for a final statement before he was shot to death, he said: "Tell my people to go West—there is no justice for them here."

Hundreds of black residents of the Memphis area heeded Thomas Moss's last words. As Wells recalled in her memoirs, which were published after her death, the "shock to the colored people who knew and loved both Moss and McDowell was beyond description." And the violence had not ended. Whites rampaged through the black neighborhood the day after the murders, and a white mob looted goods from the People's Grocery and then destroyed the contents of the building. Black reaction was swift. Like the many migrants who had left farms and sharecropping plots before them and moved west or to black towns, many city dwellers sold their property and took their families to Oklahoma Territory. Two leading pastors in the Curve community organized their entire congregations to go. Meanwhile, those that stayed instituted an informal economic boycott of white businesses and stayed off city streetcars.

Ida B. Wells went into action. She had become part-owner of the *Memphis Free Speech* newspaper in 1889, and had lost her job as a teacher when she used its pages to protest the inferior quality of schools serving black students. After the murder of her dear friend Thomas Moss, she used the newspaper to encourage the black citizens of Memphis to leave town and went to churches to urge black parishioners to support the consumer boycott of white-owned and -run streetcars. The exodus from the city did more than help African Americans escape from the racist violence that had seized Memphis. It had a very real economic impact upon whites. After the lynching, as Wells recalled in her memoirs, white people discovered a "dearth of servants to cook their meals and wash their clothes and keep their homes in order, to nurse their babies and wait on their tables, to build their houses and do all classes of laborious work."

Wells set out to become an expert on lynching and to dispel some of the myths that were popularly accepted about why lynchings occurred. Thomas Moss was an upstanding citizen who was killed because he had acquired wealth and property. But white newspapers typically claimed that lynchings occurred because of black men's criminality. They especially claimed that lynchings happened because black men sexually assaulted white women. Wells knew that Thomas Moss was neither a criminal nor a rapist, and so she questioned these allegations about lynching in general. She personally investigated every lynching that she heard about in Mississippi in the months after Thomas Moss's death. Then she published an editorial that strongly implied that when the charge behind a lynching was rape, the actual fact of the matter was that in the overwhelming number of cases a black man and white woman had agreed to have a sexual relationship with each other. In short, no rape had occurred. "Nobody in this section of the country believes the old thread bare lie that Negro men rape white women," Wells wrote in her editorial for *Free Speech* in May 1892. The charge of rape was used to cover up the real violence— that of white men against black men. And the reason for this violence was to deprive blacks of political and economic power—to keep them under the thumb of the white establishment.

When the editorial was printed, Wells was traveling in the North. She soon learned of the outcome. The same fate that had met the People's Grocery had been visited upon her newspaper office. Whites had gone to the *Free Speech* office at night, two days after the edition in which the editorial was published, and destroyed the type used to print the newspaper and all the furnishings of the office. They left a note saying that anyone who attempted to publish *Free Speech* again would be killed.

Ida B. Wells was not easily silenced. She was exiled from her home in the South because of her defense of black rights in the face of lawlessness. She took a newspaper job in the North and continued to claim for herself the right of free speech. She wrote editorials under the pen name Iola and prepared pamphlets on the lynching issue that challenged the standard view of lynchings that was presented in the white press, *North and South*. Once her writings began to be well known, she traveled widely as a lecturer, speaking on the issue of lynching to women's organizations, churches, and African-American groups.

Wells published her findings in a pamphlet called *Southern Horrors: Lynch Law in All Its Phases* in October 1892. The pamphlet was dedicated to African-American women in Manhattan and Brooklyn, because women's groups in the New York area had raised the funds to make the publication of her work possible. Victoria Earle Matthews, a freelance journalist and women's rights activist who in 1897 established the White Rose Mission, a settlement house that provided social services for black women workers and girls, and Maritcha Lyons, a Brooklyn schoolteacher, were very impressed when they read Wells's articles. They organized a series of small meetings in African-American households and church lecture rooms in which Wells presented information about lynching to groups of women. More than 250 black women attended these meetings and joined in forming a committee that organized a major fundraising event with Wells as the keynote speaker.

Though justice seemed to be sleeping in the last decades of the nineteenth century, African Americans like Wells were wide awake. Many African-American sharecroppers, like the people who had known Thomas Moss in Memphis and who decided to leave the city after his murder, migrated west, away from the lawlessness of the Deep South. Black industrial and farm workers tried forming labor and political coalitions with whites, and other individuals, like Wells and Homer A. Plessy, challenged the reversal of legal protections in court. All over the land people less well known than Wells and Plessy took their own private stands against discrimination, acting in defense of honor when personally confronted by racism. Black intellectuals wrote newspaper articles and books and gave speeches decrying injustices. And black middle-class people set about founding their own schools, churches, businesses, and self-help organizations. If the law offered no guarantee of equal access to existing institutions and services, or protection of black citizens' well-being from violence, then African Americans would create the means for achieving advancement on their own.

Self-Help: "To Hew Out His Own Path"

Johanna Bowen Redgrey was a midwife and healer who lived on a small farm on the outskirts of Tuskegee, Alabama, in the 1880s. She had been born into slavery near Richmond, Virginia, the daughter of an African-American mother and her mother's Irish-American master. When she was a teenager, her father sold her and her brothers to a white family who had a plantation in Macon County, Alabama. Johanna was a striking woman, six feet tall. She was muscular and strong from the field work she did, with a head of fiery reddish hair and a determined disposition to match her appearance. When the Civil War came, Johanna's brothers joined other young men who escaped from the plantation to try to fight for the North. She assumed they died in the attempt, because she never saw them again nor learned of their fate. She spent the latter part of the war and the early years after war's end working for wages for her former master. Then she met and married Lewis Redgrey.

Lewis Redgrey was a Native American who had spent part of his life in Mexico and spoke Spanish as well as English. He had a fifty-five-acre farm outside Tuskegee, and Johanna went to live with him there. Together they raised hogs and corn and grew a cash crop of cotton. They were both important people in the community. Johanna Bowen Redgrey had gone to school and worked with doctors, and she knew a great deal about plants and herbs and how to make medicines. She delivered babies and nursed both black and white families in times of illness or accident. She was deeply religious. She taught Sunday School and was very active with other women in the neighborhood in her own African Methodist Episcopal Zion church and in the Baptist church located on a nearby hill.

She and her husband were determined to provide good educations for their son and the other African-American children of Tuskegee. For them, making education available was the key to improving the lives of all African Americans. They were members of a committee of Tuskegee residents who worked to start a school in the town. They supported those who sent to Hampton Institute, a school in Virginia that trained African Americans for careers in nursing, teaching, farming, and trades, to find a schoolmaster to run it. They were among the group of black townspeople who gathered to greet the young teacher who came from Hampton. His name was Booker T. Washington, and he arrived in Tuskegee in June 1881. Classes in what would become Washington's famed Tuskegee Institute began a few days later, on July 4. The classes met in Johanna Bowen Redgrey's church on Zion Hill.

Church, family, neighbors, and school were at the heart of the Redgreys' lives. These connections between people were avenues for personal fulfillment, community, and mutual care. They also were means of self-expression. Strengthening and cherishing these kinds of social networks and avenues of uplift, and using their voices to present their own points of view, were crucial ways in which African Americans combated the racial injustices of the 1880s and 1890s.

The ability to worship freely, to marry and raise children without having them subject to others' control, and to learn to read and write were all freedoms that had been outside most black people's experience during slavery. This made them all the more precious to African Americans in the decades after emancipation. When it became clear in the post–Reconstruction era that the political rights and protections that had been promised after the end of the Civil War would not be theirs, African Americans set about forming their own separate institutions—schools, churches, hospitals, settlement houses, and newspapers—and making their own way. Through religion, family, and education African Americans built their own brand of freedom, working together for the good of all black people.

In developing separate institutions and systems of self-help, African Americans used the power of words, both those that were written down and those that were spoken aloud. Despite a larger society where blackness was being belittled, souls were exalted through the hymns and sermons of the black church, and children were assured of their self-worth by tales told and passed down within the black family. Black schools gave students the power of literacy, the ability to read and write, and this opened to them new economic and intellectual possibilities. Black newspapers printed the opinions of black journalists, black intellectuals spoke at public events, black writers and poets published novels and books of poetry, and black men and women gathered together in literary societies to read and debate.

People who had not had the opportunity to learn to read could listen and speak. In doing so, they carried on an oral tradition that had long sustained a rich cultural heritage among African Americans from one generation to another. Those who could read passed newspapers and books from hand to hand, or read aloud to others. Black people had a voice, and the words they used gave them hope and strength.

African Americans did not speak in one voice, however. They had many points of view. One of the biggest debates among African Americans at the turn of the century was over the best approach to providing education to black people. Tuskegee Institute and its principal were at the center of this broad discussion.

Many of them supported Booker T. Washington's philosophy of industrial or vocational education, in which students would come to school to learn a trade and find a job. Others criticized it just as strongly. Many African-American intellectuals and political activists saw Washington's vision as a way of appeasing whites who felt that blacks should be manual laborers and not strive for high intellectual achievement—or as Washington himself often put it, that they should live by their hands rather than by their wits. But for these critics, higher education for black people, in which African Americans could enter academic programs in languages and music, the arts and humanities, science and research, or prepare for a profession, was as important as training for a vocation. Thus the debate about the nature of schooling was not only about economics and education, but about how best to react to white racism.

Washington believed that the "power of the mouth is not like the power of the object lesson." That is, he felt that black people could best advance by the quiet example of their cooperation with whites, by self-development, and by their skilled contributions to their mixed-race communities, rather than by overt militancy or protest. This view was scorned by leaders such as Frederick Douglass and Ida B. Wells. Douglass and Wells were among those who used the written and spoken word to confront injustices head-on. "One farm bought, one house built, one home neatly kept, one man the largest tax-payer and depositor in the local bank, one school or church maintained, one factory running successfully, one truck garden properly cultivated, one patient cured by a Negro doctor, one sermon well preached, one office well filled, one life cleanly lived," Washington wrote in 1895, "these will tell more in our favor than all the abstract eloquence that can be summoned to plead our cause."

The academic and vocational philosophies of education developed side by side in the 1880s and 1890s. This is one of the issues on which middle-class black people and poorer African Americans, and African Americans living in the North and in the South, differed. The debate about education and the types of work for which it should prepare students was directly related to ideas about African Americans' proper expectations regarding their status in society. Middle-class and Northern blacks were more likely to identify with and promote academic programs and more intellectual—and therefore elite—types of achievement. Rather than accommodate white views of black people's secondary status, they stressed their desire for equal rights and equal opportunities, including equal access to higher education.

At the same time, less privileged African-American students sometimes rebelled against industrial education curricula because they equated acquiring an education with an escape from manual labor. But others embraced Booker T. Washington's idea that agricultural and industrial labor and other forms of skilled work with the hands should be honored, and they believed that there was dignity in this kind of work. To many blacks living in the South, Washington's brand of education had its own flavor of militancy. Separatism and equality thus became the watchwords in the 1880s and 1890s for two different strategies for black advancement. Both had power, and the two perspectives often intersected in practice.

The story of the creation of the Tuskegee Institute exemplifies this combination of approaches. It is one example of the many separate institutions that were created by or for blacks at the end of the nineteenth century. Within a few weeks of his arrival in Tuskegee, Booker T. Washington was joined by a young teacher named Olivia Davidson. Together, with the help of the Tuskegee townspeople and donations from white Northern philanthropists, they built up the school.

Olivia Davidson had started teaching when she was sixteen. She taught in Mississippi and Tennessee before she graduated from Washington's alma mater, Hampton Institute, and from the Framingham State Normal School in Massachusetts. When she came to Tuskegee in late August 1881, she immediately set about getting to know the people in the community and raising money for the institute. She went door to door and talked to the people of the town about their goals for education. With the aid of black women like Johanna Bowen Redgrey, who were eager to do anything they could to help, she organized bake sales and community potluck suppers where women contributed a dish they had prepared. Long picnic tables were covered with the donated food and the families of the town turned out to celebrate together and support the new school. Soon after classes began, Davidson organized a night of student literary entertainment, in which the students selected and memorized poems and essays and recited them to the black members of the town in an evening performance.

In June 1881 Washington began recruiting students for his new school by speaking at both the Baptist and Methodist churches, inviting anyone who was interested to come see him at his boardinghouse and enroll. He rode around Macon County and familiarized himself with the people in the countryside, reporting in his letters to friends in Virginia his shock at the impoverished conditions of share-cropper families and the lack of books and other materials in the one-room rural schools that were already in operation.

There were thirty students in the first class that began school in the Methodist church on Independence Day 1881. They varied in age from teenagers to middle-aged adults. Most of them were public school teachers who had come to receive better training so they could in turn pass that knowledge on to the rural children who were their pupils.

In time, as the result of Davidson and Washington's efforts, the school acquired land, the former Bowen plantation, and made plans to build a new building. Washington turned his mind to business, and the curriculum of the school soon combined book-learning classes with various manual labor tasks. The manual labor served two functions. It prepared students for skilled jobs in industry and agriculture, and it earned money immediately for the development of the school.

Students worked hard outside the classroom. They cleared land for a cash crop of cotton. They made bricks that would be used in the construction of Tuskegee Institute buildings or sold to local business owners for use in the town. The profits were turned back into expanding the programs and facilities of the school and hiring new teachers. Washington hoped that the kind of business relationships that would be built up between the school and the white townspeople through brick-making and other student enterprises would overcome whites' racist ideas. He also hoped that the influential white residents of Tuskegee would support the school out of self-interest because of the quality products the students produced and the value of the students' skilled employment. Thus the school served, on a small scale, as a model or experiment for Washington's philosophy of race relations, which he felt should be applied to the nation as a whole.

The ceremonies that marked the end of the Tuskegee Institute's first year were symbolic of the combination of forces that had given birth to Washington and Davidson's educational enterprise. People came from all over town, from the countryside, and from as far away as Hampton, Virginia, to meet on Zion Hill in Tuskegee.

When they paraded from the church to the new school grounds, the students and citizens of Tuskegee symbolically moved from the school's past into its future. The church building was soon replaced as the location for the school when classrooms and dormitories were built. Two years later, there were 169 students studying at the school. By 1900, when Washington published his autobiography, *Up from Slavery,* there were fourteen hundred students enrolled, and more than one hundred instructors. The Tuskegee Institute was a thriving school and economic enterprise with its own working farm, sawmill, foundry, brickyard, and blacksmith, machine, woodworking, barrelmaking, and print shops. As Washington's daughter, Portia Washington, wrote in July 1900, the industrial institute had become "really a small village," occupied and run by African Americans, and the goal of "Principal

Washington is to make it an object-lesson, or model community for the masses in general."

By the 1890s, Washington, who made extensive public speaking tours to promote the school, had become a famous and powerful man. White receptiveness to the vocational emphasis of his school had made him into a recognized spokesman on racial matters, and he wielded far-reaching political influence from behind the scenes. The little school that the Redgreys had helped begin had become the center of a social movement, with Washington at its head.

Washington turned to three different well-educated black women to share his work and his private life. During Tuskegee's first year, he married his college girlfriend, Fanny Norton Smith. Their daughter Portia was born in 1883. Fanny Washington died a year later, leaving Washington alone with the little girl. In August 1886 Olivia Davidson became Booker T. Washington's second wife. She had long been his partner in the school, teaching science classes at Tuskegee; acting as the school's Lady Principal by overseeing the female students; and making fundraising tours of the North. After their marriage she continued her work with the school. She cared for Portia and gave birth to two sons, Baker and Ernest. But disaster came. Despite her energetic work, Olivia Davidson Washington had always been frail in health. Soon after Ernest was born, the chimney in the Washingtons' house caught fire during the night, burning down the house. Booker T. Washington was away raising money for the school at the time. Olivia and the children escaped the flames, but she had been very ill after childbirth and her condition worsened after the fire. She never recovered. She died in a hospital in Boston in May 1889.

Four years later Booker T. Washington married for a third time. He turned for companionship and help with his children to Margaret (Maggie) Murray, a teacher from Mississippi who had been serving as the Lady Principal at Tuskegee since May 1890.

Margaret Murray Washington had been educated at Fisk University, in Nashville, where she was associate editor of the school newspaper and president of a campus literary society. She began teaching at Tuskegee in 1889. Like Olivia Washington, Margaret Murray Washington believed strongly in the importance of education for African-American girls and women.

The Tuskegee curriculum combined academic and vocational training for both male and female students, with an emphasis for everyone on preparing for an occupation. Tuskegee students took classes in art, music, and literature, botany, chemistry, and mathematics. In addition, they all enrolled in some program of practical training. All of these training courses were based on gaining skills for employment in occupations that already existed for black people in the South. Within Booker T. Washington's scheme, boys and girls were thought to be suited to different kinds of occupations and thus to separate sorts of classes in their education. Young men trained in agriculture or in trades such as carpentry, blacksmithing, mechanics, or furniture making. Young women were directed toward classes in housekeeping and domestic science. These courses would prepare girls for work in household service, which was the main source of wage employment for black women at the time, and also to run their own homes according to up-to-date Victorian standards. Female students could also learn advanced sewing so they could make a living as dressmakers and hatmakers.

Recognizing that women could do many kinds of agricultural work that could be turned to profit on a family farm, Margaret Murray Washington insisted that female students also be given opportunities to study agricultural methods. The "outdoor work" for women included dairying, raising poultry and livestock, and growing flowers and vegetables for market. Margaret Murray Washington considered these forms of expertise more healthy and independent options for black women in seeking a livelihood than factory work or leaving the rural areas of the South for work in cities.

The agricultural department of Tuskegee Institute as a whole was directed, beginning in 1896, by George Washington Carver. An 1894 graduate of Iowa State University, Carver was a brilliant scientist and teacher who also painted beautiful pictures of fruits and flowers. His experiments in botany and innovations in soil analysis and enrichment made the Tuskegee Institute's experimental farm into a showcase of high-yield crops. He encouraged farmers to grow crops such as sweet potatoes and peanuts in addition to cotton, and to rotate the kinds of crops grown

George Washington Carver (second from right), director of the agricultural department of Tuskegee Institute, with his students in the soil science laboratory.

in their fields to maintain the richness of the soil. He also invented industrial uses for the by-products of these diversified crops, such as the shells of peanuts. In 1899 he began what he called his "Moveable School," a large wagon equipped with farm machinery and exhibits that was drawn by mules around the dirt roads of the countryside. Carver and his assistants used the wagon to bring lessons they taught in their laboratories and classrooms to the African Americans farming throughout the county.

Many students at Tuskegee, both men and women, trained to become teachers, and Tuskegee graduates ran rural schools throughout the South and taught at other colleges. The Tuskegee Institute hospital, opened in 1892, served as a nurses' training school. The hospital and nursing program are representative of a number of black institutions that were founded between 1890 and 1930. Black women like Johanna Bowen Redgrey had long served an important function in their communities as traditionally trained lay healers, nurses, and midwives. At the end of the nineteenth century, black women and men participated in the movement to professionalize nursing, adding clinical training, hospital experience, and basic courses in nutrition, sanitation, and primary care to the kind of practical knowledge and informal apprenticeships that had trained women like Redgrey. The formation of hospitals staffed with black physicians and nurses—like the founding of schools, businesses, and community organizations—was one more important form of African-American institution-building in the post-Reconstruction period.

While she oversaw the domestic training, outdoor work, and professional education of women students in teaching and nursing at Tuskegee Institute, Margaret Murray Washington extended the principles that were being taught at the school into practice in the town. Following in the footsteps of Olivia Davidson Washington, she concentrated on ways of organizing the women of Tuskegee, especially those who worked as tenant farmers or sharecroppers and lived outside of town.

In the 1890s she devised a plan for bringing together the middle-class black women who worked as instructors at Tuskegee, or were married to male members of the faculty, and working-class or lower-class women who did not have the benefit of formal education. As she explained in an essay called "Helping the Mothers," which Booker T. Washington printed as part of his 1904 book *Working with the Hands*, the "country women, tired of the monotony of their lives, came crowding into the village every Saturday." On one Saturday, Margaret Murray Washington went into town and sent a small boy around to the women, asking them to come to a room above "a very dilapidated store which stands on the main street of the village." Six came the first night, and thus began the meetings of the Mothers' Union. Held every Saturday of the school year, the meetings attracted more than three hundred women a week by 1900.

When the women came together, Washington wrote, "we talked it all over, the needs of our women, the best ways of helping each other." Women came long

A home economics class at Hampton Institute, Hampton, Virginia. Founded in 1868, Hampton was designed to train young African Americans as teachers and leaders in the black community.

distances on foot to attend the meetings. Among them were Johanna Bowen Redgrey, who brought her young granddaughter along. Many women brought their girls with them, and soon a lending library and classes for the children were organized. Meanwhile, Margaret Washington founded the Tuskegee Women's Club for the instructors and faculty wives on the school campus. The middle-class women founded newspaper reading clubs, staffed the library, and provided Saturday day care. They also visited poor women in their homes in the country, offering advice about improving the standard of living for the farming families.

Much of this advice involved teaching middle-class ways to poor people. The sharecropper women were taught about bathing regularly and wearing more formal apparel, maintaining housekeeping and churchgoing schedules, growing vegetable gardens to supplement a diet of cornmeal and pork, and doing many of the things on the farm that women students were taught to do at the school. The Victorian values passed from middle-class to poor women extended to matters of demeanor. The well-to-do women were judgmental about the working women's conduct and believed they had the right, by their superior social standing, to correct it.

Monthly workshops were held on topics suggested by the country women, with lessons written up in pamphlet form and distributed from home to home. These booklets contained advice on parenting, manners, household repair, and farming, and "also little recipes which any woman may need in her country home, especially when there is sickness in the family." Women students joined in by establishing a house on the grounds of an old two-thousand-acre plantation where seventy-five black families lived in sharecropper cabins. A female student lived in the house and taught reading to the parents and children that were farming the land around it. Sewing, cooking, gardening, and housekeeping classes were soon added.

The kind of outreach and organization among women that Margaret Murray Washington set in motion in Tuskegee was happening among black women all around the nation. Excluded from formal social services, health care institutions, and charity organizations run by whites, black women served their communities with their own associations.

Benevolent groups in the cities and women's auxiliaries organized through churches had long provided health care to the ill and clothing and food to those who needed it. In the mid-1890s homes for black working women and for the aged, and nurseries and day care centers for the children of working mothers were established in several cities in the North. Although Margaret Murray Washington began a settlement house in a rural Southern setting, the majority of settlement houses begun in the 1890s by middle-class men and women were located in the North and Midwest. Settlement houses provided classes and job services, including literacy training and information about good nutrition and child care.

One of the most important settlements for black women was the White Rose Mission and Industrial Association, founded in 1897 by Victoria Earle Matthews, one of the women who had organized Ida B. Wells's pathbreaking public lecture in New York. The home was established to help young working women new to the city. The mission offered classes in cooking, laundry, and sewing—teaching the new migrants the city skills that could be converted into jobs in household service. Matthews also established a library of books about black history, and taught neighborhood women to be proud of their heritage.

Black settlement house residents in both the North and the South, including those at the White Rose Mission, also became involved in expanding the kindergarten movement, which in the 1890s was an innovative approach to early childhood education. Settlements and churches served as centers for community forums and lecture tours. Booker T. Washington came to speak to working women and the middle-class women organizers at the White Rose Mission, as did other prominent intellectuals and writers of the day.

In addition to attending public lectures, middle-class men and women formed literary societies that met in members' homes. These societies served a political purpose for middle-class women who were excluded from many of the public functions in which middle-class men participated. They were also one more way in which African Americans exercised the power of the word. The secular benevolent associations, church charity groups, settlement houses, and literary societies were in some ways schools for adults, especially for women. They provided a chance for middle-class women to acquire new speaking and organizing skills. Through their activism in these groups, women learned how to hold meetings, coordinate tasks among people of different backgrounds and interests, organize programs, raise funds, do publicity, and to speak with confidence to audiences and participate in group debate. Many of them would use these skills in broader forums of social and political reform.

Literary society meetings provided a chance for educated middle-class African-American men and women to discuss books and debate the current events of the day, and to give recitations and lectures to one another. The Bethel Literary and Historical Association, for example, was a key literary society in Washington, D.C. It was founded in 1881 by church activists interested in education, and it featured several black women lecturers and debaters. Topics presented at the society meetings ranged from heroes of the antislavery movement and other black history topics to discussions of music, social reform, and politics. The separate education of the sexes was one of the frequently debated issues.

The membership of literary societies, churches, and settlement programs often overlapped. One of the leaders of the Bethel Literary and Historical Association was Amanda Bowen, who also directed the Sojourner Truth Home for Working Girls of Washington, D.C., in 1895. The home was supported by the members of the Metropolitan African Methodist Episcopal Church.

The links between the Metropolitan AME Church, the literary society, and the founding of the home for girls in Washington, D.C., or between the AME Zion Church of Tuskegee, the Mothers' Clubs, and the founding of the Tuskegee Institute in Alabama, were not coincidental. These examples are indicative of the way that churches influenced the creation of black social welfare and educational institutions around the country.

The church had long been a mainstay of African-American life. Faith and spirituality were important means of maintaining and building self-worth and group support during the days of slavery. In the post–Reconstruction era, when Jim Crow practices were being made into law throughout the South, the church continued to be the focus of many African-Americans' social and inner lives. The independence of black churches within mixed-race small towns and cities, and the willingness of members to contribute money and volunteer work to their churches, made the church the strongest single institution of African-American self-help in the 1880s and 1890s.

Churches were places of worship. But they were also the primary places that African Americans used as assembly halls and community centers. Many, like the church in Tuskegee that housed the first classes of the Tuskegee Institute, were directly connected to schooling in their communities.

In the same year that Tuskegee Institute was founded in the church buildings in Tuskegee, Spelman College for women began as the Atlanta Baptist Female Seminary in the basement of the Friendship Baptist Church in Atlanta, Georgia. It began as an elementary and secondary school for adult women, offering literacy

Spelman Seminary's missionary training class of 1895. Founded in 1881 with financial help from the woman's American Baptist Home Mission Society, Spelman offered education to black women interested in becoming teachers, nurses, missionaries, and church workers.

classes to women who had not had a prior opportunity to learn to read and write, and giving religious instruction. Over the years, it broadened its programs and evolved into a full four-year college. Like Tuskegee Institute and other African-American schools, it offered classes to prepare students for occupations in teaching and household service. A nurses' training program was added in 1886.

African-American women were active as policymakers in education in addition to being students and teachers in the classrooms. The church was an important factor here as well. Beginning in the 1880s, black women church activists organized state conventions where they met to advocate support of black Baptist-owned schools for higher education and missionary work. Conventions were held in Alabama, Arkansas, Kentucky, Missouri, Mississippi, West Virginia, and other states. Many of these state conventions published their own newspapers, and their members also wrote columns on women's and educational issues for general Baptist publications. In 1887 more than forty newspapers were being produced by black Baptists. Most of these were published in the South.

The work of church members was crucial to providing social services to black people who lived nearby. Churches were also places to hold community theater productions, suppers, and programs, and to gather to discuss local issues and current events. In the midst of a larger society that denied leadership roles to African Americans, churches provided opportunities for ministers and members to speak their thoughts and hold positions of authority. Though church activities were spearheaded by the ministers who served them, and community at large looked to these preachers as spokesmen for their congregations, the community work and fund-raising was done mainly by their women members.

The black church programs, hospitals, newspapers, settlement houses, and schools that were established in the last decades of the nineteenth century left no doubt about the African American's ability to, as Booker T. Washington had put it in 1895, "hew out his [or her] own path."

Leadership: "Show Us the Way"

One of the most important moments in the life of Booker T. Washington came on the sunny late afternoon of September 18, 1895, when he walked to the front of a stage to give a speech to a huge gathering of business executives and visitors at the Cotton States and International Exposition in Atlanta, Georgia.

The audience at this big commercial event had come to celebrate the emergence of a new post–Civil War South. As Washington recalled in his autobiography, he rose to speak and faced an audience "of two thousand people, composed mostly of Southern and Northern whites." The black people in attendance sat in a separate gallery. The master of ceremonies had just introduced Washington as a great educator, with no reference to his color, but when the audience saw a tall, distinguished black man rise to give the speech, their applause wavered and died out in disapproval. Washington nevertheless strode forward and took his place on the stage.

Washington gave a short and simple oration that expressed opinions he had shared with other audiences many times before. But this time his statement was greeted in a new way. It was publicized, reprinted, and accepted among whites— and damned by some blacks—as a manifesto of black accommodation to white supremacy in the South. In preaching a message that was acceptable to white Southerners—the gradual uplift of blacks in the name of the mutual economic progress of blacks and whites, and thus of the South as a whole—Washington's speech in Atlanta set the tone for race policy and race relations in the United States for decades to come.

The speech also signaled the arrival of a new leader among African Americans. That September day in Atlanta marked the true beginning of widespread recognition of Washington as the most prominent spokesman for African Americans in his time. In his speech Washington displayed the combination of defiance and compromise that would continue to mark his leadership for the rest of his life. The statement of defiance and proclamation of black selfhood and personal authority Washington made silently—by standing up before the Atlanta audience. The compromise could be found in the openly expressed message of his words. Washington's speech symbolizes a time when new black leaders appeared in many fields of political and cultural achievement, and when themes of compromise or accommodation, self-assertion and protest, were found simultaneously in the public life and leadership of black people.

Washington began his oration by telling a story about a ship that had been lost at sea for many days. The crew was thirsty, and when they finally sighted another ship, they called out three times for water. "Cast down your bucket where you are," answered the people on the other vessel. When the thirsty sailors did lower a bucket, they were surprised to draw it back up full of fresh water. Without knowing it, they had drifted near the mouth of a river and the water that flowed under their ship was not undrinkable salt water, as they thought, but good water for drinking.

Washington's story was a metaphor for what he felt black people in the South needed to do. Instead of fleeing and looking for what they needed elsewhere, like those who had gone from Louisiana or Mississippi to Kansas, or asking for aid from without, like those who looked to the North, or trekked from the fields to the cities, he counseled that they remain in the South and find there ways to improve their condition. In his speech, Washington struck a bargain with white Southerners and Northerners in positions of power. According to this deal, black labor would remain in the South and concentrate on developing better agriculture and commerce. White businessmen and landowners would benefit from retaining the hard work and services of African Americans. They would also benefit from the commercial and industrial progress that would come with investment in the education and business enterprises of blacks. In return, both races would act, as Washington said in his speech, in "determination to administer absolute justice, in a willing obedience among all classes to the mandates of law."

The other part of the bargain that Washington suggested was the part that most disturbed black leaders who disagreed with his approach. In exchange for greater future material prosperity and the promise of more evenhanded administration of the law, African Americans, Washington implied, would not make immediate or forceful claims for equal rights and opportunities. Nor would they attempt to share in the social privileges enjoyed by whites in public and private settings. In the most famous line of the speech, which became known as the "Atlanta Compromise," Washington promised that "in all things that are purely social we can be as separate as the fingers, yet one as the hand in all things essential to mutual progress."

This metaphor of the hand and the fingers was greeted with great applause by the white audience, the very same audience that had grumbled when Washington first took the stage. The reaction of the blacks who heard Washington that day was

This montage from an 1896 publication features five of the most prominent black leaders of the era: clockwise, from top left, T. Thomas Fortune, Booker T. Washington, Ida B. Wells, I. Garland Penn, and, in the center, Frederick Douglass.

more cryptic. James Creelman, a reporter for the *New York World*, wrote on the front page of the *World*'s September 19, 1895, edition that at the speech's end "most of the Negroes in the audience were crying, perhaps without knowing just why." Whether they were shedding tears of intense pride in Washington's appearance, or tears of dismay over what his message might mean for African Americans in the future, was not recorded.

We do know how other leaders reacted. The journalist T. Thomas Fortune saw Washington's advice as a triumph of reconciliation and leadership. The black novelist Charles W. Chesnutt saw it in another way. In his 1903 article "The Disfranchisement of the Negro," he observed that "Southern white men may applaud this advice as wise, because it fits in with their purposes." But telling blacks "to go slow in seeking to enforce their civil and political rights . . . in effect, means silent submission to injustice."

Washington explained the philosophy behind his speech when he described the Atlanta event in his autobiography, *Up from Slavery*, which was published in book form in 1901 after being serialized the previous year. The book, like the speech itself, was designed to appeal primarily to a white audience. "I believe," Washington wrote, that "it is the duty of the Negro—as the greater part of the race is already doing—to deport himself modestly in regard to political claims, depending upon the slow but sure influences that proceed from the possession of property, intelligence, and high character for the full recognition of his political rights." This was a policy of appeasement.

Washington's speech symbolized a key change of personalities and techniques in the national leadership of African Americans. The 1880s and 1890s saw the deaths of many members of an older generation of African-American activists, who had led the movement to abolish slavery. The great abolitionist, orator, and women's rights advocate Sojourner Truth died in 1883. The passing of leadership from the militancy of the past to the accommodation of Washington in the present was best signified by the death of Frederick Douglass. Douglass, who had often appeared on the same platform with Sojourner Truth, had long dominated the political stage as an orator and commentator on current events. He died in Washington, D.C., on February 20, 1895, just six months before Washington spoke at the Atlanta Exposition.

In June 1895, W. E. B. Du Bois became the first African American to receive a Ph.D. degree from Harvard University. This, too, was a significant event in shaping the new standard of leadership. The young Du Bois, like Washington, would soon be recognized as one of the leaders of African-American thought.

Because of the erosion of civil rights in the late nineteenth century, black leadership had also declined in party politics and government. Although twenty-two African Americans were elected to the U.S. Congress between 1870 and the turn of the century, the post–Civil War white backlash against an integrated Republican party in the South effectively ended Republican power and Reconstruction reforms by 1877.

In the last three decades of the nineteenth century, twenty African Americans were elected to the House of Representatives. Most of these were elected in the 1870s. Eight represented districts in South Carolina, four were from North Carolina, three from Alabama, and one each was from Virginia, Georgia, Florida, Louisiana, and Mississippi. Two black men—Hiram Revels and Blanche K. Bruce—served as U.S. senators from the state of Mississippi.

Though many of these leaders were ex-slaves, a large proportion of black office-holders (in relation to the overall African-American population) were freedmen before the Civil War. Some were wealthy entrepreneurs or landowners, coming from a business class like that of many white candidates for office. (James T. Rapier of Alabama, Blanche K. Bruce, and Josiah T. Walls of Florida, were planters.) But all, regardless of their backgrounds, had an essential political base in the majority black communities in the districts they represented. Many had come to political leadership after gaining experience as leaders in black education or in the black churches in their communities or states.

After the end of Reconstruction in the late 1870s, black Republican politicians saw the need to form alliances with white Democrats and provide patronage to white constituents in order to stay in office. These compromises made it possible for some to retain their positions into the 1880s, but by the 1890s Jim Crow legal disenfranchisement crippled black political influence on the state level.

Because of the effectiveness of the disenfranchisement of black voters, the new leaders who came to the forefront in the 1880s and 1890s were not elected officials. Sometimes they were designated as representatives of African-American opinion by whites, and sometimes they rose to this stature through the esteem with which they were held by fellow African Americans who felt that they spoke what was in their own hearts and minds. The influence of leaders like Booker T. Washington, W. E. B. Du Bois, Ida B. Wells, and T. Thomas Fortune was far-reaching. Each of these leaders was involved in the formation of important organizations that reflected the needs and desires of different segments of the African-American population. And their ideas and chosen methods of activism had an impact upon African-American history well into the twentieth century.

Booker T. Washington's Tuskegee Negro Conference, first held in 1892, is an example of the kind of leadership found in that era. According to the circular advertising the meeting, Washington's aim was to "bring together for a quiet conference, not the politicians and those usually termed the 'leading colored people,' but representatives of the masses—the bone and sinew of the race—the common, hard working farmers with a few of the best ministers and teachers." There were two goals, the circular continued: "First, to find out the actual industrial, moral and educational condition of the masses. Second, to get as much light as possible on what is the most effective way for the young men and women whom the Tuskegee Institute and other institutions are educating to use their education in helping the masses of the colored people to lift themselves up." Washington expected about seventy-five farmers, educators, and preachers to come on February 23. Instead, about five hundred men and women showed up.

They spent the morning sharing with each other information about their lives, describing who owned the land in the regions where they lived, what crops were grown, what their homes were like, where they worshiped, and where their children went to school. In the afternoon they drafted a set of resolutions. The resolutions did not deal with political or civil rights. They were about methods of self-help and ways to climb the socioeconomic ladder to the middle class. They urged all to buy land, build larger houses and schools, "give more attention to the character of their leaders, especially ministers and teachers," and stay out of debt. The desire of women for greater respect and opportunities was reflected in the resolution "to treat our women better."

Tuskegee Conferences were held annually after 1892, and by 1895, the year of Washington's Atlanta Exposition address, so many people were attending that the overall conference was broken into separate conferences for farmers, teachers, and women. Long working hours and domestic violence were among the issues the women brought up as their concerns at the February 1895 conference.

The Tuskegee Negro Conferences represented discussion and change from the bottom up (although it was under the careful stewardship of Booker T. Washington and his colleagues), but the formation of the American Negro Academy represented leadership from the top down. Planned as an elite organization, the academy was founded in Washington, D.C., in 1897 and designed to be the first major learned society for African-American intellectuals. Its first president was Alexander Crummell, long an Episcopal church leader and an inspiration to many of the younger men in the group. Crummell was one of the older generation of leaders, like Frederick Douglass and Sojourner Truth, whose life spanned much of the nineteenth century. He lived and worked in Liberia, West Africa, for many years and was one of the major theorists of the early Pan-African movement, which encouraged political unity among the peoples of the African diaspora. Crummell died the year after the academy was founded.

A person could not just join the academy. Participation was restricted to the select few who were nominated and elected to membership by those who were already members. The founders included Du Bois, sociologist Kelly Miller, and poet Paul Laurence Dunbar. Only one woman, the Washington, D.C., educator and feminist theorist Anna Julia Cooper, was invited to join the men in the academy.

The purposes of the academy included the promotion of scholarly work by black Americans and the refutation of theories and beliefs that stereotyped and demeaned African Americans. In his 1897 speech "The Conservation of Races," Du Bois spelled out the academy's purposes: "It aims at once to be the epitome and expression of the intellect of the black . . . people of America, the exponent of the race ideals of one of the world's great races." Du Bois succeeded Crummell as president of the American Negro Academy in 1898.

At the same time that the academy was beginning,Du Bois was busy conducting his survey of African-American urban life in Philadelphia. Soon after finishing the survey, Du Bois became a professor at Atlanta University, where he directed the elite answer to Washington's Tuskegee conferences, the annual Atlanta Conference on Negro Problems. These conferences, held each May at Atlanta University, created a forum for African-American social scientists and other intellectuals. They gathered to exchange their research and ideas and to organize a series of sociological studies about various aspects of African-American life in the South. Studies in the 1890s focused on African-American mortality and life in the cities, and African Americans in business.

Like the Tuskegee conferences, the second Atlanta University gathering included a separate women's meeting, which focused on issues of motherhood, child rearing, and early childhood education. Educators and activists Lucy Laney and Adella Hunt Logan were among the participants who gave papers or addresses there. In 1883, Laney founded a school in Augusta, Georgia, that became the Haines Normal and Industrial Institute. She was a pioneer in kindergarten education and nurses' training. Logan was a teacher at Tuskegee Institute, beginning in 1883, and she worked closely with Olivia Davidson Washington in administering the girls' curriculum at the school. She was a founding member of the Tuskegee Women's Club and a leader in the woman suffrage movement.

The conferences for farmers at Tuskegee and for intellectuals in Atlanta were related to the formation of many new African-American professional societies and social service organizations in the 1880s and 1890s. They were also related to a long-standing method of grass-roots political debate—the holding of conventions. Black ministers, editors, business owners, and intellectuals had been holding state and national conventions to address political events since the 1830s. An important national convention was held in Louisville in 1883, and African Americans in many states—including Arkansas, Georgia, Kansas, Maryland, Rhode Island, Texas, and South Carolina—organized conventions in the 1880s and 1890s for regional black leaders to discuss political policies and conditions. Rejecting Washington's tactic of appeasement and silence on political issues, the state leaders who met at these conventions discussed the role of blacks in party politics and demanded that state legislatures and the U.S. Congress respect black people's civil and political rights.

Several rights organizations were outgrowths of the state convention movement. Among them were the National Association of Colored Men, which was organized at a convention in Detroit in January 1896. In a resolution sent to the U.S. Congress, this group announced, "We aim at nothing unattainable, nothing Utopian, not what the society of the future is seeking, but merely what other citizens of this civilization are now enjoying."

T. Thomas Fortune's National Afro-American League, formed in 1890 and revived in new form in 1898 as the Afro-American Council, was another organization that black leaders joined in order to promote equal citizenship rights.

Fortune was a close friend of Booker T. Washington for many years and he supported Washington's platform on industrial education. Washington in turn gave financial support to Fortune's newspaper, the *New York Age*. Politically, however, Fortune was much more openly militant than Washington, and in the North in the 1890s he was one of the most widely recognized advocates for African-American rights. His National Afro-American League had objectives and approaches to problems facing blacks that would be used again by civil rights organizations in the next century. Fortune made the goals of the league clear in the very first sentence of his address to its founding convention: "We are here to-day," he told the audience, "as representatives of eight million freemen, who know our rights and have the courage to defend them."

The members of the Afro-American League favored public agitation for black rights. At their first convention they demanded an end to lynching and mob violence, the convict lease system, and the suppression of black people's ability to vote in the South. They also pointed out the unfair distribution of funds to black and white schools and discrimination against black people in public transportation and in public facilities. The league emphasized the importance of black solidarity. It favored separate black economic development, including the formation of black banks, job bureaus, and cooperative business enterprises. Local leagues were founded in several states in 1889, most of them in large cities such as San Francisco and Boston, and in other areas of the Northeast and Midwest. Both men and women were urged to participate.

The National Afro-American Council came into being at a convention in Rochester, New York, in September 1898. It was important in large part for its influence and connection to other activist groups that emerged in the years immediately following. Its platform emphasizing civil rights and suffrage, for example, foreshadowed the goals of the Niagara Movement, a black intellectual group that W. E. B. Du Bois would help to found in 1905. That, in turn, led to the National Association for the Advancement of Colored People (NAACP), founded in 1910, which would serve as a major source for equal rights advocacy for decades. And, although Booker T. Washington did not participate in the founding sessions of the council, the group's policies and public statements were soon dominated by Washington and his colleagues. The National Afro-American Council remained active until 1906, but its militancy was tempered by Washington's influence, and much of the energy that had gone into its economic programs was diverted to Washington's National Negro Business League, founded in 1900 in Boston.

The need for such a business league, and the importance of black consumers buying goods and services they needed from black-owned businesses, had been voiced a few years before by Du Bois at one of the Atlanta University conferences. Du Bois later became the director of the Afro-American Council's Negro Business Bureau, where he instituted a plan to establish local business leagues around the country. But it was Washington who held more power in the council organization, and thus he who acted upon the idea for a national group to promote black commerce. The late 1880s and 1890s were a time when many new black businesses were started and when growing black urban populations brought increased business to black grocers, barbers, butchers, hotel and retail shop owners, undertakers, and real estate dealers. Black banks and insurance companies, cemeteries, and building and loan companies were also founded.

One of the issues that most concerned T. Thomas Fortune in the first year of the Afro-American Council's activism was the effect of American imperialism on people of color. He was especially concerned about the impact that the United States' war against Spain and its intervention in the Philippines in 1898 and 1899 had on Cubans, Puerto Ricans, and Filipinos.

The Spanish-American War, which began in 1895, was partly a business matter. Spanish control of territory in the New World had been gradually decreased in the late 19th century to domination of the islands of Cuba and Puerto Rico. As the end of the century approached, Cubans increasingly desired their political independence. But even as Spanish influence was waning, American business interests had invested many millions of dollars in Cuban plantations and refineries.

When the Cubans revolted against Spanish rule in 1895, the United States had a strong economic interest in controlling the outcome of events. News of the terrible suffering of Cubans who were forced from their homes and faced starvation and disease during the conflict also made many Americans favor U.S. intervention. Many African Americans sympathized with the Cuban rebels, and most cautiously supported U.S. involvement in the war. Others worried that overthrowing Spain and replacing her influence in the Caribbean with that of the United States would only result in the extension of Jim Crow racial discrimination beyond American borders. The coming of the war also raised issues about black patriotism, pointing up the irony of black soldiers serving abroad in the service of a country that did not grant them full citizenship rights at home. Nevertheless, many thousands of African Americans volunteered for service.

The Spanish-American War was one more arena in which African Americans demonstrated leadership in the 1890s. When the war against Spain began in April 1898, Charles Young, a West Point graduate, was the only black commissioned officer in the U.S. armed forces. Young was a friend of W. E. B. DuBois and had taught with him at Wilberforce University. A lieutenant when the war began, he was promoted to the rank of major (in 1916 he became a colonel). Despite severe racial discrimination within the armed services, by war's end there were more than one hundred African-American officers commissioned at the rank of first or second lieutenant. The majority of black volunteer units, including outfits from North Carolina, Massachusetts, and Illinois, had black officers in positions of command. Because the war only lasted a few months (it ended in July 1898), most of these eight thousand to ten thousand black volunteers never left military bases in the United States.

In the years between the Civil War and the Spanish-American War, four regular units of African-American soldiers, including the 9th and 10th Cavalries and the 24th and 25th Infantries, had been active in the U.S. Army in the West. These were the black regiments that were sent to Cuba in June 1898. The soldiers in these units, called "Buffalo Soldiers" by Native Americans in the West, were dubbed "Smoked Yankees" by the Cubans of African descent who met them during the war. They served with distinction in the key battles, most notably at El Caney, Las Guasimas, and San Juan Hill. In the last, they were instrumental in winning the battle for which Theodore Roosevelt and his Rough Riders gained fame. Black sailors also served aboard U.S. Navy ships, and some two thousand black men enlisted in the Navy during the war.

The question of leadership within the military became one of the largest issues of the war for African Americans. John Mitchell, Jr., the publisher of the *Richmond Planet,* a black newspaper in Virginia, coined the phrase "No officers, no fight!" It neatly summed up the African-American demand that blacks be promoted to positions of command and that black units be headed by black officers.

Blacks around the United States were well informed about the war from a black perspective because hundreds of black soldiers wrote home to African-American newspapers about their experiences. Activism through the spoken and written word was often linked through newsprint. For example, Victoria Earle Matthews invited Ida B. Wells to give her landmark speech about lynching because Matthews had read Wells's newspaper articles about lynching. Matthews, like Wells, worked as a journalist. Under the pen name Victoria Earle, she wrote for such papers as the *Brooklyn Eagle* and the *New York Times.* But more importantly, she wrote articles for some of the major African-American newspapers of the day, including the *Richmond Planet,* the *Washington Bee,* and the *Cleveland Gazette.* When she read Ida B. Wells's articles about lynching, she was working regularly for T. Thomas Fortune's *New York Age.* The influence of black newspapers was not restricted to the Northeast and the South. By 1900 more than sixty such newspapers had been founded in the states west of the Mississippi River, including Emmett J. Scott's *Texas Freeman.*

African Americans also emerged as leading figures in sports and the performing arts, and in the writing of fiction and poetry. Some of these cultural leaders achieved stature while accommodating their art to white audiences. Other leading black writers and performers chose to confront the prejudices of white audiences head-on. Some of them reacted to white racism by choosing to perform primarily for black audiences. Others used their art, performances, and writings to educate their mixed audiences about the range of black experience and to dispel negative stereotypes about black people.

Black jockeys dominated the winner's circle at the prestigious Kentucky Derby in Louisville, Kentucky, in the 1880s and 1890s. Isaac Murphy, nationally recognized as America's finest rider at that time, was the first man in history to win the

Kentucky Derby three times—in 1884, 1890, and 1891. At the same time that black athletes were excelling before large crowds in the sport of horse racing, African Americans were emerging as stars in the fields of music and musical theater. Soprano Sissieretta Jones was hailed as the "Black Patti" in tribute to the beauty of her voice, which critics compared to that of the much-acclaimed Italian opera singer Adelina Patti. Jones sang at Madison Square Garden in New York in 1892 and soon after appeared at the White House in a command performance for President Benjamin Harrison. The next year, she made a grand tour of Europe. She returned to the United States and was barred because of her race from performing at the Metropolitan Opera in New York. (The ban against blacks appearing at the nation's most prestigious opera house remained until 1955, when Marian Anderson became the first African American to perform there.)

Jones adapted to the white prejudice that excluded her from major opera houses by forming an all-black concert company called Black Patti's Troubadours. The group, with which Jones appeared as a soloist, presented arias from such operas as *Lucia de Lammermoor* and *Il Trovatore* as well as dancing and selections of popular music. The group went on tour and performed for sixteen years for black audiences in small towns and cities.

New images of blacks were also being presented to white and black audiences in other areas of musical theater and in literature. The lyricism that Sissieretta Jones was famous for portraying with her voice also filled the work of the late nineteenth century's most prominent African-American poet, Paul Laurence Dunbar. Dunbar was an elevator operator in Dayton, Ohio, when he began publishing his poetry. He had been a member of the literary society and editor of the school newspaper at Central High School in Dayton, and his first poems were published in newspapers. His first collection of poems, *Oak and Ivy,* was published in 1892, followed by *Majors and Minors* (1895), *Lyrics of Lowly Life* (1896), and *Lyrics of the Hearth-side* (1899). He also wrote short stories and novels. Dunbar's poetry received great critical acclaim. It also became very popular for African-American schoolchildren to memorize his poems and recite them in public programs, so that he was well known among both the intellectual elite and poorer people. He wrote poems in standard English and using black dialect speech, combining lyrical themes of love and death with depictions of African-American life and tributes to outstanding African-American leaders such as Frederick Douglass and Alexander Crummell.

Although most of Dunbar's work was not political in theme, he wrote what would become one of the most important protest poems in all of African-American literature. Called "We Wear the Mask," the poem talks about the dual nature of African-American existence, in which blacks exhibited a certain code of amiable outer behavior to meet white expectations, while underneath that accommodating outer demeanor, true thoughts and feelings lay hidden. Published in *Lyrics of Lowly Life,* "We Wear the Mask" goes like this:

The team of George Walker (right) and Bert Williams was one of the most popular African-American acts in vaudeville. Despite their celebrity, they faced segregation in the hotels and eating establishments of the cities where they performed. After Walker's death, Williams became the nation's first big-name African-American star as a featured performer with the Ziegfeld Follies.

We wear the mask that grins and lies,
It hides our cheeks and shades our eyes,—
This debt we pay to human guile;
With torn and bleeding hearts we smile,
And mouth with myriad subtleties

Why should the world be over-wise,
In counting all our tears and sighs?
Nay, let them only see us, while
We wear the mask.

We smile, but, O great Christ, our cries
To thee from tortured souls arise.

> We sing, but oh the clay is vile
> Beneath our feet, and long the mile;
> But let the world dream otherwise,
> We wear the mask!

In addition to writing poetry, Paul Laurence Dunbar was involved in musical theater as a songwriter. He and composer Will Marion Cook wrote an operetta called *Clorindy* in 1898. When *Clorindy* went on a tour of East Coast cities that September, it starred two of Dunbar and Cook's friends from New York, Bert Williams and George Walker. Bert Williams was born in the British West Indies and went to high school in Riverside, California. He and Walker began their career as a duo in a minstrel company in San Francisco in 1893. They developed their own comedy act, and by the mid-1890s they were leading men in New York variety productions. Walker's wife, Aida Overton Walker, had been a dancer with the Black Patti Troubadours. She appeared in all the Williams and Walker shows and choreographed their major numbers.

Williams and Walker's fame did not come without a price. Their act played to white stereotypes about blacks. Walker was the dandy, appearing in elaborately designed fancy street clothes that made fun of black consumerism and middle-class aspirations. Williams, who had never lived in the American South, played a Southern tramplike figure who sang in dialect and played the banjo. A light-skinned man, he also appeared on stage in blackface, which meant that he rubbed burnt cork on his face to make it look darker and applied makeup to exaggerate his African features. White actors had long been doing the same thing to caricature black people in minstrel and variety shows, and thus Williams's makeup fulfilled white audiences' expectations of what a black person should look like on stage. For Williams, who in real life was a dignified and quiet man, his on-stage persona was one in which he quite literally wore the mask.

The folk dialect that was used in stage by acts like Williams and Walker's, and in popular music like the songs written by Cook and Dunbar, also was used by African Americans who wrote short stories and novels. This was true for the two most prominent African-American authors of the 1890s, Charles Waddell Chesnutt and Frances Ellen Watkins Harper. Both of these writers used dialect when creating dialogue for black folk characters who were illiterate or lacked formal education. For these characters an oral, rather than a written, tradition was paramount. Educated and middle-class characters, by contrast, spoke standard English in these writers' books.

Just as Sissieretta Jones sought to present a new image of black womanhood in music, so Frances Harper's *Iola Leroy* (1892), one of the first novels published by an African-American woman, was written in part to dispel stereotypes that whites had about black women. *Iola Leroy* protested derogatory ideas that whites held about black women's social worth and morality by placing at its center an able and intelligent black woman protagonist whose actions and thoughts were full of virtue. The novel's heroine, Iola Leroy, is a well-educated, middle-class woman who devotes her life to the uplift of her people. Harper also used the story to address a series of injustices in African-American history and demonstrate ways in which elite African Americans in the decades after the Civil War developed systems of self-help.

Iola Leroy was published in the same year as two other key works written by African-American women: Ida B. Wells's *Southern Horrors,* an exposé about lynching, and Anna Julia Cooper's *A Voice from the South,* a treatise on the status of women in African-American society. Each of these works, and the lives of each of the women who wrote them, proved that African-American leadership was not just male, but female. Indeed, the 1890s produced so many extraordinary African-American women leaders and organizations that it became known as the "Woman's Era."

Woman's Era: "Strong in a Love of Justice"

In 1893, a year after her novel *Iola Leroy* was published, the veteran lecturer Frances Ellen Watkins Harper stood on the podium at the World's Congress of Representative Women in Chicago. The Women's Congress, as it was known, was held in conjunction with the World's Columbian Exposition, or Chicago World's Fair. Just as the Atlanta Exposition was held to celebrate the economic resurgence of the American South, so the Chicago World's Fair was organized to laud the industrial and cultural achievements of the Americas in the eyes of the world. Exhibition halls were set up to show advancements in many types of fields, and one hall was devoted specifically to the achievements of women. But the Lady Managers, or the board of women who had organized the women's events at the fair, largely excluded African-American women from participating.

When Harper and other black, middle-class women accepted invitations to speak at the Women's Congress, they saw themselves as representatives of all African Americans. They also came to confront the racism that had allowed the Lady Managers of the fair to present only white women's skills and creations as worthy of attention in the Women's Building.

Their speeches, like Harper's novel, Ida B. Wells's pamphlets about lynching, and Anna Julia Cooper's book *A Voice from the South,* represent the bold introduction of black women's voices into the debates within the middle-class African-American community as a whole. Their lectures also represented a defense of black womanhood, answering those who viewed black women as lacking in moral character or as secondary in importance to men. When they appeared in Chicago they challenged white women's racism both by word and example. And they gave voice to principles that they felt black people should hold dear. Among them were the right of young women to educational opportunities equal to those of young men; the right of women—black and white—to vote; and the recognition of the role that women had to play in improving society, both privately within the home and publicly as champions of justice for their race.

At the Women's Congress in Chicago in 1893, Frances Ellen Watkins Harper and the other black women who spoke summed up the issues that were in the minds of many of their sisters. Just as Booker T. Washington's Atlanta speech helped shape race relations well into the twentieth century, Harper's speech in Chicago set the agenda for middle-class black women's activism for years ahead. She also gave a name to the 1890s that reflected the rise of a generation of well-educated African-American women to positions of public leadership. She called it the "Woman's Era."

And so it was. Never before had there been so many African-American women speaking their minds in public forums, founding newspapers and schools, and shaping the world around them. In the Woman's Era, middle-class women working in their own towns and cities on behalf of working-class women and the poor developed a national momentum for positive change. Most important, black women's benevolent associations and mothers' and women's clubs joined together into regional federations, and ultimately into the National Association of Colored Women, which was founded in 1896. But the movement toward the more powerful organization of black women was happening in other ways as well—in the suffrage movement, the temperance movement, and the Baptist church.

In her speech in Chicago, Harper argued that the "world has need of all the spiritual aid that woman can give for the social advancement and moral development of the human race." Women's abilities and contributions were far too valuable to waste, and to talk only of the advancement of men and their greater opportunities was not sufficient. Harper, like her colleague Anna Julia Cooper, believed that women represented a force for good that would counteract men's tendencies toward destructiveness, war, and violence. She also argued, along with Cooper, that women should enter public and economic life. "By opening doors of labor," Harper said of black women trying to broaden the types of work they were allowed to do, "woman has become a rival claimant for at least some of the wealth monopolized by her stronger brother." She called for the "ballot in the hands of woman," which would add direct political power to the already existing influence of women in the home, the church pew, the classroom, and the press. She spoke of the male-led worlds of business and the military, the "increase of wealth, the power of armies," being nothing in contrast to the basic social needs of "good homes, of good fathers, and good mothers." She warned of the effects of heavy drinking upon families, and she castigated lynching.

In presenting this political platform, Harper echoed many of the opinions expressed by Anna Julia Cooper in *A Voice from the South*, published the previous year. Cooper, too, questioned the top-to-bottom structure of power that led one nation to attempt to conquer another, or one race to consider itself superior to another. She compared these attitudes of dominance to the ways that intellectual and political opportunities were open to men but closed to women, and to the fact that white women's prejudices against black women tarnished and limited existing movements for women's political rights. She stated that no civilization could rise higher than its women, and that the key to progress for any society was the development of its women's full rights and opportunities. She argued strongly for women's access to higher education and intellectual achievement, and for the economic independence of women that such training would permit.

Cooper, like Harper, was one of the African-American women who spoke to the international audience at the Chicago Women's Congress. She had taught school in her home state of North Carolina before graduating from the "men's" course of study with A.B. (1884) and M.A. (1887) degrees at Oberlin College—one of the first women students to do so. She headed the modern language department at Wilberforce College in Ohio—the same school where American Negro Academy leader W. E. B. Du Bois and military officer Charles Young taught. Later she moved to Washington, D.C., where she became one of the most important educators of her time. She served as principal of the famed M Street High School. She was also one of the first African-American women to obtain a Ph.D. degree, which she earned from the Sorbonne in Paris in 1925, when she was sixty-six.

At the Women's Congress, Ida B. Wells decided not to speak. Instead she protested white racism by putting together a short book, published in Chicago during the World's Fair. She called it *The Reason Why the Colored American Is Not in the World's Columbian Exposition.* Frederick Douglass, who had long supported women's right to vote and other women's causes, wrote the book's introduction.

The book included chapters about slavery, disenfranchisement, and lynching. It also chronicled African-American achievements, including a list of patents granted to black men and women and biographies of black artists, authors, and musicians. It ended with documentation of black people's exclusion from the fair by the white administrators. Wells raised the money to publish the pamphlet by arranging a series of Sunday afternoon meetings among women at different Chicago-area churches. She printed twenty thousand copies of the pamphlet, and they were distributed throughout Chicago and by mail.

The same year, Wells traveled to England and Scotland to give lectures about lynching. Frederick Douglass encouraged her to go and loaned her the money to make the trip. "It seemed like an open door in a stone wall," she wrote in her memoirs. Excluded from the South because of her newspaper writings, and having trouble getting people in the North to listen to her, she went across the Atlantic Ocean to speak in cities such as Edinburgh, Liverpool, Manchester, and London. In every speech she gave she educated white British audiences about Jim Crow laws in the American South and the realities of lynching. She succeeded in making the antilynching campaign international.

Frances Ellen Watkins Harper's speech in Chicago and Ida B. Wells's lectures abroad were both catalysts for more rigorous organization of a national black women's club movement in the mid-1890s. The movement started off with local groups in several different places. Many of these groups began in 1892–93. The Women's Loyal Union had been formed by Victoria Earle Matthews and other middle-class women activists in New York after Wells's Lyric Hall speech in 1892. The Colored Women's League of Washington, D.C., the Women's Era Club of Boston, and the Ida B. Wells Club of Chicago were formed soon after.

Mary Church Terrell, president of the Bethel Literary and Historical Society in Washington, D.C., was one of the founders of the Colored Women's League. The founding statement the league drafted, written in June 1892, summed up the spirit of the middle-class black woman's movement. "Whereas," it read, "in Union there is Strength, and Whereas, we, as a people, have been and are the subject of prejudice, proscription, and injustice, the more successful, because the lack of unity and organization, Resolved, That we, the colored women of Washington, associate ourselves together." The Colored Women's League soon expanded by opening branches in other cities, including Richmond and Norfolk, Virginia, and Newport, Rhode Island.

Journalist Josephine St. Pierre Ruffin headed the Boston Woman's Era Club. Originally called the New Era Club when it was founded in February 1893, it took the name of the Woman's Era that Frances Harper had used in her speech. In March 1894 Ruffin began publishing a monthly journal of opinion called the *Woman's Era*. Black women activists from all over the country—Mary Church Terrell of Washington, Alice Ruth Moore of New Orleans (who later married the poet Paul Laurence Dunbar, and became herself a noted literary figure under the name Alice Dunbar Nelson), Victoria Earle Matthews of New York, and Fannie Barrier Williams of Chicago—contributed to the journal, which served as a forum for the new women's movement.

One of the major concerns voiced in Anna Julia Cooper's *A Voice from the South* and many of the black women's speeches at the World's Fair was whites' habit of questioning black women's sexual morality. Ida B. Wells always made this issue a part of her lectures on lynching. Cooper spoke for the other women activists when she wrote that unwanted sexual advances were typically made by whites, not blacks. Speaking of attitudes about rape, she said that the blame had been misplaced on black people. Historically, whites were primarily responsible for sexual offenses against blacks, not vise versa. "Overtures for forced association in the past history of these two races were not made by the manacled black man, nor by the silent and suffering black woman!" she declared. Black women's outrage over this issue of their alleged immorality was a major impetus to the formation of the national black women's movement.

It happened this way. A white American journalist—a man from Missouri—wrote a letter in which he attacked Ida B. Wells's character because she had spoken out against Southern lynching on her trips abroad, and in which he demeaned the character of black women in general. Copies of the offensive letter were circulated among women activists in the antilynching movement in England and passed on to club leaders in the United States. When Josephine St. Pierre Ruffin received a copy of the letter, she decided to take action. She sent out a circular and on the editorial page of the June 1895 issue of *Woman's Era* printed a call for a big meeting of women. "To all colored women of America, members of any society or not," she wrote, "Let Us Confer Together." The result was the First National Conference of the Colored Women of America.

The conference convened in Boston at the end of July 1895. In her keynote speech, Ruffin outlined the many reasons for getting black women from all over the nation together. "In the first place," she said, "we need to feel the cheer and inspiration of meeting each other, we need to gain the courage and fresh life that comes from the mingling of congenial souls, of those working for the same ends." Ruffin also told her audience that they needed to take a united stand and make their voices heard: "Too long have we been silent under unjust and unholy charges," she said, referring to slanderous accusations against middle-class black women. The women delegates decided to form a new organization. They named it the National Federation of Afro-American Women and elected Margaret Murray Washington, the Tuskegee activist, as president.

Meanwhile, other groups were forming. The following summer, in July 1896, the National Federation of Afro-American Women and the Washington, D.C.–based National League of Colored Women merged with more than one hundred other women's clubs to form a new coalition. It was called the National Association of Colored Women (NACW). Frances Harper was at this historic meeting, a representative of older, former antislavery activists, as was the great elderly abolitionist Harriet Tubman. Frederick Douglass's only daughter, Rosetta Sprague, participated. Ida B. Wells, who had recently married and changed her name to Ida B. Wells-Barnett, came with her new baby son to chair one of the conference committees. Mary Church Terrell was elected president of the new national organization. When the NACW met for its second annual conference in 1897, it moved its meeting south to Nashville, Tennessee, and began publication of a periodical, *National Notes.*

Mary Church Terrell had graduated from Oberlin College with Anna Julia Cooper and, like Cooper, lived in Washington, D.C. She grew up in Memphis, Tennessee, and like Ida B. Wells, had been a close friend of Peoples' Grocery owner Thomas Moss. Her husband, Robert Terrell, was a close associate of Booker T. Washington and the Terrell family was well-to-do. Mary Church Terrell's election as president was questioned by some. To some of the more progressive delegates she represented an overly conservative approach to social issues and, as a very rich

The National Association of Colored Women was formed in 1896 by the merger of the National League of Colored Women and the National Federation of Afro-American Women. Representing more than a hundred women's clubs, the new coalition proved to be a powerful promoter of self-help, equity, and justice for black women.

woman, she had a sensibility that was very remote from the lives of the masses of black Americans. Nevertheless, she headed the National Association of Colored Women from its inception in 1896 until 1901.

The motto of the NACW, "Lifting As We Climb," reflected the perspective of the middle-class women who made up the movement. They saw themselves improving the conditions and behavior of lower-class women as they instituted social reforms and defended the respectability of women like themselves. The activities of the NACW were similar to the kinds of outreach that was already being done in local areas through churches, settlement houses, and women's neighborhood groups. Under Terrell's leadership the NACW members emphasized early childhood education, especially the establishment of kindergartens and day nurseries. They also actively supported the major women's progressive movements, including suffrage, temperance, self-help, and moral reform.

In a time when most black Americans lived in the South and made their living in agriculture, the leadership, and much of the membership, of the NACW was largely based in the North and among urban women. The middle-class clubwomen had economic opportunities and lifestyle choices that were not available to a majority of black women. There were also internal splits among the ranks of NACW leaders. Ideological rivalries existed between women such as Mary Church Terrell, who was often compared to Booker T. Washington in politics and temperament, and more fiery and militant members such as Ida B. Wells-Barnett. Geographic rivalries also existed between the various NACW leaders from different Northern cities, whether Boston, Chicago, Washington, D.C., or New York, each of whom had a claim to the leadership of the original club movement. But despite these internal differences, the NACW functioned as a clearinghouse for black women's community action until the 1930s.

Black women's involvement in the temperance movement straddled the line between the secular politics of the women's club movement and the religious convictions that led black women of all classes to work in their communities through their churches. The movement to moderate or ban the use of alcohol was part of the self-help aspect of black institution building. The misuse of alcohol, temperance leaders argued, drained families of needed income, took attention away from children, and led to domestic violence. Women and children often paid the emotional and physical price of men's drinking, and men who socialized at bars and pool halls were not turning their attention to more constructive things. They also helped feed white stereotypes about nonproductive black men.

As president of the NACW, Mary Church Terrell was a widely sought-after speaker. Her conservative views on social and racial issues placed her at odds with other more militant members of the group such as Ida B. Wells.

When the African Methodist Episcopal church sponsored a symposium about temperance in 1891, it was Frances Harper who gave the keynote address. Harper had long worked with the Women's Christian Temperance Union (WCTU). She was a city, state, and eventually, national WCTU organizer for temperance in black communities. In her poetry in the 1880s, she wrote about the destructive effects on families caused by the abuse of alcohol, and in 1888 she wrote an essay called "The Women's Christian Temperance Union and the Colored Woman." She told of moral influence women could have in the home and of the direct-action tactic in which "saloons were visited, hardships encountered, insults, violence and even imprisonment endured by women, brave to suffer and strong to endure."

Harper's relatively positive experience in regional chapters of the WCTU contrasted with that of Josephine St. Pierre Ruffin and Ida B. Wells, both of whom found the white leadership of the WCTU intolerably racist. Wells in particular was appalled at WCTU president Frances Willard's acceptance of the white Southern practice of lynching and negative stereotypes of both black women and men. Despite such prejudices, black women joined black auxiliaries to the white women's union. By 1898, five independent black women's state temperance unions had been founded in the South—in Arkansas, Georgia, North Carolina, Tennessee, and Texas.

The racism and the opposition of white Southern women to integration that characterized the temperance movement also limited the ability of black women to participate in the organized woman suffrage movement. Black women leaders found their own ways of furthering the cause of women's right to vote. Mary Ann Shadd Cary, a Washington, D.C., lawyer and a graduate of Howard University, founded the Colored Women's Progressive Franchise Association as an auxiliary of the predominantly white National American Woman Suffrage Association (NAWSA) on February 9, 1880. Cary's self-help group supported equal rights for women and made lobbying for suffrage its first priority. Adella Hunt Logan, who led women's sessions at the annual Tuskegee conferences and participated in the Atlanta University conferences, was a very light-skinned black person. She used this to her advantage in "passing" as white in order to attend National American Woman Suffrage Association conventions in the segregated South. She then related what had happened in the meetings to fellow black activists in Southern states. Mary Church Terrell was a life member of NAWSA in the North and appeared as a speaker at many of the organization's national meetings, including those in 1898 and 1900. Terrell was among those who used her upper-class, college-educated status as an argument for the right of others like her to vote, arguing that the franchise should not be withheld from black women of culture and learning.

While Mary Church Terrell and other conservative clubwomen were advocating the rights of privileged black women, Lucy Parsons championed the cause of working people and the poor. Parsons moved in entirely different circles from the black reformers who united into women's organizations in the 1890s. Parsons was born in Waco, Texas, of mixed African, Indian, and Mexican ancestry. She married a white man named Albert Parsons, and together they entered a life of political activism. Just as the antilynching and women's movements foreshadowed many of the issues and approaches of the civil rights and women's liberation movements of the twentieth century, Lucy Parsons's kind of activism set an example for black people's involvement in the various movements of the American Left.

Lucy Parsons was an anarchist and socialist. She and her husband lived in primarily white-ethnic, working-class neighborhoods in Chicago, where she worked as a seamstress. Albert Parsons was a leader in the International Working People's Association, and both he and Lucy were members of the Knights of Labor. Lucy Parsons wrote revolutionary essays about homelessness, violence, unemployment, and working people's rights for her husband's newspaper, *Alarm,* and she became an organizer for the Chicago Working Women's Union.

She was known for her electrifying speeches, and as part of her work with the Knights of Labor she organized mostly white Chicago women in the sewing trades in support of an eight-hour workday. In 1891, Lucy Parsons joined the ranks of black women editors when she began publishing her own newspaper, *Freedom.* Unlike the periodicals of the black woman's movement, *Freedom* put class, rather than race or gender, at the forefront of the fight for justice.

Nannie Helen Burroughs bridged the worlds between the working women whom Parsons championed and the middle-class realm of the black women's club movement. Much of her activism took place within the black church. Most of the African-American women who became involved as activists in the woman's era had experience as community workers through their churches, and much of the spirit of reform that filled the 1890s emerged originally from self-help messages within the church. It is fitting, then, that women's organization building and feminist thought in the last decade of the nineteenth century also had an impact on the way women were viewed within the black church. The growing awareness about women's abilities that had sprung from the church and blossomed in middle-class, secular organizations was plowed back in to enrich the soil of religious institutions. Nannie Helen Burroughs was only twenty-one years old when she gave a speech called "How the Sisters Are Hindered from Helping" at the annual National Baptist Convention in Richmond, Virginia, in September 1900. Her plea for a more powerful and united presence for black women within the Baptist church led to the founding of the Woman's Convention, an auxiliary to the National Baptist Convention. The Woman's Convention, with more than one million members, proved to be the largest black women's organization in America. Through it, church women set their own policies and provided their own national leaders.

In 1893, Frances Ellen Watkins Harper spoke of being on the threshold of a woman's era. In 1900, black men and women stood together on the cusp of a new century. They had as their foundation the many churches, schools, and organizations they had built, and a legacy of leadership that would carry them into the next decades. The message that the African-American activists of the 1880s and 1890s left for those in the twentieth century was a clear one. Frances Harper said it at the Chicago Women's Congress in 1893: "Demand justice, simple justice, as the right of every race."

CHAPTER 7

A Chance to Make Good

1900–1929

James R. Grossman

I n 1900, ninety percent of all African Americans lived in the South; three-fourths of these eight million people inhabited rural communities. The 880,771 black northerners, on the other hand, were decidedly urban; seventy-one percent lived in cities.

History and personal experience taught African Americans that their position in U.S. society could not be understood without understanding racism. But race was not the only basis for discrimination in American life. Nor was it the only way Americans defined themselves. Class and gender, along with religion, ethnicity, and age, also shaped lives, ideas, and dreams.

Perhaps, indeed, "the problem of the Twentieth Century is the problem of the color line," as W. E. B. Du Bois declared in 1903. But the significance and the composition of that line cannot be reduced to the biology of skin pigmentation. The meaning of race, and the practice of racism, were tightly intertwined with labor systems, ideas about family life, and assumptions about the relationship between manhood and citizenship. Du Bois recognized that it was impossible to understand the meaning of race without also understanding class. The place of African Americans in society was inseparable from their place in the economy.

In African-American history, images of victimization spring to mind as readily as notions of progress. Hope has most often bred disappointment and frequently disillusionment as well. In the early twentieth century, black Americans shared in the aspirations and expectations of their fellow citizens but did so as a people with a unique history and set of barriers to overcome.

African Americans argued among themselves as to what those barriers were made of; exactly where they were situated; how permanent they were; and whether they should be destroyed, circumvented, or hurdled. During the first three decades of the twentieth century, thousands of black men and women obliterated, removed, tiptoed around, climbed over, and even passed through these barriers. Others ignored them. Some resigned themselves to the limitations and pain these barriers produced, without accepting the notion that such obstacles were either natural or just. And still others suffered from the costs of pounding the barriers at times and in places where they were too deeply embedded in the social fabric to be breached.

Making a Living

At the dawn of the twentieth century the color line, or the separation between whites and blacks, was most clear and most rigid in the South. With ninety-five percent of African Americans living south of the Ohio River and east of central Texas, this was also where the overwhelming majority of black people lived. Before the Civil War, the Ohio River and the Mason–Dixon line (separating Pennsylvania from Maryland) had marked the line between slavery and freedom—even though "freedom" in the North was limited by employment discrimination, barriers to voting and officeholding, and racial segregation.

In 1900, thirty-five years after emancipation, this boundary remained particularly meaningful to African Americans. South of the line, citizenship guaranteed little. To describe the condition of blacks in the South, both whites and blacks used a phrase first articulated by the United States Supreme Court in the 1857 case of *Dred Scott* v. *Sanford* to limit the scope of African-American citizenship before the Civil War: blacks had "no rights which the white man was bound to respect." That was still the case in the South in 1900.

In the North, black men and women enjoyed the same legal rights as whites, but an informal color line set the races apart, limiting where blacks could work, live, and send their children to school. In the West, patterns somewhat resembled the North. In both regions African Americans lived mainly in cities. Because the black populations in Western states remained small, however, there tended to be greater flexibility and fewer restrictions. Indeed, blacks not only were barely visible in the West, but in many cases attracted less hostility than Asian and Mexican immigrants. Despite these significant variations, however, racism had become a part of American national culture. African Americans everywhere were likely to earn less than whites, work longer hours at less desirable jobs (or be unemployed), and confront limitations on where they could go and what they could do. The story of the twentieth century begins where the restrictions were the most concrete and wide ranging, and where most African Americans lived and worked: in the South.

As the century opened, four-fifths of all black Southerners lived in rural communities. Most were members of families who earned their living from the land. What they planted depended largely on where they lived. Tobacco remained important in Virginia, North Carolina, and Kentucky. Sugarcane continued to be grown in Louisiana. Through most of the South cotton still reigned. But whatever they grew and wherever they lived, most African Americans across the South worked, worshiped, rested, and partied around cycles of labor—the long hours required to plant, cultivate, and harvest a cash crop. And most operated within a system of land ownership and rental that varied considerably in its details but little in its basic framework.

By 1900, approximately one-fourth of all black Southerners who operated farms owned the soil they tilled. The number of black farm owners—and their total acreage—increased each year. Southern black leaders frequently pointed to these accomplishments as evidence of a strong work ethic among their people and of the great potential that lay in the rural South.

But the story was more complicated and less encouraging than the tale told by these statistics. Impressive increases in total acreage owned by black Southerners did testify to hard work and frugality. Many lived according to the work ethic later articulated by Alabama farmer Ned Cobb: "I didn't come in this world to rust out. If I need anything done in my field I ought to be there if time will admit it, on time. I got to work. I'm born to work."

In the opening decades of the twentieth century Cobb clawed his way up the ladder from wage laborer to sharecropper, cash renter, and finally owner. But he never was able to accumulate much, and more than once he was cheated out of his assets by white landlords or merchants. For him, as so many others, prosperity—even mere independence—remained a difficult goal to achieve and maintain.

These farms were small and seldom grew any larger. Moreover, even farmers who had not borrowed money to purchase their farms still needed some form of credit to meet a year's expenses before their crop could be harvested in the fall. Partly because the land worked by black farmers tended to be worth less than the crop that could be grown on it, local merchants and bankers would secure loans by taking a lien on the crop, guaranteeing they would have first rights to the sale of the crop, rather than a mortgage on the land. Instead of repossessing the land if a farmer failed to repay, the lender took what was due out of the sale of the crop. The farmer got what was left, and sometimes that was very little.

The holder of the lien could (and often did) require that the farmer put most of his fields into a cash crop in order to increase the likelihood of the farmer repaying his debt. Families who owned land thus had to purchase food that they otherwise might have grown themselves—and often from the same merchant who demanded that as a condition of their loan they plant most of their fields in cotton or tobacco.

With little money to invest, and working on land that was less productive than that available to renters, most black farm owners maintained an unstable grip on their independence. One or two years of bad weather or low prices for their crops could hurl them back into tenancy. The symbolic value of ownership, and the extent to which it permitted members of the family to go about their lives without thinking about a white landlord, could only multiply the pain of losing one's land.

The vast majority of black farmers rented their land, either as cash renters or sharecroppers. Most black tenants were sharecroppers, especially where cotton was the main crop. Because most sharecroppers had no source of money until the

Children provided an essential supplement to their parents when it came time to pick cotton. Schools for African-American children in the South closed when the bolls ripened.

end of the year, they had to borrow—either from the landlord or from a local merchant—in order to meet normal family expenses. These loans (often called "furnish") would be repaid after "settlement." Settlement took place at the end of the year, when the landlord (or merchant) would compare the value of the tenant's portion of the crop with the sum "advanced" to the tenant during the preceding twelve months.

Almost invariably the sharecropper came out either behind or barely even. Even the thousands of sharecroppers who were illiterate and therefore unable to challenge the accounting suspected that they seldom received their due. In 1919, for example, George Conway of Keo, Arkansas, raised twenty bales of cotton, worth $3,500. Although he knew that he had not purchased more than three hundred dollars worth of merchandise on credit from his landlord that year, he was told at settlement that he still owed forty dollars. His demand for an itemized accounting earned him only a beating. Still claiming a debt of forty dollars, the landlord seized Conway's household goods and drove him off the plantation.

The inevitability of the unfair settlement became a staple of African-American humor, with innumerable variations of a joke that has a tenant secretly withholding a bale or two of cotton at settlement time. As William Pickens, whose family sharecropped in South Carolina and Arkansas, later observed, "Who could deny it? The white man did all the reckoning. The Negro did all the work."

To complain or to threaten legal action was useless; no court would rule in favor of a black sharecropper against a white landlord. A sharecropper could carry over a debt into the next year; move to another farm with the debt built into the next contract; or quietly try to leave—to skip out on an obligation that most black Southerners considered a complete sham anyway.

Indeed the debt was even worse than a sham. By law the tenant was actually a wage laborer; the crop belonged to the landlord. But the landlord had it both ways. The sharecropper family worked, yet received no regular wages. They were paid nothing until the crop had been harvested and sold. Thus the landlord was actually the one who should have been considered the debtor. The cash—or wage—that was being withheld from the laborer was a debt, cash that the landlord owed the tenant but did not have to pay until December.

To satisfy the basic needs of their families, sharecroppers thus had to borrow at high interest rates, generally ranging from forty to seventy percent in an era when rates elsewhere generally fluctuated between four and eight percent. Even at these outrageous prices, sharecroppers could get credit to buy only what the landlord (or furnishing merchant) deemed appropriate.

Those basic needs were quite modest. The standard of living among black sharecroppers in the South was generally lower than that of mid-nineteenth-century westward pioneers. But where the pioneers' log cabins suggest to us images of upwardly mobile families clearing homesteads and carving out a living from the land, sharecroppers' log cabins represent a very different reality. These cabins, which could be constructed out of rough boards rather than logs, were dark, sometimes without windows. Where there were openings they generally lacked glass panes, and often even shutters as well. Screens were virtually unknown. Keeping the house clean, considered to be women's work, was virtually impossible.

With only three rooms or fewer, it was equally impossible to create specialized spaces for such activities as eating, sleeping, or memorizing one's school lessons. Several members of a family slept in a single room, with five or more not at all uncommon. At a time when middle- and upper-class Americans had come to expect divisions between "private" and "public" spaces in their homes, the tenant's cabin afforded no such luxury. There was no such thing as a room that had only one purpose or was the domain of a single family member.

For many sharecroppers, family life was different from that idealized by a "mainstream" middle-class family. Black families in the rural South resembled the two-parent households common elsewhere in the United States at the time, but were more likely to include older relatives as well. Perhaps the presence of other adults left husbands and fathers with less authority than their counterparts elsewhere. Many definitely had to share authority with their landlords, who drew contracts that permitted them to require family members to work the fields. Black men thus came to value their ability to relieve their wives and children of field work. Moreover, by controlling the "furnish," a landlord could influence relations within a sharecropper's family by defining the range of purchasing options—how much of each kind of clothing, how many luxuries, or what kind of food.

The sharecropper's diet was dull and often sparse. A garden could yield plenty of food, but many landlords required their tenants to grow cotton almost to the door. The Delta Farm Company, owner of 35,000 acres of land in Mound Bayou County, Mississippi, for example, prohibited its tenants from raising anything other than cotton. No chickens or vegetables were permitted. Generally, tenants tended small gardens, supplemented by what they could afford at the local store. The result was a lot of cornmeal and poor cuts of pork, all prepared with generous quantities of animal fat—another challenge to women who increasingly were being told by agricultural reformers (black and white) to be better housewives by preparing more healthful food.

Indeed, the growing movements for better farming methods and more efficient rural housekeeping bore little relevance to the realities of sharecropping. There was no incentive for tenants or owners to improve either the farm or the dwelling. Landlords were steeped in a culture committed to an agricultural economy based on cheap labor. They also were steeped in a culture which assumed that black people would have difficulty learning advanced farming methods or how to operate and maintain machinery. Landlords considered mules and cabins appropriate to the aptitudes and productivity of African Americans. A greater investment in equipment or living conditions, they thought, would neither raise the value of their property nor increase output. Moreover, the landlord would receive only a portion of any increased yield that might result from improvement.

On the tenant's side, improving the farm made even less sense. Why invest sweat or money into a home or farm that was owned by someone else? What little cash a family might accumulate was best spent in moveable items that could increase one's share of the crop next time around: a wagon, a mule, or a plow. And why accumulate household goods when in all likelihood the family would move within a few years? Little surprise that housekeeping technology seldom went far beyond water pail, washtub, and cooking kettle.

Having no investment in home or farm, and encountering constant frustration regardless of how hard they worked, sharecroppers were bound to remain alert to other possibilities. Although many families remained on a single farm for years, William Pickens's parents were more typical. By the time he had reached his nineteenth birthday in 1900, he had known more than twenty buildings that he could call "home."

At first they moved locally, from farm to farm within their rural South Carolina community. Their big chance seemed to strike in the late 1880s, when a visitor told them about Arkansas, where planters were clamoring for men to work land being brought under cultivation. The man was a "labor agent," one of many recruiters who in the late nineteenth century traveled through those parts of the South where years of growing cotton or tobacco had worn the land thin.

These agents worked for planters further south in Florida or—more frequently—further west in the Mississippi Delta or in Arkansas. With no prospects in South Carolina, Pickens's parents were prepared to listen. "The agent said that Arkansas was a tropical country of soft and balmy air, where coconuts, oranges, lemons, and bananas grew. Ordinary things like corn and cotton, with little cultivation, grew an enormous yield."

So they went. During the last two decades of the nineteenth century and the first decade of the twentieth, the system stabilized but people moved. The South's black population churned as rural people moved from plantation to plantation, county to county, state to state in quest of the holy grail of land ownership. Some, like the Pickenses, were lured by labor agents. Others, especially in hilly areas where whites already outnumbered blacks, were pushed out in a process known as "whitecapping," a term that referred to the practice of night riders pushing African Americans off their land through threat of violence. At least 239 instances of whitecapping were recorded during the two decades beginning in the late 1880s, with Mississippi the most common site. The term seems to have originated in Indiana, where night riders invading a small community or threatening an individual African-American resident would wear white caps as part of their disguise.

Despite its origins in the Midwest, whitecapping was mainly a Southern rural phenomenon. Successful black farmers were the most likely target of this kind of eviction because of the common assumption among whites that the success of some blacks might unleash unrealistic (and dangerous) aspirations among the local black population. A farmer in Alpharetta, Georgia, recognized that he "better not accumulate much, no matter how hard and honest you work for it, as they—well, you can't enjoy it." In some cases, whole communities were forced from their homes.

In areas more heavily populated by African Americans, especially the "Black Belt" stretching across the cotton-growing region of South Carolina, Georgia, Alabama, Mississippi, Louisiana, and East Texas, nature took its toll as well. The boll weevil, which devoured cotton, entered the United States from Mexico toward the end of the nineteenth century.

Some landlords responded by diversifying their farms, especially after 1910, when the weevil's impact interacted with a growing agricultural reform movement. Corn required only one-fifth as much labor as cotton, which meant that many black tenants and wage hands were suddenly thrown out of work. In other cases black farmers confronted with a weevil-infested crop headed for areas rumored to be untouched, or abandoned farming altogether.

This constant movement vexed landlords, but it was virtually built into the system. Indeed, contrary to conventional opinion among whites, the proclivity to move had little to do with what whites called "Negro character." Black Southerners did move more frequently than whites, but mainly because they were more likely to be sharecroppers—the most mobile category of farmers. Among all sharecroppers in the early-twentieth-century South, African Americans had the lowest rates of mobility; black cash renters and owners were each more stable than their white counterparts.

Moving was, in fact, the American way. The movement of labor toward opportunity is essential to the efficient operation of labor markets in a growing economy. Free labor implies the ability of workers to move from depressed locales to areas of expansion, liberating both the worker to take advantage of opportunity and the employer from any responsibility for supporting former employees.

But the rural South, especially where cotton or sugar cultivation dominated patterns of employment, was committed to a different type of economy—one dominated by the plantation, a form of production that required a tightly controlled labor force. Except in areas where new lands were being brought into cultivation, a stable labor force seemed essential to both the prosperity of individual landowners and the stability of the system itself. Complaints about a "chaotic" labor market and "restless" and "unreliable" black labor abounded. White landowners lamented the inclination of their tenants to be "controlled far more by their fancies than by their common sense."

In response, nearly all Southern states, and many localities as well, attempted to immobilize black labor by erecting legal and economic barriers to movement. Although enmeshed in a capitalist economy based on the ability of the employer to purchase—and control—only the *labor* of workers, and not the workers themselves, Southern landlords insisted on their right to limit the ability of people they called "their negroes" to change employers.

Control over land and credit provided the basis for one set of barriers to mobility. Many landowners limited the amount of land they would rent to each tenant in order to ensure that the sharecropper would cultivate the land intensively. Moreover, tenants with small plots were less likely to earn enough to permit them to advance into the ranks of landowners.

The goal was to keep black Southerners as dependent as possible on white landowners and merchants. Where the sharecropper was not dependent he could be tied down by contract. In most Southern states a sharecropping contract differed from most other contracts in that it was enforceable in criminal rather than civil courts. A sharecropper who skipped out after planting a crop would not be sued (he was not likely to have any assets anyway), but arraigned on criminal charges.

What really mattered, however, was not whether a tenant remained on a particular farm so much as whether a locality's total labor force remained stable. Local movement was expected and tolerated. Indeed, local movement provided frustrated and discontented tenants with an apparent choice of options, a reason to hope that a new chance might yield a better crop and brighter future. What was crucial was to limit the threat to the local labor supply, to ensure that come picking time there would be enough black men, women, and children to drag heavy sacks through the fields.

Assuming (incorrectly) that long-distance movement was largely the result of smooth-tongued recruiters, Southern landlords and employers went to considerable lengths to curb the "labor agent menace." States and localities across the South put considerable effort into keeping "their negroes" ignorant of outside opportunities. In 1900 the United States Supreme Court for the first time upheld the constitutionality of the laws requiring labor agents to pay licensing fees that were so high as to make it impossible to legally entice away a community's black workers. A flood of legislation followed, as state and local governments determined to protect their labor force from recruiters.

Recruitment laws had little effect, however. They were extremely difficult to enforce. Even more important, they ignored the influence of informal networks across the black South that carried information—and misinformation—about opportunities in developing sections of the region. What really kept black Southerners in place kept them not in particular communities, but in the regional economy as a whole: there were few alternatives—at least for men—beyond seasonal farm work. As the *Pee Dee Watchman,* a South Carolina black newspaper, explained in 1917, since the end of Reconstruction in the 1870s, "thousands desired to leave but could find no haven, no place where the demand for negro labor was greater than the supply."

Moreover, within the rural economy opportunities existed for employment during the slack season. A cotton crop requires spurts of intense activity—preparing the field, planting, hoeing, and harvesting—punctuated by intervals of monitoring. These intervals permitted family members who did not have primary responsibility for a crop to seek other employment.

Turpentine camps, sawmills, cottonseed-oil mills, and other industries tied to the rural economy provided young men with opportunities to earn cash wages. Young women ventured into cities and towns to earn extra cash washing, cooking, or cleaning. In most cases these individuals moved back and forth between town (or less frequently, city) and farm, with the longest interval coming after picking in the late fall and before planting time in March.

Leaving the countryside permanently, however, was a more daunting matter, especially for men. The new, expanding industries of the early-twentieth-century South offered few opportunities to black workers. Textiles, furniture, oil and gas, paper, chemicals—each contributed to the growth of Southern cities and Southern factories, each was interested only in white people as machine tenders.

Skilled positions in such new urban sectors as electrical production and streetcar transportation remained equally off-limits, while at the same time white workers were displacing blacks from nineteenth-century footholds in the skilled construction trades. Black men could find jobs in coal mines and in the iron and steel mills in the area of Birmingham, Alabama. But these represented exceptions to the general pattern of casual employment known as "negro labor." The urban economy thus meshed effectively with the rural. The plantation needed a stable labor force that could find outlets during slack periods; town and city employers looked to black workers to fill temporary needs usually involving a shovel or a broom.

Black women, on the other hand, had little difficulty finding urban employment as long as they were willing to work for a pittance. Middle- and upper-class white southerners expected black women to do their domestic chores. Wages for domestic workers were so low that even many white workers considered the availability of black "help" a part of their birthright. In contrast to Northern cities, where black servants were part of a labor market that included a large component of white European immigrants, Southern households invariably employed African Americans. And in contrast to a widespread pattern of live-in service among those immigrants, black women generally insisted on living at home. "They seem to think that it is something against their freedom if they sleep where they are employed," observed one employer whose dismissal of this sentiment stands in stark contrast to its accuracy. Nevertheless, in addition to a customary twelve- to fourteen-hour day, black women domestic workers often had to respond to demands for extra hours.

The servant's day was not only long, it was physically and emotionally difficult. Only servants for the wealthiest families could specialize as cook or nurse. "I'm looking for a nurse for my children," usually implied cleaning, cooking, and serving as well. That nurse also had to fight for her dignity in a household where as one woman noted, "The child I work for calls me girl." The man of the house could (and often did) present a very different kind of threat to a servant's dignity—pressure for sexual favors. One servant explained that she lost a job when "I refused to let the madam's husband kiss me. . . . He walked up to me, threw his arms around me, and was in the act of kissing me, when I demanded to know what he meant, and shoved him away." When the black woman's husband filed a complaint against her employer, he was arrested and fined twenty-five dollars.

Resistance to the regimen and the disrespect, however, was often more subtle than a generally useless formal complaint. Taking advantage of whites' assumptions about black women's carelessness, servants would appear to be careless. A hot iron purposely left too long on a garment could provide a fitting revenge against an employer who refused to permit a servant to take a quick trip home to visit her own children. Similarly, servants would invent holidays that their employers would grudgingly acknowledge. Whites chalked the festival up to "negro character" (they would never have used the word "culture")—something which they could never understand and felt was not worth figuring out anyway.

A woman who wanted a little more control over her time, especially to take care of her own family, would clean other people's clothes rather than their homes. The work was hard, and only slightly more remunerative than domestic service. And taking in laundry carried risks: one ruined or lost garment could bring a refusal to pay for a whole load. Like the sharecroppers whose landlord refused to pay a proper settlement, a laundress had no recourse to the courts when a dispute arose. Remarkably, washerwomen and domestics did strike, in some cases maintaining considerable solidarity. But the deck was stacked against any permanent shift in the balance of power between these women and their employers. Most women even preferred picking cotton to domestic work (it paid better), and white women in towns and cities across the "cotton belt" complained—or raised wages—when ripening cotton bolls attracted their servants to the countryside.

Residents of towns and cities were unlikely to find the countryside unfamiliar. Many had come from farms in the first place. Moreover, black urban neighborhoods in the South showed little evidence of the outpouring of services undertaken by cities of this era. African Americans generally lived on unpaved streets where such standard urban services as police, fire protection, garbage collection, and sewers were rare. As late as the mid-1920s Monroe Work, director of research at Tuskegee Institute in Alabama, could describe most of the Southern urban black population as living under "country conditions . . . just beyond the zones for water, lights, and other conveniences." Infant mortality was high, as were stillbirths. In this, as in so many other ways, the black South remained a rural world even as the proportion living in cities rose gradually from fifteen percent in 1890 to twenty-one percent twenty years later.

By the second decade of the twentieth century, cotton cultivation still employed more black Southerners than any other single activity. Men awoke at dawn and headed to the fields. Women awoke even earlier to prepare breakfast—sometimes eaten in the cabin and sometimes in the fields, where women often worked alongside their husbands. The two major slack periods in the cotton cycle—July and August, when the weeds had been hoed and the plants could be left with minimal attention, and the last two months of the year, after the cotton bolls had been picked—provided rural black Southerners with opportunities for leisure.

The first of these periods coincided with food harvests. Barbecues, religious revivals, and other community gatherings were common summer activities. The later months followed "settlement"; what little cash was realized from a year's labor could be devoted to generally secular Christmas celebrations, shopping either in town or from a mail-order catalog, and contemplating a change of scenery. Well into the 1920s, the rhythms of the black South synchronized with the patterns of cotton cultivation.

The black North and West, on the other hand, were distinctly urban. Cities housed seventy percent of all black Northerners and sixty-seven percent of black Westerners at the turn of the century. By 1910 the urbanized portion of the black population in both regions was close to eighty percent. As they did in the South, women were most likely to find work as domestic servants. Men occasionally had access to industrial jobs, but usually only as temporary strikebreakers replacing white unionists.

A small business class, complemented by an even smaller group of professionals, constituted the upper class in these communities. Craftsmen had difficulties finding employment, especially in cities with strong unions in the building trades, which generally excluded African-American workmen. In some cities, most notably on the West Coast, black men in such occupations as hotel waiters and bellmen were losing their jobs to immigrants from abroad. For most men, the tools of the trade all too often remained the familiar shovel, broom, or mop.

In many cities these workers lived in all or mostly black areas. In the largest cities, such as New York, Philadelphia, and Chicago, ghettos already had begun to emerge. But even where African Americans lived in racially mixed neighborhoods the trend was toward increased segregation. Blacks generally did not have access to housing elsewhere in the city, even if they earned enough to be more selective. Newcomers were immediately steered to districts known as "Little Africa" or the "Black Belt." African Americans who managed to circumvent efforts by real estate agents to keep blacks out of "white" areas were met with bombings or personal threats.

Black communities were diverse and included small business and professional classes. The middle class also included certain service workers. In Chicago, one of the most important judges of social standing in the black community was Julius Avendorph, whose job as personal assistant to businessman George Pullman entailed duties generally performed by a valet or a messenger. Only slightly further down the ladder stood the Pullman porters, men who worked the railroad sleeping and dining cars operated by Pullman's company. Their high status resulted in part from their relatively high job security and because many of them had high school—and in some cases even college—education.

Unlike their white counterparts, however, the black middle class—and even the minuscule black upper class—could not take advantage of the new housing available along transportation lines emerging from the city center. In a period when American cities were becoming increasingly segregated by class, African Americans remained residentially segregated by race instead.

The "White Problem"

James Weldon Johnson remembered well his introduction to the full implications of what it meant to be a black man in the United States. As a student at Atlanta University in the 1890s he recognized that "education for me meant, fundamentally, preparation to meet the tasks and exigencies of life as a Negro, a realization of the peculiar responsibilities due to my own racial group, and a comprehension of the application of American democracy to Negro citizens." The future songwriter, diplomat, writer, and civil rights leader did not learn this in the classroom; rather, he learned it on campus and around town.

Johnson, of course, already knew that he was "a Negro," and that race mattered. He had grown up in Jacksonville, Florida, after the overthrow of Reconstruction.

Although his family was better off than most African Americans (his father was a headwaiter at a hotel, his mother, a teacher), they experienced the same exclusions, acts of discrimination, and affronts to their dignity that other black Southerners suffered as white Southerners began to reestablish white supremacy. The task for black Southerners was to teach their children how to accommodate the system without accepting either the system or their place in it as natural, just, or inevitable.

In the North things were not entirely different; they simply carried a different twist. W. E. B. Du Bois described a social snub he received in the 1860s in Great Barrington, Massachusetts, at the tender age of six:

> Something put it into the boys' and girls' heads to buy gorgeous visiting-cards—ten cents a package—and exchange. The exchange was merry, till one girl, a tall newcomer, refused my card,—refused it peremptorily, with a glance. Then it dawned on me with a certain suddenness that I was different from the others; or like, mayhap, in heart and life and longing, but shut out from their world by a vast veil.

One had to learn where the color line was, what it meant, how and when to cross it, and how to maintain one's self-respect when it could not be crossed. Thousands of African Americans would spend a good part of their lives trying to destroy that line.

By the 1890s a new generation of African Americans was reaching adulthood. These young men and women had never experienced slavery. They had experienced the violent overthrow of Reconstruction only as children. Unaccustomed to timidity toward whites and without vivid memories of the disillusion and despair following Reconstruction, they did not readily settle in places defined by the racial etiquette that had emerged during the previous two decades. This was especially true in cities and towns, where black populations were increasing despite the lack of regular employment for black men.

In an era when white Southerners were writing, reading, and reminiscing about a mythical antebellum South characterized by harmony between the races brought by slavery, these seemingly rootless young African Americans could seem threatening indeed. "The negroes are being overbearing and need toning down," declared one Louisiana newspaper in 1896.

Most white Southerners continued to believe that the descendants of Africans remained at a lower stage of civilization than Europeans and their descendants. In the early twentieth century, Southern historian Ulrich B. Phillips would describe the slave plantation as a school, and most white Southerners were certain that emancipation had freed a people who had been dismissed from the school of slavery too early. Black people who did not know their place, did not acknowledge their subordinate status, and did not recognize the folly of trying to reach too high were considered dangerous.

This notion of one's "place" was central to the role of African Americans in Southern life. Place referred partly to where "the Negro" could fit in the Southern economy: mainly in agriculture. Blacks were to grow the cotton. Jobs in the industries processing the cotton into cloth were generally reserved for whites. Where the "Negro's place" was not agricultural, it was servile.

Place also referred to the location of African Americans in Southern culture, a subordinate role that was enacted and reenacted on the street, in the store, and elsewhere in the daily lives of Southerners.

The prevailing ideas about race, coupled with the inheritance of the plantation economy, contributed to the development of a legal system that left blacks peculiarly vulnerable to domination by their employers and landlords. "What could we do?" declared a black Georgian forced to work without pay to settle a fraudulent debt. "The white folks had all the courts, all the guns, all the hounds, all the railroads, all the telegraph wires, all the newspapers, all the money, and nearly all the land."

A white attorney in Mississippi explained in 1914 (six years before taking office as a judge) that "an important branch of the law here in Mississippi" was "Negro law." This law was unwritten, and at its center was the premise of African-American powerlessness.

Given how easy it was for white landlords and employers to call the shots, they considered it essential that African Americans remain in the South at the bottom of the heap—available for work that nobody else would do. Any education black Southerners received should not, as one Southern governor put it, give them aspirations "beyond the sphere of negro life."

The concern with blacks not accepting their place reveals a lasting tension within Southern white culture. On the one hand, early-twentieth-century white Southerners tended to be confident that their black workers, tenants, and servants were "amiable." African Americans thus constituted the perfect labor force: easily coerced, unlikely to organize, and readily available because they supposedly lacked the ambition and aptitude to do anything else.

Existing side by side with this confidence, however, was a set of fears. Those whites who saw blacks as a race teetering on the edge of barbarism worried about the aggressions lurking beneath the thin veneer of amiability. Moreover, white Southerners either remembered Reconstruction or had grown up hearing the recollections of their parents—recollections enveloped in myths of evil white Northerners bent on revenge and profit and allied with illiterate black legislators intent on legalizing racial intermarriage.

These memories were furthered poisoned by the myths of corruption and incompetence that hid the accomplishments of the relatively rational, clean, and progressive state governments of the Reconstruction period. But they also included accurate images of black men voting, carrying guns, and taking their landlords to court. The danger of black political participation was clear to white Southerners who wished to learn from history rather than repeat it.

White Southerners had perfectly good reason to fear that African Americans did not accept things the way they were. Black men were moving around more, finding employment in the expanding seasonal turpentine and lumber industries. Less tied to the land than their parents, young African Americans were increasingly moving to the city, especially after the depression of the 1890s sent cotton prices cascading downward. Women were welcomed as domestics but men had no settled place in the urban economy. Strikes by black domestic workers, longshoremen, lumber workers, and railroad men were unusual events, but point to an increased unwillingness among black workers to accept their place.

Black men and women were also determined to become educated. Between 1870 and 1910, the literacy rate among black Southerners increased from nineteen percent to sixty-one percent.

By the last decade of the nineteenth century, many white Southerners were growing increasingly concerned that their black neighbors, employees, servants, and tenants would not accept their place. It seemed that protocol and custom no longer held behavior in check. Even intimidation required more effort.

In cities reports of blacks resisting arrest had been on the rise since the late 1880s. Complaining of black servants referring to one another as "Miss Johnson" or "Mr. Jones," one Louisiana newspaper identified the nub of the issue: "The younger generation of negro bucks and wenches have lost that wholesome respect for the white man, without which two races, the one inferior, cannot live in peace and harmony together."

To some white Southerners the answer to this apparent threat to white supremacy lay in increased levels of intimidation. The result was an epidemic of lynching in the South, beginning in 1882 and rising to a peak a decade later.

But lynching was a disorderly way to go about maintaining order. Southern white elites—men who published newspapers, owned plantations, sat on the boards of banks and railroads, and pulled strings behind the scenes in the Democratic party—recognized that violence outside the legal system undermined the majesty of the law. Politically, however, it was unwise to condemn lynching more forcefully than a gentle chiding after each grisly murder of an African American. Lynchings, after all, were community events, festivals that parents attended with small children, holding them high in the air to afford a better view of the victim twisting in a noose or burning at the stake.

Lynchings were not only disorderly. They also gave the region bad press in the North. This was the early heyday of "yellow journalism," a new kind of newspaper publishing that attracted readers by appealing largely to their emotions. Lurid tales of Southern violence provided good copy, especially when tinged either with accusations of sexual violence or with a crowd's determination to cut off a victim's

A twin lynching in Marian, Indiana, on August 8, 1930. The Ku Klux Klan had moved to the urban North and West during the 1920s and gained its greatest influence in Indiana.

sexual organs. White Northerners, drawing on a long tradition of satisfying their consciences by expressing sympathy to black victims of Southern racism, seized on vivid descriptions of lynchings as continued evidence of Southern backwardness.

These twin threats posed by lynching—disregard for legal procedures and the possibility of federal intervention generated by outrage from the North—roused the Southern white establishment. White disorder had to be curbed, a task that required eliminating the instability and uncertainty in race relations that underlay that disorder. Blacks had to be kept in their place by other means. Across the South, state constitutions, state legislation, and city ordinances were rewritten to enshrine in law the subordinate place of black people in Southern life. Black male Southerners would no longer vote or serve on juries. Separation of the races would be required by law.

Poll taxes, property and literacy qualifications for voting, and the institution of the "white primary" were effective measures. In Mississippi, the president of the 1890 constitutional convention straightforwardly declared that "we came here to exclude the Negro," and the delegates did their job. Only black men who were economically independent or regarded by whites as "good" or "safe" Negroes remained on the voter rolls. By the turn of the century, only ten percent of black men in Mississippi were registered to vote. Forty years later that proportion had dwindled to 0.4 percent (2,000 registered voters out of approximately 500,000 possible voters). Among Alabama's 181,471 African American men of voting age in 1900, only 3,000 were registered to vote. Across the South, the proportions were similar, and black voting remained insignificant until the 1960s.

Disfranchisement, or the stripping of people's right to vote, was an attack not only on black political influence—of which there was precious little by the turn of the century—but also on black manhood. Nineteenth-century Americans tied manhood and citizenship closely together. Both hinged on independence. Cast as naturally docile, unable to control their sexual passions, and economically dependent, black men were labeled as unfit for citizenship. Denying them the ballot reinforced their exclusion from the civic community.

The logical next step was to minimize disorder by minimizing contact between the races. Between 1890 and 1915, legislators across the South, as far west as Texas and Oklahoma, enacted Jim Crow laws that ensured, regardless of how interdependent the races might be in the South, they would not inhabit the same public spaces. In the most ordinary and yet meaningful way African Americans in the South would constantly be reminded—especially in cities and towns—that they were people without social honor, people whose dignity had no official existence, people who were not a part of mainstream society.

In most cases the trains and railroad stations were the first targets of Jim Crow laws. One waiting room was marked "colored," the other "white." Next, rules of conduct were passed for streetcars—whites were seated from front to back, blacks from back to front. Some streetcar companies considered this a foolish business practice, expensive and needlessly antagonizing their large black clientele. But the laws required segregation. For the races to sit alongside each other was to imply equality; front to back versus back to front reminded one and all who belonged in front and who belonged in the back.

The legislation quickly extended to nearly all aspects of public life. Anything worth doing or building outside people's homes was worth a segregation ordinance: hotels, restaurants, restrooms, drinking fountains, parks, schools, libraries, saloons, telephone booths, theaters, doorways, stairways, prisons, cemeteries, and brothels. In some communities the ordinances even specified the size of the ubiquitous "whites only" or "colored" signs. Florida required separate storage facilities for school textbooks. In Georgia, courtrooms had two Bibles for swearing in witnesses.

This obsession with race, which reached its apex in the first decade of the twentieth century, was not unique to the South. Throughout the United States, the concept of race had become an increasingly important way of categorizing people and cultures. World atlases published during this period were less interested in economies or social systems than in the particular races inhabiting one place or another. Relying on the dominant theories in the social and physical sciences, powerful decision-makers in government and industry divided the American population into a staggering array of "races." Armenians, Gypsies, Ruthenians, Jews, Syrians, Greeks, Italians, Africans: each was a separate race, and each had its own distinct characteristics.

Northern industrialists devised hiring policies reminiscent of eighteenth-century Southern slaveholders who had been certain that Africans from one area made better slaves than men and women from another part of the continent. Thus Poles and Slavs were presumed to be suited to tasks requiring great physical exertion; Jews, Italians, and Portuguese supposedly had an aptitude for lighter, repetitive tasks that required a keen eye or nimble finger. Italians were unstable and untidy "but not destructive," noted one Milwaukee industrialist, who lamented that they drank too much (though less than the Greeks), quarreled, and did not understand modern machinery. Hungarians, although "thrifty and honest" in the view of another employer, were not clean. In most variations of this complex scheme, "Africans" were considered inefficient, incapable of mechanical labor, emotional rather than rational, oversexed, and in general a cut below everyone else.

The South differed from the rest of the country in the relative simplicity of its racial roster. There race remained largely a question of black and white. White Northerners and Westerners, although equally inclined to think in racial terms, were less likely than their Southern counterparts to translate those ideas into a system of rigid distinctions embodied in the law. They shared white Southerners' assumptions about the capabilities of the descendants of Africans, but the diversity of the population in these regions complicated the equation.

In the West, "Asiatic races," especially the Chinese, seemed a more threatening presence than the small black population. There was, of course, considerable variation. James Weldon Johnson, a performer traveling with his brother in 1905, could secure no hotel accommodations in Salt Lake City. They had considerable difficulty even finding a place to eat. A few days later in San Francisco they easily secured a room and dined without incident. Yet even in San Francisco patterns were uneven. The manager of a leading hotel there explained at the turn of the century

At the peak of its power in the 1920s, the Ku Klux Klan marches down Pennsylvania Avenue in Washington, D.C., in 1926. Its members hid behind masks and robes as they terrorized black citizens. Catholics and Jews also attracted Klan hatred during the 1920s.

that incidents seldom occurred, largely because "the colored people who travel . . . do not often place themselves or us in embarrassing positions."

In the North, race was complicated by the multiplicity of European nationalities. Blacks were not essential to the labor market. Their ability to vote generally aroused little concern because their numbers were relatively small until the 1920s. Few whites considered their presence a threat to social stability. This would begin to change in the 1920s, as social theories increasingly reduced "race" to a triad of black/white/yellow (with American Indians either a fourth race or thrown in as descendants of Asians), and as a growing black population came to play a major role in urban culture and politics. Until World War I, however, "race" as a division between two groups was largely a Southern way of thinking.

Because most Southern states by the first decade of the century had passed laws governing race and social interaction from marriage to public transportation to circus entrances and exits, it was essential to create usable definitions. How did one decide who was "a Negro"? Skin tones, after all, could suggest only so much in a society in which Africans, Europeans, and Indians—none of whom were uniformly tinted to begin with—had mingled over the centuries.

In New Orleans, for example, the population was considerably more diverse than elsewhere in the South. Because of a long history of sexual relations between people of European and African descent, skin hues ranged infinitely. A streetcar official explained why the new segregation law required clear, if arbitrary, definitions: "Our conductors are men of intelligence, but the greatest ethnologist the world ever saw would be at a loss to classify streetcar passengers in this city."

Apparently the only possible solution was to "eyeball" passengers and rely on conventional assumptions about the physical characteristics that distinguished "black" from "white." Indeed, this was the approach of the United States Bureau of the Census, which instructed its enumerators until 1920 to categorize an individual by estimating the proportion of African blood according to color and other features.

This might work for the census, but racially segregated institutions needed more exact ways of determining inclusion and exclusion. The color line had to be defined to regulate such important civic activities as school enrollments, marriage, and jury service. A question with serious social implications everywhere in the United States also had wide-ranging legal implications in the South.

Southern states divided roughly equally in how their laws defined race. Approximately half defined "a Negro" as anyone with "a trace of black ancestry." Nearly all the rest identified anyone with at least one-eighth "Negro blood" (one great-grandparent) as "colored." Yet this solution to the problem of categorization was neither inevitable nor "natural." Why should a child with one parent of European descent and one parent of African descent be a "Negro"? How much genealogical research was to be required to define someone's legal status?

Elsewhere in the Western hemisphere, societies used a broad variety of categories. Even in the United States the terms *mulatto* (half and half), *quadroon* (three white grandparents, one black) and *octoroon* (one black great-grandparent, seven white) were frequently used, both in popular speech and even (at least in the case of "mulatto") in the United States Census until 1920. Indeed, the decision to drop "mulatto" as a category that year resulted from bureau estimates that seventy-five percent of all African Americans were of "mixed blood," and eyeballing the difference between "Negroes" and "mulattoes" was impossible. Anyway, the only categories that mattered were those required by the Southern laws. "One drop" of Negro blood sullied the purity of whiteness, pushing an individual across the color line.

The legal existence and meaning of these categories was ratified by the United States Supreme Court in 1896, when it ruled in the case of *Plessy* v. *Ferguson* that state laws requiring racially segregated facilities were permissible under the Constitution as long as the facilities were "equal." They never were. But it would take nearly sixty years for American law to recognize that inequality. Not until 1954 would the Supreme Court begin dismantling Jim Crow by ruling in *Brown* v. *Board of Education* that "separate educational facilities are inherently unequal."

Building Communities

The Independent Order of St. Luke was in trouble. Founded in Maryland in 1867 to provide sickness and death benefits to dues-paying members, the order had flourished for two decades, rapidly expanding to New York and Virginia. But in 1899, in part because of the deepest economic depression the nation had yet experienced, the organization was virtually bankrupt. After 30 years in office its chief executive resigned, leaving his successor $31.61 in cash and $400 in debts.

The new Grand Worthy Secretary, Maggie Lena Walker, assumed her position at a fraction of her predecessor's salary. Under her leadership the Order of St. Luke not only survived but flourished. From fifty-seven councils with 1,080 members, it grew to 2,020 councils which enrolled more than 100,000 members in twenty-eight states. Guided by Walker's commitment to expanding economic opportunities for African Americans, the order established programs for black youth, an educational loan fund, a weekly newspaper, a department store, and a bank. Walker and her colleagues in St. Luke led a boycott against segregated streetcars in Richmond, Virginia, in 1904. The *St. Luke Herald,* the organization's paper, took positions opposing segregation, lynching, and discrimination against black job seekers.

Maggie Lena Walker was the first woman in the United States to serve as president of a bank. Born in Richmond, Virginia, in 1867, Walker graduated from that city's Colored Normal School (a teachers' college) 16 years later. By then she already had shared the work experience of most urban African-American women, helping her widowed mother with child care and with the laundry taken in to make ends meet. Her degree qualified her to teach in Richmond's segregated black schools, but she was forced to resign when she married.

Walker had joined the Independent Order of St. Luke when she was fourteen and by 1899 had held numerous leadership positions in the organization. During the next three decades she would supplement her leadership of the Order of St. Luke with active involvement in the woman suffrage movement, Richmond Council of Colored Women, Virginia State Federation of Colored Women, National Association of Wage Earners, International Council of Women of the Darker Races, National Training School for Girls, Richmond Urban League, and the National Association for the Advancement of Colored People.

Maggie Lena Walker's career suggests both the challenges faced by African-American communities in the early twentieth century and the diversity of initiatives fashioned by black leadership to meet those challenges. Although she was speaking of women in particular, Walker effectively described where African Americans as a group stood and where they had to go: "To avoid the traps and snares of life," they would have to "band themselves together, organize . . . put their mites together, put their hands and their brains together and make work and business for themselves."

Walker was calling for what her biographer has termed a "community of struggle." This community could be diverse, encompassing men, women, and children; businesspeople and domestic servants; preachers and sinners. It also could accommodate differences of opinion. But to be a community capable of moving forward it would have to encompass a people aware of their common past and shared future. The long agenda suggested by Walker's career meant that no single approach, no focus on any single organization, could define African-American leadership or purpose.

For African Americans in the early twentieth century this struggle had two related and mutually supportive components. One was to build community institutions such as schools, churches, businesses, clubs, and lodges within the African-American world. The other was to fight for integration into American institutional life, to integrate schools, workplaces, residential neighborhoods, public accommodations like hotels and restaurants, and especially councils of government. Even today these goals are often presented as alternatives, warring strategies competing for the loyalty of people forced to choose one path or the other.

Presenting these alternatives as a harsh choice is misleading. Although particular leaders and institutions did express competing visions and emphases, activism took place simultaneously at many levels. When rural black Southerners banded together to build a school, they were engaging in self-help while at the same time yielding to segregation. But they also were resisting white assumptions about the appropriate form of education for their children. They were insisting on a literacy that defied Southern white definitions of their "place." To build a school was to participate in the struggle for equality.

Yet the quest for integration did not always reflect a desire to mix with white people. Despite the ruling of the U.S. Supreme Court in *Plessy* v. *Ferguson* that separate institutions were constitutional only if they were equal, African Americans recognized that in practice separate always meant unequal. Thus blacks frequently fought for integration into white institutions in order to gain access to better services or commodities. By living among whites, a Los Angeles journalist observed, black Californians could secure "the best fire, water, and police protection."

Robert and Mary Church Terrell made the same judgment in Washington, D.C. As the first president of the National Association of Colored Women, Mary Terrell was one of the most prominent women in the United States. Robert Terrell was an attorney and eventually a federal judge. They did not necessarily want to live among white neighbors, she later recalled of their search for a house. But housing in "white" neighborhoods was "more modern" (in other words, better equipped and in better condition). It also was less expensive. Real estate agents selling homes in "Negro" neighborhoods could price properties higher because African Americans had access to only a small portion of the city's housing market. For the Terrells and others, the struggle for integration did reflect sentiment for increased contact across the color line. But even many integrationists were wary of whites, seeking integration only because the color line divided the powerful from the powerless.

Whether building community institutions or battering the walls of racial separation and discrimination, African Americans had to mobilize limited resources. These resources included a long history—dating from slavery—of community life built on families and religion. In the rural South the other major institution to emerge after emancipation was the school. In towns and cities these institutions joined with women's clubs, fraternal societies, businesses, and social service organizations to shape African-American community life and provide the basis for activism.

Other than the family, the oldest African-American institution was the church. By the beginning of the twentieth century the church brought together African Americans as no other institution possibly could. In 1906 more than half of the nearly seven million African Americans ten years or older belonged to churches, a proportion comparable to patterns among white Americans. Much more striking is the number of African Americans united in a few particular organizations. The National Baptist Convention, the largest black institution in the United States, claimed more than 2.2 million members. The African Methodist Episcopal (A.M.E.) church constituted the second largest denomination, with nearly 500,000 members.

Like most white Southerners, African-American Christians tended to be fundamentalists, men and women who read their Bibles literally and worshiped energetically. Especially in the rural South and in working-class urban churches, black Americans demanded that their ministers evoke emotional responses with powerful sermons. A pastor's ability to "shout" his congregation (to arouse a vocal expression of passion during the sermon) measured his leadership as well as his spiritual credentials.

The greatest heights of ecstasy were often reached in Holiness and Pentecostal churches, which emphasized the importance of a worshiper's personal experience with the Holy Spirit. At first attracting both black and white Southerners, Holiness and Pentecostal sects grew most rapidly after 1910. Subsequently, as Southerners moved north and west these sects expanded, especially into the urban Midwest.

African-American churches were not, however, merely places where people went for relief from the burdens of everyday life. "The social life of the Negro centres in his church," W. E. B. Du Bois observed in his 1899 study, *The Philadelphia Negro.* "Baptism, wedding and burial, gossip and courtship, friendship and intrigue—all lie within these walls." Many ministers and deacons (lay leaders) complemented their inspirational roles with political activity, or served as community spokesmen. In middle-class churches, where emotional behavior was rejected as "undecorous," a pastor might provide intellectual leadership as well.

In rural areas and small towns, churches often were the only gathering places available outside of small business establishments. People would come together in the church to discuss building a school or respond to a threatened lynching. They would share information and opinions about migration to the new "black towns" being established in Oklahoma, to agricultural areas touted by labor agents, or to Northern cities.

Although Southern cities had other gathering places, churches still functioned as one of the most important community institutions. Social services and emergency support were especially common because so many black Southerners could secure only irregular employment. A strong sense of extended family helped, providing a network of support during periods of unemployment. Beyond the family lay the church, whose members gave freely when they could and received without shame when in need.

In Atlanta, most black churches took an "after collection" each Sunday, to be distributed to members in financial distress. Fifth Street Baptist in Louisville collected and distributed clothing, paid for funerals of members unable to afford proper burial, awarded an annual college scholarship, and held annual fundraising drives for an orphanage, a home for the elderly, and a local black college.

Northern churches were likely to add to this traditional form of charity with programs influenced by early-twentieth-century progressive reform movements. Under the leadership of Reverend Reverdy Ransom, the Institutional A.M.E. Church in Chicago resembled a settlement house, providing a wide variety of social services to the neighborhood. After finding a job through Institutional's employment bureau, a black worker could leave her child at its kindergarten or day nursery. Classes in sewing, cooking, stenography, and typing taught useful skills. Leisure opportunities included concerts, lectures, a reading room, and a gymnasium.

More typical in its less ambitious program was Antioch Baptist Church in Cleveland, which sponsored boys' and girls' clubs, choral groups, and a recreation center located in two adjacent houses. Destitute members received cash assistance. North and South, black churches and denominational associations published newspapers, provided social welfare services, helped congregants find jobs, and provided recreational facilities.

These activities required time and money. In most black churches the greatest energy came from the volunteer labor of the women who raised money from communities that had little cash to spare. The role of women as church activists was particularly evident in the National Baptist Convention, where they constituted two-thirds of the membership. In 1906, forty-three percent of all female African Americans who had reached their tenth birthday belonged to the National Baptist Convention. Men, however, dominated the organization's leadership, occupied the pulpits, and controlled the finances.

Just as African Americans in general looked to the church as an institution independent of white domination, black women determined that they needed an organization within the church that would provide them with a similar degree of independence. Founded in 1900, the Woman's Convention of the National Baptist Convention quickly grew to one million members, providing many women with their introduction to community activism.

This experience in local churches and in the Women's Convention brought many black women into the emerging women's club movement. The National Association of Colored Women grew quickly, from five thousand members in the late 1890s to fifty thousand in the 1910s and one hundred thousand a decade later.

Membership in the NACW came mainly from the urban elite—generally teachers and wives of professionals, ministers, and businessmen. These women shared with their white peers a concern with upholding traditional standards of morality and respectability amid the turmoil of movement from country to city and changes in employment from farm to factory. And, like black men, they organized to challenge the increasing level of racism at the turn of the century.

Black clubwomen recognized that their destiny was inextricably intertwined with less-privileged African Americans. If they could elevate other black women to their standards of morality and manners, then the black masses would be lifted up from the gutter of poverty and degradation. At the same time they would win from white America the acceptance they deserved by dint of their middle-class values and position.

Although the NACW did achieve recognition as an affiliate of the largely white National Council of Women in 1901, black women generally encountered difficulties with major women's reform organizations at the turn of the century. As the suffrage, temperance, and women's club movements moved toward national organization, they had to consider the sensibilities of white Southerners.

The urge to participate in "white" clubs and in "white" feminist organizations did not necessarily signal a desire to turn away from the black community toward a largely white social environment. White women who worried that black women seeking to join their suffrage organizations or the Women's Christian Temperance Union sought "social equality" deluded themselves. Black women simply recognized that these larger, more broadly based organizations could provide stronger backing and more visible platforms.

Indeed, like other black institutions, black women's clubs and reform societies owed their existence only partly to exclusion from white institutions. Black communities faced problems different from those confronted by white reformers. Like their white counterparts, NACW affiliates sponsored kindergartens, day nurseries, training schools, orphanages, and clubs for mothers. But they did so in response to a community with unique needs and limited resources.

Black women's clubs represented a type of institution whose roots lay in African-American fraternal societies (lodges) and mutual benefit associations. The distinctions between the two kinds of voluntary organizations were not always clear. Generally lodges were places for recreation for their members, and membership in a lodge was considered a badge of social respectability. Mutual benefit associations, by contrast, were likely to focus more on insurance functions, especially death benefits.

By the end of the century, these organizations had increasing over-lapping functions. Nearly all provided members with burial and life insurance. Some, like the Independent Order of St. Luke, which was unusual in that it included both men and women, operated small businesses or banks. Nearly all provided opportunities for leadership.

Membership in a fraternal order could provide African-American men with a badge of respectable manhood within the community. A black man denied civic recognition in the Jim Crow South was somebody when he wore the uniform of the Elks, Knights of Pythias, Masons, Oddfellows, or any one of a number of other lodges. The largest order was the Oddfellows, with more than 300,000 members by 1904.

North and South, fraternal and sororital organizations were an integral aspect of urban culture among the mass of working-class black men and women. In the North, lodge membership provided men with political connections and stature. Robert R. Jackson, who was elected to the Illinois legislature in 1912 and was a major player in Chicago politics for two decades, belonged to approximately twenty-five fraternal orders.

There was no clear line between clubs and fraternal societies. But clubs were more likely to be exclusive and perhaps have reform or political orientations; fraternal societies were more likely to be national organizations with broad memberships. Fraternal societies were also more likely to perform business functions. Like the Order of St. Luke, most lodges took their burial and life insurance functions seriously. The first African-American insurance companies grew out of these and similar activities among church-related mutual benefit societies. Because companies controlled by whites charged blacks higher premiums—supposedly because they had higher mortality rates—black companies had a ready market for their products. So did African-American banks, since white banks seldom solicited business in the black community. Significantly, black banking and insurance companies first developed in the South, where black communities were larger and the color line was clearest.

The most dramatic example of how fraternal orders could evolve into financial institutions can be seen in the history of the Grand United Order of the True Reformers. William Washington Browne, an ex-slave and Union Army veteran, founded the organization in Richmond, Virginia, in 1881, with the intertwined goals of building a business and advancing the race. Secret ritual, regalia, a grand annual convention with a colorful parade: each provided members with opportunities for camaraderie and ceremony within an organization also dedicated to community service. At the same time, Browne's wife found a way to earn profits with a regalia factory that she established in the True Reformers' building.

From the beginning the order's mission included mutual benefit activities. The insurance business grew so rapidly that by 1888 Browne saw an opportunity in the need to deposit and invest the cash it generated. By the turn of the century, the True Reformers counted 100,000 members and had expanded into real estate, printing, and undertaking in addition to operating an old-age home and a hotel. All catered to a black clientele.

North and South, there was a noticeable rise in black business enterprise at the beginning of the twentieth century. To a considerable extent this bustling business activity was the result of the increasing segregation of African Americans into urban ghettos. But it also was part of a broader change in the social and economic life of urban black America.

In the nineteenth century black businessmen and even professionals had enjoyed a small white clientele in many cities. These men constituted an elite, an "upper crust," within their communities. Their social networks were generally distinct from those of other African Americans. In many cities, especially in the North, they worshiped at black churches (or in a few cases even predominantly white churches) affiliated with "white" denominations: Episcopalians, Presbyterians, Congregationalists. This group would remain the "upper crust" of black America, but by the turn of the century it was giving way to a new business and professional class, men and women who made their living serving an African-American clientele.

This transition in community leadership was personified in the career of John Merrick, a former slave who accumulated savings as a barber and owner of six barbershops in Durham, North Carolina. Merrick also sold insurance for the True Reformers. His prosperity, however, was due in large part to the stability and status provided by his position as personal barber to the white tobacco magnate James Buchanan Duke. He parlayed this stake into a much larger fortune during the first decade of the twentieth century, when he drew on his experience with the True Reformers to join with two other African-American entrepreneurs to form the North Carolina Mutual Life Insurance Company.

Southern cities like Durham led the way in the growth of an African-American business class catering to African-American consumers. The largest enterprises were insurance companies and banks, but small shops were the most common form of black enterprise. What mattered to the mainly black clientele was how they were treated—with respect and in a businesslike fashion. A woman could not try on a hat in a Southern downtown store; once it sat on her head it was a "Negro hat" (or worse, a "nigger hat") that the white shop owner could not in good conscience sell to a white customer. At the pharmacy a black druggist did not expect his customers to bow and scrape, or to stand aside until all the white customers were served.

Making a virtue out of necessity, many influential black Southerners declared that the race's future lay in a "group economy." Black businesses catering to black

THE GIFT OF THE GOOD FAIRY

ONCE upon a time there lived a Good Fairy whose daily thoughts were of pretty little boys and girls and of beautiful women and handsome men and of how she might make beautiful those unfortunate ones whom nature had not given long, wavy hair and a smooth, lovely complexion. So she waved her magic wand and immediately gave to those who would be beautiful a group of preparations known from that time, fifteen years ago, until to-day and at home and abroad as

MADAM C. J. WALKER'S SUPERFINE PREPARATIONS FOR THE HAIR AND FOR THE SKIN

Wonderful Hair Grower	Vanishing Cream
Glossine	Cleansing Cream
Temple Grower	Cold Cream
Tetter Salve	Antiseptic Hand Soap
Vegetable Shampoo	Complexion Soap

Superfine Face Powder (white, rose-flesh, brown)
Floral Cluster Talcum Powder
Antiseptic Dental Cream
Witch Hazel Jelly

Results from the use of our preparations especially noticeable in the hair and skin of children.

Very liberal trial treatment sent anywhere
upon receipt of a dollar and a half.

THE MADAM C. J. WALKER MFG. CO.

640 North West Street   *Dept. 1-X*   **Indianapolis, Indiana**

Madam C. J. Walker was probably the first African-American woman to become a millionaire.

customers would employ black men and women, creating a racial self-sufficiency rather than the individual self-sufficiency envisioned by so many rural black Southerners since emancipation.

In most cases, however, such businesses were precarious enterprises whose owners had little extra cash for emergencies or to tide them over during occasional slow months. The limited clientele had little to spend and often needed short-term credit to weather bouts of unemployment. Retail shops sold small items, more likely to be priced in cents than in dollars. Corner groceries, barber shops, beauty parlors: all were unstable operations. Retail businesses were especially risky because whites (often European immigrants with few other business opportunities) could open stores in black neighborhoods and compete, largely because they had greater access to borrowed money and supplies. Barbering, undertaking, and beauty shops, on the other hand, did not face competition from white entrepreneurs reluctant to deal with black bodies.

One of the manufacturing opportunities open to black entrepreneurs lay in supplying cosmetics to African-American beauticians. Among the earliest of these manufacturers was Madam C. J. Walker, a St. Louis laundress who in the 1890s developed the first commercially successful hair-straightening process. The daughter of ex-slaves, she grew up in Mississippi as Sarah Breedlove; she later took her name from her second husband, Charles Joseph Walker. By the 1910s the Madam C. J. Walker Manufacturing Company stood at the center of an empire of approximately twenty thousand managers, sales agents, clerks, and factory workers. Walker, who died in 1919, was probably the first African-American woman to join the ranks of American millionaires.

Walker's business success was unusual, but not unique. Other African Americans accumulated fortunes in the cosmetics business, in some cases opening schools to train beauticians in their particular method and, of course, tying that method to a particular line of products. Anthony Overton established the Overton Hygienic Manufacturing Company in Kansas City, Kansas, in 1898 and moved the company to Chicago in 1911. Sales of such products as High Brown Face Powder provided him with sufficient resources to diversify into real estate development and journalism. But all of this remained within a black world. Overton developed property in Chicago's South Side ghetto, known to many as "Bronzeville"; his newspaper, the *Chicago Bee,* had few white readers or advertisers.

This business class, however, remained small. With an even smaller professional class, and many businessmen barely holding on, the top of the class structure of urban black communities was extremely limited. Except at the very highest levels, status tended to depend less on wealth or on white definitions of occupational prestige than on notions of "refinement" and "respectability" maintained by the upper and middle classes. The few professionals tended to dominate the highest rungs, with the more secure businessmen (most were, in fact, men) close behind.

In northern cities, postal workers, porters serving railroad travelers in luxurious

Pullman cars, and servants employed by the best hotels and wealthiest white families constituted much of the solid middle class. Other workers with stable incomes and some education could also claim middle-class status. What often mattered most was property ownership, preferred leisure activities, and membership in an appropriate club, lodge, or church.

This group, based in black businesses and social institutions, seized the mantle of African-American leadership in most urban black communities around the turn of the century. They replaced the older elite whose commitment to integration sometimes led them to oppose building separate institutions to serve the community. In many cities, for example, it was clear that if blacks wanted a YMCA it would have to be a segregated institution. Banks, hospitals, professional baseball teams, social service institutions, political organizations—North and South, their existence often depended on the willingness of black communities to accept segregated institutions.

Baseball provides a typical example of the shift from blacks' slight access to white institutions to the establishment of a segregated black world. In the nineteenth century, a handful of black players joined white athletes on professional diamonds. By the early twentieth century they had been driven out, relegated to all-black barnstorming tours and marginally successful leagues.

Only after World War I, under the tenacious and imaginative leadership of Rube Foster, owner-manager of Chicago's American Giants, would the Negro National League establish a stable setting for black baseball. Black players flourished in this new arrangement, but they did so under conditions far inferior to their white counterparts'. Yet the teams constituted a source of pride to the black communities that they represented. Whatever their individual team loyalties, black fans pulled together on the few occasions when Negro League stars competed against white major leaguers.

These separate black institutions caused mixed feelings among black Americans. On the one hand, segregated institutions owed their existence to the exclusion of blacks from "mainstream" American life. In some cases African Americans even paid taxes for public facilities from which they were excluded. Finally, separate was almost never equal. African-American institutions such as schools, clubs, businesses, and athletic leagues nearly always lacked the facilities, money, and equipment available to their white counterparts.

At the same time, however, segregated institutions permitted community control over important cultural activities. A baseball team, a YMCA, a hospital, a retirement home—black communities could proudly claim these as their institutions maintained by and for African Americans.

Schooling for Leadership

In the early twentieth century, education was one area in which African Americans confronted the tension between the high price of segregation on the one hand and the advantages of community control on the other. Descended from slaves denied by the law any access to literacy, twentieth-century African Americans recognized the importance of education in the advancement of both individuals and the race as a whole. Black children needed schooling, and black Americans needed those schools to teach the values and skills required of a new generation of men and women who would lead the march toward equality and full citizenship.

Before the Civil War most Northern states had either excluded black children from public education or shunted them into separate schools. In some cities black communities and white abolitionists established private schools for black children. During the 1870s and 1880s, however, Northern state legislatures reversed legislation requiring segregation and even went so far as to prohibit the exclusion of children from their local school on the basis of race.

By the early twentieth century, many of the emerging ghettos in Northern cities were not yet sufficiently compact to enable white city officials to draw school district lines that would segregate neighborhood schools. In such cases black children attended schools that were predominantly, but not exclusively, African American. They were not the best schools their cities had to offer. They were housed in older buildings, often were overcrowded, and many of the white teachers looked down on their students. But they were decent schools, capable of providing students the opportunity to graduate from a high school that met the academic standards of the time. The schools were fully supported by tax dollars and taught by instructors with appropriate academic credentials.

Black Northerners valued these schools, and their children were less likely than the children of European immigrants to drop out as teenagers. They also valued integration, rising in protest whenever pressures emerged from segments of the white citizenry to segregate the schools. Most African Americans assumed, wisely, that the presence of whites guaranteed a certain degree of commitment from city politicians.

At the same time, however, Northern black communities had little control over what was taught or who stood in front of the classrooms. Nearly all school officials were white; so were the teachers, most of whom assumed that black children could not perform as well as their white peers. Some teachers simply assumed that the "white race" was more intelligent and more disciplined. Others who were more liberal extended sympathy to black children who they thought were crippled by the cultural heritage of African backwardness combined with the traumas of slavery. The cost of full integration into the system, even if not into completely integrated schools was clear: these were institutions *for* African Americans; but they were not African-American institutions.

By contrast, in most of the South black children went to schools staffed by black teachers and black principals. But the facilities varied from inadequate to abysmal. By the early twentieth century most Southern black children had some access to a public school, but in rural areas that school was likely to be open for less than six months of the year—even as little as two months in some cases. White planters wanted black children in the fields, not wasting their time sitting on the crude benches of a one-room schoolhouse.

In 1915, only fifty-eight percent of all black school-age children in the South were enrolled in school at all, compared with eighty percent of whites. City kids were the most likely to be in school. Attendance rates of black urban children lagged only slightly behind rates for whites, a remarkable comparison because few cities provided public high schools for black children.

In most Southern cities, especially in the Deep South, white civic leaders considered the education of black children an extravagance, a decision consistent with school systems that readily placed as many as sixty-five black children in dilapidated classrooms headed by a single teacher. The *Atlanta Constitution* left little doubt as to its idea of how much schooling black children needed, defending black education on the basis of its ability to "make a better cotton picker and a more efficient plowman."

By 1915, following a decade of unprecedented expansion in high school education in the South, neither Georgia, Louisiana, Mississippi, North Carolina, nor South Carolina had yet built a high school for black teenagers. The enlightened officials of Delaware, Florida, and Maryland had established a single black high school in each of these segregated states. During this period most American communities were transforming high school from a privilege available to those who could afford private school to a right funded by the taxpayers. Southern black youth were denied that right.

Tragically, black adults were among the taxpayers who supported the very school systems that allocated them only crumbs from an expanding pie. To provide better opportunities for their children, black Southerners had to mobilize their communities and do the work themselves. In effect, they paid twice—once for a public school system that allocated them a fraction of the money available to white schools and a second time to supplement those meager resources or pay tuition at a private black high school.

In many cases the additional burden was paid with labor rather than dollars, as many black Southerners had little more than their hands, tools, and skills to spare. Thousands of black public schools in the rural South were erected in the early twentieth century through donations from Chicago philanthropist Julius Rosenwald (the president of Sears, Roebuck & Company), who required that each community match his contribution dollar for dollar. In most cases public funds from white-controlled sources—that is, from taxes—amounted to less than the hard-earned cash generated within the black community.

In addition to contributing to the construction of public schools, black Southerners built private schools, especially at the high school level. At the turn of the century three-fourths of all Southern black high school students attended a private school. Coming from grossly inadequate grammar schools, many of these students required remedial classes, further straining the already precarious budgets of these institutions.

Neither public nor private schools in the South were controlled by African Americans. Public school teachers and principals had to answer to white officials, most of whom cared less about whether black children were being educated than whether they were learning anything that threatened social stability. In Palmetto, Georgia, a teacher was dismissed for merely expressing his approval when President Theodore Roosevelt invited the exceedingly moderate black leader Booker T. Washington to dinner at the White House.

African-American private schools owed a different kind of allegiance. Although by the early twentieth century nearly all of these were headed by African Americans, they still depended on the contributions of Northern white philanthropists for a considerable portion of their budget. And in rural areas they remained vulnerable to white public opinion, which tolerated a black private school only if it clearly was not educating its students out of their place. Northern philanthropists, in part because they envisioned an increasingly industrialized South with a black work force, aimed for a considerably higher level of literacy than most white Southerners thought black children would ever need.

In spite of these limits on the independence of Southern black educators, many black schools were, in fact, community institutions. Black children were taught by black teachers partly because black parents had demanded this change during the closing decades of the nineteenth century. White officials had given in to this demand for financial reasons: black teachers earned less than their white counterparts. But the large-scale entrance of African Americans into the teaching profession is significant nevertheless. These men and women played active roles in their communities, organizing women's clubs, farmers' clubs, boys' clubs, school improvement leagues, and various other self-improvement efforts.

African Americans looked upon schooling as a privilege—one that carried with it an obligation to use one's learning on behalf of the entire community. And teachers joined lawyers, social workers, librarians, nurses, doctors, and newspaper reporters and publishers as leaders of their community.

These educational institutions stood at the center of major divisions among black leaders about the role of African Americans in American society. All the schools taught the same basic values of industry, thrift, and service to the community. They recruited similar types of students. But curriculum and school leadership reflected different notions of how black Americans could attain full citizenship in a nation seemingly committed to their subordination. To what kinds of jobs should they aspire? How should they respond to the rising tide of segregation? Where should they look for allies? How hard should they push for immediate equality when few whites even considered African Americans capable of eventual equality?

Booker T. Washington's gospel of hard work, landownership, self-help, and success through small business struck genuine chords among most black Americans. To some, however, his accommodationist philosophy and the Atlanta Compromise conceded too much. John Hope, a young Southern educator and future college president, considered it "cowardly and dishonest for any of our colored men to tell white people or colored people that we are not struggling for equality."

William Monroe Trotter, editor of the *Boston Guardian* (founded in 1901), was even more scathing. Washington's willingness to accommodate to Jim Crow, along with his success in forging alliances with white businessmen, proclaimed Trotter, exposed him as "a coward" and a "self seeker." He was "the Benedict Arnold of the Negro race, the Exploiter of Exploiters, the Great Traitor," Trotter wrote.

In 1903 a more measured—and eventually more influential—challenge to Washington emerged in the form of a book, *The Souls of Black Folk,* by W. E. B. Du Bois. Du Bois, Trotter, and Hope stood out as spokesmen for a more militant response to the rising tide of racism, but they hardly stood alone. Residents of Southern cities, many of them people who admired Washington and acknowledged his distinction, participated in boycotts of Jim Crow streetcars between 1898 and 1904. In a few instances black Southerners even filed unsuccessful court suits challenging the legality of segregation ordinances.

In the North, where nineteenth-century black elites had developed ties to prominent whites and participated in a handful of integrated institutions (including high schools, colleges, political organizations, and an occasional club or philanthropic society), an older generation refused to abandon the goal of integration. The younger men and women of this class were less influential within the community than the rising class of black business and professional people catering to a black clientele. Nonetheless, many of this younger black middle class remained loyal to their parents' ideals and emerged as some of Washington's most articulate critics.

Moreover, despite Washington's ability to influence the editorial policies of most black newspapers, Trotter's was not the only militant editorial voice. Harry T. Smith, editor of the *Cleveland Gazette,* not only assailed any evidence of racial discrimination but he denounced the establishment of black facilities meant to provide services that comparable white institutions refused to provide to African Americans. He and others of like mind in Northern cities insisted that to build a black facility made it easier for the whites to maintain their policies of exclusion. Chicago's black leadership had rejected a segregated YMCA in 1889 on these principles. Smith dismissed Washington's Atlanta Compromise as a "doctrine of surrender."

For much of the African-American leadership at the beginning of the century, politics involved more than a choice between racial integration or self-help, protest or accommodation, liberal or vocational education. Alliances shifted. Lines were never neat and clean. Du Bois broke with Washington eight years after the Atlanta

Compromise speech. Mary Church Terrell publicly supported Washington while fighting for suffrage—for African Americans and for women.

Robert Abbott, editor of the *Chicago Defender,* was a graduate of the vocationally oriented Hampton Institute who believed that all black children should learn a trade and advised black Southerners to "stick to the farm." He admired Washington and praised Tuskegee as a great black institution. At the same time his headlines offered very un-Washingtonian advice to black Southerners: "WHEN THE MOB COMES AND YOU MUST DIE TAKE AT LEAST ONE WITH YOU."

Yet there were occasions when black people felt they had to line up, to take a particular position. Led by Du Bois and Trotter, a small group, nearly all from the North and mostly urban college graduates, met in 1905 to form the Niagara Movement. The movement was named for its meeting place on the Canadian side of Niagara Falls, a major terminus of the Underground Railroad. Du Bois had encountered difficulty arranging hotel accommodations on the American side. The following year the group met at Harpers Ferry, West Virginia, the site of John Brown's famous raid on behalf of abolitionism.

The Niagara Movement denounced white racism and demanded full citizenship for blacks and the abolition of all racial distinctions. At the same time it underscored the increasingly significant double bind facing African-American workers: industrial employers hired them only as temporary strikebreakers, and most unions excluded them from membership.

Two events in 1906 underscored the immediacy of the Niagara Movement's agenda, while at the same time pointing to the ineffectiveness of black protest up to this point. In August of that year President Theodore Roosevelt ordered the dishonorable discharge of three companies of black soldiers after they were accused of inciting a riot in Brownsville, Texas. Evidence of their responsibility was thin at best. They were more likely victims of violence than instigators. Their mistake, apparently, was in fighting back.

Roosevelt's "executive lynching" demonstrated that black Americans had few friends in high places. They had even fewer in the streets. In Atlanta, a month after the Brownsville incident and following a spate of local newspaper articles that fictitiously reported assaults on white women by black men, a mob of more than ten thousand white citizens freely attacked African Americans. The attacks continued for five days, and the police generally refused to interfere. The city's white establishment blamed the riot on irresponsible journalism and overreaction by lower-class whites. Nevertheless, most white Atlantans shared the mayor's conclusion that the bottom line was "black brutes [who] attempt rape upon our women." Once again, whites associated lynching with rape when in fact there had been no rape.

By 1908, the Niagara Movement's weakness was as obvious as its astute analysis of the crisis of American race relations. Few of the movement's four hundred members bothered to pay dues; most of the black press ignored it as a handful of cranky elitists hurling manifestos. Whites paid even less attention.

The Niagara Movement represents a turning point because of its view of race relations in the United States and its militant agenda for change. Its collapse coincided with an event that shocked the small portion of the Northern white population that considered racism a major "problem" in American life: lynchings and mob attacks on African Americans in Springfield, Illinois. The violence was ignited by a spark recognizable to anyone familiar with the behavior of Southern lynch mobs: a white woman had accused a black workman of rape (she later recanted, admitting that a white man whom she refused to name had beaten her). When the authorities removed the accused man from town to protect him from enraged white citizens, a mob gathered, determined to make the black community pay a price for its supposed tolerance of such criminal behavior. Five thousand soldiers were required to restore order after whites attacked black businesses, homes, and individuals.

White Northerners had condemned the Atlanta riot but had explained away the terrorism by blaming it on the peculiar backwardness of the South. But in Abraham Lincoln's hometown, on the centennial of the Great Emancipator's birth? This event pushed the minority of white reformers who already had begun to question Booker T. Washington's accommodationist agenda to consider the views of Du Bois and the "radicals."

In 1910, the remnants of the Niagara Movement joined with a small group of reformers—mostly white—who had met the previous year in response to the Springfield riot. Their new organization, the National Association for the Advancement of Colored People (NAACP), began with a straightforward agenda: to secure the basic citizenship rights guaranteed by the 14th and 15th Amendments to the United States Constitution. Most specifically this meant the end of all segregation laws, a right to equal education, and a guarantee of the right to vote.

The NAACP would publicize discrimination whenever and wherever it occurred, lobby legislatures and Congress for civil rights legislation, and file lawsuits grounded in constitutional law. It also launched a campaign against lynching, which used research and on-site reports to undermine the standard Southern defense of lynching—that its real cause was black criminality and uncontrolled sexuality. Tame by twentieth-century standards, the NAACP departed significantly from Washington's accommodationism.

Like the Niagara Movement, the NAACP was led mainly by elites. But it also sparked enthusiasm among two groups that the Niagara radicals had not tapped: the black middle and working classes, and white liberals. Although Du Bois was the only African American in the original "inner circle" of the organization, African Americans dominated the membership from the beginning. By 1918 the NAACP monthly magazine, the *Crisis* (founded and edited by Du Bois), claimed a circulation of 100,000. In the rural South many enthusiasts read and circulated the journal at considerable risk.

As African Americans like James Weldon Johnson and Walter White moved into more leadership roles after 1916 and local branches multiplied, the organi-

This cartoon, entitled "The Next Colored Delegation to the White House," appeared in *The Crisis* in 1916. It ridiculed the racist views of President Woodrow Wilson, a native of Virginia.

zation solidified its place at the center of the African-American protest movement for the next half-century.

Equally crucial—and more controversial—was the level of white involvement, especially in the early years. Disdainful of efforts that depended on white goodwill, William Monroe Trotter remained skeptical of the organization's potential and kept his distance. Men and women at the other end of the social spectrum from the Harvard-educated Trotter were probably equally skeptical.

But the great portion of black leadership was moving toward a position best articulated by Ida B. Wells. Wells identified power as the bottom line. Washington was right in arguing that it was useless to wait for whites to help. Blacks should build whatever economic power they could. And he was right, she said, to argue that it was foolish to forget that power lay in white hands and that any strategy had to recognize that blacks were playing a weak hand. But Wells took this analysis a step further. She insisted that militant protest was both possible and effective if it could reach an audience of potentially sympathetic whites. America did not have a "Negro problem," she explained. It had a white problem.

The "Second Emancipation"

On August 25, 1893, Frederick Douglass stood wearily before a large audience at the World's Columbian Exposition in Chicago. The former abolitionist, journalist, and Republican politician had been chosen to deliver the principal address on the occasion of "Colored American Day" at the fair. The "Day" itself was controversial among African Americans. Many viewed the gesture as token recognition insufficient to compensate for their exclusion from planning and presenting exhibits. Separate, unequal, and subordinate, the special day smacked of Jim Crow.

Ida B. Wells advised African Americans to stay away from the exposition completely. Douglass shared Wells's anger, but the aging orator was reluctant to pass up the chance to expose American hypocrisy on an international stage. He denounced the nation that, proud of its own freedom, denied meaningful freedom to many of its own citizens. "There is no Negro Problem," Douglass proclaimed, only the problem of Americans refusing to "live up to their own Constitution."

Douglass's long career was coming to a close in 1893. With the approach of a new century he was passing the mantle of leadership to a new generation. Wells, Booker T. Washington, and W. E. B. Du Bois had already claimed roles in this African-American vanguard. They would eventually be joined by a member of Douglass's audience, a young Georgian who would emerge as the voice of hope for tens of thousands of black Southerners, a "Black Moses," in the words of his biographer. His name was Robert Sengstacke Abbott.

Abbott came to the fair not to agitate but to entertain. Taking his place on the stage with the other three members of a vocal quartet from Hampton Institute, the twenty-five-year-old tenor was as captivated by the Windy City itself as he was by the inspiring words of Douglass and the excitement of performing at the great exposition. Like thousands of other fair visitors Abbott sensed that the future lay in Chicago.

After learning the printer's trade at Hampton, Abbott returned to Chicago in 1897, hoping to begin a career as a journalist. Ida B. Wells had resettled in Chicago two years earlier, resuming her career as a crusader against lynching and a journalist. That two ambitious young African Americans would share this interest is not surprising. The African-American press stood at the center of black American urban life and politics in the early twentieth century. Even in the rural South, religious newspapers permitted communication across county and state lines, connecting African-American communities to one another.

In the South, black newspapers filled columns with brief, but revealing, articles, usually noting when a woman—or occasionally a single man—was visiting relatives. A reader of the *Norfolk Journal and Guide*, for example, would learn that "Mr. Lonnie Jones, Norfolk, visited his parents, the Rev. and Mrs. Jones in Durham, North Carolina." These items were more than "filler"; readers wanted to know

The cartoon "Darkies' Day at the Fair" appeared in the British humor magazine *Puck*. It satirized the display of Africans at the World's Columbian Exposition in Chicago in 1893, which Frederick Douglass and other African Americans found extremely offensive.

where people came from and who they visited. The linkage of family life, generation to generation, across distances great and small had become an important part of African-American culture.

The idea of movement itself, an important theme in American history in general, has held special significance to the African-American experience. Upon emancipation many former slaves had tested their freedom by moving, if only a few miles to the next plantation. The impulse and its significance were so powerful that sixty-five years later, a woman declared an end to an interview about her early years as a slave by asserting her freedom to come and go. "I can go when I please and come back when I please. I'll come to see you, I must go home now. I am a free rooster."

Merely thinking about moving could boost the endurance of black workers who recognized that limited opportunities meant that moving along—rather than moving up—would eventually provide relief from their toil—at least until they began work someplace else.

For men, sawmills, turpentine camps, phosphate mines, and coal mines provided endless opportunities to move from place to place. Some were merely looking for work during breaks in the agricultural routine. Others sought liberation from farm life entirely. Cities promised more community life but fewer jobs, except in places like Birmingham, Alabama, where the steel mills provided unusual (though still limited) industrial opportunities. Women, always in demand as servants and laundresses, could more easily find stable employment. Families could, and did, move to the coal towns stretching across Appalachia south toward Birmingham. Some sought agricultural opportunities farther south in Florida, or—more often—west to the Mississippi Delta, Arkansas, and Texas. These destinations within the South drew African Americans who either persisted in their hopes to attain independence through land ownership or whose frustration kept them on the move but with no other apparent alternative.

Frustration and alienation, however, could also provide the foundation for hope, for faith in the ability of black people to turn their backs on their "white problem" and build their own alternatives. Some were attracted to a growing movement to establish "black towns," mainly in Oklahoma, but also as far west as Allensworth, California. The most common, and most enduring destination for potential black emigrants was Liberia, which had come to be considered a haven from American racism.

For most black Southerners, however, leaving the South meant moving north. And moving to the North meant the city. Northern farmland was expensive and most Northern rural communities expressed sympathy for oppressed blacks only as long as they remained oppressed *Southern* blacks.

Even in cities, as Robert Abbott learned, opportunities varied from nonexistent to scarce. Like other African-American craftsmen, most of whom had been trained in the South, this skilled printer found it impossible to find regular employment in a Northern city. Abbott took short-term printing jobs while attending Kent College of Law at night—the only African American in his graduating class. But the Chicago bar was no more hospitable to blacks than most of the city's neighborhood bars.

The rapidly growing metropolis of nearly two million people needed plenty of attorneys, but African-American legal business for the most part had to be generated by the small black community of thirty thousand people. An established core of black attorneys left little space for outsiders. Even within that community, Abbott found that his skin color put him at a disadvantage. A prominent African-American lawyer once curtly informed him that he was too dark to be effective in a courtroom.

Abbott returned to irregular employment as a printer, but with a larger goal in mind. On a May evening in 1905, he appeared on the streets of black Chicago selling the four-page *Chicago Defender,* which on its front page proclaimed itself "The World's Greatest Weekly." He began with virtually no money; the publisher and editor was also the reporting staff, business manager, and sales force. His landlady's kitchen table doubled as his desk.

Although the obstacles facing Robert Abbott illustrate the difficulties confronting black newcomers to Northern cities in the early years of the century, his actual experience was unusual. Black Southerners struggled mightily to provide their children with a decent education, but few young men or women reached the heights of a secondary or college degree. Moreover, Hampton, Tuskegee, and their offshoots encouraged graduates to remain in the South, to assume positions of leadership in their communities.

Black Southerners did move North during the early years of the twentieth century, but they did so in small numbers. Most came from the border states rather than such Deep South states as Abbott's native Georgia. Educated or uneducated, urban or rural, male or female, black Southerners who thought about the possibility of a better life elsewhere had to face the reality that earning a decent living in the North was close to impossible.

After building the *Defender* into a stable business, Abbott turned to the region of his birth and advised black Southerners that they should confront Southern racism rather than try to escape it. "The only wise thing to do," he declared in 1915, "is to stick to the farm." By then, however, increasing numbers of black Southerners were finding this advice difficult—if not impossible—to follow. A series of natural disasters during the preceding decade had struck with particular force in the cotton belt. In addition to boll weevils who "eat up all de cotton," drought followed by flood plagued Southern farmers. Consecutive years of poor crops in some counties had made it difficult for farmers to obtain credit, a necessity for tenants and owners of small farms. Hard times, however, were nothing new for black Southerners. They had endured Jim Crow for a generation. Most knew no life other than one of hard work with poverty as its reward. It is unlikely that a substantial number would have left the South as a result of these setbacks.

Something new was happening, however, in the North. The beginning of World War I in Europe in 1914 sent shock waves across the Atlantic, stimulating the American economy while shutting off its traditional source of industrial labor. American manufacturers could earn astronomical profits, selling first to the European combatants and, by 1916, to a domestic market on the verge of conversion to a wartime economy. But where would the additional workers be recruited? The war had stopped immigration from Europe. Within a year American entry into the war would divert thousands of men from the labor force to the armed forces. New sources of labor would have to be found.

Labor shortages hit first on the railroads, which were traditional employers of large numbers of casual laborers. By 1916 these men could find more secure and lucrative jobs in factories. Before railroad companies would turn to African Americans, however, they had to exhaust other alternatives. Some railroad executives assumed that they could recruit Mexicans to perform the regular track maintenance required every spring in the Northeast and Midwest. Other railroad executives looked to a different labor source. "By starting track work early," one executive explained, it would be possible to complete this chore with "American labor. The American hobo caught in the spring of the year will work."

Leaving aside this common assumption that the category "American" did not include African-American workers, such approaches reveal that employers considered the shortage temporary, requiring little rethinking of traditional assumptions about the ability of black men to do a "white man's job." Referring to employment patterns in Northern cities, the magazine *New Republic* observed in mid-1916 that "the Negro gets a chance to work only when there is no one else."

The notion of "no one else" depended not only on ideas about race, but also about gender. Many employers first reconsidered whether white man's work was necessarily man's work. During World War I thousands of white women moved into meat packinghouses, munitions and chemical factories, electrical industries, and other workplaces previously reserved for their husbands, fathers, and brothers. But stereotypes about gender were powerful, and employers generally considered women unsuitable for most types of industrial work.

In the packinghouses, for example, women could stuff and pack sausages but they were considered incapable of such tasks as herding animals, butchering, or lugging meat. To keep the production lines running, therefore, industrialists were forced to experiment with employing black men, generally referred to as "the Negro." The experiment spread to black women when new opportunities for white women left jobs open at the bottom of the hierarchy of female work. For the first time in American history, the nation's basic industries offered production jobs to African Americans. From New York, Boston, and Philadelphia to Pittsburgh, Chicago, Detroit, and to a lesser extent Los Angeles, factory gates opened.

Work in railroad yards, steel mills, food processing plants, garment shops, and other industries paid wages far beyond what was available in the rural or urban South. But it was more than the money that attracted black Southerners north. These jobs also represented portals into the industrial economy. These opportunities promised a new basis for claims to full citizenship—a promise that a previous generation of black Southerners had envisioned in the possibility of landownership.

Approximately 500,000 black Southerners moved between 1916 and 1919, with twice that many following during the 1920s. This movement, known as the "Great Migration," would ebb and flow until the 1970s, shifting the center of gravity of African-American culture from the rural South to the urban North. Southern cities drew increasing numbers of men and women from surrounding counties, many of whom stayed only long enough to earn enough money to move to the relative prosperity of the North. Employment in the coal mines of Appalachia drew thousands of others north as well. Smaller numbers headed west, especially toward Los Angeles, which by 1900 had surpassed San Francisco as the largest African-American community in that region. But the best opportunities and the highest wages lay in the North. What the North offered was a new start; Robert Abbott called the Great Migration a "second emancipation."

The men and women who translated the opening of new opportunities into a vast population movement had good reason for their optimism. These were not refugees blown across the winds of historical change. Rather, this was a movement of men and women who first sought information and then traveled established routes to destinations already inhabited by friends or relatives.

In the earliest months of the Great Migration—the fall and winter of 1916–17—recruiters working for Northern industry attracted attention in the South with stories of high wages and better living conditions in the North. Many of these recruiters were actually black workers visiting "home" with instructions (and cash incentives) from employers to recruit "reliable" friends and relatives.

In other cases black Southerners readily accepted offers of jobs and even free transportation only because they had already heard from other African Americans about the new opportunities and the differences in race relations. Men working in railroad yards and on trains, for example, could readily spread information along the tracks.

Chicago enjoyed a special reputation, because it was the home of the best-selling black newspaper in the South, the *Chicago Defender*. Fearless, sensational, and militant, Robert Abbott's newspaper expressed a perspective that was dangerous, if not impossible, for black Southerners to maintain in the presence of whites. Red ink announced lynchings, and readers were encouraged to fight back.

Abbott's advice shifted focus when jobs became available in Northern cities. Like other business leaders in Northern black communities he recognized that migration from the South promised opportunity not only for migrants, but also for African-American businesses and political interests. He became the primary cheerleader for "The Exodus," at one point fueling the bandwagon by setting a specific date for people to participate in a "Great Northern Drive."

Innumerable other links joined North and South, city and country. Fraternal organizations and church conventions met in different cities each year, providing opportunities to visit, see the sights, and listen to hosts brag. Returning home for weddings, funerals, or just to show off their accomplishments, migrants flaunted city clothes and spoke of voting, going to big league baseball games, and passing white people on the street without having to step into the gutter.

Alighting in a train depot downtown could stimulate exhilaration, which writer Richard Wright recalled feeling when he looked around the station for the familiar "FOR WHITE" and "FOR COLORED" signs that hung over water fountains, bathrooms, snack bars, and elsewhere in Southern terminals. He paused at a newsstand, feeling a tinge of anxiety as he exchanged coin for newspaper, "without having to wait until a white man was served."

For some, this sense of liberation was tempered by a combination of uncertainty, anxiety, and even fear. The famed musician Louis Armstrong later recalled his terror upon disembarking in a Chicago train station in 1922. He scanned the crowd, unable to locate his mentor Joe Oliver, who had made the same journey from New Orleans a few years earlier:

I saw a million people, but not Mister Joe, and I didn't give a damn who else
was there. I never seen a city that big. All those tall buildings. I thought they
were universities. I said, no, this is the wrong city. I was fixing to take the
next train back home—standing there in my box-back suit, padded shoulders, double-breasted wide-leg pants.

Armstrong's anxiety, one that characterized millions of immigrants to
American cities decades before and after he made his move, was very different from
Wright's. Armstrong worried about city life. Wright pondered the difficulty of
making the transition from a region where the rules of interaction (and separation) were spelled out and inflexible to the more ambiguous patterns of the North.

The Promise of the Cities

The Thomas family arrived in Chicago in the spring of 1917. Like thousands of
other black Southerners moving north at the time, their first task was to find a
home. For a week they pounded the pavements of the South Side ghetto. To look
elsewhere would have been futile. In Chicago the "black belt," along with a few
other scattered neighborhoods, provided the only housing available to African
Americans. The parents, their nineteen-year-old daughter, and a son two years
younger crowded into a five-room apartment—cramped, but probably larger than
the farmhouse they had left behind in Alabama.

The second task was to find work. The men went off to the stockyards; the
women turned to the familiar trade of wringing the dirt out of other people's
clothing. Optimistic about the future, the teenagers spent their evenings in night
school, hoping to improve on the grade-school education they had brought with
them from a rural Southern schoolhouse. In their free time the family explored the
leisure activities available on Chicago's South Side, carrying picnics into the park
and venturing into theaters and ice-cream parlors.

This family's experience hardly invokes the idea of a "Second Emancipation."
The Thomases struggled with the mundane aspects of everyday life that confront
anyone who leaves home to begin a new life elsewhere. For poor people this was
a particularly daunting challenge. For African Americans in the first half of the
twentieth century, most choices also were limited by racial discrimination. By
1918 migration chains linking South and North enabled thousands of Southerners
to choose destinations where they had friends or relatives to offer a welcoming
hand. A Southern town, city, or county might develop links to many Northern
cities, but a particularly strong connection usually reached toward one or two
potential destinations.

In most cases these patterns conformed to lines of longitude, largely because of
railroad routes. North and South Carolinians went to New York, Philadelphia, and
other eastern seaboard cities. Pittsburgh's African-American newcomers were
likely to hail from Alabama, Georgia, or Kentucky. From Mississippi, Louisiana,

Tennessee, and parts of Georgia and Alabama, people headed for Chicago—an especially popular destination because of the influence of the *Chicago Defender* and the long tentacles of the Illinois Central Railroad.

Arriving during a wartime housing shortage, most migrants encountered difficulty finding a home. Choices were limited. In the largest cities, emerging African-American ghettos provided obvious starting points, with New York's Harlem and Chicago's South Side especially well known among Southerners. In medium-sized cities like Cleveland, Milwaukee, and Buffalo, the process of ghettoization had begun before the Great Migration, but there was not yet a district so dominated by black residents that the neighborhood seemed segregated. In Los Angeles most blacks lived in an area that stretched thirty blocks along Central Avenue, but as late as 1919 their neighbors included Mexicans, Italians, and Russian Jews.

In some cases local geography was a crucial factor. Pittsburgh's hills and hollows, breaking toward the rivers, contrasted sharply with Chicago's flat prairie or the unbroken expanse of Manhattan Island. African-American steelworkers in the Pittsburgh area did not inhabit a single district, instead congregating in a series of steel mill communities with the largest concentration in Pittsburgh itself. Still, however, they tended to live in enclaves, in neighborhoods that became increasingly segregated during World War I and the 1920s.

In general northbound migrants entered cities where housing segregation had proceeded far enough to exclude them from most neighborhoods. But the state of flux was such that in most cases a black Northerner in 1920 was likely to have at least a few white neighbors within a couple of blocks. By 1930, that likelihood had diminished considerably, with African Americans segregated into ghettos—neighborhoods dominated by a single group excluded from other parts of the city.

Ghettos are not, however, necessarily slums. Harlem, in particular, was not a slum on the eve of the Great Migration. A middle-class neighborhood barely a decade earlier, it suffered from overcrowding during and after the war. Most urban black neighborhoods were less fortunate at the outset, with aging housing stock ill suited to the rapid influx of newcomers beginning in 1916.

Segregation by itself did not cause a decline in either housing standards or the quality of a neighborhood. What segregation meant was that neither black newcomers nor established residents could move beyond the borders of the emerging ghettos, except for gradual expansion at the fringes of these neighborhoods. The result was overcrowding and a strain on the physical capacity of buildings.

This strain was also a result of the economics of ghettoization. Contrary to popular belief, property values have not always declined as neighborhoods shifted from "white" to "black." During the Great Migration and throughout much of the twentieth century the process was more complicated. As Southerners, most of them poor and unaccustomed to urban life, moved into the least expensive and oldest neighborhoods, established residents tended to seek better housing in less crowded districts. But ghettos could expand only slowly, and only at their edges.

Real estate speculators purchased homes in these border districts, often by frightening white homeowners with the prospect of "Negro invasion." Known as "blockbusting," this tactic yielded generous profits, as the investor could sell the properties to black home buyers at inflated rates. In Los Angeles, for example the markup (in essence a race tax) went as high as one hundred percent. African-American purchasers had nowhere else to go because of the limitations defined by a dual housing market: one set of choices for whites, one (more limited) for blacks. In Northern and Western cities, African Americans generally paid more than whites would pay for equivalent living space.

At the same time, however, black workers earned less than their white counterparts. What this meant was that African Americans spent an inordinate proportion of their income on shelter. In Harlem, rents generally commanded nearly half of the earnings of African-American residents, placing a considerable burden on family budgets. There and elsewhere, the solution often lay in transforming a home into a commercial enterprise. Families rented out rooms to lodgers, often relatives or former neighbors recently arrived from the South.

Lodging, however, constituted only one type of residential overcrowding. In the long run, the deterioration of buildings probably owed more to a different way of crowding more people into limited spaces—the division of houses and apartments into smaller units by landlords eager to squeeze out more rent. Real estate investors who operated in the "white" market made profits by developing what are known as "subdivisions," large tracts of land divided into individual lots for residential construction. Building a subdivision increased the value of the land and its environs.

On the African-American side of the dual housing market, a very different kind of "subdivision" took place, one that was equally profitable but that eventually drove values down rather than up. An investor would purchase a single-family home or an apartment building and divide the structure into a rabbit warren of small apartments, known in some cities as "kitchenettes" and in others as "efficiency units." These spaces were efficient because their inhabitants (often families) slept, cooked, ate, socialized, and relaxed in a single room. The rental income from these converted buildings yielded a quick profit, thereby increasing the value of the property. But these buildings deteriorated equally rapidly, due to shoddy renovation and inadequate maintenance.

The dual housing market contributed to the deterioration of some African-American neighborhoods in other ways as well. With a captive market for their properties, landlords collected rents more assiduously than they maintained their buildings. Tenants who demanded proper maintenance (and many of them did) could usually be replaced with newcomers who either knew little about what to expect or took what they could get because choices were few.

African Americans who purchased homes often overpaid because of their inability to shop throughout the city. In some cases this left homeowners without enough money to maintain their houses adequately. Despite the continuing presence of middle-class African-American neighborhoods, invisible to whites who blithely equated slum with ghetto, the trend was downward.

During World War I and sporadically during the 1920s it was easier for black newcomers to find places to work in Northern cities than to find places to live. The Great Migration itself was catalyzed by the opening of thousands of new railroad jobs, mainly laying track and performing manual tasks around rail yards. By 1917, although still largely excluded from industrial work in the West, African Americans were working in heavy industry across the Northeast and Midwest.

On the whole these black men and women were relegated to jobs disdained by their white counterparts, who took advantage of wartime opportunities to advance into more skilled positions. Most of these jobs in steel mills, auto plants, packing-houses, and rubber factories required little skill and could be learned quickly. The hardest part for many migrants from the South was probably the adaptation to a different approach to time—an adjustment confronted by generations of rural workers around the world upon their introduction to industrial employment.

In the rural South, as in other agricultural societies, the calendar and the weather determined the rhythm of work. Planting, cultivating, and harvesting were performed at the same time each year, but with variation according to the weather. Cotton cultivation was characterized by one planter as "a series of spurts rather than by a daily grind."

But this would not work on an assembly line in Detroit. By the early twentieth century, workers in most Northern factories were punching time clocks. Arrive ten minutes late and your pay was docked one hour. On the "disassembly lines" of the packinghouses, conveyer belts moved carcasses from worker to worker, each of whom would make a single cut. Tardiness or absence could disrupt the whole process. Moreover, once the line began moving, the newcomer had no control over the pace of work.

Newcomers to industrial labor also had to accustom themselves to repeating a single task rather than completing an operation from start to finish. A man who formerly butchered a whole hog now performed only a single task among more than a hundred. A woman accustomed to picking up dirty laundry from customers and dropping it off cleaned and ironed might take a job in one of the many mechanized laundries employing thousands of black women in Northern and Southern cities. There she could spend hour after hour, day after day, only pressing cuffs, yokes, or sleeves.

Most migrants, however, not only stayed with these jobs but encouraged their friends and relatives to join them. The hard work produced rewards during the war years and the 1920s. In interviews and in letters back home, migrants spoke enthusiastically of sending their children to school, voting, sitting where they pleased on the streetcars, and other accomplishments.

Migrants to Southern cities encountered a somewhat different employment picture. With fewer basic manufacturing industries than Northern cities, places like

Louisville, Norfolk, Nashville, and Mobile provided fewer opportunities. Industries directly related to war production, especially shipyards in coastal cities, provided most of the new jobs. But where black men in the North generally held onto their foothold at the bottom of the industrial ladder until nearly the end of the 1920s, their Southern counterparts suffered the fate of black women: when the war ended most were pushed back into menial service employment.

Northern employers were willing to permit black industrial workers to keep their positions in part because they had learned during the war that these men could do the job. But the decision drew equally on two other factors: immigration restriction and the threat of unionization. Beginning in 1921 federal legislation limited immigration from nations outside the Western hemisphere to a trickle, once again forcing industrialists to look beyond European immigrants for a supply of new workers.

At the same time, union organizing campaigns in major industries during the war had convinced Northern employers that maintaining racial divisions within their work force was a strong weapon against unionization. When African-American workers passed through factory gates to their new jobs during the war, they had a reputation among white workers and employers as instinctively anti-union. This image was not entirely accurate. Black Southerners had joined unions as early as 1872 on the New Orleans docks. In cities across the South, black carpenters and bricklayers had joined segregated union locals around the turn of the century.

On the whole, however, few black workers did belong to unions, largely because most unions either excluded them from membership or simply made no attempt to organize them. In addition, most unions at the time organized mainly skilled craft workers such as carpenters, bricklayers, plumbers, printers, and cigar makers, showing little interest in the agricultural and service occupations in which most African Americans worked. Only the United Mine Workers (UMW) and the Industrial Workers of the World (IWW) systematically organized unskilled workers.

The IWW had little presence in areas populated by African Americans, although it did have some success among black dockworkers in Philadelphia and timber workers in the Louisiana forests. The UMW stood alone among major national unions in its willingness and ability to enlist African-American members. But even among the mine workers, racial divisions frequently hampered the ability of the union to maintain solidarity. Thus when white union workers went on strike, employers could—and occasionally did—tap a substantial pool of underemployed and nonunion African Americans to replace the strikers. In coal mines and packinghouses, on the railroads and in hotel restaurants, African-American workers had filled the places of white unionists on strike since the closing decades of the nineteenth century.

Between 1917 and 1921, unions undertook major organizing campaigns most notably (in terms of the role of black workers) in steel, meat packing, and coal. Except in the Appalachian coal mines these campaigns made little headway in the

South, but in major industrial centers across the Northeast and Midwest workers joined by the thousands. What made a difference was that for the first time, unions in steel and meat packing organized by *industry*, as coal miners did, rather than by *craft*, or specific occupation, as workers did in the building trades. In addition union leadership recognized that black workers were now part of the industrial labor force and would have to be included if an organizing campaign were to succeed.

Many black industrial workers did join unions during and immediately after the war, but more either dropped out quickly or never joined at all. Some black workers had difficulty appreciating the sincerity of the unions' welcome, given the record of racial exclusion and the continuing hostility among white workers and local union leadership in some areas. Others were reluctant to risk the jobs that had provided the path out of the Jim Crow South. Perhaps most important, however, was the difference in how black and white workers saw the relationship between their community and their workplace.

White industrial workers often lived in neighborhoods near the plant; unions were as much community institutions as workplace institutions. In most cities, however, African Americans lived in increasingly segregated neighborhoods away from their workplaces, which tended to be lumped with a white world dominated by white institutions. Except for the handful of African-American unions, most notably the Brotherhood of Sleeping Car Porters, founded in 1925, unions were likely to be perceived as white organizations, unable or unwilling to understand the needs of black workers.

Even though black workers identified strongly with their community and its institutions, the class differences that preceded the Great Migration remained. Indeed, these Northern urban black communities now experienced even deeper divisions. Newcomers were more likely than established residents to come from the Deep South and to work at industrial jobs that previously had played no role in the black class structure because blacks had been excluded from these workplaces. They also encountered African-American communities that encouraged migration yet held the migrants themselves at arm's length. "They didn't seem to open-arm welcome them," recalled a porter at one of Chicago's busy railroad stations, "but they seemed to welcome them."

People who called themselves "Old Philadelphians" ("O.P.'s") in one city, or "Old Settlers" in others, generally considered northbound migration to be "good for the race." The wages workers carried home increased the flow of dollars into black businesses. The votes of newcomers, most of them loyal to the Republican party, increased the clout of black politicians. Moreover their departure from the South dealt a blow to Jim Crow and proclaimed to the nation that black Southerners were not the "happy negroes" depicted by Southern white spokesmen. The Cleveland *Gazette*, echoing other African-American newspapers, cheered the exodus as evidence that black Southerners understood the folly of "depending

The future of the Negro lies in his Health.

WAR, DISEASE, FAMINE Now a MEMORY

Reconstruction in 1919 must begin with toning up the health of the individual and comunity.

The War's backwash caused Pittsburgh's death rate to increase 43% last year.

Negroes suffered greatly. The amount of sickness was appalling.

7,320 deaths in Pittsburgh from **Pneumonia** and **Influenza** last year. 630 were Negroes.

To YOU, who have recovered, Specialists say that "the after effects are as bad or worse than the disease."

Watch that weakened Heart or those Kidneys or Lungs. If in doubt —see your Doctor.

Tuberculosis kills relatively almost twice as many Negroes as white people;—if treated in time, it can be cured. Consult the Tuberculosis Dispensary at once.

Bad teeth means a bad stomach, which cause indirectly 75% of all sickness.

The Medical examination of our draftees—your sons, husbands and sweethearts has shown the alarming prevalence of Venereal diseases.

Read that Literature.

ARE YOU MOVING? READ

A Negro family moved into a house vacated by a foreigner in the East End one month ago. One week afterward the whole family, man, wife and three children were seriously ill from germs left in the house—one child died. "Nuf Sed."

Fully half of all the sickness and deaths are preventable, this means that 45 out of every 100 Negroes who died last year ought to be living.

BABIES DO NOT HAVE TO HAVE Measles, Scarlet Fever, Whooping Cough, etc.

Twice as many Negro babies die before they reach one year of age than babies of all other races in the City.

Find the nearest Baby Health Station and take your baby regularly.

The League Office will give you information on request.

IMMEDIATE STEPS.

See that your garbage and waste is moved promptly.

Don't live in or over damp basements.

In 1919, the Urban League of Pittsburgh ran its second annual Negro Health Education Campaign. It advised African Americans to seek medical attention for infectious diseases, to see their dentists regularly, and to practice good sanitation.

upon the people [white southerners] who have destroyed them in the past to aid them in the future." Instead, migrants could depend on black leadership in Northern communities to represent their interests and ease the transition to their new homes.

Black Southerners arriving in cities encountered an array of agencies committed to helping them find places in the city. The most systematically active and professionalized of these were the local branches of the National Urban League. Founded in 1911, the Urban League added dozens of branches during the decade after 1916, in a wide variety of cities across the country.

Although services varied from city to city, the Urban League developed a reputation among black Southerners preparing to leave home as an organization "that cares for Southern emigrants." This care came in the form of job and housing registries, which often dispensed advice on work habits, housekeeping, and coping with landlords and city officials. Urban League officials in Pittsburgh proudly referred to their instructions to women on "the use of gas, electricity, marketing of foods, how to purchase and prepare cheap cuts of meat."

Black branches of the Young Men's and Young Women's Christian Associations initiated cooperative programs with employers and established room registries and recreation programs. In some cases community centers, churches, and women's clubs developed day care programs, a crucial service given the unusually high level of married African-American women who held paid jobs. The husbands of black working women earned less than white men. Thus it was not unusual for these women to add wage labor to the customary housekeeping burdens of wives and mothers.

The assistance of clubs and groups like the Urban League, however, came with a double edge. Clubwomen concerned about the availability of child care for domestic workers were equally concerned about respectable housekeeping habits and public appearance. Newcomers were told not to wear head rags, scarves that Northern black women saw as symbols of servility and second-class citizenship. On a front porch shoes were a must, aprons a no-no. Like the settlement houses in white immigrant neighborhoods, YMCAs and YWCAs tried to compete with the streets and saloons for workers' leisure hours. And like the settlement houses, their efforts, though well meant, were often insulting and only partly successful.

Black newspapers printed lists of "do's and don'ts" similar to the lectures printed on Urban League brochures. Most of these lessons dealt with public behavior, reflecting anxieties about the impact of the migrants' Southern and rural habits on white images of African Americans. When newcomers were lectured not to "allow children to beg on the streets," encourage gambling, congregate in loud crowds, or "act discourteously to other people in public places," they sensed they were being talked down to. And they were.

In the North, even among African Americans, Southerners encountered a contempt for rural Southern culture. At the same time, however, these instructions reflected realistic concerns about Northern race relations and the differences between North and South. Northern whites did see African Americans as belonging to a single, unchanging, unified culture. Whatever black Northerners had accomplished in developing a community reputation could crumble under the onslaught of the new images conveyed by newcomers.

W. E. B. Du Bois recognized the dilemma of streetcar behavior in terms of the prevailing etiquette that required a male passenger to offer his seat to a female. This was something that migrants supposedly did not do, reflecting poorly on African-American manners and gentility. Southern black men were not by nature rude, observed Du Bois. But they had learned in the South to avoid interaction with white women. Even eye contact at the wrong time and place could provoke a lynching. Offering a seat to a white woman implied a social grace, a statement of manhood that was acceptable in the South only if accompanied by the kind of shuffle and deference that had no place in the North. Many black men who had recently arrived from the South took the safe—if "discourteous"—route. When a white woman boarded, they averted their glance and kept their seats.

Many newcomers responded to what they considered a cool reception by distancing themselves, especially on Sunday morning. Thousands left the big urban churches they had initially found so exciting and established smaller congregations in storefronts, often sending back home for their minister. Yet they continued to read the local black newspaper and align themselves politically with the established leaders of their communities.

This identification with the community, with the "home sphere," reflected the ways in which African Americans fit into early-twentieth-century American cities. Where they could (and could not) live related closely to race. Their children sat in classes filled mainly with other black children but with a white teacher standing in front. Whites owned the big stores; blacks, the small shops. And nearly all bosses were white. For white workers, race was taken for granted and class divisions often seemed to explain injustices and inequalities. But for black workers—and most African Americans earned working-class incomes—injustice and inequality had a distinctly racial cast. Class differences mattered, especially when thinking about the internal workings of their own community. But "their own community" was defined mainly by race.

Black Southerners who moved north hoping to leave behind the color line and racial hostilities quickly learned a harsher reality. The rules were unwritten in the North, but they were rules nevertheless. These neighborhoods were off-limits; those restaurants "don't serve Negroes." Sit where you want on the streetcar but don't be surprised if a white passenger moves away. Many teachers made no secret of their belief in the inability of black children to learn as quickly as their white peers. And there was violence.

In 1917, less than a year after industrial jobs first opened in the North, black workers in East St. Louis, Illinois (across the Mississippi River from St. Louis, Missouri), learned how dangerous their new homes could be. Thousands of black Southerners had come to work in aluminum factories, many of them recruited by employers seeking to replace striking white workers. The combination was explosive: cynical industrial managers using race to divide their workers, union organizers who raised the familiar cry of "nigger scab," corrupt white politicians, irresponsible journalists, and police inclined to look the other way when whites attacked blacks. The result was a race riot.

Nine whites and at least thirty-nine African Americans were killed; it was impossible to establish the number of black victims because their dead bodies were allegedly thrown into ditches and never recovered. The coroner was more concerned with white fatalities. Thousands of black residents were left homeless by fires set by white arsonists. Three weeks later, Du Bois, James Weldon Johnson, and other NAACP officials led a protest march down New York's Fifth Avenue. Following muffled drums, ten thousand men and women marched from Harlem through the heart of Manhattan in complete silence, with only their signs expressing their outrage.

Two years later violence erupted once more, this time in twenty-five cities and towns during a six-month period. James Weldon Johnson called it the "Red Summer," referring to the blood that flowed from racial conflict. Attacks occurred in rural Arkansas; small-town Texas; Tulsa, Oklahoma; Charleston, South Carolina; Knoxville, Tennessee; Washington, D.C.; and Omaha, Nebraska. Only the West was spared, probably because black populations were not yet large enough to pose a threat to the stability of white neighborhoods or to white men's jobs.

The worst riot was in Chicago, where black and white Chicagoans battled in the streets for five days in July, with occasional attacks punctuating an uneasy calm the following

A triumphant group of young rioters celebrates outside a damaged home during the 1919 Chicago riots.

week. Catalyzed by an attack on a black teenager who had floated onto a "white" beach, the violence was initiated by white street gangs fighting to secure their turf, their community's jobs, and their political patrons' power against the threat posed by the influx of African Americans into the city. The police stood by as blacks passing through white neighborhoods were beaten. In response black Chicagoans set upon whites as well, usually inside the boundaries of the black ghetto. Only a timely rainstorm and the Illinois National Guard restored order.

No silent marches this time. In many of these conflicts the protest had come immediately and on the field of battle. Nineteenth-century "race riots" had generally consisted of attacks on black communities while authorities looked the other way. Blacks sometimes defended themselves but seldom counterattacked. But in Longview, Texas, in 1919, blacks responded to an attempt to drive the local *Defender* agent out of town by taking out their rifles. In Chicago white peddlers and merchants in the "Black Belt" were attacked after the initial assaults on African Americans. Claude McKay's poem, "If We Must Die," published in July 1919, articulated the mood:

> If we must die, let it not be like hogs
> Hunted and penned in an inglorious spot,
> While round us bark the mad and hungry dogs,
> Making their mock at our accursed lot.

Members of the 369th Colored Infantry arrive home in New York in 1919. Every member of this unit—the first of the African-American troops to see action—received the Croix de Guerre for gallantry.

If we must die, O let us nobly die,
So that our precious blood may not be shed
In vain; then even the monsters we defy
Shall be constrained to honor us though dead!
O kinsmen! we must meet the common foe!
Though far outnumbered let us show us brave,
And for their thousand blows deal one deathblow!
What though before us lies the open grave?
Like men we'll face the murderous, cowardly pack,
Pressed to the wall, dying, but fighting back!

"New Negroes"

On February 17, 1919, less than two years after the dramatic "silent protest" parade from Harlem to downtown Manhattan, another set of disciplined marchers walked Fifth Avenue in the opposite direction. The men of the 369th Infantry Division of the United States Army had returned home from the war. They had fought hard, losing hundreds of men on the battlefield. They had fought well, becoming the only American unit to win the prized Croix de Guerre from the French, who had dubbed the unit the "Hell Fighters."

The French knew these Americans well, because the regiment had been attached to the French Army—"owing to the need for replacements in French units," according to U.S. government documents prepared after the war. The truth, however, was more complicated. Four National Guard units fought with the French. The troops were black; the officers an interracial group headed in three cases by a white colonel. Only the Illinois regiment, the pride of African Americans across the United States because of publicity from the *Chicago Defender,* had an African American in command.

Combining these regiments with white units was unthinkable to American military leaders. Nor were these generals prepared to combine the African-American units into a fully equipped all-black combat division. With the French clamoring for replacements, American commanders loaned to their allies the men they preferred not to lead into battle themselves. Appropriately, the war heroes stepped uptown in American uniforms but in French drill formation.

The decision of the United States government to enter World War I in April 1917 received a mixed reception among the American public. Many Americans opposed participation. Ethnic loyalties played a part in this opposition, as did criticism of European imperialism and a sense that Europe's troubles need not consume American lives or tax dollars. Many African Americans, questioning their role in a "white-folks' war," shared this skepticism. Most black voices, however, supported W. E. B. Du Bois's call for African Americans to "close ranks" behind the war effort. Military service, Liberty Bond purchases, diligent labor on the home front, and vocal support for the war would provide a basis upon which the black community could expect increased recognition and acceptance. As one black teacher in the South explained, his people were "soldiers of freedom. . . . When we have proved ourselves men, worthy to work and fight and die for our country, a grateful nation may gladly give us the recognition of real men, and the rights and privileges of true and loyal citizens of these United States." Democracy at home would be the reward for supporting democracy abroad.

The American military, however, had difficulty determining a potential role for black soldiers. First the army turned away black candidates for enlistment. Next, draft boards discriminated against black men seeking exemption. Grudgingly the War Department established a facility to train black officers, but the selection process weeded out many of the most qualified candidates in favor of men less likely to succeed. Black soldiers were "loaned" to the French army, whose officers were warned by American authorities that such men were potential rapists who had to be kept away from civilian populations.

In the end, 380,000 black men served, nearly half of them in Europe. Only 42,000 of these served in combat units. The rest were relegated to digging, cleaning, hauling, loading, and unloading.

Despite efforts to insult black soldiers and to remind black civilians that a war fought to "make the world safe for Democracy," as President Woodrow Wilson put it, did not necessarily mean making America itself any more democratic, African Americans drew their own lessons from the war. Writing in *The Crisis* in May 1919, Du Bois made the point:

> We *return*
> We *return from fighting.*
> We *return fighting.*
> Make way for Democracy! We saved it in France, and by the Great
> Jehovah, we will save it in the United States of America or know the
> reason why.

White Southerners wasted little time casting doubt on whether democracy had been saved at home. They lynched seventy African Americans during the year after the war. Ten of these were soldiers, some murdered in their uniforms. The riots of 1919 both punctuated this epidemic of publicly sanctioned homicide and dispelled any notions that racism and violence were unique to the South.

The riots also, however, provided a clue to an increasingly assertive sensibility spreading across black America. In some Southern cities the violence itself was sparked by white outrage at the sight of armed black veterans in uniform. In the North the riots were linked to the impact of the Great Migration, itself a statement of bold ambition and a commitment to a new role in American life. Everywhere the heightened tensions were related to an impatient mood working its way across black America. Black soldiers epitomized this sense of anticipation, this expectation that things were changing, that things had to change. Men who had fought for their country abroad had little tolerance for continued appeals to "wait" for recognition of their rights as citizens at home. This sense that they were entitled to the full rewards of American life combined with the ambition and excitement of the Great Migration to form the heart of what came to be called the "New Negro" movement.

The idea of the "New Negro" took hold in many influential black publications in the 1920s, and the term itself was used as the title of a book edited by Howard University professor Alain Locke in 1925. In his introduction Locke proposed two complementary principles underlying this new perspective. New Negroes insisted on the rights embodied in "the ideals of American institutions and democracy." They also promoted "self-respect and self-reliance" among African Americans, with a distinct emphasis on race pride.

This perspective was not as new as Locke claimed. Instead it brought together strands of Booker T. Washington's gospel of self-reliance, deep traditions of

African-American protest, ranging from abolitionism to the founding of the NAACP in 1910, and the hopes and aspirations underlying the Great Migration. What was new was a sense of expectation unequaled since emancipation and an odd combination of disillusionment, anger, militancy, and euphoria dramatized by the parades of returning veterans.

Nor was the New Negro represented by a single approach to African-American culture or the problems defined by the American color line. New Negroes moved into the arts and literature, social work and social activism, politics, the union movement, and a variety of organizations claiming to offer the solution to the dilemma of black life in a nation seemingly committed to white supremacy.

The most enduring expression of the New Negro was the literary and artistic flowering often referred to as the Harlem Renaissance. The term encompasses the work of a broad variety of novelists, poets, essayists, artists, and musicians. Their work displayed a diversity of form and content that defies simple categorization. Some, like poet Langston Hughes and folklorist and novelist Zora Neale Hurston, took street life or rural folk culture as their subject. This approach differed from older African-American literary traditions, which tended to emphasize respectability.

Others, like novelist Jessie Fauset, stuck with high culture and the black elite. Some explicitly protested against American racial oppression; others adopted racial themes but avoided overt political statements. What mattered, declared Hughes, was the inclination to write from inside the experience and to be true to one's creative muse.

By the 1920s Harlem had emerged as the cultural capital of black America, in much the same way that New York City stood at the center of mainstream American high culture. This was not an accident. The diversity of the population—a yeasty mix of New Yorkers, recent migrants from the South, and immigrants from the West Indies and Africa—played a part.

So did the efforts of Charles Johnson, an African-American sociologist who at the time was the editor of the Urban League publication *Opportunity.* Johnson, along with *Crisis* literary editor Jessie Fauset, envisioned their journals as vanguards of social change. Through the publication of short stories, poems, and essays, and the awarding of cash prizes, these two journals promoted the work of Hughes, Hurston, Countee Cullen, Jean Toomer, and countless others. Perhaps as important, the journals also provided a bridge across which African-American culture could be presented to white audiences.

And indeed, white Americans did discover African-American culture during the 1920s. A small group of white political activists, literary figures, editors, and intellectuals read the books, went to art exhibits, and even donated money for literary prizes. Few tackled the more difficult work, like Toomer's *Cane,* a series of fictional portraits connected by poetic interludes. But then again, few blacks read *Cane* either; it sold only five hundred copies. Toomer's deft manipulation of literary form to explore the rural roots of black culture and consciousness would become a classic, but it would take nearly a half-century for it to be rediscovered.

Jessie Fauset's genteel aristocrats, every bit as proper as their white counterparts but not nearly as affluent, posed a different challenge. "White readers just don't expect Negroes to be like this," explained one white editor in rejecting her manuscript. The street hustlers of Claude McKay's *Home to Harlem*, the love poems of Countee Cullen, the blues rhythms of Langston Hughes: these were easier. Charles Johnson's vision of a cultural terrain that provided a common ground for black and white Americans overestimated the interest of whites in black culture, history, or sensibilities. Whites were mainly interested in something called "The Negro," an exotic neighbor who was not bound by the narrow conventions of social morality.

It was not the literature or the art that brought white people and their money to Harlem or the South Side of Chicago. It was the nightclubs. White urbanites crowded into the clubs to listen to a new kind of music called jazz, which had emerged in the South earlier in the century. Some of these night spots, owned and operated by whites, employed black musicians and chorus girls to entertain mainly white audiences who saw Harlem and its smaller counterparts in other cities as places where they could cast aside their inhibitions and enjoy exotic entertainment. Other clubs resembled Chicago's "black and tan" cabarets, where the white downtown theater crowd mingled with the black middle class. In some cities these integrated establishments were the most likely night spots to attract police in the mood to enforce legislation enacted in the 1920s as part of the outlawing of liquor sales during Prohibition. Apparently alcohol was more dangerous when imbibed interracially. The appeal of ghetto glitz reached its apex at Harlem's Savoy Ballroom, where integrated crowds of up to four thousand danced to music provided by the most famous dance bands of the era.

Few of Harlem's residents, however, could afford the Savoy. The world of cabarets, concerts, and publication contracts that swirled around the notables of the Harlem Renaissance meant little to the majority of women who toiled daily as domestic workers, or to men carrying home a few dollars each day for pushing a broom or tending a machine. They caught their music at rent parties, all-night affairs in tightly packed apartments where a quarter at the door purchased food, drink, and live entertainment, with the proceeds used to pay the rent. Or they got music through a new phenomenon known as "race" records.

By mid-decade the strong economy had brought enough secure employment in most cities to permit many black families in cities across the country to purchase phonographs. After Okeh Records took the plunge in 1920 and issued Mamie Smith's *Crazy Blues* (which sold thousands of copies), other recording companies jumped into the market. Race records brought substantial profits to white record company owners. Black Swan Records, whose advertisements truthfully trumpeted "The Only Genuine Colored Record," enjoyed only brief success, in part because of its commitment to maintaining a catalogue of more respectable (but not profitable) classical music in addition to blues recordings.

Sustaining an African-American voice in film proved more difficult. The first attempt came in 1915 with the establishment of the Lincoln Motion Picture Company. Noble Johnson, an actor with experience at Universal Studios, made the films in Los Angeles. His brother George took care of the marketing after finishing his shift at the Omaha, Nebraska, post office. They drew support from both communities, especially in Los Angeles, with its pair of African-American hotels, a black baseball league, an "African cafe," and an active NAACP branch.

Drawing on the emerging Watts ghetto for his screenplays, Noble Johnson sought "to picture the Negro as he is in his every day life, a human being with human inclination, and one of talent and intellect." George Johnson developed strong relationships with black newspapers, and Lincoln films were able to take advantage of the wartime migration to cities to build an audience.

The story of the Johnson brothers, however, also reveals the difficulties of black enterprise and the obstacles faced by African Americans committed to using the new tools of mass culture (at that time, radio, newspapers, and motion pictures) to provide honest depictions of black life. Lack of money and restricted access to distribution networks and credit undermined the company's ability to compete with white-owned film companies.

Nor did the Johnsons reach beyond a black audience; whites showed no interest in their films. The Lincoln Motion Picture Company folded in 1921. Another independent black filmmaker, Oscar Micheaux, would continue working through the 1920s and 1930s, but on the whole the film industry would be dominated by large studios turning out films with either no black characters or African Americans appearing in stereotypical and demeaning comical roles.

Surveying the state of black America in 1925, one young African-American scholar concluded that the business of producing culture was less indicative of the power and potential of the New Negro than the culture of the black businessman. E. Franklin Frazier, at the beginning of a long career as a distinguished sociologist, stated his minority opinion in one of the essays of Alain Locke's anthology, *The New Negro*.

He urged his readers to look beyond Harlem toward Durham, North Carolina, where African Americans owned thriving insurance companies and banks. "Durham offers none of the color and creative life we find among Negroes in New York City. . . . It is not a place where men write and dream, but a place where men calculate and work." His essay pointed to black economic dynamism, not cultural achievement, as the truly important change in the 1920s. Black financiers and businessmen along with a growing industrial working class would eventually merge black America with white America. When this happened race would cease to be important; what would matter was class.

A small group of young activists argued that class already was the division that mattered. The challenge was to convince black Americans that as workers their interests were best represented not by the middle-class NAACP and National Urban League, but by the labor and socialist movements, which claimed to speak for all workers. At the same time white workers would have to be convinced that black workers were allies, rather than rivals.

Calling itself the voice of the "New Crowd Negro," a new magazine called *The Messenger* was launched in 1917 by A. Philip Randolph and Chandler Owen. Both men were college educated and had migrated from the South to Harlem. Their notion of a "New Negro" had less to do with culture than with politics—in particular socialist politics. Randolph and Owen opposed American involvement in World War I. Dismissing the war as a battle among European imperialists, they tied the oppression of African Americans to colonialism in Africa (the political and ecomonic control of most of Africa by European nations) and to the oppression of the working class around the world.

Both union activity and socialist politics were becoming increasingly visible in African-American communities in the early part of the twentieth century. The leading black socialist of that time was probably George Washington Woodbey. Born a slave in Tennessee in 1854, Woodbey educated himself after the Civil War, despite less than two years of formal schooling. He moved to San Diego in 1903 (like so many other migrants, part of a family chain—he first went there to visit his mother), where he served as a minister and as a socialist orator and pamphleteer.

Woodbey's visibility in the movement in some ways highlights socialism's weakness among African Americans. He stood out among socialists for the attention he gave in his speeches to the relationship between racial oppression and class conflict, a link that many socialists either ignored or treated superficially. Although generally less committed to white supremacy than most other white Americans, the socialists seldom directly challenged prevailing notions about race. Moreover, Woodbey's status as a minister is important. Most African Americans were likely to look within, rather than outside the black community for leadership—to their preachers, editors, business owners, lawyers, and educators.

By the end of the 1910s radical politics was developing deeper roots in some black communities, most notably Harlem. Hubert Harrison, a leading street-corner orator and Socialist party activist before World War I, broke with the party in 1917. He proclaimed the need for a combination of black nationalism and socialism, with "race first" as the cornerstone.

Harrison frequently crossed paths with Cyril Briggs, founder in 1917 of the African Blood Brotherhood. Briggs described his organization as "a revolutionary secret order" dedicated to armed resistance to lynching, opposition to all forms of racial discrimination, and voting rights for black Southerners. He also sought the unionization of black workers and African-American control of political institutions in parts of the United States where they were a majority of the population.

The brotherhood also opposed American participation in World War I and linked the struggle for black liberation in the United States to the battle against European colonization in Africa. The organization never grew beyond a few thousand, but by the early 1920s had expanded from its Harlem base to places as diverse as the West Indies and West Virginia. Like Hubert Harrison and George Washington Woodbey, the African Blood Brotherhood is significant because of its place in the broad range of African-American thought in the early twentieth century. It also is an example of the participation of black Americans in international debates about colonialism, politics, and race.

Organizing in Harlem for the nearly successful Socialist candidate for mayor in 1917, Randolph and Owen managed to attract thousands of black voters to the socialist banner. But success was short-lived and localized. In general the Socialist party failed to attract black voters, in part because it was unwilling to take a strong stand against Jim Crow.

The Communist party attracted few African Americans during the 1920s. These were mainly intellectuals impressed with its forthright stands against colonialism in Africa and racism in the United States. The party would win many black supporters for the help it lent to African Americans in civil rights and economic issues during the Great Depression of the 1930s. But in the 1920s attempts by the Communist party to organize black workers were so unsuccessful that A. Philip Randolph dismissed black Communists as a group that could meet in a phone booth.

Not that Randolph, Owen, or other African-American labor organizers had done much better. Several attempts had been made to organize unions with mainly black membership. All had failed, mostly because of resistance from white unions. By 1925, the *Messenger* was barely surviving after dropping from its peak circulation of 26,000 in 1919. Chandler Owen left to work for another publication in Chicago, and Randolph began to rethink his attitudes towards the American Federation of Labor (AFL).

The only route to black unionization seemed to be inclusion in existing labor organizations. The NAACP and the National Urban League had tried this route in 1918–19, urging black workers to join unions wherever they were accepted on an equal basis. But few unions would take blacks on an equal basis with their white members. In his earlier years as a radical Randolph had viewed the AFL as not only racist, but also too willing to accept the class structures created by capitalism. Now he decided that the AFL's approach to unionism—accepting the system and trying to secure workers a larger share of corporate profits—was the best way for black workers to move toward the standard of living that unionized white workers had attained.

Randolph began organizing an all-black union whose agenda resembled that of mainstream white craft unions: higher wages, job security, and collective bargaining. The Brotherhood of Sleeping Car Porters and Maids struggled against the Pullman company for a decade, winning partial victories in 1926 and 1929 and complete recognition in 1937. Despite considerable opposition and only after tire-less insistence on Randolph's part, the Brotherhood also became the first African-American union awarded a full charter by the American Federation of Labor. Its organizing battles and its grass-roots leadership would eventually provide the basis for a half-century of civil rights struggles in cities across the United States.

For most black Americans in the 1920s, however, unionization did not represent an option. The Harlem Renaissance was a distant phenomenon, not very impor-tant even to many Harlemites. What captured the imagination of the black masses was another movement rooted in Harlem, the Universal Negro Improvement Association (UNIA). The organization was inseparable from its founder, chief spokesman, and strategist, Marcus M. Garvey.

Garvey founded the UNIA in 1914 on his native West Indian island of Jamaica, at the time still a British colony. He attracted little support for his organization and brought his vision of a liberated Africa and a fully emancipated black population to the United States two years later. That vision and Garvey's expression of it drew heavily on the rhetoric surrounding World War I, which had been justified by the United States and its allies as a fight for "self-determination." Garvey compared his cause to that of the Irish revolutionaries fighting for independence and the Zionists struggling for a Jewish state in Palestine. His version called for the self-determina-tion of Africans across the globe—"Africa for the Africans."

"A race without authority and power is a race without respect," declared Garvey. Criticizing the NAACP's strategy of seeking justice through lawsuits and legisla-tion, he observed that "there is not justice, but strength." Blacks, therefore, had to compete. They had to establish independent nations in Africa, independent busi-nesses in the United States, and a framework of black institutions independent of white influence.

The UNIA would provide that framework. Its newspaper, the *Negro World*, attained a circulation of fifty thousand–sixty thousand in the mid-1920s. Among African-American newspapers, only the *Chicago Defender* reached a wider audi-ence. The UNIA established businesses, especially laundries and groceries, retail operations that could rely on a black clientele and employ UNIA members. Most visibly, Garvey founded the Black Star Line Steamship Company, funded by sales of stock to UNIA members. To buy shares was to invest in the race. Garvey promised profits, employment for black seamen, and transportation for African-American passengers traveling to Africa to lead that continent's struggle against European colonial domination.

At its height between 1923 and 1926 the UNIA counted more than seven hun-dred branches in thirty-eight states, in addition to a substantial body of support in the Caribbean and Central America. Some of these branches probably consisted of a handful of enthusiasts, or perhaps even a single household. Others, in large cities, numbered in the thousands. Perhaps most striking is the geographic diversity, ranging across country and city and from the Northeast to the Midwest, South, and

The charismatic Marcus Garvey promoted racial pride and economic self-sufficiency for blacks. In 1919 he founded the Black Star Line to provide black Americans with jobs, transportation, and profits.

Pacific coast. The organization claimed six million members, but 500,000 is probably a more realistic estimate. At least another half-million supporters never paid dues but counted themselves among Garvey's followers. The UNIA was easily the largest African-American mass movement the United States had ever seen.

The moment, however, was brief. The Black Star Line was a financial disaster, due in part to bad luck associated with calamitous weather on its initial freight run and in part to weak management. The company's bankruptcy provided ammunition to Garvey's enemies, a list that included nearly all of the established African-American leadership. To radicals like A. Philip Randolph and Cyril Briggs, Garvey had too much faith in capitalism. To the moderates in the NAACP he was too inflammatory. Respectable middle-class community leaders found his advice to look to Africa for salvation as foolish (actually, this was a minor part of the Garvey agenda, but one that has remained most visible in the public mind).

Editor Robert Abbott of the *Chicago Defender,* an unyielding opponent of racism but a firm believer in American institutions, hated Garvey so much that he banished mention of the UNIA from his newspaper. His readers learned absolutely nothing about the active Chicago chapter, even though it had nine thousand members. In 1922 Garvey confirmed his opponents' worst fears. He attended a meeting of the Ku Klux Klan and declared that the Klan was more honest about race in the United States than the NAACP and other black organizations. At Abbott's urging Garvey was indicted for fraud in 1923 in connection with the sale of shares in the Black Star Line. Most likely he was less guilty of fraud than of incompetence. Nevertheless, he was convicted and jailed until his deportation from the United States in 1927.

Garvey remained a hero to thousands of black Americans, especially small businesspeople and working-class men and women. Years later Malcolm X would recall accompanying his father to UNIA meetings during the 1930s, long after the movement's decline. In his autobiography, he recalled the dozen or so people packed into a living room and was struck by

> how differently they all acted, although they were the same people who jumped and shouted in church. But in these meetings both they and my father were more intense, more intelligent and down to earth. It made me feel the same way. . . . I remember how the meetings always closed with my father saying, several times, and the people chanting after him, "Up, you mighty race, you can accomplish what you will."

CHAPTER 8

From a Raw Deal to a New Deal?

1929–1945

Joe William Trotter Jr.

L ong before the stock market crash in October 1929, African Americans had experienced hard times. The "last hired and the first fired," African Americans entered the Great Depression earlier and more deeply than other racial and ethnic groups. Sociologists St. Clair Drake and Horace R. Cayton believed that the black community served as a "barometer sensitive to the approaching storm." Months before the stock market crash, the *Chicago Defender* warned that "Something is happening . . . and it should no longer go unnoticed. During the past three weeks hardly a day has ended that there has not been a report of another firm discharging its employees, many of whom have been faithful workers at these places for years."

The depression brought mass suffering to the country as a whole. National income dropped by nearly fifty percent, from $81 billion in 1929 to $40 billion in 1932; unemployment rose to an estimated twenty-five percent of the labor force; and nearly twenty million Americans turned to public and private relief agencies to prevent starvation and destitution. Still, African Americans suffered more than their white counterparts, received less from their government, and got what they called a "raw deal" rather than a "new deal."

The depression took its toll on virtually every facet of African American life. As unemployment rose, membership in churches, clubs, and fraternal orders dropped. Blacks frequently related the pain of this separation from friends and acquaintances. "I don't attend church as often as I used to. You know I am not fixed like I want to be—haven't got the clothes I need."

Blacks in the rural South faced the most devastating impact of the Great Depression. As cotton prices dropped from eighteen cents per pound to less than six cents by early 1933, an estimated two million black farmers faced hard times. The number of black sharecroppers dropped from nearly 392,000 in 1930 to under 300,000 as the depression spread. All categories of rural black labor—

The Great Depression forced growing numbers of white women to enter the work force, where they competed with black women for jobs. Here, blacks and whites work side by side at a cannery in North Carolina.

landowners, cash tenants, sharecroppers, and wage laborers—suffered from declining incomes. Mechanical devices had already reduced the number of workers needed for plowing, hoeing, and weeding, but planters now experimented with mechanical cotton pickers as well. As one black woman put it, many jobs had "gone to machines, gone to white people or gone out of style." Public and private relief efforts were virtually nonexistent in the rural South, forcing farm families to continue their trek to the city.

Despite declining opportunities to work in southern and northern cities, black migration continued during the depression years. The percentage of urban blacks rose from about forty-four percent in 1930 to nearly fifty percent during the depression years. The black population in northern cities increased by nearly twenty-five percent; the number of cities with black populations of over 100,000 increased from one in 1930 to eleven in 1935. Public social services played an increasing role in decisions to move. As the Swedish economist Gunnar Myrdal noted in his classic study of black life during the period, "It was much harder for Negroes who needed it to get relief in the South than in the North."

The increasing migration of blacks to cities intensified the poverty of established residents. Before the stock market crash of 1929, urban blacks had already faced the impact of increasing mechanization, declining demand for manufactured goods, and loss of employment to whites. The stock market crash further undercut the economic position of African Americans. By 1932, black urban unemployment reached well over fifty percent, more than twice the rate of whites. In northern and southern cities, black workers faced special difficulties trying to hold on to their jobs. In Pittsburgh, for example, some black workers were fired when they refused to give kickbacks to the foreman for being permitted to keep their jobs. At the same time, unemployed whites made increasing inroads on the so-called "Negro jobs," lower level positions that blacks had occupied during good times. Not only in factories but in street cleaning, garbage collection, and domestic service work, whites competed for the traditionally black jobs.

As the depression intensified, many white women entered the labor force for the first time. They competed with black women for jobs as maids, cooks, and housekeepers. In northern cities, unemployment and destitution forced many black women to participate in the notorious "slave market." Congregating on the sidewalks of major cities, these women offered their services to white women, who drove up in their cars seeking domestic help. Some of the employers were working-class women themselves and paid as little as five dollars weekly for full-time household workers. The work was difficult indeed. One young black woman, Millie Jones, offered a detailed description of her work for one family for five dollars a week.

> Each and every week, believe it or not, I had to wash every one of those windows [fifteen in a six-room apartment]. If that old hag found as much as the teeniest speck on any one of 'em, she'd make me do it over. I guess I would do anything rather than wash windows. On Mondays I washed and did as much of the ironing as I could. The rest waited over for Tuesday. There were two grown sons in the family and her husband. That meant that I would have at least twenty-one shirts to do every week. Yeah, and ten sheets and at least two blankets, besides. They all had to be done just so, too.

In urban factories and commercial laundries, black women also faced difficult times. In a New York laundry, black women worked fifty hours each week. According to one employee, "it was speed up, speed up, eating lunch on the fly." Women working in the starching department stood on their feet for ten hours each day, "sticking their hands into almost boiling starch." When the employees complained, the boss threatened to fire and replace them with workers from the large pool of unemployed women. But black women did not accept these conditions without a fight.

Racism and job competition helped to narrow the margin between bare survival and destitution. Evidence of racism abounded. In the South, white workers rallied around such slogans as, "No Jobs for Niggers Until Every White Man Has a Job" and "Niggers, back to the cotton fields—city jobs are for white folks." The most violent efforts to displace black workers occurred on southern railroads, where the white brotherhoods, as their unions were called, intimidated, attacked, and murdered black workers in order to take their jobs. By early 1933, nearly a dozen black firemen had lost their lives in various parts of the country. Although the Ku Klux Klan had declined by the mid-1920s, it now renewed attacks on African Americans.

The discriminatory policies of employers and labor unions also affected African Americans in northern cities. Employers maintained their views that African Americans were fit only for dirty, unpleasant, low paying, and heavy work. As blacks sought employment, employers again frequently claimed that, "We don't have a foundry in our plant and that's the kind of work Negroes are best suited for." In Milwaukee, one firm justified its exclusion of black workers in familial and paternalistic terms: "We just sort of work like a family here and to bring in Negro workers would cause confusion and cause white workers to feel that their jobs had lost in dignity if being done by Negroes." White workers reinforced and frequently demanded such policies. Twenty-four unions, ten of them affiliates of the American Federation of Labor (AFL), barred blacks completely and others practiced other forms of discrimination and exclusion. Thus, disproportionately large numbers of African Americans entered the bread lines, sold their belongings, and faced eviction from their homes.

It was a difficult time, but the Republican administration of Herbert Hoover did little to relieve the suffering. Hoover resisted proposals for aiding the nation's poor and destitute. Instead, he pursued a policy of indirect relief through the establishment of agencies like the Reconstruction Finance Corporation, which provided loans to relieve the credit problems of huge corporations like railroads, banks, and insurance companies. By "priming the pump" of big business, Hoover believed that federal aid to corporations would stimulate production, create new jobs, and increase consumer spending—that is, that wealth would "trickle down" to the rest of the economy and end the depression. Unfortunately, these policies provided little help to African Americans.

Despite their suffering under the Hoover administration, African Americans rallied to the slogan "who but Hoover" in the presidential election of 1932. Hoover had not only failed to advance effective policies for dealing with the depression; he had also offended African Americans in a variety of ways, including refusing to be photographed with black leaders. Still, he received about sixty-six percent of the black votes. Only in New York and Kansas City, Missouri, did the majority of blacks vote for Franklin Delano Roosevelt. The Republican party of Abraham Lincoln was still seen as the party of emancipation.

From the black vantage point Roosevelt looked little better than Hoover. As assistant secretary of the navy during World War I, he had supported the racial segregation of the armed forces. He had also adopted Warm Springs, Georgia, as his home and accepted the system of racial segregation in that state. Moreover, during its national convention, the Democratic party rejected an NAACP proposal for a civil rights plank, that called for an end to racial discrimination.

Unemployed blacks line up outside the State Employment Service in Memphis, Tennessee, in 1938. During the depression blacks received far less aid than their white counterparts.

Once in office, FDR did little to build confidence among African Americans. The new President depended on southern segregationists to pass and implement his "New Deal" programs. FDR saw the depression as an economic disaster, that required massive federal aid and planning. The President formulated his New Deal programs accordingly, giving close attention to the needs of big business, agriculture, and labor. Roosevelt opposed federal antilynching legislation, prevented black delegations from visiting the White House, and refused to make civil rights and racial equity a priority. FDR repeatedly justified his actions on the grounds that he needed Southern white support for his economic relief and recovery programs. In a conversation with an NAACP official, he confided that, "If I come out for the antilynching bill now, they will block every bill I ask Congress to pass to keep America from collapsing. I just can't take that risk."

African-American rights were placed on hold. Each piece of New Deal legislation failed to safeguard African Americans against racial discrimination. The National Recovery Administration (NRA), Agricultural Adjustment Administration (AAA), the Works Progress [later Projects] Administration (WPA), the Tennessee Valley Authority (TVA), the Civilian Conservation Corps (CCC), and the Federal Energy Relief Administration (FERA), to name only a few, all left blacks vulnerable to discriminatory employers, agency officials, and local whites. Despite the initiation of

New Deal relief measures, African Americans repeatedly complained of their inability to secure relief. When a father of six lost his job and sought relief in the city of Pittsburgh, relief officials denied his request. Only when he deserted his family, his wife reported, did she and the children receive aid. According to the woman's testimony: "He told me once that if he wasn't living at home the welfare people would help me and the kids, and maybe he just went away on that account." Southern state and local officials disregarded federal guidelines and paid African-American relief recipients less than their white counterparts. In Atlanta, blacks on relief received an average of $19.29 per month compared to $32.66 for whites. In Jacksonville, Florida, about five thousand whites received forty-five percent of the relief funds, while the fifteen thousand blacks on relief received the remaining fifty-five percent. Southern politicians defended the practice, arguing that the low living standard of blacks enabled them to live on less than whites.

The local Federal Emergency Relief Administration was not alone in discriminating against blacks. The Agricultural Adjustment Act paid farmers to withdraw cotton land from production, create a shortage, and drive up the price of cotton on the market. Set up to administer the law at the local level, AAA county committees excluded African Americans from participation. By depriving African Americans of representation white landowners were able to institute policies that drove black landowners into the ranks of sharecroppers and forced growing numbers of sharecroppers off the land altogether. During its first year, for example, the AAA encouraged farmers to plow under cotton that was already planted. Land owners took government checks, plowed up cotton, and denied tenants a share of the government income.

At the same time that planters removed increasing acres of land from cultivation, the largest landowners turned increasingly to scientific and mechanized farming. Tractors and cotton-picking machines rendered black labor more and more dispensable. Although their numbers dwindled, the remaining black sharecroppers earned less than their white counterparts. White sharecroppers received a mean net income of $417 per year compared to only $295 for blacks. Whites receiving hourly wages made $232 per year, compared to only $175 for blacks.

Lower earnings aggravated other forms of racial inequality. In his survey of 612 black farm families in Macon County, Alabama, the sociologist Charles S. Johnson found that more than half lived in one- and two-room weatherworn shacks. When asked if her house leaked when it rained, a black woman said, "No, it don't leak in here, it just rains in here and leaks outdoors." Another tenant complained that the landlord refused to provide lumber for repairs: "All he's give us . . . is a few planks. . . . It's nothin doin'. We just living outdoors." Food was also difficult for farm families to come by. Black tenants had good reasons to view these early years of the New Deal with skepticism.

The National Recovery Act also discriminated against black workers. Partly by exempting domestic service and unskilled laborers from its provisions, the NRA removed most blacks from its minimum wage and participatory requirements. Since over sixty percent of African Americans worked in these sectors, the measure had little meaning for most blacks, especially women. Nonetheless, other blacks who held on to their precarious footing in the industrial labor force, despite hard times, faced new pressures from employers and white workers. In 1934, the Milwaukee, Wisconsin, Urban League reported a strike at the Wehr Steel Foundry. The chief aim of the strike, the League reported, was the "dismissal of Negroes from the plant." When black workers decided to cross the picket line, police joined strikers in attacks on them. The Milwaukee Urban League reported that: "The first few days of the strike brought considerable violence between the Negroes who attempted to continue on the jobs and the white pickets. . . . Police had been summoned [by management] to protect those who cared to enter but in turn joined with the strikers in overturning an automobile filled with Negro workers."

Even on construction projects for black institutions, white workers rallied to bar African American workers. In St. Louis, for example, when the General Tile Company hired a black tile setter on the $2 million Homer Phillips Hospital for blacks, all the white AFL union men quit and delayed construction for two months. In Long Island and Manhattan, the Brotherhood of Electrical Workers and Building Service Employees' Union pursued similar practices. When African Americans were brought under the provisions of the law in southern textile firms, employers reclassified African American jobs, in order to remove them from the protection of the NRA codes. Some firms simply argued that blacks were less efficient than whites and thus deserved low wages. In Atlanta, for example, the Scripto Manufacturing company told black workers that, "This company does not base wages on color but entirely on efficiency. Our records show that the efficiency of colored help is only fifty percent of that of white help in similar plants."

Where the codes did upgrade the pay of black workers, many firms replaced their African American workforces with white employees. It is no wonder that blacks frequently called the NRA, the "Negro Run Around," "Negroes Ruined Again", and "Negro Rarely Allowed." In short, NRA legislation (particularly section 7a, which gave workers the right to collective bargaining with employers) enabled labor unions to strengthen their hand at the expense of blacks in the North and South. As late as 1935, organized white labor also blocked the inclusion of a non-discrimination clause in the National Labor Relations Act, sponsored by Senator Robert Wagner of New York. The new Wagner law gave workers and their unions extended protection in their effort to bargain collectively with management.

African Americans not only faced discrimination in industrial, agricultural, and relief programs but confronted racial bias in federal housing, social security, and regional planning and youth programs as well. The Federal Housing Administration refused to guarantee mortgages (homeloans) in racially integrated neighborhoods; the Social Security Act excluded farm laborers and domestic service employees; and the TVA and CCC developed along segregationist and unequal lines.

Established in 1933, the Tennessee Valley Authority was promoted by the Roosevelt administration as a model of social planning to improve the lives of millions of Americans in seven states in the Tennessee River Valley. It was hoped that the TVA would stimulate economic development and reduce poverty by establishing a massive program of rural electrification at dramatically reduced rates. African Americans comprised eleven percent of the two million residents of the region, and the project promised "nondiscrimination" in its official design.

African Americans took heart at the promise of benefits from TVA. Yet, the project soon accepted the racial status quo for black workers and their families in the valley. The agency barred blacks from skilled and managerial positions, excluded them from vocational training programs; and reinforced patterns of segregation in housing. When queried about the exclusion of blacks from its model town of Norris, Tennessee, TVA chairman Arthur Morgan referred to a long "lilly white" waiting list and suggested that it was unlikely that blacks would be able to move to Norris. Even more important, African Americans received inadequate benefits from the reduced rates for electrical power for their homes. In an essay on the "Plight of the Negro in the Tennessee Valley," the NAACP magazine *The Crisis* reported that: "For Negroes the introduction of cheaper electric rates into Lee County as result of the TVA power policy has meant nothing. Landlords, whether of Negro slum dwellers in Tupelo or of Negro tenant farmers in the rural section of the county, have not found it to their advantage to wire their Negro tenants' homes at the cost of $15 to $25, when already they are squeezing all the rent possible from these tenants."

In the face of blatant forms of discrimination during the early New Deal, African Americans found little to praise in the government's relief efforts. They were acutely aware that they suffered disproportionately from unemployment, but faced the greatest discrimination and received the least benefits from government relief, work, housing, and social security programs. All Americans gained increasing assistance from the federal government, but such assistance would only slowly reach African Americans and help to reverse the impact of hard times on their families and communities. By the mid-1930s, however, a variety of new forces would gradually transform the "raw deal" into a "new deal."

A New Deal, 1935–1939

Between the stock market crash of 1929 and the early years of the New Deal, the condition of African Americans moved from bad to worse. Neither the Hoover administration nor the first efforts of the Democratic regime of Franklin Roosevelt did much to lessen the suffering of African Americans. By 1935, however, a variety of forces helped to transform the relationship between blacks and the New Deal. Changes in American attitudes toward race and class, the emergence of new interracial alliances, and the growing political mobilization of African Americans themselves all put pressure on the federal government to address the needs of African Americans. In a nationwide radio broadcast, President Franklin D. Roosevelt symbolized the shift. In a speech before a conference of the Churches of Christ in America, he condemned lynching as murder: "Lynch law is murder, a deliberate and definite disobedience of the high command, 'Thou shalt not kill.' We do not excuse those in high places or low who condone lynch law." Following the President's pronouncement, the NAACP's *Crisis* magazine exclaimed that FDR was the only president to declare "frankly that lynching is murder. We all knew it, but it is unusual to have a president of the United States admit it. These things give us hope."

As the federal government increasingly affirmed its responsibility for the social welfare of all Americans, it helped to change the context of the African-American struggle for social justice. By 1939, African Americans had gradually gained a larger share of New Deal social programs and improved their economic situation. African-American income from New Deal work and relief programs—Public Works Administration, Works Progress Administration, and Civilian Conservation Corps—now nearly equaled their income from employment in agriculture and domestic service. On CCC projects, African Americans increased their percentage from less than six percent in 1935 to eleven percent in 1939. African Americans also occupied about one-third of all low income PWA housing units, obtained a rising share of Federal Farm Security Loans, and access to a variety of new WPA educational and cultural programs. Because the government spent more money on education, including the building of new facilities, black illiteracy dropped ten percent during the 1930s. The number of African Americans on relief and the amount of money available to them rose steadily. African Americans increasingly hailed such New Deal social programs as "a godsend." Some even suggested that God "will lead me" but relief "will feed me."

The changing relationship between blacks and the New Deal was not merely a matter of the government's shifting attitude toward the social welfare of all Americans. The Roosevelt administration also responded to the growing importance of the black vote on national elections, the emergence of an interracial alliance of black and white New Dealers and especially a rising core of black federal appointees. Roosevelt acted to the growing importance of the black vote by appointing increasing numbers of African Americans to federal posts. By the mid-1930s, some forty-five blacks had received appointments in various New Deal agencies and cabinet departments. The "Black Cabinet," as these black advisers were called, included Robert L. Vann, editor of the *Pittsburgh Courier,* in the office of the Attorney General; William H. Hastie, a civil rights attorney, in the Department of the Interior; Robert C. Weaver, an economist, also in the Interior Department; Lawrence A. Oxley, a social worker, in the Department of Labor; Edgar Brown, president of the United Government Employees, in the Civilian Conservation Corps; and Mary McLeod Bethune, founder of Bethune-Cookman

President Franklin Roosevelt responded to the growing importance of the black vote in national elections by appointing increasing numbers of blacks to federal posts. Members of the "Black Cabinet," as these appointees came to be called, gathered for a photograph in 1938.

College, head of the Negro Division of the National Youth Administration. The "Black Cabinet" enabled African Americans to improve their position in a variety of New Deal programs.

The first lady, Eleanor Roosevelt, played a key role in helping these black New Dealers improve the federal response to the needs of African Americans. Although Mrs. Roosevelt had little contact with African Americans before early 1933, she soon befriended Walter White of the NAACP and Mary McLeod Bethune. Through her frequent interactions with black leaders Eleanor Roosevelt gradually increased her support of civil rights issues. Following the election of 1936, for example, she endorsed legislation designed to abolish the poll tax, make lynching a federal offense, and increase aid to black institutions, particularly schools. Historians credit Mrs. Roosevelt with helping to push FDR's position on civil rights from one of caution and aloofness to one of significant support. FDR eventually allowed himself to be photographed with black leaders, conferred with civil rights delegations at the White House, and sent greetings to African American organizations.

As the White House seemed to escalate its support for racial justice, other New Dealers took heart and advanced the cause of African Americans. The policies of Harold Ickes, Secretary of Interior and administrator of the PWA; Harry Hopkins, head of the WPA; and a few others exemplified the growing support that African Americans received in some New Deal agencies. Before taking his post as Secretary of the Interior, Ickes had served as president of the Chicago chapter of the NAACP. Upon assuming his duties, he ended segregation in the department's rest rooms and cafeteria. Although local whites often ignored his policies, Ickes advocated the employment of skilled and unskilled black laborers on PWA construction projects. The secretary insisted that all PWA contractors agree to hire blacks in proportion to their percentage in the 1930 occupational census.

Under the leadership of Harry Hopkins, the WPA established policies making it illegal for any relief official to discriminate "on account of race, creed, or color." FDR had strengthened his hand, by issuing Executive Order 7046, which mandated that the WPA would assign persons "qualified by training and experience" to work projects without discrimination "on any grounds whatsoever."

Under Hopkins's leadership, the WPA also promoted black adult education, hired unemployed black professionals, and stimulated the arts within the black community. The WPA Education program employed over 5,000 blacks as leaders and supervisors, taught nearly 250,000 blacks to read and write, and trained many for skilled jobs. The Federal Music Project staged concerts involving the works of black composers; the Federal Art Project employed hundreds of black artists; and, under the direction of Hallie Flanagan, the Federal Theater Project (FTP) established an African American unit.

Supplementing the artistic work of the FTP was the Federal Writers Project. Young writers and scholars like St. Clair Drake, Horace R. Cayton, Richard Wright, and Ralph Ellison gained opportunities and early training on the Federal Writers Project. Both the FWP and FTP developed activities designed to increase interracial understanding, which provoked an investigation by the U.S. House of Representatives Un-American Activities Committee (HUAC). The HUAC helped to undercut the growth of their programs by charging them with "conspiracy and subversion" of American ideas, beliefs, and institutions.

Although most southern New Dealers resisted equal treatment for blacks, others supported efforts to improve the status of African Americans. Born in Alabama, Aubrey Willis Williams, served as Deputy Works Progress Administrator and head of the National Youth Administration (NYA). At the NYA, Williams resisted the establishment of racial differentials in wages paid to blacks and whites. He repeatedly stated the belief that African American youth should be prepared for jobs that would move them beyond the usual categories of maid and janitor. Will Alexander, director of the Farm Security Administration (FSA), was another Southern white who befriended African Americans during the period. Under his leadership, the FSA appointed a larger percentage of black supervisors than any other agency and gradually improved benefits for African Americans.

There were other reasons why federal policies toward blacks began to change for the better. Across the land, American attitudes toward race and class had begun to change. This was reflected in the emergence of new intellectual, cultural, and political currents. Increasing numbers of Americans criticized industrial elites—corporate executives, bankers, and Wall Street financiers—for eliminating their jobs and placing them in bread lines. Working Americans launched mass movements for

FARM SECURITY ADMINISTRATION AIDS THE NEGRO FARMER

THE NEGRO FARMER'S PROBLEM IS THE SOUTHERN FARMER'S PROBLEM

95 PERCENT OF NEGRO FARMERS ARE IN THE SOUTH. 47 PERCENT OF THESE ARE SHARECROPPERS.

32 PERCENT ARE TENANTS.

ONLY 21 PERCENT ARE OWNERS.

Toward

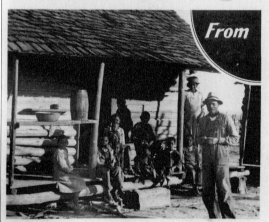

From

FARM SECURITY HELPS THROUGH ...

1. REHABILITATION LOANS FOR EQUIPMENT, LIVESTOCK, SEED, FERTILIZER.

2. TENANT PURCHASE LOANS TO MAKE OWNERS OUT OF CROPPERS AND TENANTS.

3. DEBT ADJUSTMENT TO REDUCE INTEREST, RE-SCALE PAYMENTS TO THE FARMER'S CAPACITY.

4. CO-OPERATIVE COMMUNITIES TO ENABLE SMALL FARMERS TO COMPETE WITH LARGE, MECHANIZED FARMS.

The Farm Security Administration highlights its efforts to aid black farmers in this 1939 poster. The FSA sought to increase the number of black farmers who owned the land they worked.

greater government support of their interests during the 1930s. This increased activism could be seen in the rise of the Communist party, the resurgence of organized labor, and increasing efforts to attract African Americans to the ranks of both of these types of organizations.

An unpopular minority, the Communist party was especially eager to attract black members. Although the party often used the race issue to foster its own specific ideological attacks on capitalist institutions, such as the two-party system, it nonetheless played a key role in publicizing racial injustice and placing civil rights before the nation.

Few blacks joined the Communist party, but its activities on behalf of African Americans soon got their attention. The party's most famous campaigns centered on efforts to free one of its own members, the black Communist, Angelo Henderson, from a Georgia chain gang and the attempt to win aquittal on rape charges for nine blacks held in Scottsboro, Alabama, known as the Scottsboro Boys.

The case of the Scottsboro Boys was perhaps the most infamous instance of racial injustice in the courts of the 1930s. During the depression years, blacks and whites routinely "hoboed" the nation's freight trains, traveling from place to place looking for work and the means to survive. In March 1931, a group of black and white youths boarded a freight train, southbound from Chattanooga, Tennessee, to Alabama. A fight eventually broke out and the blacks forced the whites off the train.

The white youths reported the incident to local authorities who stopped the train near Scottsboro, Alabama. Nine young black men and two white women were removed from the train by the local sheriff. Fearing arrest, the young women accused the black youths of rape at knife point. Although the black defendants pleaded "not guilty," the court failed to appoint proper legal representation for the young men. An all-white jury ignored the different versions of events on the train given in the testimony of the two women and found the defendants guilty of rape and the court sentenced all but the youngest to death in the electric chair.

The Communist party soon took up the case. The party's Central Committee issued a statement describing the sentence as a "legal lynching," and within a few days, launched a national and international crusade to save the young men. As protest rallies emerged in major cities across the nation, non-Communist organizations like the NAACP soon joined communists in demanding justice. At the same time, the party's International Labor Defense pressed the legal case through the Alabama Supreme Court, which upheld the convictions. On two separate occasions the party carried the case forward to the U. S. Supreme Court, which overturned the convictions and ordered retrials, which in both cases, *Powell* v. *Alabama* (1932), and *Norris* v. *Alabama* (1935), led not to release but to new death sentences. However, the execution dates kept being posponed and eventually all defendants were cleared of the charges brought against them. After having spent more than fifteen years in jail for a crime he did not commit, the last defendant was released after World War II.

The Communist party not only staged demonstrations and legal actions to free blacks like Herndon and the Scottsboro boys, it also carried out day to day activities designed to improve the economic status of African Americans. The party organized hunger marches, unemployed councils, farm labor unions, and rent strikes to aid unemployed and destitute workers. In Chicago, when families received eviction notices, mothers would sometimes shout to the children, "Run quick find the Reds!" On one occasion, when Communists attempted to prevent the eviction of a black family in Chicago, police shot and killed three African Americans. The communist party responded by distributing nearly five thousand leaflets, urging black and white workers to unite and demand justice for the deceased.

During the 1930s the Socialist party also campaigned against racial injustice. In 1929, the party established the United Colored Socialists of America. Socialist party head Norman Thomas appointed a special black organizer for the South and supported a resolution condemning racial discrimination by trade unions. By 1933 the Socialist party endorsed federal antilynching and anti-poll tax legislation; the party also organized sharecroppers unions, and elevated blacks to leadership positions.

Launched in 1934, the Southern Tenant Farmers Union (STFU) represented the Socialist pary's strongest effort to organize workers across racial lines. Founded near the town of Tyronza, Arkansas, the STFU resolved to organize black and white tenant farmers in the same union. Under the leadership of H. L. Mitchell, a white associate of Norman Thomas, and two ministers, Howard Lester and Claude Williams, the organization advocated both economic justice for all sharecroppers and racial justice for African Americans. A white organizer for the STFU emphasized the futility of separate organizations and appealed to what he called "belly hunger" to help erase the color line among farmers. "If we organize only a Union of Negro sharecroppers then the Negroes will be evicted and white sharecroppers from the hill country or the unemployed in Memphis will take their places. If on the other hand we organize only a Union of white sharecroppers then the white men will be evicted and Negro sharecroppers from Mississippi and the unemployed in Memphis will take their places." Although the organization failed to bring landowners to the bargaining table, it demonstrated how the American left pushed the Roosevelt administration to create a "new deal."

The economic slump of the 1930s and the Roosevelt administration's liberalized labor laws energized the organized labor movement. However, the movement split over the issue of whether to organize workers along broad industrial lines or on a narrow, craft-by-craft basis. Impatient with the exclusionary policies of the American Federation of Labor (AFL), the Committee for Industrial Organization broke from the AFL at the 1935 convention. Under the leadership of John L. Lewis, head of the United Mine Workers of America (UMW), the CIO (renamed the Congress of Industrial Organizations in 1938) embarked upon an aggressive organizing drive. This change was especially significant for blacks because they were disporoportionately represented in mass production industries.

Learning from its failure to organize southern black miners in the coal strikes of 1927, the UMW made a firm commitment to organize black and white workers. Following the "UMW formula," the CIO soon launched the Steel Workers Organizing Committee (SWOC); the Packinghouse Workers Organizing Committee (PWOC), and the United Automobile Workers (UAW). In each case, the union appealed to black organizations like the NAACP and the National Urban League; employed black organizers, placed African Americans in key union offices; and advocated an end to racially biased pay scales. Under the prodding of black labor leaders like A. Philip Randolph, competition from the emerging CIO, and the growing influence of blacks in the New Deal political coalition, the AFL also modified its position on organizing black workers. AFL president William Green eventually supported the move to free Angelo Herndon and the Scottsboro Boys, to obtain federal antilynching legislation, and to abolitish poll taxes that disfranchised black voters. By 1939, African Americans had moved into the meeting rooms of the "house of labor."

Reinforcing the lowering of racial barriers in the labor movement were new intellectual and cultural perspectives on race in American society. Scholars, artists, and the popular media gradually changed their views on race. Social scientists rejected the notion of the inborn inferiority of races and developed a new consensus. Most intellectuals and social scientists agreed that African Americans were not inferior to whites, that racism injured its victims both psychologically and socially, and that racism itself was a mental illness that damaged the health of the individual and the nation as a whole. These views gained currency in the ongoing research of Columbia University anthropologist Franz Boas, his students, and associates, who questioned the long-held assumption that racial and ethnic group differences were inherited through the genes. Boas and his associates challenged the racists to prove that African Americans suffered a lower plane of living because they were intellectually inferior to their white counterparts. In short, he forced the social scientific community, which prided itself on attending to the "facts," to recognize that it had little evidence to support some of its most cherished theories. As one scholar put it, "We do not yet know scientifically what the relative intellectual ability of the various races is. Some different tests, equally valid, might give the Negro a higher score that the white. Until we do know, probably the best thing is to *act* as if all races had equivalent mental ability."

The intellectual assault on racism reached its high point in 1937 when the Carnegie Corporation invited the Swedish economist Gunnar Myrdal to the United States to head "a comprehensive study of the Negro." The Myrdal study resulted in the publication of the monumental *An American Dilemma: The Negro Problem and Modern Democracy* (1944). Myrdal brought together numerous scholars to work on different aspects of race relations. All defined the "Negro problem" as a problem of white racism, immorality, and inequality. *An American Dilemma* concluded that "The American Negro problem is in the heart of the [white] American. It is there that the interracial tension has its focus. It is there that the decisive struggle goes on. This is the central viewpoint of this treatise. Though our study includes economic, social, and political race relations, at bottom our problem is the moral dilemma of the American—the conflict between his moral valuations on various levels of consciousness and generality."

Although legal change came only slowly, the U. S. Supreme Court also issued rulings that weakened the hold of racism in American society. As early as 1935, legal opinions on race started to change, Donald Murray, a black graduate of Amherst College in Massachusetts, applied for admission to the University of Maryland law school. When the school denied him admission based upon his race, he took the case to court and challenged racial discrimination in graduate education. Like most southern states, Maryland set up a tuition grant program that "assisted" blacks who sought graduate study and professional training by steering them elsewhere. But the Maryland Court of Appeals ordered the University of Maryland to set up a separate law school for blacks or admit them to the white one. Rather than contesting the court's decision, university officials quietly admitted blacks to the law school. In the case of *Missouri ex rel. Gaines* v. *Canada* (1938), the U.S. Supreme Court reinforced the Maryland precedent by ruling that law schools in the various states had to admit blacks or establish separate law schools.

The courts reinforced these decisions with others that slowly began to help blacks achieve full protection under the law. On two occasions (1932, 1935), the U. S. Supreme Court over-ruled the Alabama Supreme Court in the Scottsboro Case and insisted on due process of law for black defendants. In the case of *Hale* v. *Kentucky* (1938), the court noted the systematic exclusion of blacks from jury service and overturned the conviction of a black man accused of murder. Over the next three years, the U. S. Supreme Court also strengthened the economic position of African Americans. It upheld the right of African Americans to boycott businesses that discriminated in their employment practices; struck down a Georgia peonage law that permitted the virtual enslavement of blacks as sharecroppers, and upheld the elimination of unequal salaries black and white teachers in Norfolk, Virginia. In short, by 1939, the court slowly undermined the historic *Plessy* v. *Ferguson* decision of 1896, that permitted a "separate but equal" society for blacks and whites.

Despite shifting conceptions of race and the New Deal's growing response to the needs of blacks, by 1939 poverty, unemployment, and racial discrimination continued to affect the African American community. Even the most egalitarian programs experienced a huge gap in policy and practice. The Farm Securities Administration, which secured homeloans for farm families, for example, operated with limited funds and used a tought credit rating system that disqualified most

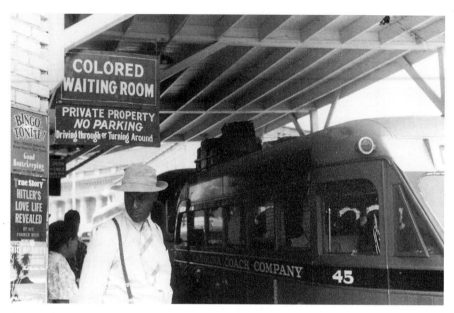

Despite the many opportunities offered to blacks by the New Deal, this sign for a "colored waiting room" at a bus station in Durham, North Carolina, attests to the racial discrimination that was still a part of daily life for the majority of blacks.

black tenants and sharecroppers from qualifiying for loans. Low-income federal housing programs reinforced the racial segregation of urban communities, adding federal policy to the ongoing historical forces—discriminatory real estate agents, restrictive covenants (regulations in many suburban neighborhoods that required resale of properties only to whites), and white neighborhood opposition—in the rise and expansion of the black ghetto.

The Works Progress Administration established regulations ending racial discrimination in its programs, but southern whites continued to evade the rules and made it more difficult for blacks than whites to gain adequate public works jobs and relief. Black women faced special forms of discrimination on WPA projects in the South. They were often forced to perform "men's jobs" at a time that white women received jobs defined as "clean" or "easy." In a South Carolina town, a local physician reported that, "The Beautification project appears to be 'For Negro Women Only.' This project is a type of work that should be assigned to men. Women are worked in 'gangs' in connection with the City's dump pile, incinerator and ditch piles. Illnesses traced to such exposure as these women must face do not entitle them to medical aid at the expense of the WPA."

By the late 1930s, as whites returned to full-time employment in private industry in growing numbers, most blacks continued to depend on public service and relief programs. Despite the various interracial alliances and growing sensitivity to the destructive impact of class and racial inequality, white Americans continued to insist that their needs be met first. While the CIO helped to organize blacks who were fortunate enough to maintain their jobs during the depression years, as the country lifted itself out of the depression it did little to promote the equitable return of employment of black and white wokers in equal numbers. For their part, although the Socialists and Communists helped to change attitudes toward inter-racial cooperation, the benefits of these efforts remained largely symbolic rather than material. Blacks continued to suffer racial injustice. African Americans, in short, would have to attend to their own interests, unite, and wage an even stronger offensive against the barriers of racial and class inequality.

Family, Community, and Politics, 1933–1939

A variety of factors shaped the experiences of African Americans during the Great Depression. The impact of economic hard times, the emergence of New Deal social programs, and changing perspectives on race and class helped to define the black experience. Despite widespread deprivation and suffering, African Americans de-veloped a variety of strategies for coping with the depression on their own. They deepened their connections with family, friends, and the African American com-munity. At the same time, they strengthened their links with organized labor and broadened their participation in the political process, particularly the New Deal coalition of the democratic party. As early as 1932, Robert Vann, editor of the *Pittsburgh Courier* had urged African Americans to abandon the party of Lincoln. "My friends, go turn Lincoln's picture to the wall. That debt has been paid in full."

As the depression took its toll on their lives, African Americans developed a variety of strategies for making ends meet. For many black women the depression was an old experience with a new name. As black men lost jobs in increasing num-bers, African-American women helped keep their families in tact by relying on black kin and friendship networks.

African-American families took in boarders, cared for each other's children, and creatively manipulated their resources. In rural areas, they maintained gardens, canned fruits and vegetables, fished, hunted, and gathered wild nuts and berries. And blacks adapted these rural responses to the realities of life in cities. In small urban spaces, for example, some continued to maintain gardens to supply certain southern staples, particularly collard greens, cabbage, potatoes, and tomatoes. Under the impact of the depression, such activities became even more important.

Since the threat of eviction weighed so heavily on the minds of urban blacks, the "rent party" represented a significant source of income. Sometimes described as "chittlin's struts," these parties had deep roots in the rural south. "Down home" food—chittlins, corn bread, collard greens, hogmaws, pig feet, and so on—was on the menu. Sponsors charged a small admission fee and sometimes offered printed or handwritten tickets.

A key component in the survival of urban blacks during the 1930s, the rent par-ties also served as a training ground for the next generation of black blues artists—

the blues men who followed in the wake of such classical blues recording artists as Bessie Smith, LeRoy Carr, Jimmy Yancey, Cripple Clarence Lofton, Big Maceo Merriweather, Sonny Boy Williamson, and Big Bill Broonzy among others moved to the fore with lyrics familiar to the house parties.

> How Long, how long has that evening train been gone
> How long, how long, baby, how long?
> Standing at the station, watch my baby leaving town
> Feeling disgusted, nowhere could she be found.
> How long, how long, baby, how long?

Such parties became even more lucrative when sponsors added gambling and liquor to food, music, and dancing. The "policy" or numbers game was also an adaptation to poverty that African American brought to the city and used to help weather the storm during the depression years the game had its roots in the mid-nineteenth century, but it gained increasing popularity among the boor because it allowed bets as low as a penny. On the South Side of Chicago, one black resident tried to imagine a world without policy. It was so important to Chicago's black community that without it he believed, "seven thousand people would be unemployed and business in general would be crippled, especially taverns and even groceries, shoestores, and many other business enterprises who depend on the buying power of the South Side."

The church provided another arena in which African Americans sought to make ends meet. Established Baptist, Methodist, and Holiness (Church of God in Christ) churches struggled to assist their parishioners to survive hard times. New religious movements also increased their following, partly as a result of their success in feeding their parishioners. For example, the Peace Mission of Father Divine (George Baker) whose efforts on behalf of the unemployed started during the 1920s, expanded dramatically during the depression. In 1932, he moved the mission from New Jersey to Harlem and gained credit for feeding the masses and offering hope in a time of widespread despair.

At the same time, Bishop Charles Emmanuel Grace, known as "Daddy Grace," established the United House of Prayer of All People with headquarters in Washington, D.C. The organization spread to more than twenty cities and provided thousands of people respite from hard times.

Black religious services featured music that sometimes resembled the music of the "rent party." It was in 1932 that the Gospel pioneer Thomas Dorsey broke from his growing reputation as a blues pianist and dedicated himself to Gospel song writing, which led to his most popular tune, "Precious Lord." Dorsey's swinging, rocking, and blueslike melodies eventually caught on and stirred the entire world. Over and over again, whether in religious or secular settings, black children of the depression recalled how their families struggled, to place food on the table and clothing on their backs.

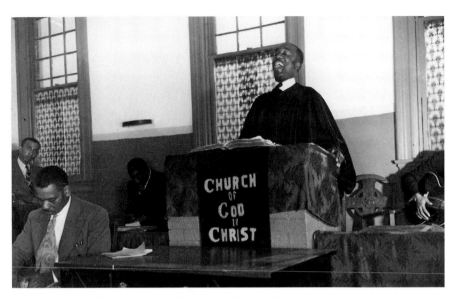

The pastor of the Church of God in Christ in Washington, D.C., preaches during a service in 1942. Black churches also featured music that mirrored the growing influence of urban life.

In order to improve the circumstances of their families and communities, African Americans also moved increasingly toward the labor movement, which had dramatically expanded under the impact of New Deal legislation. The new CIO increasingly displaced the older, more racially restrictive AFL. Under these new conditions, African Americans took the initiative to expand their place within labor's ranks. In Milwaukee, for example, LeRoy Johnson, a black butcher and packinghouse worker, became a major figure in the organization of the local United Packinghouse Union. Described by an associate as an "aggressive sort of guy and quite articulate," Johnson helped to make the CIO campaign in the city a success.

Perhaps more than any other single figure during the 1930s, however, A. Philip Randolph epitomized the persistent effort of black workers to organize in their own interest. During that decade, when new federal legislation (the Railway Labor Act of 1934) recognized the rights of workers to organize, Randolph and the Brotherhood of Sleeping Car Porters and Maids (BSCP)—which he had helped form in 1925—increased their organizing drive among black porters. Randolph's rhetoric and actions inspired the rank and file during the hard days of the depression. At one convention, he exclaimed, "The lesson that Pullman porters in particular and Negroes in general must learn is that salvation must and can only come from within."

Black pullman porters rallied to the BSCP, which, by 1933, claimed to represent some 35,000 members. Two years later the BSCP defeated a Pullman company union and gained the right to represent porters in negotiations with management, which, in 1937, signed a contract with the union. In the meantime, the AFL had grudgingly approved a full international charter for the brotherhood, placing it upon an equal footing with other member unions. The BSCP victory had extraordinary significance: It not only helped to make blacks more union conscious, but increased their influence on national labor policy, and the larger civil rights struggle.

As black workers increased their organizing activities, the major civil rights organizations also moved toward a sharper focus on the economic plight of African Americans. In 1933, the NAACP, the Urban League, and other interracial organizations formed the Joint Committee on National Recovery (JCNR). Although underfunded and illstaffed, the JCNR lobbied in Washington, D.C. on behalf of blacks and helped to publicize the plight of African Americans in the relief and recovery programs. The Urban League also formed Emergency Advisory Councils and Negro workers councils in major cities across the country and played a major role in promoting closer ties between blacks and organized labor. Although the League had earlier supported black strikebreaking activities and emphasized amicable relations with employers, it now urged black workers to organize and "get into somebody's union and stay there." For its part, the NAACP formed a Committee on Economic Problems Affecting the Negro; invited representatives of the CIO to serve on its board; and worked with organized labor to gain housing, wages, hours, and Social Security benefits for black workers.

The major civil rights organizations also supported the "Don't Buy Where You Can't Work" campaign. Aimed at white merchants who served the African American community but refused to employ blacks, "Don't Buy Where You Can't Work" galvanized the black urban community. In New York, Chicago, Washington D.C., and other cities, blacks boycotted stores that refused to hire African Americans, or hired them in only as low-paying domestic and common laborers.

New York launched its "Don't Buy Where You Can't Work" campaign under the leadership of Reverend John H. Johnson, of St. Martin's Protestant Episcopal Church. When white Harlem store owners refused to negotiate, Johnson and his supporters formed the Citizens League for Fair Play, which set up picket lines around Blumstein's Department Store, took pictures of blacks who crossed the line, and published photos in the black newspaper, the *New York Age*. After six weeks, the store gave in and hired black clerical and professional staff. As a result of such actions, New York blacks obtained the nation's first black affirmative action plan—a pattern of hiring that gave preference to previously excluded groups. In 1938, the New York Uptown Chamber of Commerce negotiated with the Greater New York Coordinating Committee for Employment and agreed to grant African Americans one-third of all retail executive, clerical, and sales jobs. The businesses would not fire whites to make room for blacks, but agreed to give blacks preference in all new openings.

Although African Americans expressed their resentment toward descrimination in formally organized and peaceful group actions, they sometimes despaired and adopted violent responses. On March 25, 1935, a race riot broke out in Harlem, when a rumor spread that a black youth had been brutally beaten and nearly killed by the police. Flyers soon appeared: "Child Brutally Beaten—near death." "One Hour Ago Negro Boy Was Brutally Beaten," "The Boy Is Near Death." Although the youth in question had been released unharmed, outrage had already spread and African Americans smashed buildings and looted stores, in a night of violence that resulted in at least one death, more than fifty injuries, and thousands of dollars worth of property damage.

In the volatile climate of the 1930s, some blacks gravitated toward the Communist and Socialist parties. They perceived radicalism as the most appropriate response to the deepening plight of African Americans. In 1931, aided by the Communist Party, blacks in rural Alabama founded the Alabama Sharecroppers Union. The organization developed an underground network of communications that enabled them to maintain secrecy. Meetings took place in black churches, where their plans were disguised as religious undertakings. The union's membership increased to an estimated three thousand in 1934. Its efforts soon attracted the attention of local authorities and violence broke out, when law officers tried to confiscate the livestock of union members, who allegedly owed money to landowners. In 1932, Ned Cobb (referred to as Nate Shaw in the published oral history of his life) joined the sharecroppers union and fought the system that oppressed him. As he recalled, he had to act because he had labored "under many rulins, just like the other Negro, that I knowed was injurious to man and displeasin to God and still I had to fall back." One cold morning in December 1932, Shaw refused to "fall back." When deputy sheriffs came to take his neighbor's livestock, he took part in a shootout with local law officers.

Nate Shaw's action underscored the increasing militancy of rural black workers. Despite violence and intimidation, black workers also took an active part in the formation of the socialist Southern Tenant Farmers Union (STFU). A black farmer helped to inspire the organization when he spoke up at the initial meeting of the group: "For a long time now the white folks and the colored folks have been fighting each other and both of us has been getting whipped all the time. We don't have nothing against one another but we got plenty against the landlord. The same chain that holds my people holds your people too. If we're chained together on the outside, ought to stay chained together in the union." When white landowners evicted sharecroppers in Arkansas, the black STFU vice president, Owen H. Whitfield, led some five hundred black and white farmers onto the main highway between Memphis and St. Louis and vowed to remain there until the federal government intervened. The Missouri State Highway patrol soon moved in and loaded families and thier possessions on to trucks and scattered them on back country roads. Although these radical actions produced few results, they highlighted the increasing activism of rural black workers in their own behalf.

A small number of blacks joined the Communist party and played a role in the party's League of Struggle for Negro Rights (LSNR). According to a recent study of the party in depression-era Alabama, blacks made up the majority of the party's membership during most of the period. The party's fight on behalf of the Scotts-boro Boys attracted local black workers.

Most African Americans, however, shunned membership in radical parties and worked hard to broaden their participation in the New Deal coalition. In 1936, African Americans formed the National Negro Congress (NNC). Spearheaded by Ralph Bunche of Howard University and John Davis, executive secretary of the Joint Committee on National Recovery, the organization aimed to unite all exist-ing organizations—political, fraternal, and religious—and press for the full socioe-conomic recovery of the black community from the ravages of the depression. Nearly six hundred organizations attended the founding meeting, which selected A. Philip Randolph as its first president.

The National Negro Congress demonstrated a new level of African-American political organization and mobilization. Because of the dramatic growth of the black population in most cities, black voter registration drives picked up momen-tum during the 1930s. The proportion of the black population that had registered to vote had risen rapidly in the major industrial cities—from less than thirty percent to sixty-six percent in Detroit. In Philadelphia the number of registered black voters rose by more than ninety percent. In Chicago the rate of black voter registration exceeded the percentage of white. In the South as well—Durham, Raleigh, Birmingham, Atlanta, Savannah, and Charleston—African Americans formed political clubs to fight for the franchise and increase the number of black voters in that region.

As Republicans continued to ignore the pleas of black voters, blacks increasing-ly turned toward the Democratic party. In the election of 1936, African Americans voted for the Democratic party in record numbers, giving Roosevelt seventy-six percent of the Northern black vote. Following that election, African Americans used their growing support of the Democratic party to demand greater considera-tion from federal policy makers.

African Americans placed justice before the law high on their list of priorities. In 1933, the NAACP organized a Writers League Against Lynching and launched a nationwide movement to secure a federal antilynching law. Sponsored in the House of Representatives by Edward Costigan of Colorado and in the Senate by Robert Wagner of New York, the antilynching bill gained little support from FDR and failed when Southern senators killed the measure in 1934, 1935, 1937, 1938, and 1940. Despite its failure, the campaign against lynchings produced results. The number of lynchings dropped from eighteen in 1935 to two in 1939. Under the leadership of black attorneys William Hastie, Charles Hamilton Houston, and Thurgood Marshall, African Americans won important cases before the U.S. Supreme Court: selection of blacks for jury duty; admission to previously all-white law schools; and greater access to employment, housing, and public accommodations. Houston, Marshall, and Hastie carefully planned an overall strategy, emphasizing test cases with broad implications for dismantling the entire segregationist system.

Missouri ex rel. Gaines v. *Canada* (1938) was one of the most celebrated of these cases. Houston's decisions to take the case represented a tactical manouver to dismantle the sparate but equal principle which the Court established in an earlier case, *Plessy* v. *Ferguson* (1896). Lloyd Gaines, a black graduate of Lincoln University in Missouri, was denied admission to the University of Missouri Law School because the school did not accept blacks. The University advised Gaines to take advantage of state funds provided to support black legal training in other states. Supported by the St. Louis chapter of the NAACP, Gaines sued, demanding access to training at the all-white law school. Houston argued the case in the Missouri courts where Gaines lost. Then Huston argued the case to the U.S. Supreme Court, where Gaines won a major victory. The Court's decision outlawed the practice of giving blacks subsidies to receive legal training at out-of-state schools. It also supported the admission of blacks to all-white shcools in the absence of fully equal facilities for blacks.

As black lawyers attacked the system of legalized racial segregation, black social scientists and artists assaulted its intellectual underpinnings. E. Franklin Frazier, W.E.B. Du Bois, Carter G. Woodson, and other black social scientists and historians had worked for years counteracting racist stereotypes. Under the leadership of Carter G. Woodson, the Association for the Study of Negro Life and History (founded in 1915) continued to promote the study of African American history, emphasizing the role of blacks in the development of the nation. While the organization continued to publish the scholarly *Journal of Negro History* founded in 1916, in 1933 it added the *Negro History Bulletin* as a publication designed for broader circulation. Launched in 1926, Negro History Week also became a regular feature of African American community life across the country.

E. Franklin Frazier conducted seminal studies of black community and family life, which culminated in the publication of his *The Negro Family in the United States* (1939). Although he underestimated the role that poor and working-class blacks played in shaping their own experience, Frazier emphasized environmental over racial factors in explaining poverty. In his scholarship on African American history, W.E.B Du Bois also called attention to the impact of class and racial discrimination in his massive reinterpretation of the emancipation period, *Black Reconstruction in America, 1860–1880* (1935). Gunnar Myrdal's *An American Dilemma* built upon the scholarship of some thirty black scholars, including young men like Charles S. Johnson, St. Clair Drake, Horace R. Cayton, and Ralph Bunche among others.

Reinforcing the work of black social scientists and historians were the contributions of black artists. Concert singer Roland Hayes, Raul Robeson, and Marian Anderson frequently appeared on stage and on national radio broadcasts. Born to a working-class family in Philadelphia in 1902, Marian Anderson had pursued advanced musical training in Europe and had performed widely in Sweden, Norway, and Denmark. As a result of her growing success in Europe, Anderson returned to the United States in 1935. *The New York Times* reported, "Marian Anderson has returned to her native land one of the great singers of our time."

In 1939 the Daughters of the American Revolution, who owned Constitution Hall in Washington, D.C., barred Anderson from giving a concert there. For her part, Eleanor Roosevelt resigned from the DAR over the incident. In her popular newspaper column, "My Day," she explained that she could no longer belong to an organization that maintained the color line. African Americans and their white allies formed a committee of protest and got permission from Secretary of the Interior Harold Ickes to hold the concert at the Lincoln Memorial. Nearly 75,000 people stood in the cold open air to hear her sing, and millions more heard her on radio. Her repertoire included Negro spirituals, bringing them to a wide audience for the first time, along with the works of classical European composers.

Richard Wright, Langston Hughes, William Attaway, and others expressed the experiences of African Americans through novels and plays. In 1938, Richard Wright won a WPA writing prize for his book *Uncle Tom's Children,* a collection of short stories on black life in the rural south. Two years later he published his most famous novel *Native Son,* which characterized the great migration of blacks to American cities and the destructive impact of racism on their lives. One observer later recalled that, "The day *Native Son* appeared, American culture was changed forever." Wright's book was a phenomenal success. It set a sales record for Harper and Brothers and soon surpassed John Steinbeck's *The Grapes of Wrath* on the best-seller lists. Born on a plantation near Natchez, Mississippi in 1908, Wright later wrote that his head was "full of a hazy notion that life could be lived with dignity, that the personalities of others should not be violated." The Mississippi-born writer William Attaway expressed similar sentiments in his powerful portrayal of black site workers in his novel, *Blood on the Forge* (1941).

Adding to the artistic portrayal of black life were the dramatic productions of black theater groups like the Rose McClendon players, the Harlem Players, and the Negro People's Theatre; the music of jazz artists like Fletcher Henderson, Duke Ellington, Bessie Smith, and Jimmie Lunceford; the paintings of Romare Bearden; and the films of the pioneer black film maker Oscar Micheaux. African Americans also gained greater access to mainstream radio and film and gradually used these media to project more positive images of themselves than was previously possible. The blues singer Ethel Waters had her own radio show and the film industry broke new ground by giving Paul Robeson the lead role in the movie version of the stage the play *The Emperor Jones,* with whites serving as supporting cast.

African Americans developed a variety of responses to life during the Great Depression. The depression offered different problems and prospects for educated black professional people on the one hand and the masses of working class and poor people on the other. Yet all were linked to each other through the persistence of racial inequality. The emergence of prizefighter Joe Louis as a folk hero for all African Americans is perhaps the most potent evidence of their sense of a common

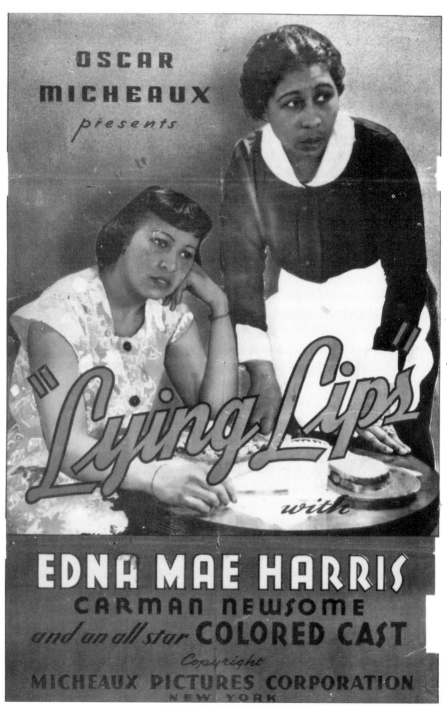

Lying Lips, a 1939 movie produced and directed by the pioneering black filmmaker Oscar Micheaux, featured an all-black cast.

plight, kinship, and future. Indeed, Joe Louis helped to unify black people during the period and gave them hope that they could topple the segregationist system. When he lost they cried, as in his first bout against the German Max Schmeling in 1936. They were especially heartbroken because Hitler preached the doctrine of Aryan supremacy, which claimed the physical and intellectual superiority of all white people, and the German people in particular.

On the other hand, when Joe Louis won, black people celebrated. After he knocked out Schmeling in the first round of their rematch, black people everywhere applauded, celebrated, and danced in the streets. Similarly, when Louis knocked out the Italian heavyweight Primo Carnera, black people were also elated and felt that they had to some degree avenged Benito Mussolini's invasion and bombing of Ethiopia in 1935. The singer Lena Horne offers a powerful statement on Joe Louis as a black folk hero: "Joe was the one invincible Negro, the one who stood up to the white man and beat him down with his fists. He in a sense carried so many of our hopes, maybe even dreams of vengeance."

The depression, New Deal, and social change sent a mixed message to African Americans. On the one hand, they experienced the gradual growth of new and more egalitarian ideas and practices on race; on the other, they suffered persistent economic deprivation and discrimination. Because they faced a dual process of poverty and progress, African-American responses were likewise complex and varied. At times, they despaired and exploded into violence, as in the Harlem riot of 1935. At other times, they gave up on mainstream institutions and turned toward alternative visions and strategies, as reflected in their growing connections with the Communist and Socialist parties. Their music also reflected a similar range of responses—blues, gospel, and jazz. Above all, however, as symbolized in the boxing career of Joe Louis, they deepened their struggle to break down barriers to their full participation in American society. They launched movements to break the back of Jim Crow and broaden their access to the larger economic, political, social, and cultural life of the nation. Their struggle would gain even greater fruits during the crisis of World War II, another epic fight that lay only a few years ahead.

World War II, 1940–1945

Under the impact of World War II, African Americans gained new industrial opportunities as the nation mobilized for war and called men into the military in rising numbers. It was during this period that African Americans regained a foothold in the industrial economy and broke the unskilled "job ceiling" and moved into semiskilled and skilled jobs. Yet, the movement of African Americans into defense industry jobs was a slow process. Employers, labor unions, and government agencies, all discriminated against blacks and undermined their participation in the war effort. The *Chicago Defender* captured the frustrations of many African Americans in an editorial. "Why die for democracy for some foreign country when we don't even have it here?

Most African Americans nonetheless supported the nation's declaration of war against Germany and Japan. Black servicemen and women fought in the European, Pacific, and Mediterranean theaters of war. Unlike World War I, however, African Americans refused to simply "close ranks" and postpone their own struggle for full citizenship and recognition of their rights at home. They now used the war emergency, as well as their growing influence in the Democratic party and the new unions, to wage a "Double V" campaign—for victory at home as well as abroad. Their campaign received its most powerful expression in the militant March on Washington, which led to the federal Fair Employment Practices Committee. By war's end African Americans and their white allies had set the stage for the emergence of the modern civil rights movement.

As the nation edged toward war in the years after 1939, African Americans continued to face a pattern of racial discrimination. Despite growing U. S. protests against the racism of Nazi Germany, African Americans confronted racial injustice at home and abroad. In the defense industries and armed services, African Americans complained of racial bias. In 1940 blacks made up less than two percent of employees in the nation's expanding aircraft industry, and management officials in that industry often stated overtly their determination to keep blacks out. At the large North American Aviation firm, for example, the company's president reported that black applicants would be considered only for janitorial jobs. In Milwaukee, the A. O. Smith Company, producer of auto frames and tanks for the military, stated that they "never did and didn't intend to employ Negroes." Black women confronted even greater difficulties gaining defense jobs than black men did. Employers expressed the belief that black women were peculiarly suited for domestic service but not for industrial jobs. Thus many African-American men and women believed that it was a waste of time to seek work in all-white defense plants.

Craft unions reinforced discrimination against black workers in defense work. Skilled black workers—plumbers, bricklayers, carpenters, electricians, cement finishers, and painters—faced exclusion from labor unions either by provisions of their bylaws or by some form of "ritual," or gentleman's agreement that blacks would not be proposed for membership. In a resolution introduced at the 1941 convention of the AFL, A. Philip Randolph pinpointed labor union discrimination against black workers in a broad range of jobs in different parts of the country. He cited the International Association of Machinists (IAM) as the union with the most conspicuous record of labor union discrimination against African Americans. By accepting only white members, the IAM reinforced the exclusion of blacks from the metal trades and the aircraft industry, including the huge Boeing Aircraft Corporation in Seattle.

Since many defense industry jobs required additional training for large numbers of white as well as black workers, the U. S. Office of Education financed such programs under the Vocational Education National Defense (VEND) Training Program. In his study of black labor during the period, economist and New Dealer Robert Weaver documented racial discrimination in the implementation of such

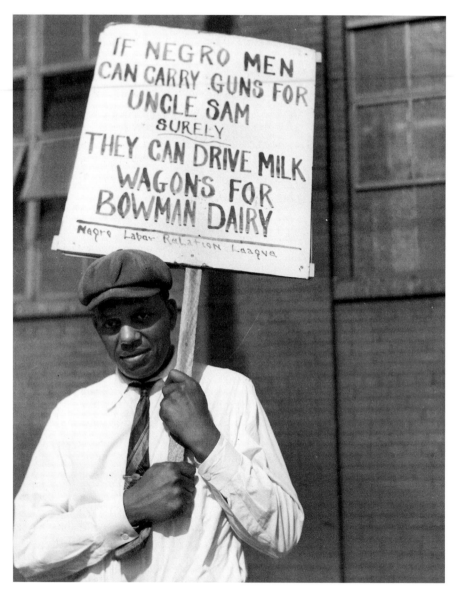

Blacks continued to struggle against racial discrimination at home, even as African-American soldiers fought and died overseas during World War II.

programs. According to Weaver, such discrimination had deep roots in earlier patterns of discrimination in federal educational programs. During the 1930s, the federal government had established a precedent for discrimination, by awarding blacks less than $4.75 per capita of federal funds, compared to $8 for whites. When the government established VEND, it continued the same practices. As Weaver put it, "This discrimination was in reality a projection of past practices. Most vocational education officials at the national, state, and local levels were not prepared

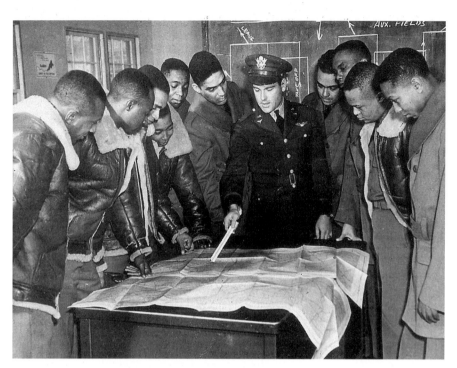

Cadets in the U.S. Army's first all-black air unit, the 99th Pursuit Squadron, were trained at Tuskegee Institute in Alabama. More than 600 black pilots were trained there during the war.

to champion new policies relative to minority groups' training." Vocational training programs reinforced a vicious cycle of black exclusion from defense jobs. When asked why blacks were not trained and employed in defense industry jobs, training school supervisors, unions, and employers conveniently blamed each other, thus passing the buck back and forth and assuring that nothing was done about their discrimination practices.

African Americans fared little better in the armed services. During the early 1940s, as the government trained white pilots to fly warplanes, the War Department barred African Americans from the U. S. Air Corps. Blacks were admitted to the U. S. Army in large numbers, but were placed in segregated service and labor units, responsible for building, maintenance, and supplies. In 1940, there were an estimated five thousand blacks in the Army, but only four black units were up to full strength and there were fewer than twelve officers in a corps of over 230,000 enlisted men and officers. At the war's outset, the Marine Corps and Coast Guard barred blacks completely, while the Department of the Navy and Coast Guard accepted them only as messmen or laborers.

Despite the existence of racial discrimination in the defense program, African Americans played a key role in the war effort. The number of blacks selected for military service increased from 2,069 in 1940 to about 370,000 in 1942, following the Japanese attack on Pearl Harbor on December 7, 1941, and the official entry of the United States into World War II. By the end of the war, nearly one million black men and women had served in the armed forces, nearly three-quarters in the U. S. Army, followed in numbers by the Navy (and Coast Guard), Marine Corps, and the Air Corps, in which only a few blacks served. At the same time, black civilians supported the war effort by purchasing war bonds and launching vigorous bond campaigns in their churches, schools, and community organizations. Despite the poverty of many, they also cooperated with the government's food conservation program and staffed United Service Organizations (USO) to boost the morale of black service men and women. The USO coordinated the social service activities of a wide range of organizations, including the YWCA, YMCA, and the Salvation Army, to name a few. In addition, African Americans served as nurses' aides, drivers in motor corps, and other voluntary but vital jobs in the Red Cross.

Nearly 500,000 African Americans saw service overseas. Most served in transportation corps, port battalions, and construction units. They moved troops and supplies, built and repaired roads and fortifications, and cleared battle zones of debris and dead and wounded soldiers. They also engaged the enemy in combat in the European, Mediterranean, and Pacific theaters, and gained recognition for their outstanding services. The 761st Tank Battalion, which served in six European countries and fought in the Battle of the Bulge, received several commendations for its bravery on the battlefield. By war's end, many of these units received the Presidential Citation for their contributions to winning the war. Several African Americans received the Navy Cross The Air Corps awarded the Distinguished Flying Cross to eighty-two African American pilots and several blacks received the Navy Cross. Messman Dorie Miller became perhaps the most renowned of these seamen. "Without previous experience [he] ... manned a machine gun in the face of serious fire during the Japanese attack on Pearl Harbor, December 7, 1941, on the Battleship *Arizona* shooting down four enemy planes."

The Air Corps awarded the Distinguished Flying Cross to eighty-two African-American pilots. This achievement was made possible by the training of black airmen at segregated institutions, like Tuskegee Institute. Although some black leaders resisted the training of blacks in segregated facilities, others accepted the arrangement as an opportunity to expand their war-and-peace-time opportunities. Tuskegee trained some six hundred black pilots who flew missions in Africa, France, Italy, Poland, Romania, and Germany. Colonel Benjamin O. Davis, a graduate of the U.S. Military Academy at West Point, became the highest ranking black officer. He flew sixty missions and won several medals for distinguished service. Other African Americans received medals of honor from the governments of France, Yugoslavia, and the Soviet Union.

African Americans served and achieved against great odds. On and off military bases, black service personnel often did not receive courteous treatment and recognition of their human and civil rights. In Durham, North Carolina, for

African-American women service a truck at Fort Huachuca, Arizona. During the war, black women, perhaps even more so than white women, performed traditionally male jobs.

example, a local jury acquitted a white bus driver who murdered a black soldier following an altercation on his route. When German prisoners of war arrived in the United States, they often received service in white establishments that denied service to African Americans.

No less than black men, black women in the military were also subject to brutality in the Jim Crow South. When they failed to move along fast enough, three black Women in the Women's Army Corps (WACS) were brutally assaulted by civilian police in a Kentucky railroad station. When African Americans resisted such treatment, racial violence erupted at Fort Bragg N.C., Fort Dix, N.J., and other military bases.

Racial discrimination in the military was part of a broader pattern of hostility toward blacks in American society. Attracted by new jobs created by the war effort, nearly 1.6 million blacks moved into the nation's cities. The percentage of blacks living in urban areas rose from less than fifty percent in 1940 to nearly sixty percent in 1945. Western cities like Los Angeles, San Francisco, and Seattle now joined established northern and southern cities as major centers of black urban population growth. Between 1940 and 1945, the black population of Los Angeles county rose from about 75,000 to 150,000. Seattle's black population leaped from 3,800 to nearly 10,000. At the same time, established midwestern and northeastern cities attracted large numbers of new blacks. In the three year period between 1940 to 1943, Detroit's black population increased by fifty thousand. As the black urban population increased, race relations deteriorated and violence broke out in several cities. One example was the so-called "zoot suit" riots in which white sailors and civilians attacked African Americans and Latino residents. Marked by their dress as well as their color—broad felt hats, pegged trousers, and pocket knives on gold chains—African American and Latino youth were assaulted in Los Angeles, San Diego, Long Beach, Chicago, Detroit, and Philadelphia.

Racial violence went well beyond the "zoot suit" confrontations. The most serious conflicts occurred in Harlem and Detroit. In 1943, a policeman shot a black soldier and touched off the Harlem riot, which resulted in at least five deaths, five hundred injuries, hundreds of arrests, and five million dollars in property damage. The actor Sidney Poitier later recalled his experience of the riot: "In a restaurant downtown where I was working I heard that there was trouble in Harlem. After work I took a train uptown, came up out of the subway, and there was chaos everywhere—cops, guns, debris and broken glass all over the street. Many stores had been set on fire, and the commercial district on 125th Street looked as if it had been bombed."

The confrontation in Detroit left behind even more deaths, injuries, and arrests. On June 20, 1943, more than 100,000 Detroiters crowded the city's Belle Isle Amusement Park to escape the sweltering summer heat. Before long, violence between blacks and whites broke out at the park's casino, ferry dock, playgrounds, and bus stops. The violence soon spilled over into the black Paradise Valley area. At a local club, a patron took the microphone and announced: "There's a riot at Belle Isle! The whites have killed a colored lady and her baby. Thrown them over a bridge. Everybody come on! There's free transportation outside!" Although the report of the death of a black woman and her child was false, by early morning African Americans had smashed windows and looted numerous white-owned stores on Hastings Avenue. Only the arrival of federal troops put down the violence, which resulted in 34 deaths, 675 injuries, nearly 1,900 arrests, and an estimated $2 million in property damage. In both the Harlem and Detroit riots, most of those killed, injured, or arrested were blacks, while the damaged property belonged almost exclusively to whites.

Racial violence in Detroit and elsewhere was intertwined with the growing residential segregation of African Americans in the urban environment. As it had during the depression years, federal housing policy reinforced patterns of residential segregation. For example, in 1941, the Federal Public Housing Authority (FPHA) approved the Sojourner Truth Housing Project. Although the project was designated for black occupancy, it was located in a predominantly white working class neighborhood. When local residents protested, federal authorities rescinded its decision and handed the project over to whites. Only the vigorous protests of the black community, organized in the Sojourner Truth Citizens Committee and supported by the United Auto Workers union, regained for African Americans ther right to live in the project.

On the other hand, the federal government soon established an all-white project at the Ford Motor Company's new Willow Run factory. Although blacks and their CIO allies tried to persuade federal officials to permit blacks and whites to occupy the units, the FPHA insisted on a policy of racial segregation. Such housing policies, along with restrictive employment practices and discrimination in the military, embittered black-white relations in the city of Detroit and fueled the underlying forces leading to the 1943 race riot.

African Americans did not passively accept racial discrimination in the defense program. They waged a militant "Double V" campaign against social injustice at home and abroad. Popularized by the *Pittsburgh Courier,* the "Double V" campaign enabled African Americans to declare their loyalty to the war effort without abandoning their thrust for equal rights at home. As early as summer 1940, the NAACP criticized the navy's policy of recruiting blacks as messmen only. The organization emphasized the injustice of using black tax dollars to finance opportunities for whites, while denying such opportunities to blacks.

The fight against discrimination in the military was not limited to male branches of the service. Under the leadership of Mabel K. Staupers, executive director of the National Association of Colored Graduate Nurses, African Americans waged a vigorous fight to integrate the Army and Navy Nurse Corps. The army established a quota on the number of black women accepted for service, while the navy barred them altogether. In her campaign to end such discrimination, Staupers tried to enlist the support of white nurses groups. Only the acute shortage of white nurses by early 1945 helped to end the army's quota system and break the barriers on black women in the navy.

African Americans also attacked racial discrimination in war industries with government contracts. On its July 1940 cover, the NAACP's *Crisis* featured an airplane factory marked, "For Whites Only," with the caption, "Warplanes—Negro Americans may not build them, repair them, or fly them, but they must help pay for them."

The African-American quest for social justice gained its most potent expression in the emergence of the militant March on Washington Movement (MOWM). Spearheaded by A. Philip Randolph, the MOWM was launched in 1941 following a meeting of civil rights groups in Chicago. The critical moment came when a black woman angrily addressed the chair: "Mr. Chairman ... we ought to throw fifty thousand Negroes around the White House, bring them from all over the country, in jalopies, in trains and any way they can get there, and throw them around the White House and keep them there until we can get some action from the White House." Randolph not only seconded the proposal but offered himself and the Brotherhood of Sleeping Car Porters as leaders: "I agree with the sister. I will be very happy to throw [in] my organization's resources and offer myself as a leader of such a movement."

By early June, the MOWM had established march headquarters in Harlem, Brooklyn, Washington D. C., Pittsburgh, Detroit, Chicago, St. Louis, and San Francisco. The movement spread through the major rail centers and soon joined forces with local NAACP and Urban League chapters, churches, and fraternal orders.

The MOWM helped to mobilize the masses of black working people as well as the middle and upper classes. According to Randolph, "It was apparent ... that some unusual, bold and gigantic effort must be made to awaken the American people and the President of the Nation to the realization that the Negroes were the victims of sharp and unbearable oppression, and that the fires of resentment were flaming higher and higher." Although the MOWM welcomed liberal white support, Randolph insisted that African Americans lead the movement. Randolph was wary of the labor movement, the major political parties, and the growing Communist influence in black organizations like the National Negro Congress (NNC). When the Communist party gained control of the NNC in early 1940, for example, Randolph resigned from the presidency and soon left the organization.

Although Roosevelt resisted the movement as long as he could, the threat of a march on Washington finally produced results. Roosevelt met with leaders A. Philip Randolph and Walter White of the NAACP on June 18, 1941. A week later, on June 24, 1941, FDR issued Executive Order 8802, banning racial discrimination in government employment, defense industries, and training programs. The order also established the Fair Employment Practices Committee (FEPC) to implement its provisions. The FEPC was empowered to receive, investigate, and address complaints of racial discrimination in the defense program.

Executive order 8802 proved to be a turning point in African-American history. It linked the struggle of African Americans even more closely to the Democratic party and helped to transform the federal government into a significant ally. African Americans used the FEPC to broaden their participation in the war effort, but it proved to be a slow process. Although an estimated 118,000 blacks were trained for industrial, professional, and clerical jobs in 1941, by the end of 1942 only a small percentage had obtained employment in defense industries. Industrial firms in the North and South dragged their feet on the putting of fair employment practices into effect. In January 1942, the FEPC cited five Milwaukee firms for racial discrimination against the city's black workers, and directed them "to give written notice" that they would end such practices. Shipyard companies in Houston, Galveston, Mobile, New Orleans, and Tampa widely advertised for white women and boys to pursue training as welders, but they resisted the FEPC's push to place black welders. Southern colleges also barred blacks from training programs supported by federal money, forcing African Americans to travel to a limited number of black training centers. In Mobile, when the FEPC pressured the Alabama

Drydock and Shipbuilders Company to upgrade some black workers to the job of welder, the company supported the walkout and a riot of some twenty thousand white workers, who quit in protest against the employment of black workers.

Southeastern railroads offered even stronger evidence of white resistance. In 1940, with the support of the National Mediation Board, the southeastern railroads and the exclusively white unions signed the notorious "Washington Agreement," designed to eliminate black firemen from employment. Black workers soon challenged the Washington Agreement under the new FEPC guidelines. The FEPC ordered the companies and unions to adjust their policies "so that all needed workers shall be hired and all company employees shall be promoted without regard to race, creed, color or national origin." When the roads and unions defied the order, African Americans took their case to court, but nothing was determined until 1944 when a U.S Supreme Court ruling, *Bester William Steele* v. *The Louisville and Nashville Company Brotherhood of Locomitive Firemen and Engineers,* upheld their claims. Every year, at the annual meetings of the AFL, A. Philip Randolph exhorted white workers to end racial bias.

Despite the persistence of discrimination, as the wartime labor shortages increased, the FEPC played a key role in helping black workers find jobs in defense plants. The number of blacks in war production increased from less than three percent in March 1942 to over eight percent in 1944. And unlike what happened during World War I, substantial numbers now moved into semiskilled and skilled positions. As St. Clair Drake and Horace R. Cayton noted in their study of Chicago during the period, "The Second World War broke the ceiling at the level of semi-skilled work and integrated thousands of Negroes as skilled laborers in the electrical and light manufacturing industries, from which they had been barred by custom, and in the vast new airplane-engine factories . . . They also began to filter into minor managerial and clerical positions in increasing numbers."

While the AFL unions and the railroad brotherhoods did much to hamper this process, the unions of the Congress of Industrial Organizations often supported the FEPC claims of black workers and helped them to break the job ceiling. At its annual convention in 1941, for example, the CIO denounced racially discriminatory hiring policies as a "direct attack against our nation's policy to build democracy in our fight against Hitlerism." A year later, the organization established its own Committee to Abolish Racial Discrimination and urged its affiliates to support national policy against discrimination. Although black workers faced ongoing obstacles in their struggle for skilled, managerial, and clerical positions, by the end of World War II they claimed the CIO, the Democratic party, and the federal government as important allies in their struggle for social change.

The "Double V" campaign for victory at home and abroad, the March on Washington Movement, and the growing use of the federal government to secure their aims helped to write a new chapter in the history of African Americans and set the stage for the modern civil rights movement of the postwar years.

CHAPTER 9

We Changed the World

1945–1970

Vincent Harding

Robin D. G. Kelley

Earl Lewis

N ear the end of World War II, Adam Clayton Powell, Jr., one of black America's most internationally conscious spokesmen, tried to place the ongoing African-American freedom movement into the context of the anticolonial struggles that were rising explosively out of the discontent of the non-white world. Already, movements for independence had begun in British colonies in West Africa and French colonies in West and Equatorial Africa. Later, colonies in North Africa and British East Africa joined the freedom struggle. Powell, who was both a flamboyant and effective congressman from Harlem and the pastor of that community's best-known Christian congregation, the Abyssinian Baptist Church, declared:

> The black man continues on his way. He plods wearily no longer—he is
> striding freedom road with the knowledge that if he hasn't got the world in
> a jug, at least he has the stopper in his hand. . . . He is ready to throw him-
> self into the struggle to make the dream of America become flesh and blood,
> bread and butter, freedom and equality. He walks conscious of the fact that
> he is no longer alone no longer a minority.

Although they might not have been able to express it in Powell's colorful lan-guage, many black Americans were quite aware of the changes taking place. There were glaring differences, for instance, between where they grew up in the South and the Northern cities where they were trying to establish themselves for the first time.

Most of the new arrivals realized that the North was not heaven, but they believed that it was a place where they could escape some of the most hellish aspects of their life in the South. For instance, they did not expect ever again to have to see the bodies of men hanging from trees after they had been riddled with

A member of the 12th Armored Division stands guard over Nazi prisoners who were captured by U.S. forces in 1945.

bullets and often mutilated. They did not expect that women would be vulnerable to rape and exploitation simply because they were black and defenseless. In the Northern cities they did not expect to have to teach their children to move out of the path when white people were approaching.

Blacks also migrated to the West and settled in cities such as Los Angeles and Seattle. One of the most exciting gifts that these new locales offered was the opportunity for black people to vote as free men and free women for the first time in their lives. Registering to vote in Philadelphia, Detroit, or Oakland did not mean risking your life and the lives of your family, risking your job or your home. In those postwar years, black people took significant advantage of this new freedom and became voters in even larger proportions than white Southerners who had migrated North. As a result, black voters in some Northern cities like Chicago and New York held the balance of power in close municipal elections.

This new political involvement brought with it another change. In most of the Northern cities where the black Southerners settled, the political structures were largely dominated by the Democratic party. Generally, the men who controlled these tightly organized political machines were eager to add the newly arrived black people to their voting tallies as long as they thought they could control their votes. And, in fact, millions of African Americans eventually broke away from their generations-long allegiance to the Republican party, the party of Lincoln, the Great

Emancipator. Ironically enough, this transfer of allegiance meant that Northern blacks were now aligned with the same Democratic party that had long been dominated on the national scene by the white racist sons of the slaveholders, men who kept their control of the party largely through terrorist acts to deny black voting rights in the South. In the North, black voters were now part of that Democratic party structure and were in a position to begin to challenge its worst traditions.

Despite such rewards as finding better jobs and educational opportunities, and gaining the right to vote, this liberating movement into the Northern cities carried some clear penalties. Racism lived in many white urban neighborhoods and postwar suburbs. The rising black middle class, anxious to buy property in a "nice" neighborhood with good schools and efficient services, often bumped up against a threatening white mob and its racist rhetoric. Sometimes white resistance to black neighbors turned deadly. In Chicago, Los Angeles, Detroit, and several other cities (in both the North and the South), newly purchased homes were burned, vandalized, or had crosses burned on their lawns—a common tactic adopted by white supremacist organizations, notably the Ku Klux Klan.

Of course, there were real estate agents and white residents who insisted that their form of segregation was not racist but driven by economic realities. They claimed to have nothing against black people but were simply worried about their homes declining in value. Sadly, their arguments were tacitly backed by the federal government, notably the Federal Housing Administration (FHA), the agency that insured homeowners' loans to low-income Americans and set housing standards. Indeed, after World War II, the FHA refused to provide mortgages to blacks moving into white neighborhoods and claimed that African Americans were regarded as poor risks for loans. The FHA also claimed that the future value of homes owned by blacks was uncertain.

Most of the new migrants could not afford to buy homes immediately, especially in the sprawling suburbs. No matter where they ended up, however, primarily the inner areas of urban centers like Chicago and Detroit, they sought to create the rich sense of community they had left behind. For even in the midst of harsh white oppression and poverty, black people, nurtured by their extended families and by their churches, had managed to build astonishing reservoirs of love, faith, and hope in the South. Such support was not readily available in the North.

Reflecting on his own Harlem childhood in *Nobody Knows My Name* (1961), James Baldwin caught some of the perplexing dilemma of a city block in the long-anticipated "Promised Land" of the North.

> They work in the white man's world all day and come home in the evening to this fetid block. They struggle to instill in their children some private sense of honor or dignity which will help the child to survive. This means, of course, that they must struggle, stolidly, incessantly, to keep this sense alive in themselves, in spite of the insults, the indifference, and the cruelty

they are certain to encounter in their working day. They patiently browbeat the landlord into fixing the heat, the plaster, the plumbing; this demands prodigious patience, nor is patience usually enough.... Such frustration so long endured, is driving many strong, admirable men and women whose only crime is color to the very gates of paranoia....

It required the sensitivity and skills of gifted artists to capture the complexities of the changes that millions of black women, men and children were experiencing in their movement North. Baldwin was only one of the writers who tried to explain that complexity to the world. Ann Petry provided a painfully honest account of a young woman's encounter with the Northern urban reality in her novel *The Street*. Ralph Ellison's classic novel *Invisible Man* reflected the humor, anger, hope, and the search for new beginnings that the urban experience represented for the transplanted black Southerners. Ellison's protagonist discovers a major difference between the South and the North when he first arrives in Harlem and begins to mingle with the evening crowds who have gathered to listen to the street-corner teachers and lecturers. Most of the rousing speeches eventually turn to the injustices of white people against people of color at home and abroad, and the young man in the novel, who has come North from Alabama, says, "I never saw so many Negroes angry in public before."

The expanding ability to be angry in public was a major part of the change that black people found in the North. In his novels, short stories, and essays, Richard Wright, who had originally gone to Chicago from Mississippi in the twenties, expressed this anger and its consequences more vividly and consistently than anyone else in his novel *Native Son* (1940).

Still, there were emotions and experiences that could never be captured by the written word. The music surging out of black communities became a powerful vehicle for communicating these feelings. The blues that had come up with the solitary old guitars from Memphis and the Mississippi Delta took on the new electricity and complexity of the cities, eventually becoming the music of small combos and big bands, pressing on toward what would soon be known as rhythm and blues. At the same time, out of the familiar settings of classic African-American jazz, piercing new sounds began to break through, offering unexpected, unresolved, and often jagged tonal edges in place of the smoother flows of the music from which it sprang. This was called "bebop" or "bop" for short. The names of its practitioners—Thelonious Monk, Dizzy Gillespie, Charlie ("Yardbird") Parker, and the young Miles Davis—and the boldness of their lifestyles soon became as well known in the black community and among white jazz fans as their predecessors Lester Young, Louis Armstrong, and Coleman Hawkins.

Whatever else bop was, it was the music of change. Everything in it sounded protest, marked a determination to break out of the older, predictable harmonies. Based in places like Minton's Playhouse in Harlem, the 52nd Street jazz strip further downtown in New York City, and Los Angeles's famed Central Avenue, the irrepressible music grew out of the urgency of a postwar generation to sing its new songs, to wail and scream when necessary.

Nowhere were the songs more important than in the thousands of black churches in the Northern cities. Following the lead of vibrant women vocalists such as Mahalia Jackson, Sallie and Roberta Martin, and Sister Rosetta Tharpe, supplied with a stream of songs by the prolific gospel songwriter Rev. Thomas A. Dorsey, the churches were filled with resounding, rhythmic witness to the new time, as gospel singers shouted, "There's been a great change since I been born."

In the decade following World War II, more than sixty percent of the black population was still living in the South, however. And the nation's attention focused on that region as the African-American community won a series of significant battles in the courts and at the executive level of the federal government. In 1946, for example, the Supreme Court ruled that segregation on buses was unconstitutional. Two years later, the Court outlawed the use of "restrictive covenants"—codicils added on to a deed to limit the sale of a home to specific racial groups. Restrictive covenants were generally used to keep African Americans from buying homes in all-white neighborhoods. Although these gains were long overdue, they were partial outgrowths of national and international circumstances that forced President Harry S. Truman and the Democrats to pay attention to blacks.

First, Truman, his cabinet, and Congress were all concerned about America's image abroad, especially now that the United States was competing with the Soviet Union for influence over the new nations in Asia and Africa, for example, created by the collapse of European colonialism. They could not promote their version of democracy abroad as long as the United States treated its own black citizens so badly. Second, Truman's reelection in 1948 depended on black votes more than ever. This time around, the Democratic party was in utter disarray. On one side stood former Vice President Henry Wallace, who decided to run for President as a member of the newly formed Progressive party. Wallace was highly regarded in the black community; his civil rights record was impeccable, and he sought to bring the cold war with the Soviet Union to an end through cooperation rather than military threats.

On the other side were the Southern Democrats led by South Carolina senator Strom Thurmond. Their break from the Democrats further divided the vote, creating a situation in which black voters would have a decisive role in the elections. Calling themselves the States' Rights party (also known as the Dixiecrats), these Southern Democrats believed Truman's civil rights agenda had gone too far.

Because Truman had to respond to African-American and international pressure, he and his cabinet contributed to the Southern white flight from the Democratic party. The main catalyst was Truman's decision to create the first Civil Rights Commission. The commission's report, *To Secure These Rights* (1947), proposed some specific ways in which the federal government might respond to the demands of the postwar black community. For example, the report called for the establishment of a permanent federal civil rights commissiona bold and progressive proposal in those days. The report urged an end to segregation in the U.S. armed forces and pressed for laws to protect the voting rights of black people.

To Secure These Rights provided solid evidence to black people that their needs were finally being dealt with at the highest level of U.S. political life. Meanwhile, almost every year in the crucial postwar decade seemed to produce new, affirming responses from the federal courts to the dozens of challenges to segregation and disenfranchisement that the NAACP and thousands of black plaintiffs were pressing in the courts.

One of the most important of these cases, *Morgan* v. *Virginia,* was heard by the U.S. Supreme Court in 1946. Irene Morgan had firmly refused to move to the back of a Virginia-to-Baltimore Greyhound bus, as Virginia law required. She was convicted of a misdemeanor. The Court declared that the practice of segregated seating in interstate public transportation was unconstitutional and that black people traveling across state lines could not be legally forced into segregated rear seats when they arrived in a Southern state. The "back of the bus" experience was one of the most humiliating and widely known manifestations of legalized white supremacy, so word of the decision was welcomed in the nation's black communities. Irene Morgan became a hero among black Americans. But a Supreme Court decision did not guarantee change. Neither the bus companies nor the Southern states leaped to comply with the ruling. So others had to take up Irene Morgan's initiative and move it forward.

That was precisely what happened in the spring of 1947 when a group of sixteen men, evenly divided between black and white, began what they called a Journey of Reconciliation. The trip was organized by a Chicago-based interracial organization known as the Congress of Racial Equality, or CORE. A relatively new offshoot from the Fellowship of Reconciliation (FOR)—a Christian pacifist organization, founded during World War I, that advocated nonviolent social change through civil disobedience—CORE was deeply committed to nonviolent direct action. Its members took inspiration from the spirit of the Indian nationalist leader Mahatma Gandhi in their quest for racial justice and reconciliation. At the same time, with the black members of the team sitting in front and the whites in back of the two Greyhound and Trailways buses that they rode from Washington, D.C., to stops in Virginia, North Carolina, and Kentucky, they were testing compliance with the recent *Morgan* decision and urging federal enforcement of the ruling. The major immediate result of the journey was that some other black passengers felt encouraged to move toward the front of the buses. In one incident during the fifteen-city trip through the South, three members of the CORE team were arrested and sentenced to twenty-one days of hard labor on a North Carolina prison farm. The Journey of Reconciliation provided the model for the later Freedom Rides in 1961.

Probably no legal victory of the immediate postwar years could match the overall significance of the 1944 Supreme Court decision in *Smith* v. *Allwright.* This decision essentially destroyed one of the major legal obstacles to black political participation in the South—the white primaries of the Democratic party.

Earlier in the twentieth century, having claimed that their party primary voting process was the activity of private associations, Democrats managed to exclude African Americans from participating in this "private" activity. As a result, black citizens were left with little voice in government, since the Southern Democratic primaries often determined the outcome of the general elections. African Americans refused to accept this situation, and in state after state they brought lawsuits challenging these exclusively white primaries.

In July 1940, Lonnie Smith, an African-American resident of Harris County, Texas, was stopped from voting in the Democratic party's primary election. Though he met all the legal requirements to vote, Smith was forbidden to vote because of his race. With the assistance of an NAACP legal team that included attorney Thurgood Marshall, Smith sued election judge Allwright. Finally, in *Smith* v. *Allwright,* the Supreme Court responded to the black challengers with a judgment outlawing the white primary process. When that happened, everyone knew that a new era was beginning: blacks across the South took that decision regarding the Texas primary as a signal to expand and intensify their voter registration activity.

With the help of a ruling by a South Carolina federal judge, J. Waties Waring, black plaintiffs won a crucial victory in that state. When South Carolina attempted to circumvent the *Smith* v. *Allwright* decision by removing all statutes relating to primaries—on the assumption that without state involvement, the Democratic primaries would be a private matter—George Elmore challenged the state's move. In the case of *Rice* v. *Elmore* (1947), Waring ruled that as long as the Democratic primary constituted the only real election in the state, blacks were entitled to participate in it.

In many places this was a dangerous resolve to take, especially in the rural South's "Black Belt"—a line of counties stretching from North Carolina to Texas, where the flat and fertile land had been dominated by cotton plantations. There, the legacy of plantation-based slavery had created counties where black people outnumbered whites in proportions of three-, four-, and five-to-one—sometimes more. The obvious implications of this human arithmetic were clearly stated by one distressed white cotton gin owner. Speaking to a *New York Times* reporter, he tried to imagine what would happen if black people gained full access to the ballot box in his Tennessee county: "The niggers would take over the county if they could vote in full numbers. They'd stick together and vote blacks into every office in the county. Why you'd have a nigger judge, nigger sheriff, a nigger tax assessor—think what the black SOB's would do to you."

Ever since the days of slavery such fears were common to many white Southerners who wondered what black people would do if the racial tables were turned. Many whites found it easy to rally around the virulently racist rhetoric of a politician like Theodore G. Bilbo, U.S. senator from Mississippi. He voiced the fears of many Southern whites, especially the poorer ones, when he declared that World

War II "and all of its great victories will not in any way or in any manner change the views and sentiments of white America on the question of social equality . . . of the negro and white race." In a time when so much was changing, Bilbo and his fellow white supremacists were seeking guarantees that they would continue to dominate.

Throughout the South, white supremacists were desperate to preserve an old world that was coming to an end. They had no intention of giving up their control of the region and would use all legal means of undermining the constitutional defenses that black people increasingly depended on. Many also conspired to use illegal means, from economic coercion to acts of terrorism, to keep their black fellow Southerners "in their place."

Nowhere was this new world more evident than in the ranks of the thousands of African Americans who returned from the battlegrounds of World War II. They were the ones who seemed most ready to demonstrate the truth of Adam Clayton Powell's statement that black people were "ready to throw [themselves] into the struggle to make the dream of America become flesh and blood." A recently discharged army corporal from Alabama spoke for many of his black comrades in 1945 when he declared, "I spent four years in the army to free a bunch of Dutchmen and Frenchmen, and I'm hanged if I'm going to let the Alabama version of the Germans kick me around when I get home. No sirree-bob! I went into the Army a nigger; I'm comin' out a man."

Among those determined to win voting rights for blacks in the South was a solid core of veterans who felt like they had earned the right to vote after risking their lives for democracy overseas. In 1946, brothers Charles and Medgar Evers returned home from the war to their town of Decatur, Mississippi, determined to vote. But they were driven away from the registrar's desk, and one of the white men predicted that there would be "trouble" if these black citizens persisted in their attempts to register and vote. But he could never have guessed the nature of the coming trouble. For the Evers brothers and thousands like them would return all over the South to challenge the keepers of the old terror.

The powerful thrusts of postwar change were not confined to politics. A remarkable change in the world of sports captured the attention of the rest of the nation. Jackie Robinson, another veteran of the war and a baseball player with the Kansas City Monarchs of the segregated Negro Leagues, was signed by the Brooklyn Dodgers in 1945. The action broke the racial barrier in major league baseball, the "national pastime." An outstanding athlete who had lettered in baseball, basketball, track, and football at the University of California at Los Angeles, an outspoken critic of America's racial betrayals of democracy, the twenty-eight-year-old Robinson spent a year with the Dodgers' farm team in Montreal before finally joining the Brooklyn lineup in the spring of 1947. Black people were ecstatic.

The black community followed local and national developments in civil rights by reading African-American newspapers such as the *Pittsburgh Courier,* the

Chicago Defender, the *Baltimore Afro-American,* and the *Norfolk Journal and Guide.* These papers were circulated through many hands in households, barbershops, beauty parlors, churches, and restaurants. In the hands of Pullman car porters, they found their way into the Deep South as well.

By reading the papers, black people followed the anticolonial, independence-oriented exploits of the darker-skinned majority of the world in places like India, Africa, and China. There were constant references to Gandhi, who had spent decades challenging his people in India to wage a nonviolent struggle for independence against the great British empire that governed them. Repeatedly, the black newspapers carried letters and editorials contending that Gandhi's movement offered a model for black America, especially in the South. Mordecai Johnson, president of Howard University in Washington, D.C.; Howard Thurman, mystically oriented preacher and dean of Howard University's chapel; and Benjamin Mays, president of Morehouse College in Atlanta, were some of the best known black Americans who had made the pilgrimage to the ashrams, the humble communal villages where Gandhi based himself.

Gandhi's life and teaching mirrored some of the best African-American traditions. Like the 19th-century abolitionists David Walker and Frederick Douglass, like W. E. B. Du Bois, Ida B. Wells-Barnett, and Howard Thurman, Gandhi believed that the despised of the earth actually carried within their own lives and history the seeds of healing transformation for themselves, their oppressors, and their world. So when black Americans identified their struggle as part of a larger, worldwide movement, it was not simply the idea "that [we are] no longer alone" that compelled them. It was also the vision that as the rising children of their enslaved forbears, they—like Gandhi's masses—might have some liberating gift to offer to the world.

While blacks were developing an understanding of worldwide repression, the U.S. government seemed to be, in some instances, supporting that repression. On the one hand, U.S. foreign policy appeared to link the United States with the interests and points of view of its white, Western allies, such as England, France, Portugal, and white South Africa, countries still identified with colonial domination. On the other hand, as part of the deepening cold war against the Soviet Union, the United States was also projecting itself as "the leader of the free world," avowedly concerned for the rights of oppressed people everywhere, especially people of color who might be tempted to turn to the Soviet Union and to other socialist and communist movements for assistance in their freedom struggles.

So when black leaders with socialist sympathies, such as W. E. B. Du Bois and the politically active actor, singer, and scholar Paul Robeson, spoke out on behalf of the nonwhite peoples and their freedom struggles, when they articulated too positive a view of the Russian Revolution's social and economic ambitions, when they sharply criticized U. S. foreign and domestic policy, the U.S. government considered them un-American and dangerous. The passports of both men were confiscated to prevent them from traveling and speaking abroad on behalf of the anticolonial movements and against the reign of white supremacy in America. Still, both men continued to speak out. But the price they paid was very high. Robeson essentially lost his lucrative concert career, and ultimately his health. Du Bois, in the fearful climate of anticommunism in America, found himself deserted by many people who had benefited from his decades of unstinting service to the cause of freedom, justice, and democratic hope, and he moved permanently to Africa.

Anticommunist fervor virtually crushed these two intellectual giants, but it could not crush the movement. In the streets and in the courts, black activists forced the federal government to admit that segregation was wrong and must be remedied. By 1954, it became evident to all that African Americans, like their counterparts in the colonial world, would no longer wait for the birth of a new freedom.

Jim Crow Must Go!: The Road from Brown to Montgomery

Revolutions always exact a price from their participants. People have lost their livelihoods, lost friends and family, lost their connection to community, even lost their lives. The movement to end segregation and press America to live up to its creed of justice for all was no different. Nowhere was this personal cost more obvious than in the five legal cases that would force their way into the U.S. Supreme Court and become known collectively as *Brown* v. *Board of Education*. The case known as *Briggs* v. *Elliott* provided the legal bedrock on which the entire set of *Brown* cases was built.

The setting for this initial drama was Clarendon County, South Carolina, known for its bitter resistance to any attempts at changing the brutal traditions of white supremacy. There, love for their children drove black parents to take the simple but dangerous risk of confronting the school board with their children's need for bus transportation to their segregated school. The white children had several buses, while the black children, who outnumbered the others, had no buses at all. Of course, the black parents and their supporters were also aware that the all-white school board spent more money on each white child in the county than on each black one. What the adults had to figure out was how to deal with the rude and re peated rebuffs from the school board and its chairman, R. W. Elliott, who said at a meeting with black people, "We ain't got no money to buy a bus for your nigger children."

Then Rev. J. A. Delaine, a local black pastor and school superintendent in Summerton, met Rev. James A. Hinton, a regional representative for the NAACP, at a meeting at Allen College, one of the black colleges in Columbia, about sixty miles from Summerton. Hinton told the gathering that the NAACP was trying to find men and women to become plaintiffs in a case that would challenge the legality of the segregated schools. Delaine knew after the meeting that he had to become the bridge between the unrelenting but frustrated neighbor parents and the national organization.

Delaine and his wife worked for the school board they were suing, and both lost their jobs. They also lost their home and their church when the buildings were burned to the ground. Meanwhile, in Farmville, Virginia, in 1951, a courageous sixteen-year-old high school junior organized her fellow students to fight for equal facilities for black schools. Under Barbara Rose Johns's dynamic leadership, the black students at the woefully inadequate Moton High not only went on strike but arranged with the NAACP to file a desegregation lawsuit in their county. That suit was eventually tied to the one initiated by Oliver Brown of Topeka, Kansas, on behalf of his daughter Linda and all the black children of their city.

The Topeka school board had denied Linda Brown admission to a school just five blocks from her home, forcing her to make a long commute across town, because her neighborhood school was for whites only. Charles Houston and Thurgood Marshall of the NAACP Legal Defense and Education Fund were the attorneys for the Browns. In his Supreme Court argument, Marshall presented evidence that separating black and white students placed the blacks at a great disadvantage. Marshall's strategy was to force the Supreme Court to overturn the 1896 *Plessy* v. *Ferguson* ruling, which upheld the legality of segregation as long as states provided "separate but equal" facilities to African Americans. Such practices, he said, violated the 14th Amendment to the Constitution, which guarantees equal protection of the laws. Once he was able to get the Court to overturn *Plessy*, Marshall did not have to prove that facilities set aside for "colored only" were unequal to those set aside for whites. To buttress his argument, Marshall brought in pioneering black psychologists Mamie and Kenneth Clark, whose research demonstrated that African-American children in inferior, segregated schools had a negative self-image and generally performed poorly as a result.

When the Supreme Court handed down its unanimous decision in *Brown* on Monday, May 17, 1954, it was a stunning accomplishment. All eyes focused on the solemn announcement that "in the field of public education the doctrine of 'separate but equal' has no place." After more than half a century of determined struggle, black people and their allies had finally turned the Supreme Court around. Two days after *Brown*, the *Washington Post* declared, "It is not too much to speak of the court's decision as a new birth of freedom."

Perhaps it was only the opening of a new chapter in the long black struggle for authentic democracy in America. But it forced individual men and women to make hard, exciting choices about how they would lead their own lives. In Boston, Martin Luther King, Jr., and his new bride, the former Coretta Scott, had been facing such choices together ever since their marriage in June 1953, and his completion of the coursework for his doctorate in theology at Boston University. Soon Coretta would complete her three years of work in music education at the New England Conservatory of Music, and the choices they had been wrestling with were now leading to a move from Boston to Montgomery, Alabama.

Born in Atlanta in January 1929, Martin was the beloved first son of Martin Luther King, Sr., one of that city's leading Baptist ministers, and his wife, Alberta

Williams King, whose father had been the founding pastor of Ebenezer Baptist Church, the congregation now headed by King Senior. The younger King entered Morehouse College in Atlanta, one of the most respected black colleges in the nation, when he was only fifteen. He became a popular student leader and a serious student.

When he was eighteen, not long before he graduated from Morehouse with a B.A. in sociology, King decided to stop resisting an inner calling to the Christian ministry. So his father proudly ordained the young man who had finally decided that he would not take the path of law or medicine, possibilities that had intrigued him for a while. At that point in his life young "M.L." was often torn between the image of ministry he saw in his father, a pietistic man with an engaging, emotionally charged approach, and the one he found in Benjamin Mays, Morehouse's president. Mays's combination of profound spirituality, intellect, and commitment to social justice left a deep mark on the lives of many of his "Morehouse Men."

Martin King, Jr., left Atlanta in 1948 to enroll at Crozer Theological Seminary in Chester, Pennsylvania (one of the few white theological schools that accepted more than one or two black men in each entering class). He carried with him a profound sense of identity with the black church, community, and extended family that had done so much to shape and nurture him. Although he knew that he did not want to be the kind of preacher that his father was, King was deeply appreciative of the older man's unwavering religious faith and his readiness to confront racism.

So although Crozer was King's first extended experience in an overwhelmingly white institution, he was spiritually and mentally prepared for it. By now the young Atlantan, whose eloquence was praised by his professors, was firmly grounded in the way of thinking that marked the lives of many young black people in those days. He knew that his life and career were not simply matters of personal success and advancement. Instead, he recognized and acknowledged an inextricable connection to the "cause" of black advancement, to the responsibility he bore for fighting for "the uplift of the race." King graduated from Crozer in 1951 as valedictorian of his class and received a coveted fellowship to pursue his doctorate at Boston University. The decision to do doctoral work reflected King's continuing exploration of the possibility that he might somehow combine his love for academic work with his passion for the Christian ministry.

In Boston, King was introduced to Coretta Scott, a bright, attractive young woman who had grown up not far from Selma, Alabama. Living in the rural South of the thirties and forties, Coretta saw many instances of violently enforced white domination, including the beating of her father. With these disturbing memories of the past and her own professional ambitions on her mind, Coretta King was strongly inclined to stay out of the South. And King was attracted by invitations to consider positions in the North. But, King later remembered, "The south, after all, was our home. Despite its shortcomings we loved it as home. . . ." At the same time,

Martin and Coretta King were part of the long black Southern tradition that called on its educated young people to work to change the South they had known.

So Coretta was neither very surprised nor very resistant when her husband finally declared that they were going to live in the South. By the spring of 1954 King had accepted an invitation to the pastorate of Dexter Avenue Baptist Church in Montgomery, Alabama, the city known as "The Cradle of the Confederacy." Montgomery was where Jefferson Davis had been sworn in as president of the pro-slavery states that seceded from the Union in 1861. By the time King began his official tenure as pastor of Dexter's middle-class congregation in September 1954, it was clear that the city's black population of close to fifty thousand was on the brink of a new time.

Like their counterparts throughout the South, many of the most activist-oriented members of Montgomery's black population had been prodded into new forms of organizing. For instance, the expanding, state-by-state defeat of the segregated white primary system inspired the creation of a number of voter registration organizations and campaigns in Montgomery. It also encouraged a variety of risky experiments to challenge the humiliating segregation of everyday life.

One of the most important of these experiments was the formation of the Women's Political Council (WPC), a well-organized group of black, middle-class women. They developed an important telephone communications link (called a "telephone tree" in those days) among their members, initially used for voter registration campaigns. But eventually the group expanded its concerns to other issues faced by a black community in a white-dominated segregated city. In the early fifties these issues ranged from black citizens' seeking access to the public parks that their taxes helped to maintain to the constantly vexing matter of the harsh treatment black people received on the local buses.

It was not long before King discovered that the creative and outspoken chairperson of the WPC, JoAnn Robinson, a faculty member at Alabama State College, the local black college, was a member of Dexter's congregation. He quickly recruited her to lead the church's Social and Political Action Committee, which he had organized. In turn, as Robinson and her conscientious group of women took their concerns into the chambers of the Montgomery City Council, she often called on her young pastor to go with them to add his sharp mind, eloquent voice, and passionate commitment to justice to their arguments for change.

In Montgomery, as elsewhere in the South, those black citizens demanding justice included many military veterans. The Reverend Ralph David Abernathy, pastor of First Baptist Church, was one of the best known of these veterans. He had served with the U.S. Army in Europe, then returned to study at Montgomery's Alabama State College and earn his master's degree in sociology at Atlanta University. As Abernathy later recalled of those days in Montgomery, "Many of the older clergy were in favor of sweeping social change, but they were willing for it to come about slowly, when white society was ready to accept it." He also remembered that "those of us in our twenties were less patient and less afraid of making trouble. . . . As we talked with one another, we began saying that we were willing to help tear down the old walls, even if it meant a genuine uprising."

Another highly regarded veteran freedom worker who was ready for change was E. D. Nixon, the gruff-voiced, outspoken Pullman car porter who had worked for years with the legendary A. Philip Randolph organizing the Brotherhood of Sleeping Car Porters. Now in his fifties, Nixon was probably best known for his role as president of the Alabama branch of the NAACP and as an unrelenting campaigner for black citizenship rights, especially the right to vote. In his NAACP role, Nixon was quietly and efficiently assisted by a highly respected woman in her early forties who served as secretary to the local NAACP branch and as adviser to the organization's youth council. A seamstress by profession, she was named Rosa Parks, and she turned out to be less patient than she sometimes seemed.

By 1955, it was not just Montgomery's black pastors, NAACP members, and community leaders who sensed with Martin and Coretta King that something remarkable was happening. Many of the city's ordinary black citizens recognized that they were entering a new time.

Of course, they (and the rest of the nation, even the world) also knew about the brutal lynching of fourteen-year-old Emmett Till, who was beaten and killed in Mississippi in 1955 by two white men after Till made the mistake of speaking familiarly to a white woman, the wife of one of the men. The black newspapers and journals spread the word (and the photos) of the murdered teenager whose Chicago upbringing had not prepared him for the proper approach to a white woman in rural Mississippi. The papers also reported that black congressman Charles Diggs, Jr., of Michigan, and national NAACP officials went to Money, Mississippi, to attend the trial of Till's accused killers, along with Till's mother, Mamie Till, who helped to turn the tragedy of her son's death into a rallying point for the civil rights movement. Because she insisted on an open casket, and allowed photographs, people nationwide saw firsthand the horrors of Southern lynching.

In spite of the predictable not-guilty verdict in the Till murder case that summer, the black people of Montgomery realized they had seen signals of a new time: In the heart of Bilbo's Mississippi, keepers of the past had been forced to hold a trial and to face a black member of the U.S. House of Representatives; they had been pressed to recognize the rising power of an inflamed black community at home and to answer hard questions from people of color and of conscience from around the world.

For many ordinary black citizens, some of their most painful and consistently humiliating encounters with white power and injustice took place in public, especially on city buses. In the mid-fifties the automobile had not yet become the ubiquitous presence that it is now especially not for the thousands of black people in Montgomery who earned their living as maids, cooks, janitors, porters, and the like. High school and college students were also part of the seventeen thousand or so black people who made up some seventy-five percent of the passengers on the segregated buses. During their daily rides, blacks were relegated to the often-crowded back area and were forbidden to take vacant seats in the forward white section, even if no white passengers were present. Beyond this were the all-too-common encounters with rude and hostile white bus drivers (there were no black ones) who often called their black passengers "apes," "niggers," "black cows," and other demeaning names. Often they demanded that blacks get up and surrender their seats to white passengers when the white section was full. Black passengers were also required to pay their fare in front and then get off to re-board through the rear door.

Such practices were common on the buses in cities all over the South, but that did not make them any more palatable. In the spring of 1955 a teen-aged Montgomery high school student named Claudette Colvin loudly resisted both the driver's orders to give up her seat and the police who were called to arrest her. Colvin's screams and curses were not quite what leaders like Robinson and Nixon had in mind as they searched for a case that could be used to challenge the constitutionality of Montgomery's segregated seating. Their aim was to rally the black community to experiment with a brief boycott of the buses that would focus not only on the segregated seating but on the humiliating treatment. Colvin was not the test case they needed, but Nixon and the waiting WPC forces knew that someone else would eventually be pressed beyond the limit and would resist. Evicted in the early forties for sitting too far forward, Rosa Parks, who had long served as a freedom worker, provided the opportunity that Nixon and the WPC needed.

On December 1, 1955, quiet, soft-spoken Rosa Parks did what she had to do. After all, she was a veteran freedom worker and in many ways one of the most prepared for this historic moment. During the previous decade, she had served as secretary of the Montgomery branch of the NAACP, worked on voter registration campaigns, and had run the local NAACP Youth Council. Because of her earlier challenge to bus segregation ordinances, a few bus drivers refused to stop for her. Perhaps she remembered how right she had felt the previous summer at the Tennessee training center for social change called Highlander Folk School, as she talked with other black and white participants about Montgomery and what was needed there. They talked about their South and how they might contribute to the powerful transformation unfolding everywhere. Perhaps she remembered the young people of her NAACP Youth Council and the models they needed.

So when a bus driver told Parks and three other black people in her row to get up and relinquish their seats to a white man who was standing, she had to say no. There were no shouts, no curses, no accusations, just an inwardly powerful woman sensing the strength of her conviction and refusing to move. When, inevitably, policemen boarded the bus and one ordered her to get up, she still had to say no, realizing that arrest would be the next step. Rosa Parks, the magnificently proper and respectable church member, prepared to go to jail, in a time when such people

Rosa Parks, who refused to give up her bus seat to a white man in Montgomery, was accompanied by NAACP activist E. D. Nixon (second from left) as she appealed her conviction.

did not go to such places. But first she responded to the policeman who asked her why she did not obey the driver. She said, "I didn't think I should have to." Then she asked the officer, "Why do you push us around?" His response may have been the only one he could give: "I don't know." Yet he revealed his own entrapment in the system: "But the law is the law, and you are under arrest." And he took Rosa Parks to the police station.

At the station Parks called her friend and NAACP coworker, E. D. Nixon. For the veteran freedom worker, the shock of Parks's arrest was immediately mixed with the conviction that this was the test case that would challenge the city's bus segregation laws. After informing Parks's husband, Raymond, and her mother, Nixon immediately contacted two local whites he knew he could depend on, Clifford and Virginia Durr. Clifford Durr was a white lawyer in private practice, and he and Nixon went to the station to bail out Rosa Parks. Immediately they began discussing with her the possibility that her arrest could develop into the test case they all needed, and that she needed to recognize the physical and economic risks this might entail. After some hesitation on the part of her husband, Parks and her family were ready.

But history, JoAnn Robinson, and the black people of Montgomery soon overtook those original plans. For when Robinson heard the news of Parks's adventure she realized that the arrest of her friend was potentially more powerful than a legal case. She began to use the telephone tree that her WPC had developed for its voter registration work, and soon dozens of black people knew that the highly respected Rosa Parks had been arrested for refusing to cooperate with the humiliating bus segregation practices that troubled them all. Working all that night and into the next morning, Robinson managed to compose, type the stencil, and run off more than thirty thousand mimeographed copies of a leaflet that said:

> Another Negro woman has been arrested and thrown in jail because she refused to get up out of her seat on the bus for a white person to sit down. It is the second time since the Claudette Colvin case that a Negro woman has been arrested for the same thing. This has to be stopped. Negroes have rights, too, for if Negroes did not ride the buses, they could not operate. Three-fourths of the riders are Negroes, yet we are arrested, or have to stand over empty seats. If we do not do something to stop these arrests, they will continue. The next time it may be you, or your daughter, or mother. This woman's case will come up on Monday. We are, therefore, asking every Negro to stay off the buses Monday in protest of the arrest and trial. Don't ride the bus to work, to town, to school, or anywhere on Monday. You can afford to stay out of school for one day if you have no other way to go except by bus. You can also afford to stay out of town for one day. If you work, take a cab, or walk. But please, children and grown-ups, don't ride the bus at all on Monday. Please stay off all buses Monday.

That morning, Friday, December 2, with the assistance of some of her students and WPC coworkers, Robinson blanketed the black community with the leaflets. By then, Nixon had begun to mobilize the traditional black community leaders, especially the ministers. It soon became clear that both his and Robinson's best instincts had been right: there was a powerful and positive reaction to the call for the leaders to meet and respond both to Parks's arrest and to Robinson's call for a boycott.

By that evening the local community leaders, including King, had decided to confirm Robinson's initiative and agreed that the next Monday, December 5, would be the day for a one-day experimental boycott. Since that was also the day for which Parks's trial was scheduled, it seemed logical to call for a mass community meeting that evening. In order to spread the word of Monday's boycott and mass meeting, the leadership group was depending upon another leaflet, many phone calls, and crucially, the dozens of black church services scheduled for Sunday, December 4. Then, when one of the leaflets got into the hands of a white employer and was passed on to the *Montgomery Advertiser,* the city's daily newspaper, a great gift of publicity was handed to the planners: a Sunday morning front page story on the planned boycott and mass meeting.

Of course, no one could be certain how the black community would respond to the call. There was significant fear among the leaders, including King, that a combination of apathy and fear might overwhelm the sense of righteous indignation that people felt. Nor could anyone predict how white people, especially the more rigid and violence-prone segregationists, would respond. All over the South, many white men and women had been eagerly rallying to the calls of the White Citizens Council to defend segregation by any means necessary. The local Ku Klux Klan was also very much alive and well, carrying on its periodic marches and car caravans through Montgomery's black community, knowing that their reputation for lynchings, beatings, and bombings was enough to drive most blacks off the streets and porches behind the relative safety of closed doors. It was clear to blacks that there was real physical danger involved in the simple act of not riding the buses. But for a lot of black riders there might also be economic danger if their employers objected to such black initiative and protest.

As a result, it was impossible to predict what the results of the boycott attempt would be. The leaders of the courageous experiment felt the action would be successful if sixty percent of the riders stayed off the buses. That cold and cloudy morning, as Martin and Coretta King looked out their front window toward a nearby bus stop, the uncertain victory now seemed clear. Most of the buses moving by were empty. Neither apathy nor fear had prevailed. Then, as King went out to drive along the black community bus routes, he saw an extraordinary scene: everywhere, black people were walking, thumbing rides, walking, riding mules, walking, resurrecting old horse and buggy contraptions, taking taxis. Some older men and women were walking more than five miles each way, at times saying, "I'm walking for my grandchildren." Meanwhile, all the buses from the black communities were at least ninety-five percent empty.

King recognized instinctively that more than bus seating, more than painful memories of humiliation, even more than solidarity with Rosa Parks was at stake here. As he said later, "A miracle had taken place. The once dormant and quiescent Negro community was now fully awake." At the same time, King's own personal awakening, inextricably tied to the rising of the people of Montgomery, was still in process. That Monday afternoon, he gathered with twenty or so other local leaders to assess and celebrate the overwhelming success of the almost spontaneous boycott and to plan for the evening's mass meeting. King was then surprised to find himself—one of the youngest and newest community leaders—nominated and elected president of the new organization that they had just brought into being at that session, the Montgomery Improvement Association (MIA).

The immediate task of the new MIA leaders was to build on the powerful momentum of the one-day boycott. They decided to move rather slowly, to focus first on the simple need for more courteous and humane treatment of black bus riders. They also called for what Coretta King and later others ruefully described as "a more humane form of segregation," which would allow white riders to fill the buses from the front to the middle, black riders from back to middle, with no need for anyone to have to give up a seat. They also pressed for the hiring of black drivers in black neighborhoods. The new MIA leadership decided to call for black people to continue the boycott until these changes were made.

That night at the first mass meeting at the large Holt Street Baptist Church, the leaders immediately recognized that an extraordinary spirit was taking hold. The crowd was so dense and animated that King and the other speakers had a hard time pushing their way to the pulpit. One of the few white reporters on hand, Joe Azbell of the *Advertiser,* was almost awestruck by the experience he witnessed, including the consideration shown to him as a white person. The next day he wrote, "The meeting was much like an old-fashioned revival with loud applause added. . . . It proved beyond any doubt that there was a discipline among Negroes that many whites had doubted. It was almost a military discipline combined with emotion."

As the new MIA president and featured speaker, King had to decide how to position himself in the midst of the dynamic power he had recognized among the people since early in the morning. The twenty-six-year-old pastor later described his struggle to figure out the correct approach:

> How could I make a speech that would be militant enough to keep my people aroused to positive action and yet moderate enough to keep this fervor within controllable and Christian bounds? I knew that many of the Negro people were victims of bitterness that could easily rise to flood proportions. What could I say to keep them courageous and prepared for positive action and yet devoid of hate and resentment? Could the militant and the moderate be combined in a single speech?

In what might be called a freedom sermon, combining the vivid preaching style found in the black churches with the content of the freedom movement, the young pastor set the people and their movement in their largest context that night. He identified them "first and foremost" as American citizens, citizens who had the right and the responsibility to protest injustice and to work for a better society. At every point he grounded himself in the concrete experience of Montgomery's black people and their experiences on the buses and elsewhere in their unjust, humiliating and segregated city. So there was constant enthusiastic and empathetic verbal response all through his presentation, particularly when King uttered the words, "There comes a time when people get tired of being trampled over by the iron feet of oppression." He pushed even further, pressing on the audience a sense of identity beyond their status as victims of oppression, declaring, "I want to say that we're not here advocating violence. . . . We have never done that. . . . I want it to be known throughout Montgomery and throughout this nation that we are a Christian people. . . . We believe in the Christian religion. We believe in the teachings of Jesus. The only weapon that we have in our hands this evening is the weapon of protest." All through that statement of their central religious identity the people shouted and applauded, moved with King, pressed him forward even as he urged them toward their own best possibilities. He said, "We, the disinherited of this land, we who have been oppressed so long, are tired of going through the long night of captivity. And now we are reaching out for the daybreak of freedom and justice and equality."

So the issue was already far beyond the buses, encompassing freedom, justice, and equality. Calling upon the people to continue to work together for much more than a desegregated bus seat, King set an example for the freedom movement leadership. For he declared to his community:

> Right here in Montgomery, when the history books are written in the future . . . somebody will have to say, "There lived a race of people . . . who had the moral courage to stand up for their rights. . . . And thereby they injected a new meaning into the veins of history and of civilization." And we're going to do that. God grant that we will do it before it is too late.

The excited, inspired people hardly had time to consider this grand calling to be the bearers of new universal values when they were brought right back to the concrete realities of their new movement. Right there in the meeting they were called upon to vote their approval of the proposals the MIA leadership was using as a basis for their negotiating with the city administration and the bus company. They were also told that private automobiles and black-owned taxis had to be volunteered, along with drivers, for use in a car pool that would soon become the most highly organized element of the boycott movement. And, of course, money had to be collected, for gas, for maintenance, and for all the other expenses connected to the development of an essentially volunteer organization. So the marvelously ordinary black men and women who were just being called upon by King to inject "a new meaning into the veins of history and of civilization" were also being asked to drop their hard-earned quarters and dollars into the MIA collection baskets.

The sense that something new was being born in Montgomery's black churches had drawn black leaders from other parts of Alabama to the initial meeting that night. They came from such places as Birmingham, Mobile, Tuskegee, and Tuscaloosa, both to encourage the people of Montgomery and to gain new inspiration for their own struggles. Still, it is quite possible that the expansion of the boycott's inspiring potential might have simply been confined to Alabama if its white opponents had not made a series of mistakes, mistakes based on their stubborn refusal to realize that a new time and a new black community were emerging.

First, in the earliest attempts at negotiation, the representatives of the city and the bus company refused to make even the slightest accommodation to the relatively modest changes the MIA leadership was proposing. This stiff resistance on the part of the white leaders helped to steel the resolve of the aroused and walking people. Then the city commissioners inaugurated what they called a "get tough" policy with the boycotters and their leadership. Legal harassment of the crucial cabs and car pool, and an unjustified arrest of King for speeding were part of the strategy of intimidation. This was soon followed by a publicly announced decision by all three city commissioners to join the local White Citizens Council, a slightly more respectable version of the Klan.

Such actions only compelled black Montgomery to form a deeper resolve to stay off the buses. Then the most important of the early opposition mistakes took place on Monday night, January 30, 1956, almost two months into the boycott. That night, while King was at one of the mass meetings, his wife and young child were at home accompanied by a member of Dexter church. The two women heard something hit the front porch. They ran to the back room where three-month-old Yolanda Denise was sleeping. What they had heard was a stick of dynamite landing on the front porch, and its explosion blew a hole in the porch floor, shattered four windows, and damaged a porch column. Running to the back had saved Coretta King and her friend from possible injury.

Called out of the mass meeting, King arrived at his house some fifteen minutes after the blast. There he found hundreds of angry black people, some of them armed, milling around his front porch. After determining that his family was safe, he came back out to address the crowd, some of whom were fiercely challenging the chief of police and the mayor to match them gun for gun, and defiantly refusing to obey police orders to disperse. "Getting tough" was obviously an approach that had epidemic possibilities, but when King appeared he maintained an extraordinary and crucial composure that transformed the situation. After assuring the crowd that his family had not been harmed, he said,

> We believe in law and order. Don't get panicky. . . . Don't get your weapons. He who lives by the sword will perish by the sword. Remember, that is what God said. We are not advocating violence. We want to love our enemies. Be good to them. Love them and let them know you love them.

After urging that stern and demanding post-dynamite discipline upon himself and the crowd, pressing them to apply the tenets of their religion to the crisis of that night, King went on to remind the quieting crowd, "I did not start this boycott. I was asked by you to serve as your spokesman." Then he added, "I want it to be known the length and breadth of this land that if I am stopped this movement will not stop. . . . What we are doing is just. And God is with us." The gathered people responded by spontaneously breaking into song, including hymns and "My country 'tis of thee, sweet land of liberty, of thee I sing."

It was the terrorist bombing and King's mature and challenging response to it that effectively began to push the Montgomery story beyond the confines of the African-American press and the local newspapers into the nation's mainstream mass media and into the consciousness (and consciences) of hundred of thousands of its citizens, irrespective of color.

Meanwhile, the white defenders of Montgomery continued to misread the times and the people they were dealing with. Shortly after the dynamite attack on King's house, a bomb was thrown into the front yard of MIA treasurer and movement stalwart E. D. Nixon. Two weeks later eleven thousand white people gathered in Montgomery for a White Citizens Council rally, where they cheered the mayor and police chief for holding the line in the cause of bus segregation. Perhaps encouraged by their own mass meeting, the city officials decided to ask a grand jury to indict nearly one hundred leaders of the MIA on charges of conspiracy. That broadside approach and the refusal of the MIA leadership to be intimidated by it only intensified the national media interest in Montgomery and in King.

The first time that the Montgomery story appeared on the front page of the internationally respected *New York Times* and *New York Herald Tribune* was when these papers reported the mass meeting held the evening after the leaders were arrested, and immediately bailed out, on the conspiracy charge. Readers around the world were able to catch the spirit of determined, nonviolent resistance as thousands of boycotters gathered to hear the news from the courtroom and to stand in solidarity with their leaders. Thus the nation received King's message: "This is not a war between the white and the Negro but a conflict between justice and injustice." Expanding his vision to include the largest possible participation, King went on, "If our victory is won—and it will be won—it will be a victory for Negroes, a victory for justice, a victory for free people, and a victory for democracy." In a sense, there were hundreds of thousands of distant listeners as he proclaimed, "If we are arrested every day, if we are exploited every day, if we are trampled over every day, don't ever let anyone pull you so low as to hate them. We must use the weapon of love."

The nation began to respond in a variety of ways. The proprietor of Sadie's Beauty Shop in the black community of Gastonia, North Carolina, took up a collection in her shop for Montgomery's walkers. The first African-American winner of the Nobel Peace Prize, Ralph Bunche, who served as an official of the United Nations, wrote to praise and encourage King and the people of the movement: "Your patient determination, your wisdom and quiet courage are constituting an inspiring chapter in the history of human dignity." In hundreds of black churches across the country the combination of praying and organizing produced scenes like the one in Concord Baptist Church in Brooklyn, New York, where a collection of four thousand dollars was taken up for Montgomery in trash cans and cake boxes after the collection plates were filled.

This vital connection between King and Montgomery's church-based movement and the black churches throughout the country was crucial in transforming the nation after World War II. Supplementing the news that came from black newspapers and magazines like *Jet, Ebony,* and *Sepia,* as well as from the newly attentive white-owned media, black churches served as a massive network for information and mobilization regarding Montgomery. Other committed groups—the skycaps at Newark airport and some longshoremen in San Francisco, for example—made their own contributions, sometimes just an hour's pay.

King and the movement attracted the attention of two of the most important religiously based pacifist groups in the country: the Fellowship of Reconciliation (FOR) and the American Friends Service Committee, better known as Quakers. Many of their members had hoped and worked for a long time to see Mahatma Gandhi's religiously inspired organizing combined with the courageous, nonviolent spirit of Jesus in the cause of racial justice and equality in the United States. Though predominantly white, they were often joined and even led by a number of African Americans, such as Howard and Sue Thurman, Benjamin Mays, Mordecai Johnson, and Bayard Rustin, the radical Quaker and peace activist. Indeed, when Montgomery broke into the mainstream news, the national chairman of the FOR was Charles Lawrence, a 1936 Morehouse College graduate who was then teaching sociology at Brooklyn College in New York. Lawrence, a firm, articulate, and jovial believer in the nonviolent struggle for justice, wrote to King as soon as he saw the newspaper reports on the post-indictment mass meeting and claimed that he found the stories "among the most thrilling documents I have ever read." He wrote, "Who knows? Providence may have given the Negroes of Montgomery the historic mission of demonstrating to the world the practical power of Christianity, the unmatched vitality of a nonviolent loving approach to social protest."

Inspired by such grand hopes, Lawrence and his FOR colleagues sent their national field secretary, Glenn Smiley, on an exploratory visit to Montgomery that winter. Smiley, a white Texan who was an ordained minister in the Southern Methodist Church, had been involved with the Fellowship since the early forties and had been a conscientious objector on religious grounds during World War II. According to Lawrence's instructions, Smiley's FOR mission in Montgomery would be "primarily that of finding out what those of you who are involved directly would have those of us who are 'on the outside' do."

Meanwhile, Rustin, one of the best-known activists in the pacifist movement, also went independently to offer his services to King and the Montgomery struggle. A personable, brilliant, nonviolent strategist and writer, Rustin did not, unfortunately, stay long in Montgomery. Ironically, in the eyes of some of the MIA officers, Rustin's past involvement with communist-related organizations and his prior arrest for a homosexual liaison made him more of a risk than Smiley. Nevertheless, both men helped King on what he later called his "pilgrimage to nonviolence," introducing him to leading religious pacifists, such as Howard Thurman and Harry Emerson Fosdick; introducing him to the classic published writings on nonviolence, such as Fosdick's *Hope of the World*; and assisting the MIA in developing its own training workshops in nonviolence. Rustin, in particular, helped King prepare important articles on the Montgomery struggle for a number of religious journals.

By the end of the winter of 1956, as the boycott moved into its fourth month, King's picture had appeared on the cover of a number of national magazines, and his name and message were familiar in many other parts of the world. He carried the message across the nation, his powerful baritone voice reverberating in scores of large churches, on college and university campuses, in municipal auditoriums, at conventions of the NAACP and the National Urban League, at fraternal and religious conventions, even at a black funeral directors' convention.

By the fall of 1956 Montgomery had become the unmistakable symbol of transformation in the nation, a symbol of its African-American citizens and its Southern-based traditions of legal segregation, white domination, and the subversion of democratic hope. That symbol belonged to all the licensed practical nurses, the maids and skycaps, the scholars and Nobel laureates, the prisoners, students, artists, and pastors who would eventually create their own versions of Montgomery across the nation.

By this time the Montgomery movement had also provided a crucial set of opportunities for King and his co-workers to experiment with Gandhian nonviolent action (or "passive resistance," as King sometimes described it) on behalf of freedom and justice. King could now announce with confidence, "We in Montgomery have discovered a method that can be used by the Negroes in their fight for political and economic equality.... We fight injustice with passive resistance.... Mohandas Gandhi ... used it to topple the British military machine.... Let's now use this method in the United States."

At the same time, while he increasingly referred to Gandhi, King kept returning to his fundamental grounding in the black church experience. "The spirit of passive resistance came to me from the Bible," he said, "from the teachings of Jesus. The techniques came from Gandhi." Summing up what the events in Montgomery meant for a religiously sensitive region and nation, King continued to affirm that "This is a spiritual movement, depending on moral and spiritual forces."

But such a spiritual vision did not exclude the use of practical methods. For instance, the white authorities' unwillingness to negotiate and the continued harassment and violence directed at the black community compelled the MIA leaders to take their struggle into the courts. In consultation with the local and national NAACP lawyers, the MIA initiated a legal suit to challenge the constitutionality of Montgomery's segregated bus system. They had moved far beyond the initial quest for "a more humane form of segregation." Now they were challenging the Jim Crow transportation system itself. The case was identified as *Gayle* v. *Browder* (1956). And when the U.S. Supreme Court ruled in favor of the black citizens of Montgomery, it was clear the South was about to change forever.

The Court's ruling in *Gayle* v. *Browder* was announced on November 13, 1956, but no one knew when the official papers of notification would reach Montgomery. The city commission refused to allow the bus company to make any changes in its practices until the court documents actually arrived in their offices. But the people of the movement prepared themselves for the next phase of the journey they had begun on December 5, 1955. On the night when the Supreme Court decision was announced, a caravan of forty cars of Klan members drove through the city's black neighborhoods. But no one ran into their houses. No one pulled down the shades. Instead, many "New Negroes" stood and watched calmly. Some even waved to the disconcerted white-robed visitors, and soon the visitors drove away.

The next night there were two mass meetings to accommodate all the people full of courage who had come to give thanks for the past and plan for the future. It was natural that the MIA executive committee called on King to address the meetings that night. Speaking at Holt Street Church, where they had begun together, King said, "These eleven months have not all been easy. . . . We have lived with this protest so long that we have learned the meaning of sacrifice and suffering. But somehow we feel that our suffering is redemptive." Forever the teacher, King felt that he had to encourage the people to consider what it would mean to "press on" to their next steps "in the spirit of the movement." For him, two elements were crucial. One was the need to avoid arrogance as they made their victorious return to the buses. Taking on a personal tone, he said to the people, "I would be terribly disappointed if anybody goes back to the buses bragging about, we, the Negroes, have won a victory over the white people." Instead, King called on them to remember the need to open both the struggle and the victory beyond racial lines. So he said that when the legal papers finally arrived, "it will be a victory for justice and a victory for goodwill and a victory for the forces of light. So let us not limit this decision to a victory for Negroes. Let us go back to the buses in all humility and with gratitude to the Almighty God for making this [court] decision possible."

Even at such a high point in their struggle, King knew that he was pressing his people toward a fiercely demanding discipline. He said, "I know it's hard" but kept pushing: "the strong man is the man . . . who can stand up for his rights and yet not hit back."

King knew they were on a dangerous path. They were poised at a crucial moment in history, a moment that required disciplined courage and disciplined love, especially in the light of the South's long history of violence against black attempts to gain justice. Finally, King faced his people with the ultimate encouragement—his willingness to sacrifice his own life. Normally not given to this kind of self-focus, it was a clear sign that he saw the moment as a moment of crisis, one similar to that January night on his bombed-out porch. So he said to the visibly moved assembly:

> I'm not telling you something that I don't live. [Someone yelled, "That's right!"] I'm aware of the fact that the Ku Klux Klan is riding in Montgomery. I'm aware of the fact that a week never passes that somebody's not telling me to get out of town, or that I'm going to be killed next place I move. But I don't have any guns in my pockets. I don't have any guards on my side.

> But I have the God of the Universe on my side. I'm serious about that. I
> can walk the streets of Montgomery without fear. I don't worry about a
> thing. They can bomb my house. They can kill my body. But they can never
> kill the spirit of freedom that is in my people.

Finally, on December 20, the Supreme Court mandate made its way to
Montgomery, affirming the people and their audacious struggle. The next morning a restrained but happy group, including King, Abernathy, and Smiley, boarded
the first desegregated bus, beginning a new phase of the long journey toward freedom and justice for all.

Old Order, New Order

By the time the victory was won in Montgomery, the struggle had lasted for more
than a year. All along the way there were dramatic, compelling new events, bombings, indictments, rallies in other cities, and courtroom trials reminding people,
especially black people, that the Montgomery movement was alive. Black folks had
stuck together and grown together in the longest sustained campaign for justice
that the nation had ever seen.

And, of course, the movement's prime symbol, Martin Luther King, Jr., seemed
to be everywhere, proclaiming and exemplifying the emergence of a new people
and a new time. By the time the legal victory was announced in Montgomery, it
appeared that King was right: It was far more than a victory for the black walkers
of Montgomery (although *that* victory certainly needed to be savored and celebrated), and wherever people claimed the fruits of the long ordeal, a powerful energy of hope and a sense of new possibilities appeared.

Sometimes the Montgomery connections to other places in the nation was
obvious. In cities such as Mobile and Birmingham, Alabama, and nearby Tallahassee, Florida, ministers tried to repeat the Montgomery success with their own
bus boycotts. In January 1957 King and the Fellowship of Reconciliation brought
together some sixty representatives of these and other boycott movements to a
conference in Atlanta. They discussed the possibility of forming a regional organization based on the Montgomery experience. Before the summer of 1957 was over,
King and his fellow black ministers had established the Southern Christian
Leadership Conference (SCLC).

The major early accomplishments of SCLC were the sponsorship of several conferences and organizing, with Bayard Rustin and A. Philip Randolph, a "prayer pilgrimage" of about twenty thousand people in Washington, D.C., who were calling
for civil rights legislation. SCLC also hoped to undertake a "Crusade for Citizenship," projected as a massive Southwide voter registration campaign based in the
black churches. Due to lack of personnel, planning, and finances, this campaign
never materialized.

Even with its provocative founding announcement that "we have come to
redeem the soul of America" and the predictable choice of King as president, the

mostly Baptist group was not, however, able to focus and mobilize the new energies in the ways that King, his Alabama comrades, and his Northern allies had
hoped. This was partly because the approximately one hundred men (there were
only men in mainstream black church leadership) who formed the core of the
SCLC were only a small minority of the black ministers of the South. And, besides,
SCLC's ministers had had no real experience in forming a regional organization
that would be both flexible and open to new strategies yet also structured enough
to mount a sustained challenge to the system of legal segregation.

So for a number of years after the Montgomery victory, the energies that were
released there had to be channeled into less obvious places than the Southern black
churches that had anchored the celebrated boycott. As a result, the expansion of the
Southern freedom movement depended on unlikely groups of people, emerging
from unexpected places.

For instance, there was the teenager John Lewis, a short, slightly built, slow-
speaking country boy from Troy, Alabama, who had first heard King's pre-boycott
preaching on a local black radio station. The unassuming but religiously rooted
Lewis had been training himself for his own calling by preaching to the livestock in his family's yard, and baptizing some of them too. Regardless of his uncon-
ventional training and practice congregation, Lewis knew that there was work for
him to do, and King and the people of Montgomery were his models. Throughout the post-Montgomery decade, John Lewis took that work and those models
into some of the most dangerous frontiers of the Southern-based struggle for freedom, accumulating many scars and much honor in the process. As a Freedom
Rider in 1961, Lewis rode buses throughout the South, testing the law that made
segregated buses and station facilities illegal. He became the first Freedom Rider
to meet with violence when he was struck by some white men as he attempted
to go through the white entrance to the Rock Hill, South Carolina, Greyhound
bus station.

In the same way, few people would have predicted that a matronly, middle-aged
black South Carolinian named Septima Poinsette Clark would be one of the most
effective carriers of Montgomery's best spirit. In her fifties when the victory was
won, the Charleston woman was not too old to be a "new Negro." A veteran teacher
in the public school system of Charleston, she had led important struggles for the
equalizing of salaries for black and white teachers.

Then, on April 19, 1956, a law was passed prohibiting state and city employees
from having an affiliation with any civil rights group, including the NAACP. Clark
refused to obey the law and lost her job. She now joined forces with the white
Southerners who had founded the Highlander Folk School in the mountains of
eastern Tennessee. Highlander was established in the thirties as a nontraditional
educational center to encourage local citizens and others to build a more just and
democratic society across racial lines.

At Highlander the soft-spoken but iron-willed Clark created a program based
on work she had been doing for decades. She called it Citizenship Education, and

it involved an informal but carefully crafted workshop combination of storytelling, political analysis, American and African-American history, religious education, autobiographical sharing, careful study of arcane voter registration laws and forms, and much singing and mutual encouragement. With such deceptively simple methods, Clark and her expanding group of co-workers performed an almost unbelievable task. They helped thousands of marginally literate (and sometimes illiterate) black people not only learn to read and write their way to voter registration skills, but also to teach others, and to become committed believers in the freedom movement.

By that time many people had discovered that the path blazed by Rosa Parks, Martin Luther King, Jr., and the Montgomery boycotters was not meant to be duplicated exactly. That was clear not only in efforts of people like John Lewis and Septima Clark. It could also be seen in the failed attempts to build Montgomery copycat boycotts in places like Mobile and Tallahassee, failures that inspired people to search for other methods. Indeed when King had declared near the close of the Montgomery boycott that "nothing can kill the spirit of my people," he probably understood that the spirit needed to take many different forms.

That spirit was seen, for instance, in the fiery determination of Fred Shuttlesworth, the Birmingham pastor who became a staunch comrade to Martin King in the next stages of the Southern freedom movement. A contrast to King in almost every conceivable way, Shuttlesworth was a native of Alabama's backwoods—a wiry, volatile, and gritty man. Before he answered the inner call to the Christian ministry, he had been a truck driver, cement worker, and operator of the family's whiskey still. Indeed, he was just the kind of utterly courageous, sharp-tongued, quick-tempered believer in nonviolence that the movement needed. Though profoundly inspired by King and Montgomery, Shuttlesworth was his own man. When white-led governments across the South responded to black assertiveness by banning established organizations such as the NAACP, Shuttlesworth's independence proved invaluable.

In Alabama the white authorities formally blamed the national organization and its local branches for organizing an illegal boycott by black residents of Montgomery and used that as their excuse for outlawing the organization in the state. The state demanded its membership lists (a demand that the NAACP managed successfully to resist for the eight years that it took to get the state action reversed in federal courts). Just a few days after the NAACP ban went into effect, Fred Shuttlesworth angered the local authorities when he formed a new, replacement organization from his Birmingham base, calling it the Alabama Christian Movement for Human Rights (ACMHR). Led essentially (and somewhat autocratically) by Shuttlesworth, the ACMHR became one of the most vital affiliates of the Southern Christian Leadership Conference, temporarily providing a mass movement–oriented substitute for the NAACP and eventually carrying the spirit of Montgomery to another level of confrontation. The ACMHR fought against bus segregation in December 1956 and October 1958, using direct-action tactics. It also tried to integrate Birmingham schools and train stations in 1957.

In other states, such as Mississippi and Florida, courageous NAACP officials and those who tried to stand with them were sometimes run out of the state or assassinated. On Christmas night 1951, Harry T. Moore, executive secretary of NAACP branches in Florida, and his wife were killed when their house was bombed in Mims, Florida. Shuttlesworth himself was subjected to everything from midday beatings by mobs of white segregationists to the nighttime bombing of his house and church. The attacks intensified after the intrepid pastor insisted on personally desegregating the Birmingham city buses and on trying to enroll his children in an all-white school in the stubbornly segregated city school system.

Indeed, public opinion polls revealed that eighty percent of white Southerners were opposed to school desegregation in the immediate post-*Brown* period. Although the terms of opposition were framed in various ways, so much finally came down to the basic truth that South Carolina governor James Byrnes had expressed. If taken seriously, desegregation marked "the beginning of the end of civilization in the South" as white people, especially privileged white people, had known it. In the same way, there was no room for misinterpreting the so-called "Southern manifesto" that had been signed in March 1956 by ninety Southern members of the House of Representatives and by all of the senators except Estes Kefauver and Albert Gore of Tennessee and Senate majority leader Lyndon Johnson. In this document these respected senators and representatives denied that the Supreme Court had a right to rule on racial issues in the realm of public education, as it had in the *Brown* decision, and called upon their constituents to disobey the court's order, offering "massive resistance" to the ruling.

In addition, the person who might have been expected to provide some firm guidance to the nation in this crucial time of transition was offering a version of his own resistance. The widely admired military hero Dwight D. Eisenhower had been elected President in 1952 and again in 1956. He probably had more leverage to lead the nation down the path of peaceful change than any other public figure, but he never really came to the aid of African Americans. Rather, the President chose to condemn what he called "the extremists on both sides" of the school desegregation question, thereby equating courageous children and their communities who were working for democratic change with men and women who defied the Supreme Court, dynamited buildings, and assassinated leaders.

Though Eisenhower never made a clear public statement of opposition to the Court's action in *Brown,* neither did he ever publicly support it. He felt that "forcing" desegregation would raise white resistance. But as the nature of the battle for desegregation progressed, Eisenhower was forced to take action on behalf of the federal government.

Faced with such a range of opposition midnight bombers, an uncommitted President, members of Congress urging "massive resistance," and the Supreme

Court's own ambiguous 1955 call for school districts to move to implement the *Brown* decision not by any certain date but "with all deliberate speed," it would not have been surprising if Southern blacks had given up the quest for desegregated schools. But they were constantly reminding each other that "we've come too far to turn back."

Children, ranging in ages from six to seventeen, were on the front lines of this phase of the struggle. In hundreds of schools across the South, the children had to face hatred, ignorance, and fear. As they arrived at newly desegregated schools, they had to face screaming, cursing, threatening presences of white men, children, and women who had appointed themselves as protectors of the social and educational bastions of white supremacy.

Still, the black children went into the schools—sometimes to the accompaniment of white rioting in the streets, sometimes under the protection of federal marshals or troops.

Eventually, all the possibilities and complications of the post-Montgomery struggles for a desegregated nation seemed to gather around Little Rock's Central High. Little Rock was considered a city that was reasonably open to the powerful surges of change that were mounting in the South, and in 1954 it had been the first Southern city to respond positively to the *Brown* decision. Less than a week after the decision was announced, the Little Rock school board declared its intention to voluntarily desegregate its public schools, beginning with the two-thousand-student Central High, located in a working-class white neighborhood. However, it was not until 1957 that the board announced that it would actually begin the desegregation process on a rather timid level that fall. Then seventy-five students volunteered to lead the way. Of those, twenty-five were chosen. The all-white school board, worried about a brewing politically inspired white reaction, soon pared the number down to nine. Six young women and three young men were chosen to "carry the banner."

Unfortunately, the white community of Little Rock and the state of Arkansas once again lacked the kind of courageous moral leadership that would have helped guide them. Instead the confused and searching citizens were subjected to the mercurial and election-driven performance of Governor Orville Faubus. A racial "moderate" in pre-1954 Southern white terms, he had become convinced that in order to be reelected, he had to respond to the worst fears of the white parents and politicians who were busy galvanizing opposition to the school board's modest desegregation plan. This led to the spectacle of Faubus calling out the Arkansas National Guard that fall to block the way of the black students as they—with amazing poise—moved past a crowd of screaming adults and young people and tried to enter Central High.

Such a use of state troops to resist a U.S. Supreme Court order, carried out in front of national network television cameras, finally pushed Eisenhower to action. But his initial attempt to use his personal powers of persuasion on Faubus turned

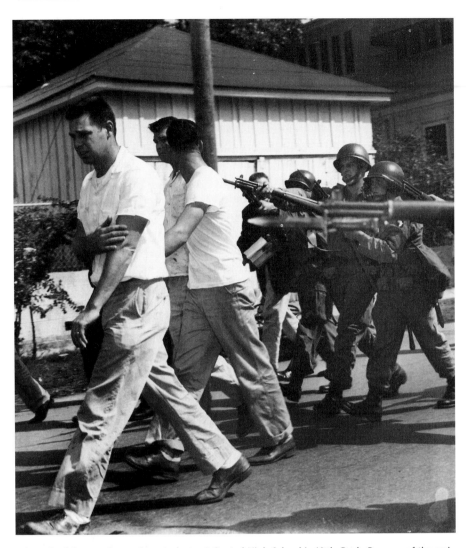

Armed soldiers confront white students at Central High School in Little Rock. Because of the serious challenge to federal authority in Arkansas, President Eisenhower sent one thousand U.S. Army troops to protect the nine black students who had defied white protests and threats of violence to enroll at the school.

out to be too little too late and served only to help heighten the crisis. Ten days after the beginning of the Little Rock crisis, Eisenhower summoned Faubus to a private conference. The governor left his conversation with the President to return to Little Rock and pull away the Arkansas National Guard, leaving only the local police to deal with the constantly expanding crowd of white adult opponents at the school building. Their hysterical calls for resistance to integration finally erupted into violence against several black journalists. At the same time there were reckless threats from the mob to lynch one or more of the black students. The scenes of white crowds surging against the overwhelmed and under-committed local police moved across the nation's television screens. (The medium was new, and the black struggle for freedom in the South was its first major ongoing story.) Many people also saw the electrifying image of Elizabeth Eckford, one of the black students in Little Rock, accidentally cut off from the rest of the group of students, surrounded by the hostile mob, moving in silent, terrified dignity, finally joined by a tall white woman, Grace Lorch, who stood by her side and then helped her board a bus to safety.

Eisenhower finally did what he had pledged never to do: send federal troops to Little Rock "to aid in the execution of federal law," he said to the nation. But he also sent more than a thousand riot-trained troops from the 101st Airborne Division to protect the right of nine young citizens to make use of the opportunity that the Supreme Court had guaranteed to them.

The Little Rock pioneers stayed the course, managed to live through an academic year of hateful taunts and actual assaults, managed also to find a few friends. For a while each student was accompanied in the school by a soldier, but these military companions could not go into locker rooms, lavatories, classrooms, the cafeteria, and other spaces that had become danger spots. There came a time when one of the nine, Minnie Jean Brown, finally gave in to the deep frustration they were all feeling and one day poured her bowl of chili on the head of a persistent tormenter. Her unexpected action evoked a spontaneous round of applause from the black cafeteria workers, but it also led to a suspension from school, and Minnie Jean finished her academic year in New York City. Meanwhile the other students continued, making their way through Central High's school year, carrying the banner—and the pain—all the way. Crucial to their endurance was the community support that they found.

Many people in both the South and the North, however, were not convinced that a just and humane new nation could be born on this bloody ground. These reluctant unbelievers simply could not convince themselves that American democracy could ever become a reality for black people.

As a matter of fact, even as the Little Rock struggle was going on in the 1957–58 academic year, in Monroe, North Carolina, a rather different scenario was developing. Ex-Marine Robert Williams, who had been so ecstatic with hope at the time of the *Brown* decision, had returned to his hometown of Monroe after the Korean War. He soon became president of the local branch of the NAACP and also became convinced that his military training provided a better alternative for dealing with the terrorists of the Klan and other white groups than King's way of nonviolent resistance. With the help of the National Rifle Association, Williams created a rifle club within his NAACP branch and began talking of the need to "meet lynching with lynching." But by the middle of 1959 Williams found himself attacked and disowned by the national NAACP organization and hounded as a fugitive by local and national law enforcement agencies. Two years later, he was forced to flee the country altogether as a result of trumped-up kidnapping charges. Eventually he became an exile from the land that once inspired his hope, finding political asylum in Cuba, which had just undergone its own socialist revolution. He later went to China and then the East African nation of Tanzania before returning to America almost a decade later.

Nevertheless, Williams's demand for an alternative to nonviolent resistance did not end with his departure. His calls for armed self-defense and physical retaliation were familiar themes in the traditions of black American resistance. Indeed, even then an important variation on this theme was rising up in the northern cities of the nation.

When all eyes seemed to be on Montgomery, in the black communities of Detroit, New York, Chicago, Los Angeles, and elsewhere a growing number of young black men, impeccably dressed in suits and bow ties, and young women, wrapped in long, flowing white dresses, became a regular part of the urban landscape. These quiet, dignified, disciplined black folk were practicing Muslims, members of the Nation of Islam (NOI). The NOI was founded by an obscure self-styled prophet named W. D. Fard in the thirties. Fard and his handpicked successor, Elijah Poole (who would later take the name Elijah Muhammad), preached a modified version of Islam. It combined claims of black racial supremacy (such as the idea that black people were the original people and whites were "devils" invented by a mad scientist named Yacub) with elements of the orthodox Islamic tradition and borrowed heavily from the style and structure of black Christian churches. Despite their reputation for being a radical sect, the NOI promoted fairly conservative ideas and values. It sought to "uplift" the race by establishing black-owned businesses and "teaching" black ghetto dwellers the importance of discipline, self-help, and cleanliness. It imposed strict rules about personal behavior: alcohol, drugs, tobacco, gambling, dancing, adultery, premarital sex, profanity, or watching movies with sex or "coarse speech," for example, were simply not allowed. The NOI even impressed black conservative George Schuyler, managing editor of the New York office of the black-owned *Pittsburgh Courier,* who praised them for their values and moral vision. "Mr. Muhammad may be a rogue and a charlatan," wrote Schuyler in 1959, "but when anybody can get tens of thousands of Negroes to practice economic solidarity, respect their women, alter their atrocious diet, give up liquor, stop crime, juvenile delinquency and adultery, he is doing more for the Negro's welfare than any current Negro leader I know." Although the NOI officially stayed out of politics, focusing its energies on the spiritual uplift of African Americans and offering an alternative to the "white man's religion," it did practice self-defense and did not shy away from violence. During the thirties in Detroit, for example, Black Muslims, as members of the NOI were known, attracted attention

The Nation of Islam attracted thousands of urban blacks to the disciplined life of abstinence, prayer, and black self-determination.

during a bloody shootout with police. And under Fard's leadership, the NOI even established a paramilitary organization known as the Fruit of Islam. They kept order at big gatherings, served as bodyguards for "the Messenger" (Muhammad), and were trained to defend NOI institutions at any cost.

The NOI remained a fairly small religious sect until World War II. Its membership began to increase after Elijah Muhammad and about one hundred other Muslims were jailed for resisting the draft. As a result, the NOI not only garnered more national publicity but it began to recruit members from the ranks of black prisoners. One of those prisoners who discovered the Nation was Malcolm Little, whose name was changed to Malcolm X by Elijah Muhammad. He wrote in his autobiography that he received the X from the Nation of Islam as a symbol of his unknown African ancestry. More than any other figure, Malcolm X was responsible for turning the NOI into a national force to be reckoned with. And more than anyone else, he embodied the NOI's militant, uncompromising, and, when needed, violent image, one that would scare many white liberals and nurture a new generation of black radicals.

The son of Earl Little, a Baptist preacher, and his wife, Louisa, Malcolm and his siblings experienced dramatic confrontations with racism. According to his autobiography, hooded Klansmen burned their home in Lansing, Michigan. Earl Little was killed under mysterious circumstances, welfare agencies split up the children and eventually had Louisa Little committed to a mental institution, and Malcolm was forced to live in a detention home run by a racist white couple. By the eighth grade he had left school, moved to Boston to live with his half-sister Ella, and discovered the underground world of African-American hipsters and petty criminals. His downward spiral ended in 1946, when he was sentenced to ten years in jail for burglary.

After discovering Islam, Malcolm Little submitted to the discipline and guidance of the NOI and became a voracious reader of the Koran and the Bible. He also immersed himself in works of literature and history in the prison library. Upon his release in 1952, Malcolm X, a devoted follower of Elijah Muhammad, rose quickly within the NOI ranks, serving as minister of Harlem's Temple No. 7, where he went in 1954. He later ministered to temples in Detroit and Philadelphia. Through speaking engagements, television appearances, and by establishing *Muhammad Speaks*—the NOI's first nationally distributed newspaper—Malcolm X called America's attention to the Nation of Islam. His criticisms of civil rights leaders for advocating integration into white society instead of building black institutions and defending themselves from racist violence generated opposition from both conservatives and liberals.

But Malcolm showed signs of independence from the NOI line. During the mid–fifties, for example, he privately scoffed at Elijah Muhammad's interpretation of the genesis of the "white race" and seemed uncomfortable with the idea that all white people were literally devils. More significantly, Malcolm clearly disagreed with the NOI's policy of not participating in politics. He not only believed that political mobilization was indispensable but occasionally defied the rule by supporting boycotts and other forms of protest. He had begun developing a Third World political perspective during the fifties, when anticolonial wars and decolonization were pressing public issues. Indeed, Africa remained his primary political interest outside black America: in 1959 he toured Egypt, Sudan, Nigeria, and Ghana to develop ties between African Americans and the newly independent African states.

African Americans had long seen themselves as part of a larger world, as more than "minorities" within the confines of the United States. But there was never a time like this, when every corner of the earth seemed engaged in a struggle for freedom, and the black freedom movement in America seemed to be at the eye of the international storm.

Freedom Now!: The Student Revolutionaries

On a Sunday morning late in November 1959, Martin Luther King, Jr., announced to his congregation at Dexter Avenue Baptist Church in Montgomery, Alabama, that he had decided to leave the city and return to his native Atlanta. The major reason was the need to connect himself more firmly to the Southern Christian Leadership Conference, which had been headquartered in Atlanta since its founding in 1957. In the years since its establishment, SCLC had been having a hard time getting organized. In the statement he made to the Dexter congregation that Sunday, King seemed to be trying to rally himself, his organization, and the larger developing freedom movement to a new state of activity. He said, "The time has come for a broad, bold advance of the Southern campaign for equality.... Not only will it include a stepped-up campaign of voter registration, but a full-scale assault will be made upon discrimination and segregation in all forms.... We must employ new methods of struggle involving the masses of our people."

In this "bold advance" King envisioned SCLC as a crucial force, and he was convinced that a great deal of the energy that was needed would come from black young people. Indeed, King said, "We must train our youth ... in the techniques of social change through nonviolent resistance." It is likely that King was envisioning a youth movement that would be firmly based in the SCLC organization. But by the time King moved to Atlanta in January 1960, SCLC had not yet done anything to organize a youth movement. Fortunately, the young people were not waiting. Beginning independently from several Southern bases, an ever-expanding nonviolent army of black young people and their white allies began to put an indelible mark on the sixties.

On January 31, 1960, at North Carolina Agricultural and Technical College (known as A&T), one of the South's many black colleges, four freshmen decided to move from words to deeds. Ezell Blair, Jr., Joseph McNeil, Franklin McClain, and David Richmond decided that they were going to confront one of the most demeaning symbols of segregation: the all-white lunch counter at the local Woolworth's department store. Like all the chain stores in the South, the Greensboro store accepted the money of its African-American customers at the various merchandise counters, but the lunch counter was a different story. Black people were not permitted to sit for a snack, a meal, or even a drink of water. Usually, such segregationist practices were enforced by local ordinances, state laws, and coercion by whites acting almost out of habit. Whites considered public space theirs to control and define, and they were especially sensitive about public eating places, where white employees might be perceived as serving blacks (as opposed to merely accepting their payments at other store counters).

The young men from A&T planned to go into Woolworth's on Monday morning, February 1, shop for some small items in other parts of the store, and then go to the lunch counter. They would sit there quietly, with dignity and with a firm insistence on their right to be served. For these students the central issue was not the hamburgers or Cokes. The issues were justice, human dignity, fairness, equality, and freedom. They were all driven by the desire to reach the fundamental goal: "Jim Crow Must Go."

The three young men who had grown up in Greensboro (McNeil came from Wilmington) were fully aware of a strong local tradition of challenging segregation. They and their parents had been active in the NAACP, and they had heard of blacks who fought to desegregate the local schools. They attended NAACP-sponsored public presentations by black student pioneers of the effort to desegregate Central High in Little Rock. And, of course, they all had as an example the noble actions of Rosa Parks and Martin Luther King, Jr., the best-known public heroes of the successful Montgomery bus boycott. When King spoke in Greensboro in 1959, Ezell Blair, Jr., remembered that his sermon was "so strong" that "I could feel my heart palpitating. It brought tears to my eyes." The young men knew that they could go to jail. Or there could be violence. So it was not surprising that David Richmond later recalled that "all of us were afraid" that Sunday night before their planned action; yet, he added, "We went ahead and did it."

Monday morning, February 1, 1960, was the day they "did it." When they sat down and asked clearly for coffee and snacks and were told that they could not be served, they refused to get up from their seats. Like Rosa Parks, they believed that holding their seats was essential to affirming their dignity and their place as citizens. So Blair, their chosen spokesman, responded to the refusal of service with a polite but probing inquiry: "I beg your pardon," he said, "but you just served us [at the other counters], why can't we be served here?"

By that time other customers were noticing the four neatly dressed, quietly determined young black men. The manager asked them to leave, but they refused, still quiet, still polite. As a matter of fact, not only did they say they would stay until the store closed, but they announced that they would return again the next day, and the days after that, until they were served, until all black people could be served and their humanity duly recognized—at least at that lunch counter.

When McClain recalled that first sit-in in an interview more than twenty years later, he reported, "If it's possible to know what it means to have your soul cleansed, I felt pretty clean at that time. I probably felt better on that day than I've ever felt in my life. . . . I felt as though I had gained my manhood, so to speak, and not only gained it, but had developed quite a lot of respect for it."

That afternoon's action concluded when the manager ordered the store closed. By the time the four freshmen returned to the campus, word of their action had streaked through the classrooms, dormitories, dining halls, and gymnasiums. Many of their fellow students soon pledged their determination to return to the lunch counter the next day.

The example set by the freshmen was so powerful that the new excitement could not be confined to one campus or one city. The students at Bennett College, a private, black women's school nearby, heard the news and joined the fight. Within a few days this powerful moral action had also become a challenge to local white undergraduates, starting with students at the elite Women's College of the University of North Carolina, located in Greensboro. Beginning on Thursday, February 4, small groups of them decided to join the demonstration and risk all the protection of their whiteness, to risk their social and family connections, and to reconsider the meaning of democracy, Christianity, and human dignity.

Before the week was over, the relatively low-key action of the four sit-in leaders

To occupy their time while they were waiting to be served, students participating in sit-ins did their home-work and wrote letters.

had escalated to unexpected levels. Nineteen students came to Woolworth's on the second day, and more than eighty were present on Wednesday. Now there were more students ready to sit in than there were seats at Woolworth's lunch counter. So, the nearby S. H. Kress store became the next target, and by Saturday of that first week hundreds of students from A&T were streaming into the downtown area to participate in what had become a kind of student crusade. Even members of the A&T football team—including a quarterback named Jesse Jackson—abandoned the apolitical, disengaged stance that marked so many college athletes. They were on the scene when gangs of young white men, waving Confederate flags, began to harass the black students, attempting to block their access to the lunch counters. On at least one occasion, members of the A&T football team, waving small U.S. flags, opened a path through the threatening white crowd for the sit-in squads.

By the next week the new, youth-led movement had spilled over into other North Carolina cities, as students in Durham, Winston-Salem, Charlotte, Chapel Hill, and elsewhere began their own sit-in campaigns. In Chapel Hill, as in other cities, there were demonstrators with picket signs on the streets as well as students sitting at the lunch counters. Several of the Chapel Hill demonstrators carried signs that expressed the message they wanted all Americans to hear: "We do not picket just because we want to eat. We can eat at home or walking down the street. We do picket to protest the lack of dignity and respect shown to us as human beings."

None of this activity had been pre-planned or coordinated. But, as one Charlotte student put it, the sit-ins provided a "means of expressing something that had been on our minds for a long time." Speaking for his generation of activists, Greensboro's Joseph McNeil said, "I guess everybody was pretty well fed up at the same time."

By the middle of February 1960, the nation had begun to discover that "everybody" really meant *everybody* and not just the North Carolina students. Within weeks the sit-ins had become a powerful social movement, ranging across the South and evoking imaginative responses of support from many places in the North. Students organized sit-ins at the New York affiliates of Woolworth's, for example. Longtime black social activist Bayard Rustin and singer and actor Harry Belafonte helped organize the Struggle for Freedom in the South, which raised funds to cover legal fees of arrested sit-in participants. Television helped to spread what people called "sit-in fever" across the South and demanded the nation's attention. But there were also human networks that carried the news. All over the South, adult veterans of the long struggle for justice and equality made phone calls, wrote letters, traveled by car to make sure that others knew what had begun in North Carolina and encouraged them to consider what needed to be done in their own communities.

The students themselves contacted friends, relatives, and members of their fraternities and sororities on other campuses in other states. Lunch counters were usually the focus of the action, but the students soon turned their attention to other forms of public accommodations as well. They created "wade-ins" at segregated public pools and beaches, "kneel-ins" at churches, "read-ins" at public libraries, and "bowl-ins" and "skate-ins" at segregated recreation centers. Usually, the students combined those nonviolent "direct action" challenges with marches and picketing at local city halls, seeking negotiations, demanding that the white elected officials take responsibility and take action to change the segregation statutes.

After the initial white surprise at these challenges to the laws and traditions of segregation, resistance to the student actions became very real. In some places it came in the form of arrests by the local police. In other situations the police stood by as white citizens took affairs in their own hands. Angry, frightened, and determined to maintain their historic positions of domination and control, white people frequently attacked the students. Sometimes sit-in participants were dragged from the lunch-counter stools and beaten. Ketchup was poured on their heads. Lighted cigarettes were pressed into their hair and on their exposed necks and shoulders. Women swung handbags at them, and men and boys used sticks and bats. Consistently, the students refused to allow themselves to be diverted from their central purpose or from their nonviolent stance, and they chose not to strike back at their attackers.

In Atlanta, one of the early targets of the demonstrating black students was the cafeteria in City Hall, where a sign announced, "Public Is Welcome." Julian Bond, a Morehouse College student leader and son of Dr. Horace Mann Bond, an internationally known scholar, led a student contingent into the cafeteria on March 15, 1960. There, they were greeted by the manager, who asked, "What do you want?" When Bond replied, "We want to eat," the manager's response was, "We can't serve you here." Bond then said, "The sign outside says the public is welcome and we're the public and we want to eat." They got their food, but the cashier refused to take their money. Bond and seventy-five of his companions did not get a meal in the public cafeteria that day but a cell in the nearby city jail. However, when they were bailed out of jail the next day, the group immediately organized themselves and other students in the Atlanta University complex (which included Spelman College, Clark College, Gammon Theological Seminary, Morehouse, and Morris Brown College) into what became known as the Committee on an Appeal for Human Rights. This turned out to be the first step toward its emergence as one of the most important student movement groups in the South. Its eloquent and thoughtful "Appeal for Human Rights" eventually appeared in the *Congressional Record*, the *New York Times*, and publications in many other parts of the world:

> We . . . have joined our hearts, minds, and bodies in the cause of gaining those rights which are inherently ours as members of the human race and as citizens of the United States.
>
> We do not intend to wait placidly for those rights which are already legally and morally ours to be meted out to us one at a time. . . . We want to state clearly and unequivocally that we cannot tolerate, in a nation professing democracy and among people professing Christianity, the discriminatory conditions under which the Negro is living today in Atlanta, Georgia.

People who knew Southern black communities of that time would have expected Georgia's capital city to produce a significant student movement. Its six black institutions of higher education, the presence of Martin Luther King, Jr., and the SCLC, the tradition of a distinguished and relatively progressive African-American middle class, and the existence of a white leadership group that was concerned about maintaining its reputation for moderation (exemplified by Ralph McGill and his *Atlanta Constitution*, the best-known Southern newspaper)—all of these factors could have led contemporary observers to predict that Atlanta students would rise to the occasion of the new movement. They did, but it was actually the student sit-in leadership of Nashville, Tennessee, not Atlanta, that provided the focal point for the emerging student movement.

Nashville was home to one of the nation's oldest and best-known black schools,

Fisk University, alma mater of W. E. B. Du Bois. In the largely segregated city, black students were also enrolled at Meharry Medical School, the American Baptist Theological Seminary, and Tennessee Agricultural and Industrial College, a large, all-black state school. But it was one of the first black students at Vanderbilt University who played the central role. James Lawson, son of a Methodist minister and a strong and devout mother, had originally gone to Nashville from Ohio in 1958 as Southern field secretary for the Fellowship of Reconciliation. The FOR was a mostly white organization of religious pacifists that had long been involved in a quiet search for nonviolent methods of fighting for racial justice in America. Lawson first met Martin Luther King, Jr., when King was visiting Oberlin College in Ohio and Lawson was one of its older undergraduates. When King learned about the impressive personal history and Gandhian commitments of the articulate, self-assured, and spiritually grounded young man, he urged Lawson to come South and work with him in the expanding freedom movement.

Lawson, a year older than King, had already explored many aspects of the world of nonviolent action. In 1951, while active in organized Methodist youth work, Lawson had refused to register for the military draft that was then gathering young men for service in the Korean War. Basing his objection to participation in the war on the nonviolent teachings of Jesus, Gandhi, and his own mother, Lawson had been arrested for resisting the draft after he was denied conscientious objector status. He spent more than a year in jail. While in prison he met other black and white men who were refusing military service based on their religious and philosophical commitment to pacifism and nonviolence. Eventually, Lawson was released on parole in the care of the Methodist Board of Overseas Missions, and he spent three years as a Christian fraternal worker in India under the board's auspices. During this time, while teaching and coaching sports in Methodist schools, Lawson was able to explore more deeply his strong interest in Gandhian nonviolent action. He had already decided that he wanted to help create an American version of Gandhi's spiritually based liberation movement when he happened to see the first story about the Montgomery bus boycott in an Indian newspaper. As he read the article, Lawson literally jumped for joy and vowed to deepen his own commitment to work for racial justice and reconciliation in the United States. So King's later invitation was a powerful affirmation of what Jim Lawson had long been preparing for.

Responding to King's challenge, Lawson decided to explore an earlier invitation from the Fellowship of Reconciliation to become its Southern field secretary, possibly based in Nashville. Lawson also accepted an invitation to develop workshops on nonviolence from the Nashville Christian Leadership Conference (NCLC), an affiliate of King's SCLC that was led by the outspoken black Baptist pastor Kelly Miller Smith. Joined by his white FOR colleague and fellow Methodist minister Glenn Smiley, Lawson began his Nashville responsibilities by leading a workshop on nonviolent action for the NCLC in March 1958. By the fall of that year, he had decided to enroll as a student at the Divinity School of Nashville's all-white, Methodist-affiliated Vanderbilt University. He was soon offering extended versions of his initial workshop, focused now on ways in which Nashville's segregated world of public accommodations could be challenged and changed by well-trained, committed teams of nonviolent volunteers.

By the beginning of 1960 there were some seventy-five regular participants in Lawson's weekly workshops at First Baptist Church. Some of them had even experimented with sitting in at some of the downtown lunch counters and then leaving when refused service. They set up role-playing situations, anticipating what they would do and say when they encountered the expected violent opposition in words or deeds.

Then the word came from North Carolina. It appeared as if the action they were preparing for in Nashville had actually begun several hundred miles away. That Friday night at their usual meeting time, the regular Nashville participants were overwhelmed by some five hundred students and adults who wanted to join the fight. Because Lawson's corps of nonviolent trainees had been getting ready, they quickly decided to sit in at the segregated Nashville outlets of Woolworth's and Kress, and they wanted to begin the next morning, Saturday, February 6.

The students who became the heart of the Nashville movement included Marion Barry, a Mississippi native who was a graduate student in chemistry at Fisk University (and later became mayor of Washington, D.C.); Diane Nash and Angela Butler, two student leaders from the Fisk campus; and a trio of students from the all-black American Baptist Seminary, James Bevel, John Lewis, and Bernard Lafayette. After two weeks of almost daily sit-ins without arrests, attacks, or lunch-counter service, they began to hear that the police were ready to begin arresting them and that local white troublemakers were prepared to attack them physically. Undeterred, the Nashville students (joined by several white exchange students on their campuses) were determined to continue their campaign.

When the Nashville students went back downtown, at the start of the third week, the jailing, the ridicule, the spit, the fierce attacks were all waiting for them— and eventually the world saw it. Perhaps even more important, the black community began to experience a new level of solidarity. Adults rallied to the side of their children and students. Such solidarity became one of the hallmarks of the sit-in phase of the movement, providing an important source of strength for the ongoing freedom struggle. Thousands of black citizens showed their willingness to come forward with every needed kind of assistance, from bail money, to food for the imprisoned students, to the impassioned offering of long and deep prayers on behalf of their young freedom fighters.

At the same time, there were some black adults who thought the students were too brash, too uncompromising, too dangerously provocative, and these various points of view led to significant tensions. But the college students' spirit of bold, nonviolent defiance was infectious, and its effect on an even younger generation may have been at least as significant as its challenge to the elders. One of Nashville's high school students from those days later recalled that when the sit-ins began, he paid relatively little attention to them, for he was very wrapped up in his private ambition of becoming a famous and wealthy rock star. So even when the college students started marching right past his high school, Cordell Reagon was still "unconscious," as he put it. Then, Reagon said, "One day they came by, and just on impulse I got some friends together and said, 'Let's go.' We weren't committed to the cause or anything. We just wanted to see what they were up to—it looked exciting."

That day the marching students had a stop to make on their way to the lunch counters, a stop that opened new possibilities for young Cordell Reagon's life. He said,

> They were marching to the jail, where Diane Nash, one of the main student leaders in the movement, was being kept. We go down to the jail, and we're all singing. There up in the jail cell we could see Diane. And everyone was shouting and waving. And I'm just looking. There is something amazing—a black woman only a couple of years older than me, up in this cell. There was some spirit, some power there, I had never seen before. Suddenly, I realized that everyone had marched down the street, and I was all alone staring at the cell. I ran down and caught up with the end of the march. But I figured then I better not let these people go. There is some power here that I never experienced before.

Responding to that power, holding on to those people, Reagon eventually moved toward the center of the movement, becoming one of the first full-time field secretaries for the Student Nonviolent Coordinating Committee (SNCC, pronounced "snick"). He was also a member of SNCC's Freedom Singers, carrying the music, the stories, and the action of the movement around the world. There were young people like Cordell Reagon all over the South. Not long after Reagon caught up with the end of the powerful line in Nashville, students in downtown Orangeburg, South Carolina, demonstrated. There, they faced tear gas, high-powered fire hoses, and police beatings. In Tallahassee, Florida, the students from Florida Agricultural and Mechanical College also encountered tear gas and violence, but they met up at the lunch counters with white students from neighboring Florida State University who had pledged to arrive before them and to share their food if the black students were refused service.

Everywhere in the South black students were meeting these mixed realities: harsh resistance, some overly cautious elders, new self-confidence and transformation, the emergence of new, sometimes unexpectedly courageous white allies, the beginning of some desegregation victories, and a fresh sense of themselves and the meaning of their movement. At the same time, in spite of the growing sense of solidarity, other black adults were troubled and frightened by the unprecedented boldness of the student action. Too familiar with the world of white violence and intimidation, these adults wondered what harsh reactions the student uprising would bring. What jobs would be lost, what homes and churches bombed, what bank loans canceled, what licenses revoked, which young careers aborted, which lives lost? Because of such understandably adult concerns, the students especially appreciated the consistent support and encouragement from Martin King's public statements.

Indeed, it seemed as if King clearly recognized that these students embodied some of his own best dreams for the future of a nonviolent, mass-based freedom movement. So he offered great encouragement to their activities whenever possible and tried to interpret them to the world. Speaking in Durham, North Carolina, King said, "What is fresh, what is new in your fight is the fact that it was initiated, led and sustained by students. What is new is that American students have come of age. You now take your honored places in the world-wide struggle for freedom."

Then he urged them to move ahead and "fill up the jails." Ever since the days of Gandhi in India, resistance leaders had issued the call to fill up the jails as both a personal and strategic challenge. On the personal level in America, it urged nonviolent warriors to overcome their justifiable fear of dangerous Southern jails as well as the sense of shame that respectable families experienced when their children ended up there. On the strategic level, it was a call to present so many challengers to the legal system that its machinery would be blocked, making it difficult to carry on business as usual.

By the end of the winter of 1960 the mostly black contingent of Southern students was taking King—and their own consciences—seriously; their sit-ins were reaching into every Southern state except Mississippi, which was too harsh in its resistance; they were filling up at least some of the jails of the region, and their sophisticated political consciousness and courageous action were catching the attention of the nation and the world. In March some of the leaders of the local movements got a much-needed opportunity to meet together for the first time to catch their breath. The occasion was what had originally been an annual conference of mostly white Southern college student activists. The 1960 session at Highlander Folk School in Tennessee reflected the rapidly changing nature of the Southern student leadership scene. Now, more than half of the eighty-five participants in the Annual Leadership Workshop for College Students were black student sit-in leaders.

Highlander Folk School, established in the thirties, was run by a white couple, Myles and Zilphia Horton. Highlander's adult education programs, sometimes conducted by an interracial staff, included interracial conferences and workshops to train citizens to work for social change. It was an extraordinary and risky set of activities in the South in those days.

As a result of its nonconformist agenda and its left-wing friends, the school had experienced much harassment and persecution from local and state government authorities. Nevertheless, the Hortons persisted in their work, making Highlander a well-known resource center for labor movement organizers and for Southern freedom movement workers such as Septima Clark of Charleston, E. D. Nixon, Rosa Parks, Martin Luther King, Jr., and Fred Shuttlesworth.

Since 1953 Highlander had held an annual workshop for college student leaders. For the 1960 workshop, the Hortons chose a new, post-Greensboro theme: "The New Generation Fights for Equality." In that retreatlike mountainside setting, leaders from the sit-in movements and their potential white allies shared experiences, exchanged strategies, and recognized fellow pioneers. They considered long-range goals, explored new meanings of nonviolence, and talked about not only surviving but prevailing while in jail.

And there was time for singing, singing, singing—the flooding soulful glue that held everything and everyone together. By now it was obvious that this was to be a singing movement, especially as it developed in Nashville, where James Bevel, Bernard Lafayette, and the young Cordell Reagon had taken their love for rhythm and blues street-corner singing and moved right into the hymns and spirituals of their home churches.

At Highlander, Zilphia Horton had discovered anew the power of song in social movements. In her work with union organizers, she had heard the old nineteenth-century African-American religious song "I'll Be Alright," which became "I Will Overcome." Then she heard the song transformed by black women labor organizers in the forties, who took it to the picket lines of the justice-seeking Food and Tobacco Workers Union in Charleston, South Carolina, as a great rallying call: "We shall overcome. . . . Oh yes, down in my heart I do believe, we shall overcome some day." Eventually, it became a kind of community anthem at Highlander. Spontaneously developing new verses out of their own sit-in experiences ("We are not afraid; We shall live in peace; Black and White together"), students sang it into the night, feeling the power of the expanding interracial band of sisters and brothers.

The gathering at Highlander was a valuable development in the necessary process of turning a set of semi-spontaneous, creative, youthful challenges into a powerful, sustained, insurgent mass movement that would eventually break the decades-old bondage of legal segregation in the South. Indeed, some adult veterans of the long black struggle for freedom had already begun to plan for a more formal meeting of the sit-in leaders.

Central among the movement veterans was Ella Baker, a native North Carolinian who in the twenties had dreamed of becoming a medical missionary. Unfortunately, the financial pressures of the Great Depresssion made her medical school dream unattainable. So after graduation from Shaw University, a black Baptist institution in Raleigh, North Carolina, she moved to Harlem. Soon, she became involved in a number of political and economic organizing activities. These included the development of a consumers' cooperative organization and attempts at organizing African-American domestic workers, who badly needed better wages and working conditions. By the beginning of the forties, Baker was on the national staff of the NAACP, serving an important and often dangerous role as a roving organizer of NAACP chapters in the hostile South.

Later, when the Montgomery movement began to catch the attention of the world, Baker became part of a small group of New York–based social activists who called themselves "In Friendship." They initially focused their attention on raising funds to assist black and white Southerners who had suffered economic losses because of their freedom movement activities or sympathies. As a result of her work with "In Friendship," Baker met King and was later encouraged by her New York colleagues—including Bayard Rustin—to return to the South and help SCLC as its temporary executive director, operating from its Atlanta office.

A brilliant grass-roots organizer, Baker was also an articulate and outspoken woman with a feminist consciousness far ahead of her time. Baker therefore found it difficult to work effectively in a leadership role in an organization made up of black pastors who were too often accustomed to seeing women only as compliant subordinates. Nevertheless, as a result of her SCLC position, Baker was strategically located when the Southern student sit-in movement erupted. And as soon as she began to grasp what was happening among the young people, she decided to find a way to bring their leaders together.

Later Baker said that she wanted to encourage their interests "not in being leaders as much as in developing leadership among other people." So she convinced administrators at Shaw University that they should host a conference of the sit-in leaders. She convinced Martin Luther King, Jr., and other SCLC leaders that the organization should put up eight hundred dollars to cover the basic expenses for what was officially called a Southwide Youth Leadership Conference on Nonviolence, to be held April 15–17, 1960, the Easter weekend break.

Baker and King signed a letter of invitation and sent it out to student activists and their allies all over the nation. The letter called the sit-in movement and its accompanying nonviolent actions "tremendously significant developments in the drive for Freedom and Human Dignity in America." (Many of the more active leaders and grass-roots participants in the Southern movement used "freedom" and "human dignity" to describe the goals of their struggle much more often than "civil rights.") Now, according to King and Baker, it was time to come together for an evaluation of the burgeoning movement, "in terms of where do we go from here."

The young student leaders were ready for such a gathering. Responding to letters, phone calls, and other personal contacts, more than two hundred students and adult observers made their way to Raleigh. Of these, about one hundred twenty came from more than fifty black colleges and high schools in twelve Southern states. They brought with them a rich treasury of experiences and stories about organizing, about marching, about opposition forces and their weapons, about nonviolent resistance, about jails, about the jokes that made it possible for them to laugh in some of the most perilous situations. And of course they brought their songs of defiance, of empowerment, of hope.

In an opening address to the conference on Friday night, April 15, the eloquent and insightful Baker spoke pointedly to the adults present when she said, "The younger generation is challenging you and me. . . . They are asking us to forget our laziness and doubt and fear, and follow our dedication to the truth to the bitter end." King, who was only thirty-one years old himself, picked up a similar theme in another address when he declared that the student movement "is also a revolt against the apathy and complacency of adults in the Negro community; against Negroes in the middle class who indulge in buying cars and homes instead of taking on the great cause that will really solve their problems; against those who have become so afraid they have yielded to the system." In the post-Raleigh years, this double-edged role of the young warriors would continue: inspiration *and* tough challenge to the adult community.

Because he was the freedom movement leader best known to the press, King was initially the focus of attention for the small press contingent at Shaw. But in the course of the first evening's speeches, they had to deal with the powerful presences of James Lawson and Ella Baker. Baker was acknowledged by the students as their prime mentor. Lawson, the official coordinator of the conference, and Baker both encouraged the students to think about forming an independent organization of their own. By the time the evening was over, the students had become the center of the weekend.

And they were eager to seize the opportunities presented to them. Well-attended workshops ranged from discussions of nonviolence to the political and economic implications of their crusade. They discussed and debated proposals for future organizational structure and spent much time and energy exploring the moral and strategic significance of refusing bail. One of the ten discussion groups that day focused on the role of "white supporters" in the rising movement. From the heart of that discussion a powerful insight emerged, one that would mark the student-led campaigns for several years. According to the notes kept by one of the participants, the workshop participants declared that "This movement should not be considered one for Negroes but one for people who consider this a movement against injustice. This would include members of all races."

By welcoming idealistic, non-black participants into their struggle, blacks confirmed one of the best self-definitions of the Southern-based freedom movement: freedom for black Americans freed all Americans. This vision was a central reason why so many socially committed whites were attracted to the movement at large and particularly to the politically conscious and religiously motivated nonviolent student workers. It was not surprising to find among the "observers" at Shaw representatives from such groups as the ecumenical National Council of Churches; the

Northern-based Congress of Racial Equality (CORE), which fought for integration; the Fellowship of Reconciliation (FOR); and the overwhelmingly white National Students Association, which represented college students.

The conference concluded with the birth of the Student Nonviolent Coordinating Committee. Conferees elected Marion Barry the new organization's first chairman. Barry held that post through the fall of 1961, when he returned to graduate school in Nashville. During his brief tenure, he established a tone that characterized the group well into the late sixties. He professed SNCC's intention of directly and forcefully confronting segregation and injustice, even vowing to go to jail to achieve results.

The Arduous Task: Rooting Out Fear and Getting Out Votes

In one of his characteristically insightful essays on the American condition, Ralph Ellison wrote, "The business of being an American is an arduous task." In the context of the African-American struggles of the sixties, this was perhaps an understatement. For what emerged from the Southern freedom struggle by the beginning of the sixties was the clear recognition that the arduous task for black people would be redefining what it means to be an American. Nowhere was this work of re-creation more evident than in the battles for justice that took place in Alabama, Georgia, and Mississippi in 1961.

In May of that year, CORE organized an interracial group of activists to challenge a Supreme Court order outlawing segregation in bus terminals. Calling themselves Freedom Riders, they set out across the South to see if they could integrate all bus terminal facilities, including lunch counters, waiting rooms, and rest rooms. They began their ride in Washington, D.C., and originally hoped to end it in New Orleans. Where they failed, they hoped to draw attention to the continued racism in the South and the need for federal intervention to protect black rights. All was relatively peaceful until they entered Alabama. But the riders met with violence in almost every city they stopped in throughout that state. In Anniston, for example, mobs actually threw a bomb on the bus and set it on fire.

As a result of international publicity, President John F. Kennedy and Attorney General Robert Kennedy tried to persuade the riders to stop their journey. When they refused, the Kennedys struck a deal with Mississippi officials, allowing them to maintain segregated facilities as long as the Freedom Riders were not harmed. Instead of being attacked, riders in Mississippi were simply arrested. Altogether, at least 328 Freedom Riders served time in Mississippi's jails. Realizing that the negative publicity would not die down and that CORE would continue to challenge segregation, Robert Kennedy asked the Interstate Commerce Commission (ICC) to issue an order banning segregation in terminals that catered to interstate transportation. That September, the ICC complied with the attorney general's request, issuing a statement that all interstate facilities must obey the Supreme Court ruling.

The next battle took place in Albany, Georgia, a city of approximately sixty thousand people that was intimately shaped by its agricultural setting and the racial attitudes of its Black Belt location. Bernice Johnson, who later married Cordell Reagon, was one of the most powerful participants in the Albany movement. She was a student at the segregated Albany State College in 1961 when the emerging Southern movement began to take hold in Albany.

As an officer of the Youth Council of the local NAACP, Johnson had been one of the students who marched in 1961 on the college president's house to protest the administration's failure to develop adequate security measures against white intruders from town. Such men regularly harassed students on the campus and more than once sneaked into women's dormitories in an attempt to intimidate and sexually threaten the students.

So Johnson, many of her fellow students, and some of their parents were already preparing to challenge the system when representatives of SNCC appeared in Albany that fall of 1961. Recognizing that it was really not able to coordinate a widely scattered Southern student movement that had already begun to change its character, the fledgling organization had decided to become essentially a committed group of antisegregation organizers. More than a dozen of the core group of SNCC people announced late that spring and summer that they were dropping out of school for a year in order to commit themselves to the struggle for justice, dignity, and hope. It was also during this summer of 1961 that the group decided that it would send out "field secretaries" to do grass-roots organizing, especially educating and preparing potential voters across the South, working for SNCC at subsistence wages of twenty-five to forty dollars per week, depending on whether they were single or married. It was during that same period that the young freedom workers engaged in a series of very long and piercing debates with each other about whether the organization should continue to commit itself to nonviolent direct action or focus instead on voter registration in the Deep South.

SNCC's ongoing internal debates became so heated at times during that summer of 1961 that the new organization seemed in danger of breaking apart. One of the major forces pushing the organization to focus on voter registration was President John F. Kennedy and his brother, Robert, the U.S. attorney general. They were urging the Southern freedom movement organizations to take their primary action "out of the street" and focus on what the Kennedy brothers assumed would be a less volatile, and therefore less internationally embarrassing, action of registering black voters. As a part of their proposal, the Kennedys promised to round up foundation funds for the voter registration campaigns and to ensure federal protection for its participants. Of course, not only were the Kennedys and their friends hoping to get the movement off the front pages of the world's newspapers, but they expected that the vast majority of any new black registered voters would be ready to cast their votes for the Democratic party, especially if that party appeared to be committed to securing their rights.

Many of SNCC's young people brought a high level of moral sensitivity and political savvy to their work. So it was not surprising that in the course of the long meetings, many of them thought they saw political and financial bribery at work in the Kennedys' offers. For some who had recently come out of the terror of the Freedom Rides and the resultant rigors of Mississippi's Parchman Penitentiary, any call to turn away from such direct action was a call to betray their history. So the internal battle was a hard one, and it was only the wisdom of their trusted mentor, Ella Baker, that finally led the students to the decision that avoided a split. The "band of brothers," as they had begun to call themselves, reflecting both the sexism of the time and the deep love and respect these young men and women shared for each other, decided to set up a "direct action" project and a "voter registration" project within the one organization.

That fall two SNCC voter registration organizers headed into Southwest Georgia, considered by black people to be a region of the state most resistant to such activities. SNCC had already begun to develop its risky practice of choosing the most difficult and dangerous places to start its projects, working on the assumption that once the "hardest nuts" in a state were cracked, it would be possible to assure local people and their own members that they could take on anything else. But "Terrible" Terrell County, SNCC's chosen starting point, proved to be too much at first. It was a place too filled with the fear and the bloody memories of its black people and the brutality of its white citizens to be ready for the voter registration action that Charles Sherrod and Cordell Reagon had in mind. Sherrod was a seminary student from Virginia who had left school to join SNCC's crusade. His eighteen-year-old companion was the same Cordell Reagon who had been drawn out of his Nashville classroom the previous year by the sheer power of that city's student movement.

So they turned toward Albany, the largest town in the area. Because an order of the Interstate Commerce Commission banning segregation in all interstate travel facilities (notably, bus terminals and train stations) was scheduled to take effect on November 1, 1961, Sherrod and Reagon decided that they should encourage the local black young people of Albany to test the ICC mandate. In this way they could take "direct action."

As the first SNCC people on the scene in Albany, Sherrod and Reagon had to improvise in organizing the black people there. The two men also had to figure out a way to reach the most receptive young people in the African-American community without seeming to compete with the local NAACP chapter and its own Youth Council. Reagon later remembered: "We would sit in the student union building on the college campus all day long, drinking soda, talking with the students, trying to convince them to test the public accommodations at the bus station." SNCC organizers like Reagon and Sherrod were key in bringing teenagers into the center of the freedom movement of the sixties.

The SNCC workers and their young student compatriots appeared at the Trailways bus terminal in Albany on November 1, 1961, ready to test the new federal desegregation mandate. On that same day, other bus terminals in scores of Southern and border cities were tested in a CORE-inspired follow-up to the Freedom Rides. The Albany action that day marked the beginning of a rising tide of student-led nonviolent confrontations with the city's police force as blacks met an incoming train carrying an interracial group of Freedom Riders. Although the passengers disembarked without incident, the confrontation inspired the formation of a coalition among SNCC, the local NAACP, a local ministers group, and others, which became known as the Albany Movement.

Albany's young people staged their challenge to the bus system on Wednesday, November 22, the day before Thanksgiving. Normally, on that day, Albany State's many out-of-town students would file dutifully into the "colored" side of the bus and train terminals to travel home for the holiday break. This time, even before the crowd of college students arrived, three high school students from the SNCC-revived NAACP Youth Council walked into the white side of the bus terminal. When the police ordered them to move, they refused, and were arrested. Although they were quickly bailed out by the head of the local NAACP branch, who was not happy about the path on which Reagon and Sherrod were leading his youth, their audacious action was like the first crack in a dam.

Before long the college students arrived at the terminal. They had heard about the arrest of the high school students, and their college dean was there to try to make sure his students were not carried away by their new sense of duty. He directed them to the "colored" side. Nevertheless, two Albany State students from the SNCC workshop, Bertha Gober and Blanton Hall, refused. A detective informed them that their presence in the white ticket line was creating a disturbance, and when Gober and Hall did not leave, they were arrested.

Their presence in Albany's dirty jail over the holiday became the magnet that drew the larger black community of the city together. Not only did people bring Gober and Hall a steady stream of Thanksgiving dinners, but the Albany Movement leaders took the arrests, along with those of the high school students, as a sign that they had to join their children in the challenge to the old ways. The city and its youth-inspired movement caught the attention of the national press, and the Albany Movement held its first Montgomery-like mass meeting on the Saturday evening after Thanksgiving, November 25. By then Gober and Hall had been bailed out of jail, but they had also been suspended from college by their easily intimidated administrators, a decision that only solidified black community support for the students. At the Saturday night mass meeting, all the religious fervor of Albany's black people was poured into the songs that the students had brought out of their workshops and their jail cells and transformed for the occasion. The Albany Singers, including Bernice Johnson, were principally responsible for defining the music of the civil rights movement. Later, Johnson founded the women's singing group Sweet Honey in the Rock.

By now the people at the meeting were ready to do more than sing and listen to testimonies. They were prepared to march on City Hall to demand enforcement of federal law, the reinstatement of the Albany State students, and the end of segregation. Over the next two weeks, at least three groups marched, praying for and demanding change, and when they did, they were arrested in scores. The steady rising of their inspired people actually surprised the leaders of the Albany Movement, among them movement president Dr. William Anderson, a local osteopath, and vice president Slater King, a local realtor. They were not prepared for a situation in which nearly a thousand people, including parents and breadwinners, were at one point stranded in jail with no bail money available and no significant response to their call for desegregation of public transportation facilities.

It was at this point that some of the leadership, especially Anderson, decided that they needed the help of Martin Luther King, Jr. Anderson was a college friend of Ralph Abernathy and a fraternity brother of King. He decided to use these connections to bring in the best-known hero of the Southern movement to see if his presence could bring greater national attention to their struggle, and thereby shake the resistance of the white establishment.

This determination to call in King and SCLC widened divisions that were already present in the Albany Movement leadership. For instance, additional SNCC forces had come in to help Sherrod and Reagon as the work expanded, and SNCC adamantly opposed calling in King and SCLC. Its leaders argued that the media attention King would attract might well suffocate the creative development of a local grass-roots leadership and that they could become too dependent on the star of the freedom struggle.

Nevertheless, King, Abernathy, and some of their SCLC staff arrived in Albany for a December 16 mass meeting that they understood to be a one-night inspirational event. But at the meeting Anderson publicly maneuvered King into leading a march the next day. As a result, King and his organization became enmeshed in a very difficult situation.

Increasingly, Albany attracted black and white allies from across the nation. Religious communities were especially attracted to the strong church component of the movement's mass meetings, marches, and mass jailing. But Albany's black leaders, now joined by King and the SCLC, were working for something that had never been attempted in the South before. They had moved beyond the immediate confrontational settings of the bus and train terminals and were pressing for the desegregation of the entire city, beginning with its municipally owned public accommodations and its local bus lines. Such a development was a necessary and inevitable step in the burgeoning Southern struggle, but no one knew how to organize for it or to develop a citywide strategy.

The movement's task was complicated by the fact that Laurie Pritchett, the chief of police, was not a volatile loose cannon like some of his counterparts in other

Southern communities. Instead, Pritchett was very concerned about public relations and insisted that his officers rein in their tendencies toward violent treatment of the black community, especially when they were under the scrutiny of the mass media. This strategy was meant to deprive the movement of emotional rallying points and to deprive an already recalcitrant federal government of any reasons for entering the Albany situation. Partly because of Pritchett's strategy, partly because of divisions within the Albany Movement, partly because of the unprecedented demands that they were pressing on the segregated city, and partly because of their own inexperience with such a setting, King, SNCC, and the Albany Movement leaders were unable to reach their immediate goals of achieving the desegregation of public facilities. Pritchett undermined the very basis of nonviolent passive resistance by refusing to respond with violence. There were no dramatic images of activists being attacked or beaten by mobs. Instead, they were peacefully arrested for breaking the law.

There was no victorious breakthrough in Albany for several reasons. The Kennedy administration agreed not to intervene directly, either to enforce the ICC ruling or to protect the civil rights activists, as long as the Albany authorities could keep the peace. Pritchett succeeded not only in keeping the peace and reducing publicity, but in defeating the movement there. By the end of 1962, a year after the Albany campaign started, SCLC called the campaign off, although SNCC activists remained in Albany for another six years. Segregation was still firmly in place, and only a handful of African Americans could vote.

Nevertheless, even in failure, the movement gained a new vision, a new voice. Partly by accident it had chosen to try to challenge the segregation patterns of an entire Southern city. This was the first time in the post-Montgomery years of the freedom movement that young people and their elders had marched and gone to jail together, had together shaped an organization to challenge segregation. As important, the movement had discovered its capacity to take on more than a boycott, or a sit-in, or a voter registration project. It had learned something through failure. These lessons would be important when King and the forces of SCLC eventually responded to the invitation from their fearless comrade, Fred Shuttlesworth, and moved in the spring of 1963 toward Birmingham, perhaps the toughest, most terrifying city in America in which to stage a fight for desegregation.

The road to Birmingham was not the only path that the Southern movement took in those years following the sit-ins and the Freedom Rides. Even while the Albany Movement was at its height, a small but steady stream of SNCC's voter registration workers arrived in the counties that Sherrod and Reagon had originally targeted. As the Albany campaign slowed down in 1962, Sherrod himself went back into the nearby rural areas to lead the work on the voter registration project in Baker, Terrell, Lee, and Dougherty counties.

Although it rarely received the same kind of media attention as the dramatic public confrontation of marches, demonstrations, and sit-ins, this sort of tedious, demanding, unglamorous, and dangerous day-to-day work of voter registration was an essential step in providing blacks with the tools, and the power, to transform the nation.

The work of these voter registration campaigners began simply: they made themselves known in the local black community—where they were often identified as "Freedom Riders." They visited homes, churches, schools, individuals, and families, and they sought out black community leaders. Central to their strategy was always the work of "canvassing." Moving on foot, on bicycles, in cars, on mules, the young men and women went from house to house, often at night, asking if people were registered or if they wanted to register, telling them about the benefits of voting, letting them know that classes were being set up to help people deal with the intentionally complicated registration process, and calming their fears.

The atmosphere of confrontation and overcoming fear became most evident in a meeting in Sasser, a country town in Terrell County. On Monday night, July 25, 1962, Sherrod, some of his interracial SNCC comrades, and several of the local black leaders and participants were carrying on their weekly voter registration meeting at Mount Olive Baptist Church. There were some thirty or thirty-five people in the building. Attendance was lower than usual partly because of a threat from whites that the gathering would be broken up.

But the meeting went on, likely encouraged by the presence of three national newspaper reporters who had also heard about the threat. The session began, as usual, with a hymn, a prayer, and a Bible reading, the necessary ingredients for starting a meeting anywhere in the black South. Sherrod was in charge of this part of the meeting. The anxiety level was higher than usual that night, but the SNCC organizer kept his voice even and calm as he opened the session. They sang, "Pass me not/O gentle Savior," and then repeated the Lord's Prayer together. Sherrod led them in repeating the Twenty-third Psalm, slowing down on the words, "Yea, though I walk through the valley of the shadow of death, I will fear no evil." Just then they heard the sound of car doors slamming in the driveway.

Sherrod had begun to read one of his favorite passages from the New Testament. When he heard the car doors, he said quietly, firmly, "They are standing just outside now. If they come in I'm going to read this over again." He read from Romans 8:31, "If God be for us, then who can be against us?" At that point about fifteen white men from Sasser walked in, including one in a deputy sheriff's uniform, along with Sheriff Mathews, in plain clothes. They lined up against the wall in the back of the church while Sherrod completed the reading. Then, without missing a beat, the young freedom minister began to pray: "Into thy hand do we commend our minds and souls and our lives every day. . . . We've been abused so long. . . . We've been down so long." The "Amens" and "Uh-huhs" of the people had begun to roll into place between his phrases, and they came again when Sherrod went on.

"All we want," he said, "is for our white brothers to understand that Thou who made us, made us all.... And in Thy sight we are all one." Sheriff Mathews had bowed his head and closed his eyes.

Sherrod led the strangely mixed congregation in the Lord's Prayer, and then someone began singing, "We are climbing Jacob's ladder." Soon after the song began, the men in the back filed out. At the end of the song Sheriff Mathews, accompanied by two of his deputies and the sheriff of neighboring Sumter County, walked back in. One deputy now had a large revolver holstered on his belt, and the other one was brandishing a two-foot-long flashlight, a familiar weapon.

By this time, Lucius Holloway, the local chairman of the voter registration drive, had begun to lead the meeting, and he called out to the lawmen, "Everybody is welcome. This is a voter registration meeting." Sheriff Mathews responded:

> We are a little fed up with this registering business. Niggers down here have been happy for a hundred years, and now this has started. We want our colored people to live like they've been living. There never was any trouble before all this started. It's caused great dislike between colored and white.

Then the deputies began taking the names of everyone present, and they told the local black people that they did not need the outsiders from SNCC in order to register. They also issued ominous threats about what could happen to blacks after their outsider allies left the area. In the midst of the lawmen's performance, someone began humming "We Shall Overcome." Others picked up the song. The lawmen retreated to the back of the church and the people continued their meeting, giving reports of registration attempts, testimonies of beatings, and statements of hope.

At the end of the meeting, they gathered in a circle at the church door to sing "We are not afraid." That night there was no violence, except to the tires of one of the reporters' cars. But several nights later, the church was burned to the ground. Eventually, most of the SNCC workers and community leaders who were at the meeting found themselves thrown in jail, and beaten, as usual. Still, the organizing and overcoming continued in Terrell County and elsewhere in the Deep South.

In these settings it had usually been so long since black people had voted that many local black people did not even know that the nation's laws guaranteed them that right. Voting and politics generally were considered "white folks' business," and there were terrible memories that reminded them of what could happen to blacks who tried to participate in that business. In addition to the physical terror that stood between African Americans and the ballot box, everyone knew of the economic intimidation that was often used against them, sometimes forcing them off the land they were farming as sharecroppers, putting them out of the miserable shacks they lived in, making it impossible to get jobs with local employers, ultimately forcing them to leave the area. These were the settings that had produced black registered voting percentages of zero to five percent in many places where black people made up more than fifty percent of the population.

But in every such setting, there were always people willing to work for a new day. That was certainly what Bob Moses found when he went into Mississippi. Moses had been working in Atlanta as a volunteer in the SNCC office staff in the summer of 1960. He was sent to Alabama and Mississippi that summer to recruit participants for the next SNCC organizing conference, scheduled for the fall. In preparation for the trip, Ella Baker supplied Moses with the names of people she had worked with during her days as an NAACP organizer in the South.

One such person was Amzie Moore, president of the local, somewhat bedraggled NAACP chapter in Cleveland, Mississippi. When Moses met Moore, the forty-nine-year-old Mississippi movement veteran was farming part-time, working a few hours each day in the local post office, and running his own gas station. Because Moore had insisted on trying to develop a voter registration campaign in Cleveland in the mid-fifties, and because he refused to put up the legally required "colored" and "white" signs in his station, he had almost lost his business and his life. But he was still there when Moses arrived, looking for recruits for SNCC.

Moore convinced Moses that what Mississippi needed more than a group of young SNCC-like recruits going off to Atlanta was a band of SNCC's arduous freedom workers coming to Mississippi to create a major voter registration campaign, starting right there in Cleveland. Moses said he would take the message back to Atlanta. But Moses promised that regardless of what SNCC formally decided, he would personally return to Cleveland the following summer. When Moses returned South in the summer of 1961, much had changed throughout the nation. Most important among the changes was the influence of the Freedom Rides and the hope they inspired. And in Mississippi itself, Medgar Evers, the head of that state's NAACP organization, was openly calling for the city government of Jackson, the capital city, to desegregate public facilities.

But the time was still not quite right for a voter registration campaign in Moore's Delta area. White reaction to black assertiveness was swift and violently brutal, federal protection could not be assured, and many blacks questioned the wisdom of "stirring up trouble." Instead, some local NAACP leaders in Southwest Mississippi had heard about the possibility of a SNCC team coming to the state to work on voter registration, and they asked their friend Moore to put them in touch with Moses. As a result, SNCC's voter education wing began its Mississippi development in a small town called McComb, near another town named Liberty. Courageous older NAACP veterans from the area, like C. C. Bryant, E. W. Steptoe, and Webb Owens helped to open the way for Moses, who was soon joined by two former Freedom Riders, John Hardy and Reginald Robinson.

The SNCC forces started in the usual way. With the help of the committed older men and women in the town, they began to introduce themselves to other local

Poll taxes, literacy tests, and citizenship exams—as well as other, more brutal methods—were routinely used to keep blacks away from the polls in the South.

leaders and soon sought out the young people as well. Many of the teenage group were fascinated by the fact that these activists had come to their town, and they were ready for any kind of exciting direct action. Their elders, however, knew that people in their area had been beaten, killed, or driven out of town for trying to register to vote. So when Moses and his team began to set up a "school" to help people prepare for the intimidating moment when they might face a hostile registrar, the response was slow. Moses made it a practice never to pressure local people to register, because he knew, and they also knew, that he was asking them to risk their lives, a decision that they had to make themselves.

But when the first group of three local volunteers, an older man and two middle-aged women, were finally ready, it was Moses whose life was most at risk. After helping his frightened candidates break their silence as they faced the registrar, Moses was attacked on the main street of McComb by a man who was the sheriff's cousin. He split Moses's scalp with the heavy handle of a hunting knife. About a week later Moses felt a different kind of pain when he had to identify the body of Herbert Lee, a black farmer who had risked his life to volunteer as a driver for the SNCC voter registration team. Because of his Movement association, Lee had been shot to death in daylight by a white segregationist—a Mississippi state legislator.

Meanwhile in McComb, the committed high school students were too young to register and too impatient to wait. They wanted to enter the freedom struggle more directly than by teaching older people to read the registration materials. By now, SNCC people from the "direct action" contingent, like Marion Barry and Diane Nash, had also begun to gather in McComb, and they were leading workshops for the teenagers on nonviolent direct action. As soon as they could, the students put their training into action with a sit-in at a local lunch counter, the first in that part of Mississippi, an action that SNCC had not planned for. The sit-in squad was put in jail, and some of them were suspended from school. That led to a student-organized walkout from their school and a march to City Hall.

Sensing that the teenagers were moving into a dangerous action that they could not handle, Moses and some of his co-workers decided to march with them. The youngsters decided that they wanted to pray on the steps of City Hall. The police thought prayers belonged only in churches or homes, and they began to arrest the young people. The students were repeating the Lord's Prayer, and each time one was interrupted and arrested, another walked up the steps to continue the prayer. Finally, the police arrested more than one hundred young people and took them to jail. By then the spectacle had attracted a crowd of curious and angry white people.

Moses and his two SNCC companions offered a striking testimony to the spirit of SNCC. One of them was Charles "Chuck" McDew, an Ohio-born black college student who became a sit-in leader at South Carolina State College in Orangeburg. The other was Bob Zellner, the organization's first full-time field secretary assigned to recruiting white students. A native of Alabama, Zellner was the son of a white Southern Methodist minister, and he went to McComb instead of traveling to white campuses because he wanted to know what SNCC was actually doing in order to be an effective recruiter for the cause.

However, the white people of McComb wanted to know what *he* was doing there in the midst of the black troublemakers. Here, and in many future situations, Zellner was considered "a traitor to the white race." So as he came down the City Hall steps on his way to jail, several men rushed to attack him. There were many beatings and jailings in McComb that fall. At one point, all but one of the SNCC organizers were in jail. But it was the death of Herbert Lee that haunted people more than anything else. Despite the harsh white resistance that had forced the adults of McComb to temporarily slow down their attempts at voter registration, leading to SNCC's temporary withdrawal, still no one could miss the tremors of change throughout the state.

In 1962, the most spectacular tremor in Mississippi was the decision of black Air Force veteran James Meredith, with the support of the NAACP, to apply for admission to Ole Miss. Few institutions were considered more quintessentially white Mississippian, more worthy of defense against the black challenge than the University of Mississippi at Oxford. When Meredith first tried to enroll in the university, Governor Ross Barnett barred him from admission, a power that a federal court ruled Barnett did not possess. Barnett then encouraged white people in the state to believe that their active, armed resistance—even to a court-ordered change—could halt desegregation.

So by the end of September 1962, when it was time for Meredith to appear on campus to register for his first classes, thousands of white Mississippians—both students and others—believed that they could physically guard the university against the newly defined black presence that Meredith represented. Students and their segregationist allies rioted against the federal marshals who had slipped Meredith onto the campus the Sunday afternoon before registration. The rioters hurled rocks, bricks, lead pipes, and tear gas at the marshals, and finally even shot at them in a one-sided battle in which the marshals were ordered not to return the fire. In the course of the uproar, a foreign reporter and a local white worker were shot and killed, and some 350 others, mostly marshals, were wounded. The Kennedys had been trying to negotiate their way to a settlement with Barnett that would not require them to send in federal troops to protect Meredith's rights. However, in the end, the Kennedys decided they had to send in the troops. Though late, this federal intervention finally ended the white resistance.

The next day, James Meredith finally registered as the first black student at Ole Miss and became a powerful symbol to the black people of the nation.

As the SNCC workers reflected on their experiences in southwest Georgia and southwest Mississippi, they moved to the northwest area of Mississippi, known as the Delta. They stopped in Jackson to work out the details of a new coalition. Now they would coordinate their work with the activities of the NAACP, SCLC, and CORE, and together they formed the Council of Federated Organizations (COFO). This coalition was largely Bob Moses' idea, and it served as an important pipeline for the funds that supported registration work.

Ultimately, this united front was important for the morale of Mississippi's black people, providing them with a sense of the joint strength that was needed to break open the "closed society" of their state. Nevertheless, the essential energies and people power of the next stages of the COFO campaign came from SNCC, which was the heart of COFO. SNCC realized that the dangerous and essentially underground work of registering blacks had to become more visible to the world, not only to provide protection and build morale but also to prod the federal government into action.

From the spring of 1962 to the fall of 1963 the Mississippi voting rights work was focused on the Delta region. It was known as one of the most terror-filled sections of a violence-prone state. Partly because of this reputation, partly because this was the area where Amzie Moore lived, Bob Moses, as the new COFO program director, took his voter registration forces there, working to make Moore's old dream come true.

The reality of voter registration in the Delta was harsher than the dreams, however. Once again, the violence was persistent and nerve-wracking. As in every other voter registration campaign in the Black Belt, however, SNCC and other groups were constantly meeting such men and women as Fannie Lou Hamer of Ruleville, a town not far from Greenwood. The forty-seven-year-old sharecropper with a sixth-grade education went to a mass meeting one night in 1962 and heard James Bevel, the charismatic leader who had emerged from the Nashville student move-ment, holding forth like an evangelist, calling people to a new life of struggle for freedom. Hamer later said, "Until then I'd never heard of no mass meeting and I didn't know that a Negro could register and vote." But when she found out, she was one of the first volunteers to go to the courthouse the next day.

Hamer knew she was volunteering for danger, and later she said, "I guess if I'd had any sense I'd a-been a little scared, but what was the point of being scared. The only thing they could do to me was kill me and it seemed like they'd been trying to do that a little bit at a time ever since I could remember." From that day on Hamer was at the heart of the movement.

While in Greenwood, Bob Moses wrote about how to face the long, hard, dan-gerous times when it was easy to give in to fear:

> You dig into yourself and the community and prepare to wage psychologi-cal warfare; you combat your own fears about beatings, shootings, and pos-sible mob violence; you stymie by your own physical presence the anxious fear of the Negro community ... you organize, pound by pound, small bands of people who gradually focus in the eyes of Negroes and whites as people tied up in "that mess"; you create a small striking force capable of moving out when the time comes, which it must, whether we help it or not.

Of course no one could predict how and when the time would come, again and again, in these life-changing campaigns. But for people on the front lines, like Moses, the testing time was always nearby. This was the testimony of one of his co-workers, Marian Wright, a Spelman College graduate who was taking some time from her Yale Law School studies to join the forces of hope in Greenwood. She wrote,

> I had been with Bob Moses one evening and dogs kept following us down the street. Bob was saying that he wasn't used to dogs, that he wasn't brought up around dogs, and he was really afraid of them. Then came the march, and the dogs growling and the police pushing us back. And there was Bob, refus-ing to move back, walking, walking towards the dogs.

Neither Moses nor the dogs backed down, and one of the animals tore a piece out of his trousers before the dog's police handler finally pulled him away. Bob Moses kept walking.

In Greenwood, in 1962 and early 1963, no one knew how long they would have to walk and work, facing dogs, facing death, facing fear. But one thing began to be clear: they were not walking alone. For instance, in response to appeals from SNCC, communities in the North were donating truckloads of food and clothing for desperate Delta families. Dick Gregory, the socially concerned comedian, came to stand in solidarity and mordant humor with the people who continued to walk toward the courthouse and the registrar's office. Folksinger Bob Dylan arrived for his baptism in the work of the movement, sharing his songs and hope.

In the early spring of 1963, many of the full-time SNCC workers took time out from Greenwood's battleground to attend the annual SNCC staff meeting in Atlanta. The organization's full-time staff was now up to sixty people, and they came in from all over the South. Some 350 people attended the April gathering held at one of Atlanta's black theological schools, Gammon Seminary.

Reflecting later on the session, James Forman, who was the organization's indefatigable executive secretary during those crucial years, summed up the spirit and meaning of the experience: "The meeting was permeated by an intense comradeship, born of sacrifice and suffering and a commitment to the future, and out of a knowledge that our basic strength rested in the energy, love, and warmth of the group. The band of sisters and brothers, in a circle of trust, felt complete at last."

In the midst of a throbbing social movement nothing remained "complete" for long. Even as the SNCC meeting was going on, its companion and slightly elder organization, SCLC, was opening another front of the expanding Southern freedom movement. Responding to repeated invitations from Fred Shuttlesworth, leader of the Birmingham civil rights movement, and determined to learn crucial lessons from the many difficulties and experiments in Albany, in the spring of 1963 Martin Luther King, Jr., and his staff had gone to Birmingham, Alabama.

Birmingham: The Days beyond "Forever"

When SCLC decided to challenge segregation in Birmingham, it was taking on a city with one of the worst records of anti-labor and anti–civil rights violence in the country. Because of its surrounding coal and steel industries, the city had always attracted labor organizing activities. In 1931, the police force established the "Red Squad" to handle communist and other left-wing organizers with force, and from then on Birmingham's law enforcement agencies—with much assistance from private citizens—were infamous for their brutal tactics. During the thirties, many black and white labor organizers were arrested, kidnapped, beaten, or even killed. And in 1941, Birmingham experienced a wave of police killings and beatings. The best-known incidents involved the deaths of two young black men, O'Dee Henderson and John Jackson. Henderson, who was arrested and jailed for merely arguing with a white man, was found handcuffed and shot the next morning in his jail cell. A few weeks later, Jackson, a metalworker in his early twenties, was shot to death as he lay in the backseat of a police car. He had made the fatal mistake of arguing with the arresting officers in front of a crowd of blacks lined up outside a movie theater.

After World II, blacks often referred to the rigidly segregated city as "Bomb-ingham." The name called attention to the frequent bombings of the homes and churches of those African Americans who dared to take even tentative steps toward the establishment of racial justice. This was the setting in which Birmingham minister Fred Shuttlesworth and his family had been beaten, bombed, attacked, and jailed. Many people agreed with Martin Luther King, Jr., when he said, "As Birmingham goes, so goes the South." Later, when he reflected on the Birmingham campaign, King wrote:

> We believed that while a campaign in Birmingham would surely be the toughest fight of our civil-rights careers, it could, if successful, break the back of segregation all over the nation. This city had been the country's chief symbol of racial intolerance. A victory there might well set forces in motion to change the entire course of the drive for freedom and justice.

After exploring the situation, SCLC moved into action in Birmingham during the first days of April 1963. This was a period of intense freedom movement activity all across the South, with thousands of demonstrators challenging segregation from Maryland to Louisiana. In Birmingham, SCLC and Shuttlesworth's Alabama Christian Movement for Human Rights (ACMHR) focused on breaking the hold of legalized segregation in all the public facilities, starting with its downtown stores and its municipal facilities, such as city-owned parks, pools, and drinking fountains. They also hoped to open up the police force to black officers. To work out details and to keep the process moving beyond the demonstrations, the black organizations pressed for the establishment of a city-sponsored biracial committee.

In light of Birmingham's history—and in the presence of Alabama's new governor, George Wallace, who had declared in his 1963 inaugural address, "Segregation now! Segregation tomorrow! Segregation forever!"—this relatively modest set of goals appeared to most white residents to be undesirable, and impossible. Complicating the situation was the fact that the white leadership of Birmingham was deeply divided. When SCLC came on the scene that spring, the city was awaiting a judicial decision concerning a recent, disputed municipal election. The decision would either establish Bull Connor, the police commissioner, as mayor or place in office a more moderate segregationist named Albert Boutwell. At the same time there was a white business community of expanding influence whose members were greatly concerned about their city's image, an image they were trying to refurbish "to look like Atlanta," the liberal showcase city of the region. But in the midst of all of this the Ku Klux Klan and its adherents were still dangerously active, rallying behind their new governor.

For most of April, SCLC's challenge to Birmingham seemed to have a hard time capturing the full energy and interest of local black people or the national press. Even when King and Abernathy were arrested and jailed for marching on Good Friday, April 12, the best of the nightly mass meetings could not produce more than 50 or 60 volunteers for the next morning's demonstrations, which were designed to demand an immediate end to racist employment practices and segregation in public accommodations.

It was important to note who did show up to march. At the outset of the campaign it was the older people who stepped forward. Eventually, the Birmingham grandchildren would respond to the elders.

While King sat in the isolation cell of Bull Connor's jail, one of his lawyers managed to smuggle in some newspapers. In one of the Birmingham papers King came across a statement signed by a group of local white clergymen who considered themselves friends of black people and open to "moderate" racial change. Expressing concern that the desegregation campaign could play into Bull Connor's hands, they urged King and SCLC to leave Birmingham's future in the hands of its moderate black and white leaders. King seized the opportunity to respond. After a yellow, legal-sized pad was passed on to him, King ended up with a lengthy handwritten document that attempted to lay out the justification for his presence in Birmingham, to express the meaning and purpose of nonviolent direct action, and to provide a statement concerning the role of the churches in the quest for racial justice. However, the single most powerful section of his long letter arose out of his determination to let the white clergymen—and any other readers— know something about what it meant to be a black person in the segregated South, and what it meant to be told by white "friends" and Christian brothers to wait for a more convenient time to protest and challenge the injustice and inhumanity of segregation.

King wrote, "I guess it is easy for those who have never felt the stinging darts of segregation to say, 'Wait.'" Then in the longest sentence he had ever written, or would ever write again, he poured out a statement that was more than a moan or a plea for understanding.

> When you have seen vicious mobs lynch your mothers and fathers at will and drown your sisters and brothers at whim, when you have seen hate-filled policemen curse, kick, brutalize and even kill your black brothers and sisters with impunity, when you see the vast majority of your twenty million Negro brothers smothering in an air-tight cage of poverty in the midst of an affluent society; when you suddenly find your tongue twisted and your speech stammering as you seek to explain to your six-year-old daughter why she can't go to the public amusement park that has just been advertised on television, and see tears welling up in her little eyes when she is told that Funtown is closed to colored children, and see the depressing clouds of inferiority begin to form in her little mental sky, and see her begin to distort her little personality by unconsciously developing a bitterness toward white people; when you have to concoct an answer for a five-year-old son asking in agonizing pathos, 'Daddy, why do white people treat colored people so

mean?'; when you take a cross-country drive and find it necessary to sleep night after night in the uncomfortable corners of your automobile because no motel will accept you; when you are humiliated day in and day out by nagging signs reading "white" and "colored"; when your first name becomes "nigger" and your middle name becomes "boy" (no matter how old you are) and your last name becomes "John," and when your wife and mother are never given the respected title "Mrs."; when you are harried by day and haunted by night by the fact that you are a Negro, living constantly at a tip-toe stance, never quite knowing what to expect next, and plagued with inner fears and outer resentments; when you are forever fighting a degenerating sense of "nobodiness"; then you will understand why we find it difficult to wait.

King's *Letter from Birmingham Jail,* one of the classic statements of the freedom movement, did not begin to reach the outside world until more than a month after it was written. It was published in a number of newspapers and magazines and in book form in 1964 as *Why We Can't Wait.*

As the Birmingham demonstrations grew larger and more public, young people were eager to join in. Soon, young people regularly attended the nightly mass meetings and begged their parents to let them join the marches. But the movement leaders debated about encouraging students to miss school for an almost certain rendezvous with prison, or worse. Marchers were attacked by police dogs, shot with high-power water hoses, and beaten with clubs. In that debate the views of SNCC leaders Diane Nash Bevel and her husband, SCLC staff member James Bevel, prevailed. James Bevel, who played a major role as a strategist for the Birmingham protests, argued that since the young people did not carry the burden of their family's economic responsibilities on them, they were free to meet the challenge of going to jail. But the situation soon became more complicated. For as soon as the announcement was made in mass meeting that Thursday, May 2, 1963, would be the day for high school demonstrations, dozens of elementary school children declared their own readiness to march.

Now there was another debate among the leaders. What should be the minimum age for their freedom marchers? They decided that anyone who was old enough to volunteer to become a church member should be old enough to volunteer to become a member of the freedom corps. In that black Baptist-dominated setting, such a decision meant that children as young as six might be on the marching line when Thursday morning came.

That morning Sixteenth Street Baptist Church, the usual meeting place, was filled with hundreds of children. Shuttlesworth offered the morning send-off prayers, and the recently released King told the young people how important they were. Before the day was over, more than six hundred of the children discovered that the way to freedom led directly through Birmingham's jail.

The Birmingham fire hoses knocked protesters to the ground with enough force to take the bark off trees.

Bull Connor had been caught off-guard on Thursday by the surge of young marchers, moving around the police lines. He did not intend to be upstaged again by a flood of singing black children. So on Friday, May 3, when the young marchers came singing down the steps of Sixteenth Street Church, they saw fire trucks in the park facing the church. Andrew Young, who oversaw SCLC's fledgling voter registration drive and was a chief negotiator in the Birmingham campaign, later described what happened:

> As groups of kids marched past the park headed for downtown, Connor issued the order to the firemen to uncoil their hoses. Police dogs had been seen before, and once again they were brought to the front of the barricades, straining at their leashes. But until now, the fire trucks had remained on the sidelines. Suddenly fire hoses didn't seem like fun anymore, and the kids watched with trepidation as the firehoses were unwound. They kept marching and their voices grew stronger with the comforting tunes of the freedom songs. It never ceased to amaze me, the strength that people drew from the singing of those old songs. . . . Suddenly, Connor ordered the firemen to open the hoses on both the marchers and the large crowd of onlookers who had gathered in the park. The water was so powerful it knocked people down and the line began to break as marchers ran screaming through the park to escape the water. Connor then ordered the police to

pursue the terrified kids with angry dogs, and to our horror actually unleashed some of them. The police ran through the park, swinging their billy clubs at marchers, onlookers, and newsmen—anyone in the way.

As the tension escalated, an international audience watched. By now it was clear that the nation's leaders could not continue to avoid direct engagement with the situation in Birmingham and still claim to be "leaders of the free world." The Kennedys, after some initial annoyance with SCLC's timing and methods, let it be known, first privately, then publicly, that they believed a negotiated way should be found through Birmingham's troubles. They sent personal emissaries to the city, especially to urge the business leaders to take responsibility for moving toward desegregation. Robert Kennedy himself made dozens of phone calls to corporate leaders nationwide whose Southern subsidiaries were located in the Birmingham area. He urged them to put pressure on their local people to cooperate with the movement's demands for desegregation.

With the rising pressure of the federal government, negotiations based on the movement's basic demands were finally begun. The negotiations were difficult, but they lasted less than a week. They led to an agreement that was announced on May 7, 1963, about a month after the demonstrations had begun. Under the agreement, an irreversible process of desegregation was begun in public accommodations and municipal facilities. SCLC won its demands for desegregated lunch counters, rest rooms, fitting rooms, and drinking fountains. Downtown store owners agreed to hire African-American clerks. Expanded hiring and promotion of black people was begun throughout the industrial community of Birmingham. All the imprisoned demonstrators were released on bail that was supplied from various local and national sources, and the cases against the released prisoners were soon dismissed. But there was a compromise: SCLC agreed to a timetable of planned stages rather than demanding that these changes take place immediately. It also agreed to the release of arrested demonstrators on bail rather than insist that the charges be dismissed outright.

But it would not be a simple matter to extricate Birmingham from its past. On the evening after the announcement, the Ku Klux Klan leadership bitterly condemned the arrangement at a rally on the edge of the city. Later that night a bomb badly damaged the home of A. D. King, Martin's younger brother, who was an activist pastor in the city and a participant in the movement. Soon, a second bomb exploded at the Gaston Motel, practically demolishing Room 30, the modest suite that King normally used as his headquarters. Fortunately, A. D. King's family was not hurt, Martin King had already left the city, and no one else was injured at the motel. But the bombings drew hundreds of outraged black people into the streets. Without waiting for a request from the new mayor, Albert Boutwell, Governor Wallace sent in state troopers to maintain order. However, the pushing, attacking, cursing troopers seemed intent on provoking the leaderless crowd into violence. In response, black people threw rocks and bottles and set some stores and cars on fire. For a moment it seemed as if a major explosion would blow apart the new agreement. Instead, some of the SCLC and local Birmingham leaders were able to work out a truce between the enraged black people and the brutally aggressive troopers.

The Birmingham campaign, saved from catastrophe, had not only energized the civil rights movement, but it had made the world aware of segregation's ugliness. Television was a critical factor. The new technology enabled millions of viewers to watch with rapt horror as the police attacked the youthful demonstrators. There was no mistaking the haunting scenes of Birmingham police dogs snapping at the legs of children. Nor could even the most casual viewer ignore the fire department's role in the daily confrontations.

It became clear to the White House that the civil rights activists would not abandon their cause without fundamental changes. An angry encounter between Attorney General Robert Kennedy and African Americans gathered by black writer James Baldwin highlighted the rawness of race relations in the country. Blacks bluntly told Kennedy that they expected more from him and his brother, the President. Robert Kennedy left the room angered by their demands, yet he later reflected that the encounter forever changed his views about race and the race problem in American life. Even the politically pragmatic John Kennedy would understand very soon that he could not shrink from the demands for full inclusion. To his credit, President Kennedy tried to get a new civil rights bill through the Congress. The new bill was stronger than all previous ones. It would end discrimination in all interstate transportation, at hotels, and in other public places; it ensured all who had a sixth-grade education the right to vote; and it gave the attorney general the power to cut off government funds to states and communities that continued to practice racial discrimination. It would be more than a year before Congress passed the Civil Rights Act of 1964. In the meantime, President Kennedy worried that any further demonstrations threatened his ability to secure sufficient bipartisan support for the legislation.

King and others sensed that it was time to bring the strategies of the Southern civil rights movement to the nation's capital. In a private conversation with friends Stanley Levison and Clarence Jones, recorded by an FBI wiretap, King broached the idea of a huge, 100,000-person march on Washington. The FBI had begun to tap King's phone lines after FBI director J. Edgar Hoover convinced Robert Kennedy that Levison, who was white, was a member of the Communist Party and had too much influence over King. Hoover, in fact, had a difficult time believing that blacks had initiated the movement and that it was led by blacks. Unaware that others were listening, King and his friends added other names to the list of possible organizers, including the venerable labor leader A. Philip Randolph, whose earlier threats to march on Washington had led President Franklin D. Roosevelt to issue Executive Order 8802, which banned hiring discrimination at military facilities and government agencies during World War II.

The planning committee brought together representatives from civil rights organizations and the labor movement, interested clergy, and entertainment figures. The logistics of putting together the August 28, 1963, event were an enormous challenge. Organizers had to plan, for example, for inclement weather, medical emergencies, transportation, sanitation, drinking water, and food. They also needed to coordinate speakers and to mobilize members of black communities nationwide who would attend. In the meantime, ever worried by the prospect of social disturbances, President Kennedy readied several thousand soldiers for riot control.

The response from Americans staggered the organizers. By the morning of the march, more than a quarter million people had descended on Washington from every state in the Union. They arrived in twenty-one chartered trains, in caravans of buses and cars, on bicycles, and on foot. One fellow rollerskated to the march from Chicago. Men and women, old and young, black and white, made their way to the summertime shadows of the Washington Monument. Although the occasion was sometimes festive, the mood was serious. Few knew of the behind-the-scenes crisis threatening to destroy the semblance of unity among sometimes rival civil rights groups.

But as folk singers such as Joan Baez, Odetta, Peter, Paul, and Mary, and Bob Dylan entertained the estimated quarter of a million people who assembled, march organizers worked to get SNCC leader John Lewis to temper his speech. Lewis's prepared text bristled with anger. In a shorthand fashion he recalled the painful lessons sandwiched between the Birmingham campaign and the Washington march. In that period bombs had exploded in Birmingham; civil rights workers June Johnson, Annell Ponder, and Fannie Lou Hamer endured a tortuous beating at the hands of Winona, Mississippi, police; Mississippi NAACP leader Medgar Evers was assassinated in his own driveway; and the Highlander Folk School in Tennessee was burned to the ground.

Lewis eventually agreed to the pleadings of Randolph, not because Washington area clergy threatened to boycott the affair, but because he respected and understood the power of the moment. Nonetheless Lewis advised those watching and listening that blacks would not go slow. He told the gathering, "We shall crack the South into a thousand pieces and put them back together in the image of democracy."

Though Lewis offered perhaps the most forceful message of the day, it was Martin Luther King, Jr.'s speech that became a sort of national motto. Fusing classical philosophy to the oral traditions of the black Baptist Church, King preached that day about an America that could be. He shared his dream of a day when race did not matter: "I have a dream that my four little children will one day live in a nation where they will not be judged by the color of their skin but by the content of their character. I have a dream today!"

King's speech—and the entire march—energized the black community with the hope of justice. Then on Sunday, September 15, 1963, little more than two weeks after the March on Washington, a package of dynamite ripped through the Sixteenth Street Baptist Church in Birmingham while worshipers were preparing for church services. When the smoke cleared, four young girls—ages eleven to fourteen—lay dead. Addie Mae Collins, Denise McNair, Carole Robertson, and Cynthia Wesley had not taken part in earlier demonstrations, but their young faces, appearing in newspapers worldwide, became instant symbols of both the tragedy of racism and the hope of the civil rights struggle.

Two months later, violence of another kind erupted in Dallas, and the victim this time was President Kennedy, who had gone to Texas to shore up his Southern base in the Democratic party. The 1964 election was a year away, and signs indicated that the Republicans might nominate the very conservative Barry Goldwater, a senator from Arizona. As his motorcade traveled the streets of Dallas on November 22, the sound of rifle fire rang out. The open limousine carrying Kennedy made him a ready target.

With Kennedy's death, Lyndon Baines Johnson, a Texan and former majority leader in the Senate, was sworn in as the country's new President. Among his first acts was to call for passage of the Civil Rights Act proposed by Kennedy. He told a joint session of Congress, "No memorial or eulogy could more eloquently honor President Kennedy's memory than the earliest possible passage of the civil rights bill for which he fought."

As Congress debated the merits of the legislation, blacks in Mississippi were continuing to demand their voting rights. In the fall of 1963, activists launched a Freedom Vote campaign to register voters statewide and to demonstrate the importance of black electoral participation. With help from sixty white students drawn from Northern colleges, canvassers went door-to-door, enduring beatings, intimidation, and the fear of physical injury, to get black Mississippians to vote in a mock election. Nearly 100,000 voted for a Freedom Party slate, thereby indicating what they could do if they had the right to vote.

Following this campaign, longtime SNCC worker Bob Moses proposed an expansion of the earlier effort. He and others had in mind a Freedom Summer, during which white college students, in alliance with local black leadership and blacks active in SNCC, would canvass Mississippi, registering voters and teaching in Freedom Schools. Moses had in mind something other than another mock vote; this time he would register blacks for the coming Presidential election in November 1964. Freedom Summer lasted three months, June, July, and August. About one thousand volunteers participated, three-quarters of whom were white and three hundred of whom were women. The students hailed from Western and Northern colleges and universities. After spending a week in a training session directed by SNCC executive director James Forman in Oxford, Ohio, the first two hundred volunteers embarked for Mississippi and the forty-three project sites scattered across the state.

Tragically, within the first two days of Freedom Summer, law enforcement officials in Philadelphia, Mississippi, added three new names to the list of martyrs who made the supreme sacrifice on behalf of civil rights. Andrew Goodman was a college student at Queens College in New York and a Freedom Summer volunteer. Michael Schwerner had recently opened the CORE office in Meridian with his wife, Rita. CORE worker James Chaney was the only one who was black and a native Mississippian.

On June 21, 1964, the three had set out for Lawndale to investigate another church burning. Near Philadelphia they were arrested for speeding, but the police let them go. That was the last time anyone other than their murderers saw them alive. One hundred fifty FBI agents, aided by sailors, searched woods and rivers. Investigators did not locate the three men until August 4, after they received a tip from an informant motivated by a thirty thousand dollar reward. The three decomposed bodies were found buried under a manmade dam. Later testimony revealed that the bulldozer operator at the dam had been paid by Klan members to hide the bodies there. Each had been shot by a .38-caliber gun; and clearly Chaney had been severely beaten before being shot. The U.S. Justice Department indicted nineteen men, including police officers and Klansmen, for the murders; only seven were found guilty.

The horrifying events caused a few volunteers to drop out, but not many. Many would later recall that the summer of 1964 was a pivotal time in their lives. Many whites experienced the warm fellowship of local black Southerners, who freely adopted them into their lives and communities. Black and white participants struggled with the perceptions and realities of power. Some SNCC and CORE activists complained, for example, that white volunteers too quickly assumed they were experts and leaders. Each group had to be educated and reeducated about the other's abilities and sensibilities. But the politics of leadership was no small matter. The tension soon grew into calls for black control of civil rights groups.

More than anything, however, Freedom Summer highlighted the potential political empowerment of black Mississippians. And it turned the national spotlight on racial violence and voting injustices in the state, forcing the federal government to respond. As August came to a close, more than eighty thousand blacks joined the new Mississippi Freedom Democratic party (MFDP). They would use this new strength to wrest changes from the national Democratic party, forcing the national body to undo, reluctantly, the practice of locking blacks out of the Mississippi party.

The Fire This Time

President Lyndon B. Johnson signed the Civil Rights Act into law on July 2, 1964. It not only outlawed segregation in public accommodations of every kind throughout the country, but it laid the foundation for federal affirmative action policy. Affirmative action programs were meant to ensure that victims of past discrimination would have greater opportunities to find jobs, earn promotions, and gain admission to colleges and universities. In particular, Title VII of the Civil Rights

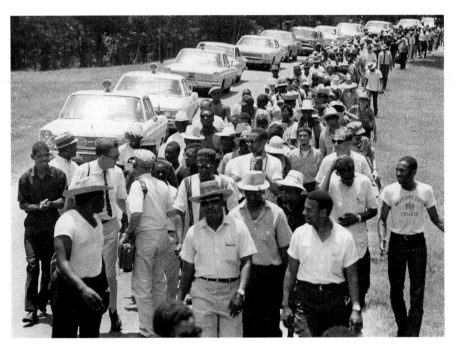

The 1966 "March against Fear" in Mississippi was initiated by James Meredith. After Meredith was shot, Martin Luther King, Jr., (front center) and others took over the march. Black militants denounced their tactics of nonviolence and urged blacks to defend themselves against attack.

Act outlawed employment discrimination by creating the Equal Employment Opportunity Commission (EEOC) to enforce the law. It not only applied to both governmental and nongovernmental employers but covered labor unions and employment agencies as well. Workers who believed they were discriminated against in the workplace because of their race, sex, creed, color, or religion could file a complaint with the federal government.

But the new law did not dismantle the obstacles to voting that blacks in the South still faced. In the summer of 1964, the Mississippi Freedom Democratic party (MFDP) filed a lawsuit against the Democratic party for discrimination and used the television cameras to take their story to the nation. Fannie Lou Hamer told the world how she had been beaten and tortured by white supremacists simply because "we want to register," and she pointed out that the white Democrats were not even loyal to President Lyndon B. Johnson. Those Democrats vehemently attacked Johnson's candidacy because of his commitment to civil rights and equal opportunity for all. Yet, while Johnson agreed with the MFDP's assessment, he and his party would not recognize its delegates as the legitimate representatives of the state of Mississippi at the Democratic National Convention.

Questioning both the horrors at home and the Democratic party's refusal to take their delegation seriously, Hamer asked, "Is this America? The land of the free and the home of the brave?" Johnson's response was to strike a deal: he signaled that he was prepared to select the liberal Minnesota senator Hubert H. Humphrey as his running mate, if MFDP delegates and their surrogates cooperated by allowing the delegation to remain intact, with one modification. Two members of the MFDP would sit as members of the Mississippi delegation, while other MFDP delegates would attend the convention as observers. Although Martin Luther King, Roy Wilkins, executive secretary of the NAACP, and several mainstream black leaders urged the MFDP to accept the compromise, they refused. Most MFDP delegates felt the compromise minimized their claim of truly representing Democrats in Mississippi.

When election day arrived, all of Mississippi's electoral votes went to archconservative Republican Barry Goldwater. Indeed, the Republican party made history, not only winning the state of Mississippi for the first time but also declaring victories in Alabama, Georgia, South Carolina, and Louisiana. The Democratic party's failure to fully embrace Mississippi's black voters signaled the beginning of the end of the solid Democratic South.

Johnson won by a landslide, but the failure of the capital-D Democratic party to support small-d democratic forces in the South and the willingness of Martin Luther King and other national civil rights figures to go along with Johnson struck a blow to the movement. Increasingly, local activists in the rural South, SNCC activists, and urban activists associated compromise with weakness.

Less than a year later King supported another compromise that would further damage and divide the movement. It involved a struggle in Selma, Alabama, where SNCC activists had been locked in a battle with local forces and Governor George Wallace, who used brutal violence to suppress the movement there. After SNCC organizer Jimmie Lee Jackson was shot by a state trooper as he tried to shield his mother from officers' billy clubs during a civil rights demonstration, SNCC and SCLC decided to hold a march from Selma to Montgomery on March 7, 1965. After calling for the march, however, King reconsidered after a tortuous conversation with Attorney General Nicholas Katzenbach. It was clear that President Johnson did not want the march to happen, because the potential violence would generate bad publicity and, from his perspective, jeopardize his relations with Southern Democrats. Worried that his defiance of Johnson's wishes might undermine the goal of passing a voting rights bill, King decided to cancel the march at the very last minute. He and Ralph Abernathy left town, announcing that they had to minister to their congregations.

But the young people of SNCC were not about to postpone the march. They convinced SCLC leader Hosea Williams to go on with it, with or without King. (Many marchers, however, did not know what had happened and were surprised by King's absence.) But they never made it; the police and state troopers brutally attacked the racially mixed crowd as it reached the Edmund Pettus Bridge, forcing the marchers to turn back. Three days later, amidst criticism for his absence, King decided to lead another group of three thousand people, who had answered the call to go to Selma and complete the march, across the bridge. But unbeknownst to the crowd he had made a secret agreement with Attorney General Katzenbach to retreat as soon as they came up against the state troopers. So when King and the march leaders got within fifty feet of the troopers' blockade, they kneeled, prayed, and, as they rose, called on the marchers to retreat. Angry and confused, the marchers did what they were told. The march was eventually held a few weeks later, after much negotiation with the Johnson administration and Governor Wallace.

Despite its fits and starts, the Selma march contributed to the passage of an important piece of legislation by the federal government: the Voting Rights Act of 1965. Signed into law on August 6, 1965, the act prohibited states from imposing literacy requirements, poll taxes, and similar obstacles to the registration of black voters. Of course, the 15th Amendment to the Constitution, passed almost a century earlier, was supposed to guarantee this right to vote, but a federal system of "states' rights" had allowed Southern states to deny black people voting privileges through such measures as the poll tax, literacy tests, and grandfather clauses (until 1939).

With the Voting Rights Act, however, blacks could not be denied the vote any more. Federal examiners were now sent South to safeguard black citizens' right to register and vote. The impact of the act was dramatic: between 1964 and 1969, the number of black adults registered to vote increased from 19.3 percent to 61.3 percent in Alabama, 27.4 percent to 60.4 percent in Georgia, and 6.7 percent to 66.5 percent in Mississippi. It took several more years before blacks turned the right to vote into electoral might.

The victory was bittersweet. King's role in the Selma march tarnished his reputation in the eyes of his followers. As respect for King's ideas and strategies began to wane among young people, groups such as SNCC began to envision new, more militant strategies. It became clear—from the failure of the MFDP at the 1964 Democratic National Convention to the Selma fiasco—that African Americans could not always rely on the federal government for support. A new generation of activists realized that black people needed more than friends in high places; they needed power.

Within SNCC, a recent Howard University graduate named Stokely Carmichael quickly emerged as a voice of uncompromising militancy and, later, black nationalism. Born in Trinidad and raised in New York City, Carmichael had been associated with interracial radical movements since high school. Like many of his contemporaries, he joined the civil rights movement but never fully embraced the philosophy of nonviolence. He and several other SNCC activists began carrying guns to protect themselves from violence. Carmichael led a militant voter registration campaign, organizing open rallies and marches for black rights in the heart of the Black Belt—with its long history of white violence and terrorism against black sharecroppers. In Lowndes County, Alabama, in 1965, he founded the Lowndes County Freedom Organization (LCFO). An all-black group (mainly because whites would not join), the LCFO adopted the symbol of the black panther because, according to its chairman, John Hulett, the panther will come out fighting for its life when cornered.

The LCFO was only the beginning of the new black militancy. A few months later, a group of black SNCC activists in Atlanta circulated a position paper calling on white members to leave the organization and devote their attention to organizing white people in their own communities. Although most SNCC members, black and white, opposed this position, it became clear to many white activists that the character of the movement had changed profoundly. Several leading white figures resigned voluntarily or were forced to leave because, in their view at least, the political climate had become intolerable. Carmichael had successfully contested John Lewis for the chairmanship of SNCC and he, along with other SNCC militants such as veteran organizer Willie Ricks, began questioning the movement's integrationist agenda. Then, during the summer of 1966, the slogan Black Power emerged full-blown within SNCC as well as within the Congress of Racial Equality (CORE).

On June 5, James Meredith, the first black student admitted to the University of Mississippi, initiated a march from Memphis, Tennessee, to Jackson, Mississippi, in order to mobilize black Mississippians to register to vote. A few hours into the march, however, Meredith was shot and the march came to an abrupt end. Martin Luther King, Jr., Carmichael, and CORE leader Floyd McKissick decided to go to Memphis in order to finish the march to Jackson. From the very beginning, however, tensions between King and Carmichael created tensions within the ranks. Carmichael insisted that the Deacons for Defense, an armed black self-defense group based in Louisiana, provide cover for the marchers, a request to which King reluctantly agreed. At the same time, SNCC activist Willie Ricks began to promote the slogan Black Power among the membership, who seemed to embrace it enthusiastically. While King called it "an unfortunate choice of words," McKissick embraced it. As he explained, "Black Power is not Black supremacy; it is a united Black voice reflecting racial pride in the tradition of our heterogeneous nation. Black Power does not mean the exclusion of White Americans from the Negro Revolution; it means the inclusion of all men in a common moral and political struggle."

Not everyone agreed with this definition, of course, but it quickly became clear during the summer of 1966 that the issue of Black Power would transform the movement in multiple ways. Tired and impatient with the slow pace of the civil rights establishment, a new attitude overtook the movement: no more compromise, no more "deals" with white liberals, no more subordinating the movement to the needs of the Democratic party. Out of bitter disappointment rose this new slogan.

The Black Power of the sixties had roots in the Southern freedom movement, in the many compromises made by mainstream leaders, and in the recognition that ending Jim Crow was not enough to win full equality or political power. It also had roots in the increasingly black cities of the North and South, where poverty and police brutality were becoming increasingly visible. And it was nourished by the growing popularity of black nationalism—the idea that black people constitute a single community, if not a "nation," within the United States and therefore have a right to determine their destiny—as expressed by people such as former North Carolina NAACP leader Robert Williams, as well as SNCC leaders such as H. Rap Brown and Stokely Carmichael.

Perhaps *the* most important and controversial progenitor of the Black Power movement was Malcolm X. For many young people, particularly those in the civil rights movement, Malcolm's uncompromising stance toward white supremacy and his plainspoken oratory on black history, culture, and racism deeply affected a new generation of activists. Even efforts to portray Malcolm in a negative light, such as the special 1959 television documentary on the Nation of Islam called "The Hate That Hate Produced" revealed to many black viewers Malcolm's critique of nonviolence and of the strategy to ally with white liberals. He clearly saw the need for a movement in the urban North, one that would focus on the needs of the poor and deal with pressing issues such as police brutality, crumbling schools, and the lack of jobs. While preaching black self-reliance, he also attacked mainstream civil rights leaders for being sellouts. "The black masses," he argued, "are tired of following these hand-picked Negro 'leaders' who sound like professional beggars, as they cry year after year for white America to accept us as first-class citizens."

These civil rights leaders, Malcolm said, were leading a nonviolent Negro revolution, when what was needed was a black revolution. Whereas the Negro wants to desegregate, he said, the black demands land, power, and freedom. Whereas the Negro adopts a Christian philosophy of "love thy enemy," the black has no love or respect for the oppressor.

As long as Malcolm remained in the Nation of Islam, he was compelled to conceal his differences with Elijah Muhammad. But as Malcolm became more popular, the tensions between the two men became increasingly evident. The final blow came when Malcolm discovered that the NOI's moral and spiritual leader had fathered children by two former secretaries. The tensions became publicly visible when Muhammad silenced Malcolm for remarking after the assassination of President John F. Kennedy that it was a case of the "chickens coming home to roost." Malcolm's point was that the federal government's inaction toward racist violence in the South had come back to strike the President. When Malcolm learned that Muhammad had planned to have him assassinated, he decided to leave the NOI. On March 8, 1964, he announced his resignation and formed the Muslim Mosque, Inc., an Islamic movement devoted to working in the political sphere and cooperating with civil rights leaders. Despite his criticisms of black leadership,

Martin Luther King, Jr., and Malcolm X met accidentally and amicably in Washington, D.C., in 1964. Despite their differences in style and philosophy, they shared many of the concerns, goals, and risks involved in freedom movement leadership.

Malcolm had always said that he should be actively involved in the struggles in the South and elsewhere, but Elijah Muhammad's rule that NOI members not participate in politics had hampered Malcolm. Free of the Nation of Islam, Malcolm sought alliances with those willing to work with him.

That same year he made his first pilgrimage to Mecca—the holy city of Islam, in Saudi Arabia. During his trip he changed his name to El-Hajj Malik El-Shabazz and embraced the multiracial Islam he found during his pilgrimage. He publicly acknowledged that whites were no longer devils, though he still remained a black nationalist and staunch believer in black self-determination and self-organization.

During the summer of 1964 Malcolm formed the Organization of Afro-American Unity (OAAU). Inspired by the Organization of African Unity, made up of the independent African states, the OAAU's program combined advocacy for independent black institutions (for example, schools and cultural centers) with support for black participation in mainstream politics, including electoral campaigns. Following the example of Paul Robeson and W. E. B. Du Bois, who had submitted a petition to the United Nations in 1948 claiming that black people in the United States were victims of genocide, Malcolm planned to submit a similar petition in 1965. The UN petition documented human rights violations and acts of genocide against African Americans. Unfortunately, Malcolm and members of the OAAU never had a chance to submit the petition: on February 21, 1965, he was assassinated by gunmen affiliated with the NOI.

Malcolm had known he was in danger ever since he had left the NOI. He received regular death threats and was constantly followed by suspicious characters. One week before his murder, his home in Queens, New York, was firebombed. He had even begun to carry a gun for protection. But on Sunday, February 21, as he took the stage to speak to a small audience at the Audubon Ballroom in Harlem, two gunmen stood up and opened fire. One got away, but the crowd stopped the other, a Muslim named Talmadge Hayer. (One year later, Hayer was convicted of the murder of Malcolm.) The OAAU died with Malcolm X.

Although Malcolm left no permanent organizations (the Muslim Mosque, Inc., collapsed soon after his death), he did exert a notable impact on the civil rights movement in the last year of his life. Black activists in SNCC and CORE who had heard him speak to organizers in Selma just weeks before his death began to support some of his ideas, especially on armed self-defense, racial pride, and the creation of black-run institutions. Ironically, Malcolm's impact on black politics and culture was greater after his death than before it. In fact, not long thereafter, the Black Power movement and his ideas about community control, African liberation, and race pride became extremely influential. His autobiography, written with Alex Haley—the future author of *Roots*—become a movement standard. Malcolm's life story proved to movements such as the Black Panther party, founded in 1966, that ex-criminals and hustlers can be turned into revolutionaries. And arguments in favor of armed self-defense—certainly not a new idea in African-American communities—were renewed by the publication of Malcolm's autobiography and speeches.

One of the first radical organizations to be inspired by Malcolm's ideas was the Revolutionary Action Movement (RAM). It originated neither in the South nor in the Northeast. Rather, its founders were a group of black Ohio students at Case Western Reserve University in Cleveland, Central State College, and Wilberforce University. Active in SNCC, CORE, and local chapters of Students for a Democratic Society (SDS), a predominantly white national student group that emerged during the Vietnam War protests, this gathering began meeting in 1961 to discuss the significance of Robert Williams's armed self-defense campaign in North Carolina and his subsequent flight to Cuba. Led by Donald Freeman, a student at Case Western Reserve, the group agreed that armed self-defense was a necessary component of the black freedom movement and that activists had to link themselves to anticolonial movements around the world. Freeman was influenced by Malcolm X's speeches and the writings of an independent black Marxist intellectual named Harold Cruse, who argued that African Americans themselves lived under colonialism inside the United States. Freeman hoped to transform the group into a revolutionary movement akin to the Nation of Islam but one that would adopt the direct action tactics of SNCC. By the spring of 1962, they became the Revolutionary Action Movement (RAM).

Although RAM's leaders decided to organize it as an underground movement, it did attract activists across the nation. In the South, RAM built a small but significant following at Fisk University in Nashville, the training ground for many leading SNCC activists. In northern California, RAM grew primarily out of the Afro-American Association, a student group founded in 1962 based at Oakland's Merritt College and the University of California at Berkeley. Never a mass movement, RAM had a radical agenda that anticipated many of the goals of the left wing of the Black Power movement. Its twelve-point program called for the development of freedom schools, national black student organizations, rifle clubs, a guerrilla army made up of youth and the unemployed, and black farmer cooperatives not just for economic development but to keep "community and guerrilla forces going for a while." They also pledged support for national liberation movements in Africa, Asia, and Latin America as well as the adoption of socialism to replace capitalism across the globe.

After RAM spent years as an underground organization, a series of "exposés" that ran in *Life* magazine and *Esquire* in 1966 identified it as one of the leading extremist groups "Plotting a War on 'Whitey.'" RAM members were not only considered armed and dangerous but "impressively well read in revolutionary literature." Not surprisingly, these highly publicized articles were followed by a series of police raids on the homes of RAM members in Philadelphia and New York City. In June 1967, RAM members were rounded up and charged with conspiracy to instigate a riot, poison police officers with potassium cyanide, and assassinate NAACP leader Roy Wilkins and National Urban League director Whitney Young. Though the charges did not stick, the FBI's surveillance of RAM intensified. By 1969, RAM had essentially dissolved itself, though its members opted to infiltrate existing black organizations, continue to push the twelve-point program, and develop study groups that focused on the "Science of Black Internationalism."

RAM's movement was, in part, based on the assumption that black people had the potential to launch a war against the U.S. government. Writing in exile from Cuba and later China, Robert Williams anticipated black urban uprisings in a spring 1964 edition of *The Crusader,* a publication RAM members regarded as an unofficial organ of their movement. Entitled "USA: The Potential of a Minority Revolution," Williams's article announced, "This year, 1964 is going to be a violent one, the storm will reach hurricane proportions by 1965 and the eye of the hurricane will hover over America by 1966. America is a house on fire—FREEDOM NOW!—or let it burn, let it burn. Praise the Lord and pass the ammunition!!"

Williams was not alone in this assessment. A year earlier, the writer James Baldwin had predicted that in the coming years race riots would "spread to every metropolitan center in the nation which has a significant Negro population." The next six years proved them right. With riots erupting in the black communities of

Rochester, New York City, Jersey City, and Philadelphia, 1964 was indeed a "violent" year. By 1965, these revolts had indeed reached "hurricane proportions."

The hurricane also touched the West Coast in the black Los Angeles community of Watts. Sparked when a resident witnessed a black driver being harrassed by white police officers, a frequent occurrence on the streets of Los Angeles, the Watts rebellion turned out to be the worst urban disturbance in nearly twenty years. When the smoke cleared, thirty-four people had died, and more than $35 million in property had been destroyed or damaged. The remainder of the decade witnessed the spread of this hurricane across America: violence erupted in some three hundred cities, including Chicago; Washington, D.C.; Cambridge, Maryland; Providence, Rhode Island; Hartford, Conneticut; San Francisco; and Phoenix. Altogether, the urban uprisings involved close to half a million African Americans, resulted in millions of dollars in property damage, and left 250 people (mostly African Americans) dead, 10,000 seriously injured, and countless black people homeless. Police and the National Guard turned black neighborhoods into war zones, arresting at least sixty thousand people and employing tanks, machine guns, and tear gas to pacify the community. In Detroit in 1967, for instance, forty-three people were killed, two thousand were wounded, and five thousand watched their homes destroyed by flames that engulfed fourteen square miles of the inner city.

Robert Williams was not too far off the mark: a real war erupted in America's inner cities. Elected officials, from the mayor's office to the Oval Office, must have seen these uprisings as a war of sorts because they responded to the crisis with military might at first. Later they turned to a battery of social science investigators, community programs, and short-lived economic development projects to pacify urban blacks. Just as the American military advisers in Southeast Asia could not understand why so many North Vietnamese supported the communists, liberal social scientists wanted to find out why African Americans rioted. Why burn buildings in "their own" communities? What did they want? Were these "disturbances" merely a series of violent orgies led by young hoodlums out for television sets and a good time, or were they protest movements? To the surprise of several research teams, those who rioted tended to be better educated and more politically aware than those who did not. One survey of Detroit black residents after the 1967 riot revealed that eighty-six percent of the respondents identified discrimination and deprivation as the main reasons behind the uprising. Hostility to police brutality was at the top of the list.

Although Robert Williams, James Baldwin, and many African Americans who survived each day in the crumbling ghettoes of North America knew the storm was on the horizon, government officials and policymakers were unprepared. After all, things seemed to be looking up for black folk: between 1964 and 1969, the median black family income rose from $5,921 to $8,074; the percentage of black families below the poverty line declined from 48.1 percent in 1959 to 27.9 percent in 1969. However, these statistics also reveal a growing chasm between members of a black middle class who were beginning to benefit from integration, affirmative action policies, and a strong economy, and the black poor left behind in deteriorating urban centers. Dilapidated, rat-infested housing, poor and overcrowded schools, the lack of city services, and the disappearance of high-wage jobs in inner-city communities all contributed to the expansion of urban poverty and deprivation. But there is more to the story: the black freedom movement and the hope it engendered in black communities convinced many blacks that change was inevitable. Some historians have called it "rising expectations"; others simply identified it as "rights consciousness." Either way, an increasing number of African Americans, including the poor, adopted a new attitude for a new day. They demanded respect and basic human rights, expected decent housing and decent jobs as a matter of rights, and understood that social movements and protests were the way to achieve these things. This attitude manifested itself in the daily interactions between blacks and whites. For example, after buses had been desegregated in the South, white residents complained frequently of the growing impudence and discourtesy of black passengers. As one white Birmingham woman complained, "Can't get on the bus and ride to town because the colored have taken the buses."

But the same circumstances that unleashed such fervent opposition to segregation and emboldened ordinary black people to assert their rights also unleashed a more sustained effort on the part of the police to put things back in order. Police repression reached an all-time high between 1963 and the early seventies and black male youths from poor communities were involved in the majority of incidents.

There is a similar paradox evident in the growth in the number of welfare recipients during the sixties. In 1960, 745,000 families received assistance; by 1968 that figure had grown to 1.5 million. The most dramatic increase took place between 1968 and 1972, when the welfare rolls grew to three million. On the one hand, the surge in the welfare rolls reflects the expansion of poverty amidst plenty, the growing numbers of poor people (particularly among minority women and children) who needed assistance to survive. But the growth also reflects a "rights consciousness" among welfare recipients inspired by the civil rights and Black Power movements of the period. In 1966, the former associate director of CORE, George Wiley, created the Poverty Rights Action Center (PRAC) in order to help coordinate the activities of numerous local welfare rights organizations that had begun appearing during the early sixties. Out of discussions within PRAC, Wiley helped found the National Welfare Rights Organization (NWRO) a year later. Led primarily by black female welfare recipients, the NWRO educated the poor about eligibility for assistance under existing laws and pressured welfare agencies to provide benefits without stigmatizing applicants. They demanded adequate day-care facilities and criticized poorly planned job training programs. They attacked degrading, low-wage employment and the practice of scrutinizing women's lives as a precondition for support (such as investigations to determine whether recipients were unwed mothers, had a man living with them, or spent their meager welfare check on things a social worker might find unnecessary, such as makeup). Moreover, they viewed welfare not merely as a gift from the government or a handout but as a right. By emphasizing that welfare was a right, the NWRO stripped welfare of its stigma in the eyes of many poor women and convinced them that they could receive assistance and retain their dignity.

The NWRO was not the only advocate for the increased demands of the black poor. Under President Lyndon Johnson, the federal government launched a "War on Poverty" as part of his overall vision of transforming America into a "Great Society." Most of the programs that fell under the broad title of the "War on Poverty" were created by the Economic Opportunity Act of 1964. Agencies such as the Job Corps, administered by the Department of Labor, sought to create employment opportunities for the poor. And through the newly created Office of Economic Opportunity (OEO), agencies such as the Legal Services Corporation, to provide civil legal assistance; the Community Action Program; Head Start, a preschool education program; and Volunteers in Service to America (VISTA) sought to provide services for the poor and incorporate them in the decision-making and policymaking process at the local level. The OEO's director, Sargent Shriver, called for the "maximum feasible participation" of the poor in these agencies and, more generally, in the process of solving the problems of poverty.

The only program that actively tried to implement "maximum feasible participation" was the Community Action Program (CAP). CAP's mission was to coordinate the work of more than a thousand federally funded, neighborhood-based antipoverty agencies and to make new services more accessible to the poor. Unlike other antipoverty agencies, CAP focused its efforts on rehabilitating the entire community rather than poor families or individuals who happened to fall below the poverty line. Although CAP quickly earned a reputation for "stirring up the poor," it mainly worked with prosperous local blacks and established black middle-class leadership. Indeed, despite directives from on high calling for maximum feasible participation, urban rebellions from below turned out to be what got the black activists and community people into the antipoverty agencies.

The bureaucrats and planners who implemented these poverty programs conceived of "maximum feasible participation" very differently from groups like the NWRO or leaders of the civil rights movement. After all, they were planned almost entirely by middle-class white men in the Johnson administration who set out to provide "a hand up" to the poorest segment of society, from the ghetto residents in America's sprawling cities, to the Mexican migrants on farms and in barrios in the Southwest, to the poor whites scratching out a living in Appalachia.

Overall, Johnson's Great Society programs did begin to reduce poverty ever so slightly. Ironically, the greatest successes were not products of the Equal Opportunity Act of 1964 but of other programs, notably the expansion of the food stamp program, free school meals and other nutrition projects, and the creation of Medicaid and Medicare programs (which provided the poor and elderly with free health care). But Johnson's War on Poverty fell short of the mark. First, agencies such as the Job Corps focused on job training rather than creating new, decent-paying jobs. Second, Johnson refused to raise taxes in order to pay for these programs, which proved disastrous because he had given the middle class a huge tax cut in 1964 and there was not enough money available. Besides, the cost of fighting the Vietnam War steadily drained federal resources away from the War on Poverty and contributed to rising inflation. Third, the War on Poverty operated from a very limited definition of poverty, one that included only families who fell below a fixed poverty line. The goal was not to change the structure of poverty, to reduce income inequality or help the working poor earn more money; rather, it was to change the behaviors that officials believed led to poverty by providing educational, legal, and job training services to the very poor in order to give them the resources to rise up out of poverty. In other words, the Johnson administration believed the causes of poverty to be culture and behavior rather than political and economic forces. Rather than deal with issues such as low wages, a shortage of well-paying jobs, and blatant racism in employment and labor unions, the proponents of the War on Poverty sought to "correct" poor people's behavior or improve their social skills. The administrators and intellectuals working in these federal programs saw their task in terms of reversing "community pathology," breaking the the "culture of poverty," or restoring the "broken family." The poor, especially the black poor, were considered "disadvantaged."

Most black activists did not believe liberal goodwill, as they viewed it, could eliminate poverty. They viewed the problem in terms of power and unequal distribution of wealth. As NWRO leader George Wiley put it: "I am not at all convinced that comfortable, affluent, middle-class Americans are going to move over and share their wealth and resources with the people who have none. But I do have faith that if the poor people who have the problems can organize, can exert their political muscle, they can have a chance to have their voices and their weight felt in the political process of this country, and there is hope."

Martin Luther King, Jr., concurred. In his book *Where Do We Go From Here?*, King wrote: "The plantation and the ghetto were created by those who had power both to confine those who had no power and to perpetuate their powerlessness. The problem of transforming the ghetto is, therefore, a problem of power."

So King and the Southern Christian Leadership Conference took the movement to the urban North, settling in Chicago in 1966. They initially tried to build a grassroots union of poor black residents rather than opening their efforts with a direct-action campaign that would draw media attention, as King and his associates had done in Birmingham three years earlier. When the organizing drive failed to generate much support, King decided to lead a march through a white Chicago neighborhood to demand an end to racial discrimination in housing. King and the SCLC had gone there to appeal to the city, the state, and the nation for open housing for all, and to use the power of love to persuade white racists that segregation was immoral. Instead, King met an angry white crowd raining rocks and bottles on the protesters. In all of his years fighting racism and injustice in the South, he had never seen anything like this before.

The Chicago campaign marked another failure for King. To compound matters, his increasing opposition to the Vietnam War drew fire from nearly every major older mainstream black leader in the country, who feared alienating the volatile President, and further distanced him from the Johnson administration.

Given King's deep and abiding commitment to nonviolence, he was bound to come out openly against the war. And militants in CORE and SNCC had begun issuing antiwar statements as early as 1966. SNCC openly endorsed resistance to the draft. It declared: "Vietnamese are being murdered because the United States is pursuing an aggressive policy in violation of international law." King understood the link between the war abroad and the failure to wage a real war on poverty at home. He pointed out that the United States was spending close to $500,000 to kill each enemy soldier but spent only a paltry thirty-five dollars a year to help a needy American in poverty. The more he criticized the war, the more isolated he became in mainstream civil rights circles. His longtime allies Bayard Rustin, Roy Wilkins, and Whitney Young denounced him publicly, and they were joined by a chorus of distinguished black spokesmen, including Ralph Bunche, Massachusetts senator Edward Brooke, and former baseball star Jackie Robinson. And, of course, this diminished his standing with the White House. But King's national, and international, reputation after winning the 1964 Nobel Peace Prize meant he could not be ignored entirely.

As he endured criticism from white and black friends, King became more radical in key respects. He became more committed than ever to organizing the poor and he openly rejected liberal reform as the strategy for change. King and his aides at SCLC planned a massive Poor People's Campaign on Washington to take place in the spring of 1968. The march was to bring thousands of poor people from all ethnic and racial backgrounds to demand, among other things, a federally supported guaranteed income policy.

Despite plans for a new campaign, the movement and the criticisms had taken their toll on King. Many friends and associates described him as tired and depressed. He talked openly of death, his own death. As he fretted in the first months of 1968, behind the scenes King and his associates vigorously debated the wisdom of the Poor People's Campaign in Washington. A few encouraged King to support their call for a civil disobedience campaign that would close key streets in the nation's capital. Bayard Rustin, among others, considered such a strategy pure folly, given the outbreaks of violence that had marred the public landscape since 1965. King, moreover, worried that too little had been done to recruit those of all races who were very poor and chronically unemployed.

Meanwhile, in February 1968, in Memphis, another battle erupted, this one between municipal workers who sought union recognition and city officials who refused such recognition. Black garbage collectors in the city fumed when twenty-two of them were sent home without pay due to bad weather, while white workers were allowed to stay and were paid. The 1,300 members of AFSCME Local 1733, a nearly all-black local representing the sanitation workers, refused to let the issue die; they demanded that the city acknowledge their union and refused to work otherwise. Memphis Mayor Henry Loeb refused to negotiate with the men or anyone else. Residents of the black community joined the men, boycotting downtown merchants and triggering a thirty-five percent loss of profit. Still the mayor refused to budge. And following an unsuccessful public meeting, a confrontation with police resulted in an ugly moment of violence, onlookers overturned police cars, and the police indiscriminately maced and clubbed everyone in their way.

Seeking to dramatize the plight of black workers and force the city to the bargaining table, longtime civil rights activist and minister of Centenary Methodist Church James Lawson placed a call to King for assistance. The fusing of race and economics had by now been a chief concern for King for several years. Still he put Lawson off at first, pleading fatigue and a tight schedule. King did go to Memphis and addressed more than fifteen thousand on the evening of March 18. He then promised to return the next week, a promise broken only by a rare foot of snow that forced a postponement of the march he was to have joined. In the interim, further negoitations with city officials produced little. On March 28 he did return, prepared to fight until victory was won.

Speaking before a black audience on April 3, King predicted that the Memphis sanitation workers' struggle would succeed. But in midstream, when the audience rose with his inspirational tone, King's speech changed rather abruptly. Sweat pouring down his face, he closed with these famous and fateful words:

> I don't know what will happen now. But it really doesn't matter to me now. Because I've been to the mountaintop. I won't mind. Like anybody, I would like to live a long life. Longevity has its place. But I'm not concerned about that now. I just want to do God's will. And He's allowed me to go up to the mountain. And I've looked over, and I've seen the promised land. . . . I may not get there with you but I want you to know tonight that we as a people will get to the promised land. So I'm happy tonight. I'm not worried about anything. I'm not fearing any man. "Mine eyes have seen the glory of the coming of the Lord."

The following evening, April 4, 1968, King was fatally shot by a white man named James Earl Ray. For some inexplicable reason, the police who had been guarding King's hotel happened to be absent at the time of his assassination. Although they caught the assailant, America lost a visionary.

The response to King's death was immediate and varied. Some white students at the University of Texas at Arlington screamed with glee, joyous that an assassin's bullet had taken out the "troublemaker" King. At the same time the *New York Times* editorialized, "Dr. King's murder is a national disaster." And that it was: major riots engulfed Washington, D.C., Baltimore, and Chicago. All told, more than one hundred cities suffered from rioting after the assassination of King, leaving thirty-nine people dead and millions of dollars' worth of property destroyed. President Johnson declared April 7, 1968, a day of mourning, and in tribute to the man whose death brought condolences from leaders and citizens around the world, the country flew its flag at half mast. Between King's death and his funeral on April 9, Coretta Scott King and her children led a silent, peaceful march through the streets of Memphis.

On the hot, humid April day of the funeral, thousands of schoolchildren sat transfixed as black-and-white televisions were hauled into classrooms so that the nation could collectively mourn King's passing. What they witnessed that day was a unique assembly. In the Ebenezer Baptist Church in Atlanta sat Vice President Hubert Humphrey, Presidential aspirants Democrat Robert Kennedy and Republican Richard Nixon, civil rights warriors young and old, Jacqueline Kennedy, who a few years earlier had suffered the loss of her own husband, as well as an assortment of friends, acquaintances, and loved ones. Ralph David Abernathy eulogized his old and dear friend. At Coretta King's insistence, Martin offered his own eulogy, too, as a tape recording of his "A Drum Major for Justice" sermon played for all to hear. That voice, deep and rich, so full of vitality, reminded all of the man who was made by the needs of his time.

A simple cart pulled by two mules hauled King's draped casket to its final resting place. His grave marker told the world what his life had come to symbolize:

> FREE AT LAST, FREE AT LAST
> THANK GOD ALMIGHTY
> I'M FREE AT LAST.

Where Do We Go from Here?

One year before his murder in 1968, Martin Luther King, Jr., published the book *Where Do We Go From Here: Chaos or Community?* More than the title itself, the subtitle captured what the year 1968 felt like to many Americans. With increasing regularity young men were fleeing the nation to escape the draft or returning from Vietnam in body bags.

Thousands of miles from that war, American support for a declining Portugal as it struggled to hang on to its African colonies in Mozambique, Angola, and Guinea-Bissau produced another kind of chaos. For those African Americans paying attention to liberation campaigns on the African continent, the support revealed the degree to which the United States would resort to violence to prop up an aging colonial power. The U.S. government supplied the Portuguese with military advisors and many weapons, including napalm bombs that were dropped on towns and villages where African nationalists had established bases.

Back in the United States, 1968 was a year of unprecedented chaos and considerable violence. Inner-city neighborhoods, such as Washington, D.C., Chicago, and Memphis, visited by race riots, continued to burn; incidents of police brutality rose steadily; dozens of black activists committed to protecting their communities from police violence were embroiled in several shoot-outs with law enforcement officials; and political assassinations continued. Just weeks after the country watched the burial of Martin Luther King, Jr., a gunman named Sirhan Sirhan fatally shot Democratic party Presidential candidate Robert F. Kennedy.

Liberals sought to turn this chaos into "community," to stem the country's division into two nations, one black and the other white. This was certainly the goal outlined in the report of the National Advisory Commission on Civil Disorders, a Presidentially appointed committee whose study of the causes of urban uprisings was also published in 1968. Better known as the Kerner Commission (named after Ohio governor Otto Kerner, the commission's head), its report acknowledged the urgent need for the government to bridge the widening gulf between blacks and whites. The report recommended massive job training and employment programs, educational improvements, an overhaul of the welfare system, and a plan for integrating blacks into the nation's mainstream.

The authors of the report, a predominantly white group of liberal social scientists and policymakers committed to racial integration and ending poverty, made what seemed to many Americans a bold and startling claim: that racism was endemic to U.S. society. Racism was not merely the bad behavior of a few individuals but operated through institutions and forces of power. Thus in order to eliminate racism, massive changes in American institutions needed to take place. As the authors wrote, "The essential fact is that neither existing conditions nor the garrison state [referring to the massive numbers of police and National Guardsmen in riot-plagued communities] offered acceptable alternatives for the future of this country. Only a greatly enlarged commitment to national action, compassionate, massive, and sustained, backed by the will and resources of the most powerful and the richest nation on this earth, can shape a future that is compatible with the historic ideals of American society."

While the Kerner Commission proposed a plan to turn "chaos" into "community," African-American activists who embraced the politics of Black Power saw themselves already as community builders. They had previously viewed racism as institutionalized, and most had lost faith in the American creed of justice for all, the goal of integration, or the kindness of white liberals. Instead, they sought to build alternative institutions within black communities, to strengthen the black community itself, and to fight for political and economic power. Of course, precisely what Black Power meant was always open to debate. For some it was a movement for black political power with the hope of making American democracy more open and inclusive for all. For others it meant building black businesses. For many grass-roots activists, Black Power meant creating separate, autonomous institutions within black communities.

The leadership of the Congress of Racial Equality (CORE), a leading force in the civil rights movement, had begun to embrace Black Power around the same time it shifted its focus from large, highly visible direct-action campaigns against segregation to less visible community organizing in poor African-American neighborhoodsespecially in the urban North. CORE underwent a change in leadership when Floyd McKissick replaced James Farmer as executive director in January 1966. Farmer, who had been a charter member of the group and took over its leadership in 1961, had been a longtime proponent of integration and direct action, while McKissick had been among the early advocates of Black Power.

With the shift to a focus on building up black communities, CORE's black membership increased dramatically. Some of the increase can be attributed to McKissick. Among his many symbolic and substantive actions, he moved the national office from downtown New York City to Harlem. There, he combined an interest in economic development and an appreciation of cultural training, especially the teaching of African languages. Though he never advocated complete racial separation, CORE's new leader did preach a message of black autonomy and self-determination.

It was Roy Innis, who took over CORE in 1968, who linked black self-determination and black capitalism, that is, getting a fair share of the economic pie, especially control of businesses in urban ghettos. In some ways he saw the black community as a colony within the United States that could become independent only if it had a strong economic base. Innis therefore called for federal funds to establish black businesses. He envisioned a federal system in which black communities would be linked together in a federation, constituting a black "nation within a nation." The U.S. Constitution made no allowances for such a possibility, however. Innis eventually lost faith in black nationalism as a strategy of liberation. By 1972, he had thrown his support behind conservative Republican Richard Nixon and promoted a limited strategy of black enterprise and assimilation.

Others embraced a more conventional, if not conservative, form of economic black nationalism. A small but dominant group came from the rising black middle class. Many college-educated blacks who were nonetheless concerned about affairs within black communities interpreted Black Power to mean black capitalism. In fact, in an age when Black Power evoked fears of bomb-throwing militants and radicals with Afro hairstyles, it is interesting to note that the first Black Power conference was organized by conservative Republican Nathan Wright, and the second was cosponsored by Clairol, a manufacturer of hair care products. Even Republican Richard Nixon, who won the 1968 Presidential election, praised Black Power, since he, like the conservative business daily the *Wall Street Journal,* connected Black Power to black economic self-sufficiency.

Nixon was not the only symbol of the white mainstream who embraced black capitalism. A number of corporations promoted a black managerial class and supported black capitalism: Xerox sponsored the TV series "Of Black America"; Chrysler put a little money in a black-owned bank; and the lumber and paper products giant Crown Zellerbach set up subsidiaries run by black management.

Companies that to date had viewed blacks as no more than consumers even modified their lending policies in the years between 1968 and 1970. Prudential, the large life insurance conglomerate, made more than $85 million in loans to blacks in urban communities, after much of the property it owned and insured in Newark, New Jersey, was destroyed after the 1967 rebellion. Throughout 1968 and 1969, Nixon and other white conservatives supported black economic advancement as an alternative to rebellion or revolution. They believed if people had a real stake in society they would be less inclined to seek its overthrow.

In 1968 and 1969 the federal government and many average citizens openly worried about the overthrow of the government. Many saw chaos and feared true anarchy. College campuses, especially, were sites of antiwar demonstrations, calls for changes in curriculum, attempts to ban the Reserve Officers Training Corps (ROTC, a military training program), and other actions. Campuses became a cauldron of black protest, too. In the years 1968–69, fifty-seven percent of all campus protests involved black students. This level reflects both the growing numbers of black students on campuses and the increasing numbers who ended up at predominantly white colleges. Between 1964 and 1970, the number of black college students nearly doubled, from 234,000 to half a million, while the percentage attending black colleges dropped from fifty-one to thirty-four percent.

Black students often faced attacks from some white students who were uncomfortable with their increasing numbers on previously nearly all-white campuses; they found the campus environment hostile, given their small numbers, isolation from other students, discrimination by various student groups, and lack of African-American faculty and administrators; and they judged their classes as lacking relevance to their own lives.

Out of this atmosphere emerged the black studies movement. On campuses nationwide, Black Student Unions (BSUs) were formed to advocate further social and curricular changes, especially the introduction of black studies programs. Of course, scholars at many of these institutions and at historically black colleges have taught some aspects of African-American history or studies, but no department committed to developing a broad curriculum based on the lives of African peoples had ever been established. Students took the initiative, first forming political and cultural organizations such as the Afro-American Students Association at Berkeley and Merritt College in Oakland, California, and the Black Student Congress at Columbia University in New York. As early as 1967 students at Howard University called for the creation of a concentrated program in the study of African Americans.

Black students at Cornell University in 1969 launched their own effort to force substantial curricular changes. Since 1967, scores of colleges and universities, both black- and white-dominated, had to address the demands of blacks. In fact, between 1960 and 1969, the scene of the sit-in shifted from the lunch counter to the university president's office. Protests visited campuses as varied as the University of Massachusetts, Duke, Harvard, Columbia, Yale, Simmons College, and Antioch.

At Cornell, a particularly dramatic episode transfixed the nation. Through the mid-sixties Cornell had had a dismal record of attracting and graduating African-American students. But beginning around mid-decade the school began in earnest to recruit blacks. Once there, however, the black students complained of overtly racist acts and general alienation. They also sought to institute a black studies department. After a series of incidents, including the tossing of a burning cross into a dormitory, tensions reached a critical phase, and black students took over part of the student union during Parents Week in April. Fearing more violence, especially given their small numbers (only 250 of the more than 10,000 students on campus were black), a few black students managed to smuggle guns into the union. After long negotiations, which ultimately led to Cornell's first black studies program, the students filed out peacefully and ended the standoff. When the incident ended without loss of life, the country recalled only the image of gun-toting black students. What many outside commentators failed to realize was that students wanted more than freedom by 1969; they wanted liberation, and they were willing to fight for their demands, educational or otherwise.

The link between liberation and education was not confined to the university. By 1968 the struggle for Black Power in education had reached down to public schools in many locales. More and more community activists began demanding control over local schools. Black parents and teachers objected to a curriculum that excluded Third World cultural perspectives. They objected, too, to the tracking of their children into remedial and special education classrooms, which they considered just another form of segregation; and they objected to the failure to funnel blacks and Latinos into college preparatory classes. More than anything, they objected to the fact that they had so little control over what their children learned.

For some blacks, the fight to transform education was merely a small part of a larger revolutionary movement. Organizations sprang up during this period that sought to transform the whole country, to eliminate all forms of inequality and racial discrimination. Perhaps the best-known of the radical black organizations was the Black Panther party (BPP). Although it is often identified as a proponent of Black Power, the BPP was essentially a Marxist organization. Embracing the ideology of the nineteenth-century German political philosopher Karl Marx, BPP members believed that the poor and oppressed peoples of the world would eventually mount a revolution to overthrow capitalism.

Calling itself the Black Panther Party for Self-Defense, it was founded in October 1966 in Oakland, California. The group was led by Huey P. Newton and Bobby Seale, former student activists at Merritt College in Oakland. At its founding, the party issued a ten-point program calling for, among other things, full employment, decent housing, relevant education, black exemption from military service, an end to police brutality, freedom for all black prisoners, and trials with juries of their peers. Seeing themselves as part of a global liberation movement, the Panthers also spoke of the black community as a colony inside the United States.

A 1968 Black Panther rally in New York. Carrying guns and wearing their trademark berets, the Panthers believed blacks should arm themselves against police brutality. Over the next few years, shootouts with police officers and FBI agents were frequent.

Yet, unlike many other black or interracial radical groups of their day, they never advocated secession or the creation of a separate state. Instead, they preferred interracial coalitions when possible. They joined forces with the predominantly white Peace and Freedom party (a third party of socialists and peace activists) and developed strong ties with Students for a Democratic Society (SDS).

In alliance with the Peace and Freedom party, the Black Panther party put up candidates in both the national and California state elections of 1968. The coalition's Presidential candidate was Eldridge Cleaver, an ex-prisoner who wrote the best-selling book *Soul on Ice* (1968). He had joined the party in February 1967. As a writer and speaker, Cleaver emerged as the main spokesperson for the Panthers after Bobby Seale was arrested for armed invasion of the State Assembly chamber in Sacramento and Newton was jailed for allegedly shooting an Oakland police officer. The charges against Newton were eventually dropped, but only after a long national campaign to free him.

The Black Panthers felt that armed struggle was the only way to defend the black community from police repression. By carrying loaded firearms in public (which was legal in California at the time), the Panthers drew a great deal of attention from the media and wrath from the police and FBI. Perhaps because of their notoriety, their ranks grew; by 1970 Panther chapters had taken root in nineteen states and in more than thirty cities, and eventually in England, Israel, and France.

A deft combination of style and substance accounted for the party's popularity. Early BPP members looked sharp in their all-black outfits of jeans, shirt, beret, and sunglasses. They affected a politics of style, making themselves look daring, mysterious, dangerous, and powerful. But style alone would fail, they quickly realized. As a result, the Panthers sponsored several community-based initiatives in most cities in the country, including clothing drives, a community day-care center, a Panther school, and a free breakfast program. Their free breakfast program provided meals to 200,000 children daily. Most amazingly, they proved that grass-roots movements could make a difference, even when the U.S. government vowed to eliminate the organization by any means necessary.

Federal law enforcement officers, especially the FBI, targeted a growing list of black-run organizations in the late sixties. Since the mid-sixties the agency had spied on Martin Luther King, Jr., Malcolm X, and other notable black leaders. By 1968 spying had come to include an active policy of group infiltration, in which FBI informants posed as members of radical or militant organizations. Local and federal police began a crackdown. In 1969, for example, police arrested 348 Panthers for a range of offenses, among them murder, rape, robbery, and assault.

The FBI and local police declared war on the Panthers. In 1968 alone, at least eight Black Panthers were killed by police in Los Angeles, Oakland, and Seattle. And the during the following year, two Chicago Panther leaders, Mark Clark and Fred Hampton, were killed in their sleep during an early morning police raid. The violence and constant surveillance by the FBI reflected the position of FBI director J. Edgar Hoover: the only good Panther was a dead Panther. Without question, the FBI helped destroy the Black Panther party.

Yet it was much more difficult to snuff out all who were swayed by the appeal of Black Power. In Detroit, for example, radical Black Power ideology influenced one of the most militant labor movements in the country. Eventually calling themselves the League of Revolutionary Black Workers (LRBW), the group was founded by several young black auto workers, many of whom worked at Detroit's Dodge Main Plant. Led by activists such as Luke Tripp, General Baker, John Watson, Mike Hamlin, and Ken Cockrel, they were a unique bunch. All had been students at Wayne State University and had worked together in a black nationalist organization called Uhuru (Swahili for "Freedom"). Uhuru had been loosely associated with RAM—the same organization from which several founding members of the Black Panther party came.

Two events spurred the creation of the league. The first was the Detroit riots of 1967, which revealed the degree of unrest, poverty, and police brutality in the "Motor City." The Detroit chapter of the NAACP was flooded with complaints about police treatment of African Americans. Even black police officers were subjected to brutality.

The second event was more immediate: on May 2,1968, General Baker and several other black militants in the Dodge Main Plant led a walkout of four thousand workers, the first in that factory in fourteen years and the first organized and led entirely by black workers. The strike was over a speedup of the assembly line, which in the previous week had increased from forty-nine to fifty-eight cars per hour. Out of this strike emerged the Dodge Revolutionary Union Movement (DRUM). It was the first of several Revolutionary Union Movements (RUMs) that popped up at auto plants in and around Detroit, and which subsequently led to the formation of the League of Revolutionary Black Workers.

DRUM's specific demands, safer workplaces, lower production demands, an end to racist hiring practices, echoed past grievances. Of course they wanted to win better working conditions and wages for black workers, but their ultimate goal was freedom for all workers, and that meant, in their view, the end of capitalism. DRUM members knew that racism limited the ability of workers to unite, and that white workers, as well as black workers, were hurt by this. But they also argued that white workers benefited from racism in the form of higher wages, cleaner and safer jobs, and greater union representation.

Not everyone in the league agreed as to the best way to achieve Black Power and workers' power. One group, led by General Baker, believed the movement should focus on shop-floor struggles, while Watson, Hamlin, and Cockrel felt that the league needed to organize black communities beyond the factories. Thus, the latter got together and organized the Black Economic Development Conference (BEDC) in the spring of 1969. At the urging of former SNCC leader James Forman, who had recently arrived in Detroit, the league became heavily involved in the planning and running of the conference.

Out of BEDC came Forman's proposal for a Black Manifesto, which demanded, among other things, $500,000,000 in reparations from white churches and synagogues to be used to purchase land in the South, fund black publishing companies, a research skills center, a black Southern university, and a national black labor strike fund. The work in BEDC took the league leadership, of which Forman was now a part, away from its local emphasis. Their efforts led to the founding of the Black Workers Congress (BWC) in 1970. The BWC called for workers' control over the economy and the state to be brought about through cooperatives, neighborhood centers, student organizations, and ultimately a revolutionary party. And they demanded better wages and working conditions for all workers.

Meanwhile, the league's local base began to disintegrate. Dodge had fired several league activists, including General Baker. The General Policy Statement of the league, which based everything on the need for vibrant DRUM-type organizations, seemed to have fallen by the wayside. Divisions between the leadership groups were so entrenched that no one could cooperate any more.

Influenced by events on the factory floor and in the universities, writers laid claim to their own interpretations of Black Power. Starting with John Oliver Killen's 1954 novel *Youngblood,* and increasing in frequency by the mid-sixties, black writers debated whether there was something distinctive about black culture, something that made it different from "white" or European-American culture. The debate had less to do with whether black writers would write about black life—

they had been doing so since the days of the first slave narratives in the United States—and more to do with a universal definition of a black aesthetic. In the midst of the debates and disagreements that ensued, some sense of a general consensus did emerge. Black was not only powerful, it was beautiful. And it was up to black people to express and celebrate both the power and the beauty.

Thus, the political revolution in black America was accompanied by a profound cultural revolution. A new generation of artists created literature, art, and music that celebrated black people and promoted rebellion against racism and poverty throughout the world. They encouraged African Americans to celebrate their African heritage and to embrace their blackness not as a mark of shame but as a symbol of beauty.

To understand this revolution, however, we need to go back to the fifties, when Africans declared war on European colonialism and began to win their independence. Inspired by Africa's example, jazz pianist Randy Weston recorded the album *Uhuru Afrika* (1960); drummer Max Roach brought together African and African-American musicians to produce *We Insist: Freedom Now Suite* (1960); and the brilliant saxophonist John Coltrane recorded songs such as "Dahomey Dance" (1961), "Africa" (1961), and "Liberia" (1964). African Americans even began to emulate African styles or create new styles that, in their mind, represented African culture. During the early sixties a number of black women artists, most notably the folk singer Odetta, the jazz vocalist Abby Lincoln, and the exiled South African singer Miriam Makeba, styled their hair in medium to short Afros. They refused to straighten their hair and instead allowed it to grow naturally.

All of these independent cultural developments emerging out of the late fifties and early sixties began to coalesce into a full-blown movement just when America's cities began to explode. In 1965, following the assassination of Malcolm X, the poet and playwright Leroi Jones and several other black writers, namely Larry Neal, Clarence Reed, and Askia Muhammad Toure, founded the Black Arts Repertory Theater School (BART) in an old brownstone building on 130th Street in Harlem. With meager support from federal War on Poverty programs, they held classes for Harlem residents and launched a summer arts and culture program that brought music, drama, and the visual arts to the community virtually every day of the week.

Like many artists of his generation, Leroi Jones could not ignore the black freedom movement in his midst. Before founding BART, he was the senior member of the downtown New York literary scene. Born to a working-class family in Newark, New Jersey, Jones attended Howard University (a historically black college), served briefly in the air force, and ended up a struggling writer in New York's Greenwich Village. After the success of his first book of poetry, *Preface to a Twenty Volume Suicide Note* (1961), his first book of prose, *Blues People: Negro Music in White America* (1963), and his first play, *Dutchman* (1964), he no longer had to struggle. Indeed *Dutchman*, a surreal encounter between an educated black man and a white woman who, as a symbolic representative of the racist state, taunts the man and eventually kills him, earned him many awards and accolades. After *Dutchman,* Jones could have pursued a lucrative career as a writer but chose instead to use his artistic insights to build a political movement.

In 1966, a year after founding BART, Jones moved back to his hometown of Newark, started a similar institution called Spirit House, and changed his name to Imamu Amiri Baraka. Although Spirit House also sponsored community arts programs, it developed a more explicit political orientation after Newark's ghettos exploded in 1967. In the aftermath of the riots, Spirit House held a Black Power conference that attracted several national black leaders, including Stokely Carmichael, H. Rap Brown, Huey P. Newton of the Black Panther party, and Imari Obadele of the newly formed Republic of New Africa (a black nationalist organization that demanded land on which African Americans could settle and form an independent nation, and was partly an outgrowth of RAM). Shortly thereafter, Spirit House became the base for the Committee for a Unified Newark (CFUN). In addition to attracting black nationalists, Black Muslims, and even a few Marxists, CFUN bore the mark of Ron Karenga's US Organization.

Karenga, originally a West Coast leader of RAM, insisted that the crisis facing black America was first and foremost a cultural crisis. He envisioned "US" as a movement of cultural reconstruction, creating a new synthesis between traditional African culture and African-American culture. Drawing on African religions, philosophies, and ideas about family and kin relations, US attempted to create a political movement rooted in communal ties between people of African descent rather than competition or individualism. Although tensions arose between Karenga and some of the Newark activists over his treatment of women and the overly centralized leadership structure CFUN had imported from the US Organization, the movement continued to grow.

In this setting, the search for artistic expression became known as the Black Arts Movement. In addition to Baraka, other leading lights included poets Nikki Giovanni, Don L. Lee (Haki Madhubuti), Jayne Cortez, and Sonia Sanchez; playwrights Ed Bullins, Ben Caldwell, and Jimmy Garrett, to name a few. Although openly critical of whites and brutally critical of blacks who seemed to go along with a system of white supremacy, the members of the Black Arts Movement were important for the innovations they introduced in literary form. Determined to bring poetry and prose to the people, they experimented with freer forms and drew heavily on jazz rhythms and the everyday vernacular language of black folk. They often turned the hip, cool phrases of black youth into hot, angry declarations of war against American racism and exploitation.

While literary artists made an appeal for the hearts and souls of the black majority, it was musicians who achieved mass appeal in the late sixties, a time of intense experimentation and political expression. Some of them, such as James

Brown (known as the "godfather of soul") and poet/singer Gil Scott-Heron, adopted a Black Power stance more clearly than others. Within jazz circles, artists such as saxo phonists Ornette Coleman, John Coltrane, Albert Ayler, and Archie Shepp, pianists Cecil Taylor and Sun Ra, and many others, lauded a new sound, variously known as "free jazz," "the new thing," the "jazz avant-garde," or the "new black music." Detractors, on the other hand, called the music "anti-jazz" or "nihilism." Essentially, the new jazz musicians began playing free form, breaking out of traditional harmonies, rhythms, and song structures. Inspired by music from Africa and Asia, they often improvised freely over a single musical phrase. Furthermore, many of these musicians identified with the black arts movement; Ayler, Shepp, Sun Ra, and others performed frequently at BART, and the jazz avant-garde even had its own publications calling for the creation of revolutionary music. The key journal at the time was called the *Gracle: Improvised Music in Transition*. In the *Gracle,* black musicians debated the music's relationship to the movement, thought about ways to fuse music and literature, and discussed the importance of political education for black artists.

Although the jazz avant-garde sought to establish direct ties to black communities, its music never achieved the popularity of "soul" music. The creators of soul consciously searched for black roots; their products reflected gospel's major influence. Aretha Franklin's early music, for example, was characterized by gospel-style piano playing.

A product of mid- to late sixties transformations, soul was also much more political than rock and roll. Its themes have to do with more than equality; they deal with conditions in the urban North such as poverty, the powerlessness of black folk, and drug use. The titles tell the story: James Carr's "Freedom Train," the Chi-Lites' "Give More Power to the People," and Tony Clarke's "Ghetto Man."

Still, there was no single ideology of Black Power in soul music. Singers Curtis Mayfield and James Brown simultaneously promoted reform of the system and acceptance into it. While recording songs promoting black pride like "Say it Loud, I'm Black and I'm Proud," and "Soul Brother No. 1," Brown also came out with the patriotic assimilationist tune "America is My Home." After King was assassinated and riots began erupting, Brown went on national television to urge blacks to go back home. He even came out in support of the conservative and sometimes openly racist President Richard Nixon, mainly because of Nixon's advocacy of black capitalism as a way of achieving racial equality.

The Temptations and Marvin Gaye were also politically conscious, but unlike Mayfield, whose songs were of hope and possibility, theirs were songs of pessimism: Gaye's "Inner City Blues," "What's Goin' On?" and the Temptations' "Message from a Black Man," "Cloud Nine," and "Ball of Confusion." In the last, before the chorus, "Ball of Confusion, that's what the world is today," we hear a baritone voice singing "And the band plays on," signaling business-as-usual politics, indifference, and apathy. The "band" is symbolically drowning out the noise of poverty and resistance. The irony of this world as described by the Temptations is captured in the line "The only safe place to live is on an Indian reservation."

As millions of black Americans tuned in to the sounds of soul and jazz, they also tuned in to the dramatic television broadcast from the 1968 Mexico City Olympics. What happened there represented the most international expression of Black Power. To call attention to racism in sports here and abroad, former San Jose State basketball and track and field star Harry Edwards formed the Olympic Project for Human Rights. Its intent was to organize an international boycott of the 1968 games.

Edwards hoped to draw attention both to the treatment of black athletes as well as to the general condition of black people throughout the world. As he put it, "What value is it to a black man to win a medal if he returns to the hell of Harlem?" Specifically, he and others sought to ban athletes from South Africa and Southern Rhodesia (both at the time were white-dominated African countries that segregated and exploited the African population) from the Olympics, the appointment of a black member to the U.S. Olympic Committee, appointment of an additional black coach on the U.S. team, the desegregation of the New York Athletic Club, and the removal of the International Olympic Committee's president, Avery Brundage. Among other things, Brundage was quoted as saying he would sell his exclusive Santa Barbara, California, country club membership before admitting "niggers and kikes" as members.

Instead of boycotting the Olympics, however, black athletes decided to use the event as a way to draw attention to racism and the black struggle. They agreed to wear black armbands and developed strategies to protest during the victory ceremonies. The most famous demonstration involved track stars Tommie Smith and John Carlos, who mounted the awards platform wearing knee-length black socks, no shoes, and a black glove on one hand (Smith also wore a black scarf around his neck). When the band played the U.S. national anthem, they bowed their heads and raised their gloved fists toward the sky in the Black Power salute. In an interview with sportscaster Howard Cosell, the pair explained that the closed-fisted salute symbolized black power and unity; the socks with no shoes represented the poverty most black people must endure; and Smith's scarf symbolized black pride. They bowed their heads in memory of fallen warriors in the black liberation movement, notably Malcolm X and Martin Luther King, Jr.

Although their actions did not harm anyone or incite violence, the U.S. Olympic Committee decided to suspend Smith and Carlos from the games and strip them of their medals for being overtly political. Angered by the decision, many of their fellow black athletes continued to protest. The three U.S. medalists who swept the four-hundred-meter dash wore black berets on the victory stand, as did the 1600-meter relay team (which also broke the world record). Bob Beamon and Ralph

Boston, medal winners in the long jump, wore black socks without shoes to protest both the condition of black people and the treatment of their teammates. And Wyomia Tyus, anchor in the women's four-hundred-meter relay team, dedicated her gold medal to Carlos and Smith.

The political stance of black athletes in Mexico City combined with other examples of forceful advocacy of Black Power to provoke fear and a backlash. By 1969, after passage of the Civil Rights Act of 1964, the Voting Rights Act of 1965, and the Fair Housing Act of 1968, many white Americans began to ask: What more does the Negro want? Dissatisfied with the responses they heard to that question, more and more whites found their own answers in the politics of rage endorsed first by George Wallace and then by Richard Nixon.

George Wallace had surfaced as a national political force in the early sixties, after he made a highly publicized effort to block the desegregation of the University of Alabama. He had been active in Alabama politics since before the start of World War II. Steeped in the traditions of Alabama and the South, he held views on race that were neither enlightened nor particularly regressive. Each race had its own genius and place in the life of country, he asserted at the time. To him this was less a disputable fact than merely an obvious truth.

He held fast to that view through the Alabama gubernatorial campaign of his mentor "Big Jim" Folsom in the mid-fifties. With the *Brown* v. *Board of Education* decision fresh in people's minds, with Montgomery roiling from the effects of the bus boycott and news of similar boycotts forming across the region, Wallace staked out a new political image. It was an image that distanced him from his mentor, ensured his own selection as governor of Alabama in 1962, and forever solidified his reputation as the embodiment of Southern obstruction of black rights.

But it was Wallace the Presidential candidate rather than Wallace the governor who attracted more attention. George Wallace's ascendancy as a legitimate third-party candidate in 1968 signaled a clear backlash. He openly courted whites who felt disenfranchised by governmental policy. For his efforts he won five Southern states in 1968 and between eight and fifteen percent of the vote in more than a dozen Northern and Western states. Before an assassin's bullet nearly killed him in 1972, Wallace had received nearly as many popular votes in the Democratic Presidential primaries as George McGovern, the Democratic party's eventual candidate. Wallace's most important influence, however, may have been inspiring the Republican party to adopt a strategy that catered to white fears of social equality for blacks.

Richard Nixon quickly moved into the political space Wallace had created. Aided by the conservative push in his own party, the electoral appeal of law and order themes in 1968, and his own realization that Republicans could use race as an issue to drive Southern whites into their party, he outlined a plan for what became the Republican party's Southern strategy. Heading into the spring of 1968, polls showed Nixon tying either Robert F. Kennedy or Hubert H. Humphrey, the two leading contenders for the Democratic nomination. Kennedy's assassination left Humphrey, the old liberal now too closely aligned with Lyndon Johnson's failed social and military policies. Nixon won the election in part due to his ability to channel a racial backlash. This backlash came just as black Americans intensified their demands for social, economic, and political action.

Despite backlash politics and the rising tide of racism, this was also the moment Black Power in some ways entered the realm of electoral politics. Nearly a generation after a new wave of black migrants moved into urban areas, during what became known as the Second Great Migration, their numbers had grown sufficiently—and whites had fled city centers in large enough numbers—to give blacks electoral majorities, or at the very least working margins. This change in the racial makeup of cities improved the likelihood that African Americans could gain a stronger political foothold in major urban centers. In some cases, they were successful. The mayoral victories of Carl Stokes in Cleveland and Richard Hatcher in Gary, Indiana, in 1967 raised black hopes that electoral politics might offer real opportunities, at least at the municipal level. However, despite a growing black electorate in the nation's cities, African Americans held few really important political offices.

During the early seventies, for example, black elected officials tended to hold low-level city and county jobs, especially in law enforcement, on school boards, and on some city councils. Most of these black elected officials were in the South. The lack of more significant black political representation in big Northern cities where African Americans made up forty to fifty percent of the population was particularly striking. To pave the way for participation at higher levels of city government, black political leaders worked hard on devising strategies to win local elections.

When the clock ticked off the last minute of 1969 and African Americans took stock of the last few years, they thought not only about the changes they had witnessed but also about the ones they still hoped to see. They knew they were the caretakers of King's dream of living in a nation where character was more important than color. And they knew they had to take charge of their community. After all, the civil rights and Black Power eras had forged change through community action. Although many blacks may have sensed that all progress was tempered by the social, economic, and political realities of a government and a white public often resistant to change, they could not ignore the power of their own past actions. America in 1969 was not the America of 1960 or 1965. At the end of the decade, a chorus could be heard rising from the black community proclaiming, "We changed the world."

CHAPTER 10

Into the Fire

1970 to the Present

Robin D. G. Kelley

A nyone strolling through the black ghettos of Chicago, Newark, or Los Angeles in 1973 probably noticed posters advertising Oscar Williams's new film, *Five on the Black Hand Side,* pasted along the sides of temporary plywood walls or on abandoned buildings. You could tell by the poster's cartoon illustrations that this was a comedy. In the center is a conservatively dressed black businessman surrounded by dozens of crazy-looking people: some are protesting, some are fighting, some are simply enjoying each other's company. Even though the characters in the poster are decked out in bell bottoms, platform shoes, and serious Afro puffs, this film is not another action-packed ghetto drama about pimps, hipsters, and black crime-fighters, like the ever-popular *Superfly* or *Shaft.* Instead it is a comedy about the trials and tribulations of the black middle class. Challenging the more common films about hustlers and ghetto violence, the text of the poster summons us all to the theater: "You've been coffy-tized, blacula-rized and super-flied—but now you're gonna be glorified, unified and filled-with-pride . . . when you see *Five On the Black Hand Side.*"

The poster, like the film itself, marked a transition taking place in black political attitudes. During the early to mid-seventies, there was a little less talk of revolution and more emphasis on winning local elections. The push for black pride and black unity we often associate with the "sixties generation" did not die, however. On the contrary, the ideas of the Black Power movement reached its apex in the seventies. Black was in. Afros and African garments were not only in style but had become even more popular among ordinary African Americans. The slogan "Black is Beautiful" lingered well after the decline of Black Power. Militant black nationalist organizations, such as the Black Panther party, the Republic of New Afrika, and the Black Liberation Front, continued to gain local support in urban neighborhoods for their advocacy of armed self-defense, black control over political and economic institutions, and efforts to build black pride and self-esteem. Yet, with legal segregation finally gone, thanks to the civil rights movement, upwardly

One of the goals of Oscar Williams's *Five on the Black Hand Side* was to explore the trials and tribulations of the black middle-class—a subject most black action films, such as *Shaft* and *Superfly*, avoided.

mobile black families headed for the suburbs, and many working-class parents believed their children would enjoy a better life than they had.

The vast majority of African Americans who could not afford the luxury of suburban life were left behind in America's overcrowded ghettoes. But if leaving was not an option, fighting back certainly was. The first year of the new decade, 1970, was marked by violence, militant campaigns, racial tensions, and new movements demanding social justice. Urban rebellions and police-community violence continued to be a source of tension in several cities, including Philadelphia; New Orleans; New Bedford, Massachusetts; and Hartford, Connecticut. The issue of school desegregation was hardly settled, particularly after court-ordered busing was proposed as a solution to integrate public schools. Throughout the country, white opponents of school integration frequently turned to violence to defend all-white schools. In September 1970, the Black Panther party and activists from the women's and gay liberation movements organized the Revolutionary People's Constitutional Convention, which attracted some six thousand people to the city of Philadelphia with the goal of rewriting the U.S. Constitution.

In spite of these events, few black activists and perhaps fewer inner-city residents believed change was inevitable or that the government was on their side. The person African Americans overwhelmingly voted *against* in the 1968 Presidential election, the conservative Republican Richard M. Nixon, was now in the White House. Nixon attacked welfare mothers, blamed the black poor for their own poverty, and tried to link the social movements of the sixties to criminals and drug addicts. Nixon's conservative agenda was a far cry from the civil rights movement's vision of a country without poverty or race hatred, a view noticed and articulated by the man whom Nixon replaced in the White House, Lyndon Baines Johnson.

Yet Nixon was surprised when he failed to attract black votes during his reelection campaign in 1972. After all, he had appointed a handful of African Americans to mid-level federal posts, and he even called himself a supporter of Black Power when he proposed reducing welfare in favor of grants and tax cuts for black-owned businesses. Despite these measures, very few African Americans trusted Nixon. His cabinet was openly less concerned about racism than the Johnson administration had been. Indeed his domestic advisor, Daniel P. Moynihan, passed on a confidential memo proposing "the time may have come when the issue of race could benefit from a period of 'benign neglect.'" Moynihan felt that enough progress had been made and there was no need to actively combat racial inequities. More important, Nixon and his advisers understood that the Republicans' success came in part because of their attacks on radical social movements, such as the Black Panthers, and on liberal policies, such as Johnson's War on Poverty.

A large segment of the white middle class believed that African Americans, especially the poor, received too many government handouts, and they were tired of "paying the bill." They believed that African Americans had nothing to complain about because, in their view at least, racism no longer existed. They were tired of the Vietnam War and felt besieged by the constant protests by hippies, ghetto residents, feminists, and welfare rights activists. Fearing that ghetto rebellions would spill into their suburbs and that too much of their taxes was going to support welfare, the overwhelming white vote for Nixon partly reflected an anti-black backlash.

One of Nixon's campaign promises was to get rid of "troublemakers," especially militant black nationalist organizations like the Republic of New Afrika, the National Committee to Combat Fascism, the Black Liberation Front, and the Black Panther party—whom FBI director J. Edgar Hoover once called "the greatest threat to the internal security of this country." During the Nixon years, the FBI and local police forces intensified their efforts to squelch dissent of any kind. And it did not matter if their tactics were legal or not. In Chicago, for example, local police not only raided the headquarters and homes of black activists frequently but they also kept files on prominent outspoken African Americans, including future Presidential candidate the Reverend Jesse Jackson. At the time, Jackson led Operation PUSH (People United to Save Humanity), a fairly mainstream grass-roots organization that sought to help African Americans get off welfare, find jobs, and motivate poor children to stay in school.

Jailings, beatings, and constant surveillance conducted by local police and the FBI were part and parcel of what most political movements during this era had to contend with.

One very important case centered around the Reverend Benjamin Chavis, a young black minister of the United Church of Christ who would eventually serve a brief stint as executive director of the National Association for the Advancement of Colored People. It all began when Chavis tried to organize a nonviolent campaign in Wilmington, North Carolina, to improve education for African-American children. The campaign was still in its early stages when, in February 1971, a white-owned store was burned in the midst of the campaign. Chavis, along with eight black student leaders and one white woman activist, was charged and convicted of arson and conspiracy. Altogether, their combined sentences totaled 282 years; the twenty-four-year-old Chavis received thirty-four of those years. Human rights activists from around the world questioned the convictions from the very beginning. Not only was there no solid evidence against them, but it was revealed that at least one jurist was a member of the Ku Klux Klan. Even Amnesty International, a worldwide organization dedicated to monitoring human rights abuses, called Benjamin Chavis and his fellow inmates "political prisoners." They quickly became known as the Wilmington Ten.

Despite many appeals, the Wilmington Ten remained in prison throughout most of the decade. Then, in 1977, one of the key witnesses for the state admitted that he had been pressured into lying on the stand. Another witness said he was given a job at a local service station and a minibike in exchange for testimony that would lead to a conviction. Yet, in spite of these new developments in the case, the judge would not reverse the decision. He insisted that the defendants' constitutional rights had not been violated. Yet because of increasingly negative publicity surrounding the case, the governor of North Carolina persuaded prison administrators to parole Chavis in 1979. A year later, the U.S. Court of Appeals overturned the original decision, ruling that the Wilmington Ten had been denied a fair trial.

Many African Americans and movement sympathizers believed that federal, state, and local governments arrested activists on false charges in order to stop them from protesting and organizing. While this may seem to contradict American ideals of freedom, the release of secret files of the FBI's Counter Intelligence Program (COINTELPRO) and the voluminous files local police departments kept on suspected dissidents revealed that some activists were indeed jailed and harassed because of their politics. The FBI devoted much of its energies to collecting information on "radical" organizations. Under COINTELPRO, FBI agents also used fake press releases to spread false rumors about social activists; hired undercover agents to commit crimes in the name of the more militant Black Power movements; violently attacked competing organizations; and created an atmosphere of tension, confusion, and division within the organizations under surveillance. COINTEL-PRO was finally disbanded in 1972 after the death of J. Edgar Hoover. A congressional investigation of the program not only revealed that Hoover had kept tabs on many prominent African Americans—including political leaders Martin Luther King, Jr., Roy Wilkins, and Whitney Young; athletes Muhammad Ali, Joe Louis, Jesse Owens, and Jackie Robinson; and cultural figures such as Lena Horne, Paul Robeson, and James Baldwin—but that President Nixon himself used the FBI to attack his enemies and wage war against alleged dissidents.

Clearly the most celebrated "political prisoner" of the early seventies was Angela Davis. "Free Angela" posters, buttons, and T-shirts became as much a part of the changing urban landscape as liquor stores and "soul food" restaurants. Tall, lean, with a raised fist and an Afro, a flashing smile, and an aura of confidence, Angela Davis offered the African-American community a striking image to rally around. To her many supporters—young and old, male and female—she was a young, beautiful, militant intellectual boldly challenging "the system."

Born and raised in Birmingham, Alabama, Angela Davis was the daughter of schoolteacher and early civil rights activist Sallye Davis. The oldest of three children, Angela Davis lived a fairly comfortable life in some respects, but segregation and racial tensions also made for a very dangerous environment. Two of her friends were killed in a church bombing in September 1963. The bombing was orchestrated by white supremacists retaliating for the civil rights demonstrations in Birmingham. And as a very young child, she lived in a neighborhood where black-owned homes were firebombed so frequently that it was nicknamed "dynamite hill." The bombings were the work of white residents attempting to keep black families out of that section of Birmingham.

Anxious to leave Birmingham (or "Bombingham" as black residents began calling it), Davis moved to New York City when she was fifteen to attend Elisabeth Irwin High School, a renowned experimental private school in Greenwich Village. She went on to Brandeis University, the Sorbonne in Paris, and Goethe University in Frankfurt; in 1967 she moved to California to work toward a Ph.D. in philosophy. Always concerned about the plight of African Americans, she soon became active in the Student Nonviolent Coordinating Committee.

As a SNCC activist, Davis saw both the possibilities and limitations of the organization. She not only encountered sexist attitudes on the part of several male leaders, but she realized that SNCC and other Black Power organizations did not have an adequate explanation for why people remained poor. Insisting that the "free market" exploits workers by paying them poorly and making them dependent on the marketplace and wages to survive, she regarded the capitalist economy as the source of many social ills. Many of her ideas were based on the writings of Karl Marx and Frederick Engels, two nineteenth-century German radical thinkers whom Davis was introduced to in high school. Reading Marx and Engels'

Communist Manifesto (1848) as a teenager changed her life. "Like an expert sur-geon," she wrote in her autobiography,

> this document cut away cataracts from my eyes. . . . What had seemed a per-sonal hatred of me, an inexplicable refusal of Southern whites to confront their own emotions, and a stubborn willingness of Blacks to acquiesce, became the inevitable consequence of a ruthless system which kept itself alive and well by encouraging spite, competition and the oppression of one group by another. Profit was the word: the cold and constant motive for the behavior, the contempt and the despair I had seen.

Although there are different varieties of Marxism, adherents generally argue that all wealth is created by labor. Capitalists, or the owners of businesses, are able to exploit labor by denying workers access to other sources of income through the private ownership of land and factories. Thus workers have no choice but to work for wages to survive, a condition which breeds conflict and resentment between those who own wealth and those who do not. Marxists believe that this conflict between workers and owners is a fundamental aspect of capitalist society. To resolve it, they advocate replacing capitalism with "socialism"—a system whereby working people, in theory, share the fruits of their labor. The land and factories would not be owned by private individuals but by the people who work them. The goal of labor would not be to enrich the few but to improve the quality of life for all. Quality education and health care would not be things one would pay for indi-vidually but would be paid for by and available to all members of society. Of course, there have been attempts to create such a system in places like China and the former Soviet Union, but in these countries it never worked in practice the way it was imagined to work in theory. Nevertheless, in the minds of many Marxists and liberals who sympathized with the Marxist point of view, the failure of social-ism in other countries did not diminish the fact that capitalism made some peo-ple's lives miserable while making a handful of people very wealthy.

As a Marxist, Davis was convinced that the building of a new socialist society would go a long way toward creating the kind of equality many labor, student, and civil rights activists dreamed of. Thus in 1969 she made the fateful decision to join the Communist Party of the United States (CPUSA), longtime advocates of social-ism whose origins go back to 1919. That same year the University of California at Los Angeles hired her to teach philosophy. However, once her party membership became public knowledge, the California Board of Regents and Governor Ronald Reagan fired her, citing a state law that banned communists from teaching at state universities.

Davis and the many who rallied to her defense were undoubtedly upset over her dismissal. She challenged the decision in court, arguing on the basis of the First Amendment that she had the right to freedom of expression. The jury and judge agreed; the law was overturned and the regents were forced to reinstate her. Nevertheless, they eventually succeeded in forcing her out of the University of California system by censuring Davis for her political activism and closely monitoring her classes. Losing her job did not keep her from organizing. She became actively involved with the Black Panther party and worked with radical black prisoners—most notably George Jackson.

George Jackson had been an inmate at Soledad prison in California for nearly a decade when he first came into contact with Davis. After spending the first fourteen years of his life in a Chicago ghetto, in 1957 he moved with his family to South Central Los Angeles, where he fell in with neighborhood gangs. He was constantly in trouble with the law; he was arrested several times as a juvenile for theft, burglary, and robbery. At age fifteen he was sentenced to eight months at a California Youth Authority camp—a state-run juvenile detention center. He escaped twice from the camp, once fleeing to Illinois, where he was involved in a knifing and subsequently returned to California in chains. Paroled after sixteen months, Jackson continued to pursue a life of crime. In February 1961 he was arrested for being an accessory to armed robbery of a gas station in Bakersfield, California. Because no one was hurt and only seventy dollars was taken, the public defender persuaded Jackson to plead guilty in exchange for a light sentence. To his surprise, the judge sentenced him to "one year to life." He was nineteen years old.

Jackson was initially sentenced to San Quentin, where he gained a reputation as one of the meanest, toughest inmates in the prison yard. He participated in prison gangs, received disciplinary action at least forty-seven times for assaulting guards, and was feared by most of his fellow inmates. But by the fifth or sixth year of his sentence, Jackson began to undergo a dramatic change. He began reading books he had never read in school, and he eventually linked up with the Black Panther party. In his quest to understand why so many of his fellow inmates were black men, why so many were driven to steal, Jackson studied the writings of revolutionary leaders from across the globe and read broadly in the fields of history, sociology, and politics. He came to the conclusion that racism, the economy, and the government's covert efforts to put a lid on black rebellion were the main reasons for the rise in African-American prisoners. In one sense, he argued, virtually all of the inmates were "political prisoners":

> There are still some blacks here who consider themselves criminals—but not many. Believe me, my friend, with the time and incentive that these brothers have to read, study, and think, you will find no class or category more aware, more embittered, desperate, or dedicated to the ultimate remedy—revolution. . . . They live like there was no tomorrow.

By the late sixties, Jackson emerged as one of Soledad's most outspoken radicals. He introduced fellow prisoners to a variety of radical ideas, including Marxism and black nationalism. Influenced by the various protest movements erupting outside prison walls, Jackson and a few of his fellow convicts set out to "transform the black criminal mentality into a black revolutionary mentality." Quickly, prison authorities identified him as a serious threat when he attempted to organize the inmates to fight for better conditions.

In 1969, the activities and plight of George Jackson became nationally known after he and two fellow inmates, Fleeta Drumgo and John Clutchette, were accused of murdering a prison guard. Since the state had very little evidence against the three men, most of their supporters believed they were being framed for political reasons. Jackson, Drumgo, and Clutchette were well known in Soledad for their political activism. Once the case went public, they became known as the Soledad Brothers. Throughout the country, student activists, black militants, and people concerned about prisoners' rights organized demonstrations demanding the release of the Soledad Brothers. Donations for their legal defense came from all over the country. Leading publications, including the *New York Times Magazine,* carried articles about Jackson and the others. Within a few months, they were celebrities. Their most vocal defenders included actress Jane Fonda, child psychiatrist Benjamin Spock, and poet Allen Ginsberg.

The Soledad Brothers' most dedicated advocate turned out to be George Jackson's younger brother Jonathan, also a close acquaintance of Angela Davis's. On August 7, 1970, the younger Jackson, barely seventeen years old, somehow smuggled several guns into the Marin County (California) Courthouse during the trial of James McClain, another black Soledad prisoner accused of stabbing a guard. After watching the proceedings from the audience for a while, Jonathan Jackson rose to his feet, drew a sawed-off shotgun from under his coat and announced, "All right, gentlemen. I'm taking over now." He then passed the other guns he had concealed to McClain and Ruchell Magee, a Soledad inmate who had been brought to trial as a witness to the stabbing. They took the judge, the deputy district attorney, and three jurors hostage in a van parked outside. As they left the courthouse, according to one witness, McClain shouted, "Free or Release the Soledad Brothers by twelve thirty or they all die!" The police and San Quentin guards in the area responded promptly. Remaining true to their "no hostage" policy, the guards opened fire on the van as it pulled off. When the smoke cleared Jonathan, along with two prisoners and the judge, lay dead. (Soon after the Soledad Brothers were acquitted of murder, prison guards killed George Jackson during an alleged escape attempt. The guards claimed Jackson had hidden a gun in his Afro.)

Young Jonathan Jackson's actions directly affected Angela Davis. The guns he used were hers—firearms he had taken without permission. Because Davis owned the guns and because she was a noted radical activist in California, the FBI issued a warrant for her arrest and placed her on its "Ten Most Wanted" list. Following her capture, an international campaign demanding her release was born. Even the celebrated soul singer Aretha Franklin offered to pay her bail: "I'm going to set Angela free . . . not because I believe in communism but because she's a Black woman who wants freedom for all Black people." After spending eighteen months in jail, she was finally released in February 1972 on $102,000 bail. She was eventually acquitted of all charges.

The decade of the seventies, therefore, was hardly the end of a militant era. The violent repression and jailings of black radicals no doubt transformed the movements they led, sometimes making leaders ineffective, other times turning them into martyrs. New debates and new circumstances compelled African-American activists to think about politics in new ways. African-American women activists began to chart their own course, creating a dynamic black feminist movement that challenged male-dominated black nationalism and white-dominated women's rights organizations. Moreover, black elected officials joined community activists and artists to develop a new approach to the ballot.

"It's Nation Time!": From Black Feminism to Black Caucus

Black community activist Margaret Wright was tired of being told by male leaders in the Black Power movement that black women oppressed black men, that black women were domineering, that successful black women stripped black men of their manhood. "Black women aren't oppressing them," she announced in a 1970 interview. "We're helping them get their liberation. It's the white man who's oppressing, not us. All we ever did was scrub floors so they could get their little selves together!" The very idea that black women kept black men down made her even more angry when she thought about the role most black women had to play in the civil rights and black liberation movements. "We run errands, lick stamps, mail letters, and do the door-to-door. But when it comes to the speaker's platform, it's all men up there blowing their souls, you dig."

Margaret Wright knew the truth. Black women, in general, were not only more exploited and oppressed than black men but they were often oppressed *by* black men. As an activist in the Los Angeles–based group Women Against Repression, she confronted issues ranging from wife battering to inequities in household chores. Most black women not only worked for wages but were responsible for child care, cooking, and cleaning. And when it came to participating in political movements, black women were often shunted aside or told that the struggle for liberation is "a man's job." While she acknowledged that black men and white women were also oppressed, she wanted both groups to understand how they unintentionally contributed to the exploitation of black women:

> Black women have been doubly oppressed. On the job, we're low women on the totem pole. White women have their problems. They're interviewed for secretarial instead of the executive thing. But we're interviewed for mopping floors and stuff like that. Sometimes we have to take what's left over in Miss

Ann's refrigerator. This is all exploitation. And when we get home from work, the old man is wondering why his greens aren't cooked on time.

Margaret Wright voiced the opinions of a growing number of African-American women, some of whom joined forces with the feminist movement that had reemerged in the sixties. While there was no single definition of feminism, most feminists agreed that male domination—in the family and the government—pushed women into an inferior status in society. They argued that women were paid less for the same job, underrepresented in positions of power and authority, and expected to take responsibility for housework and other domestic duties, not because they were less able than men, but because they were discriminated against.

Even the culture women lived in contributed to their subordination. Women were portrayed as passive and weak or as sex objects for male pleasure. Feminists did not merely want to take men's places in positions of power, to substitute male dominance with female dominance; they fought to replace male domination with a more just, equitable society.

Ironically, this new wave of black feminism was partly a response to male chauvinism within the civil rights, Black Power, and student movements of the period. Many cultural nationalists—activists who believed that black people in the United States should adopt traditional African cultures—emphasized that women ought to remain in "their place." One pamphlet distributed by a nationalist organization in Newark laid out, in no uncertain terms, what men and women's roles should be: "It is only reasonable that the man be the head of the house because he is able to defend and protect the development of his home. . . . Women cannot do the same things as men—they are made by nature to function differently. Equality of men and women is something that cannot happen even in the abstract world." Of course, not all male advocates of black nationalism were hopelessly sexist; on the contrary, some opposed statements such as these. Moreover, not all black women active in nationalist movements agreed with this sort of logic. Women frequently challenged such remarks. Nevertheless, the overall tenor of the Black Power movement emphasized the struggle for power, equality, and rights as a struggle for "manhood."

Concerned about the rising tide of black male sexism and chauvinism, many African-American women active in political and social movements spoke out. Toni Cade Bambara, a writer and activist who edited an important anthology in 1970 titled *The Black Woman*, wrote: "We rap about being correct but ignore the danger of having one of our population regard the other with such condescension and perhaps fear that that half finds it necessary to 'reclaim his manhood' by denying her her peoplehood." Some African-American women were drawn to mainstream feminist organizations, such as the National Organization for Women (NOW), or small radical feminist groups such as the Redstockings and WITCH. However, during the early to mid-seventies, most black feminists avoided the predominantly white women's movement. Several leading white feminists, including Susan Brownmiller, Jo Freeman, and Kathie Sarachild, had cut their political teeth in the civil rights struggles of the early to mid-sixties and compared the oppression of women with the oppression of African Americans. But many black feminists found their white counterparts unaware of the importance of race and racism, and some resented the way white women equated their plight with black people. When white women appealed to sisterhood, African-American women were quick to point out that historically their relations with one another had been as domestic servants (or other employees) to employers. More important, most black women activists did not separate their fight for women's rights from issues affecting the entire black community. The majority of black feminists did not believe, as many of their white counterparts did, that all men were the enemy.

In 1973 several African-American women's groups were founded, the most important of which was the National Black Feminist Organization (NBFO). The first NBFO conference was held in New York City and was attended by approximately four hundred African-American women. The atmosphere was electric; no one attending the conference had ever witnessed such a large gathering of black women speaking about issues that directly affected them. It became clear from the speeches that the NBFO's emphasis would be on combating sexist and racist discrimination against black women and struggling for greater involvement in the political process. Many journalists and activists took special note of the diversity of participants—black women from all walks of life, from domestic workers to lawyers, welfare rights organizers to polished elected officials. Although the different backgrounds of these women enriched the discussion from the floor, it also created tensions. After its first year, black women active in the welfare rights movements began to feel that the NBFO sidestepped the problems of poor women, and many African-American lesbians criticized the NBFO for ignoring homophobia and for speaking only to issues affecting heterosexual women. Partly in response to the NBFO's shortcomings, new black women's groups were formed to address issues that the NBFO did not choose to address, such as homophobia and the replacement of capitalism with socialism.

Despite such differences, black politics in the seventies—as in the sixties—emphasized unity above all else. With unity came strength, black political leaders argued, and with strength came real power. Nowhere was the potential for real power more evident than in electoral politics. After the Voting Rights Act of 1965 was passed, and organizations like SNCC waged massive voter registration campaigns, the ballot seemed to be an increasingly powerful weapon. Changes in the racial makeup of cities, in particular, improved chances for African Americans to gain a stronger political foothold in major urban centers.

With the formation of the Congressional Black Caucus (CBC) in 1971, a group of black members of Congress committed themselves to working jointly in the interests of African Americans. The origins of the CBC go back to 1969, when

Congressman Charles Diggs of Detroit led a committee of nine black representatives to oppose President Nixon's policies. The CBC initially worked for reforms
in job training, health care, welfare and social services, and other areas of social
policy that directly affected African-American communities. It also tried to fashion
a national strategy to increase black political representation. The formation of the
CBC attracted a wide range of political activists, including cultural nationalists
such as Imamu Amiri Baraka, the popular playwright and poet whose Newark,
New Jersey–based movement, New Ark, had just played a key role in electing that
city's first black mayor in 1970. Like many other progressives, Baraka believed
that the CBC and black voters could pressure the Democratic party into becoming more accountable to black people. For Baraka and other radical supporters
of the CBC, however, the ultimate goal was not to have more influence over the
Democratic party. Rather, they wanted to build an independent black political
movement.

The idea of a national black political campaign generated a lot of excitement
among black artists as well as among elected officials and community activists.
Although black writers, musicians, and visual artists had a long tradition of linking politics and art, the generation of black artists that emerged in the sixties and
seventies set a new standard for their direct political involvement and community
activism. Poets such as Baraka, Don L. Lee (Haki Madhubuti), Mari Evans, Kalamu
ya Salaam, and Sonia Sanchez were among the leading voices calling for a coordinated black political movement. Thus, prompted by Baraka and Richard Hatcher,
mayor of Gary, Indiana, several African-American political leaders organized a
national convention to create a black agenda and to discuss possible strategies for
gaining greater black political power. The idea proved enormously popular, and
throughout the fall and winter of 1971, grass-roots political movements elected
delegates, people raised money for transportation, and political activists passed out
leaflets informing local communities about the event.

In March 1972, some eight thousand African Americans (three thousand of
whom were official delegates) arrived in Gary, Indiana, to attend the first convention of the National Black Political Assembly, which was more commonly known
as the "Gary Convention." The roll call, the tall floor signs identifying each state's
delegates, the constant calls to order were much like the Democratic or Republican
conventions we see on television. But the comparison stopped there; at Gary all the
faces were black and many were working-class. And this sea of eight thousand
black faces was chanting, "It's Nation Time! It's Nation Time!" No one in that room
had ever seen anything like this before.

The feeling among the delegates that it was, indeed, "Nation Time" captures the
political sensibilities dominating the convention. The radical black nationalists
clearly won the day; moderates who supported integration and backed the Democratic party were in the minority. Most of the delegates—at least the most vocal
ones—agreed that African-American communities faced a social and economic

crisis, and that nothing short of fundamental changes in the political and economic system could bring an end to this crisis. As the famous Gary Declaration put it:

> A Black political convention, indeed all truly Black politics, must begin from this truth: *The American system does not work for the masses of our people, and it cannot be made to work without radical, fundamental changes.* (Indeed, this system does not really work in favor of the humanity of anyone in America.) . . .
>
> The challenge is thrown to us here in Gary. *It is the challenge to consolidate and organize our own Black role as the vanguard in the struggle for a new society.* To accept that challenge is to move to independent Black politics. There can be no equivocation on that issue. History leaves us no other choice. White politics has not and cannot bring the changes we need.

The convention's agenda included a bill that would expand voter registration and provisions to ensure community control over such institutions as police, government, and city services.

To arrive at such a radical document was not easy. From the very outset local issues clashed with efforts to create a national agenda, and delegates representing different outlooks had trouble compromising. Indeed, part of the Michigan delegation walked out of the convention to protest the separatist tone of the resolutions. Most elected officials also believed the delegates had gone too far: resolutions were passed calling for the creation of independent black schools and opposing court-ordered busing. And, as politicians active in the Democratic party, they strongly rejected the pledge to create an independent black political party.

Gary was an amazing example of democracy at work. Most mainstream political leaders and elected officials did not expect such a radical agenda to come out of this convention. But the three thousand official delegates and the additional five thousand in the audience believed they had a voice, a right to express their thoughts on black liberation.

Unfortunately, the vision created in Gary was soon abandoned. First, grassroots activists committed to the Gary Declaration did not have national visibility. Black elected officials and leaders who did have that visibility were concerned with being reelected or losing white allies. Therefore, most black elected officials did not dare echo Gary's call for revolutionary changes in American society. Besides, many black politicians felt betrayed by the convention. They dismissed the delegates for being insensitive to and ignorant of the kind of "hard-nosed" negotiations black elected officials must participate in. Real politics, they argued, involved compromising and coalition building, not demands for revolutionary change.

By the time the 1972 Presidential election campaign was well under way, the historic Gary Convention seemed to be but a faint echo in the world of electoral politics. Most black politicians scrambled to endorse white Democrats, either Hubert

Shirley Chisholm thanks her supporters after her failed bid for the Presidency during the 1972 Democratic National Convention in Miami.

Humphrey or George McGovern, for the Presidential nomination. Others, like Floyd McKissick, a Black Power proponent and head of the Congress of Racial Equality, joined fellow CORE leaders and endorsed Republican Richard Nixon. In particular, Nixon's support for black business and his advocacy of self-help appealed to CORE leaders, whose politics had grown increasingly conservative. Meanwhile, amid the backroom negotiating and political deals being made between white men and black men, an African-American congresswoman from New York stepped to the fore and sought the Democratic party's nomination for President. Shirley Chisholm's bid for President surprised everyone. She certainly did not develop a reputation as a radical outside the political process. Indeed, she joined those who abandoned the original goals of the National Black Political Assembly, and in fact felt betrayed by parts of the Gary Declaration. And yet, she was not your typical politician. Born Shirley St. Hill in Brooklyn in 1924 and raised by working-class Barbadian parents, Chisholm earned a bachelor's degree from Brooklyn College and an M.A. in early childhood education from Columbia University. After several frustrating years as an active member of the Democratic party in the Bedford-Stuyvesant section of Brooklyn, in 1968 she ran against former CORE leader James Farmer (who by then had joined the Republican party) for a newly created congressional seat representing Brooklyn. She soundly beat Farmer, becoming the first black woman elected to the House of Representatives. Her active support for equal rights, affirmative action policies, and women's liberation attracted the attention of both women's organizations and civil rights advocates. She turned out to be among the most outspoken feminists in Congress, serving as an active member of the National Organization for Women, a founder of the National Women's Political Caucus, and member of the National Abortion Rights Action League. In a memorable speech delivered at the Conference on Women's

Employment organized by the Congressional Committee on Education and Labor, Chisholm called on women to "rebel."

> Women in this country must become revolutionaries. We must refuse to accept the old, the traditional roles and stereotypes.... We must replace the old, negative thoughts about our femininity with positive thoughts and positive action affirming it, and more. But we must also remember that we will be breaking with tradition, and so we must prepare ourselves educationally, economically, and psychologically in order that we will be able to accept and bear with the sanctions that society will immediately impose upon us.

When Chisholm made her bid for the Presidency in 1972, she was poised, experienced, and knowledgeable about issues affecting African Americans and women. And she earned supporters. On the first ballot she garnered over 150 votes at the Democratic National Convention. But, to her surprise and disappointment, very few white women's organizations, black male politicians, or black organizations led by men came out in support of her candidacy. Chisholm was disillusioned by black male politicians who refused to take her campaign seriously precisely because she was a woman. The only major black political organization to endorse her candidacy was the Black Panther party, which by then had a substantial number of women in leadership positions.

Chisholm lost the nomination to George McGovern, who was then summarily crushed in the 1972 election. Nixon's popularity had soared, especially among white working- and middle-class voters. After all, he promised to be tough on crime and extra hard on dissidents. Ironically, Nixon's own administration harbored a number of crooks, and the President himself seemed to be the ringleader. Less than a year after his reelection a Senate investigation revealed that Nixon directed or had knowledge about a whole litany of crimes against political rivals, including the June 1972 break-in at the campaign headquarters of the Democratic National Committee. On August 9, 1974, just before the House of Representatives was to vote on impeachment, Nixon resigned. The Watergate affair ended in the first resignation of a President in U.S. history, the imprisonment of twenty-five Nixon aides, and a crisis in American politics.

Watergate was a serious blow to the rising hopes that many African Americans had placed in electoral politics. For others it confirmed what they already believed: the white-dominated political system was corrupt and completely bankrupt. A few activists tried to resurrect the political spirit of the Gary Convention by continuing to support a path independent of the Democrats and Republicans. But the very idea of an independent black political party, which had inspired the Gary Convention in the first place, was no longer a goal. Indeed, it would be another four years before a national black independent political party was formed. The National Black Political Assembly drew only one thousand delegates to its third national convention in 1976. One year later, its membership had shrunk to a paltry three hundred. Political apathy and cynicism was also evident in the declining number of African Americans willing to vote. The percentage of voting-age blacks who actually went to the polls dropped from 52.1 percent in 1972 to 49 percent in 1976.

By the time the United States geared up for its bicentennial celebration in 1976, African Americans had reason to look upon the democratic process with mixed feelings. They had certainly made progress in the electoral sphere. In 1969, 994 black men and 131 black women held public office nationwide; by 1975 the number of black elected officials grew to 2,973 men and 530 women. Black politicians won mayoral races in several major cities, including Los Angeles, Atlanta, New Orleans, Philadelphia, and Washington, D.C. By 1974, more than two hundred African Americans served as state legislators, and seventeen sat in Congress— including four women: Shirley Chisholm, Cardiss Collins of Illinois, Barbara Jordan of Texas, and Yvonne Brathwaite Burke of California. For all the pessimism surrounding Presidential races, municipal victories were greeted with optimism.

These were victories for black politics, for sure, but bittersweet ones. Once the victory parties were over, many residents still had a difficult time obtaining city services, affordable housing, or improved schools. In some cases, local politicians consciously tied their fate to big business. Some black citizens began to question whether having an African American in city hall even made a difference. But most black mayors really wanted to help the communities that put them into office. What they had not counted on was a reduction in federal spending on cities, white and black middle-class flight to the suburbs, a rapid growth in urban poverty and unemployment, and one of the most severe economic recessions in U.S. history.

Inner City Blues: Urban Poverty in the Seventies

North Lawndale was once a thriving Chicago community made up of European immigrants and U.S.-born whites and blacks. A community of working-class neighborhoods, North Lawndale before 1970 was home to people who worked for International Harvester, Western Electric, Sears Roebuck, Zenith, Sunbeam, or any one of several other factories and retail outlets in the area. By 1980, most of these firms had closed up shop, leaving empty lots and burned-out buildings in their wake. The dominant retail outlets by the early eighties were bars and liquor stores. In less than a generation, North Lawndale's economy had evaporated, leaving fifty-eight percent of its able-bodied workers unemployed and half of its population on welfare. As jobs disappeared, so did most of the white and black middle-class residents. Once a thriving industrial hub, North Lawndale became one of the poorest black ghettos in Chicago.

The story of North Lawndale was repeated in almost every major city in the United States after 1970. What are the reasons for such economic devastation? Why has the collapse of the urban economy had such a profound impact on African Americans? To answer these questions, we need to first acknowledge that the economies under the free enterprise system have always had their ups and downs. Sometimes manufacturers produce more than the market can absorb, which not only results in lower prices but leads many companies to fire excess workers. Other times new technology intended to make production faster and more efficient leads to layoffs or reduced wages because new machinery often requires workers with less skill. These and other worldwide economic conditions have caused the U.S. economy to swing between economic surges and periods of economic recessions or outright depressions. And in virtually every case of recession, African-American workers were the "last hired and first fired."

But by the mid-seventies, parts of the U.S. economy appeared to be in a permanent crisis. Ironically, just as programs were being implemented to correct racial imbalances in the workplace, and laws barring discrimination in hiring were being enforced a little more vigorously than before, much of the manufacturing part of the economy began a downward cycle from which it never seemed to recover. Even if protection for black workers improved slightly, changes in the global economy created massive unemployment and led to an expansion of poverty among African Americans not seen since the Great Depression of the thirties.

A series of events and policies during the early seventies contributed to the decline of the U.S. economy, especially its heavy industry—steelmaking and the manufacture of automobiles, tires, textiles, and machines of various kinds. In 1973, the Organization of Petroleum Exporting Countries (OPEC), an alliance of mostly Arab oil-producing countries that joined together in 1960 to reduce competition and set higher oil prices, declared an embargo on oil shipments to the United States and Western Europe to protest Israel's war with its Arab neighbors. Because the United States had become dependent on foreign oil supplies, the embargo had a devastating impact on the economy, making it difficult for individual consumers and big business to obtain inexpensive fuels. Plants shut down in large numbers. In 1974 alone, sales and manufacturing of American automobiles declined drastically, unemployment nearly doubled, and inflation more than doubled. Over the next ten years the economy never really recovered; the value of imported manufactured goods from places like Japan and Western Europe grew from less than fourteen percent of the U.S. domestic economy in 1970 to almost forty percent in 1979, while at the same time inflation sharply increased. With increased inflation came a steady loss in the standard of living for all Americans.

President Nixon tried to control inflation, but his policies actually made matters worse, especially for the poor. First, in August 1971 he temporarily froze wages, prices, and rents. But because prices and rents were already high, those earning low wages found themselves in the same situation as before. Second, Nixon placed a tariff on Japanese-made cars. This was intended to reduce competition between Japanese auto manufacturers and American manufacturers, but all it did was increase the price of otherwise affordable Japanese economy cars. American-made cars, for the most part, were still rather expensive and tended to use more gas than foreign cars. And in an economy in which oil prices were rising faster than just about any other item, cars that required less gas continued to be popular in the United States.

In spite of Nixon's measures, inflation continued to rise rapidly and low wages and growing unemployment made it impossible for large numbers of consumers to buy American products, no matter how much the government tried to protect the market with tariffs. Moreover, massive military spending exacerbated the country's economic woes. It dramatically increased the national debt and redirected much-needed investment away from roads, schools, and industries unrelated to the military buildup. Just months before President Nixon signed a peace agreement withdrawing U.S. troops from Vietnam, the national deficit had grown to $40 billion.

President Gerald Ford continued Nixon's economic policies, and when Democrat Jimmy Carter took over the Presidency in 1976, the situation for African Americans improved only slightly. He appointed Patricia Harris, an African-American woman, as Secretary of Housing and Urban Development, and Andrew Young, a black veteran of the civil rights movement, as ambassador to the United Nations. The Carter administration did little to lessen unemployment, and the jobless rate for African Americans increased during his first two years in office. Like the Republican presidents before him, Carter gave corporations a big tax cut, reduced financial aid to black colleges and universities, provided minuscule support for the nation's declining cities, and slashed federal spending for social programs—notably welfare, free lunch programs for children, and health services. He even backpedaled on his promise to reduce defense spending: the military budget for 1978 reached $111.8 billion, the highest level in U.S. history up to that point.

The creation of multinational corporations in the post–World War II era was the most important change in the new global economy. These multinational corporations no longer had a stake in staying in a particular country or region. Instead, they moved their firms wherever labor and taxes were cheaper, pollution laws were less stringent, and labor unions were either weak or nonexistent. Some manufacturers moved from the Midwest and Northeast to the southern United States in search of cheaper labor with weaker unions, although the South hardly experienced an economic boom during the seventies. The more common trend was for big companies to set up shop in countries like Mexico, Brazil, and South Africa, leaving in their wake empty American factories and huge numbers of unemployed workers. By 1979, for example, ninety-four percent of the profits of the Ford Motor Company and sixty-three percent of the profits from Coca-Cola came from overseas operations. Between 1973 and 1980, at least four million U.S. jobs were lost when firms moved their operations to foreign countries. And during the decade of the seventies, at least 32 million jobs were lost as a result of shutdowns, relocations, and scaling-back operations.

The decline of manufacturing jobs in steel, rubber, auto, and other heavy industries had a devastating impact on black workers. Although black joblessness had been about twice that of whites since the end of World War II, black unemployment rates increased even more rapidly, especially after 1971. During these economic downturns, white unemployment tended to be temporary, with a higher

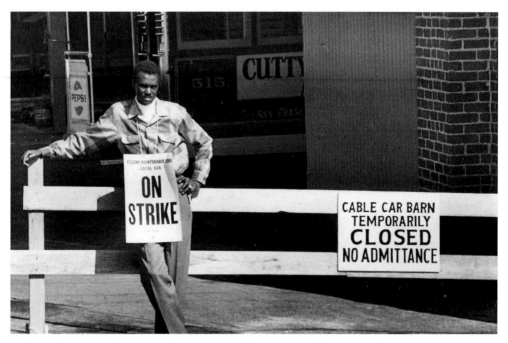

A city employee on strike outside a San Francisco cable car barn in 1970. During the 1970s, many blacks looked to labor unions to protect their rights and advance their interests.

percentage of white workers returning to work. For blacks, layoffs were often permanent. While the number of unemployed white workers declined by 562,000 between 1975 and 1980, the number of black unemployed *increased* by 200,000 during this period—the widest unemployment gap between blacks and whites since the government started keeping such statistics.

The loss of well-paying industrial jobs affected not only African Americans but the entire working class. Some workers looked to labor unions affiliated with the AFL-CIO to battle factory closures and wage reductions. At the height of the recession in the seventies, however, most labor unions were on the defensive, fighting desperately to hold on to the gains they had made a decade earlier. To make matters worse, many black industrial workers felt that white labor leaders were not very responsive to their needs. These leaders did not actively promote African Americans to leadership positions within the unions. In 1982, for example, the AFL-CIO's thirty-five member Executive Council had only two black members, a figure that fell far short of representing actual black membership. Indeed, African Americans tended to have higher rates of participation than whites in union activities: by 1983, more than twenty-seven percent of black workers were union members, compared to about nineteen percent of white workers.

Politically, the AFL-CIO leadership took stands that openly went against the interests of the majority of black workers. In 1972 George Meany supported

Nixon's bid for the Presidency, which was interpreted by black rank-and-file members as a clear sign that the AFL-CIO was deserting African Americans. In response, a group of black trade union activists formed the Coalition of Black Trade Unionists (CBTU) in 1972. Under the leadership of veteran labor organizer William Lucy, secretary-treasurer of the American Federation of State, County, and Municipal Employees (AFSCME), the CBTU not only condemned the Nixon administration for what it felt were racist policies but also attacked AFL-CIO president George Meany for endorsing Nixon. The CBTU also issued a statement critical of union leaders who did not actively oppose discrimination and support minority and rank-and-file efforts to have a greater voice in the affairs of the union.

The loss of manufacturing positions was accompanied by an expansion of low-wage service jobs. The more common service jobs included retail clerks, janitors, maids, data processors, security guards, waitresses, and cooks—jobs with little or no union representation. Not everyone who was laid off in the seventies and eighties got these kinds of jobs, and those who did experienced substantial reductions in their income. Many of these new service jobs paid much less than manufacturing jobs. They tended to be part-time and offered very little in the way of health or retirement benefits.

Black men and women who were laid off from auto plants and steel mills in the Midwest and South suddenly found themselves working at fast food and sanitation jobs to make ends meet. Young people entering the job market for the first time quickly discovered that the opportunities their parents once had were fading quickly. Many African-American youths without the option to go to college chose the military as an alternative to low-wage service work. As the United States pulled out of Vietnam, the military became one of the biggest employers of African Americans: the percentage of blacks in the armed forces rose from eighteen percent in 1972 to thirty-three percent in 1979.

These dramatic changes in the economy meant greater poverty for African Americans. One of the most striking features of the seventies was the widening income gap between blacks and whites. At the beginning of the decade, African Americans in the northeastern United States made about seventy-one cents for every dollar whites made; by 1979 that ratio dropped to fifty-eight cents. In 1978, 30.6 percent of black families earned income below the official poverty line, compared with 8.7 percent of white families.

Black women and children were the hardest hit by the economic crisis. Hemmed in by limited job opportunities, more and more working-class black women found themselves having to raise children without the benefit of a spouse to help pay the bills or participate in child care. The number of black homes without male wage earners rose from twenty-two percent in 1960 to thirty-five percent in 1975. Since black women, especially those in their teens and twenties, were the lowest paid and had the highest unemployment rate, it is not an accident that black single-mother households headed the list of families below the poverty line. In 1969, fifty-four percent of all black families below the poverty line were headed by women; in 1974 this figure rose to sixty-seven percent.

Several politicians and academics blame the rising number of "female-headed households" for the decline of inner cities and the rise of black crime and violence. This crisis of the black family, they argue, is new and unprecedented. They insist that the inability of single mothers to control and discipline their children, combined with the lack of male role models, has led to a whole generation of out-of-control youth. But a lot of these claims are based on misinformation. First of all, single-mother families are not a uniquely "black" crisis; between 1970 and 1987 the birth rate for white unwed mothers rose by seventy-seven percent. Second, out-of-wedlock births are not entirely new to African-American communities. Studies have shown that at least since the days of slavery black women are more likely than white women to bear children outside of marriage and to marry at later ages, after becoming mothers. Part of the reason has to do with the fact that black families have tended not to ostracize women for out-of-wedlock births.

Why have the number of female-headed households grown, and what impact has it had on the social and economic fabric of black communities? First, the declining number of employed black men has contributed to the growth of single-parent households. Aside from a rapid increase in permanently unemployed black men who suddenly cannot support their families as they had in the past, black men have a higher chance of dying young than any other male population in the United States. They are more often victims of occupational accidents, fatal diseases, and homicides than other men. And throughout the seventies and eighties, the black male prison population increased threefold; by 1989, twenty-three percent of black males ages twenty to twenty-nine, or almost one out of every four, were either behind bars or on legal probation or parole. Another important factor is that African Americans have a higher divorce and separation rate than whites. High unemployment for black males certainly contributes to marital instability among poor families, but welfare policies also play a major role. In at least twenty-five states, two-parent families are ineligible for Aid to Families with Dependent Children (AFDC), and in many cases black men have to leave the household in order for the women and children to have access to welfare and Medicaid.

Although single-parent families (including those run by males) tended to suffer more than two-parent families because they lacked a second wage earner, the structure of the family was not the *cause* of poverty. Most of these households were poor not because the women were unmarried but because of the lack of employment opportunities for women, lower levels of education, and the gross inequality in wages as a result of race and sex discrimination. One study shows, for example, that while seventy-five percent of unemployed black women heading families were poor in 1977, only twenty-seven percent of employed black women heading families were poor. Besides, the vast majority of women who ended up as single parents were poor *before* they had children or experienced divorce, separation, or the death of their husband.

Finally, single-parent families are not always the product of economic deprivation. Oftentimes they reflect the efforts of black women to escape abusive situations and to raise their children in a more supportive environment. As Barbara Omolade, an African-American scholar and activist, explained it: "My children and other children of Black single mothers are better people because they do not have to live in families where violence, sexual abuse, and emotional estrangement are the daily, hidden reality.... In a society where men are taught to dominate and women to follow, we all have a lot to overcome in learning to build relationships, with each other and with our children, based on love and justice. For many Black single mothers, this is what the struggle is about."

Because many families headed by single women are poor, they frequently must turn to welfare to survive. The amount of financial support available to welfare recipients in most states barely allowed families to make ends meet. In a recent study of welfare in the eighties, for example, one researcher met a divorced mother of two whose combined cash aid and food stamps amounted to a mere twelve dollars per day. "This is probably about the lowest point in my life," she admitted, "and I hope I never reach it again. Because this is where you're just up against a wall. You can't make a move. You can't buy anything that you want for your home. You can't go on vacation. You can't take a weekend off and go see things because it costs too much." The stigma attached to welfare made matters worse. Using food stamps often brought stares and whispers of disgust from clerks and consumers standing by.

The majority of single black mothers who received welfare during the eighties, however, did so for an average of only six months, and most had to supplement aid with odd jobs in order to make ends meet. Besides, not all poor African Americans received public assistance, nor were they the primary beneficiaries of welfare. In 1991, sixty-one percent of all people on welfare were white. Blacks, by comparison, made up only thirty-three percent of welfare recipients. And many who did qualify for some form of public assistance did not always receive it. A 1979 study revealed that seventy percent of all unemployed blacks never received any unemployment benefits; more than half of all poor black households received no AFDC or General Assistance; half of all black welfare households received no Medicaid coverage and fifty-eight percent of all poor black households received benefits from only one or two of the seven income programs available to assist the poor. There are many reasons why a substantial number of poor people did not receive full benefits. In some cases, the lengthy application process discouraged applicants; in other instances, computer errors, misplaced files, or unsympathetic or ill-informed case workers were to blame. But in many cases, black men and women living below the poverty line were simply too proud to accept welfare.

Living the Dream? The Black Middle Class

To the residents of Philadelphia, July 1976 must have felt like the hottest month in that city's history. Throngs of people from all over the country and throughout the world invaded the "City of Brotherly Love" to celebrate the 200th birthday of the Declaration of Independence. Waving overpriced flags and wearing red, white, and blue outfits, they came to examine the famous crack in the Liberty Bell and see firsthand the document that announced the beginning of this country's democratic journey.

In the neighborhoods just north, west, and south of the celebrations, a growing number of jobless and working-poor African Americans were fighting to survive. While the patriotic celebrations of the moment cast a shadow over Philadelphia's dark ghettos, hiding much of the recent devastation that would characterize the next two decades, a group of African-American leaders was trying to get the bicentennial committee to acknowledge the black presence in the past two hundred years of history. The fact that the majority of Africans in America were still slaves when the Declaration of Independence was signed made many bicentennial organizers uncomfortable. Instead, they tried to integrate the celebrations by highlighting black achievement in business, politics, the arts and entertainment, sciences, and education.

By emphasizing black achievement and paying less attention to the crumbling ghettos in earshot of the Liberty Bell, the organizers of the bicentennial were not being entirely dishonest. Just as the majority of African Americans experienced immense poverty, segregation, violence, and rising racism, some black professionals and entrepreneurs were reaping the fruits of integration. Of course, there had always been middle- and upper-class blacks, but in the past they succeeded in a segregated economy, lived in segregated neighborhoods, and had to operate in an atmosphere of outright racial discrimination. Although discrimination did not disappear entirely, the civil rights struggles of the previous two decades helped usher in affirmative action programs that gave minorities and women preference in hiring and college admission to compensate for past and present discrimination.

"We were all . . . children of the civil rights movement: the nation had changed its laws and, in some respects, its ways during our childhoods and adolescences. We were living the opportunities for which generations of black folk had fought and died. Walking paths wet with the blood of our martyrs, we felt an uneasy fear that taking advantage of those opportunities was changing us."

These words were written in 1991 by Yale law professor and best-selling author Stephen L. Carter. Carter exemplifies what it meant for a generation of young people to live the American Dream. A graduate of Yale Law School, Carter turned out to be a gifted legal scholar and talented writer. In another era, a black person of his considerable talents might not have had the chance to attend Yale or to accept a major professorship at his alma mater. But affirmative action policies and an aggressive recruitment effort to attract African Americans to the school opened doors for him that had been closed to previous generations. He is clearly one of those who "made it." Between his salaries, royalties on his book sales, and fees for speaking engagements, Professor Carter makes more than enough money to live a comfortable middle- or upper-middle-class existence.

And yet, Carter is somewhat ambivalent about how his success and the particular road he had to take to achieve it has changed him and other black professionals. Everywhere he turned, his white colleagues hinted that he did not make it on his own merit; that every college and every law firm opened doors to him because he was black, not because he was good. Some days he believed this argument. Other days he felt enraged that so many of his colleagues viewed him as the representative of a race rather than as an individual. Occasionally he convinced himself that his success was entirely the result of his own initiative and hard work. Indeed, there were moments when Carter believed that the old racial barriers of the past had been completely destroyed. But just when life seemed good, the handsomely attired and articulate scholar would be reminded of his race. "When in New York, for example, if I am traveling with a white person, I frequently swallow my pride and allow my companion to summon the taxi as I hang back—for to stand up for my rights and raise the arm myself would buy only a tired arm and no ride. For a black male, blue jeans in New York are a guarantee of ill-treatment. There are the jewelry-store buzzers that will not ring, the counter clerks who will not say 'Sir,' the men's departments with no staff to be found."

Carter's mixed feelings about his success are characteristic of a rapidly expanding class of black urban and suburban professionals who came of age during the fifties and sixties. Their numbers increased substantially during the seventies. In 1970, 15.7 percent of black families had incomes over $35,000; by 1986 the percentage had grown to 21.2 percent. Likewise, black families earning more than $50,000 almost doubled, increasing from 4.7 percent in 1970 to 8.8 percent in 1986. And like Carter, their rapid success can be partially attributed to antidiscrimination laws and affirmative action programs first established in the sixties and expanded under President Jimmy Carter during the mid- to late-seventies.

The roots of recent affirmative action policies can be traced to the Civil Rights Act of 1964 and the establishment of the Equal Employment Opportunity Commission (EEOC) and the Office of Federal Contract Compliance (OFCC). Both of these agencies were created to monitor employment discrimination and enforce the law. Unfortunately, the staff at the EEOC and the OFCC was small relative to the number of cases it received each year.

While lack of personnel within these institutions has led to a huge backlog of cases and limited their effectiveness, the EEOC, especially, has put pressure on firms to hire more women and minorities. For example, in 1973 the EEOC successfully sued the U.S. Steel Corporation for failing to promote black workers at its Fairfield, Alabama, plant. The court ordered U.S. Steel to expand job opportunities for its African-American workers. The EEOC discovered blatant incidents of white workers with less seniority being promoted to better jobs—mainly skilled machinist, clerical, technical, and managerial occupations. The court ruling required equal hiring of black and white apprentices and black and white clerical and technical employees until African Americans held about a quarter of these jobs.

Soon thereafter, the Detroit Edison Company was fined $4 million in punitive damages for discriminating against African-American employees, and a Detroit union local of the Utility Workers of America (UWA) was slapped with a $250,000 fine. The suit was initiated by a group of black Detroit Edison workers after the UWA and the International Brotherhood of Electrical Workers refused to file their grievance for them. Their primary complaint was that Detroit Edison employed very few black workers, turned down a large number of qualified black applicants, and kept blacks in the lowest-paid jobs. The judge in the case ordered the company to increase the proportion of black employees from eight percent to thirty percent and to set hiring guidelines that would ultimately place more black workers in higher-paying jobs with more authority.

Affirmative action policies were also responsible for briefly increasing black enrollment at major colleges and universities starting in the late sixties. Black enrollment rates rose from twenty-seven percent in 1972 to thirty-four percent in 1976, before dropping steadily during the next decade. Many leading black scholars and corporate leaders who came of age in the 1950s and sixties benefited from affirmative action initiatives. Because such policies were more strongly enforced at the federal, state, and municipal levels, African Americans employed in the public sector gained the most. By 1970, twenty-eight percent of all employed African Americans held government jobs, and approximately sixty percent of all black professional workers were employed by governmental bodies. This is particularly striking when we consider that in 1970 African Americans held only one percent of the managerial and administrative jobs in manufacturing. Thus, the expansion of public sector jobs for minorities has been largely responsible for the growth of the black middle class.

However, the inclusion of African Americans in public sector jobs and managerial positions did not always translate into big salary increases. Many black families reporting middle-class incomes were often the result of two parents working full-time for fairly low or moderate wages. Besides, in 1979, eighteen percent of all black female managers and thirteen percent of all black male managers actually earned wages below the poverty line. Many middle-class black families who had purchased suburban homes during the seventies lived from paycheck to paycheck; one layoff could mean the loss of their home. In fact, all economic indicators show that middle-class blacks, on average, possess substantially less "wealth" (savings, money invested in buying a home, stocks, bonds, retirement accounts, etc., minus debts) than middle-class whites who earn the same income.

Much of African-American wealth is concentrated in the hands of independent entrepreneurs, some of whom also benefited from affirmative action initiatives to provide more minority firms with government contracts and loans. The purpose of such programs was not to provide a handout to struggling businesses. Rather, they sought to rectify policies that had kept minority firms from obtaining government contracts in the first place and to improve the economic status of all African Americans by establishing a strong foundation for "black capitalism." The Nixon administration, for example, created several subsidy programs to assist black businesses, including the Office of Minority Business Enterprise, the Manpower Development and Training Program, and the Minority Enterprise Small Business Investment Company. Although these programs might have been effective if properly funded, they were never given much of a chance: after Ronald Reagan was elected President in 1980, virtually all of these programs were cut back.

Between 1972 and 1977, the number of black-owned firms and their proportion of total industry revenue declined for the most part. The number of black-owned auto dealerships fell by twenty-four percent; black-owned hotel and lodging facilities dropped by twenty-one percent; and the number of food and eating establishments declined by ten percent. In 1977, black-owned firms made up only three percent of all businesses in the country. By 1980, more than eighty percent of all black-owned firms did not have a single paid employee aside from the owner, and at least one-third of these firms failed within twelve months of opening.

Competition with other businesses only partly explains the failure of certain black-owned ventures. Black entrepreneurs have had more difficulty securing loans for their businesses than their white counterparts. A recent survey of five hundred black entrepreneurs with an annual revenue of $100,000 or more revealed that ninety percent had been turned down by banks when they applied for business loans. Of those surveyed, seventy percent had to rely on personal savings to finance their business. Often, black business people have to turn to black-owned community banks for help.

Not all black business suffered during the seventies recessions and Reagan-era cutbacks. On the contrary, the last decades of the twentieth century are filled with remarkable stories of black entrepreneurship. One rising corporate star during the seventies was Naomi Sims, a high-fashion model originally from Oxford, Mississippi. After earning a degree in psychology from New York University and studying at the Fashion Institute of Technology, Sims quickly emerged as one of the most popular black women models in the country, making several magazine-cover and television appearances. In 1973, she helped develop a new fiber for a line of wigs and founded the Naomi Sims Collection, selling cosmetics and hair-care products nationwide. By 1977, her firm reported annual revenues of about four million dollars.

Reginald F. Lewis's road to success was a bit more traditional. Born in Baltimore, Maryland, Lewis was helped by affirmative action policies that enabled him to earn a law degree from Harvard in 1968. After working for one of New York's most prestigious corporate law firms, Lewis, with fellow attorney Charles Clarkson, started his own law firm on Wall Street in 1970. His firm helped minority-owned businesses obtain financing and structure deals. In 1983, Lewis launched the TLC Group, an aggressive investment firm with the specific purpose of acquiring companies. And acquire he did: in 1984 TLC bought McCall's Pattern Company (a manufacturer of sewing patterns) for $25 million—and sold it for $90 million three years later. Then in 1987, the TLC Group made history by purchasing BCI Holdings, the former international division of the Chicago-based Beatrice Foods. Comprised of sixty-four companies operating in thirty-one countries, BCI Holdings manufactured and distributed a wide range of food products, including ice cream, meats, chocolates, and soft drinks. Lewis's firm paid $985 million for BCI Holdings, making it the largest leveraged buyout of an overseas operation in the history of American business up to that time.

The year before Lewis's death in 1993, TLC Beatrice had revenues of $1.54 billion and Lewis himself had amassed assets of more than $300 million, making him the wealthiest African American in U.S. history.

Perhaps the best-known black millionaire is publishing magnate John H. Johnson, founder of *Ebony* and *Jet* magazines. Born in Arkansas in 1918, he migrated to Chicago with his mother at age fifteen. While working for the black-owned Supreme Liberty Life Insurance Company in 1942, twenty-four-year-old Johnson decided to launch *Negro Digest,* a small magazine summarizing longer articles for and about African Americans. Raising the money was hard. "Most people had seen *Reader's Digest* and *Time*," he recalled, "but nobody had seen a successful black commercial magazine. And nobody was willing to risk a penny on a twenty-four-year-old insurance worker." That is, except for the Citizens Loan Corporation of Chicago, one of the few financial institutions willing to loan money to African Americans. They loaned him $500, but only after Johnson's mother offered to put up all of her new furniture as collateral. It was a good investment, for within eight months of its founding *Negro Digest* was selling fifty thousand copies a month nationally. Three years later, Johnson launched *Ebony* magazine, a photo magazine modeled after *Life.* By 1991, the Johnson companies reported

John H. Johnson, the founder of *Ebony* and *Jet* magazines, headed a publishing empire that recorded total gross sales of $252 million in 1991.

total gross sales of $252 million. According to *Forbes* magazine, Johnson headed one of the four hundred richest families in the United States.

The combination of higher incomes and the dismantling of legal segregation enabled many rising middle-class black families to flee collapsing ghettos and move out to the suburbs or to lavish townhouses and brownstones in wealthy urban communities. The trend is reflected in the rapid suburbanization of the African-American population during the seventies and eighties: between 1970 and 1986, the black suburban population grew from 3.6 million to 7.1 million. Although they often left behind deteriorating neighborhoods, a growing drug economy, and a rapidly expanding army of unemployed men and women, most blacks could not escape bigotry. To their surprise, some middle-class black families who moved into predominantly white suburbs discovered burning crosses on their lawns, hate mail, and letters from property owners' associations concerned that their presence would lower property values.

Potential black homebuyers also had to deal with real estate agents who deliberately steered them to poorer, predominantly black neighborhoods, and with financial institutions that blatantly discriminated against African Americans. The evidence of discrimination against African Americans in housing is overwhelming. Numerous studies conducted in major metropolitan areas since the sixties demonstrated that real estate agents frequently showed black home buyers different properties, withheld information, or simply lied about the status of the property in question. This practice of steering black home buyers toward nonwhite neighborhoods is a form of discrimination known as "redlining." Similarly, a massive study of ten million applications to savings and loan associations between 1983 and 1988 revealed that the rejection rate for blacks applying for home mortgages was more than twice that of whites, and that high-income African Americans were rejected more than low-income whites.

What is clear from such stories of discrimination is that the dismantling of legal barriers to segregation has not been completely effective. Indeed, by some measures racial segregation has increased in the urban North during the last three decades. Despite evidence that middle- and upper-income African Americans were the greatest beneficiaries of integration, it is interesting to note that in some major cities African Americans earning more than $50,000 were as segregated as those making less than $2,500 annually. Of course, in a few cases middle-class blacks have chosen predominantly black suburban enclaves in well-to-do communities such as Prince George's County, Maryland (just outside of Washington, D.C.), or sections of Westchester County, a community north of New York City. Their decision is understandable given the history of violence and discrimination directed at African Americans who try to integrate all-white suburban communities. But fear of racist attacks and the desire for respectful neighbors indicate the narrowness of choices that are offered to blacks compared to whites.

School integration, another component of African Americans' desire to reach for the American Dream, quickly became one of the most contested racial battlefields during the post–civil rights era. A quarter of a century after the landmark case of *Brown* v. *Board of Education of Topeka, Kansas* (1954), the nation's public schools looked as segregated as they had ever been. Although black children made up about one-fifth of the total public school enrollment, almost two-thirds went to schools with at least fifty percent minority enrollment. This pattern is even more striking in major cities, where African-American children attended underfunded public schools while many white students, often the children of urban professionals, have deserted the public school system for private institutions. By 1980, for example, whites made up only four percent of public school enrollment in Washington, D.C., eight percent in Atlanta, nine percent in Newark, and twelve percent in Detroit.

Drastic measures were needed to remedy this situation, especially since middle-class families who had migrated to the suburbs took precious tax dollars needed to run city schools. With fewer well-paid, property-owning families living in urban areas, the property taxes so essential to funding education and other city services declined considerably. Under pressure from black families who wanted to send their children to better-funded schools in the suburbs and civil rights groups that believed the nation should live up to the *Brown* decision, school boards across the country tried to achieve racial balance by busing students to schools in different neighborhoods.

The nation was sharply divided over the issue of busing. President Nixon vehemently opposed court-ordered busing, officials in the Department of Health, Education and Welfare thought it was a good idea, and the Supreme Court remained unsure whether it was constitutional or not. The clearest expression of resistance to mandatory busing came from white parents who believed the addition of black children from the inner city would bring down the quality of education. Indeed, in some cities busing programs were met with militant protests that frequently led to violence. Throughout the early to mid-seventies, organized resistance erupted in cities throughout the country, including Pontiac, Michigan; Louisville, Kentucky; Pasadena, California; and Kansas City, Missouri. The best-known clashes were in Boston, where most public schools had been racially segregated until an NAACP-led campaign won a court order in 1975 to bus children from predominantly black and poor Roxbury to Charlestown, a largely working-class Irish community. Over the course of the next three years, Boston police were called in to protect black children from white mobs screaming racial epithets and occasionally throwing bricks and fists.

The Boston busing controversy died down by the early eighties, partly because liberal black and white politicians created a coalition that elected more supporters of integration to the city council and to the Board of Education. Besides, proponents of school integration could hardly claim a victory. By 1980, white flight to the suburbs and a decrease in the use of busing by conservative judges caused a resegregation of most big city school systems.

In the area of higher education, the backlash against affirmative action policies and financial aid for minorities took on many forms. During the late seventies and through the eighties, the number of reported racial assaults and acts of intimidation against blacks on college campuses showed a marked increase. The specific cases are chilling.

At Wesleyan University in 1981, black students found racist graffiti and flyers riddled with epithets and threats, including a leaflet advertising a fraternity "dedicated to wiping all goddamned niggers off the face of the earth." Ten years later, a white sorority at the University of Alabama hosted a party at which pledges painted their faces black and dressed as pregnant welfare mothers. Usually white backlash is much more subtle. One black college administrator vividly described the attitudes of white freshmen toward African Americans at his university: "Somebody will have the idea that the dorm is exclusively theirs, so therefore we can't have these 'germy, diseasey, dirty, filthy,' black kids live in their dormitory. . . . Black kids are seen as a gang now. They must be on drugs or crazy or something."

By far the most devastating form of white backlash in higher education was the partial dismantling of affirmative action initiatives. In the case of *Regents of the University of California* v. *Bakke* (1978), Allan Bakke, an unsuccessful white applicant, claimed that he was discriminated against because the University of California, Davis, admitted African Americans with lower test scores than his in order to meet their quota of minority students. The Supreme Court ruled that Bakke had been unfairly denied admission to the medical school. The court did not overturn all forms of affirmative action, but it did argue that quotas—setting aside a specific number of slots for designated groups—were unconstitutional. The medical school's denial of admission to Bakke in order to increase the number of minority students was regarded by the court's majority opinion as "reverse discrimination."

Although Bakke won the case, the unspoken facts behind U.C. Davis's admissions policy call into question the court's opinion that he was a victim of reverse discrimination. First, the sons and daughters of influential white families—potential donors or friends of the dean of the medical school—were also admitted over Bakke despite lower test scores. As had been the case historically, the dean controlled a handful of slots to admit special cases. Second, most minority applicants had higher scores than Bakke. This is an important fact, for the Bakke case left many observers with the incorrect impression that U.C. Davis admitted unqualified minorities. Most importantly, the decision was a major setback for efforts to achieve racial equality through social policy. Justice Thurgood Marshall, the first African American to serve on the Supreme Court, dissented from the majority opinion. Marshall, who viewed the Bakke decision as a tragedy, did not believe that America was even close to becoming a color-blind society. "The dream of America as a great melting pot," he wrote in his dissenting opinion in the Bakke case, "has not been realized for the Negro; because of his skin color he never even made it into the pot."

Most African Americans who stood at the threshold of the Reagan era knew they had entered the worst of times. *Equal opportunity, welfare, civil rights,* and *Black Power* became bad words in the national vocabulary. Most white Americans believed they had given all they could give, and that any form of government support would be nothing more than a handout. A small but growing contingent of black conservatives agreed. And if this was not enough, the crumbling cities that African Americans and other minorities had inherited turned out not to be the utopia they had hoped for. They were dangerous, difficult places where racist police officers still roamed and well-paying jobs fled the city limits. Despite the rising number of black mayors, it became clear by the eighties that a new freedom movement was needed.

"How We Gonna Make A Black Nation Rise?": The Struggle for Political Power

In December 1979, Arthur McDuffie, a thirty-three-year-old black insurance executive, was beaten to death by police officers in Dade County, Florida. The police said he was driving recklessly and had resisted arrest, but eyewitnesses believed it was a clear-cut case of brutality. African Americans who had followed the case closely knew who the real criminals were, and McDuffie was not one of them. To everyone's shock and dismay, however, in May 1980 an all-white jury returned a not-guilty verdict for all of the officers involved. That night black Miami exploded. Many inhabitants of the predominantly black and poor communities of Liberty City, Brownsville, Overton, and Coconut Grove took to the streets—turning over cars, setting fire to buildings, looting, throwing rocks and bottles at police and National Guardsmen. When the smoke cleared, Miami's losses exceeded $250 million; at least 400 people were injured and several were killed; more than 1,250 were arrested; and a 52-square-mile area of Dade County was placed under curfew from 8:00 p.m. to 6:00 a.m.

On closer inspection, it is clear that the Miami rebellion was not just a spontaneous response to an unfair verdict. It was a product of black frustrations caused by joblessness, economic deprivation, and immigration policies that clearly favored white Cubans over black Haitians, added to a string of incidents of police brutality and racial harassment that had gone unchecked during the seventies prior to McDuffie's death. It also marked the most dramatic example of the growing feeling of political powerlessness among poor and working-class African Americans. In an age when the number of black elected officials had increased dramatically and civil rights leaders achieved tremendous influence in national policy-making, Miami's black rebels displayed distrust toward their "leaders." When Andrew Young, former U.N. ambassador under President Carter and veteran civil rights

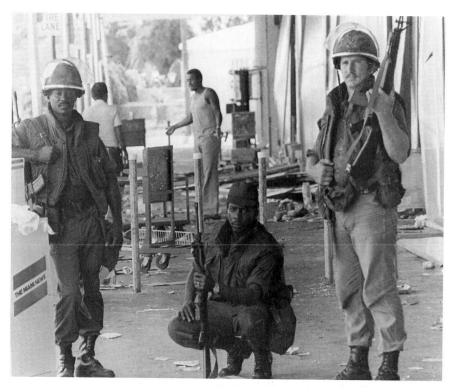

In May 1980, riots erupted in Miami after a jury found four policemen not guilty in the beating death of a prominent black businessman. After the riots members of the Florida National Guard stand watch outside a looted store.

leader, attempted to talk to black youths, he was shunned. As historian and social activist Manning Marable put it, "History and black people had pushed their so-called leaders aside."

The Miami uprising and the failure of black leadership was just a foreshadowing of the dark days yet to come. Throughout the country, African Americans had become the most likely victims of police violence. According to one study, African Americans constituted forty-six percent of people killed by police in 1975. By the end of the seventies, police killings and nonlethal acts of brutality emerged as a central political issue among African Americans.

Racist violence was clearly on the rise in the eighties. The number of racially motivated assaults rose dramatically, many of them on college campuses. Between 1982 and 1989, the number of hate crimes reported annually in the United States grew threefold.

Other signs pointing to a resurgence of racism in the eighties include the proliferation of white supremacist organizations such as the Ku Klux Klan. By the late seventies the Klan had tripled its membership and waged a nationwide campaign of intimidation against African Americans. In 1978–79, Klansmen initiated a reign of terror against black people, which included the firebombing of homes, churches, and schools in more than one hundred towns and rural areas, and drive-by shootings into the homes of NAACP leaders. Very few of these incidents led to convictions. The Klan and other white supremacist organizations also gained influence in electoral politics. In 1980 Tom Metzger, the "Grand Dragon" of the Ku Klux Klan, garnered enough votes to win the Democratic primary in Southern California's 43rd congressional district. Similarly, David Duke, former Klansman and founder of the National Association for the Advancement of White People, was elected to the Louisiana House of Representatives.

Although racists like Duke and Metzger were in the minority, their electoral wins signaled a changed mood in the eighties in the United States toward African Americans and other racial minorities. A new conservative movement emerged that strongly opposed affirmative action, immigration, and welfare. Even if this so-called "New Right" did not condone the resurgence of racism in the United States, its policies ultimately had a negative impact on African Americans. In particular, the election of former California governor Ronald Reagan to the White House in 1980 had disastrous consequences for black Americans, especially the poor. Reagan was a staunch believer in the "trickle down" economic theory—the idea that building big business would benefit everyone because its profits would somehow "trickle down" to the poor and middle class. With this philosophy as justification, the Reagan administration cut back social programs in favor of corporate investments and tax breaks to the wealthy. During his two terms in office, military spending increased by forty-six percent while funding for housing was slashed by seventy-seven percent and education by seventy percent. Money for Aid to Families with Dependent Children and the Food Stamp program were also cut back substantially.

By the time Reagan began his second term in 1985, the living conditions of poor and working-class blacks were worse than they had been at the height of the 1973–75 recession. In 1985, about one out of every three African Americans, most of whom were women and children, lived below the poverty line, and the official black unemployment rates hovered around fifteen percent nationwide. In midwestern cities such as Chicago, Detroit, and Milwaukee, the percentage of blacks without jobs ranged from twenty-five to thirty percent.

Reagan-era spending cuts were especially hard on cities, where the vast majority of African Americans lived. In addition to closing down the Neighborhood Self-Help and Planning Assistance program, which allotted $55 million to assist inner cities in 1981, aid to cities was reduced to a fraction of what it had been under President Nixon a decade earlier. City governments were forced to cut their budgets as well, leading to massive layoffs of low- and mid-level city workers. Because blacks held many of these government jobs, they were hardest hit by these cutbacks.

Most of the black mayors elected since the late sixties inherited this new urban crisis. With shrinking tax revenues caused by tax revolts and the flight of the middle class to the suburbs and almost no support from the federal government, most big city black mayors sought out whoever had money—which often turned out to be real estate developers and investors interested in building downtown financial centers. Coleman Young in Detroit, Maynard Jackson and Andrew Young in Atlanta, Ernest Morial in New Orleans, Carl Stokes in Cleveland, W. Wilson Goode in Philadelphia, to name a few, all faced this dilemma.

Perhaps the most telling example of this problem occurred in Los Angeles under Mayor Tom Bradley, a former Los Angeles police officer who was elected to the city council in 1963 and mayor in 1973. During his twenty-year tenure as mayor, from 1973 to 1993, Bradley promoted policies that favored the development of the downtown business district at the expense of poor communities in South Central Los Angeles that put him in office.

Because of the shutdown during the late seventies and eighties of numerous steel and rubber plants that had employed many African Americans in these neighborhoods, in some ways the decline of South Central was beyond Bradley's control. Economic conditions in South Central deteriorated faster than in any other L.A. community. A 1982 report from the California legislature revealed that South Central neighborhoods experienced a fifty percent rise in unemployment while purchasing power dropped by one-third. The 1982 median income for South Central L.A.'s residents was a paltry $5,900—that is, $2,500 below the median income for the black population *in the late seventies.* Youths were the hardest hit. For all of Los Angeles County, the unemployment rate of black youth remained at about forty-five percent.

Just when no one thought life in South Central Los Angeles could get any worse, crack cocaine entered the illegal drug scene in the mid-eighties. Crack, or "rock," was a cheap, highly addictive version of powdered cocaine that is smoked rather than inhaled through the nose. When this new drug hit the streets, it had an immediate and devastating impact on South Central Los Angeles as well as on other inner-city communities across the country. During 1984–85, emergency room admissions for cocaine trauma doubled and the number of juvenile arrests for drug dealing and related crimes increased fivefold. Violence also intensified as old gangs and new groups of peddlers battled for control of the crack market.

In spite of the violence, the constant threat of arrest, and the devastating health crisis generated by the drug, for many black youngsters selling crack was the only way to make a good income. Although the crack market might have put money into some people's pockets, for the majority it turned their neighborhoods into small war zones. Police helicopters, complex electronic surveillance, even small tanks armed with battering rams became increasingly familiar additions to the landscape of black Los Angeles. Housing projects were renovated along the lines of minimum security prisons and equipped with fortified fencing and mini-police stations. Some housing project residents were required to carry identity cards and visitors were routinely searched.

The intensive "law-and-order" policies of the Los Angeles Police Department were duplicated in most U.S. cities, with mixed results. Some black citizens complained that their communities were turning into police states. In Philadelphia, for example, tensions between police and civilians escalated into one of the most brutal episodes of violence in at least a decade. After Wilson Goode was elected the first black mayor in Philadelphia's history in 1983, he immediately found himself caught between a white constituency who wanted a law-and-order mayor and a police force with a legacy of corruption and brutality. In fact, in 1986 a federal grand jury indicted seven Philadelphia police officers who had worked in the narcotics division for racketeering and extorting at least $400,000 plus quantities of cocaine from drug dealers.

But the key event was Goode's decision to allow the police to bomb the headquarters of a Black nationalist organization called MOVE in May of 1985. Located in a Philadelphia neighborhood called Powelton Village, MOVE was mostly a militant black back-to-nature movement that had attempted to create a rural, communal environment in the middle of the city. As a result of complaints from neighbors and MOVE members' hostile attitude toward police, mayor Frank Rizzo tried to root them out in 1978, culminating in a shoot-out that left one officer dead and several injured on both sides. In a similar standoff seven years later, Goode authorized the dropping of an aerial bomb which killed 11 people, including 5 children, destroyed 61 homes, and left 250 people homeless. The MOVE bombing marred Goode's administration and his relations with Philadelphia's black community until he left office in 1991. Perhaps the biggest blow to Goode's administration was that the commission appointed to investigate the bombing concluded that racism strongly influenced the actions of the Philadelphia police force. This was crystal clear from the first words spoken by Philadelphia Police Commissioner Gregore J. Sambor, who announced over the bullhorn at the beginning of the assault: "Attention MOVE! This is America!"

Increasingly, African Americans began to realize that putting a black person in the mayor's office was not enough to solve the problems facing black America. Unlike the days of the civil rights movement, when politics appeared to be clearly etched in black and white, the political landscape of the eighties became more complicated. The appearance of a strong, vocal contingent of black pro-Reagan conservatives added to the confusion. Black conservatism was not new. The legacy of black conservatives advocating self-help and free-market economics goes back at least to the mid-nineteenth century. But during the Reagan years, black conservatives gained greater visibility in national politics and federal policy, distinguishing themselves for their advocacy of Reagan's "trickle down" theory and staunch opposition to affirmative action policies. (Ironically, most of these intellectuals had benefited from affirmative action in education and hiring.)

The most important spokesperson for this group, economist Thomas Sowell of the Hoover Institution at Stanford University, insisted that the problem of poor African Americans was one of values and the lack of a work ethic. He believed welfare and affirmative action policies undermined middle-class values of hard work and thrift and forced African Americans to become too dependent on government assistance. Black Harvard economist Glen Loury made similar arguments, insisting that racial preferences and equal opportunity legislation are worthless since the problems of the black poor are largely products of weak cultural values, broken families, and irresponsible parenting.

While many African Americans agreed with aspects of what the black Right had to say, particularly its insistence on self-sufficiency and its critique of welfare, most rejected neo-conservatism as a strategy to solve the black community's problems. A 1982 public opinion survey revealed that eighty-five percent of African Americans opposed Reagan-era policies of cutting back social welfare programs. On the other hand, while most polls conducted in the eighties indicated that African Americans supported increased government spending on the disadvantaged and endorsed affirmative action programs, they also revealed strong conservative views toward issues such as abortion and crime. Some African Americans, therefore, looked to political organizations and social movements that combined conservative social policy with racial militancy. The most potent example of this trend was the Nation of Islam, which grew dramatically during the eighties.

The NOI had undergone a dramatic change after the death of Elijah Muhammad in 1975. As soon as Wallace D. Muhammad, Elijah's son, took over the leadership of the NOI, he denounced his father's earlier teachings that the white man was the devil and that white people were created by an evil black scientist. Wallace, a respected Muslim scholar who had studied Arabic in Egypt, adopted an orthodox approach to Islam, changing the name of the organization to the World Community of al-Islam in the West. He even invited whites to join the group. In 1978, Louis Farrakhan, a devoted follower of Elijah Muhammad, broke from the World Community and reestablished the old NOI under Elijah's original beliefs. Under Farrakhan's leadership, the reconstituted Nation of Islam attracted a huge following among young people, many of whom were in search of solutions to joblessness, drug addiction, and the inability of poor African Americans to effect change in the political structure. Ironically, the Nation for the most part continued to distance itself from direct political participation and supported a fairly conservative agenda. Its policies centered on self-help, the creation of black business, and the maintenance of traditional relations between men and women.

The popularity of the NOI stems in part from its efforts to root out drug dealers from inner-city communities and its emphasis on community economic development. Through its economic wing, People Organized and Working for Economic Rebirth (POWER), the NOI has tried to create a nationwide cooperative of black businesses so that consumers and entrepreneurs can coordinate a massive "buy black" campaign. POWER has also introduced its own products, from soaps and shampoos to food items, which it markets through black stores or street corner vendors. By encouraging young, jobless African Americans to sell POWER products, they sought to create alternatives to crime and drug dealing and instill in them a sense of entrepreneurship.

Despite its conservative social policies and its tendency to stay out of electoral politics (an important exception being its support for Jesse Jackson's 1984 bid for the Presidency), the NOI is still regarded by many as an extremist organization. The Central Intelligence Agency and the Reagan administration remained convinced that the NOI maintained ties to Arab terrorist organizations, especially after Libyan president Muammar Qaddafi extended a five million dollar interest-free loan to the Nation to help start POWER. Furthermore, the NOI developed a reputation as a proponent of anti-Semitism because of several remarks made by Farrakhan and other NOI leaders. In 1983, for example, Farrakhan caused a national controversy when he described Nazi leader Adolf Hitler as "wickedly great." Although his point was to show how greatness could be used in the service of evil, the press reports interpreted Farrakhan's remark as praise for Hitler.

Although more radical black political activists rejected the NOI's conservatism, they agreed that African Americans needed to develop a road to political power independent of either the Democrats or the Republicans. Indeed, they had tried to build such a movement back in 1972, when the National Black Political Assembly first met in Gary, Indiana. But as more and more black elected officials became integrated into the Democratic party machine (and to a lesser extent, the Republican party), the idea of an independent road lost its appeal during the late seventies. However, the failure of the Carter administration to respond to black needs, followed by the election of Reagan, compelled black political activists to reopen the discussion of an independent movement.

Thus in 1980, the National Black Independent Political Party (NBIPP) was formed to meet the challenge. Conceived as a democratic, mass-based political movement capable of embracing a range of organizations and ideas without suppressing differences, NBIPP attracted between 1,500 and 2,000 delegates to its founding convention in November 1980. NBIPP's constitution called for strategies to work within the electoral arena and the development of community institutions that would involve ordinary people in local decision-making and ultimately shape public policy. Perhaps NBIPP's most revolutionary proposal was to put in place mechanisms that would ensure gender equality throughout the organization. Among other things, its charter and constitution called for equal gender representation in all leadership positions.

Unfortunately, NBIPP could not compete with the Democratic party, which continued to attract the vast majority of black voters. Nevertheless, it did set the stage for two historic political campaigns: Harold Washington's 1983 mayoral race in Chicago and Jesse Jackson's bid for President in 1984. Although both of these

Chicago mayor Harold Washington at a press conference announcing funding for a community center in 1986. As Chicago's first black mayor, Washington struggled against the entrenched power structure, which had long denied access to blacks.

campaigns took place within the Democratic party, they can be characterized as "independent" since they drew more on grass-roots organizing than mainstream party support.

No one believed Harold Washington could win when he announced his candidacy for mayor in 1983. Chicago had never had a black mayor, and given its long history of racial animosity and its well-entrenched Democratic political machine in city hall as well as in Congress, a black challenger was viewed as a long shot. Chicago did not have a black majority, and the percentage of African Americans who went to the polls had not been very high. To win such an election, Washington would have to appeal to a significant proportion of white and Latino voters and convince hundreds of thousands of complacent, frustrated black adults to register and come out to the polls.

A veteran of Chicago politics and a native of the city, Harold Washington understood what he had to do. After earning a B.A. from Roosevelt University in 1949 and a J.D. from Northwestern University Law School in 1952, Washington worked as assistant city prosecutor in Chicago until he was able to establish his own private law practice. As a Democrat, Washington became a rising star in state politics, serving in the state House of Representatives from 1965 to 1976 and the

Illinois State Senate from 1977 to 1980. In 1980, campaigning on a progressive agenda of racial equality and justice for working people and the poor, Washington was elected to the U.S. House of Representatives.

By 1983, Washington felt the time had come to make a bid for mayor of Chicago. African Americans, in particular, were frustrated with the incumbent, Jane Byrne, whose policies did little to help the poor, provide jobs, or place blacks in appointed positions within city hall. In opposition to the Byrne administration, local black and Latino activists began to mobilize support for Washington's campaign. The movement not only waged successful voter registration campaigns, increasing the number of black voters by 180,000 in 1982, but enjoyed substantial support from liberal whites.

In a hotly contested primary election in which the white vote was split between Byrne and Richard M. Daley, the son of former mayor Richard Daley, Washington scored a narrow victory. Last-minute Byrne campaign propaganda played on the racial fears of Chicago's white voters, subtly warning that a black mayor would undermine white privilege. Such fears were made even more explicit in the general election, especially after Byrne briefly announced her intention to run as a write-in candidate in order to save a "fragile" city that, in her words, was "slipping." When Byrne realized this tactic would not work, however, she withdrew. Despite heightened racial tensions and a very nasty campaign, Washington also beat his Republican challenger, Robert Epton, in yet another close election.

Once in office, however, Washington soon discovered that he was a long way from "victory." Members of the city council tied to the old Chicago machine opposed virtually everything the Washington administration tried to do. Yet, in spite of this opposition, he created the Commission on Women's Affairs, successfully pushed for a state law giving public employees the right to form labor unions, and implemented affirmative action policies to increase the number of women and minorities in government.

Yet, like all big-city mayors, Washington faced problems beyond his control. The Chicago Police Department still had a reputation for brutality and terrorism against minorities. Big business was reluctant to increase investment in Chicago since Washington was labeled a radical and his ability to govern in opposition to the machine was constantly being questioned. Moreover, he spent much of his time trying to clean up generations of mismanagement, corruption, graft, and budget deficits. He was reelected in 1987, but his reform efforts came to a halt when he died of a heart attack soon after returning to work.

Meanwhile, as Harold Washington launched his historic campaign for mayor, a group of black activists—mainly independents, Democrats, and labor organizers—began debating the pros and cons of running an African American in the 1984 Presidential elections. Most agreed on the futility of running an independent, especially in light of NBIP's inability to become a powerful force in politics. Instead, they wanted to run someone within the Democratic party who could pressure mainstream white candidates to be more responsive to black needs. Black elected officials and other party supporters were afraid that the Democrats were promoting more conservative policies in order to attract white working-class voters who had voted for Reagan in 1980. A black candidate, it was argued, could not only show how valuable blacks were to the party but could run on a more liberal and even radical agenda. Such a candidate would not merely espouse racial justice and civil rights; rather, he or she would focus on workers' rights, the environment, nuclear disarmament, and issues affecting women, Latinos, Asian Americans, and gays and lesbians.

Few established black politicians in the early eighties believed such a campaign could be anything but symbolic, and few were in the mood for symbolism. Even before a candidate was named, several African-American leaders opposed the plan.

However, one of the strongest supporters of a black Presidential candidate was Jesse Jackson. Because Jackson was so outspoken about the need to run a black candidate, he quickly emerged as the movement's spokesman. In no time, the media dubbed him the next Presidential candidate, a label Jackson himself did little to dispel. By the spring of 1983, opinion polls revealed that Jackson ranked third among the potential slate of Democratic candidates.

Jesse Jackson turned out to be an ideal choice. Born in Greenville, South Carolina, in 1941, he left South Carolina to attend the University of Illinois in 1959, hoping that life in the North would prove less humiliating than life in the segregated South. It wasn't true. Following several bouts with racism, he returned to the South to attend North Carolina Agricultural and Technical College, where he starred on the football team and quickly emerged as a leader in the civil rights sit-ins in Greensboro, North Carolina. After earning a bachelor's degree in sociology, Jackson entered Chicago Theological Seminary, where he was ordained as a Baptist minister in 1968. An activist in the Southern Christian Leadership Conference since 1965, Jackson founded Operation PUSH (People United to Save Humanity) in 1971 in order to further the cause of human rights around the globe and to help the poor develop strategies to rise out of poverty.

Although Jackson was consistently described by the media as representing a "black agenda," his campaign and platform reflected the interests of many different groups. His staff included environmentalists, feminists, and labor organizers as well as black and Latino grass-roots community activists. The campaign encompassed so many different issues and different ethnic groups that Jackson dubbed it the "Rainbow Coalition." Most importantly, Jackson brought to the Presidential race a vision for a new America that challenged politics as usual. In a speech before the Democratic National Convention in 1984, he issued the following challenge to a new generation of Americans:

> Young people, dream of a new value system. Dream of teachers, but teachers who will teach for life, not just for a living. Dream of doctors, but doc-

tors who are more concerned with public health than personal wealth. Dream of lawyers, but lawyers who are more concerned with justice than a judgeship ... of authentic leaders who will mold public opinion against a headwind, not just ride the tailwinds of opinion polls.

In spite of Jackson's vision, support from mainstream black politicians within the Democratic party was slow in coming because many believed a vote for Jackson would undermine efforts to beat the incumbent, Ronald Reagan. Jackson also maintained strained relations with the Jewish community, partly because he supported the right of Palestinians in Israel to have a homeland and because he would not repudiate his relationship with the Nation of Islam, especially NOI leader Louis Farrakhan. But the most damaging incident occurred with the publication of an anti-Semitic remark Jackson made in private, which virtually destroyed whatever Jewish support he had in 1984.

Despite these and other problems, Jackson ran a respectable campaign, winning several state primaries and caucuses and garnering 3.5 million popular votes. He lost the nomination to Walter Mondale (who was subsequently crushed by Ronald Reagan in a landslide election), but Jackson's Rainbow Coalition made some very important strides. Its massive voter registration drive brought hundreds of thousands of new voters—notably African Americans and Latinos—into the Democratic party. He also gave the struggle against apartheid in South Africa far more visibility than it had had before and sharply criticized U.S. military intervention in Central America and the Caribbean.

By the time the 1988 election rolled around, more and more Democrats had come to realize that Jackson was a serious candidate. In spite of several impressive showings in a number of states, he again lost the nomination—this time to Michael Dukakis, the governor of Massachusetts. Dukakis was in turn defeated by George Bush, Ronald Reagan's Vice President. In one of the most viciously race-tainted campaigns in U.S history, Bush attacked Dukakis as "soft on crime" because under Dukakis's administration in Massachusetts a black man named Willie Horton had been paroled from prison and subsequently committed a rape. The image of black men as criminal rapists out to violate white women was an old theme that tapped into the already heightened racial fears of white Americans. The infamous Willie Horton ads not only helped secure Bush's victory but proved once again the power of race to shape American politics.

"One Nation under a Groove": African-American Culture since 1970

As the seventies opened, the cultural revolution born in the sixties had reached its height then slowly sputtered out. Afros and dashikis—loose shirts made of bright African fabrics—were the style of the day. The music was soul, and James Brown was still the Godfather—even if his record sales had declined a bit from his peak

Afrika Bambaataa (front), pictured here with his group, the Soul Sonic Force, was an early pioneer of rap music, integrating European electronic dance music with South Bronx hip-hop. He also founded the Zulu Nation in the 1970s—a politically conscious organization of rappers, break dancers, graffiti artists, and others associated with hip-hop culture.

years in the late sixties. Even the "ghetto" was a place to be proud of, a place where pure soul could be found. By the end of the decade, however, things got to be a lot more complicated. As the language of soul and Black Power began to fade, black music crossed over to white listeners and more black faces appeared on television shows about family life.

As in virtually every previous era, African-American culture stood at the center of American life. But more than ever, this culture was extremely diverse, reflecting generational and class differences within black communities. In the late twentieth century, there seemed to be less agreement about "how to be black" than at any other period since the first generation of African captives—with their many different cultural and linguistic backgrounds—arrived on these shores.

Black popular music in the seventies is often described as "crossover" because it either adopted elements of other nonblack musical styles or was deliberately produced in a way that would attract white audiences. In a period when the sounds and scenes of urban rebellion slowly faded from the evening news, and when at least some sections of American society were becoming more and more racially integrated, the very idea of "crossover" seemed to be a fitting label. Of course, black popular music has always "crossed over"—from the popularity of jazz among urban whites in the twenties to the irreverent sounds of Chuck Berry and Little Richard in the fifties.

From 1968 to the early seventies, one of the most revolutionary "crossover" bands was Sly and the Family Stone. The first major pop band to be integrated by race and sex, it combined the heavy-bass line associated with James Brown (also known as funk music) with rock to create a new sound that appealed to black and white audiences. The lyrics explored political themes, particularly in songs such as "Everyday People," "Thank You for Talkin' to Me Africa," and "Stand!"

An even more poignant example of a crossover musician is Jimi Hendrix, the Seattle-born master of the electric guitar. Although he died quite young in 1970, Hendrix paved the way for greater black involvement in heavy metal. A major figure in the heavy metal and psychedelic rock movements, Hendrix did not shy away from political themes; his instrumental version of "The Star Spangled Banner," which evoked powerful images of war, suffering, and anger within the United States, is still a classic example of late-sixties protest music.

As the militant mood of the late sixties died down, and as black radio stations attracted more and more white listeners, black artists developed styles that reflected the changing times. The Philadelphia-based songwriting team of Kenny Gamble and Leon Huff gave birth to a new musical format known as "soft soul." Utilizing orchestral arrangements, lots of ballads, and a very smooth rhythmic pulse, they created a pop sound that quickly became popular in discotheques—dance clubs where records replaced live bands—across the country. Some of the more famous examples of the Gamble and Huff sound include Harold Melvin and the Blue Notes' "If You Don't Know Me By Now," and the O'Jays' "Love Train."

Disco had its roots in black and Latino dance music, and its strongest links were to the gay community. Indeed, the rise of disco coincided with the gay liberation movement and the push for open expressions of homosexuality. One of the most important places for "coming out" happened to be the multiracial underground dance clubs and ballroom dancing dance halls. These were places where performers such as Sylvester, a black gay disco singer, adopted feminine or "camp" stage presences much like Little Richard had done two decades before. The Village People, a multiracial group of gay men, made a big splash parodying macho culture and attitudes. While these performers made it big well beyond the gay community, lesser known artists who were even more explicit about their sexuality rarely got contracts with big record companies. In fact, the first major record label to release a disco song with an explicitly gay theme was Motown; in 1978 it recorded Carl Bean's "I Was Born This Way."

Initially, early disco artists did not get much air time on the radio, although their music was popular in the clubs. The first groups to cross over into radio include the Hues Corporation with "Rock the Boat" (1974) and the extremely popular Donna Summer tune, "Love to Love you Baby" (1975). As disco became more popular among whites, it also became "upscale" and trendier. New York disco clubs moved to expensive downtown locations that often refused to admit poor black and Puerto Rican youths. By the late seventies, however, disco had become so much a part of the white mainstream that the media ultimately dubbed the Bee Gees, a British group, the kings of disco.

The irony for black artists and audiences was that, while black musicians were losing precious radio airplay to disco music performed by whites, all dance music began declining in popularity. As more and more radio stations specializing in heavy metal adopted anti-disco slogans, the fortunes of black performers declined considerably in the larger world of popular music. A telling case in point is Music Television, better known as MTV. Launched in 1981, when the disco craze was beginning to wane, MTV started out playing only rock music videos, which targeted MTV's main audience of suburban white youth. In 1983, only sixteen of the eight hundred videos in rotation were by black artists—mainly performers like Prince, who had a large rock-fan following. MTV executives began to rethink their strategy after Michael Jackson released *Thriller,* which sold 33 million albums worldwide, and Prince released a succession of big-selling albums. It was the massive popularity of rap music, however, that compelled MTV to place more black artists in rotation. In the process, the corporate executives and marketing experts finally realized that their "target audience" was more diverse in both background and tastes than they had realized.

Meanwhile, as disco moved up from the underground and artists like Prince moved "crossover" music to still another level of sophistication, the African-American underground scene took on new dimensions. George Clinton revolutionized black music despite the fact that he had virtually no big sellers or Top 40 hits. Leading groups like Parliament and Funkadelic, Clinton expanded Sly Stone's fusion of rock and soul and built on James Brown's funk style to create music whose impact was still being felt two decades later. With albums such as *Maggot Brain, Chocolate City, America Eats Its Young,* and *One Nation Under a Groove,* the

Parliament/Funkadelic family not only introduced a complex, improvisational style to pop music but retained a black nationalist edge that had all but disappeared in the mid-seventies.

Some of George Clinton's biggest followers could be found in the parks and school yards of New York, among poor African-American, West Indian, and Puerto Rican kids who were themselves at the forefront of a cultural revolution. Known to the world at large as hip-hop, this predominantly black and Latino youth culture included rap music, graffiti art, and break dancing, as well as the language and dress styles that have come to be associated with the hip-hop generation.

The oldest component of hip-hop culture is graffiti. Of course, wall writing goes back centuries, from political slogans and gang markings to romantic declarations. But the aerosol art movement was quite different. Calling themselves writers, graffiti artists, aerosol artists, and subterranean guerrilla artists, the kids who started this art form in the early seventies came from a variety of different ethnic groups and neighborhoods throughout the city of New York. Subway trains provided the most popular canvases. Writers often "bombed" the interiors of trains with "tags"—quickly executed and highly stylized signatures, often made with fat markers rather than spray cans. Outside the trains they created "masterpieces," elaborate works of art carefully conceived and designed ahead of time. Incorporating logos and images borrowed from TV and comic books, stylistic signatures, and inventive lettering techniques—bubble letters, angular machine letters, and the very complex "wild style"—the best aerosol artists produced complicated compositions using a vast array of colors.

By the late seventies, the Metropolitan Transit Authority in New York City was spending $400,000 per year cleaning the trains and added 24 million dollars worth of ribbon wire fencing designed to ensnare and shred the body or object attempting to cross it. Ironically, while the MTA largely succeeded in keeping the trains graffiti-free, aerosol art exploded throughout other parts of the city and spread across the world during the eighties and 1990s. Tags became commonplace in most cities and masterpieces continued to pop up on the sides of housing projects, school yards, abandoned buildings and plants, under bridges, and inside tunnels that service commuter trains.

Rap music is clearly the most enduring and profitable component of hip-hop culture. Although rap music as we know it originated in New York during the seventies, it has a long prehistory in African-American culture that can be traced back to preaching, singing the blues, the rhyming styles of black radio DJs, and toasting (oral stories performed in rhyme that are usually humorous but often filled with explicit sex and violence). But what made hip-hop music unique was the technology: DJs and producers transformed oral traditions by adding electronic drum machines, turntables, mixers, and, later, digital samplers. (Sampling is the practice of incorporating portions of other records, or different sounds, into a new recording.)

Soon the parks, school yards, and underground clubs throughout New York were overrun with DJs. One important figure was Grandmaster Flash, who is credited with inventing "scratching" or back-cueing records on the turntable to create a new percussive sound. The DJs were followed by MCs (meaning "masters of ceremony," though they were much more than that) whose job was to keep the crowd moving and the parties "jumping." The early MCs often relied on call and response from the audience. A common phrase might be, "Just throw ya hands in the air / and wave 'em like ya just don't care / if your man has on clean underwear / somebody say 'oh yea.'" These simple party phrases became more complicated rhymes, and by the late seventies MCs, or rappers, were as much a part of hip-hop music as the DJs themselves. By 1977, Harlem and the Bronx claimed several pioneering rap groups: Double Trouble, The Treacherous Three, The Funky Four Plus One, Grandmaster Flash and the Furious Five, and Afrika Bambaata and his various groups. However, the first commercial rap hit, "Rapper's Delight" by the Sugar Hill Gang, was not recorded until 1979.

Women had been part of the hip-hop underground from its origins. Some of the pioneering New York women rappers include Lady B, Sweet T, Lisa Lee, Sha Rock, the Mercedes Ladies, Sula, and Sequence. But popular women artists such as Sequence or Roxanne Shante were often treated as novelty groups instead of legitimate rappers, despite the fact that the first wave of women rappers displayed skills equal to the best of the male rappers. Because rap was portrayed as "the voice of the ghetto," the tough street culture associated with men, women were discriminated against by promoters who believed they could not sell many records. It was not until the appearance of Salt N' Pepa, and later MC Lyte and Queen Latifah, that women rappers gained legitimacy and respect. Like female MCs who came after and before them, they challenged the notion that boasting and profanity were distinctly "men's talk."

Although early rap artists were known for their humorous or boasting lyrics, groups such as Grandmaster Flash also recorded songs such as "White Lines" and "The Message" that critiqued contemporary racism, poverty, police brutality, and drug use. Out of that tradition emerged dozens of rap groups devoted to radical political themes, including Public Enemy, KRS-1, Brand Nubians, and the X-Clan. Other groups, such as the so-called "gangsta rappers" dominant on the West Coast, produced chilling stories of modern "bad men," tales of street life, police brutality, crime, and domination over women.

Though not all rappers were driven by political and social themes, the use of profanity and sexually explicit lyrics pushed several rap groups into the center of controversy. In 1990, for instance, 2-Live Crew became a symbol for those who wanted to protect freedom of speech under the First Amendment after obscenity laws were vigorously enforced in several states to ban sale of their recordings as well as live performances. In 1993, several black community groups, led by the Reverend Calvin Butts of the Abyssinian Baptist Church in New York and representatives of various African-American women's organizations, denounced "gangsta rap" for its offensive, violent, and sexist lyrics. The backlash against rap music, in fact, spurred congressional hearings to investigate the matter.

Despite these attacks, hip-hop was clearly a dominant force in American popular music by the millennium's end. It had grown in several different directions and developed its own subgroups, incorporating elements of Jamaican reggae, jazz, punk rock, and heavy metal. Hip-hop even sparked a literary revival among young people, causing an explosion in "spoken word" performances all over the world. Black and Latino poets such as Tracie Morris, Saul Williams, Carl Hancock Rux, and Jessica Care Moore rose directly out of hip-hop culture to publish, perform, and record works that have earned international acclaim.

Hip-hop might be the newest addition to the world of black music, but it is successful precisely because it draws on what came before. Jazz continued to be a mainstay in African-American culture, and its popularity seemed to have skyrocketed in the eighties and nineties. Modern jazz experienced a kind of renaissance with the overnight success of trumpeter Wynton Marsalis and his brother, saxophonist Branford Marsalis, and the return of trumpeter and jazz pioneer Miles Davis (who had retired in 1975). Despite its renewed success, by the early nineties the jazz world was sharply divided. On one side stood the "purists," strong advocates of more traditional jazz forms, or what is often called "repertory jazz." The strongest voice for the maintenance of tradition has been the Jazz at Lincoln Center Orchestra and the Smithsonian Jazz Masterpiece Ensemble. These ensembles highlight the music of major jazz composers, notably Louis Armstrong, Duke Ellington, and Thelonious Monk.

On the other side stood musicians who experiment with "free jazz" or incorporate rock, funk, and hip-hop in their music. Artists as varied as saxaphonists Steve Coleman, Ravi Coltrane, and David Murray, pianist Geri Allen, trombonist Craig Harris, clarinetist Don Byron, cornetist Graham Haynes, and vocalist Cassandra Wilson continued to work in the jazz tradition but were not afraid to mix musical genres. Composers such as Anthony Davis, T. J. Anderson, and Olly Wilson ushered in a revolution by bringing together jazz, blues, and other black musical forms with opera and symphonic music. Working with librettist/poet/novelist Thulani Davis, Anthony Davis won international acclaim for operas such as *X: The Life and Times of Malcolm X*(1985) and *Amistad* (1998). Greg Osby and Joshua Redman were among the more prominent young artists to fuse jazz and hip-hop, although some veterans, including vibist Roy Ayers, trumpeter Donald Byrd, and drummer Max Roach, had also moved in this direction.

Musicians such as Graham Haynes, Don Byron, and Geri Allen represented a new generation of black artists who resisted categories, who embraced all kinds of music from classical to rock. They joined other like-minded artists in the Black Rock Coalition (BRC). Founded in 1985 by guitarist Vernon Reid (formerly of Living Colour), writer Greg Tate, and artist/manager Konda Mason, the BRC attracted a wide range of musicians, writers, and artists committed to working collectively, improving conditions for black performers in the music industry, and breaking down barriers that limit black musicians to certain genres (jazz, soul, hip-hop, for example). BRC members were activists, as well. According to their founding manifesto, they vowed to oppose "those racist and reactionary forces within the American music industry which deny Black artists the expressive freedom and economic rewards that our Caucasian counterparts enjoy as a matter of course."

Film and television has had a profound impact on race relations in the United States. In an age when segregation was becoming more entrenched, most Americans confronted black people through the big screen or their home television sets. The images of African Americans as violent, oversexed, lazy, and ignorant are as much a product of modern media as of old-fashioned racism. And yet, the same media can take credit for breaking down old stereotypes, for changing our ideas about history and creating a more complex image of what it means—or meant—to be black in the United States.

In the early seventies films about black ghetto life became extremely popular among black and white audiences alike. Often called "blaxploitation cinema," these films were less a response to black political radicalism of the era than the film industry's realization that African-American consumers were a potentially profitable market, particularly in urban areas where white flight to the suburbs left inner city theaters empty unless they catered to local audiences.

The signature film of that era was clearly Melvin Van Peebles's *Sweet Sweetback's Badasss Song* (1971). Shot on a shoestring budget in nineteen days, *Sweetback* quickly became the largest-grossing independent production up to that point—an amazing accomplishment when we consider the fact that it was rated X. In this film, Van Peebles plays a regular hustler whose bout with the police forces him to flee Los Angeles, always staying one step ahead of the cops, vigilantes, and attack dogs. His flight, assisted by ordinary community people, ultimately turns him into a rebel. Despite the mass appeal in the black community, *Sweetback* was attacked by black and white critics alike, who called it degrading, self-hating, and invidious.

What made *Sweetback* and films like it so popular to poor and working-class black audiences? Van Peebles and such black filmmakers as Gordon Parks, Sr., Gordon Parks, Jr., and Ivan Dixon generally focused on the lives of ghetto residents and emphasized racial pride, community solidarity, and Black Power. No matter how stereotyped the characters were, the people in "the streets" were constantly fighting back and winning. The police and government were the source of corruption, and even pimps, dope dealers, and petty criminals showed more morals than white authority.

Not all dramatic films about African Americans were set in the ghetto or emphasized violent revenge. *Sounder* (1972) was a "coming of age" film set in the rural South. Starring Cicely Tyson, Paul Winfield, and Kevin Hooks, it tells the story of a poor sharecropping family during the thirties struggling to make ends meet. Also

Gordon Parks, Sr., a noted photographer and writer, was the first African American to direct full-length feature films for a major Hollywood studio. His best known films are *Shaft* (1971), about a suave black detective, and *The Learning Tree* (1969), which Parks also wrote as a novel.

noteworthy was the highly acclaimed *Lady Sings the Blues* (1972), the moving story of jazz singer Billie Holiday's descent from being one of the most brilliant vocal stylists of the century to a heroin addict. And black cinema had its share of deeply sensitive love stories, such as *Claudine* and *Sparkle* (1976). Taken together, these films at least challenged the one-dimensional portrayal of African Americans created by the overload of blaxploitation cinema.

By the eighties, as the number of black-oriented films declined, the possible range of roles actually widened. Now black characters—mainly men—had more supporting roles in films where their race was incidental. Roles written with white actors in mind, such as Lou Gossett, Jr.'s part as a Marine drill sergeant in *An Officer and a Gentleman,* created new opportunities for black actors to reach a wider audience. Actors such as Billy Dee Williams, Richard Pryor, Morgan Freeman, Eddie Murphy, Denzel Washington, Alfre Woodard, and Whoopi Goldberg achieved superstardom in this new era. *A Soldier's Story* (1984), an intricate tale centering on the murder of an unpopular black army sergeant on a Louisiana military base during World War II, and *The Color Purple* (1985), a film about domestic violence, black male exploitation of black women, and lesbian encounters among black women, were two notable films of this era.

By the late eighties Hollywood's relationship with black films shifted yet again. One cause of this change was the appearance in 1986 of Spike Lee, a young black independent filmmaker just out of New York University's film school whose first feature film turned out to be a box-office smash. *She's Gotta Have It* was a comedy about a young black woman's search for romance and sexual freedom in the eighties and the three very different men to whom she was attracted.

The success of *She's Gotta Have It* and Lee's subsequent films did not suddenly compel Hollywood to take chances on young black filmmakers. What *did* make a difference was the rapid popularity of hip-hop in American culture, which convinced advertisers and the film industry alike that there was big money to be made in the music and styles of black urban youth. Rap producers were called in to make soundtracks and the ghetto, once again, became the favored backdrop for a new wave of films. But unlike the blaxploitation films of the seventies, the cult status of Spike Lee placed a greater premium on having young, black, and especially male directors.

Called by some critics the major example of the "new ghetto aesthetic," the film that opened up this new era was made by none other than Mario Van Peebles, the son of Melvin Van Peebles. *New Jack City* was not young Van Peebles' first film, but up to that point it was clearly his most successful, grossing over $40 million at the box office. In *New Jack City,* the story of the rise of a Harlem drug cartel and the crack cocaine industry it created, Van Peebles literally reverses his father's message of two decades before: in this story the black community is the problem and the police are the solution. The only black woman filmmaker to merit entrance into what otherwise is a boys' club of new directors was Leslie Harris, whose funny and gritty *Just Another Girl on the IRT* was underdistributed and largely ignored by the critics.

By the mid- to late nineties, the "new ghetto aesthetic" began to slowly give way to more complicated, epic films drawing on African-American history. Spike Lee's *Malcolm X* (1994), starring Denzel Washington, gave viewers a spectacular visual history of postwar urban America and the Nation of Islam. Steven Spielberg explored the depths of the transatlantic slave trade and the heroic traditions of American abolitionism in *Amistad* (1997), and the following year Jonathan Demme put Toni Morrison's magical and terrifying Pulitzer Prize–winning novel *Beloved* on the big screen. All of these films generated debates over questions of historical accuracy, historical and contemporary representations of black people, the ability of white filmmakers to make "black films," and the willingness of nonblack audiences to see films about black subjects. Although the subject of slavery has been a central theme in American history—a theme that has affected all Americans—many viewers insisted that these films were primarily intended for black audiences.

The blaxploitation film craze did not translate to television so easily. Attempts to turn blaxploitation films into TV serials, notably "Get Christie Love" (1974–75), "Shaft" (1973–74), and "Tenafly" (1973–74), were flops. "The Flip Wilson Show" (1970–74), the first popular black show of the decade, was created with white audiences in mind. Using a comedy/variety show format, Wilson often played characters that relied on common stereotypes of African Americans. Sitcoms popular during the seventies, such as "Good Times," "What's Happenin'," "That's My Mama," and "Sanford and Son" focused on black working-class life, offering a slightly more sympathetic account of humor and perseverance in an age of rising unemployment, poverty, and violence.

The successful dramatic shows rarely appeared as serials. Rather, TV specials such as "The Autobiography of Miss Jane Pittman" (1974), the personal saga of an elderly black woman who lived most of her life under segregation, and the miniseries "Roots" (1977) based on Alex Haley's historical novel tracing his family from slavery to freedom, captured the attention of broad television audiences.

However one TV series, "The Cosby Show," which premiered in 1984, dramatically changed black television. Against TV executives' assumptions, Bill Cosby created a black middle-class family free of old stereotypes, yet capable of entertaining millions of Americans of all ethnic and racial backgrounds. The show centered around Cosby, who played a congenial doctor named Cliff Huxtable, his five children, and his wife Claire, a successful attorney played by Phylicia Rashad. Though "The Cosby Show" was often criticized for ignoring race or painting too rosy a picture of black life, it subtly introduced issues such as the civil rights movement and apartheid in South Africa without making them central to the story. Moreover, given the then-dominant images of African Americans as an "underclass" with broken families, it is no accident that the show emphasized black middle-class success, a stable and unified black family, and high morals. And by dealing with universal issues, notably the problems of parenting, it invited audiences from different backgrounds to identify with the Huxtables.

For black writers and artists, "What is black?" has been a never-ending question. The post-1970 generation of fiction writers continued to turn to African-American history for ideas, inspiration, and insights into contemporary issues they wished to explore in their art. But many more began recovering the dark side of black life—domestic violence, psychological trauma, the internal conflicts that rarely show up in heroic stories of black achievement. Others turned to satire, laughing at aspects of black culture and the absurdity of race.

Though this sort of self-criticism is hardly new to black literature, it became more visible in the post–civil rights era. Like most African Americans, black artists were products of a rapidly changing world in which defining one's culture or identity seemed more complicated than ever. An increasing number of middle-class African Americans raised their children in integrated settings. West Indians and Latinos of African descent, many of whom migrated to the United States after 1965, reminded other African Americans that all black people do not share the same ethnic heritage. Black gays and lesbians began to come out publicly, insisting on basic civil rights, respect and recognition for their sexual orientation, and a place in African-American history and culture. Black feminists grew increasingly vocal in African-American political, cultural, and intellectual life.

Partly an outgrowth of the resurgence of black feminism, black women writers such as Toni Cade Bambara, Rita Dove, Audre Lorde, Toni Morrison, Gloria Naylor, Ntozake Shange, Alice Walker, and Sherley Anne Williams brilliantly approached the subjects of sexism, domestic violence, and other forms of women's oppression. Through fiction, poetry, and political essays, these writers gave voice to the concerns and experiences of women, literally writing them into history. They challenged the trend among the previous generation of black nationalist writers to focus on men. And they revealed a complicated history of gender and family conflict that rarely found its way into history books, let alone African-American fiction.

In the process, these women writers set new standards for creative writing. Gloria Naylor won the American Book Award for her first novel, *Women of Brewster Place* (1983); Ntozake Shange's highly acclaimed play, *For Colored Girls Who Have Considered Suicide/When the Rainbow is Enuf* (1976), received several awards, including the coveted Obie Award; Alice Walker's *The Color Purple* (1982) won both the American Book Award and the Pulitzer Prize.

Out of this generation of black women writers emerged one of the late twentieth century's most celebrated novelists, Pulitzer Prize winner and Nobel Laureate Toni Morrison. Born Chloe Anthony Wofford in 1931, Morrison grew up in Lorain, Ohio. After earning a B.A. from Howard University and a master's degree in literature from Cornell University, she taught briefly at Texas Southern University in Houston and then returned to Howard University in 1957. In 1966 she left academia to become an editor at Random House, spending whatever free time she had on her fiction writing. *Beloved* (1987), her fifth novel, was a masterpiece— one of the most important literary achievements of the century. This beautifully written and very complicated novel about slavery, family life, and memory won the Pulitzer Prize for fiction. Throughout her writing, Morrison has turned to black culture and history as a way to explore the diversity of the human experience in the context of both love and hate, degradation and defiance, community and individualism. In 1993 she received the Nobel Prize for Literature.

Since the seventies and eighties, several black writers have finally been recognized in genres in which African Americans have tended to be overlooked. By the early nineties, for example, one of the country's most popular crime-detective novelists was black, Los Angeles author Walter Mosley. Each of the books in his trilogy, *White Butterfly, A Red Death,* and *Devil in a Blue Dress,* were instant successes. In the field of science fiction, Samuel Delany and Octavia Butler won major literary prizes for their work. They turned to the future rather than the past to explore issues of race, gender, and sexuality in contemporary society. Delany, a prolific author of sixteen novels and novellas and at least five nonfiction books, twice won the coveted Nebula Award from the Science Fiction Writers of America. Octavia Butler published nine novels between 1976 and 1989, and her novella, *Bloodchild,* won both the Hugo Award and the Nebula Award in 1985. Her first series of novels actually linked the ancient African past to the future; its central characters include African healers, a four-thousand-year-old Nubian "psychic vampire," and a variety of powerful, independent black women.

In the world of visual arts, earlier generations of artists—collagist Romare Bearden, painters Jacob Lawrence, Elizabeth Catlett, Robert Colescott, and sculptor Martin Puryear—continued to have a huge influence on the American art scene throughout the seventies and eighties. More recently, black artists have deliberately broken with traditional conventions like painting and sculpture. Acclaimed sculptor David Hammons playfully used objects such as human hair, chicken parts, watermelon, and elephant dung to comment on racial stereotypes and African-American culture. Faith Ringgold, a Harlem-born painter and political activist, turned to the older "folk" tradition of quilting as her primary medium in the early eighties. Adrian Piper has used photography, as well as drawings, texts, collage, and video technology, to bring out and thoroughly challenge her audience's racial fears and attitudes. A fair-skinned African-American woman who can sometimes "pass" as white, Piper made use of her own body to question people's assumptions about who is black and who is not.

The nineties witnessed the emergence of a younger generation of artists who turned to photography, painting, collage, sculpture, video, and performance to explore controversial aspects of race, gender, and sexuality. By revisiting stereotypes, exploring diversity within black communities, and turning to the interior, often hidden dimensions of black life, artists such as Dawoud Bey, Michael Ray Charles, Ellen Gallagher, Lyle Ashton Harris, Kerry James Marshall, Alison Saar, Gary Simmons, Lorna Simpson, Kara Walker, and Carrie Mae Weems have expanded what it means to be black in America.

Called by one critic "the post-soul era," black culture since the seventies seems limitless in range and depth. Never before have there been so many different ways to be black, so much so that even those who mimic African-American culture have had a difficult time trying to decide what to copy. The history of black culture in the late twentieth century is living proof that "blackness" has been—and will continue to be—multicultural.

"Ain't No Stopping Us Now": Black Politics at the End of the Century

For African Americans, the end of the twentieth century looks very much like the end of the nineteenth century. The sixties and seventies, like the eighteen-sixties and seventies, were decades of immense struggle and high expectations. Emancipation of sorts had been achieved and black communities looked to each other, and occasionally to the federal government, to help them secure their freedom. Most black people were optimistic. And they had a right to be, especially as they approached the nineties. The successful mayoral bids by Michael White in Cleveland, Sharon Pratt Dixon in Washington, D.C., and David Dinkins in New York City were not only indicative of the growing political strength of African Americans in major metropolitan areas but proved that black politicians were capable of winning over large numbers of white voters. This was certainly the case with Douglas Wilder's historic election as governor of Virginia in 1989; he became the first African American elected governor of any state. The same can be said of the successful mayoral campaigns of Norman Rice in Seattle, the Reverend Emmanuel Cleaver in Kansas City, and Wellington Webb in Denver. In all three cities, the majority of voters were white.

Yet despite these impressive gains, in 1988 blacks comprised only 1.5 percent of all elected officials, more than half of whom served on local school boards or city or town councils. Moreover, in many other respects the situation for African Americans actually worsened. Aside from the economic disaster caused by the loss of decent-paying jobs, reductions in social spending, and the decline in government subsidies to cities, racism and racist violence against African Americans actually intensified.

Since 1990, black customers and employees have filed suits against several nationally known restaurants for discrimination. In December 1991, for example, a group of black college students successfully sued an International House of Pancakes in Milwaukee, Wisconsin, for refusing to seat them. They were told that the restaurant was closed, though white customers were allowed in. The most notorious case involved Denny's restaurants. After the U.S. Department of Justice discovered a pattern of discrimination in the Denny's chain in 1993, Denny's corporate executives agreed to provide its employees with special training in nondiscriminatory behavior and to include more minorities in its advertising. Yet, in spite of these attempts to change its corporate behavior, Denny's continued to discriminate against black customers. In one striking case that led to a separate lawsuit, six black Secret Service agents patronizing a Denny's in Annapolis, Maryland, waited an hour for service while the white customers, including their fellow white agents, were served promptly. Other instances of discrimination frequently encountered by African Americans occur when shop owners refuse to open their doors to black customers.

Some of the Denny's employees who testified suggested that this kind of treat-

ment of black customers was part of the company's rational efforts to reduce rob-
beries and disruptive behavior. The fear of crime and the presumption that black
people are more likely than whites to commit crime, regardless of their age or class
background, has led retail outlets to adopt blatantly discriminatory measures. For
example, in several cities, one must ring a buzzer in order to be admitted to certain
stores during business hours. If the customer looks legitimate, the salesperson,
manager, or security guard admits him or her. Not surprisingly, African-American
patrons are frequently left outside to window shop.

Such incidents, compounded by the impoverishment of a large segment of the
black population, compelled African Americans to question the costs and benefits
of integration. This never-ending battle with white racism convinced some former
advocates of integration to turn inward, to build separate black institutions. Others
believed integration has failed precisely because the new generation of black youth
did not have a sense of history and pride in their cultural heritage. They insisted
that the perspectives and experiences of African Americans be represented in classrooms, boardrooms, and political arenas. They saw no contradiction in celebrating
their African heritage and participating as equals in the white world.

Not surprisingly, black nationalism has made a comeback among the nineties
generation—the sons and daughters of the sixties generation. The militant nationalist and Muslim leader Malcolm X emerged as the decade's central black hero.
Kinte cloth (a colorful and intricately woven West African fabric), beads, and
leather medallions with outlines of Africa became popular consumer items. On
many college campuses more and more young people could be seen wearing
dreadlocks (twists of hair worn long and uncombed) and sporting T-shirts bearing such slogans as "Black by Popular Demand" or "Black to the Future." Membership in the Nation of Islam and other black Muslim groups rose dramatically
during the late eighties and nineties.

In fact, during much of the 1990s, Minister Louis Farrakhan of the Nation of
Islam enjoyed an upsurge of national and international popularity. He not only
became a political force to be reckoned with among black leaders, but on October
16, 1995, he did what many said could not be done: he drew nearly one million
African-American men to the nation's capital to pray, be in fellowship with one
another, atone for their sins, and pledge to take responsibility for leadership in
their communities and families. As Minister Farrakhan explained, the main purpose of the march was to "declare to the Government of America and the world
that we are ready to take our place as the head of our families and our communities and that we, as Black men, are ready to take responsibility for being the main-
tainers of our women and children and the builders of our communities." While it
would be inaccurate to call the Million Man March a "protest," some of the speeches did criticize racism in the U.S. and lamented the erosion of the welfare system,
and Farrakhan himself explained that the increase in the black prison population
is related to the fact that prisons have become big business.

Even if the march did not produce a clear and concise political agenda, its powerful spiritual and emotional impact was undeniable. At the very least, the march spurred many men to become active in political organizations, trade unions, and community groups, and prompted a dialogue throughout African-American communities about the state of gender relations. It also inspired a Million Woman March in Philadelphia (October 25, 1997), and a Million Youth March in Atlanta and Harlem (September 5 and 25, 1998). Neither one of these gatherings attracted as many participants as the Million Man March, but they each articulated a more explicit political agenda. The women's gathering provided a forum to discuss, among other things, federal policies that adversely affect poor women, human rights abuses, and the need to establish more independent black schools. The youth march, led in New York by controversial ex-NOI minister Khalid Muhammad, was conceived both as an act of atonement as well as a political mobilization to protest racism, the deterioration of neighborhoods and schools, the decline in job opportunities, and police brutality. This otherwise peaceful event ended in violence when new York Mayor Rudolf Giuliani ordered the police to attack the crowd. Khalid Muhammad, who had exacerbated tensions between the crowd and police by inciting black youth to "take their guns" and then rushing from the scene of the protest, lost some respect among many of his young followers. When he attempted to organize another march one year later, it turned out to be a dismal failure. Nevertheless, taken together these marches proved that African Americans were prepared to come together for the sake of the entire community; it demonstrated the capacity for a renewed black grassroots social movement.

One important outgrowth of the upsurge in black nationalist sentiment has been the popularity of "Afrocentrism." Although there are many varieties of Afrocentric thought, the concept might best be described as a way of thinking and a type of scholarship that looks at the world from an African/African-American perspective. A good deal of Afrocentric scholarship argues that black people have a distinctive way of doing things, a set of cultural values and practices that are unique to their African heritage. Some scholars, such as Temple University professor Molefi Asante, locate the origins of this distinctive African culture in the ancient African civilization of Egypt, and offer prescriptions for maintaining this Afrocentric way of life. Some black educators and parents have called for the incorporation of an Afrocentric curriculum in public schools. Others have turned to independent schools emphasizing Afrocentrism. The number of such schools has grown dramatically during the eighties and nineties, particularly in major cities such as Detroit, Washington, D.C., Los Angeles, and Oakland.

Though Afrocentrism and varieties of black nationalism are associated with radicalism, these philosophies share much in common with those of conservatives. Molefi Asante, for example, has been sharply criticized for arguing that an Afrocentric lifestyle includes distinct roles for men and women and that homosexuality is a form of deviance. Black Christian conservatives agree. Organizations such as Project 21, Concerned Citizens for Traditional Family Values, and the Traditional

Values Coalition, and publications such as the *Black Chronicle* have mobilized conservative African Americans to protest legislation that would protect gay and lesbian rights and to attack the NAACP and the National Urban League for defending the rights of homosexuals.

Black feminists too have been attacked by Afrocentrists, black nationalists, and black conservatives who have called for a return to traditional male-female roles and placed a good deal of blame for the behavior of young black males squarely on the shoulders of single mothers, whom they characterize as irresponsible and incapable of disciplining their sons. One of the most controversial and best-known books to attack African-American feminists was *The Blackman's Guide to Understanding the Blackwoman* (1989). Written by a woman, Shahrazad Ali, a formerly unknown black street vendor of Afrocentric products, this vastly popular book caricatured black women as selfish, power-hungry, aggressive, manipulating, and even dirty. Ali argued that true liberation required that black women return to their traditional African roles as child-care givers and supporters of black men.

The backlash against poor black women has had an even greater impact on social policies. The image of poor black women as promiscuous, highly irresponsible single mothers who spend years and years receiving welfare became increasingly popular in the late eighties and nineties. Although studies show that most women receive assistance for very short periods of time as a transitional stage between jobs, and many who do receive aid must nevertheless work part-time to make ends meet, the image of welfare cheats and overweight, indulgent, lazy black mothers was far more common among white voters. It was so pervasive that many liberal Democrats joined forces with Republicans to call for dramatic changes in public assistance. In fact, some of the most far-reaching changes in social welfare were initiated after George Bush was defeated by Democrat Bill Clinton in the 1992 Presidential race.

In 1996 Clinton signed into law the Personal Responsibility and Work Opportunity Reconciliation Act, which replaced Aid to Families with Dependent Children (AFDC) with state block grants, denied benefits to legal immigrants, and cut funding for low-income programs, such as food stamps and Supplemental Security Income (SSI)—a program targeted to the elderly and disabled poor. The law was intended to force welfare recipients into the labor market, but it did not take into account the needs of children. Under the new law, for example, recipients whose youngest child is more than a year old must do some form of paid or unpaid work after twenty-four months of receiving benefits or lose their benefits altogether. And those who fail to find jobs within two months of receiving assistance are required to enroll in a mandatory workfare program. The Personal Resposibility Act does not include higher education in its definition of work or "training programs"; rather, welfare recipients are limited to vocational programs approved by the state. Furthermore, anyone convicted of a drug felony cannot receive direct aid or welfare for life.

The simmering backlash against African-American women and the efforts on the part of black feminists to reverse the trend were powerfully dramatized by a single event: the confirmation of Supreme Court Justice Clarence Thomas. A story of race, sex, and political intrigue, it was perhaps the biggest media spectacle of 1991. What began as a fairly routine and friendly hearing suddenly became a national scandal when the Senate Judiciary Committee called University of Oklahoma law professor Anita Hill to testify. Hill had worked for Thomas when he was with the Department of Education and later when he headed the Equal Employment Opportunities Commission. During the questioning, she revealed that Thomas had sexually harassed her—pestering her to go out on dates, bragging about his sexual prowess, and making explicit references to pornography.

Thomas's description of himself as a God-fearing, hard-working, self-made black man contrasted sharply with Hill's characterization of him as an avid consumer of pornography. Born in the little rural town of Pin Point, Georgia, he was raised by grandparents and attended Catholic schools most of his life. After earning a bachelor's degree from Holy Cross and a law degree from Yale University, he was hired as assistant attorney general for the state of Missouri in 1974, and in 1981 was appointed assistant secretary in the Office of Civil Rights in the Department of Education. In 1982 he accepted the chairmanship of the EEOC, which he held until 1990. The Reagan administration chose Thomas for these two important posts precisely because he opposed affirmative action and had criticized established civil rights leadership. His leadership of the EEOC effectively weakened the commission's role in combating discrimination on the basis of race, age, and sex.

Thomas's appointment to the Supreme Court was especially important for African Americans because he was to replace retiring Justice Thurgood Marshall— the first African American to serve on the Court. The Congressional Black Caucus and several other black leaders outside of the government came out strongly against Thomas because of his lack of judicial and intellectual qualifications and his staunch conservatism. Though himself a beneficiary of Yale University's affirmative action initiative to recruit more minority law students, Thomas opposed affirmative action, supported cutbacks in social programs geared to help the poor, and consistently attacked civil rights leadership.

When the confirmation hearings began, most black voters knew very little about Thomas or his views. Many African Americans who backed the confirmation of Thomas, for example, did not know that his actions within the EEOC eroded black civil rights substantially. Thomas's initial testimony and the White House press releases focused on his personal biography, emphasizing how he worked his way up from rural poverty to a successful career as an attorney and a judge. But lack of information is only part of the story. Many African Americans sided with Thomas simply because he was a black man about to hold one of the most powerful positions in the country. By emphasizing his impoverished rural upbringing he gained a sympathetic hearing from blacks eager to see a black man succeed. More importantly, he gained a sympathetic hearing from Democratic senators who were afraid to ask critical questions about his views on affirmative action and civil rights. Whenever these issues came up, Thomas would insist that he had an especially sensitive understanding of them because of his life as a black man from segregated Georgia.

While Anita Hill's allegations could have disgraced Thomas and cost him the nomination, they actually worked in his favor. Many African Americans dismissed Professor Hill as a spurned lover or a black woman out to destroy a black man's career—a characterization not unlike Shahrazad Ali's bizarre assertion in *The Blackman's Guide to Understanding the Blackwoman* that black women sabotaged the upward mobility of black men. Tragically, the alleged victim of sexual harassment was turned into the villain. On the other hand, several polls and interviews reveal that a majority of African Americans believed both Thomas and Hill were victims of white racism. They believed that Hill was being used by the Senate committee to keep a black man from occupying one of the most powerful positions in the federal government. Thomas manipulated these underlying feelings by testifying before the Senate Judiciary Committee that the hearings were a "high tech lynching for uppity blacks who in any way deign to think for themselves." On October 16, 1991, the Senate voted 52–48 to confirm Clarence Thomas as an associate justice of the Supreme Court.

In spite of a high black approval rating for Thomas as measured by polls, many black people—especially women—were outraged by Thomas's confirmation. Several black feminist organizations and activist groups publicly criticized the appointment and used the hearings to draw attention to the issue of sexual harassment and the general backlash against women in the United States. Sixteen hundred black women signed a three-quarter page advertisement in *The New York Times* denouncing the appointment and explaining the significance of the hearings for black women. The ad highlighted the long history of racial and sexual abuse black women have had to endure, the lack of protection against such violations, and the perpetuation of stereotypes that continue to represent black women as sexually promiscuous and immoral.

Throughout the country, the Senate Judiciary Committee's behavior during the Hill-Thomas hearings sparked women's organizations to promote more women to run for public office. In 1992, more women ran for office than ever before, and the percentage of women who went to the polls rose markedly, representing fifty-four percent of the American electorate.

One woman inspired by the Hill-Thomas hearings to run for the U.S. Senate from the state of Illinois was Carol Moseley-Braun. Born in Chicago in 1947, Braun earned a bachelor's degree from the University of Illinois and a law degree from the University of Chicago in 1972. Upon graduation she worked as assistant U.S. attorney for the Northern District of Illinois, and later she won a seat in the Illinois state legislature and was elected Cook County recorder of deeds. Although she had very little money and an understaffed campaign team, Moseley-Braun beat incumbent Alan Dixon (who voted for Thomas's confirmation) in her 1992 U.S. Senate race, thereby becoming the first black woman to be elected to the U.S. Senate.

Though Moseley-Braun's election certainly benefited from women's response to the Hill-Thomas hearings, black women had already begun to have a greater presence in national politics in the late eighties. Perhaps the most dynamic and uncompromising black elected official to emerge on the national scene in this period was California congresswoman Maxine Waters. Born one of thirteen siblings in a housing project in St. Louis, Missouri, in 1938, she graduated from high school, got married, and took a number of low-paying jobs in order to make ends meet. She and her husband eventually moved to Los Angeles, where she worked in a garment factory and then for the telephone company. In the late sixties, Waters enrolled at California State University in Los Angeles, where she studied sociology, and then went on to teach in the Head Start program—a federally funded preschool program geared especially for poor and minority children.

Largely through her community work, Waters became involved in politics, winning a seat representing South Central Los Angeles in the state assembly in 1976. Her constant battles on the assembly floor produced some important pieces of legislation, including withdrawing investments of the California state pension fund from companies with ties to South Africa. Waters also established a vocational and education center in her district and increased access to social services for housing project residents in the Watts district. During this same period, she became active in national Democratic politics, serving as a key advisor to Jesse Jackson's 1984 Presidential campaign.

In 1990 Waters was elected to the U.S. Congress from the 29th district of California, becoming one of the most vocal African Americans in the House of Representatives. In 1991 she fought attempts to weaken laws requiring banks and savings and loans to service minority and low-income communities. In the aftermath of the riots that tore through Los Angeles in 1992, she emerged as the key spokeswoman for aggrieved residents of South Central Los Angeles. She and her staff organized residents of housing projects into carpools in order to get needed food, water, and other supplies that were unavailable during the uprising. Although she lamented the loss of life and destruction of property, she kept the issues surrounding the rebellion focused on the deteriorating social and economic conditions of African Americans and Latinos.

Not all significant political battles fought by African-American women took place in the sphere of electoral politics. Nor were they national in scope. Throughout the country poor, working-class, and some middle-class black women built and sustained community organizations that registered voters, patrolled the streets, challenged neighborhood drug dealers, and fought vigorously for improvements in housing, city services, health care, and public assistance. There was nothing new about black women taking the lead in community-based organizing. A century earlier, black women's clubs not only helped the less fortunate but played a key role in the political life of the African-American community. Even a generation earlier, when militant, predominantly male organizations like the Black Panther party and the Black Liberation Army received a great deal of press, black women carried on the tradition of community-based organizing. If one looked only at South Central Los Angeles in the mid-sixties, one would find well over a dozen such organizations, including the Watts Women's Association, the Avalon-Carver Community Center, the Mothers of Watts Community Action Council, Mothers Anonymous, the Welfare Recipients Union, the Welfare Rights Organization, the Central City Community Mental Health Center, the Neighborhood Organizations of Watts, and the South Central Volunteer Bureau of Los Angeles.

Black women activists continued the tradition of community organizing, but in the eighties and nineties they confronted new problems. Of the new battlegrounds, one of the most important has been the fight against toxic dumping in poor black communities. Calling themselves the movement against environmental racism or, alternately, the movement for environmental justice, local African-American, Latino, and Native American groups, led largely by women, have fought against companies and government institutions responsible for placing landfills, hazardous waste sites, and chemical manufacturers dangerously close to low-income minority communities.

The evidence that poor African-American and other minority communities are singled out for toxic waste sites is overwhelming. One study released in 1987 estimated that three out of five African Americans live perilously close to abandoned toxic waste sites and hazardous commercial waste landfills. The study also revealed that the largest hazardous waste landfill in the country is located in Emelle, Alabama, whose population is 78.9 percent black, and that the greatest concentration of hazardous waste sites is in the mostly black and Latino south side of Chicago. A 1992 study concluded that polluters based in minority areas are treated less severely by government agencies than those in largely white communities. Also, according to the report, federally sponsored toxic cleanup programs take longer and are less thorough in minority neighborhoods.

The effects of these policies have been devastating. Cases of asthma and other respiratory diseases as well as cancer have been traced to toxic waste. Accidents involving the mishandling of hazardous chemicals have ravaged some poor black communities, often with little or no publicity.

The roots of the environmental justice movement go back to 1982, when black and Native American residents tried to block state authorities from building a chemical disposal site in Warren County, North Carolina. Since then, dozens of local movements have followed suit, including the Concerned Citizens of South Central (Los Angeles), and the North Richmond West County Toxics Coalition (near Oakland, California). By demonstrating, holding hearings and public workshops, conducting research, and filing suits against local and state governments, these groups have tried to draw attention to the racial and class biases that determine how hazardous waste sites are selected.

In the political arena, the nineties for African Americans have truly been the best of times and the worst of times. Black gains in the electoral sphere accompanied growing incidents of racism in public places; successful grass-roots organizing followed discoveries of more toxic waste dumps; the spectacular rise of black women in national politics coincided with a vicious backlash against women in the society as a whole. And if this was not enough to complicate matters, the old order of black versus white was fast becoming obsolete. With the recent wave of immigration from nonwhite countries, African Americans found themselves surrounded by new neighbors, new cultures, and new issues with which they had to contend.

Black to the Future: Immigration and the New Realities of Race

While the decade of the nineties was a period of resurgent black nationalism, it also was a period when what it meant to be "black" no longer was a simple matter. By the eighties, the increase in black *immigrants* to the United States, most of whom came from the Caribbean, profoundly changed the cultural makeup of black communities.

Black immigration from the Caribbean did not begin in the eighties; there had been vibrant West Indian communities, especially in New York City, at least as early as the twenties. However, several factors contributed to the massive influx of West Indians to the United States in the late twentieth century. First, the easing of restrictions on immigration to the United States after 1965 enabled greater numbers of West Indians to enter the country. Second, Britain imposed severe restrictions on immigrants from its own former colonies in 1962. Third, rising unemployment and poverty in the Caribbean during the seventies and eighties forced many West Indians to search for work in the United States. Thus, by the early eighties approximately fifty thousand legal immigrants from the English-speaking Caribbean and some six thousand to eight thousand Haitians were entering the United States annually, about half of whom settled in New York City.

Despite myths of West Indian affluence and financial success as a result of thrift and hard work, the majority of immigrants were very poor and worked mainly in service sector jobs, such as janitors, cooks, secretaries, and clerical work. Some established independent businesses—small groceries, taxi services, restaurants—but most of these are small, family-run enterprises. Haitians have faced the most difficulties because many are extremely poor refugees fleeing desperate poverty and political violence. To make matters worse, during the administrations of Presidents Reagan and Bush many Haitian refugees were detained by the Immigration and Naturalization Service and either deported or held in camps or prisons until they received a hearing.

There have been tensions between these new black immigrants and native-born African Americans, especially because they competed against each other in a shrinking labor market. Even during the first wave of immigration after World War I, most West Indians have been fiercely independent in terms of maintaining their unique cultural heritage and not identifying more generally with "black Americans." As their communities grew, West Indians became even more distinctive, creating cultural institutions and political organizations that encouraged loyalty to their home island, and carving out a separate niche for themselves in black America.

On the whole, however, relations between West Indians and native-born African Americans have been good. Caribbean music, cuisine, and even dialects have been an integral part of African-American culture, especially on the East Coast. Caribbean youth were key contributors to the development of rap music.

The growth of Rastafarianism in the United States illustrates the impact black West Indian immigrants have had on African-American culture as a whole. Rastas, or members of the Rastafarian religious faith, regard the late Ethiopian emperor Haile Selassie as God. While preaching peace and love between the races, they also warn that some kind of race war is imminent. What made Rastafarianism appealing, aside from its highly spiritual form of black nationalism, was the culture surrounding it. Rastas tend to be vegetarians, do not drink alcohol, and wear their hair in dreadlocks. Their locks are never cut because hair is considered part of the spirit. The popularity of reggae music, in particular, was responsible for introducing Rastafarianism to American audiences. By 1990, there were about one million Rastas in the United States, at least eighty thousand of whom resided in New York City.

In the realm of politics, native-born African-American and Caribbean communities have worked collectively to fight racism in New York City, and some West Indians have even risen to important leadership roles in traditional civil rights organizations. (The Congress on Racial Equality has been headed by Virgin Islands native Roy Innis, although his Republican party affiliation has limited his political base among both West Indians and African Americans.) Similarly, African-American political leaders have maintained a longstanding interest in Caribbean politics. They have tended to support democratic political movements in the Caribbean and pushed for a more progressive U.S. policy toward that region. Some actively backed the struggle for independence from colonial rule back in the fifties and sixties.

As the number of Caribbean-born immigrants to the United States grows, what happens in the Caribbean takes on even greater importance in black politics. When President Reagan called for the invasion of the tiny island of Grenada in 1983, African Americans organized massive protests. Similarly, African-American political leaders have been among the most vocal supporters of Haitian refugees. After the democratically elected president of Haiti, Jean-Bertrand Aristide, was overthrown by the military and exiled in 1992, African Americans and West Indians consistently called for his return to power. Black political leaders have protested the Bush administration's harsh immigration policies toward Haiti, which often resulted in refusing entry to refugees fleeing political violence and starvation. Protests were also directed at the Clinton administration to develop a more active policy toward Haiti that would help restore democratic rule. As a result of demonstrations by several black members of Congress and a dramatic hunger strike waged by Randall Robinson, the president of a lobbying group called TransAfrica, President Clinton appointed former congressman Bill Gray as special envoy to Haiti. In October 1994, Clinton went even further, pressuring the Haitian military to relinquish power and dispatching U.S. troops to restore Aristide to the presidency.

America's changing cultural and ethnic landscape not only calls into question the longstanding (and always false) presumption that the country was divided into two races—black and white. It transformed the meaning of race relations in America's inner cities. Before 1965, Jews were probably the most visible ethnic group with whom urban blacks had contact who did not simply fall into the category of "white." Relations between blacks and Jews in the past had always been mixed, running the gamut from allies in radical organizations to economic competitors. Because some Jews owned small retail outlets in African-American communities—largely because anti-Semitism kept them from establishing businesses elsewhere—blacks and Jews sometimes dealt with each other on the basis of a consumer/proprietor relationship. In the aftermath of the urban riots of the late sixties, however, most Jewish merchants sold off their businesses and the few still residing in the ghetto moved out. Except for places like Brooklyn's Crown Heights community, where tensions between blacks (mostly West Indians) and Hasidic Jews erupted in a major riot in 1991, few inner city blacks live in close proximity to Jews.

But as the Jews moved out of the inner city, new groups of immigrants moved in. The most prominent of the post-1965 wave of immigrants settling in or near African-American communities were Asians from Korea, Vietnam, Cambodia, the Philippines and Samoa, and Latinos from Central America, Cuba, Mexico, and the Dominican Republic.

The combination of economic competition, declining opportunities, scarce public resources, and racist attitudes led to a marked increase in interethnic conflict. In South Central Los Angeles, once an all-black community, Latinos made up about one-fourth of the population in 1992. Job and housing competition between Latinos (most of whom are Central American and Mexican immigrants) and African Americans created enormous tensions between these two groups. Black residents, who in the past had been indifferent to immigration, began supporting measures to limit the entry of Latinos into the United States.

On the other hand, Koreans have been singled out by both blacks and Latinos because a handful own retail establishments and rental property in the poorer sections of South Central Los Angeles. African-American and Latino residents believed the federal government favored Korean immigrants by offering them low interest loans and grants. The fact is, however, that few Korean merchants received federal aid. The majority in Los Angeles and elsewhere ran small family businesses—mainly liquor stores, groceries, discount markets, and specialized shops such as hair care and manicure supply outlets. Often investing what little capital they brought with them from their home country, Koreans relied on family labor and maintained businesses with very low profit margins. Moreover, the idea that Koreans were denying blacks the opportunity to "own their own" businesses ignores the fact that most Korean establishments (particularly liquor stores) were purchased at enormously high prices from African Americans, who in turn had bought these businesses at high prices from Jews fleeing South Central in the late sixties and early seventies.

Last, and perhaps most important, the vast majority of Koreans were neither merchants nor landlords; they were low-wage workers. Nevertheless, blacks and Latinos perceived Koreans as thriving newcomers, backed by a white racist government, taking money and opportunities away from the residents. These perceptions were intensified by the myth that all Asian immigrants were "model minorities," hard-working and successful entrepreneurs who settled comfortably in the United States, and by a general anti-Asian sentiment that had swept the country after the recessions of the seventies and eighties.

But these interethnic tensions were not based entirely on myths. The daily interactions between blacks and Latinos and Korean merchants generated enormous hostility. A common complaint in Los Angeles and elsewhere (most notably, New York) was that Korean merchants treated black and Latino consumers disrespectfully. Fearful of crime, some Korean store owners have been known to follow customers down the aisles, ask to inspect customers' handbags, and refuse entry to young black males who they think looked "suspicious."

By the early nineties, tensions between African Americans and Korean merchants escalated to the point of violence. In one six-month period in 1991, at least three African Americans and two Koreans were killed as a result of customer/proprietor disputes. The most dramatic encounter was the fatal shooting of fifteen-year-old Latasha Harlins in Los Angeles by Korean grocer Soon Ja Du, which was captured on videotape and played on network news programs throughout the country. The incident began when Du accused Harlins of stealing a $1.79 bottle of orange juice in spite of the fact that she held the bottle in clear view and had not attempted to leave the store. Angered by the accusation, Harlins exchanged harsh words with Du, and they engaged in some mutual shoving. As soon as Harlins struck a final blow and began to walk out of the store, Soon Ja Du pulled out a pistol from behind the counter and shot her in the back of the head.

African Americans were shocked and saddened by the shooting. Harlins's family pointed out that Latasha was an honor student at Compton High School and had no history of trouble. Local organizations called for boycotts of Korean-owned businesses, and tensions between merchants and community residents escalated

After her 1990 election to the U.S. House of Representatives, Maxine Waters became one of the most vocal African Americans in Congress. Here, with Jesse Jackson, she speaks to reporters after meeting with the U.S. attorney general to discuss the Rodney King case.

even further. But black anger over the shooting turned to outrage when Judge Joyce Karlin sentenced Du to five years probation, a five hundred dollar fine, and community service, prompting a long-uttered lament among African Americans that a black person's life was of minimal value in the United States. Insult was added to injury when, five days after Du's sentencing, a black man from nearby Glendale, California, was sentenced to thirty days in jail for beating his dog.

The combination of interethnic tensions, white racism, and immense poverty exploded on April 29, 1992, when Los Angeles experienced the most widespread and devastating urban uprising in the history of the United States. The spark for the rebellion was a police brutality trial that ended in the acquittal of four officers who had savagely beaten a black motorist named Rodney King thirteen months earlier. Unlike most incidents of police brutality, this one was captured on videotape by George Holliday, a white plumbing company manager. Holliday tried to report the incident to Los Angeles Police Department officials, but he was rebuffed. Instead, he sold the videotape to a local television station and it soon became national news. The entire nation watched King writhe in pain as he absorbed fifty-six blows in a span of eighty-one seconds. In addition to punching, kicking, and whacking King with a wooden baton, police shocked him twice with a high voltage stun gun. When it was all over, King was left with a broken cheekbone, nine skull fractures, a shattered eye socket, and a broken ankle and needed twenty stitches in his face.

For most viewers, regardless of race, the videotape proved beyond a shadow of a doubt that the officers involved in the beating used excessive force. Thus, when the all-white jury handed down a not-guilty verdict on April 29, 1992, African Americans were shocked, saddened, and then very angry. Throughout Los Angeles, from South Central to downtown, groups of black people began to vent their rage. They were soon joined by Latinos and whites who were also shocked by the verdict. But as the violence unfolded, it became very clear that these riots were not just about the injustice meted out to Rodney King. As one black L.A. resident explained, "It wasn't just the Rodney King verdict. It's the whole thing, the shooting of Latasha Harlins and the lack of jail time for that Korean woman." In some neighborhoods, therefore, blacks and Latinos attacked Korean-owned businesses, white motorists, and each other rather than the police. Among the biggest targets were liquor stores, long seen as the cause of many of the black community's woes. And in the midst of chaos, virtually everyone went after property, seizing furniture, appliances, clothes, and most of all, food.

Unlike previous "race riots," the events in Los Angeles were multiethnic and not limited to the predominantly black ghettoes. Buildings burned from West Los Angeles and Watts to Koreatown, Long Beach, and Santa Monica. Of the first five thousand people arrested, fifty-two percent were Latino and only thirty-nine percent were African American. When the smoke finally began to clear on May 2, at least fifty-eight people were killed (twenty-six African Americans, eighteen Latinos, ten whites, two Asians, two unknown) and thousands were injured. The fires left more than five thousand buildings destroyed or badly damaged. The estimated property damage totaled a staggering $785 million.

More than any other event, the L.A. uprising dramatized to the rest of the country the tragic plight of urban America. And because it occurred during a Presidential election year, there was enormous pressure on President George Bush to offer a prompt response. He proposed Operation Weed and Seed, an urban policy that would provide big tax breaks to entrepreneurs willing to invest in inner cities, some limited programs for disadvantaged children, and a massive buildup of the police and criminal justice system. Indeed, the real emphasis was on the "weed" rather than the "seed" component; nearly eighty percent of the proposed $500 million allocation was earmarked for policing. Bush's proposals were severely criticized by liberal black political leaders and scholars. They felt that the "law-and-order" emphasis was misplaced and that giving tax breaks to companies was not enough to attract capital to South Central L.A. Attempts to do the same thing in the past have failed. On the other hand, black elected officials responded to the rebellion by holding meetings and conferences, and by visiting communities damaged by the riots. Established black leaders criticized the Bush administration's proposals but few proposed policies of their own. One exception was Representative Maxine Waters, who tried desperately but failed to get Congress to pass a sweeping and much-needed urban aid bill.

Ironically, one of the clearest and most comprehensive proposals came from leaders of the two largest black street gangs in Los Angeles. After a long and violent rivalry, leaders of the Bloods and the Crips called a truce and drafted a document called "Give Us the Hammer and the Nails and We Will Rebuild the City." The proposal asked for $2 billion to rebuild deteriorating and damaged neighborhoods; $1 billion to establish hospitals and health-care clinics to South Central Los Angeles; $700 million to improve public education and refurbish schools; $20 million in

A few days after the riots of late April, 1992, ended in Los Angeles, members of several rival gangs called a press conference to announce a truce.

low-interest loans for minority businesses; $6 million to fund a new law enforcement program that would allow ex-gang members, with the proper training, to accompany the LAPD patrols of the community. If these demands were met, the authors promised to rid Los Angeles of drug dealers and provide matching funds for an AIDS research and awareness center. Of course, some of these same gangs were involved in the drug trade themselves, suggesting that their proposal would eliminate an important source of their own revenue. Besides, it is doubtful that the Bloods and the Crips could raise matching funds. In any event, their efforts were to no avail; the mayor and the city council completely ignored the gang members' proposal.

Despite a deluge of plans and proposals, black Los Angeles remained pretty much unchanged in 1994. Two years after the riots, unemployment was still sky high, job opportunities were scarce, and the historic truce between the Crips and the Bloods had begun to unravel locally. Nevertheless, what happened in Los Angeles represented a kind of crossroads for the United States. It vividly called into question the idea that race relations in this country can be viewed as "black and white." It also underscored the extent of desperation in cities generated by the new global economy. The days when jobs were plentiful, even if they were low-wage jobs, are gone. Now America's inner city has an army of permanently unemployed men and women who have little or no hope of living the American Dream. Most keep pushing on. A handful turn to the underground, the illegal economy of bartering stolen goods and drugs. In some neighborhoods, that is all that is left. Meanwhile, the police deal with this tragedy by placing virtually every black person under siege.

Indeed, by the end of the century police harassment and brutality became the leading source of protest for African Americans, irrespective of class. The problem of police use of excessive force was dramatized by a series of high-profile beatings and shootings, including the 1997 assault on Haitian immigrant Abner Louima. New York police officers arrested, handcuffed, beat, and sexually assaulted Louima in the bathroom of a Brooklyn precinct house. After shoving a broken broomstick into Louima's rectum, officer Justin Volpe threatened to kill him if he told anyone about the assault. Louima did press charges, however, which resulted in Volpe's conviction and more investigations into other cases of racism and excessive force in the New York Police Department.

Less than two years later, members of the same NYPD Street Crimes Unit summarily shot to death another black immigrant, twenty-two-year-old street vendor Amadou Diallo. Despite the fact that he was unarmed, had no criminal record, and looked nothing like the alleged suspect in a Bronx rape case, four officers discharged forty-one bullets on him—nineteen of which entered his body. The Diallo killing prompted the largest police brutality protest in New York's history. Tens of thousands of protestors representing the entire spectrum of race, ethnicity, and age blocked the streets around City Hall and engaged in civil disobedience that resulted in hundreds of arrests. Unfortunately, the Diallo killing and Louima beating were just the tip of the iceberg. During the first six months of 1999, for example, literally dozens of others in New York and across the nation were killed or badly beaten by police under dubious circumstances.

The most notable case highlighting racism in the criminal justice system centers around jailed journalist and activist Mumia Abu-Jamal. A former Black Panther party member whose exposés on police misconduct and racial discrimination in Philadelphia won awards and national acclaim, Mumia had been convicted of first-degree murder and sentenced to death for the alleged shooting of a white police officer on December 9, 1981. He had no prior criminal record, despite being subject to FBI surveillance since he was sixteen years old, and the evidence against Mumia was questionable, to say the least. An international movement, endorsed by many leading celebrities, lawyers, and social justice activists, arose demanding that he receive a new trial. A documentary film entitled *A Case for Reasonable Doubt* revealed a pattern of illegal behavior on the part of the Philadelphia police department, including suppressing evidence, intimidating witnesses, and paying off and threatening individuals to give false testimony, among other things. Even the secretary-general of Amnesty International expressed concern in a 1997 statement that "Mumia Abu-Jamal's original trial may have been contaminated by the deep-rooted racism that appears to taint the application of the death penalty in Pennsylvania." In late 1999, under a stay of execution, Mumia remained in prison fighting for a new trial.

Many black citizens were moved by these dramatic cases of police abuse, and some took to the streets in protest. But unequal police practices also affected ordinary African Americans directly in the form of "racial profiling," or what has been called "Driving While Black" (DWB). These are routine traffic stops by police used as a pretext to search for evidence. This practice is used ostensibly to target drug dealers and is based on the premise that most drug offenses are committed by people of color (mainly blacks and Latinos). Although the premise is factually untrue, the vast majority of motorists routinely stopped as alleged drug carriers are African Americans and Latinos. Between January 1995 and September 1996, the Maryland State Police stopped and searched 823 motorists on Interstate 95, of which 600 were black. Only 19.7 percent of those searched in this corridor were white. Some cases were highly publicized. In 1997 San Diego Chargers football player Shawn Lee and his girlfriend were pulled over, handcuffed, and detained by police for half an hour. The officer claimed that Lee's Jeep Cherokee fit the description of a vehicle stolen earlier that day. Records later revealed that the stolen vehicle was a Honda sedan. In 1998, a Liberian student named Nelson Walker was driving along I-95 in Maryland when he was pulled over by state police for not wearing a seatbelt. The officers proceeded to search his car for illegal drugs, weapons, or other contraband, to the point of dismantling a door panel, a seat panel, and part of the sunroof, but they found nothing. The overwhelming number of incidents like these became evident when victims began to sue and concerned politicians began promoting legislation to outlaw racial profiling. The state of New Jersey alone paid out over $800,000 in out-of-court settlements to victims of racial profiling. Nevertheless, as a result of systematic harassment and surveillance, few African Americans feel safe around the police. Christopher Darden, a black attorney who gained notoriety as a prosecutor in the O.J. Simpson murder case, said that in order to survive routine stops, he had to learn "the rules of the game. . . . Don't move. Don't turn around. Don't give some rookie an excuse to shoot you."

In other words, even those who live on the outskirts of America's crumbling ghettos at times feel like they are living in a police state. Yet, while they have their share of nightmares, of racist humiliation, of invisible barriers, even of violence, they are a little safer, a little more secure, and a lot richer. At moments they are as distant from ghetto residents as white farmers in Iowa. At other times they are as close as kin. In a strange way, the L.A. rebellion simultaneously brought them together and tore them apart. They shared the experience of racial humiliation, of realizing that black life, no matter how much money one has, is valued less than white life. The experience tore them apart because it underscored the growing chasm dividing rich and poor.

The generation that came of age in the '70s, '80s, and '90s had been called a lot of things: the post-soul generation, the post–civil rights generation, the postindustrial generation. But few standing "at the edge of history," to use the language of the Gary Declaration, thought in terms of being "post" anything. Rather, they entered a new period with tremendous efforts toward racial integration. For others is was the hope for greater political and social control of their lives. For most African Americans it was a combination of both with a little fun and pleasure thrown in for good measure.

Few anticipated the economic, social, and political crises poor urban blacks would have to face, and fewer still imagined the plush black suburbs of Prince Georges County, Maryland, or that several black-owned companies might one day dwarf Motown Records. Although each difficult day questioned their faith in this country, young mothers and fathers hoped that racism would diminish a little and life for their children would be much easier. In some cases their lives *were* much easier; in other cases a racist police officer's bullet or the fists, sticks, and stones of skinheads cut their young lives short.

But this story is not finished yet, and it need not have a tragic ending. The chapters to come will be written by all of us still living, including you who hold this book in your hands. What we add to this story depends, to a large degree, on us . . . all of us: black and white, Latino and Asian, Native American and Arab American, Jew and Gentile, women and men, rich and poor. If there is one thing we have learned from this book, it is that the problems facing African Americans are not simply outgrowths of a crisis in *black* America. They are products of America's crisis. We must constantly remind ourselves that America's future is bound up with the descendants of slaves and the circumstances they must endure. As police brutality victim Rodney King put it in his memorable press conference following the Los Angeles uprising, "We're all stuck here for a while."

Chronology

1441

Portuguese explorers capture Africans off the coast of Mauritania, signaling the start of a European trade in African slaves.

1479

Spain and Portugal sign the Treaty of Aláçovas, granting Portugal the right to supply the Spaniards with all the African slaves they needed.

1494

The first Africans arrive in Hispaniola with Christopher Columbus. They were free persons.

1502

African slavery introduced in Hispaniola, thereby inaugurating the institution in the Americas.

1522

First rebellion by African slaves in the Americas occurs in Hispaniola.

1539

The black explorer Esteban encounters the Zuni Indians in New Mexico and is killed.

1542

The Spanish Crown abolishes Indian slavery and the *encomienda* system.

1550

First slaves to arrive in Brazil directly from Africa disembark at the city of Salvador.

1565

Africans help construct St. Augustine in Spanish Florida, the oldest non-Indian town in North America.

1586

Francis Drake frees Africans in the Spanish Caribbean but fails to make them part of England's colony at Roanoke.

1595

Spanish Crown awards the first *Asiento*, or monopoly contract, to supply the colonists with slaves.

1609

Runaway slaves in Mexico, led by Yanga, sign a truce with the Spaniards and obtain their freedom and a town of their own.

1617

The town of San Lorenzo de los Negros receives its charter in Mexico, becoming the first officially recognized free settlement for blacks in the Americas.

615

1619

About twenty Africans disembark from a Dutch ship at Jamestown, Virginia.

1644

For the first time, New England merchants send three ships to Africa to trade for gold dust and Negroes.

1662

Virginia statute declares that all children born in the colony are to inherit the status of the mother.

1663

England creates the Company of Royal Adventurers into Africa, replaced in 1672 by the Royal Africa Company.

1700

Slavery becomes legally sanctioned in the colonies of Pennsylvania and Rhode Island.

1708

Africans in South Carolina are more numerous than Europeans, making it the only English mainland colony with a black majority.

1731

African-born Samba Bambara plans slave revolt in French Louisiana and is executed with his co-conspirators.

1733

The Spanish king issues an edict granting freedom to any English slaves escaping to St. Augustine, Florida.

1739

Slaves kill their masters in Stono Rebellion in South Carolina, but their efforts to reach Florida fail.

1765

Anti–Stamp Act demonstrations in Charleston, South Carolina, lead to rumors of a slave plot and black calls for liberty.

1770

Black sailor Crispus Attucks leads an attack on British soldiers and is killed in the Boston Massacre.

1772

The decision of Lord Mansfield in the Somerset Case puts slavery on the road to extinction in England.

1773

African-born Phillis Wheatley, age nineteen, publishes her book, *Poems on Various Subjects, Religious and Moral.*

1775

Virginia governor, Lord Dunmore, issues a proclamation offering freedom to slaves joining the British cause against the colonists.

One of the first independent black Baptist congregations develops in Silver Bluff, South Carolina.

1776

American Declaration of Independence proclaims that all men are created equal.

1777

Blacks in Massachusetts and New Hampshire petition for freedom based upon principles of the Declaration of Independence.

1778

Black businessman Paul Cuffe and his brother John refuse to pay taxes, claiming taxation without representation.

1780

Pennsylvania enacts first gradual emancipation law.

Blacks in Newport, Rhode Island, form the first Free African Union Society.

1783

Massachusetts outlaws slavery by court decision in the Quok Walker case.

1786

Black Poor Committee formed in London to aid needy African-American immigrants.

1787

British abolitionists found the Society for the Abolition of the Slave Trade, and British reformers establish the colony of Sierra Leone to receive black American immigrants in London and other freed slaves.

American Constitutional Convention develops a new government protecting slavery.

Northwest Ordinance forbids slavery in American territory north of the Ohio river and east of the Mississippi.

Richard Allen and Absalom Jones form the Free African Society in Philadelphia.

1788

Massachusetts prohibits all foreign blacks, except those from Morocco, from living in the state for more than two months.

1790

Charleston's free black people organize the Brown Fellowship Society.

1791

Haitian revolution begins.

1793

Eli Whitney's cotton gin spurs economic expansion and tightens the bonds of slavery.

1794

Slavery is abolished in the French Empire.

In Philadelphia, the St. Thomas African Episcopal Church opens its doors, and Richard Allen establishes Bethel African Methodist church.

1798

Toussaint-Louverture expels the British and becomes the most powerful leader in French colony of Saint Domingue (Haiti).

1799

New York's manumission law frees the children of slaves born after July 4.

1800

Gabriel Prosser's planned revolt against slavery in Virginia fails; Prosser and his followers are hanged.

1802

Napoleon reinstitutes slavery in the French Empire.

1804

New Jersey becomes the last northern state to pass a manumission act.

Haiti becomes an independent nation.

1808

The foreign slave trade is closed; Africans are no longer legally imported into the United States.

1811

Led by enslaved leader Charles Deslondes, about four hundred slaves revolt and flee plantations in St. Charles and St. John the Baptist parishes in Louisiana.

1816

The American Colonization Society is formed by white Americans. Their aim is to send African Americans back to Africa.

1817–18

African Americans join the Seminole Indians in their fight to keep their Florida homelands.

1820

The Missouri Compromise allows Missouri to enter the United States as a slave state but outlaws slavery north of the 36th parallel.

1822

Denmark Vesey, a free African American, plans a revolt against the arsenal at Charleston and surrounding plantations. He is betrayed before the revolt begins, and Vesey and his followers are hanged.

The American Colonization Society buys land in western Africa for the few blacks who want to return; the nation is called Liberia.

1827

Freedom's Journal, the first African-American newspaper, is published by Samuel Cornish and John Russworm.

1829

David Walker issues his *Appeal,* in which he denounces slavery and calls on African Americans to rise up and throw off the yoke of slavery.

More than half of the black people of Cincinnati flee the city in response to white mob violence. Riots in other northern and western cities force blacks to migrate to Canada and elsewhere.

1830

African-American delegates from New York, Pennsylvania, Maryland, Delaware, and Virginia meet in Philadelphia in what was the first of many conventions to devise ways of bettering the condition of free and enslaved blacks.

1831

Nat Turner leads about seventy fellow slaves in uprising against the slaveholders of Southampton, Virginia. He and his followers are captured and hanged after they kill about sixty whites.

1833

The predominantly white American Anti-Slavery Society is formed, signaling the beginning of organized white protest against slavery.

1835

Fugitive slaves join the Seminoles against the militias of Florida, Georgia, and Tennessee to keep their homelands.

1847

Frederick Douglass publishes abolitionist newspaper the *North Star.*

1850

The Compromise of 1850 is passed with the most repressive fugitive slave law ever put into effect in the United States.

1852

Black activist and abolitionist Martin Delany publishes *The Condition, Elevation, Emigration, and Destiny of the Colored People of the United States,* in which he argues that emigration to Central or South America or some area in the American West offers the best prospects for black freedom.

1854

The Republican Party is formed on the premise that slavery must be kept out of the western territories.

1857

In *Scott* v. *Sandford*, the Supreme Court rules that blacks are not citizens and therefore have no legal rights, that blacks are property, and that whites who possess such property can treat them however they please and can take them wherever they want.

1859

White abolitionist John Brown leads a slave revolt against the federal arsenal at Harpers Ferry, Virginia. Brown is captured and hanged. Revolt spreads fear among slaveholders across the nation.

1860

Arkansas expels all free blacks from the state. Other Southern states had debated expulsion of free blacks but only Arkansas passes an expulsion law.

Abraham Lincoln is elected President on the Republican platform of non-extension of slavery. Seven Southern states secede in reaction to his election.

April 12, 1861

Civil war begins when Confederates fire on a U.S. ship sent to resupply Fort Sumter, in South Carolina. Four more Southern states secede and join the Confederacy.

August 6, 1861

First Confiscation Act prevents slave owners from reenslaving runaways.

April 16, 1862

Slavery is abolished in Washington, D.C.

July 17, 1862

Congress permits the enlistment of black soldiers.

January 1, 1863

Lincoln's Emancipation Proclamation goes into effect.

July 13, 1863

Draft riots begin in New York.

April 12, 1864

Fort Pillow, Tennessee, massacre of Union soldiers, including blacks.

June 15, 1864

Congress approves equal pay to African-American soldiers.

March 3, 1865

Congress establishes Bureau of Refugees, Freedmen, and Abandoned Lands.

April 9, 1865

General Robert E. Lee surrenders to General Ulysses S. Grant at the town of Appomattox Court House, Virginia.

April 14, 1965

Lincoln is assassinated; Vice President Andrew Johnson becomes President.

April 1, 1866

First national Ku Klux Klan convention.

April 9, 1866

Congress passes Civil Rights Bill.

1868

President Andrew Johnson is impeached by the House of Representatives, but the Senate votes not to remove him from office.

July 28, 1868

14th Amendment, granting citizenship to freed people, is adopted.

February 25, 1870

Hiram Revels of Mississippi is elected to the U.S. Senate and takes the seat once held by Jefferson Davis.

May 30, 1870

15th Amendment, granting freedmen but not women the right to vote, is ratified.

December 11, 1872

Pinckney B. S. Pinchback becomes governor of Louisiana.

March 1, 1875

Congress passes Civil Rights Act.

1877

Rutherford B. Hayes becomes President with agreement to remove federal troops from the South.

1879–1881

First major migration of African Americans from the South to Kansas and western territories occurs.

July 4, 1881

Booker T. Washington opens Tuskegee Institute in Tuskegee, Alabama.

October 15, 1883

In *Civil Rights Cases*, the U.S. Supreme Court reverses the 1875 Civil Rights Act.

May 1884

Schoolteacher Ida B. Wells is removed from the Chesapeake, Ohio, and Southwestern Railroad and begins her lawsuit against the racial segregation of railway transportation.

1886

The Knights of Labor reaches its peak membership at 700,000, including between 60,000 and 90,000 African Americans.

March 1888

The Colored Farmers' National Alliance and Cooperative Union is founded in Lovejoy, Texas.

1889

The federal government opens Oklahoma Territory to settlement, and some seven thousand African Americans participate in the land rush.

1890

The National Afro-American League is founded by T. Thomas Fortune.

The all-black town of Langston, Oklahoma Territory, is founded.

1892

Anna Julia Cooper publishes a set of theoretical essays, *A Voice from the South,* and Frances Ellen Watkins Harper publishes her novel *Iola Leroy.*

The Populist, or People's, Party emerges as an independent political party with the support of black and white farmers and laborers.

October 1892

Ida B. Wells gives landmark speech about lynching at New York City's Lyric Hall and publishes *Southern Horrors: Lynch Law in All Its Phases.*

1893

Black women leaders address the Women's Congress at the World's Columbian Exposition in Chicago.

Ida B. Wells makes antilynching lecture tour of Great Britain.

June 1895

W. E. B. Du Bois receives his Ph.D. from Harvard University, the first African American to do so.

September 18, 1895

Booker T. Washington delivers "Atlanta Compromise" speech at the Cotton States and International Exposition in Atlanta, Georgia.

May 18, 1896

In *Plessy* v. *Ferguson,* U.S. Supreme Court establishes principle that racial segregation is constitutional as long as "separate but equal" facilities are provided

July 21, 1896

The National Association of Colored Women is organized in Washington, D.C.

July 1898

Black troops participate in the Spanish-American War.

August 23–24, 1900

The National Negro Business League is formed in Boston.

September 1900

Nannie Helen Burroughs leads the founding of the Women's Convention of the National Baptist Convention in Richmond, Virginia.

1901

Publication of *Up from Slavery* by Booker T. Washington.

William Monroe Trotter establishes the *Boston Guardian.*

1903

Publication of *The Souls of Black Folk* by W. E. B. Du Bois.

1905

Robert S. Abbott establishes the *Chicago Defender.*

July 1905

Niagara Movement founded to demand full citizenship for blacks and the abolition of all racial distinctions.

September 1906

Race riot in Atlanta.

1910

Founding of the National Association for the Advancement of Colored People.

1914

World War I begins.

The Universal Negro Improvement Association is founded in Jamaica.

1916

Great Migration of blacks from the South to the North begins.

April 1917

United States enters World War I.

November 1918

World War I ends.

1919

Race riots break out in twenty-six cities across the United States.

1920

20th Amendment to the Constitution ratified, providing women the right to vote. Black women in the South, like black men, remain largely disfranchised.

Negro National League in baseball is founded.

1921–22

Shuffle Along, a musical written, produced by, and starring African Americans, is the most popular show on Broadway.

1923

Marcus Garvey is imprisoned for mail fraud.

1925

The Brotherhood of Sleeping Car Porters and Maids is founded.

Publication of *The New Negro*, edited by Alain Locke.

1928

Oscar DePriest (Republican, Chicago) becomes the first African American elected to Congress from a district north of the Mason-Dixon line.

October 24, 1929

Stock market crashes; Great Depression begins.

1931

Communist party assists in the formation of the Alabama Sharecroppers Union.

March 1931

Eight of the nine Scottsboro Boys are tried and convicted of rape in an Alabama court.

1932

U.S. Supreme Court overturns conviction of Scottsboro Boys in *Powell* v. *Alabama.*

November 1932

Franklin D. Roosevelt elected President.

1933

The National Association for the Advancement of Colored People, the National Urban League, and other civil rights organizations organize the Joint Committee on National Recovery.

Negro History Bulletin begins publication under Carter G. Woodson.

1934

Socialist party organizes the Southern Tenant Farmers Union.

1935

In *Pearson* v. *Murray,* the Maryland Court of Appeals orders the University of Maryland to admit African Americans to the state's all-white law school or to set up a separate law school for blacks; the University of Maryland chooses to admit its first African-American students.

Brotherhood of Sleeping Car Porters and Maids receives an international charter from the American Federation of Labor.

Race riot breaks out in Harlem. National Labor Relations Act (Wagner Act) is passed by Congress; National Labor Relations Board established.

U.S. Supreme Court again overturns convictions of Scottsboro Boys, in *Norris* v. *Alabama.*

1936

Nearly six hundred black organizations form the National Negro Congress; A. Philip Randolph is elected its first president.

1937

Brotherhood of Sleeping Car Porters and Maids signs its first contract with the Pullman Company.

1938

Joe Louis defeats German boxer Max Schmeling.

1940

Righard Wright's novel *Native Son* is published.

June 1941

A. Philip Randolph organizes March on Washington.

June 24, 1941

Franklin Roosevelt issues Executive Order 8802, establishing the Fair Employment Practices Committee.

December 7, 1941

Japan attacks Pearl Harbor; United States enters World War II the next day.

1943

Race riots break out in Harlem and Detroit.

1944

Swedish economist Gunnar Myrdal publishes *An American Dilemma: The Negro Problem and Modern Democracy.*

August 14, 1945

World War II ends; nearly one million African Americans served in the U.S. armed forces during the war.

June 3, 1946

U.S. Supreme Court bans segregation in interstate bus travel in *Morgan* v. *Virginia.*

April 9, 1947

Civil rights groups organize the first Freedom Rides to test compliance with bus integration law.

April 10, 1947

Jackie Robinson of the Brooklyn Dodgers becomes the first African American to play major league baseball.

July 26, 1948

President Harry S. Truman signs an executive order ending segregation of the armed forces.

May 17, 1954

U.S. Supreme Court rules in *Brown* v. *Board of Education* that school segregation is illegal.

December 1, 1955

In Montgomery, Alabama, a bus boycott begins after Rosa Parks is arrested for refusing to give up her seat on a bus to a white man.

November 13, 1956

U.S. Supreme Court rules in *Gayle* v. *Browder* that segregation in Montgomery's buses is illegal.

September 1957

President Dwight D. Eisenhower orders federal troops to enforce school desegregation in Little Rock, Arkansas.

February 1960

Students stage a sit-in to protest segregated lunch counters in Greensboro, North Carolina.

September 30, 1962

Riots erupt after James Meredith becomes the first black student to enroll at the University of Mississippi.

May 3, 1963

Police in Birmingham, Alabama, use dogs and fire hoses to attack civil rights marchers.

June 11, 1963

Governor George Wallace stands in the door of the University of Alabama to prevent a black student from enrolling.

June 12, 1963

Civil rights leader Medgar Evers is slain in Jackson, Mississippi.

August 28, 1963

Martin Luther King, Jr., leads 250,000 Americans in the March on Washington, D.C.

September 15, 1963

Four schoolgirls are killed when a bomb explodes at the Sixteenth Street Baptist Church in Birmingham.

November 22, 1963

President John F. Kennedy is assassinated in Dallas, Texas.

June 20, 1964

During Freedom Summer, one thousand civil rights volunteers go to Mississippi.

July 2, 1964

President Lyndon Johnson signs Civil Rights Act.

August 20, 1964

President Lyndon Johnson signs the Economic Opportunity Act.

December 10, 1964

Martin Luther King, Jr., receives the Nobel Peace Prize.

February 1965

Malcolm X is shot and killed in New York City.

March 7, 1965

Civil rights marchers in Selma, Alabama, are clubbed and gassed by police.

March 9, 1965

Under the protection of federal troops, civil rights marchers complete the trek from Selma to Montgomery.

August 11, 1965

Rebellion in the Watts section of Los Angeles results in thirty-four people dead and $35 million in property damage.

June 26, 1966

At a civil rights rally in Mississippi, Stokely Carmichael launches the Black Power movement.

July 1967

Riots in urban areas leave scores dead and many neighborhoods in ruins.

October 2, 1967

Thurgood Marshall is sworn in as the first African-American justice of the U.S. Supreme Court.

February 29, 1968

The Kerner Commission warns that America is becoming "two societies—one black, one white—separate and unequal."

April 4, 1968

Martin Luther King, Jr., is assassinated in Memphis, Tennessee.

June 19, 1968

The Poor People's Campaign brings fifty thousand demonstrators to Washington.

1970

Race riots erupt in several cities, including Philadelphia; New Orleans; New Bedford, Massachusetts; and Hartford, Connecticut.

September 1970

Black Panther party, along with women's and gay liberation activists, holds the Revolutionary People's Constitutional Convention in Philadelphia.

October 13, 1970

Angela Davis arrested and charged with murder, kidnapping, and conspiracy; case prompts an international campaign to free her. Two years later, she is found not guilty.

1971

Congressional Black Caucus is founded.

1972

Shirley Chisholm becomes first African American in history to seek the Democratic party's Presidential nomination.

Coalition of Black Trade Unionists is founded.

March 1972

National Black Political Assembly holds its founding convention in Gary, Indiana.

1973

National Black Feminist Organization is founded.

Tom Bradley is elected first black mayor of Los Angeles.

1973–75

United States experiences worst economic recession in decades.

1975

NAACP wins court order to integrate Boston schools by busing black children from Roxbury to predominantly white schools in Charlestown; the transition is marred by violence.

Wallace D. Muhammad takes over Nation of Islam after death of his father, Elijah Muhammad. He denounces his father's teachings, adopts orthodox Islam, and changes the name of the organization to the World Community of al-Islam in the West.

February 1977

Television miniseries "Roots," based on Alex Haley's best-selling novel, is watched by a record 130 million viewers, sparking a national debate about race and African-American history.

1978

Black unemployment rate is nearly 2.5 times higher than white; this is the largest gap since the federal government began keeping such statistics.

Allan Bakke's charge of "reverse discrimination" against the University of California, Davis, Medical School weakens affirmative action policies when the Supreme Court rules in *Regents of the University of California* v. *Bakke* that he had been denied "equal protection of the laws" as required by the 14th Amendment.

Louis Farrakhan breaks with Wallace D. Muhammad and reestablishes the Nation of Islam under Elijah Muhammad's original beliefs.

1979

The Sugar Hill Gang releases the first commercially successful rap single.

May 1980

African Americans in Liberty City, Florida, riot after police officers are acquitted for killing an unarmed black man.

November 1980

National Black Independent Political party is founded.

1982

Alice Walker publishes *The Color Purple,* which received the American Book Award and the Pulitzer Prize.

The struggle to block a toxic waste dump in Warren County, North Carolina, launches a national movement against environmental racism.

1983

Harold Washington is elected first black mayor of Chicago.

1984

Jesse Jackson makes first bid for the Democratic party's Presidential nomination, receiving about 3.5 million popular votes in the primaries.

"The Cosby Show" makes its debut, becoming the most popular regular program on television.

May 1985

Black Philadelphia mayor Wilson Goode directs the police to bomb the headquarters of MOVE, a local black nationalist organization. The bombing leaves 11 people dead and 250 people homeless.

September 1985

U.S. Census Bureau reports that one out of three African Americans is living below the poverty line.

1986

Spike Lee releases his first feature film, *She's Gotta Have It,* igniting Hollywood's interest in young black male filmmakers.

1988

Jesse Jackson seeks Democratic Presidential nomination for a second time; he receives seven million votes and is Michael Dukakis's strongest challenger for the nomination.

The Black Women Mayor's Caucus is founded.

1989

Douglas L. Wilder is elected governor of Virginia and becomes the first African American elected governor of any state.

1990

Sharon Pratt Kelly (formerly Dixon) is elected mayor of Washington, D.C. She is the first African American and first native of the district to hold that post.

1991

Julie Dash releases *Daughters of the Dust,* the first feature film by an African-American woman.

October 1991

Anita Hill's testimony during the confirmation hearings of Supreme Court Justice Clarence Thomas launches a nationwide discussion of sexual harassment.

1992

Carol Moseley-Braun becomes first African-American woman elected to the U.S. Senate.

April 29–May 1, 1992

Acquittal of four Los Angeles police officers accused of using excessive force on black motorist Rodney King sparks the largest, most costly urban rebellion in U.S. history.

1993

Novelist Toni Morrison wins Nobel Prize for literature.

May 1994

Class-action suit forces Denny's restaurant chain to pay $54 million in damages for systematically discriminating against African-American customers.

1996

President Bill Clinton signs into law the Personal Responsibility and Work Opportunity Reconciliation Act, which replaced Aid to Families with Dependent Children (AFDC) with state block grants and cut funding for programs to help the poor.

1997

New York police officers beat and sexually assault Haitian immigrant Abner Louima; high-profile case calls attention to the problem of police brutality.

February 4, 1999

New York police officers discharge forty-one bullets at black immigrant Amadou Diallo; the killing prompts the largest police brutality protest in New York's history.

Further Reading

General African-American History

Anderson, James D. *The Education of Blacks in the South, 1860–1935.* Chapel Hill: University of North Carolina Press, 1988.

Aptheker, Herbert, ed. *A Documentary History of the Negro People in the United States.* Vols. 1–2. New York: Citadel Press, 1951.

Aptheker, Herbert, ed. *A Documentary History of the Negro People in the United States.* Vols. 5–7. Secaucus, N.J.: Carol Publishing, 1994.

Bennett, Lerone, Jr. *Before the Mayflower: A History of Black America.* 6th rev. ed. New York: Viking Penguin, 1988.

———. *The Shaping of Black America.* New York: Viking Penguin, 1993.

Berry, Mary Frances, and John W. Blassingame. *Long Memory: The Black Experience in America.* New York: Oxford University Press, 1982.

Blackburn, Robin. *The Overthrow of Colonial Slavery, 1776–1848.* New York: Verso, 1988.

Boles, John B. *Black Southerners, 1619–1869.* Lexington: University Press of Kentucky, 1983.

Conniff, Michael, and Thomas J. Davis. *Africans in the Americas: A History of the Black Diaspora.* New York: St. Martin's, 1993.

Cooper, Anna Julia. *A Voice from the South.* 1892. Reprint, New York: Oxford University Press, 1988.

Foner, Philip S. *History of Black Americans: From Africa to the Emergence of the Cotton Kingdom.* Westport, Conn.: Greenwood, 1975.

Franklin, John Hope, and August Meier, eds. *Black Leaders of the Twentieth Century.* Urbana: University of Illinois Press, 1982.

Franklin, John H., and Alfred A. Moss, Jr. *From Slavery to Freedom: A History of African Americans.* 8th ed. Boston: McGraw-Hill, 1999.

Garwood, Alfred N., comp., *Black Americans: A Statistical Sourcebook 1992.* Boulder, Colo.: Numbers and Concepts, 1993.

Gates, Henry L., Jr. *A Chronology of African-American History from 1445–1980.* New York: Amistad, 1980.

Genovese, Eugene. *From Rebellion to Revolution: Afro-American Slave Revolts in the Making of the Atlantic World.* Baton Rouge: Louisiana State University Press, 1979.

Giddings, Paula. *When and Where I Enter: The Impact of Black Women on Race and Sex in America*. New York: Bantam, 1984.

Gutman, Herbert G. *The Black Family in Slavery and Freedom, 1750–1925*. New York: Vintage, 1977.

Harding, Vincent. *There Is a River: The Black Struggle for Freedom in America*. San Diego: Harcourt Brace, 1981.

Harris, William H. *The Harder We Run: Black Workers Since the Civil War*. New York: Oxford University Press, 1982.

Hine, Darlene C., et al., eds. *Black Women in America*. Brooklyn, N.Y.: Carlson, 1993.

Hornsby, Alton, Jr. *Chronology of African-American History: Significant Events and People from 1619 to the Present*. Detroit: Gale Research, 1991.

Jaynes, Gerald David, and Robin M. Williams, Jr., *A Common Destiny: Blacks and American Society*. Washington, D.C.: National Academy Press, 1989.

Jones, Jacqueline. *Labor of Love, Labor of Sorrow: Black Women, Work, and the Family from Slavery to the Present*. New York: Basic Books, 1985.

Levine, Lawrence. *Black Culture and Black Consciousness: Afro-American Folk Thought from Slavery to Freedom*. New York: Oxford University Press, 1977.

Litwack, Leon, and August Meier. *Black Leaders of the 19th Century*. Urbana: University of Illinois Press, 1988.

Mintz, Sidney W., and Richard Price. *The Birth of African- American Culture: An Anthropological Perspective*. Boston: Beacon, 1992.

Nash, Gary B. *Red, White, and Black: The Peoples of Early America*. Englewood Cliffs, N.J.: Prentice-Hall, 1992.

Quarles, Benjamin. *The Negro in the Making of America*. 3rd ed. New York: Macmillan, 1987.

Rice, C. Duncan. *The Rise and Fall of Black Slavery*. Baton Rouge: Louisiana State University Press, 1975.

Salzman, Jack, David Lionel Smith, and Cornel West, eds. *Encyclopedia of African-American Culture and History*. 5 vols. New York: Simon & Schuster Macmillan, 1996.

Savage, William Sherman. *Blacks in the West*. Westport, Conn.: Greenwood Press, 1976.

Chapter 1
Histories and Accounts of Africa and the Americas

Curtin, Philip D., ed. *Africa Remembered: Narratives by West Africans from the Era of the Slave Trade*. Madison: University of Wisconsin Press, 1968.

Curtin, Philip D., Steven Feierman, Leonard Thompson, and Jan Vansina. *African History*. New York: Longman, 1978.

Knight, Franklin. *The Caribbean: The Genesis of a Fragmented Nationalism*. 2nd ed. New York: Oxford University Press, 1990.

Lockhart, James. *Spanish Peru, 1532–1560: A Colonial Society*. Madison: University of Wisconsin Press, 1967.

Lockhart, James, and Stuart Schwartz. *Early Latin America: A History of Colonial Spanish America and Brazil*. New York: Cambridge University Press, 1983.

Palmer, Colin A. *Slaves of the White God: Blacks in Mexico, 1570–1650*. Cambridge: Harvard University Press, 1976.

Rodney, Walter. *How Europe Underdeveloped Africa.* Rev. ed. Washington, D.C.: Howard University Press, 1982.

Rout, Leslie B. *The African Experience in Spanish America, 1502 to the Present Day.* New York: Cambridge University Press, 1976.

Schwartz, Stuart B. *Sugar Plantations in the Formation of Brazilian Society: Bahia 1550–1835.* New York: Cambridge University Press, 1986.

Thornton, John. *Africa and Africans in the Formation of the Atlantic World, 1400–1680.* New York: Cambridge University Press, 1992.

Van Sertima, Ivan. *They Came Before Columbus.* New York: Random House, 1976.

Slavery and the Slave Trade

Bowser, Frederick P. *The African Slave in Colonial Peru, 1524–1650.* Stanford, Calif.: Stanford University Press, 1974.

Curtin, Philip D. *The Atlantic Slave Trade: A Census.* Madison: University of Wisconsin Press, 1972.

Davidson, Basil. *The African Slave Trade.* New York: Little, Brown, 1988.

Donnan, Elizabeth, ed. *Documents Illustrative of the Slave Trade to America.* 4 vols. Washington, D.C.: Carnegie Institution, 1930–35.

Equiano, Olaudah. *The Interesting Narrative of the Life of Olaudah Equiano, or Gustavus Vasa the African.* Edited by Paul Edwards. 2 vols. London: Heinemann, 1967.

Genovese, Eugene. *From Rebellion to Revolution: Afro-American Slave Revolts in the Making of the Modern World.* Baton Rouge: Louisiana State University Press, 1979.

Klein, Herbert. *African Slavery in Latin America and the Caribbean.* New York: Oxford University Press, 1986.

Lovejoy, Paul E. *Transformations in Slavery: A History of Slavery in Africa.* New York: Cambridge University Press, 1983.

Phillips, William D., Jr. *Slavery from Roman Times to the Early Atlantic Slave Trade.* Minneapolis: University of Minnesota Press, 1985.

Rawley, James A. *The Transatlantic Slave Trade.* New York: Norton, 1981.

Reynolds, Edward. *Stand the Storm: A History of the Atlantic Slave Trade.* Chicago: Ivan R. Dee, 1993.

Schwartz, Stuart B. *Slaves, Peasants, and Rebels: Reconsidering Brazilian Slavery.* Urbana: University of Illinois Press, 1992.

Thomas, Hugh. *The Slave Trade.* New York: Simon & Schuster, 1997.

Watson, Alan. *Slave Law in the Americas.* Athens: University of Georgia Press, 1989.

Chapter 2
Slavery and Slave Culture

Aptheker, Herbert. *American Negro Slave Revolts.* New York: Columbia University Press, 1943.

Berlin, Ira. *Many Thousands Gone: The First Two Centuries of Slavery in North America.* Cambridge: Harvard University Press, 1998.

Burnside, Madeleine, and Rosemarie Robotham. *Spirits of the Passage: the Transatlantic Slave Trade in the Seventeenth Century.* New York: Simon & Schuster, 1997.

Ferguson, Leland. *Uncommon Ground: Archaeology and Early African America, 1650–1800.* Washington, D.C.: Smithsonian Institution Press, 1992.

Franklin, John Hope, and Loren Schweninger. *Runaway Slaves: Rebels on the Plantation.* New York: Oxford University Press, 1999.

Frey, Sylvia. *Water from the Rock: Black Resistance in a Revolutionary Age.* Princeton, N.J.: Princeton University Press, 1991.

Frey, Sylvia, and Betty Wood. *Come Shouting to Zion: African American Protestantism in the American South and British Caribbean to 1830.* Chapel Hill: University of North Carolina Press, 1998.

Gomez, Michael A. *Exchanging Our Country Marks: The Transformation of African Identities in the Colonial and Antebellum South.* Chapel Hill: University of North Carolina Press, 1998.

Higginbotham, A. Leon, Jr. *In the Matter of Color: Race and the American Legal Process: The Colonial Period.* New York: Oxford University Press, 1978.

Holloway, Joseph E., ed. *Africanisms in American Culture.* Bloomington: Indiana University Press, 1990.

Johnson, Charles, Patricia Smith, and the WGBH Research Team. *Africans in America: America's Journey Through Slavery.* New York: Harcourt Brace, 1998.

Jordan, Winthrop D. *White Over Black: American Attitudes toward the Negro, 1550–1812.* Chapel Hill: University of North Carolina Press, 1968.

Kaplan, Sidney, and Emma Nogrady Kaplan. *The Black Presence in the Era of the American Revolution.* Rev. ed. Amherst: University of Massachusetts Press, 1989.

Kolchin, Peter. *American Slavery, 1619–1877.* New York: Hill & Wang, 1993.

Mullin, Michael. *Africa in America: Slave Acculturation and Resistance in the American South and the British Caribbean, 1736–1831.* Urbana: University of Illinois Press, 1992.

Piersen, William D. *From Africa to America: African American History from the Colonial Era to the Early Republic, 1526–1790.* New York: Twayne, 1996.

Raboteau, Albert J. *Slave Religion: The "Invisible Institution" in the Antebellum South.* New York: Oxford University Press, 1978.

Scherer, Lester B. *Slavery and the Churches in Early America, 1619–1819.* Grand Rapids, Mich.: William B. Eerdmans, 1975.

Smith, Billy G., and Richard Wojtowicz. *Blacks Who Stole Themselves: Advertisements for Runaways in the Pennsylvania Gazette, 1728–1790.* Philadelphia: University of Pennsylvania Press, 1989.

Stuckey, Sterling. *Slave Culture: Nationalist Theory and the Foundations of Black America.* New York: Oxford University Press, 1987.

Thomas, Hugh. *The Slave Trade.* New York: Simon & Schuster, 1997.

Regional Studies

Breen, T. H., and Stephen Innes. *"Myne Owne Ground": Race and Freedom on Virginia's Eastern Shore, 1640–1676.* New York: Oxford University Press, 1980.

Greene, Lorenzo Johnston. *The Negro in Colonial New England.* New York: Columbia University Press, 1942.

Hall, Gwendolyn Midlo. *Africans in Colonial Louisiana: The Development of Afro-Creole Culture in the Eighteenth Century.* Baton Rouge: Louisiana State University Press, 1992.

Hanger, Kimberly S. *Bounded Lives, Bounded Places: Free Black Society in Colonial New Orleans, 1769–1803.* Durham, N.C.: Duke University Press, 1997.

Hodges, Graham Russell. *Slavery and Freedom in the Rural North: African Americans in Monmouth County, New Jersey, 1665–1865.* Madison, Wis.: Madison House, 1997.

Holton, Woody. *Forced Founders: Indians, Debtors, Slaves, and the Making of the American Revolution in Virginia.* Chapel Hill: University of North Carolina Press, 1999.

Ingersall, Thomas N. *Mammon and Manon in Early New Orleans: The First Slave Society in the Deep South, 1718–1819.* Knoxville: University of Tennessee Press, 1999.

Landers, Jane. *Black Society in Spanish Florida.* Urbana: University of Illinois Press, 1999.

Littlefield, Daniel. *Rice and Slaves: Ethnicity and the Slave Trade in Colonial South Carolina.* Baton Rouge: Louisiana State University Press, 1981.

Morgan, Edmund S. *American Slavery, American Freedom: The Ordeal of Colonial Virginia.* New York: Norton, 1975.

Morgan, Philip D. *Slave Counterpoint: Black Culture in the Eighteenth-Century Chesapeake and Lowcountry.* Chapel Hill: University of North Carolina Press, 1998.

Olwell, Robert. *Masters, Slaves, and Subjects: The Culture of Power in the South Carolina Low Country, 1740–1790.* Ithaca, N.Y.: Cornell University Press, 1998.

Piersen, William D. *Black Yankees: The Development of an Afro-American Subculture in Eighteenth-Century New England.* Amherst: University of Massachusetts Press, 1988.

Sensbach, Jon F. *A Separate Canaan: The Making of an Afro-Moravian World in North Carolina, 1763–1840.* Chapel Hill: University of North Carolina Press, 1998.

Sobel, Mechal. *The World They Made Together: Black and White Values in Eighteenth-Century Virginia.* Princeton, N.J.: Princeton University Press, 1987.

Tate, Thad W., Jr. *The Negro in Eighteenth-Century Williamsburg.* Charlottesville: University Press of Virginia, 1966.

Usner, Daniel H., Jr., *Indians, Settlers, and Slaves in a Frontier Exchange Economy: The Lower Mississippi Valley Before 1783.* Chapel Hill: University of North Carolina Press, 1992.

Williams, William H. *Slavery and Freedom in Delaware, 1639–1865.* Wilmington, Del.: Scholarly Resources, 1996.

Wood, Betty. *Slavery in Colonial Georgia, 1730–1775.* Athens: University of Georgia Press, 1984.

Wood, Peter H. *Black Majority: Negroes in Colonial South Carolina from 1670 through the Stono Rebellion.* New York: Knopf, 1974.

Biographies and Literature

Edwards, Paul, ed. *Equiano's Travels.* London: Heinemann, 1967.

Gordon-Reed, Annette. *Thomas Jefferson and Sally Hemings: An American Controversy.* Charlottesville: University Press of Virginia, 1997.

Grant, Douglas. *The Fortunate Slave: An Illustration of African Slavery in the Early Eighteenth Century.* New York: Oxford University Press, 1968.

Shields, John C., ed. *The Collected Works of Phillis Wheatley.* New York: Oxford University Press, 1988.

Yates, Elizabeth. *Amos Fortune, Free Man.* New York: Dutton, 1950.

Chapter 3
The American Revolution

Berlin, Ira. *Many Thousands Gone: The First Two Centuries of Slavery in North America.* Cambridge: Harvard University Press, 1998.

Berlin, Ira, and Ronald Hoffman, eds. *Slavery and Freedom in the Age of the American Revolution.* Charlottesville: University Press of Virginia, 1983.

Davis, David Brion. *The Problem of Slavery in the Age of Revolution, 1770–1823.* Ithaca, N.Y.: Cornell University Press, 1975.

Flexner, James T. *George Washington: Anguish and Farewell (1793–1799).* Boston: Little, Brown, 1972.

———. *George Washington in the American Revolution (1775–1783).* Boston: Little, Brown, 1968.

Frey, Sylvia R. *Water from the Rock: Black Resistance in a Revolutionary Age.* Princeton, N.J.: Princeton University Press, 1991.

Greene, Jack P. *All Men are Created Equal: Some Reflections on the Character of the American Revolution.* Oxford: Clarendon Press, 1976.

Hirschfeld, Fritz. *George Washington and Slavery: A Documentary Portrayal.* Columbia: University of Missouri Press, 1997.

Horton, James Oliver, and Lois E. Horton. *In Hope of Liberty: Culture, Community, and Protest Among Northern Free Blacks, 1700–1860.* New York: Oxford University Press, 1997.

Kaplan, Sidney, and Emma Nogrady Kaplan. *The Black Presence in the Era of the American Revolution.* Amherst: University of Massachusetts Press, 1989.

Morgan, Edmund S. *The Birth of the Republic, 1763–89.* Chicago: University of Chicago Press, 1992.

Nash, Gary. *Race and Revolution.* Madison, Wis.: Madison House, 1990.

Quarles, Benjamin. *The Negro in the American Revolution.* Chapel Hill: University of North Carolina Press, 1961.

Wood, Gordon. *The Creation of the American Republic, 1776–1787.* Chapel Hill: University of North Carolina Press, 1969.

Revolution in France and Haiti

Cole, Hubert. *Christophe: King of Haiti.* London: Eyre & Spottiswoode, 1967.

Fick, Carolyn E. *The Making of Haiti: The Saint Domingue Revolution from Below.* Knoxville: University of Tennessee Press, 1990.

Geggus, David P. *Slavery, War, and Revolution: The British Occupation of Saint Domingue, 1793–1798.* Oxford: Clarendon Press, 1982.

Hunt, Alfred N. *Haiti's Influence on Antebellum America: Slumbering Volcano in the Caribbean.* Baton Rouge: Louisiana State University Press, 1988.

James, C. L. R. *The Black Jacobins: Toussaint L'Ouverture and the San Domingo Revolution.* Rev. ed. London: Allison & Busby, 1980.

Korngold, Ralph. *Citizen Toussaint: A Biography.* New York: Hill & Wang, 1965.

Logan, Rayford W. *The Diplomatic Relations of the United States with Haiti, 1776–1891.* Chapel Hill: University of North Carolina Press, 1941.

McCloy, Shelby T. *The Negro in the French West Indies.* Lexington: University of Kentucky Press, 1966.

Ott, Thomas O. *The Haitian Revolution, 1789–1804.* Knoxville: University of Tennessee Press, 1973.

Rude, George. *Revolutionary Europe, 1783–1815.* New York: Harper, 1964.

African-American Culture and Society

Andrews, William L. *To Tell a Free Story: The First Century of Afro-American Autobiography, 1760–1865.* Urbana: University of Illinois Press, 1986.

Berlin, Ira. *Slaves without Masters: The Free Negro in the Antebellum South.* New York: Oxford University Press, 1974.

Bolster, W. Jeffrey. *Black Jacks: African American Seamen in the Age of Sail.* Cambridge: Harvard University Press, 1997.

Chaplin, Joyce E. *An Anxious Pursuit: Agricultural Innovation and Modernity in the Lower South, 1730–1815.* Chapel Hill: University of North Carolina Press, 1993.

Egerton, Douglas R. *Gabriel's Rebellion: The Virginia Slave Conspiracies of 1800 and 1802.* Chapel Hill: University of North Carolina Press, 1993.

Fitts, Leroy. *A History of Black Baptists.* Nashville, Tenn.: Broadman Press, 1984.

Fitts, Leroy, and Charles T. Davis. *The Slave's Narrative.* New York: Oxford University Press, 1985.

Gewehr, Wesley M. *The Great Awakening in Virginia, 1740–1790.* Gloucester, Mass.: Peter Smith, 1965.

Hall, Gwendolyn Midlo. *Africans in Colonial Louisiana: The Development of Afro-Creole Culture in the Eighteenth Century.* Baton Rouge: Louisiana State University Press, 1992.

Hatch, Nathan O. *The Democratization of American Christianity.* New Haven: Yale University Press, 1989.

Hodges, Graham Russell. *Root and Branch: African Americans in New York and East Jersey, 1613–1863.* Chapel Hill: University of North Carolina Press, 1999.

———. *Slavery and Freedom in the Rural North: African Americans in Monmouth County, New Jersey, 1665–1865.* Madison, Wis.: Madison House, 1997.

Isaac, Rhys. *The Transformation of Virginia: Community, Religion, and Authority, 1740–1790.* Chapel Hill: University of North Carolina Press, 1982.

Jordan, Winthrop D. *White Over Black: American Attitudes Toward the Negro, 1550–1812.* Chapel Hill: University of North Carolina Press, 1968.

Kulikoff, Allan. *Tobacco and Slaves: The Development of Southern Cultures in the Chesapeake, 1680–1800.* Chapel Hill: University of North Carolina Press, 1986.

Littlefield, Daniel C. *Rice and Slaves: Ethnicity and the Slave Trade in Colonial South Carolina.* Baton Rouge: Louisiana State University Press, 1981.

Miller, Floyd J. *The Search for a Black Nationality: Black Colonization and Emigration, 1787–1863.* Urbana: University of Illinois Press, 1975.

Morton, Louis. *Robert Carter of Nomini Hall: A Virginia Tobacco Planter of the Eighteenth Century.* Charlottesville: University Press of Virginia, 1941.

Mullin, Gerald W. *Flight and Rebellion: Slave Resistance in Eighteenth-Century Virginia.* New York: Oxford University Press, 1972.

Mullin, Michael. *Africa in America: Slave Acculturation and Resistance in the American South and the British Caribbean, 1736–1831.* Urbana: University of Illinois Press, 1992.

Nash, Gary B. *Forging Freedom: The Formation of Philadelphia's Black Community, 1720–1840.* Cambridge: Harvard University Press, 1988.

Nell, William C. *The Colored Patriots of the American Revolution.* 1855. Reprint, Salem, N.H.: Ayer, 1986.

Payne, Daniel A. *History of the African Methodist Episcopal Church.* 1891. Reprint, New York: Arno, 1969.

Porter, Dorothy, ed. *Early Negro Writing, 1760–1837.* Boston: Beacon Press, 1971.

———. *Negro Protest Pamphlets: A Compendium.* New York: Arno, 1969.

Raboteau, Albert J. *Slave Religion: The "Invisible Institution" in the Antebellum South.* New York: Oxford University Press, 1978.

Robinson, William H. *Black New England Letters: The Uses of Writings in Black New England.* Boston: Trustees of the Public Library, 1977.

———. *Early Black American Prose: Selections with Biographical Introductions.* Dubuque, Iowa: William C. Brown, 1971.

Ruchames, Louis. *Racial Thought in America: A Documentary History. Volume I: From the Puritans to Abraham Lincoln.* Amherst: University of Massachusetts Press, 1969.

Sernett, Milton C. *Black Religion and American Evangelicalism: White Protestants, Plantation Missions, and the Flowering of Negro Christianity, 1787–1865.* Metuchen, N.J.: Scarecrow Press, 1975.

Sidbury, James. *Ploughshares into Swords: Race, Rebellion, and Identity in Gabriel's Virginia, 1730–1810.* New York: Cambridge University Press, 1997.

Simms, James M. *The First Colored Baptist Church in North America. Constituted at Savannah, Georgia, January 20, A.D. 1788.* 1888. Reprint, New York: Negro Universities Press, 1969.

Smith, Charles S. *A History of the African Methodist Episcopal Church.* New York: Johnson Reprint, 1968.

Sobel, Mechal. *Trabelin' on: The Slave Journey to an Afro-Baptist Faith.* Westport, Conn.: Greenwood Press, 1979.

Stuckey, Sterling. *Slave Culture: Nationalist Theory and the Foundations of Black America.* New York: Oxford University Press, 1987.

Walls, William J. *The African Methodist Episcopal Zion Church: Reality of the Black Church.* Charlotte, N.C.: A.M.E. Zion Publishing House, 1974.

Wilmore, Gayraud S. *Black Religion and Black Radicalism: An Interpretation of the Religious History of Afro-American People.* 2nd ed., revised and enlarged. Maryknoll, N.Y.: Orbis, 1983.

Wood, Gordon S. *The Radicalism of the American Revolution.* New York: Knopf, 1992.

Yentsch, Anne Elizabeth. *A Chesapeake Family and their Slaves; A Study in Historical Archaeology.* New York: Cambridge University Press, 1994.

Slavery and the British Empire

Drescher, Seymour. *Capitalism and Antislavery: British Mobilization in Comparative Perspective.* New York: Oxford University Press, 1987.

Fyfe, Christopher. *A History of Sierra Leone.* London: Oxford University Press, 1962.

Porter, Dale H. *The Abolition of the Slave Trade in England, 1784–1807.* New York: Archon Books, 1970.

Wilson, Ellen Gibson. *The Loyal Blacks.* New York: G. P. Putnam, 1976.

Winks, Robin W. *The Blacks in Canada: A History.* New Haven: Yale University Press, 1971.

Biographies

Bedini, Silvio A. *The Life of Benjamin Banneker.* New York: Scribner, 1972.

Crawford, George W. *Prince Hall and His Followers. Being a Monograph on the Legitimacy of Negro Masonry.* 1914. Reprint, New York: AMS Press, 1971.

George, Carol V. R. *Segregated Sabbaths: Richard Allen and the Rise of Independent Black Churches, 1760–1840.* New York: Oxford University Press, 1973.

Hodges, Graham. *Black Itinerants of the Gospel: The Narratives of John Jea and George White.* Madison, Wis.: Madison House, 1993.

Robinson, William H. *Phillis Wheatley and Her Writings.* New York: Garland, 1984.

Thomas, Lamont D. *Rise to Be a People: A Biography of Paul Cuffe.* Urbana: University of Illinois Press, 1986.

Chapter 4
Slavery and Free Blacks

Berlin, Ira. *Slaves Without Masters: The Free Negro in the Antebellum South.* New York: Random House, 1974.

Blassingame, John W. *The Slave Community: Plantation Life in the Antebellum South.* Rev. ed. New York: Oxford University Press, 1979.

Botkin, B. A., ed. *Lay My Burden Down: A Folk History of Slavery.* Chicago: University of Chicago Press, 1945.

Genovese, Eugene. *Roll, Jordan, Roll: The World the Slaves Made.* New York: Random House, 1974.

Gutman, Herbert. *The Black Family in Slavery and Freedom, 1750–1925.* New York: Pantheon, 1976.

Johnson, Michael, and James L. Roark. *Black Masters: A Free Family of Color in the Old South.* New York: Norton, 1984.

Kolchin, Peter. *American Slavery 1619–1877.* New York: Hill & Wang, 1993.

Lebsock, Suzanne. *The Free Women of Petersburg: Status and Culture in a Southern Town, 1784–1860.* New York: Norton, 1984.

Litwack, Leon F. *North of Slavery: The Negro in the Free States, 1790–1860.* Chicago: University of Chicago Press, 1961.

Meier, August, and Elliot M. Rudwick. *From Plantation to Ghetto: An Interpretive History of American Negroes.* 3rd ed. New York: Hill & Wang, 1976.

Nash, Gary B. *Forging Freedom: The Formation of Philadelphia's Black Community, 1720–1840.* Cambridge: Harvard University Press, 1988.

Osofsky, Gilbert, ed. *Puttin' On Ole Massa. The Slave Narratives of Henry Bibb, William Wells Brown and Solomon Northup.* New York: Harper & Row, 1969.

Richardson, Marilyn, ed. *Maria W. Stewart, America's First Black Woman Political Writer: Essays and Speeches.* Bloomington: Indiana University Press, 1987.

Sweet, Leonard L. *Black Images of America, 1784–1870.* New York: Norton, 1976.

White, Deborah Gray. *Ar'n't I a Woman? Female Slaves in the Plantation South.* New York: Norton, 1985.

Williamson, Joel. *New People: Miscegenation and Mulattoes in the United States.* New York: Free Press, 1980.

Biographies and Autobiographies

Andrews, William L., ed. *The Oxford Frederick Douglass Reader.* New York: Oxford University Press, 1996.

Douglass, Frederick. *Narrative of the Life of Frederick Douglass, an American Slave.* New York: St. Martin's, 1993.

Gilbert, Olive. *Narrative of Sojourner Truth.* New York: Oxford University Press, 1991.

McFeely, William S. *Frederick Douglass.* New York: Norton, 1991.

Chapter 5
General Histories of the Civil War and Reconstruction

Edwards, Laura F. *Gendered Strife and Confusion: The Political Culture of Reconstruction.* Urbana: University of Illinois Press, 1997.

Foner, Eric. *Reconstruction: America's Unfinished Revolution, 1863–1877.* New York: Harper & Row, 1988.

McPherson, James M. *Battle Cry of Freedom: The Civil War Era.* New York: Oxford University Press, 1988.

African Americans During the Civil War Era

Bardaglio, Peter. "The Children of Jubilee: African American Childhood in Wartime." In *Divided Houses: Gender and the Civil War,* edited by Catherine Clinton and Nina Silber. New York: Oxford University Press, 1992.

Berlin, Ira, et. al. *Free At Last: A Documentary History of Slavery, Freedom, and the Civil War.* New York: New Press, 1992.

Billington, Ray Allen, ed. *The Journal of Charlotte L. Forten: A Free Negro in the Slave Era.* New York: Dryden Press, 1953.

Daniels, Douglas Henry. *Pioneer Urbanites: A Social and Cultural History of Black San Francisco.* Philadelphia; Temple University Press, 1980.

Davis, Ronald L. F. *Good and Faithful Labor: From Slavery to Sharecropping in the Natchez District, 1860–1890.* Westport, Conn.: Greenwood, 1982.

Du Bois, William E. B. *Black Reconstruction in America, 1860–1880.* New York: Atheneum, 1962.

Foner, Eric. *Freedom's Lawmakers: A Directory of Black Officeholders During Reconstruction.* New York: Oxford University Press, 1993.

Frankel, Noralee. *Freedom's Women: Black Women and Families in Civil War Era Mississippi.* Bloomington: Indiana University Press, 1999.

Franklin, John Hope. *Reconstruction After the Civil War.* Chicago: University of Chicago Press, 1961.

Gerteis, Louis S. *From Contraband to Freedman: Federal Policy toward Southern Blacks, 1861–1865.* Westport, Conn.: Greenwood, 1973.

Glatthaar, Joseph I. *Forged in Battle: The Civil Alliance of Black Soldiers and White Officers.* New York: Free Press, 1990.

Holt, Thomas. *Black over White: Negro Political Leadership in South Carolina during Reconstruction.* Urbana: University of Illinois Press, 1977.

Horton, James Oliver, and Louis E. Horton. *Black Bostonians: Family Life and Community Struggle in the Antebellum North.* New York: Holmes & Meier, 1979.

Jaynes, Gerald David. *Branches Without Roots: Genesis of the Black Working Class in the American South, 1862–1882.* New York: Oxford University Press, 1986.

Katzman, David M. *Before the Ghetto: Black Detroit in the Nineteenth Century.* Urbana: University of Illinois Press, 1973.

Kolchin, Peter. *First Freedom: The Responses of Alabama's Blacks to Emancipation and Reconstruction.* Westport, Conn.: Greenwood, 1972.

Leckie, William H. *The Buffalo Soldiers: A Narrative of the Negro Cavalry in the West.* Norman: University of Oklahoma Press, 1967.

Litwack, Leon E. *Been in the Storm So Long: The Aftermath of Slavery.* New York: Knopf, 1979.

McPherson, James M. *Marching toward Freedom: Blacks in the Civil War, 1861–1865.* New York: Facts on File, 1991.

———. *The Negro's Civil War: How American Negroes Felt and Acted during the War for the Union.* New York: Vintage, 1965.

Miller, Edward A. *Gullah Statesman: Robert Smalls from Slavery to Congress, 1839–1915.* Columbia: University of South Carolina Press, 1995.

Mohr, Clarence L. *On the Threshold of Freedom: Masters and Slaves in Civil War Georgia.* Athens: University of Georgia Press, 1886.

Pearson, Elizabeth Ware, ed. *Letters from Port Royal, 1862–1868.* New York: Arno, 1969.

Quarles, Benjamin. *The Negro in the Civil War.* Boston: Little, Brown, 1969.

Rabinowitz, Howard N. *Race Relations in the Urban South, 1865–1890.* New York: Oxford University Press, 1978.

Ransom, Robert L., and Richard Sutch. *One Kind of Freedom: The Economic Consequences of Emancipation.* New York: Cambridge University Press, 1977.

Rawich, George P. *The American Slave: A Composite Autobiography.* Westport, Conn.: Greenwood, 1972.

Schwalm, Leslie. *A Hard Fight For We, Women's Transition from Slavery to Freedom in South Carolina.* Urbana: University of Illinois Press, 1997.

Chapter 6
Black Migration, Land Use, Labor, and Black Towns

Arneson, Eric. *Waterfront Workers of New Orleans: Race, Class, and Politics, 1863–1923.* New York: Oxford University Press, 1991.

Foner, Philip S., and Ronald L. Lewis, eds. *Black Workers: A Documentary History from Colonial Times to the Present.* Philadelphia: Temple University Press, 1989.

Fortune, T. Thomas. *Black and White: Land, Labor, and Politics in the South.* 1884. Reprint, New York: Arno, 1968.

Gutman, Herbert G. "The Negro and the United Mine Workers of America: The Career and Letters of Richard L. Davis and Something of their Meaning, 1890–1900" in *The Negro and the American Labor Movement*. Edited by Julius Jacobson. Garden City, N.J.: Anchor/Doubleday, 1968, 42–127.

Hamilton, Kenneth Marvin. *Black Towns and Profit: Promotion and Development in the Trans-Appalacian West, 1877–1915*. Urbana: University of Illinois Press, 1991.

Harris, William H. *The Harder We Run: Black Workers since the Civil War*. New York: Oxford University Press, 1982.

Hunter, Tera W. To 'Joy My Freedom: Southern Black Women's Lives and Labors after the Civil War. Cambridge: Harvard University Press, 1997.

Lewis, Ronald L. Black Coal Miners in America: Race, Class, and Community Conflict 1780–1980. Lexington: University Press of Kentucky, 1987.

Painter, Nell Irvin. *Exodusters: Black Migration to Kansas after Reconstruction*. New York: Knopf, 1976.

Rachleff, Peter. *Black Labor in Richmond, 1865–1890*. Urbana: University of Illinois Press, 1989.

Stokes, Melvyn, and Rick Halpern, eds. *Race and Class in the American South since 1890*. Providence, R.I.: Berg Press, 1994.

Social and Political Histories

Ayers, Edward L. *Vengeance and Justice: Crime and Publishment in the 19th-Century American South*. New York: Oxford University Press, 1984.

Bederman, Gail. *Manliness and Civilization: A Cultural History of Gender and Race in the United States, 1880–1917*. Chicago: University of Chicago Press, 1995.

Foner, Jack. *Blacks and the Military in American History*. New York: Praeger, 1974.

Gatewood, Willard B. Jr. *"Smoked Yankees" and the Struggle for Empire: Letters from Negro Soldiers, 1898–1902*. Urbana: University of Illinois Press, 1971.

Gunning, Sandra. *Race, Rape, and Lynching: The Red Record of American Literature, 1890–1912*. New York: Oxford University Press, 1996.

Gutman, Herbert. *The Black Family in Slavery and Freedom*. New York: Pantheon, 1976.

Harris, Trudier. *Exorcising Blackness: Historical and Literary Lynching and Burning Rituals*. Bloomington: Indiana University Press, 1984.

Jaynes, Gerald David. *Branches without Roots: Genesis of the Black Working Class in the American South, 1862–1882*. New York: Oxford University Press, 1986.

Katz, William Loren. *The Black West*. Garden City, N.Y.: Doubleday, 1971.

Lofgren, Charles. *The Plessy Case: A Legal Historical Interpretation*. New York: Oxford University Press, 1987.

Moss, Alfred Jr. *The American Negro Academy: Voice of the Talented Tenth*. Baton Rouge: Louisiana State University Press, 1981.

Painter, Nell Irvin. *Standing at Armageddon: The United States, 1877–1919*. New York: Norton, 1977.

Rabinowitz, Howard N. *Race Relations in the Urban South, 1865–1890*. New York: Oxford University Press, 1978.

Redkey, Edwin S. *Black Exodus: Black Nationalist and Back-to-Africa Movements, 1890–1910*. New Haven: Yale University Press, 1969.

Shapiro, Herbert. *White Violence and Black Response: From Reconstruction to Montgomery.* Amherst: University of Massachusetts Press, 1988.

Taylor, Quintard. *In Search of the Racial Frontier: African Americans in the American West, 1528–1990.* New York: Norton, 1998.

Thomas, Brook, ed. *Plessy* v. *Ferguson: A Brief History with Documents.* Boston: Bedford Books, 1997.

Urban Histories

Borchert, James. *Alley Life in Washington.* Urbana: University of Illinois Press, 1980.

Brown, Elsa Barkley. "Mapping the Terrain of Black Richmond." *Journal of Urban History* 21, no. 3 (March 1995): 296–347.

Du Bois, W. E. B. *The Philadelphia Negro.* 1899. Reprint, New York: Schocken, 1967.

Lane, Roger. *William Dorsey's Philadelphia and Ours.* New York: Oxford University Press, 1991.

————. *Roots of Violence in Black Philadelphia, 1869–1900.* Cambridge: Harvard University Press, 1986.

Pleck, Elizabeth. *Black Migration and Poverty: Boston 1865–1900.* New York: Academic Press, 1979.

Biographies and Autobiographies

Ashbaugh, Carolyn. *Lucy Parsons: American Revolutionary.* Chicago: Charles H. Kerr, 1976.

Boyd, Melba Joyce. *Discarded Legacy: Politics and Poetics in the Life of Frances E. W. Harper, 1825–1911.* Detroit: Wayne State University Press, 1994.

Chall, Malca, interviewer. "Frances Mary Albrier: Determined Advocate for Racial Equality." University of California, Berkeley, Bancroft Library, and the Schlesinger Library, Radcliffe College, Cambridge, Mass., 1977–78.

DeCosta-Willis, Miriam. *The Memphis Diary of Ida B. Wells.* Boston: Beacon Press, 1995.

Duster, Alfreda, ed. *Crusade for Justice: The Autobiography of Ida B. Wells.* Chicago: University of Chicago Press, 1970.

Foner, Philip, ed. *Life and Writings of Frederick Douglass.* New York: International Publishers, 1955.

Harlan, Louis. *Booker T. Washington, the Making of a Black Leader, 1856–1901.* New York: Oxford University Press, 1975.

Harlan, Louis, Stuart B. Kaufman, et. al, eds. *The Booker T. Washington Papers,* vols. 2, 3, 4. Urbana: University of Illinois Press, 1972, 1974, 1975.

Harris, Trudier. *The Selected Works of Ida B. Wells-Barnett.* New York: Oxford University Press, 1991.

Jones, Beverly Washington. *Quest for Equality: The Life and Writings of Mary Eliza Church Terrell, 1863–1954.* Brooklyn, N.Y.: Carlson, 1990.

Lewis, David Levering. *W. E. B. Du Bois: Biography of a Race, 1868–1919.* New York: Holt, 1993.

McMurry, Linda D. *To Keep the Waters Troubled: The Life of Ida B. Wells.* New York: Oxford University Press, 1998.

Sterling, Dorothy. *Black Foremothers: Three Lives.* Old Westbury, N.Y.: Feminist Press, 1979.

Thompson, Mildred. *Ida B. Wells-Barnett: An Exploratory Study of an American Black Woman, 1893–1930*. Brooklyn, N.Y.: Carlson, 1990.

Thornbrough, Emma Lou. *Booker T. Washington*. Englewood Cliffs, N.J.: Prentice-Hall, 1969.

———. *T. Thomas Fortune: Militant Journalist*. Chicago: University of Chicago Press, 1972.

Washington, Booker T. *Up from Slavery: An Autobiography*. 1900. Reprint, New York: Oxford University Press, 1995.

———. *Working with the Hands: Being a Sequel to Up From Slavery Covering the Author's Experiences in Industrial Training at Tuskegee*. 1904. Reprint, Salem, N.H.: Ayer, 1970.

African-American Women's History

Aptheker, Bettina. *Woman's Legacy: Essays on Race, Sex, and Class in American History*. Amherst: University of Massachusetts Press, 1982.

Brody, Jennefer DeVere. *Impossible Purities: Blackness, Femininity, and Victorian Culture*. Durham, N.C.: Duke University Press, 1998.

Cooper, Anna Julia. *A Voice from the South*. 1892. Reprint, New York: Oxford University Press, 1988.

Davis, Angela. *Women, Race and Class*. New York: Vintage, 1983.

Giddings, Paula. *When and Where I Enter: The Impact of Black Women on Race and Sex in America*. New York: William Morrow, 1984.

Guy-Sheftall, Beverly. *Daughters of Sorrow: Attitudes toward Black Women, 1880–1920*. Brooklyn, N.Y.: Carlson, 1990.

Higginbotham, Evelyn Brooks. *Righteous Discontent: The Women's Movement in the Black Baptist Church, 1880–1920*. Cambridge: Harvard University Press, 1993.

Hine, Darlene Clark. *Black Women in White: Racial Conflict and Cooperation in the Nursing Profession, 1890–1950*. Bloomington: Indiana University Press, 1989.

Lerner, Gerda, ed. *Black Women in White America: A Documentary History*. New York: Vintage, 1973.

Shaw, Stephanie J. *What A Woman Ought to Be and Do: Black Professional Women Workers During the Jim Crow Era*. Chicago: University of Chicago Press, 1996.

White, Deborah Gray. *Too Heavy A Load: Black Women in Defense of Themselves, 1894–1994*. New York: Norton, 1999.

Literary Sources

Carby, Hazel. *Reconstructing Womanhood: The Emergence of the Afro-American Woman Novelist*. New York: Oxford University Press, 1987.

Chesnutt, Charles W. *The Conjure Woman*. 1899. Reprint, Ann Arbor: University of Michigan Press, 1969.

Dunbar, Paul Laurence. *The Complete Poems of Paul Laurence Dunbar*. 1913. Reprint, New York: Dodd, Mead, 1970.

Harper, Frances Ellen Watkins. *Iola Leroy*. 1892. Reprint, Boston: Beacon Press, 1987.

———. *Complete Poems of Frances E. W. Harper*. Compiled by Maryemma Graham. New York: Oxford University Press, 1988.

Goss, Linda, and Marian E. Barnes, eds. *Talk that Talk: An Anthology of African-American Storytelling*. New York: Simon and Schuster, 1989.

Salem, Dorothy. *To Better Our World: Black Women in Organized Reform, 1890–1920.* Brooklyn, N.Y.: Carlson, 1990.

Chapter 7
Leadership and Institutional Development

Anderson, James. *The Education of Blacks in the South, 1880–1935.* Chapel Hill: University of North Carolina Press, 1988.

Brown, Elsa Barkley. "Womanist Consciousness: Maggie Lena Walker and the Independent Order of Saint Luke," *Signs,* vol. 14, no. 3 (1989): 610–633.

Du Bois, William Edward Burkhardt. *The Souls of Black Folk.* 1903. Reprint, New York: Vintage, 1990.

Garvey, Amy Jacques. *The Philosophy and Opinions of Marcus Garvey, with an Introduction by Robert A. Hill.* New York: 1992.

Harlan, Lewis R. *Booker T. Washington: The Wizard of Tuskegee, 1901–1915.* New York: Oxford University Press, 1983.

Higginbotham, Evelyn Brooks. *Righteous Discontent: The Women's Movement in the Black Baptist Church, 1880–1920.* Cambridge: Harvard University Press, 1993.

Ottley, Roi. *The Lonely Warrior: The Life and Times of Robert S. Abbott.* Chicago: Henry Regnery, 1955.

Salem, Dorothy. *To Better Our World: Black Women in Organized Reform, 1890–1920.* Brooklyn, N.Y.: Carlson, 1990.

Shaw, Stephanie. *What a Woman Ought to Be and to Do: Black Professional Women Workers during the Jim Crow Era.* Chicago: University of Chicago Press, 1996.

Biographies and Autobiographies

Johnson, James Weldon. *Along This Way: The Autobiography of James Weldon Johnson.* New York: Viking Press, 1933.

Johnson, Lyman T. *The Rest of the Dream: The Black Odyssey of Lyman Johnson.* Edited by Wade Hall. Lexington: University of Kentucky Press, 1988.

Pickens, William. *Bursting Bonds: The Heir of Slaves.* Boston: Jordan & More, 1923.

Rosengarten, Theodore. *All God's Dangers: The Life of Nate Shaw.* New York: Knopf, 1975.

Tarry, Ellen. *The Third Door: The Autobiography of an American Negro Woman.* Expanded ed. New York: Guild Press, 1966.

Washington, Booker T. *Up from Slavery: An Autobiography.* 1900. Reprint, New York: Oxford University Press, 1995.

Wright, Richard. *Black Boy: A Record of Childhood and Youth.* New York: Harper & Row, 1937.

African-American Culture

Cripps, Thomas. *Slow Fade to Black: The Negro in American Film, 1900–1942.* New York: Oxford University Press, 1977.

Huggins, Nathan I. *Harlem Renaissance.* New York: Oxford University Press, 1971.

———. *Voices from the Harlem Renaissance.* New York: Oxford University Press, 1976.

Johnson-Feelings, Dianne, ed. *The Best of* The Brownies' Book. New York: Oxford University Press, 1996.

Levine, Lawrence L. *Black Culture and Black Consciousness: Afro-American Folk Thought from Slavery to Freedom.* New York: Oxford University Press, 1977.

Lewis, David Levering. *When Harlem Was in Vogue.* New York: Knopf, 1981.

Locke, Alain. *The New Negro: An Interpretation.* 1925. Reprint, New York: Arno, 1968.

The Studio Museum in Harlem. *Harlem Renaissance: Art of Black America.* New York: Abrams, 1987.

Watson, Steven. *The Harlem Renaissance: Hub of African-American Culture, 1920–1930.* New York: Pantheon, 1995.

Community Studies

Daniels, Douglas Henry. *Black Pioneers: A Social and Cultural History of Black San Francisco.* Philadelphia: Temple University Press, 1980.

Du Bois, William Edward Burkhardt. *The Philadelphia Negro: A Social Study.* 1899. Reprint, New York: Benjamin Blom, 1967.

Kusmer, Kenneth L. *A Ghetto Takes Shape: Black Cleveland, 1870–1930.* Urbana: University of Illinois Press, 1976.

Lewis, Earl. *In Their Own Interests: Race, Class, and Power in Twentieth-Century Norfolk, Virginia.* Berkeley: University of California Press, 1991.

Spear, Allan H. *Black Chicago: The Making of a Negro Ghetto, 1890–1920.* Chicago: University of Chicago Press, 1967.

Taylor, Quintard. *The Forging of a Black Community: Seattle's Central District from 1870 through the Civil Rights Era.* Seattle: University of Washington Press, 1994.

Trotter, Joe William. *Black Milwaukee: The Making of the Industrial Proletariat, 1915–1945.* Urbana: University of Illinois Press, 1985.

Wright, George. *Life Behind a Veil: Blacks in Louisville, Kentucky, 1865–1930.* Baton Rouge: Louisiana State University Press, 1985.

The Great Migration and World War I

Adero, Malaika ed., *Up South: Stories, Studies, and Letters of the Century's Black Migrations.* New York: New Press, 1993.

Crew, Spencer R. *Field to Factory: Afro-American Migration 1915–1940.* Washington, D.C.: National Museum of American History, Smithsonian Institution, 1987.

Gottlieb, Peter. *Making Their Own Way: Southern Blacks' Migration to Pittsburgh, 1916–1930.* Urbana: University of Illinois Press, 1987.

Grossman, James R. *Land of Hope: Chicago, Black Southerners, and the Great Migration.* Chicago: University of Chicago Press, 1989.

Henri, Florette, and Arthur Barbeau. *The Unknown Soldiers: Black American Troops in World War I.* Philadelphia: Temple University Press, 1974.

Trotter, Joe W., ed. *The Great Migration in Historical Perspective: New Dimensions of Race, Class and Gender.* Bloomington: Indiana University Press, 1991.

Race Relations

Ayers, Edward L. *The Promise of the New South: Life After Reconstruction.* New York: Oxford University Press, 1993.

Dittmer, John. *Black Georgia in the Progressive Era, 1900–1920.* Urbana: University of Illinois Press, 1977.

Hair, William Ivy. *Carnival of Fury: Robert Charles and the New Orleans Race Riot of 1900.* Baton Rouge: Louisiana State University Press, 1976.

McMillen, Neil. *Dark Journey: Black Mississippians in the Age of Jim Crow.* Urbana: University of Illinois Press, 1989.

Tuttle, William M., Jr. *Race Riot: Chicago in the Red Summer of 1919.* New York: Atheneum, 1970.

Williamson, Joel. *A Rage for Order: Black/White Relations in the American South since Emancipation.* New York: Oxford University Press, 1986.

Work and the Economy

Clark-Lewis, Elizabeth. *Living In, Living Out: African American Domestics in Washington, D.C., 1910–1940.* Washington, D.C.: Smithsonian Institution Press, 1994.

Harris, William H. *The Harder We Run: Black Workers since the Civil War.* New York: Oxford University Press, 1982.

Jones, Jacqueline. *The Dispossessed: America's Underclass from the Civil War to the Present.* New York: Basic Books, 1992.

Trotter, Joe William. *Coal, Class, and Color: Blacks in Southern West Virginia, 1915–32.* Urbana: University of Illinois Press, 1990.

Wright, Gavin. *Old South, New South: Revolutions in the Southern Economy since the Civil War.* New York: Basic Books, 1986.

Chapter 8
The Depression and World War II

Kusmer, Kenneth L., ed. *Depression, War, and the New Migration, 1930–1960.* Vol. 6 of *Black Communities and Urban Development in America, 1720–1960.* New York: Garland, 1991.

McElvaine, Robert S. *The Great Depression: America, 1929–1941.* New York: Times Books, 1984.

Nash, Gerald D. *The Crucial Era: The Great Depression and World War II, 1929–1945.* 2nd ed. New York: St. Martin's, 1992.

Sitkoff, Harvard. *A New Deal for Blacks: The Emergence of Civil Rights as a National Issue: The Depression Decade.* New York: Oxford University Press, 1978.

Sternsher, Bernard, ed. *The Negro in Depression and War: Prelude to Revolution, 1930–1945.* Chicago: Quadrangle, 1969.

Wright, Richard, and Edwin Rosskam. *12 Million Black Voices.* New York: Thunder's Mouth, 1941.

African-American Culture and Institutions

Frazier, E. Franklin. *The Negro Church in America.* New York: Schocken, 1963.

Hazard-Gordon, Katrina. *Jookin': The Rise of Social Dance Formations in African-American Culture.* Philadelphia: Temple University Press, 1990.

Jones, LeRoi (Amiri Baraka). *Blues People: The Negro Experience in White America and the Music That Developed from It.* New York: Morrow, 1963.

Levine, Lawrence. *Black Culture and Black Consciousness: Afro-American Folk Thoughts from Slavery to Freedom*. New York: Oxford University Press, 1977.

Southern, Eileen. *The Music of Black Americans: A History*. 3rd ed. New York: Norton, 1997.

Tucker, Mark, ed. *The Duke Ellington Reader*. New York: Oxford University Press, 1993.

Black Community Studies

Broussard, Albert S. *Black San Francisco: The Struggle for Racial Equality in the West, 1900–1954*. Lawrence: University Press of Kansas, 1993.

Daniels, Douglas Henry. *Pioneer Urbanites: A Social and Cultural History of Black San Francisco*. Philadelphia: Temple University Press, 1980.

Drake, St. Clair, and Horace R. Cayton. *Black Metropolis: A Study of Negro Life in a Northern City*. 2 vols. 1944. Reprint, New York: Harcourt, Brace & World, 1962.

Greenberg, Cheryl Lynn. *Or Does it Explode? Black Harlem in the Great Depression*. New York: Oxford University Press, 1991.

Lewis, Earl. *In Their Own Interests: Race, Class and Power in Twentieth Century Norfolk*. Berkeley: University of California Press, 1991.

Taylor, Quintard. *The Forging of a Black Community: Seattle's Central District from 1870 through the Civil Rights Era*. Seattle: University of Washington Press, 1994.

Trotter, Joe William, Jr. *Black Milwaukee: The Making of an Industrial Proletariat, 1915–45*. Urbana: University of Illinois Press, 1985.

Politics, Leadership, and Race Relations

Anderson, Jervis. *A. Philip Randolph: A Biographical Portrait*. Berkeley: University of California Press, 1986.

Grant, Nancy L. *TVA and Black Americans: Planning for the Status Quo*. Philadelphia: Temple University Press, 1990.

Kelley, Robin D. G. *Hammer and Hoe: Alabama Communists during the Great Depression*. Chapel Hill: University of North Carolina Press, 1990.

Kirby, John B. *Black Americans in the Roosevelt Era: Liberalism and Race*. Knoxville: University of Tennessee Press, 1992.

Mintz, Sidney W., and Richard Price. *The Birth of African-American Culture: An Anthropological Perspective*. Boston: Beacon Press, 1992.

Myrdal, Gunnar. *An American Dilemma: The Negro Problem and Modern Democracy*. 2 vols. 1944. Reprint, New York: Pantheon, 1962.

Naison, Mark. *Communists in Harlem During the Depression*. Urbana: University of Illinois Press, 1983.

Nieman, Donald G. *Promises to Keep: African-Americans and the Constitutional Order, 1776 to the Present*. New York: Oxford University Press, 1991.

Shapiro, Herbert. *White Violence and Black Response: From Reconstruction to Montgomery*. Amherst: University of Massachusetts Press, 1988.

Urquhart, Brian. *Ralph Bunche*. New York: Norton, 1993.

Wolters, Raymond. *Negroes and the Great Depression: The Problem of Economic Recovery*. Westport, Conn.: Greenwood, 1970.

Work and Labor Relations

Dickerson, Dennis C. *Out of the Crucible: Black Steelworkers in Western Pennsylvania, 1875–1980.* Albany: State University of New York Press, 1986.

Foner, Philip S. *Organized Labor and the Black Workers, 1619–1981.* New York: International Publishers, 1982.

Harris, William H. *Keeping the Faith: A. Philip Randolph, Milton P. Webster, and the Brotherhood of Sleeping Car Porters, 1925–37.* Urbana: University of Illinois Press, 1977.

———. *The Harder We Run: Black Workers Since the Civil War.* New York: Oxford University Press, 1982.

Meier, August, and Elliot Rudwick. *Black Detroit and the Rise of the UAW.* New York: Oxford University Press, 1979.

Painter, Nell Irvin. *The Narrative of Hosea Hudson: His Life as a Communist.* Cambridge: Harvard University Press, 1979.

Rosengarten, Theodore. *All God's Dangers: The Life of Nate Shaw.* New York: Knopf, 1975.

Trotter, Joe William, Jr. *Coal, Class, and Color: Blacks in Southern West Virginia, 1915–32.* Urbana: University of Illinois Press, 1990.

African-American Women

Gray, Brenda Clegg. *Black Female Domestics during the Depression in New York City, 1930–1940.* New York: Garland, 1993.

Hawks, Joanne V., and Sheila L. Skemp, eds. *Sex, Race, and the Role of Women in the South.* Jackson: University Press of Mississippi, 1983.

Hine, Darlene Clark. *Black Women in White: Racial Conflict and Cooperation in the Nursing Profession, 1890–1950.* Bloomington: Indiana University Press, 1989.

Lerner, Gerda, ed. *Black Women in White America: A Documentary History.* New York: Vintage, 1973.

Chapter 9

The Civil Rights Era

Lincoln, C. Eric. *The Black Muslims in America.* Grand Rapids, Mich.: Eerdmans, 1994.

Patterson, James T. *Grand Expectations: The United States, 1945–1974.* New York: Oxford University Press, 1996.

Wofford, Harris. *Of Kennedys and Kings: Making Sense of the Sixties.* New York: Farrar Straus & Giroux, 1980.

Civil Rights Movement

Archer, Jules. *They Had a Dream: The Civil Rights Struggle, from Frederick Douglass to Marcus Garvey to Martin Luther King, Jr. and Malcolm X.* New York: Viking, 1993.

Branch, Taylor. *Parting the Waters: America in the King Years, 1954–1963.* New York: Simon & Schuster, 1988.

———. *Pillar of Fire: America in the King Years, 1963–1965.* New York: Simon & Schuster, 1998.

Bullard, Sara. *Free at Last: A History of the Civil Rights Movement and Those Who Died in the Struggle.* New York: Oxford University Press, 1993.

Carawan, Guy, and Candie Carawan. *Freedom Is a Constant Struggle: Songs of the Freedom Movement.* New York: Oak Publications, 1968.

Carson, Claybourne. *In Struggle: SNCC and the Black Awakening of the 1960s.* Cambridge: Harvard University Press, 1981.

Carson, Claybourne, et al. *The Eyes on the Prize Civil Rights Reader.* New York: Penguin, 1991.

Chafe, William H. *Civilities and Civil Rights: Greensboro, North Carolina, and the Black Struggle for Freedom.* New York: Oxford University Press, 1980.

Cleghorn, Reese, and Pat Watters. *Climbing Jacob's Ladder: The Arrival of Negroes in Southern Politics.* New York: Harcourt, Brace & World, 1967.

Couto, Richard A. *Ain't Gonna Let Nobody Turn Me Round: The Pursuit of Racial Justice in the Rural South.* Philadelphia: Temple University Press, 1991.

Crawford, Vicki, Jacqueline Anne Rouse, and Barbara Woods, eds. *Women in the Civil Rights Movement: Trailblazers and Torchbearers, 1941–1965.* Bloomington: Indiana University Press, 1993.

Egerton, John. *Speak Now Against the Day: The Generation Before the Civil Rights Movement in the South.* New York: Knopf, 1994.

Fairclough, Adam. *To Redeem the Soul of America: The Southern Christian Leadership Conference and Martin Luther King, Jr.* Athens: University of Georgia Press, 1987.

Forman, James. *The Making of Black Revolutionaries.* New York: Macmillan, 1972.

Grant, Joanne, ed. *Black Protest: History, Documents, and Analyses, 1619 to the Present.* New York: St. Martin's, 1970.

Hampton, Henry, and Steve Fayer, with Sarah Flynn. *Voices of Freedom: An Oral History of the Civil Rights Movement from the 1950s through the 1980s.* New York: Bantam, 1990.

Harding, Vincent. *Hope and History: Why We Must Share the Story of the Movement.* Maryknoll, N.Y.: Orbis, 1990.

Hughes, Langston. *Fight for Freedom: The Story of the NAACP.* New York: Berkley, 1962.

Kapur, Sudarshan. *Raising Up a Prophet: The African-American Encounter With Gandhi.* Boston: Beacon Press, 1992.

King, Martin Luther, Jr. *Stride Toward Freedom.* New York: Harper & Row, 1958.

———. *Trumpet of Conscience.* New York: Harper & Row, 1968.

———. *Where Do We Go from Here: Chaos or Community?* New York: Harper & Row, 1967.

———. *Why We Can't Wait.* New York: Harper & Row, 1964.

Kluger, Richard. *Simple Justice: The History of Brown v. Board of Education and Black America's Struggle for Equality.* New York: Knopf, 1975.

Lawson, Stephen. *Running for Freedom: Civil Rights and Black Politics in America Since 1941.* New York: McGraw-Hill, 1991.

Lewis, Anthony. *Portrait of a Decade: The Second American Revolution.* New York: Random House, 1964.

Lomax, Louis E. *The Negro Revolt.* New York: Harper & Row, 1962.

Lowery, Charles D., and John F. Marszalek, eds. *Encyclopedia of African-American Civil Rights.* New York: Greenwood, 1992.

Lyon, Danny. *Memories of the Southern Civil Rights Movement.* Chapel Hill: University of North Carolina Press, 1992.

Meier, August, and Elliot Rudwick. *CORE: A Study in the Civil Rights Movement, 1942–1968.* New York: Oxford University Press, 1973.

Morris, Aldon D. *The Origins of the Civil Rights Movement.* New York: Free Press, 1984.

O'Reilly, Kenneth. *"Racial Matters": The FBI's Secret File on Black America, 1960–1972.* New York: Free Press, 1989.

Payne, Charles M. *I've Got the Light of Freedom.* Berkeley: University of California Press, 1995.

Peck, James. *Freedom Ride.* New York: Simon & Schuster, 1962.

President's Committee on Civil Rights. *To Secure These Rights.* Washington: U.S. Government Printing Office, 1947.

Raines, Howell. *My Soul is Rested: The Story of the Civil Rights Movement in the Deep South.* New York: Viking Penguin, 1977.

Reiser, Bob, and Pete Seeger. *Everybody Says Freedom: A History of the Civil Rights Movement in Songs and Pictures.* New York: Norton, 1989.

Sitkoff, Harvard. *The Struggle for Black Equality.* New York: Hill & Wang, 1993.

Skolnick, Jerome. *The Politics of Protest.* New York: Ballantine, 1969.

Sugarman, Tracy. *Stranger at the Gates: A Summer in Mississippi.* New York: Hill & Wang, 1966.

Weisbrot, Robert. *Freedom Bound: A History of America's Civil Rights Movement.* New York: Norton, 1990.

Williams, Juan. *Eyes on the Prize: America's Civil Rights Years, 1954–1965.* New York: Penguin, 1988.

Young, Andrew. *An Easy Burden: The Civil Rights Movement and the Transformation of America.* New York: HarperCollins, 1996.

Zinn, Howard. *SNCC: The New Abolitionists.* Boston: Beacon Press, 1964.

Autobiographies and Biographies

Anderson, Jervis. *Bayard Rustin: Troubles I've Seen, a Biography.* New York: HarperCollins, 1997.

Baraka, Amiri. *The Autobiography of LeRoi Jones/Amiri Baraka.* New York: Freundlich Books, 1984.

Bennett, Lerone, Jr. *What Manner of Man: A Biography of Martin Luther King, Jr.* Chicago: Johnson, 1964.

Burner, Eric. *And Gently He Shall Lead Them: Robert Parris Moses and Civil Rights In Mississippi.* New York: New York University Press, 1994.

Carmichael, Stokely. *Black Power: The Politics of Liberation in America.* New York: Vintage, 1992.

Carson, Clayborne. *Malcolm X, The FBI File.* New York: Carroll & Graf, 1991.

Carson, Clayborne, ed. *The Papers of Martin Luther King, Jr.* Berkeley: University of California Press, 1992, 1994.

Clark, Septima P. *Echo In My Soul.* New York: Dutton, 1962.

———. *Ready From Within.* Navarro, Calif.: Wild Trees Press, 1986.

Cone, James. *Martin and Malcolm and America.* Maryknoll, N.Y.: Orbis, 1991.

Farmer, James. *Lay Bare the Heart: An Autobiography of the Civil Rights Movement.* Forth Worth: Texas Christian University Press, 1998.

Garrow, David. *Bearing the Cross: Martin Luther King, Jr., and the Southern Christian Leadership Conference.* New York: Morrow, 1986.

Goldman, Peter. *The Death and Life of Malcolm X.* New York: Harper & Row, 1973.

Grant, Joanne. *Ella Baker: Freedom Bound.* New York: Wiley, 1998.

Hamilton, Charles V. *Adam Clayton Powell, Jr.* New York: Atheneum, 1991.

Harding, Vincent. *Martin Luther King: The Inconvenient Hero.* Maryknoll, N.Y.: Orbis, 1996.

King, Coretta Scott. *My Life With Martin Luther King, Jr.* New York: Holt, Rinehart & Winston, 1969.

King, Martin Luther, Sr., with Clayton Riley. *Daddy King.* New York: Morrow, 1980.

Lewis, David L. *King: A Critical Biography.* New York: Praeger, 1970.

Malcolm X, with the assistance of Alex Haley. *The Autobiography of Malcolm X.* New York: Grove Press, 1965.

Mills, Kay. *This Little Light of Mine: The Life of Fannie Lou Hamer.* New York: Dutton, 1993.

Oates, Stephen B. *Let the Trumpet Sound: The Life of Martin Luther King, Jr.* New York: Harper & Row, 1982.

Rowan, Carl Thomas. *Dream Makers, Dream Breakers: The World of Justice Thurgood Marshall.* Boston: Little, Brown, 1993.

Washington, James M. *A Testament of Hope: The Essential Writings of Martin Luther King, Jr.* New York: Harper & Row, 1986.

Wilkins, Roy, with Tom Mathews. *Standing Fast: The Autobiography of Roy Wilkins.* New York: Viking, 1982.

Chapter 10
General Histories of the United States Since 1970

Amott, Teresa L., and Julie A. Matthaei. *Race, Gender, and Work: A Multicultural History of Women in the United States.* Boston: South End Press, 1991.

Carroll, Peter N. *It Seemed Like Nothing Happened: The Tragedy and Promise of America in the 1970s.* New York: Holt, Rinehart and Winston, 1982.

Coontz, Stephanie. *The Way We Never Were: American Families and the Nostalgia Trap.* New York: Basic Books, 1992.

Edsall, Thomas Byrne. *Chain Reaction: The Impact of Race, Rights, and Taxes on American Politics.* New York: Norton, 1991.

Evans, Sara M. *Born for Liberty: A History of Women in America.* New York: Free Press, 1989.

Omi, Michael, and Howard Winant. *Racial Formation in the United States: From the 1960s to the 1990s.* 2nd ed. New York: Norton, 2000.

Piven, Frances Fox. *The New Class War: Reagan's Attack on the Welfare State and its Consequences.* New York: Pantheon, 1982.

Plummer, Brenda Gayle. *Rising Wind: Black Americans and U.S. Foreign Affairs, 1935–1960.* Chapel Hill: University of North Carolina Press, 1996.

Siegel, Frederick F. *Troubled Journey: From Pearl Harbor to Ronald Reagan.* New York: Hill & Wang, 1984.

Stacey, Judith. *Brave New Families: Stories of Domestic Upheaval in Late Twentieth Century America.* New York: Basic Books, 1990.

von Eschen, Penny. *Race Against Empire: Black Americans and Anticolonialsim, 1937–1957.* Ithaca: Cornell University Press, 1997.

African-American Politics

Bell, Derrick. *And We Are Not Saved: The Elusive Quest for Racial Justice.* New York: Basic Books, 1987.

Collins, Sheila D. *The Rainbow Challenge: The Jackson Campaign and the Future of U.S. Politics.* New York: Monthly Review Press, 1986.

Davis, Angela. *Women, Culture, and Politics.* New York: Random House, 1989.

Harding, Vincent. *Hope and History: Why We Must Share the Story of the Movement.* Maryknoll, N.Y.: Orbis, 1990.

Hatch, Roger D., and Frank E. Watkins, eds. *Reverend Jesse L. Jackson: Straight from the Heart.* Philadelphia: Fortress Press, 1987.

Henry, Charles P. *Culture and African-American Politics.* Bloomington: Indiana University Press, 1990.

Horne, Gerald. *The Fire This Time: The Watts Uprising and the 1960s.* Charlottesville: University Press of Virginia, 1995.

James, Joy. *Transcending the Talented Tenth: Black Leaders and American Intellectuals.* New York: Routledge, 1997.

Lawson, Steven F. *Running for Freedom: Civil Rights and Black Politics in America Since 1941.* Philadelphia: Temple University Press, 1991.

Lusane, Clarence. *African Americans at the Crossroads: The Restructuring of Black Leadership in the 1992 Elections.* Boston: South End Press, 1994.

Marable, Manning. *Race, Reform, and Rebellion: The Second Reconstruction in Black America, 1945–1990.* 2nd ed. Jackson: University Press of Mississippi, 1991.

Morrison, Toni, ed. *Race-ing Justice, En-gendering Power: Essays on Anita Hill, Clarence Thomas and the Construction of Social Reality.* New York: Pantheon, 1992.

West, Cornel. *Race Matters.* Boston: Beacon Press, 1993.

African-American Social and Economic Conditions

Banner-Haley, Charles T. *The Fruits of Integration: Black Middle-Class Ideology and Culture, 1960–1990.* Jackson: University Press of Mississippi, 1994.

Billingsley, Andrew. *Climbing Jacob's Ladder: The Enduring Legacy of African-American Families.* New York: Simon & Schuster, 1992.

Bush, Rod. *We Are Not What We Seem: Black Nationalism and Class Struggle in the American Century.* New York: New York University Press, 1999.

Davis, Mike. *City of Quartz: Excavating the Future in Los Angeles.* London: Verso, 1990.

Feagin, Joe R., and Melvin P. Sikes. *Living with Racism: The Black Middle-Class Experience.* Boston: Beacon Press, 1994.

Gill, Gerald. *Meanness Mania: The Changed Mood.* Washington, D.C.: Howard University Press, 1980.

Glasgow, Douglas G. *The Black Underclass: Poverty, Unemployment, and Entrapment of Ghetto Youth.* New York: Vintage, 1981.

Jones, Jacqueline. *The Dispossessed: America's Underclasses from the Civil War to the Present.* New York: Basic Books, 1992.

Kasinitz, Philip. *Caribbean New York: Black Immigrants and the Politics of Race.* Ithaca, N.Y.: Cornell University Press, 1992.

Kelley, Robin. *Race Rebels: Culture, Politics, and the Black Working Class.* New York: Free Press, 1994.

Landry, Bart. *The New Black Middle Class.* Berkeley: University of California Press, 1987.

Lusane, Clarence. *Pipe Dream Blues: Racism and the War on Drugs.* Boston: South End Press, 1991.

Madhubuti, Haki R., ed. *Why L.A. Happened: Implications of the '92 Los Angeles Rebellion.* Chicago: Third World Press, 1993.

Massey, Douglas S., and Nancy A. Denton. *American Apartheid: Segregation and the Making of the Underclass.* Cambridge: Harvard University Press, 1993.

Quandango, Jill. *The Color of Welfare: How Racism Undermined the War on Poverty.* New York: Oxford University Press, 1994.

Rank, Mark Robert. *Living on the Edge: The Realities of Welfare in America.* New York: Columbia University Press, 1994.

Simms, Margaret C., and Julianne Malveaux, eds. *Slipping Through the Cracks: The Status of Black Women.* New Brunswick, N.J.: Transaction Books, 1986.

Wilson, William Julius. *The Truly Disadvantaged: The Inner City, the Underclass, and Public Policy.* Chicago: University of Chicago Press, 1987.

———. *When Work Disappears: The World of the New Urban Poor.* New York: Knopf, 1996.

African-American Culture

Castleman, Craig. *Getting Up: Subway Graffiti in New York.* Cambridge: MIT Press, 1982.

Cross, Brian. *It's Not About a Salary . . . Rap, Race and Resistance in Los Angeles.* London: Verso, 1993.

Dates, Jannette L., and William Barlow, eds. *Split Image: African Americans in the Mass Media.* 2nd ed. Washington, D.C.: Howard University Press, 1993.

Dent, Gina, ed. *Black Popular Culture.* Seattle: Bay Press, 1992.

Eure, Joseph G., and James G. Spady. *Nation Conscious Rap.* Brooklyn, N.Y.: P.C. International Press, 1991.

Franklin, V. P. *Black Self-Determination: A Cultural History of African American Resistance.* Brooklyn, N.Y.: Lawrence Hill, 1992.

Gaines, Kevin. *Uplifting the Race: Black Leadership, Politics, and Culture in the Twentieth Century.* Chapel Hill: University of North Carolina Press, 1996.

George, Nelson. *The Death of Rhythm and Blues.* New York: Plume, 1988.

———. *Hip Hop America.* New York: Penguin, 1998.

Guerrero, Ed. *Framing Blackness: The African-American Image in Film.* Philadelphia: Temple University Press, 1993.

Hazzard-Gordon, Katrina. *Jookin': The Rise of Social Dance Formations in African-American Culture.* Philadelphia: Temple University Press, 1990.

Kelley, Robin D. G. *Yo' Mama's Disfunktional!: Fighting the Culture Wars in Urban America.* Boston: Beacon Press, 1994.

Lippard, Lucy R. *Mixed Blessings: New Art in a Multicultural America.* New York: Pantheon, 1990.

Lipsitz, George. *The Possessive Investment in Whiteness.* Philadelphia: Temple University Press, 1998.

MacDonald, J. Fred. *Blacks and White TV: Afro-Americans in Television since 1948.* Chicago: Nelson-Hall, 1983.

Rose, Tricia. *Black Noise: Rap Music and Black Culture in Contemporary America.* Middletown, Conn.: Wesleyan University Press, 1994.

Stuckey, Sterling. *Slave Culture: Nationalist Theory and the Foundations of Black America.* New York: Oxford University Press, 1987.

Tate, Greg. *Flyboy in the Buttermilk: Essays on Contemporary America.* New York: Simon & Schuster, 1992.

Van Deburg, William L. *New Day in Babylon: The Black Power Movement and American Culture, 1965–1975.* Chicago: University of Chicago Press, 1992.

Ward, Brian. *Just My Soul Responding: Rhythm and Blues, Black Consciousness, and Race Relations.* Berkeley: University of California Press, 1998.

African-American Women and Politics

Carby, Hazel. *Reconstructing Black Womanhood.* New York: Oxford University Press, 1987.

Collins, Patricia Hill. *Fighting Words: Black Women and the Search for Justice.* Minneapolis: University of Minnesota Press, 1998.

Davis, Angela Y. *Blues Legacies and Black Feminism: Gertrude "Ma" Rainey, Bessie Smith and Billie Holiday.* New York: Pantheon, 1998.

Guy-Sheftall, Beverly, ed. *Words of Fire: An Anthology of African-American Feminist Thought.* New York: New Press, 1995.

hooks, bell. *Ain't I a Woman: Black Women and Feminism.* Boston: South End Press, 1983.

Hull, Gloria T., Patricia Bell Scott, and Barbara Smith, eds. *All the Women Are White, All the Blacks Are Men, But Some of Us Are Brave.* Old Westbury, N.Y.: Feminist Press, 1982.

Hunter, Tera. *To 'Joy My Freedom: Southern Black Women's Lives and Labors After the Civil War.* Cambridge: Harvard University Press, 1997.

Smith, Barbara, ed. *Home Girls: A Black Feminist Anthology.* New York: Kitchen Table Press, 1983.

Steady, Filomina, ed. *The Black Woman Cross-Culturally.* Cambridge: Schenkman, 1981.

Memoirs, Biographies, Autobiographies, Oral Histories

Carter, Stephen L. *Reflections of an Affirmative Action Baby.* New York: Basic Books, 1991.

Chisholm, Shirley. *The Good Fight.* New York: Harper & Row, 1973.

Delany, Samuel R. *The Motion of Light in Water.* New York: William Morrow, 1988.

Griffith, Farah Jasmine. *Who Set You Flowin'?: The African-American Migration Narrative.* New York: Oxford University Press, 1995.

Gwaltney, John Langston. *Drylongso: A Self-Portrait of Black America.* New York: Vintage, 1981.

Lanker, Brian. *I Dream a World: Portraits of Black Women Who Changed America.* New York: Stewart, Tabori, and Chang, 1989.

Lewis, Reginald, and Blair S. Walker. *Why Should White Guys Have all the Fun?* New York: Wiley, 1995.

Lorde, Audre. *Zami: A New Spelling of My Name.* Trumansberg, N.Y.: The Crossing Press, 1982.

McCall, Nathan. *Makes Me Wanna Holler: A Young Black Man in America.* New York: Random House, 1994.

Shakur, Sanyika ["Monster" Kody Scott]. *Monster: The Autobiography of an L.A. Gang Member.* New York: Penguin, 1993.

Tarpley, Natasha, ed. *Testimony: Young African Americans on Self-Discovery and Black Identity.* Boston: Beacon Press, 1994.

Terkel, Studs. *Race: How Blacks and Whites Think and Feel About the American Obsession.* New York: New Press, 1992.

Thomas, Arthur E. *Like It Is: Arthur E. Thomas Interviews Leaders on Black America.* Edited by Emily Rovetch. New York: Dutton, 1981.

Tyson, Timothy B. *Radio Free Dixie: Robert Williams and the Roots of Black Power.* Chapel Hill: University of North Carolina Press, 1998.

Williams, Patricia. *The Alchemy of Race and Rights: Diary of a Law Professor.* Cambridge: Harvard University Press, 1991.

Woodard, Komozi. *A Nation Within a Nation: Amiri Baraka (Leroi Jones) and Black Power Politics.* Chapel Hill: University of North Carolina Press, 1998.

Fiction

Butler, Octavia E. *Imago.* New York: Warner Books, 1989.

Danticat, Edwidge. *Breath, Eyes, Memory: A Novel.* New York: Soho Press, 1994.

Delany, Samuel R. *Dahlgren.* New York: Bantam, 1975.

Guy, Rosa. *And I Heard a Bird Sing.* New York: Delacorte Press, 1987.

———. *New Guys Around the Block.* London: Gollancz, 1983.

Morrison, Toni. *Beloved.* New York: Random House, 1987.

———. *Jazz.* New York: Random House, 1992.

Mosley, Walter. *Devil in a Blue Dress.* New York: Norton, 1990.

Mowry, Jess. *Way Past Cool.* New York: Farrar, Straus & Giroux, 1992.

Shange, Ntozake. *For Colored Girls Who Have Considered Suicide, When the Rainbow is Enuf: A Choreopoem.* New York: Bantam, 1980.

———. *Sassafrass, Cypress & Indigo.* New York: St. Martin's, 1982.

Walker, Alice. *The Color Purple.* New York: Harcourt Brace, 1982.

Woodson, Jacqueline. *Between Madison & Palmetto.* New York: Delacorte, 1993.

Picture Credits

Courtesy American Antiquarian Society: 96; Archivo General de la Nación de México: 32; Courtesy of the Billy Graham Center: 188; Boston Athenaeum: 211; By Permission of the British Library: 167; Chicago Historical Society: 64, 83, 174, 200, 222, 232, 397, 580; Courtesy of the Charleston Museum, Charleston, S.C.: 202; Everett Collection: 438; Florida Photographic Collection, Florida State Archives: 348, 574; Giraudon/Art Resource, NY: 43; Courtesy of Hampton University Archives: 318; Courtesy of the John Carter Brown Library at Brown University: 115; Library Company of Philadelphia: 21, 126, 191, 324; Library of Congress: ii, 28, 70, 87, 91, 110, 111, 130, 152, 177, 241, 249, 269, 272, 284, 287, 316, 341, 360, 363, 372, 381, 383, 407, 413, 418, 420, 425, 428, 434, 437, 478, 520, 556; Maryland Historical Society, Baltimore, Md.: 157; Metropolitan Museum of Art, Rogers Fund, 1942 (42.95.19): 147; Museum of Modern Art, Film Stills Archive: 544; Moorland-Spingarn Research Center, Howard University Archives: 274; Museo de América, Madrid: 46; Museum of the City of New York: 333; National Archives: 398, 440, 446, 569, 591; Collection of the New-York Historical Society: 100, 184, 185; New York Public Library, I.N. Phelps Stokes Collection, Miriam and Ira D. Wallach Division of Art, Prints and Photographs: 35, 61; North Carolina State Archives: 410; Reuters/Corbis-Bettman: 608, 610; Schomburg Center for Research in Black Culture, New York Public Library, Astor, Lenox, and Tilden Foundations: viii, 73 (Slavery-Documents Collection), 164, 170 (Slavery-Labor Collection), 230, 407 (Organizations-U.N.I.A.), 482 (Black Experience in America Collection), 509 (Black Experience in America Collection); Smithsonian Institution: 340; Courtesy Spelman College, Atlanta, Ga.: 321; Courtesy Tommy Boy Records: 584; Courtesy Gary Tong: 6, 12; University of Chicago Library: 307; University of Pittsburgh, Archives of Industrial Society, Urban League of Pittsburgh Collection: 394; UPI/Bettman Newsphotos: 561; UPI/Corbis-Bettman: 460, 475, 518, 534; Valentine Museum, Richmond, Va.: 294; Walter P. Reuther Library, Wayne State University: 262.

Contributors

The Editors

Robin D. G. Kelley is professor of history and Africana studies at New York University. He previously taught history and African-American studies at the University of Michigan. He is the author of *Hammer and Hoe: Alabama Communists during the Great Depression*, which was named Outstanding Book on Human Rights by the Gustavus Myers Center for the Study of Human Rights in the United States. Professor Kelley is also the author of *Race Rebels: Culture, Politics, and the Black Working Class*, and *Yo' Mama's DisFunktional!: Fighting the Culture Wars in Urban America*.

Earl Lewis is vice provost and dean of the graduate school and professor of history and Afroamerican studies at the University of Michigan. He served as director of the university's Center for Afroamerican and African Studies from 1990 to 1993 and has been dean since 1998. Professor Lewis is the author of *In Their Own Interests: Race, Class and Power in Twentieth Century Norfolk* and co-author of *Blacks in the Industrial Age: A Documentary History*.

The Authors

Barbara Bair is a documentary editor with the Jane Addams Papers Project, sponsored by the history department, Duke University. She is an associate and contributing editor of *The Marcus Garvey and Universal Negro Improvement Association Papers*, and a member of the editorial board of the Marshall Cavendish *African American Encyclopedia*. She received her Ph.D. from Brown University.

Noralee Frankel is assistant director on women, minorities, and teaching at the American Historical Association. She is co-editor of *Gender, Class, Race, and Reform in the Progressive Era* and author of *Freedom's Women: Black Women and Families in Civil War Era Mississippi*. In addition, she has published several articles dealing with the issues of race and gender.

James R. Grossman is vice president for research and education at the Newberry Library and senior lecturer in history at the University of Chicago. He is the author of *Land of*

Hope: Chicago, Black Southerners, and the Great Migration, editor of *The Frontier in American Culture,* and co-editor of the series "Historical Studies of Urban America."

Vincent Harding is professor of religion and social transformation at the Iliff School of Theology at the University of Denver. Harding has been director of the Martin Luther King, Jr., Memorial Center in Atlanta and the Institute of the Black World, which he helped to found. He was senior academic adviser to the PBS television series "Eyes on the Prize," about the civil rights movement, and he is author of many publications, including *There Is a River, Hope and History,* and *Martin Luther King: The Inconvenient Hero.* .

Daniel C. Littlefield is Carolina Professor of History at the University of South Carolina. He is the author of *Rice and Slaves: Ethnicity and the Slave Trade in Colonial South Carolina.*

Colin A. Palmer is Distinguished Professor of History at the Graduate School and University Center of the City University of New York. He was previously the William Rand Kenan, Jr., Professor of History at the University of North Carolina at Chapel Hill, where he chaired the history department, and African and Afro-American. He is the author of *Passageways: A History of Black America to 1865; Slaves of the White God: Blacks in Mexico, 1570–1650;* and the forthcoming *Africa's Children: The Pre-emancipation Experiences of Blacks in the Americas,* among other publications.

Joe William Trotter Jr. is Mellon Professor of History and director of the Center for African-American Urban Studies and the Economy at Carnegie-Mellon University. He holds a Ph.D. from the University of Minnesota. In addition to other edited and co-edited volumes, Professor Trotter is the author of *River Jordan: African American Urban Life in the Ohio Valley; Coal, Class, and Color: Blacks in Southern West Virginia, 1915–1932;* and *Black Milwaukee: The Making of an Industrial Proletariat, 1915–1945.*

Deborah Gray White is professor of history at Rutgers University. She holds a Ph.D. from the University of Illinois at Chicago. Dr. White is the author of *"Ar'n't I A Woman?" Female Slaves in the Plantation South,* for which she won the Letitia Brown Memorial Book Prize, and *Too Heavy a Load: Black Women in Defense of Themselves, 1894–1994.* She has also contributed articles to *Before Freedom Came: African-American Life in the Antebellum South,* and *Visible Women: New Essays on American Activism.*

Peter H. Wood is a professor of history at Duke University. He holds a Ph.D. from Harvard University and spent two years at Oxford University on a Rhodes scholarship. Dr. Wood is the author of *Black Majority: Negroes in Colonial South Carolina from 1670 through the Stono Rebellion,* which was nominated for the National Book Award. He is also the co-author of *Winslow Homer's Images of Blacks* and co-editor of *Powhatan's Mantle: Indians in the Colonial Southeast.*

Index